SECOND EDITION

Health Psychology

A Cultural Approach

Regan A. R. Gurung
University of Wisconsin, Green Bay

WADSWORTH
CENGAGE Learning™

Australia • Brazil • Japan • Korea • Mexico • Singapore • Spain • United Kingdom • United States

WADSWORTH
CENGAGE Learning™

Health Psychology: A Cultural Approach, Second Edition
Regan A. R. Gurung

Senior Publisher: Linda Schreiber,
Michele Sordi

Senior Sponsoring Editor: Jane Potter

Associate Development Editor:
Tali Beesley

Assistant Editor: Trina Tom

Editorial Assistant: Nicolas Albert

Associate Media Editor: Rachel Guzman

Marketing Manager: Kim Russell

Marketing Coordinator: Molly Felz

Marketing Communications Manager:
Talia Wise

Project Manager, Editorial Production:
Charlene M. Carpentier

Creative Director: Rob Hugel

Art Director: Vernon Boes

Print Buyer: Paula Vang

Permissions Editor: Timothy Sisler

Production Service: Pre-PressPMG

Photo Researcher: Pre-PressPMG

Copy Editor: Shanin Dockrey

Illustrator: Pre-PressPMG

Cover Designer: Lisa Henry

Cover Image: Stéphan Daigle/Images.com

Compositor: Pre-PressPMG

For product information and technology assistance, contact us at
Cengage Learning Customer & Sales Support, 1-800-354-9706.

For permission to use material from this text or product,
submit all requests online at **www.cengage.com/permissions.**
Further permissions questions can be e-mailed to
permissionrequest@cengage.com.

Library of Congress Control Number: 2008931516
ISBN-13: 978-0-495-60079-4
ISBN-10: 0-495-60079-2

Wadsworth
10 Davis Drive
Belmont, CA 94002-3098
USA

Cengage Learning is a leading provider of customized learning solutions with office locations around the globe, including Singapore, the United Kingdom, Australia, Mexico, Brazil, and Japan. Locate your local office at **www.cengage.com/international**.

Cengage Learning products are represented in Canada by Nelson Education, Ltd.

To learn more about Wadsworth, visit **www.cengage.com/Wadsworth**

Purchase any of our products at your local college store or at our preferred online store **www.ichapters.com.**

Printed in the United States of America
1 2 3 4 5 6 7 12 11 10 09

In memory of my nana, Carmelina Fernandes: You will always be a part of us. In celebration of her namesake, Melina Ann Raj Gurung: Welcome to the jungle.

BRIEF CONTENTS

v

CONTENTS

11 Psychoneuroimmunology and HIV   341

PREFACE

PHILOSOPHY

Culture is more important now than it has ever been. The 2008 presidential race often evoked cultural dimensions—both the race card and the sex card. World politics is rife with the clashing of cultural factions. Shias and Shiites in the Middle East. Hindus and Muslims in India. Caste and tribal genocide in Africa. Through this all, the disparities between different cultural groups—especially the rich and the poor—relate to significant health disparities. There are significant differences in health behaviors and the incidence in illnesses such as coronary heart disease and cancer across ethnic groups. These cultural differences are crucial to acknowledge and catalyzed me to present an introduction to health psychology with a cultural approach. In this second edition, I have had a chance to fine-tune the cultural focus and explain more thoroughly how culture is an important predictor of health. I also have the opportunity to reveal to you the two major changes in the field of health psychology: a greater focus on evidence-based treatment and the use of health behavior codes. Of course, with the multitude of new and exciting research in the field published monthly, this second edition offers an opportunity to update you and keep you informed.

We often discount the importance of culture, perhaps because we rarely acknowledge its many dimensions. For example, what do your mother, your best friends, and God have in common? They each constitute the major socialization forces of culture. Take parents for example. Whether we do something because they told us to ("Eat your greens!") or exactly because they told us *not to* ("Don't smoke!"), parents have a strong influence on us. In the same way, if our friends exercise, we are more likely to exercise also. As another example, consider religions, which have different prescriptions for what individuals should or should not do. Muslims cannot eat pork or drink alcohol. Hindus cannot eat beef. Unfortunately, textbooks often limit discussions of culture to race or ethnicity, when a broader discussion is required to fully understand the precedents of health and health behaviors. Culture is not just race or ethnicity; it also includes religion, age, gender, family values, the region of the country in which one was raised, and many other features. Understanding the dynamic interplay of the cultural forces acting on us can greatly enhance how we face the world and how we optimize our way of life.

THIS EDITION

The goals of this second edition are to examine how the areas of health, illness, and medicine can be studied from a psychological and cultural perspective and to introduce the main topics and issues in the area of health psychology. This is in combination with providing training to judge the scientific quality of research on psychology and medicine. I begin by describing what health psychology is all about, giving you a sense of what culture is, and highlighting research methods. I build on these basics with a revealing chapter on cultural variations in health beliefs and behaviors (how do shamans, acupuncture, yoga, and sweat lodges fit into health?). Our physiology is an important determinant of health. The new Chapter 3 describes essential physiological systems and processes that will aid your understanding of the different topics discussed later in the book. I then unravel the mysteries of stress and the ways to cope. In chapters 4 and 5, I discuss the theories explaining stress and the many practical ways to alleviate it. Armed with tools to make everyday life stress-free, I turn to another common aspect: health behaviors that many of us do (or try to do more often) and those we try not to do. Chapter 6 describes some of the theories predicting health behaviors, and Chapter 7 describes some of the behaviors in detail. The second half of the book turns to topics relating to sickness, such as factors that surround illness (such as adherence and patient-practitioner interactions; Chapter 8), pain (Chapter 9), and chronic illnesses, terminal illness, and death (Chapter 10), before examining some of the major health concerns and illnesses plaguing society today—HIV, cancer, and cardiovascular disease (chapters 11 to 13). Finally, I identify the major challenges faced by those in the field of health psychology (and provide some avenues for future exploration and training in this area).

Each chapter prepares you with an outline of the topics covered as well as a clear preamble to the main topics of the chapter. Each chapter ends with a summary to help you review the major points and a list of the key terms, concepts, and people. To understand the material more clearly, each chapter contains sections called "Synthesize, Evaluate, Apply." These questions serve to break up the chapters into easy, manageable segments and allow you to test your knowledge. In addition, each chapter ends with ten multiple-choice questions to help further your comprehension. To help you learn, the answers to these questions are provided in the back of the book. Finally, I have provided a short list of *absolute must-reads*—a selection of essential readings comprising classic articles in the field or *hot-off-the-press* research studies that are some of the material most cited by health psychologists. These are essentially the articles that are most likely to be used in any writing on the topic, and I think you will enjoy being involved in the field while reading them. There are also a set of annotated Web links for you to explore.

If you think I have missed something, if you have a suggestion for how this book can be improved, if you want to share a way that your culture has influenced your health, or even if you want to share that you really enjoyed learning about health psychology using this book (that's my goal), you may contact me by email at gurungr@uwgb.edu.

WHAT ELSE IS NEW?

Most importantly, I have ensured that you get to read the most updated information—there are over 1,000 new research articles cited (yes, I have been busy reading up on the literature for this revision). Additionally, as a testament to my commitment to providing you with a robust scientific introduction to the field, I enforce the chapter discussions with relevant and interesting citations. Numerous changes have been made to this edition. The following are some examples:

Chapter 1
- Additional material on biopsychosocial model and culture added.
- Table 1.3 updated to show 2008 publication examples.
- Expanded discussion of SES with special discussion of variations across ethnic groups in America.
- Additional information and research on sex differences added.
- Specific examples of health behaviors (i.e., smoking) used to explain the biopsychosocial model.
- Inclusion of explicit discussion of international classification of diseases (ICD-9), clinical health psychology, and evidence-based treatments with relevance for health psychology.
- Greatly expanded section on research methods with a discussion of major statistics used in health psychology (logistic regression, odds ratios, effect size, ANOVA, MANOVA, etc.), and the major health longitudinal studies students will encounter frequently (such as women's health initiative).
- FOCUS section includes discussion of 2008 presidential race and relevance.
- All references to contemporary culture and recent research updated.

Chapter 2
- Addition of discussion of variance in international understandings of health and well-being.
- Expanded discussion of ethnic differences and variations in North America.
- Additional discussion of the role of religion in cultural approaches to health: expansion of Hindu and Muslim religions' philosophy of health and wellness.
- Further empirical evidence added for the effectiveness of traditional Chinese medicine with discussion of special challenges for the use of the scientific method for testing some alternative medicines.

- Additional material added on Ayurveda with a focus on mental health.
- Inclusion of additional citations for Latino medicine section with a completely new section on empirical studies.
- Details on variations in American Indian medicine across different tribes added.
- Addition of new material on African American medicine.
- Expansion of section on discussion of complementary and alternative medicines with more information on use and tests of effectiveness of different types.
- All references to contemporary culture and recent research updated.
- Greater detail added to tables and figures.
- Additional essential readings added and list updated.

Chapter 3

- Entirely new chapter focused on physiological systems with all previous physiological material pulled from chapters and consolidated in one place.
- Addition of discussion of digestive, respiratory, endocrine, and renal systems.
- Additional essential readings added.
- New FOCUS section on the effect of video games on physiology.

Chapter 4

- Physiology information moved to new Chapter 3.
- Addition of new large section on Taylor et al.'s Tend and Befriend theory of stress.
- Additional discussion of sex differences in stress, especially within different cultural groups.
- Expanded and updated section on the role of culture on appraisals.
- New section on stress and psychopathology (the diathesis model).
- Expanded discussion of stress across culture with brand new section on discrimination.
- Streamlined discussion of perceived stress.
- Streamlined discussion of outdated measures of stress (e.g., social readjustment scale).
- New section on stress resulting from Hurricane Katrina and effects of the same.
- New section on Post-traumatic Stress Disorder.
- New FOCUS section on the effect of perceived stress added.
- All references to contemporary culture and recent research updated.

Chapter 5

- Expanded section on coping and culture.
- New sections on role of ethnic identity and acculturation.
- Clarification of section on mediation and moderation with additional examples and in-depth coverage of recent research from the 2008 supplement of *Health Psychology*.
- Addition of recent research with biological outcomes related to better coping.

- Expansion of discussion of mastery and hostility.
- New material on resilience.
- Additional material on social support across cultures.
- All references to contemporary culture and recent research updated.

Chapter 6
- New section on additional theories of health behavior change.
- Expanded discussion of interventions.
- New cultural examples.
- Addition of recent research on interventions and personality and health.
- Expanded discussion of health people program and healthy people 2020 program.
- Expanded discussion of pros and cons of models of health behavior change.
- Additional empirical examples added to discussion of interventions.
- All references to contemporary culture and recent research updated.

Chapter 7
- Expanded discussion of obesity and children.
- Additional examples of interventions aimed to change exercise, eating, and smoking.
- Expanded section on eating disorders, especially incorporating cultural differences.
- Additional discussion of how recommendations for exercise came about.
- Brand new FOCUS section on the "Freshman Fifteen" (college weight gain).
- All references to contemporary culture and recent research updated.

Chapter 8
- New section on emerging area of environmental health psychology.
- New section on cultural competency in hospitals.
- Expanded section on behavioral involvement.
- Expanded section on adherence to better capture current work.
- New section on shared medical decision making reflecting emerging work in behavioral medicine.
- All references to contemporary culture and recent research updated.
- Major reorganization of chapter to improve flow and understanding.
- Figures revised for better learning.
- New photos that are more relevant and better break up sections.

Chapter 9
- Additional information on sex differences in pain experience.
- Additional information on Latin Americans.
- Developmental differences streamlined and incorporated into cultural difference section.
- New measures of pain and patient-practitioner issues with pain management added.
- Addition of important new information on racism in pain measurement and treatment.

- New section on use of virtual reality treatments for pain.
- Section on acupuncture and pain expanded.
- Hospital treatments of pain expanded to give students more complete picture of pain treatment.
- All references to contemporary culture and recent research updated.
- Major reorganization of sections in the chapter to enable better flow and a more coherent discussion of topics.

Chapter 10

- Entire section on death across the lifespan added.
- Additional detail to cultural differences in life expectancy with new data.
- Expanded section on quality of life with more cultural differences and discussion of counter-intuitive findings.
- New information on life expectancy projections as well as cost to nation of chronic illnesses.
- New research on the role of additional personal characteristics and chronic illnesses added.
- More detail on how families vary added.
- More information on role of prejudice and discrimination in chronic illnesses.
- Expanded section on social support and culture.
- New details on interventions and chronic illnesses reflecting recently published summative work.
- All references to contemporary culture and recent research updated.
- Major reorganization of sections in the chapter to enable better flow and a more coherent discussion of topics.
- New tables added to better explain differences between groups.

Chapter 11

- Physiological information moved to Chapter 3, a brand new chapter that focuses on human physiology related to health psychology.
- All references to contemporary culture and recent research updated.
- Additional material on examples of autoimmune diseases such as Multiple Sclerosis.
- Expanded discussion of the field of psychoneuroimmunology (PNI).
- Clear examples of research studies designed to help showcase the research in the field of PNI added.
- Inclusion of August, 2008 CDC methodology changes for measuring HIV incidence and 2008 recommendations.
- Expansion of information on psychosocial correlates of HIV including personality factors and factors influencing progression.
- Additional material on ethnic-specific interventions.
- Additional material on culture, social support, and HIV.
- Additional material on models of health behavior change and interventions to change risky sexual behavior.
- New section on stress management interventions.

Chapter 12
- Physiological information moved to Chapter 3.
- All references to contemporary culture and recent research updated.
- Additional information on diets and cancer.
- Additional information on interventions.

Chapter 13
- Physiological information moved to Chapter 3.
- All references to contemporary culture and recent research updated.
- Expanded information (and figure) on international rates of cardiovascular disease.
- Greatly expanded sections on cultural differences and the link between culture, biology, and cardiovascular disease.
- Additional information on sex differences.
- More on the role of hostility.
- More on social support.
- Additional information on diets, physical activity, and tobacco.

Chapter 14
- Expanded information on health disparities.
- Greatly expanded sections on health and behavioral codes and the politics surrounding them.
- New section on evidence-based treatment.
- Expanded section on biopsychosocial model.
- New information on the role of the Internet in health.
- Additional information on sex differences.
- All new figures and photos to help visually enhance the chapter.
- All references to contemporary culture and recent research updated.

ACKNOWLEDGMENTS

Together with those who fueled my passion for health psychology (acknowledged in my first edition, but Shelley Taylor, Christine Dunkel-Schetter, and Margaret Kemeny at UCLA in particular) and those who first helped me get this project off the ground (especially Michele Sordi), I am grateful to the wonderful students I have had the pleasure to teach using this book. They have helped me make this second edition even stronger. The many colleagues who used this book have also been wonderful resources, providing useful suggestions for improvement.

Tali Beesley, my editor at Cengage, has been a joy to work with on this revision. Thank you Tali. I would also like to thank Vernon Boes, Karna Gunasekaran, both their staff members, and all the Cengage staff who worked behind the scenes in bringing this book to life. I also thank Stacie Herzog and Carrie Norton who went over the entire book with a fine-toothed comb.

A number of dedicated reviewers read draft chapters and the first edition and suggested insightful improvements. In particular the following people provided invaluable comments: Lisa Armistead, Georgia State University; Lisa K. Comer, University of Northern Colorado; Sussie Eshun, East Stroudsburg University; Ephrem Fernandez, Southern Methodist University; Deborah Jones, Barry University; Scott F. Madey, Shippensburg University; Charlotte Markey, Rutgers University; Cathleen McGreal, Michigan State University; Deborah Fish Ragin, Montclair State University; Christy Scott, Tennessee State University; Elizabeth E. Seebach, Saint Mary's University of Minnesota; Aurora Sherman, Brandeis University; Holly Tatum, Colby-Sawyer College; Debra VanderVoort, University of Hawaii at Hilo; John M. Velasquez, University of the Incarnate Word; Susan Walch, University of West Florida; and Michael Wohl, Carleton University.

I am particularly grateful to my wife Martha Ahrendt for her patience during the entire process and my son for putting up with my distraction.

ABOUT THE AUTHOR

REGAN A. R. GURUNG is chair of the Human Development Department and Professor of Human Development and Psychology at the University of Wisconsin, Green Bay.

Born and raised in Bombay, India, Dr. Gurung received a bachelor of arts in psychology at Carleton College (Minnesota) and master's and Ph.D. degrees in social and personality psychology at the University of Washington (Washington). He followed with three years at the University of California, Los Angeles, as a National Institute of Mental Health (NIMH) research fellow.

His early work focused on social support and close relationships, in which he studied how perceptions of support from close others influence relationship satisfaction. His later work investigated cultural differences in coping with stressors such as HIV infection, pregnancy, and smoking cessation. He continues to explore cultural differences in health and is heavily involved in pedagogical research directed toward improving teaching and student learning.

He has received numerous local, state, and national grants for his research in health psychology and social psychology regarding cultural differences in stress, social support, smoking cessation, body image, and impression formation. He has published articles in a variety of scholarly journals, including *Psychological Review* and *Personality and Social Psychology Bulletin,* and is a frequent presenter at national and international conferences. He is the author of *Optimizing Teaching and Learning: Pedagogical Research in Practice* (2009, with Beth Schwartz), and is editor of three books: *Culture & Mental Health: Sociocultural Influences on Mental Health* (2009, with Sussie Eshun); *Getting Culture: Incorporating Diversity across the Curriculum* (2009, with Loreto Prieto); and *Exploring Signature Pedagogies: Approaches* to *Teaching Disciplinary Habits of Mind* (2009, with Nancy Chick and Aeron Haynie). Dr. Gurung is also a dedicated teacher and has interests in enhancing faculty development and student understanding. He is co-director of the University of Wisconsin System Teaching Scholars Program, has been a UWGB teaching fellow and a UW System teaching scholar, and is winner of the Founder's Award for Excellence in Teaching and the Founder's Award for Excellence in Scholarship. He also has won the UW Teaching at Its Best, Creative Teaching, and Featured Faculty awards. He has organized statewide and national teaching conferences and is an active member of the Society for the Teaching of Psychology (APA-Division 2) and was elected fellow of the American Psychological Association. Dr. Gurung is also the current Chair of the Health Psychology (APA, Division 38) Education and Training committee.

When not reading, writing, or helping people stay calm, Dr. Gurung enjoys culinary explorations, travel, and inventing "Pookie Adventures" (and other exciting pursuits) for his son Liam. He is also preparing to raise his newborn daughter.

Health Psychology: Setting the Stage

Are you healthy? Sounds like a simple question to answer, right? Take a moment to consider it. What is your answer? If you are like most people, you probably think that you are reasonably healthy. Even if you do not think you are like most people, you may be more like most people than you know (most people do not think that they are like most other people). How did you arrive at your answer? Did you quickly drop down on the floor and see how many push-ups or sit-ups you could perform and how fatigued the exercises made you? Did you put down this book and time how long it took you to sprint to the corner and back? Maybe you put a finger on your wrist and took your pulse. More than likely, if you do not presently have a cold or other illness, if you have not recently stumbled and twisted an ankle, or if you do not have any other physical ailment, you probably answered the opening question with a statement like, "Yes, pretty healthy, I guess."

For most people living in the United States, basic indicators of good health include the absence of disease, injury, illness, a slow pulse, the ability to perform many physical exercises, or the ability to run fast. You may be surprised to learn that these all represent only one general way of being healthy, the one supported by Western medicine and as seen on television in such popular shows as Grey's Anatomy and ER. The definition of what is healthy varies from person to person and is strongly influenced by his or her way of thinking and his or her upbringing. For some, being happy signifies good health. For others, being spiritually satisfied signifies good health. Are some people right and others wrong? What are the best ways to measure

© Bob Llewellyn/ImageState/Jupiter Images

Different Pictures of Health

These individuals may seem healthy to the naked eye. It is important to also look beyond mere physiological health and the lack of disease and consider mental, spiritual, and emotional health.

health and what are the different factors that influence how healthy we will be? In particular, what are the psychological and sociocultural factors that influence health?

The United States is a diverse nation with approximately 303 million citizens (Census Bureau, 2008). Many of these Americans will have different answers to questions about health. For example, ask a child what being "healthy" is, and it is almost certain that his or her answer will be different from that of an older person. Someone earning less than $13,000 a year will probably answer differently than someone making more than $100,000 a year. A Catholic will probably answer differently than a Buddhist. Essentially, a person's cultural background makes a substantial difference in how he or she answers. Furthermore, our many different actions influence our health—things that often vary by culture as well. The amount of carbonated beverages that you drink can make a difference; younger people tend to drink more of these types of beverages than older people do. What you eat, including the amount of fast food you eat, makes a difference too. As with beverage consumption, some cultural groups tend to eat more fast food than other groups.

In fact, the answer to the simple question, are you healthy? can vary according to where you live, how old you are, what your parents and friends think constitutes health, what your religious or ethnic background is, and what a variety of other factors indicate about you. If you live in California, where the sun shines most of the time, your health habits are probably different than if you live in Wisconsin, where it is often chilly (Nelson et al., 2002).

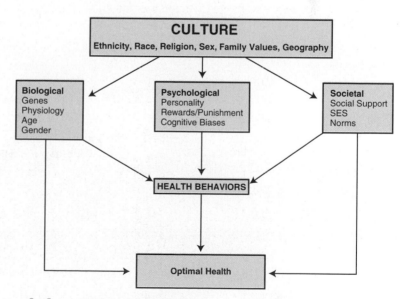

FIGURE **1.1** Health and Its Correlates

Our cultural backgrounds, our biology, and our health behaviors all influence whether we will be healthy or not.

Though both states are leading producers of dairy products in the United States, statistically, Wisconsinites tend to weigh significantly more than Californians (Is it the cheese? Is it the lack of sun?). Factors such as where you live, your age, or your ethnicity, interacts with others to influence what you do and how healthy you will be. "Culture" is the term that adequately captures all these different elements that influence health. Thus, the focus of this book is on how our cultural backgrounds influence our health, shape healthy behaviors, prevent illness, and enhance our health and well-being.

The schematic diagram in Figure 1.1 provides a map for the course we will take in this book. Notice how many different pathways can determine health and how culture is often the basis of biological, psychological, and societal differences. In fact, many of the health disparities, "differences in health that are not only unnecessary and avoidable, but in addition, are considered unfair and unjust" (Whitehead, 1992, p. 433), are due to cultural factors (Braveman, 2006; National Research Council, 2004). See Table 1.1 for examples of major cultural differences in health. Consequently, this book takes a cultural approach to discussing health psychology.

To begin, this chapter discusses the dissimilar ways we define and measure health and culture. Next, the discussion introduces you to the field of

TABLE **1.1**

Age-Adjusted Death Rates for Blacks and Whites for Three Causes of Death, and Racial Disparities, 1950–2000

Cause	1950	1960	1970	1980	1990	2000
Homicide						
White	2.6	2.7	4.7	6.7	5.5	3.6
Black	28.3	26.0	44.0	39.0	36.3	20.5
Difference	25.7	23.3	39.3	32.3	30.8	16.9
Ratio	10.9	9.6	9.4	5.8	6.6	5.7
Heart Disease						
White	584.8	559.0	492.2	409.4	317.0	253.4
Black	586.7	548.3	512.0	455.3	391.5	324.8
Difference	1.9	−10.7	19.8	45.9	74.5	71.4
Ratio	1.0	1.0	1.0	1.1	1.2	1.3
Cancer						
White	194.6	193.1	196.7	204.2	211.6	197.2
Black	176.4	199.1	225.3	256.4	279.5	248.5
Difference	−18.2	6.0	28.6	52.2	67.9	51.3
Ratio	0.9	1.0	1.2	1.3	1.3	1.3

Notes: Deaths per 100,000 population. "Difference" is calculated as black death rates minus white death rates for each cause of death. "Ratio" refers to the ratio of black deaths to white deaths. http://www.naccho.org/topics/justice/documents/NACCHO_Handbook_hyperlinks_000.pdf

Source: National Center for Health Statistics, Health, United States, 2003.

Key Health Behaviors

Getting six to eight hours of sleep, being physically active, eating a nutritional meal, and not smoking are all important health behaviors that can prolong life.

health psychology and provides an overview of what health psychology covers. Finally, the chapter concludes with a profile of a multicultural America, a look at how each of us is "multicultural," especially focusing on differences in family structure, and how sociodemographic variables such as gender and income level are critical aspects of culture.

WHAT IS HEALTH?

Newspaper headlines scream the latest health findings almost every day. Drinking soda can give you gout (Choi & Curhan, 2008); diets are not the answer to the obesity crisis (Mann et al., 2007). Not only do news agencies report on countless research every day, but much of the information presented is contradictory. Much of the media blitz capitalizes on the fact that people, in general, seem to be paying more attention to attaining healthier lifestyles. Supermarket shelves overflow with supplements to enhance one's quality of life, and bookstores brim with recommendations on how to live better. The answer to the question, what is health? depends on who you ask. Let's start with the **WHO** (World Health Organization). This organization defines **health** as a state of complete physical, mental, and social well-being (WHO, 1979, 2003).

As you can see, this is a general definition and encompasses almost every aspect of life. One aspect that could be added is "spiritual." Definitions such as this one are relatively common when we look at books or magazines that cover health in a nonspecific way. One way to see health is as a continuum with optimal health (broadly defined) at one end and poor health at the other, sitting on two ends of a great big teeter-totter (Figure 1.2). The number of healthy things we do in life determines our relative position (closer to optimal health or closer to death) at a particular moment in time. The healthy things we do (e.g., eat and sleep well, exercise, and take time to relax) make the optimal health side of the teeter-totter heavier. The unhealthy things we do (e.g., get stressed, smoke, and drink excessively) make us tilt toward the poor

FIGURE **1.2** Health is a Continuum
The sum of the different health behaviors we perform influence where we stand on the balance of health. This is a dynamic process, and although good health behaviors can compensate for some bad ones, you can optimize your health by loading the balance in your favor by practicing as many healthy behaviors as possible.

health side of the balance. This imagery also captures how we sometimes rationalize some unhealthy behaviors by practicing some healthy behaviors to ensure the teeter-totter is leaning in the right direction and we are moving toward the optimal end of the spectrum. Of course, this analogy can only go so far: If you have smoked for 20 or 30 years, it will be quite difficult to compensate the balance. Furthermore, it is difficult to compare the extent to which different behaviors translate into longevity. Just because you do not smoke does not mean that you can drink excessively. Just because you may exercise a lot does not mean you can afford to avoid a nutritional diet. Keeping your life tilted toward optimal health is a daily challenge and a dynamic process.

CROSS-CULTURAL DEFINITIONS OF HEALTH

In Western medical circles, health is commonly defined as "the state in which disease is absent" (Galanti, 2004). Of course, this definition focuses primarily on the physical or biological aspect of life and correspondingly, this approach taken by Western medicine is often referred to as the **biomedical approach** to health. This author refers to this as the Western approach because many other societies have a different understanding of health. For example, in **Traditional Chinese Medicine** (TCM), health is the balance of yin and yang, the two complementary forces in the universe (Kaptchuk, 2000). Yin and yang are often translated into hot and cold (two clear opposites), referring to qualities and not temperatures. To be healthy, what you eat and drink and the way you live your life should have equal amounts of hot qualities and cold qualities. Balancing hot and cold is a critical element of many different cultures (e.g., Chinese, Indian, and even Mexican), although the foods that constitute each may vary across cultures. Some "hot" foods include beef, garlic, ginger, and alcohol. Some "cold" foods include honey, most greens, potatoes, and some fruits (e.g., melons, pears). This book covers a complete description of diverse approaches to health in Chapter 2.

Other cultures also believe that health is the balance of different qualities (Table 1.2) (Galanti, 2004). Similarly, ancient Indian scholars and doctors defined health as the state in which "the three main biological units— enzymes, tissues, and excretory functions— are in harmonious condition and when the mind and senses are cheerful." Referred to as **Ayurveda,** or "Knowledge of Life," this ancient system of medicine focuses on the body, the sense organs, the mind, and the soul (Chopra & Doiphode, 2002; Dash, Junius, & Dash, 1997). Another way of looking at health is the approach of Mexican Americans, one of the largest ethnic groups in the United States. Mexican Americans believe that there are both natural biological causes for illness (similar to Western biomedicine) and spiritual causes (Trotter & Chavira, 1997). Though Mexican American patients may go to a Western doctor to cure a biological problem, only *curanderos*, or healers, can be trusted to cure spiritual problems.

American Indians do not even draw distinctions between physical, spiritual, and social entities or between religion and medicine (Cohen, 2003). Instead, most tribes (especially the Navajo) strive to achieve a balance between human beings and the spiritual world (Alvord & Van Pelt, 2000). The trees, the animals, the earth, the sky, and the winds are all players in the same game of life. Most of the world's cultures use a more global and widespread approach to assessing health instead of just looking at whether or not disease is absent to determine health (as the biomedical model and most Western approaches do). We will discuss each of these different approaches to health in more detail in the next chapter.

TABLE **1.2**
Some Cross-Cultural Definitions of Health

Culture	Definition
Western	Absence of disease
Chinese	Balance of yin and yang Balance of hot and cold
Indian	Balance of mind, body, and spirit
Mexican	Balance of body types and energies
American Indian	Spiritual, mental, and physical harmony Harmony with nature
Hmong	Preventing soul loss
Ethiopian	Preventing spirit possession

- How has our view of the mind-body connection changed over time?
- What is the best way to view health? What do you feel is the best definition?
- How do different cultures vary in their definition of health?

Common Rubrics for Health

Regardless of which one we consider, each definition of health is broad and ambiguous. How can we measure mental, spiritual, and social health? Does simply the absence of physical problems or disease equate to health? Can anyone even measure a balanced yin and yang? The answer is no, not really, or at least not by any measure that we know of or use in the United States or in the scientific community and not in a way on which we can all agree. To understand what keeps us healthy, it is important to start with a good measurement of health. As you learn about the field of health psychology, you will see that although most researchers will use a common understanding and relatively broad definition of health to guide their general thinking (e.g., a general state of well-being), every researcher uses a different specific measure of health to help understand what makes us healthy. Take a quick look at the major research journals that report on health psychological research, and you will see that different studies use slightly different measures. The main categories of measures vary with each journal. For example, *Health Psychology*, is the leading journal in the field and publishes the results of studies on the topic of health psychology. This journal features many studies that define health in terms of the extent to which health-improving behaviors are practiced (e.g., how much did the participants in the study exercise in a week?) or in terms of psychological well-being (e.g., what were the participants' scores on the Profile of Mood States, a common measure of mood?). You will also see many studies that assess the extent to which health-diminishing behaviors are practiced. For example, how much does a person smoke? What predicts the amount of alcohol consumed? Other journals, such as *The Annals of the Society for Behavioral Medicine* and *Psychosomatic Medicine*, measure many specific physiological outcomes. For example, what are the levels of immune cells in the blood? Table 1.3 shows sample contents from the three major journals. The bottom line is that, we determine if people are healthy by measuring a variety of aspects, such as: basic physiological levels of their bodies' various systems (e.g., blood pressure, heart rate, or cholesterol level); how much they practice healthy behaviors (e.g., exercising); their psychological well-being (e.g., levels of depression or optimism); and how well they practice "healthy" psychological ways (e.g., good coping skills).

WHY IS CULTURE IMPORTANT?

One easy answer is "to explain why there are significant differences in the health of European Americans and non-European Americans" (National Center on Minority Health and Health Disparities, 2005). However, that is not all.

TABLE **1.3**

Sample Contents from the Major Health Psychology Journals

Health Psychology (2008, Volume, 27)	Annals of Behavioral Medicine (2008, Volume 35)	Psychosomatic Medicine (2008, Volume 70)
• Perceived group devaluation, depression, and HIV-risk behavior among Asian gay men • A quasi-experimental investigation of message appeal variations on organ donor registration rates • Asking questions changes behavior: Mere measurement effects on frequency of blood donation • Healthcare provider cultural competency: Development and initial validation of a patient report measure	• What Types of Evidence are Most Needed to Advance Behavioral Medicine? • Cognitive–Behavioral Stress Management Interventions for Persons Living with HIV: A Review and Critique of the Literature • Mediation of Adult Fruit and Vegetable Consumption in the National 5 A Day for Better Health Community Studies	• Early Socioeconomic Status is Associated With Adult Nighttime Blood Pressure Dipping • Social Networks and Incident Stroke Among Women With Suspected Myocardial Ischemia • Overweight and Obesity Are Associated With Psychiatric Disorders: Results From the National Epidemiologic Survey on Alcohol and Related Conditions • Course of Anxiety Symptoms Over an 18-Month Period in Exhausted Patients Post Percutancous Coronary Intervention

What do your mother, your best friend, and your religion have in common? They each constitute a way that you learn about acceptable behaviors. Take parents, for example. Whether we do something because they told us to (e.g., "Eat your greens!") or exactly because they told us not to (e.g., "Don't smoke!"), they have a strong influence on us. If our friends exercise, we will be more likely to exercise. Similarly, religions have different prescriptions for what individuals should and should not do. Muslims should not eat pork or drink alcohol. Hindus are prohibited from eating beef. Even where we live can determine our habits and can help predict the diseases we may die from as studied in detail by the area of health geography (Andrews, 2002). Parents, peers, religion, and geography are a few of the key determinants of our behaviors and are examples of what makes up our culture.

Dimensions of Culture

If you think that there are many ways to describe health, then prepare for the challenge of defining culture. At first, it does not seem too difficult, but both trained psychologists and laypeople often mean different things when they discuss culture. Many use the words culture, ethnicity, and race interchangeably. Beyond these specific examples, people also think culture represents a set of ideals or beliefs or sometimes a set of behaviors. Behaviors and beliefs are other accurate components of what culture is. Take the popular *Austin Powers* movies. The actor Mike Myers plays a spy from the late 1960s and early 1970s. The movies rely on the fact that Austin's period had a recognizable set of behaviors considered to be part of a certain carefree type of culture.

Sometimes referred to as the "culture of free love," the late 1960s and early 1970s had some clear stereotypes. For example, people during this cultural period had specific ways of dressing (e.g., flared pants and shirts with wide collars), grooming (e.g., the Beatles-like mop-top haircuts), and behaving (e.g., sexual activity was seen in a different light than it is today). Identifying as a member of a certain culture also entails sharing the beliefs and values of others in that culture.

Although we rarely acknowledge it, culture has many dimensions. Many of us limit discussions of culture to race or ethnicity. Look at what happens if you ask someone what she thinks the dominant culture around her is. In most cases, she will identify an ethnic category. Someone in Miami may respond with Cuban. Someone in Minnesota may respond with Scandinavian. When the question is posed in Green Bay, Wisconsin, people often respond Hispanic or Hmong (people from Laos near Vietnam). They sometimes say American Indian because they think that they are being asked which ethnic group is most visible in town. In reality, culture can be a variety of things. The dominant culture in Green Bay is Catholic, but people rarely realize that religion constitutes a form of culture as well. Is there an "American" culture? The Focus section at the end of this chapter will address that question.

Defining Culture

A broader discussion and definition of culture is important for a full understanding of the precedents of health behaviors and health. Culture includes ethnicity, race, religion, age, sex, family values, the region of the country, and many other features. Adolescents belong to a different culture than do college students. Even in college, there are different cultures. Some students live in dorms, and some live in off-campus apartments. On campus, also, there are athletes and musicians, and each group provides different prescriptions for what is correct behavior. For instance, it is normal for the athletes to exercise a lot. Aspects of the specific culture we belong to correspondingly influence each of our health behaviors. Understanding the dynamic interplay of cultural forces acting on us can greatly enhance how we face the world and how we optimize our way of life. This book will describe how such cultural backgrounds influence the different behaviors we follow that can influence our health.

There are probably as many different definitions for culture as there are for health. A good way to comprehend the breadth of culture is to see if you know what your own is. For the next 30 seconds, think of all the ways that you would answer the question, who am I? Write down or just think of every response that comes to mind.

You will notice that you use many labels for yourself. Social psychologists call this the "Who am I?" test (not a very inventive name, obviously) and use it to measure how people describe themselves. You probably generated a number of different descriptors for yourself, and your responses provide a number of different clues about yourself and your culture. Your answers may have included your religious background (e.g., I am Lutheran), your sex (e.g., I am male), or your major roles (e.g., I am a student, a daughter, or a friend). You may have even mentioned your nationality (e.g., I am American) or your ethnicity (e.g., I am Latino). Therefore, if you really took the 30 seconds suggested, you should be staggering under the realization that you actually have a lot more culture than you previously expected. Before doing this listing exercise, many European Americans have said things like, "I do not have any culture; I'm just White." Part of the exciting thing about life is that every one of us has different experiences and backgrounds, and we will keep these backgrounds at center stage as we discuss health behaviors and health.

CONTEXT AND LEVEL OF ANALYSIS

The order in which the different descriptors came to your mind gives you a good idea of the aspects of yourself that are most important to you right now. It also alerts us to two critical factors for measuring culture. First, the order in which we use words to describe ourselves often depends on the **context** or the environment in which we are. If you are male and are answering the "Who am I?" question sitting in a room full of women, the answer, I am a man is likely to be near the top of your list. Even if you did not answer with, I am American, your nationality probably would be one of the first descriptors that would come to mind if you were on a holiday abroad, say checking out the Tower of London, surrounded by a group of local British citizens.

Even though the context can influence our ordering, it does not mean it changes the content of our self-views. This is where the **level of analysis** is important. This means that our views of ourselves reside at different levels of conscious awareness. Although you may think of yourself as a "runner," this description may be far down on the list you generated and correspondingly we would have to go to a deeper level of analysis to uncover it. If we really want to get a good sense of a person and his or her culture, we have to remember that many different levels could be important and that the context in which we make our assessment can make a world of difference. Look at the example shown in Figure 1.3 and notice how the order of ways Manish describes himself varies depending on the context in which he is.

Having culture can offer a person many things. Think about what you may get from being part of a certain culture. Like someone in the army or someone on an athletic team (both cultures of their own), the culture in which you live influences ideas about what to do, what to wear, how to behave, and even how to feel. These prescriptions of how to be form the basis of the way culture has been defined in the scientific literature. There are many definitions of culture. Soudijn, Hutschemaekers, and Van de Vijver (1990) analyzed 128 definitions. Next, we provide a comprehensive definition of culture that shows you how culture can influence our health behaviors and our health in general.

Culture can be defined as a dynamic, yet stable, set of goals, beliefs, and attitudes shared by a group of people (Matsumoto, 2009). Culture can also include similar physical characteristics (e.g., skin color), psychological characteristics (e.g., levels of hostility), and common superficial features (e.g., hairstyle and clothing). Culture is dynamic because some of the beliefs held

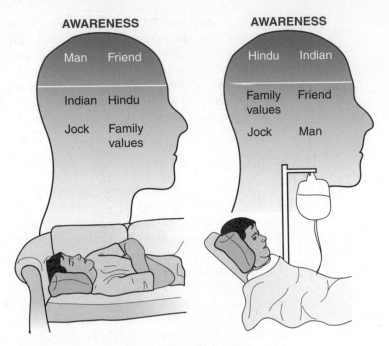

FIGURE **1.3** Levels of Analysis and Context

The context we are in can influence the things that first come to mind when we are asked to describe ourselves. If Manish were awakened from a nap and asked to describe himself, the order of things that would come up would be very different from those if he had an accident and were taken to the hospital. The context (the hospital) would bring different things to the level of consciousness. Being Hindu in a Western hospital may make those aspects of his self-concept more salient.

by members in a culture can change with time. However, the general level of culture maintains stability because the individuals change together. The beliefs and attitudes can be implicit, learned by observation, and passed on by word of mouth, or they can be explicit, written down as laws or rules for the group to follow. The most commonly described objective cultural groups consist of grouping by ethnicity, race, sex, and age. Look at Figure 1.4 for a summary of the different types of cultures and characteristics. There are more subjective aspects of culture that cannot be seen or easily linked to physical characteristics. For example, nationality, sex/gender, religion, and geography also constitute different cultural groups, each with its own set of prescriptions for behavior.

Two Major "Cultures"

Two of the most important aspects that define cultural groups are **socioeconomic status** (SES) and sex. This book features frequently both aspects throughout. Socioeconomic status is becoming one of the most important and widely studied constructs in health psychology (Adler & Rehkopf, 2008; Adler et al., 2008). Almost any study done on this topic shows that poverty

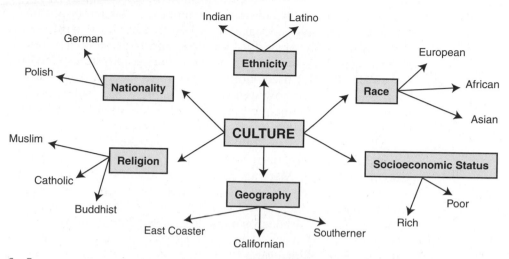

FIGURE **1.4** The Variety of Cultures and Associated Behaviors

There are many different aspects to the definition of culture. The term culture can imply many different things.

and illness tend to go together, often linked by factors such as access to health care and insurance. The poor (those with a yearly income equal to or less than $21,000 for a family of four (Federal Registry, U.S. DHHS, 2008) make up a large percentage of Americans without health insurance.

Of particular importance to taking a cultural approach to health is that the cultural make-up of those considered "poor" is changing. For example, Indiana's Manchester College and Massachusetts's Bentley College examined poverty rates and income levels from 1995–2006 for several groups in the U.S. population. They found that the disparity in poverty rates between European Americans and other ethnic groups decreased seven of the last eleven years, dropping 23 percent overall since 1995. Whereas European American poverty is remaining relatively stable (8.2% in 2006 versus 8.5% in 1995), the African American poverty rate dropped from 29.3 percent to 24.2 percent; Hispanics dropped from 30.2 percent to 20.6 percent; and Asians/Pacific Islanders dropped from 14.6 percent to 10.1 percent (Wollman, Yoder, Brumbaugh-Smith, & Haynes, 2007). Such changes can influence usage of health services and consequently a number of other factors that health psychologists study.

Socioeconomic status is related to a higher occurrence of most chronic and infectious disorders and to higher rates of nearly all major causes of mortality and morbidity (Adler, Boyce, Chesney, Folkman, & Syme, 1993; Macintyre, 1997; Williams & Collins, 1995). Even the neighborhood in which you live can be important. Neighborhood SES has been associated with poorer health practices (Petridou et al., 1997) and a variety of other health conditions such as coronary heart disease (Diez-Roux et al., 2001; Robert, 1999). The relationship between SES and health is also direct: the more money you have, the better your health. This relationship is seen in children and in older adults alike. Several ways of measuring SES have been proposed but most include some quantification of family income, parental education, and occupational status. Research shows that SES is associated with a wide array of health, cognitive, and socioemotional outcomes with effects beginning before birth and continuing into adulthood (Bradley & Corwyn, 2002; Gottfried, Gottfried, Bathurst, Guerin, & Parramore, 2003). Even perceptions of how well-off your family is (i.e., subjective perceptions of familial socioeconomic status) have been found to influence health (Goodman, Huang, Schafer-Kalkhoff, & Adler, 2007).

Many differences in health are due to **sex**—an innate, biological characteristic. For instance, men and women react differently to hospitalization (Suominen-Taipale, Martelin, Koskinen, Holmen, & Johnsen, 2006; Volicer, Isenberg, & Burns, 1977), in their need for health information (Stewart, Abbey, Shnek, Irvine, & Grace, 2004) and to illness in general (Westbrook & Viney, 1983). Although women live longer than men (WHO, 2008), they report symptoms of illness more frequently and utilize health services to a greater extent (Nathanson, 1977; Waldron, 1991), and the once common belief that women have poorer health in general than men has been challenged (Macintyre, Hunt, & Sweeting, 1996). There are both pros and cons to being female. The female sex hormone estrogen has a protective effect against cardiovascular illness in women younger than age 50 (Orth-Gomer, Chesney, & Wegner, 1998). On the other hand, women are more likely to be victims of violence and sexual assault (Risberg, 1994; U.S. Department of Justice, 2006) and have body image, eating, and diet problems (Chesney & Ozer, 1995; Harrison, Taylor, & Marske, 2006). Boys and men are not always better off. Boys have body image issues as well, often spurred on by the media in general and some media (e.g., video gaming magazines) in particular (Harrison & Bond, 2007). Sometimes these differences are due to gender, behaviors determined by socialization, and learning of social roles. For example, sociological factors related to gender include the extra demands of balancing different roles (e.g., being the primary caregiver for children and going to work, Repetti, 1998). Most studies acknowledge these differences by statistically controlling for sex and implicitly (and sometimes explicitly) treating biological sex as a proxy for gender. Remember that sex and gender are not identical constructs, although the two are often treated interchangeably (Pryzgoda & Chrisler, 2000).

Our culture has a major impact on behaviors that influence our health. Culture influences some explicit health behaviors. For example, how much do we exercise? Do we drink or smoke? Do we eat well? Culture also influences a whole range of behaviors that indirectly influence our health. For example, how do we form relationships? How many close friends do we have and do we call on them when we are under stress or in need?

SYNTHESIZE, EVALUATE, APPLY	• What are the components of a good definition of culture? • What aspects of life are influenced by culture? How is culture transferred? • What factors can influence responses to the "Who am I?" test? • Why are cultural differences important in the context of health? • How can context and level of analysis play a role in describing culture?

SOME IMPORTANT WARNINGS

Whenever we talk about culture, we often tend to emphasize cultural differences. To some extent, this is a natural human phenomenon. Even if people who are relatively identical in age, ethnicity, and intelligence were to be randomly separated into two groups and forced to compete with each other, members of each group would tend to believe that they are better than those of the other group (e.g., the minimal subgroup paradigm, an important social psychological effect considered in later chapters). Even if we are not competing for resources we still emphasize how we are different from other people. There are two major problems here. First, this emphasis on differences often leads us to treat some groups better than others (factors such as prejudice are discussed later in this book). For example, we may be more likely to help people who look like us. We may be less likely to give information to someone who is not from a social group to which we belong. Second, whenever we deal with an individual from a culture with which we are not familiar, we are likely to use the key ways that he or she is different and generalize from that one person to the entire culture (this book later discusses the dangers of stereotyping as well). By focusing on major group differences, we often forget that differences exist within a group as often as between groups. Let's review an example.

Look at the two bell-shaped curves in Figure 1.5. The horizontal x-axis represents the number of push-ups a person can do, and the vertical y-axis

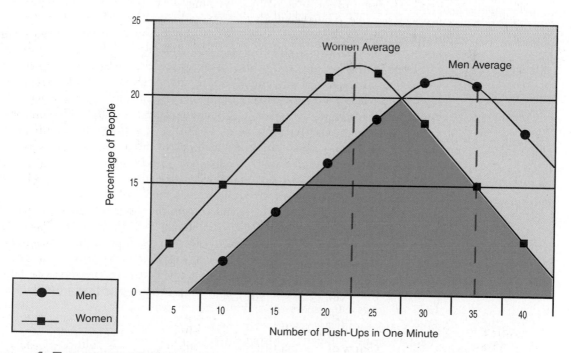

FIGURE **1.5** People within Cultures Vary Too

Although men may be able to do more push-ups than women on average, many women can do more push-ups than a number of men. Notice the number of men and women (shaded) that can do the same number.

represents the number of people who can do each number of push-ups. Now suppose we walk around town for a few days, and we ask every man and woman we see to get down on the pavement and do as many push-ups as he or she can in one minute. We continue this odd request until we speak to 100 men and 100 women. Each curve you see represents one of the two sexes. Therefore, the point of the curve for women above the number 10 means that of all the women we talked to (and who agreed to our strange request), 15 could do 10 push-ups. Now you will probably notice that the two curves are slightly set apart from each other. If we were to ask one of the most commonly asked questions in much of psychology, "Are there significant sex differences?" it is easy to see that the answer is yes. The average number of push-ups men can do is significantly higher than the average number of push-ups women can do. You can also see that there are more men who can do 30 or more push-ups than women, and more women than men who can only do 10 or fewer push-ups in one minute.

There are two critical things to notice about those two overlapping curves. First, even though there are men who can do more push-ups than women and women who can do fewer push-ups than any man, notice how many men and women can do the same number of push-ups. The entire center portions of each curve overlap (the shaded part). At the heart of all this, we are all much more similar than we are dissimilar. Excluding unfortunate and unpredictable circumstances, we all have two eyes, two legs, a nose, and two ears. We all look pretty much the same. We all need to eat, drink, and sleep to live. So why then do we often look at either end of the curves or focus on group differences only? We do so because differences are more noticeable and provide a way to distinguish groups.

Even though we all need to eat, drink, and sleep to live, we vary in how we accomplish each, and how much food, drink, or sleep we need. These variations often make the difference between illness and health. This book will draw your attention to these variations. All humans have about 32,000 genes (compare that number with the fruit fly at 18,000 or the worm at 12,000), but a variety of environmental and cultural factors can influence the kind of organisms those genes transcribe onto (Collins, 2007). Humans share 99.8 percent of their genes, but that 0.02 percent of a difference is very important. In short, even though we should always remember that there are more similarities than differences, sometimes we can learn much from the differences.

There is something else to notice in Figure 1.5. Look at each curve by itself. Notice that there is a lot of diversity in push-up ability *even within each sex*. The average number of push-ups women can do provides a sense of general ability, but notice the number of women at different stages of ability level. A lot of diversity is seen among women. This is a critical observation to hold on to as we discuss the many different topics in this book. No matter how many significant group differences we see, we must also remember that there are many differences within each culture as well. This basic understanding of the differences *within* versus *between* cultures applies to every culture we discuss. We can be talking about men and women as in the lighter push-up example above, or we can be comparing young and old, rich and poor, or Mexican American and African American. To make it easier to understand the

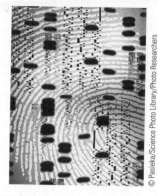

© Pasieka/Science Photo Library/Photo Researchers

© Cristina Pedrazzini/Science Photo Library/ Photo Researchers

© PhotoDisc/Getty Images

The Biopsychosocial Determinants of Health

Our genes, our psychological states, and our friends and social environments are some of the many factors that influence our health and health behaviors.

different aspects of health psychology, this book will highlight how groups differ. Every time it does, keep these two overlapping curves at the back of your mind and always remember that these are average group differences only.

HEALTH PSYCHOLOGY'S BIOPSYCHOSOCIAL APPROACH

An understanding of the different definitions of culture becomes a useful aid to study health and examine why we do or do not do things that are good for us. Most behaviors that influence health—whether healthy ones such as physical activity and eating nutritionally balanced diets or unhealthy ones such as smoking or drinking excessively—depend heavily on the culture in which we grew up. If both of your parents exercised, there is a high probability that you will exercise as well. The fact that behavior is influenced by many different factors outside of the individual is a critical aspect on which health psychologists focus. We will discuss the exact ways that culture influences our development and health behaviors in more detail throughout this book.

How does the culture that we come from and surround ourselves with influence our health and behaviors? Answering this question with a concerted look at sources of influence outside a person (i.e., not just his or her biology or psychology) is a distinctive feature of the approach taken by health psychologists in studying health. In contrast to the biomedical approach of Western medicine described previously, health psychologists use a **biopsychosocial approach**. Most terms used in psychology reflect common sense, and this term is no exception. This type of approach focuses on the biology or physiology underlying health, the psychology or thoughts, feelings, and behaviors influencing health, and the ways that society and culture influence health. This approach goes beyond defining health as simply the absence of disease and instead forces us to focus on the broader range of the critical determinants of health (Suls & Rothman, 2004).

Smoking provides a good example of how the biopsychosocial model is useful. People may start smoking for psychological reasons such as thinking it makes them less stressed or because of personality traits (extroverts are more likely to smoke). People may start to smoke due to pressure from their social networks or because of perceived cultural norms. Finally, addictions have a strong biological component in terms of their heritability.

The Evolution of Health Psychology

The first two components of the biopsychosocial approach—focusing on biology and psychology—represent a current resolution to an ancient debate. For centuries researchers, thinkers, and philosophers have questioned if and how the mind (and psychology) and the body (and our biology) are related and whether this relationship influences health. Is the mind connected to the body? Does it reside in the body? Where is the soul? Philosophers and scientists alike have debated these questions for eons. Modern health psychology has roots in philosophy, nineteenth-century scientific discovery, medical and clinical psychology, epidemiology and public health, medical sociology and anthropology, and psychosomatic medicine (Friedman & Adler, 2007).

The earliest evidence, such as oral traditions and pictorial evidence from early civilizations, suggests that the mind and body were originally considered to be one (Ellenberger, 1970). Spirits invading the body were thought to cause illness and gruesome solutions such as trephination—the poking of holes in the skull to release spirits—were practiced to make people healthy. This was not a highly successful method (nor was it likely to have been extremely popular with people developing illnesses).

Many of the world's early philosophies seemed to share the view that the mind and the body were intimately connected, and close to 5,000 years ago, both the ancient Chinese Taoist sages and the ancient Indian practitioners of Ayurveda wrote about various ways the mind could calm the body and vice versa (Dash & Junius, 1983; Kaptchuk, 2000; Svoboda, 1992). It is also certain that the rich traditions of medical practice in Egypt and the Middle East around 2000 BC (e.g., Mesopotamia, present-day Iraq) also focused on this connection (Udwadia, 2000). Greek philosophers around 300 to 400 BC challenged this notion and proposed that the mind and the body were separate. Reason and rational thought, basic components of the Greek approach to life, were valued more than the biology of the body, but basic bodily substances were hypothesized to cause different diseases. For example, the Greek philosopher Hippocrates's rational explanation of why people get sick concerned the balance of four major bodily fluids (something that he borrowed from Alcmaeon of Crete). He argued that people got sick or showed different symptoms if the amount of one fluid exceeded that of the others. If you had a lot of blood, you would be cheerful; if you had a lot of black bile, you would be sad or melancholic. Hippocrates made many other contributions to the biological study of illness and is considered the father of Western biomedicine. In fact, all doctors take some form of the Hippocratic Oath before they practice medicine (Table 1.4).

The French philosopher René Descartes (famous for his exclamation, "I think therefore I am"—*Ergo summa cogito*) strengthened many centuries later the Greek idea about the separation of the mind from the body. The hundreds of years that people believed that the mind was separate from

TABLE **1.4**
The Hippocratic Oath

I swear by Apollo Physician and Asclepius and Hygieia and Panaceia and all the gods and goddesses, making them my witnesses, that I will fulfil according to my ability and judgment this oath and this covenant: To hold him who has taught me this art as equal to my parents and to live my life in partnership with him, and if he is in need of money to give him a share of mine, and to regard his offspring as equal to my brothers in male lineage and to teach them this art—if they desire to learn it—without fee and covenant; to give a share of precepts and oral instruction and all the other learning to my sons and to the sons of him who has instructed me and to pupils who have signed the covenant and have taken an oath according to the medical law, but no one else. I will apply dietetic measures for the benefit of the sick according to my ability and judgment; I will keep them from harm and injustice. I will neither give a deadly drug to anybody who asked for it, nor will I make a suggestion to this effect. Similarly I will not give to a woman an abortive remedy. In purity and holiness I will guard my life and my art. I will not use the knife, not even on sufferers from stone, but will withdraw in favor of such men as are engaged in this work.

Whatever houses I may visit, I will come for the benefit of the sick, remaining free of all intentional injustice, of all mischief and in particular of sexual relations with both female and male persons, be they free or slaves. What I may see or hear in the course of the treatment or even outside of the treatment in regard to the life of men, which on no account one must spread abroad, I will keep to myself, holding such things shameful to be spoken about. If I fulfil this oath and do not violate it, may it be granted to me to enjoy life and art, being honored with fame among all men for all time to come; if I transgress it and swear falsely, may the opposite of all this be my lot.

Source: Translation from the Greek by Ludwig Edelstein. From Edelstein, L. (1943). *The Hippocratic Oath: Text, translation, and interpretation.* Baltimore: Johns Hopkins Press.

the body helped medical science develop as scientists dissected dead bodies and increased our knowledge of human anatomy. The Greek Galen first pioneered the examination of the dead to find the cause of disease although he worked primarily on animals. Centuries later, the study of human anatomy was fine tuned by Andreas Vesalius (1514–1564) and the Italian artist (and the prototypical Renaissance man) Leonardo Da Vinci. Both drew detailed diagrams of the construction of the human body. Human dissections were conducted rarely and were explicitly banned by the Roman Catholic Church, which deemed dissections unholy. Finally, Descartes brokered a deal with the church resulting from a complex set of sociopolitical factors. Active antagonism had existed between the church and science, but the declining power of the church and the draining of church resources due to the Inquisition, made it easier for Descartes to convince the Holy Father to allow dissections. Descartes essentially argued that because the mind and body were separate, the mind and soul of a person left the body when the person died. Hence, only the biological body was left behind, and it was unimportant. The church accepted this explanation, and human dissections began in earnest.

Cultural Influences on Behavior

Our own health behaviors are largely dependent on the health behaviors of other individuals who share our cultural group.

In the early twentieth century, psychology started to play a part in the examination of health. Part of the reason this involvement came so late is that psychology was not a field of study in its own right until that time. Thinking back to your introductory psychology class, you probably remember that the German William Wundt founded the first psychology laboratory in 1879. The first book in psychology, *Principles of Psychology* by Harvard University psychologist William James, was published in 1897. In a precursor of sorts to the biopsychosocial model, James also wrote *Varieties of Religious Experience* (1902) that referred to spirituality, health, and psychology. Also in the late 1890s, Sigmund Freud first generated his ideas about the structure of the human mind. When one mentions Freud's name, people quickly think of couches, bearded psychologists, and other stereotypical Freudian artifacts. Yes, Freud did have clients lie on his couch while he sat behind them and listened to them speak. Yes, we often see pictures of him in a beard and most movie psychoanalysts are similarly bearded (e.g., Billy Crystal in *Analyze This*). These tidbits aside, Freud was one of the earliest health psychologists, though few would call him such.

How did Freud revolutionize the way we look at illness? Freud was the first to draw attention to the possibility that illness could have psychological causes. Trained as a neuroscientist, Freud had a strong biological background. He was perplexed by clients who reported strong symptoms of illness but who lacked physical evidence of illness. He also noticed the work of Pierre Janet and Franz Anton Mesmer, who cured cases of hysteria with hypnosis. In talking to his clients, Freud discovered that many of their physical illnesses were due to psychological issues. Once these issues were resolved, the physical symptoms disappeared. This focus on the workings of the mind in disease was continued later in the twentieth century by the psychoanalysts Franz Alexander and Helen Flanders Dunbar. Together they established the first formal gathering of individuals interested in studying the influences of the mind on health. This movement within the mainstream medical establishment was coined **psychosomatic medicine**.

Galen

Descartes

Freud

Dunbar

Key Figures in the History of Health Psychology

The new field of psychosomatic medicine had many supporters, which led to the formation of the first society specifically dedicated to the study of mind and body connections. The American Psychosomatic Society (APS) was formed to "promote and advance the scientific understanding of the interrelationships among biological, psychological, social, and behavioral factors in human health and disease, and the integration of the fields of science that separately examine each, and to foster the application of this understanding in education and improved health care" (APS, 2001). In 1936, the New York Academy of Medicine's joint committee on Religion and Medicine headed by Dunbar assembled a collection of the psychosomatic medical literature, together with publications examining the relationship of religion to health. Dunbar's early collection of articles led her to organize the publishing in 1939 of the first journal for this field, *Psychosomatic Medicine*, which still publishes research today. Although the early movement faltered and received mixed attention because it was based heavily on Freudian ideas and case study methods of research, the APS survives and is still active with annual meetings and active members.

Another movement within the field of medicine, called **behavioral medicine**, looks at nonbiological influences on health. Doctors and health care specialists within the medical community were probably always aware that changes in behavior and lifestyle improve health, prevent illness, and reduce symptoms of illness, although they did not focus on this fact. The Society of Behavioral Medicine (SBM), a multidisciplinary, nonprofit organization founded in 1978, is dedicated to studying the influences of behavior on health and well-being. This organization brings together different disciplines—nursing, psychology, medicine, and public health—to form an interdisciplinary team. The society's explicit mission is to "foster the development and application of knowledge concerning the interrelationships of health, illness, and behavior" (Society of Behavioral Medicine, 2001). Like *Psychosomatic Medicine* for the APS, the SBM also has its own journal, *The Annals of Behavioral Medicine*. Another important resource for health psychology and clinical health psychologists in particular is the *International Classification of Diseases, Ninth Revision (ICD-9)*, a classification of diseases and disorders. The connection between

Breathing a vein.

The National Library of Medicine

The National Library of Medicine

Early Cures for Illness

Many bizarre remedies for illness, such as bloodletting and leeches, were used experimentally prior to the discovery of modern medicine.

health psychology and medicine is strong. Even today, health psychology and clinical health psychologists play an important role in the practice of medicine and management of disease (Bennett Johnson, Perry, & Rozensky, 2002).

Other groups of individuals also began to draw attention to the fact that health issues needed to be addressed by a broader approach than the point of view taken by the medical establishment. Medical anthropologists are individuals who are committed to improving public health in societies in economically poor nations. Based on the biological and sociocultural roots of anthropology, medical anthropologists have long considered health and medical care within the context of cultural systems although not necessarily using the tools or theoretical approaches of psychologists. Similarly, medical sociologists are individuals working within the framework of the medical model, focusing on the role of culture and a person's environment in health and illness. There are many fascinating studies of health and behavior conducted within these different fields that we will refer to in this book. These fields and health psychology share common interests and terms. For example, health psychology and medical sociology both are influenced by the field of **epidemiology**—a branch of medicine that studies the frequency, distribution, and causes of different diseases with an emphasis on the role of the physical and social environment. We will also be paying close attention to clear-cut outcome measures used by epidemiologists. For example, we shall look at how different biopsychosocial factors relate to the number of cases of a disease that exist at a given point in time, or **morbidity**, and to the number of deaths related to a specific cause, or **mortality**.

Even within mainstream psychology, researchers in social psychology, personality psychology, cognitive psychology, and clinical psychology realize that the basic theories that they derived to describe and predict behavior easily could be applied in the study of health and well-being. Beyond simply explaining what many laypeople (especially senators in Congress during the late 1960s who begrudged the use of government money to fund psychological studies) considered commonsensical and mundane issues, psychological theorizing can actually save lives! As we will soon discover, social psychological theories form one of the core foundations of health psychological research, and many social phenomena can explain why we do what we do. Are children likely to start smoking? What makes a person more or less likely to exercise or eat well? The answers to each of these questions come from theories derived from basic social psychological research.

WHAT IS HEALTH PSYCHOLOGY?

Health psychology is an interdisciplinary subspecialty of psychology dedicated to promoting and maintaining health and preventing and treating illness (Leventhal, Weinman, Leventhal, & Phillips, 2008; Matarazzo, 1982; Taylor, 1990). Health psychologists pay close attention to the way that thoughts, feelings, behavior, and biological processes all interact with each other to influence health and illness (Belar, McIntyre, & Matarazzo, 2003). In many ways, health psychology is greater than a subfield within the discipline of psychology, as it is built on theoretical ideas and research findings from many other areas in psychology. For example, many of the ways to understand the causes of stress and how we cope come from social and personality psychology. As previously discussed, in the evolution of psychology, even clinical psychologists such as Freud, Alexander, and Dunbar contributed to the development of the field. The biological bases of health have been studied by physiological psychologists. As we discuss in later chapters the ways in which health psychologists try to change behaviors, the influence of behaviorists such as Skinner and Watson will become apparent. Applying basic behaviorist theories (e.g., classical and operant conditioning) can help someone to stop smoking or help you to eat better or exercise more.

Whenever we refer to Health Psychology (with the capital letters) we refer to the subdivision of the American Psychological Association (**APA Division 38**) that is dedicated to:

1. Advancing the contributions of psychology to the understanding of health and illness through basic and clinical research.
2. Encouraging the integration of biomedical information about health and illness with current psychological knowledge.
3. Promoting education and services in the psychology of health and illness.
4. Informing the psychological and biomedical community and the general public about the results of current research and service activities in this area (APA, 2001).

Unlike the Society of Behavioral Medicine or the American Psychosomatic Society, whose members are overwhelmingly physicians, APA's Division of Health Psychology is a group specifically for psychologists. That fact aside, it is also open to (and is driven to foster collaborations with) members of the other health care professions who are interested in the psychological aspects of physical and mental health. The Division's main goals are to (1) understand the etiology and promotion and maintenance of health; (2) prevent, diagnose, treat, and rehabilitate physical and mental illness; (3) study psychological, social, emotional, and behavioral factors in physical and mental illness; and (4) improve the health care system and formulation of health policy.

SYNTHESIZE, EVALUATE, APPLY	• What are the different areas of knowledge/psychology that play a role in health psychology?

- What are the different areas of knowledge/psychology that play a role in health psychology?
- A nine-year study (Berkman & Syme, 1979) showed that people who practiced more healthy behaviors lived longer, but examined men and women over the age of 45 only. What aspect of this finding is a challenge for health psychologists (as we try to change the behaviors of younger adults)?
- How are the three main organizations for health psychology different from each other?
- Contrast the two approaches used by medicine and health psychology. What are components of each?

Main Areas in Health Psychology

The field of health psychology, as well as the contents of this book, is naturally segmented into three areas: (1) stress and coping, (2) health behaviors, and (3) issues in health care. One major area under the umbrella of health psychology is **clinical health psychology**, a broad specialty in professional psychology, that spans the three main segments and in which clinical practitioners work (Belar, 2008). Many health psychologists are clinicians and, although we will discuss clinical issues throughout this book, especially **Evidence-Based Treatments** (Davidson, Trudeau, & Smith, 2006), our focus is on the wider field of health psychology. At the psychological roots of this area of study, the first part of this book will examine the biopsychosocial determinants of stress and then investigate how these same factors can influence coping style. The next part of the book will primarily describe the main health psychological theories relating to why we act in various healthy ways using different health behaviors as examples. We will look at the good (e.g., physical activity), the bad (e.g., eating too much fast food), and the ugly (e.g., seeing what smoking can do to a person's teeth and lungs). The last part of the book will focus on different factors relating to health care. These include the complexities of dealing with chronic and terminal illnesses and the different psychological factors influencing the quality of interactions between doctors and patients. We will begin by discussing how different theories of human development and cultural variations can help us understand our health-related behaviors and our health. We will also demonstrate how cultural differences in development (e.g., parenting styles) can influence health behaviors and health. As you continue studying the book, you will also learn about some of the fascinating ways that different cultures approach health and illness.

A RESEARCH PRIMER

Health psychology relies firmly on the scientific method. The key elements of a science are (1) that it is empirical (relying on sense observations and data) and (2) that it is theory driven. The data or empirical evidence is collected in ethical, rigorously controlled, and standardized ways whether you are identifying causes of stress or testing the psychological effects of an intervention to reduce smoking. The research enterprise is a fascinating one and to get a good feel for the results of research (discussed throughout this book), you should have a good idea of the main research designs and data collection methods (courses in experimental methods and statistics are great companions or foundations for the health psychology course). Understanding the common research methods used by health psychologists and knowing how to interpret some common statistical results will also enable you to make better sense of peer-reviewed journal articles, the source of the information used in writing this book. Even if you learn of results of research on the radio, television, or via the Internet, it is always good practice to go to the original published article to substantiate the results. You will be surprised how often media outlets "spin" a finding to amplify the possible implications. Reading the original sources for yourself (and understanding them) will make you a better consumer of science. Most of you should have already encountered research methods in your introductory psychology courses; therefore, we will discuss briefly the major research designs and their basic issues here and then move on to more complex material, such as distinctive terms, methods, and statistics commonly used in health psychology research.

Major Research Designs

Correlational Studies

The most basic form of research describes relationships between variables. Are heavier people more at risk for cardiovascular disease? Do poorer people smoke more? A **correlation coefficient** is the statistical measure of the association. Correlations range from –1.00 to +1.00 with values closer to 1 (regardless of sign) signifying stronger associations. Positive correlations indicate variables that change in the same direction (e.g., higher weight correlates with higher risk of cardiovascular disease). Negative correlations indicate variables that change in opposite directions (e.g., lower socioeconomic status correlates with higher smoking rates). Most journal articles in health psychology will report correlations between variables. These will either be zero-order or **direct correlations**, in which the relationship between two variables is tested (distress correlated with coping style), or **partial correlations**, where the relationship between two variables is tested while controlling for a third variable (or more). For example, researchers often statistically control for a research participant's age when assessing correlations, which essentially acknowledges the fact that the association between the variables of interest (e.g., distress and coping style) could vary for people of different ages.

A Note on Statistics

As you read journal articles, do not be surprised to see emphasis about correlations around the .2 to .3 level. If 1.00 is the highest, .2 and .3 seem low. They are, but given that there are many factors accounting for any behavior or result, a *statistically significant* correlation in the .2 to .3 range between any two variables suggests a worthy relationship. The "results" section of a journal article will report the significance level of any findings. Statistical analyses with p-values (probability values) less than .05, .01, or .001 (reported as $p < .05$, $p < .01$, or $p < .001$) are significant. A probability value of less than 0.05 suggests that the probability of getting the same result by chance is less than 5 in 100. You can see why $p < 0.001$ is a-significant level.

Be aware: Just as not all change may be statistically significant, not all statistically significant change may be *meaningful* change. We can launch a philosophical debate around the topic of what constitutes meaningful change in learning. However, there is one simple answer that is hard to negate: statistically significant changes that could not have taken place by chance are important. That said, there are some simple factors that can artificially create statistical significance. The most critical to consider is the number of participants being studied (or the sample size). Researchers perform many health psychological studies on hundreds or thousands of participants. Increasing the sample size can make previously insignificant changes significant. There are some safeguards and limiting factors. For example, only phenomena that have a large *effect size* will be significant when the sample size increases. If the psychological intervention or the drug tested or a cognitive behavioral change was not effectual (a simple paraphrase of effect size that adequately conveys its intended meaning), many more participants may not make results significant. Most journal articles report effect size (look for it as one of many Greek letters representing a variety of effect size calculations).

Together with looking at correlational coefficients (reported using the italicized letter r) and effect sizes, the other major statistical tests you will encounter are **analyses of variance (ANOVAs)**, **multivariate analyses of variance (MANOVAs)**, and regression analyses. Both ANOVAs and MANOVAs test for differences between group means. Is the weight loss in one group different from the weight loss in another group (ANOVAs)? If you want to test for differences between a number of variables that are related to each other, you would use a MANOVA (hence, the multivariate). The good news is that just like for a correlation, you are paying attention to the p-value of the statistical test. Look for if it is significant. **Regression analyses** are used to predict the likelihood of an outcome from a list of variables. If you want to predict depressed mood from ethnicity, sex, coping style, and HIV status, you could use a multiple regression analyses (Gurung, Taylor, Kemeny, & Myers, 2004). In regressions, you can actually get a sense of how much of the variance in the dependent variable your predictor variables account for(i.e., variance in the dependent variable equals how the dependent variable is different for different people—why are some people more depressed than others?).

One other statistical test that is relatively common in health psychology articles is the **logistic regression**. This analysis predicts the probability of the occurrence of an event. Articles will often report an **odds ratio**, which is the ratio of the odds of an event occurring in one group to the odds of it occurring in another group. Are men more likely to have a heart attack than women? (See Chapter 13 for the answer). An odds ratio of 1 suggests the phenomenon (e.g., a heart attack) is equally likely in both groups. An odds ratio greater than 1 suggests the phenomenon is more likely to occur in the first group. Being comfortable with some commonly used statistics and analyses will make you a much better consumer of health psychology research and a better health psychologist (see Field, 2005, for a good intro-duction to statistics and for more details on the terms discussed above).

Experimental and Quasi-Experimental Designs

Correlational studies do not allow us to draw causal conclusions. This does not stop the casual reader or the uninformed and can sometimes lead to mild panic where none is warranted. For example, a study found that oral sex was correlated with incidences of mouth cancer (Alberg et al., 2004). Does this mean that practicing oral sex causes mouth cancer? If the study was correla-tional, it does not. In fact, the study also showed that oral sex was highly cor-related with smoking and drinking, two behaviors more likely to cause mouth cancer. **Experimental designs** help us determine causality. In experiments, the researcher manipulates the variable that is believed to be important—the **independent variable**—and measures how changes in this variable influence another variable—the **dependent variable**.

Experiments have two or more groups, each of which experience different levels of the independent variable. If the participants are randomly sampled (everyone in the population has an equal chance of being in the study) and extraneous variables (other variables that may influence the outcome of interest such as socioeconomic status or other health behaviors) are controlled for, then one can be fairly certain that changes in the dependent variable are due to changes in the independent variable. Cause can be determined.

To test whether exercise is good for concentration you can have one group of people exercise (the independent variable) three times a week and the other not exercise. You can then see if the two groups vary in concentra-tion (the dependent variable). In health psychological research, it is often impractical and unethical to manipulate key variables of interest (e.g., making people smoke or have oral sex) so groups that naturally vary in the variable of interest are used instead (e.g., compare groups of people who vary in how much they smoke or have oral sex). Because using naturally occurring groups is not a perfect experiment, such designs are referred to as **quasi-experimental designs**, and the independent variables are called subject variables. Examples of common subject variables are age, sex, ethnicity, personality type, occupa-tion, socioeconomic status, and disease state (level or presence of).

You will also hear about **randomized, controlled, or clinical trials (RCTs)**, in which one group gets an experimental drug or intervention treat-ment and a second group unknowingly gets a **placebo** (an inactive substance that appears similar to the experimental drug) or nothing (the control group). A large number of evidence-based treatment reviews and clinical interventions use RCTs (e.g., Barrera, Strycker, MacKinnon, & Toobert, 2008). Perhaps one of the best examples of an RCT is the Women's Health Initiative study that was launched in 1991 and in which over 161,000 healthy postmenopausal women were given hormone replacement pills or a placebo. Researchers stopped the study before completion because the results indicated that women taking the pills were actually more at risk for heart disease (Manson et al., 2003). To make matters worse, recent results suggest that even after stopping the study, women who received the hormone replacement pills still had a higher risk of heart disease (Heiss et al., 2008).

Cross-Sectional and Longitudinal Designs

Research can also be **cross-sectional**, conducted at one point in time, or **longitudinal**, conducted over a period of time and often involving many measures of the key variables. Cross-sectional studies often sample a large number of people and examine different cultural groups in the sample comparing men and women, and people of different ethnicities.

Research can be **prospective**, following disease-free participants over a period to determine whether certain variables (e.g., eating too much fast food) predict disease, or **retrospective**, studying participants with a disease and tracing their histories of health behaviors to determine what caused the disease.

There are a number of well-known prospective studies. One study is the Women's Health Initiative described previously. Another study that you will see many references to in the media and in health psychology research, is the Nurses' Health Study (NHS). Started in 1976, the NHS and the NHS II are among the largest prospective studies of the risk factors for major chronic diseases in women (e.g., Tamimi et al., 2005). Approximately 122,000 registered nurses in 11 states were followed over time and findings shed light on a variety of health issues ranging from preventing premenopausal colorectal cancer and breast cancer to the impact of weight on cancer risk (Nurses' Health Study, 2008).

Other Key Terms

Epidemiological studies often report **prevalence rates**, the proportion of the population that has a particular disease at a particular time (commonly reported as cases per 1,000 or 100,000 people), and **incidence rates**, the frequency of new cases of the disease during a year. Other important terms to watch for in the reporting of health psychological research are **relative risk**, the ratio of incidence or prevalence of a disease in an exposed group to the incidence or prevalence of the disease in an unexposed group, and **absolute risk**, a person's chance of developing a disease independent of any risk that other people may have.

SYNTHESIZE, EVALUATE, APPLY

- What are the pros and cons of different research designs?
- What are some constraints you might experience doing health psychology research?

FOCUS ON CURRENT ISSUES

Profile of a Multicultural America

What does it mean to be American? The presidential race of 2008 brought race and sex, two of the most salient and visible forms of cultural diversity, to the fore. For the first time in the history of the United States, an African American man, Barack Hussein Obama, and a woman, Hillary Rodham Clinton, were on the national stage prominently poised to be democratic candidates for president. The months of campaigning were often accompanied by discussion of

(continues)

FOCUS ON CURRENT ISSUES *(continued)*

not just their positions and platforms, but their race and sex. For the first time in many years people had to confront the fact that for all of America's history, presidents have been European American men. Is that profile what it means to be American? Does being American mean being White? Of course, it does not. American citizens have many different skin colors, religions, and styles of dressing, and that is only the beginning of our country's diversity. America consists of a variety of cultural groups, and it is critical to remind ourselves that not only is the country multicultural, but we ourselves are also all multicultural.

The most recent census data lists the population of the United States at approximately 302 million. That number can be broken down along different cultural lines. An example of a "cultural group" that most people tend to think of first is ethnicity. Of that 302-million population, approximately 13 percent are African American or Black, approximately 4 percent are Asian American (including Americans of different Asian backgrounds such as Chinese, Japanese, Korean, and Indian), and approximately 1 percent are American Indians or Native Americans. The remaining 82 percent of the population are considered European American or White and include people of Latin American and Spanish ancestry. Commonly referred to as Latinos, the preferred term, or Hispanic (a term applied to this ethnic group by the U.S. government in the 1980 Census), the truth is that people in this same group have their own names for their groups depending on which part of the United States they live in and their specific country of origin. For example, *Hispanic* is preferred in the Southeast and much of Texas, New Yorkers use both *Hispanic* and *Latino*, and in Chicago, *Latino* is preferred (Shorris, 1992). Ethnicity is just one way to divide cultural lines.

A second type of "culture" is religion. Of the 302 million Americans, the majority are Christians, accounting for 84 percent (57 percent Protestant and 27 percent Catholic). You may be surprised by the next largest percentage: Eight percent of Americans do not have any religious affiliation. It is difficult to say whether they are nonbelievers or just practice some personal form of religion. Of the remaining, 2 percent are Jewish. Importantly, some popular religious groups are not present in large numbers. Testifying to the fact that we as human beings tend to overestimate the actual occurrence of something just based on the extent to which we hear about it (referred to as the availability heuristic), Muslims only constitute a minute part of the U.S. population (between 3.5 and 6 million). Because of political events (e.g., trouble in the Middle East and the War on Terrorism in Afghanistan and Iraq, areas whose populations are predominantly Muslim), many Americans believe that there are many Muslims in the United States (and unfortunately have prejudices against them), when in fact they are a very small minority.

We can also think about culture in terms of ethnicity, different age groups, SES, or different geographical regions. Your gender and biological sex contribute in large part to your sense of self. Different age groups—children, adolescents, teenagers, young adults, or older adults—may experience different stressors. When you break down the United States population along these different lines, you realize that there are many such groups and that each has its own specific health issues. The numbers in each of these groups also change over time. For example, in 2001, there were 35 million people in the United States above age 65. In 1990, there were only 31 million in this age group. This difference in the age profile can have implications for health care. People living in different parts of the country may have different health behaviors (e.g. the southeastern states such as Kentucky and Virginia show some of the highest levels of smoking). A person's SES can have many implications for his or her health. If you have money, you can afford healthy food and higher quality health services. In 2001, the median or normative household income level was $42,228 (Census Bureau), but 30 percent of American households were making less than $25,000 a year. That is not much money on which to support a family. As you can see, America is multicultural indeed, and we will soon see how these different aspects of culture interact to influence behaviors and health.

SUMMARY

- There are many different definitions of health, each varying in its culture of origin. Western medicine sees health more as the absence of disease whereas other cultures see health more as a balance of opposing forces or spiritual harmony. The most common definition is that used by the World Health Organization.
- Culture is broadly defined and includes ethnicity, sex, religion, gender, and nationality. Various dimensions of culture shape our health behaviors and our general health. Individualism and collectivism are examples of basic cultural dimensions. Socioeconomic status and sex are two of the most important cultural variables, each leading to a variety of health differences.
- Health psychology uses a biopsychosocial approach. This approach focuses on the biological, psychological, and sociocultural factors that influence health and health behaviors.
- Theorizing about the extent to which the mind and the body are connected has varied over time and across cultures. The ancient Chinese and Indians saw the two as connected, but the Greeks and other Europeans saw the mind and body as separate. Today we recognize that the two are clearly interconnected, and this connection is critical to understanding health and illness.
- Freud was the first psychologist to link the mind and body together and hypothesize psychological bases for physiological problems. His early views led to the formation of the first organization of behavioral medicine in the late 1930s followed by further growth in the late 1960s.
- Health psychology as a unique area of psychology came to the forefront in the 1970s and has since grown. Its main goals are the prevention of illness, the promotion of health, the understanding of the biopsychosocial aspects of physical and mental illness, and the improvement of the health care system. The main areas of health psychology are stress and coping, health behaviors, and issues in health care.
- Three major organizations cater to those using the biopsychosocial model.
- There are many different types of research design and data collection methods. Research is primarily correlational or experimental in nature. Correlations are the assessment of association between variables. In experiments, researchers manipulate key variables (independent variables) to see the effects on others (dependent variables).

TEST YOURSELF

Check your understanding of the topics in this chapter by answering the following questions. Answers appear in the Appendix.

1. The most comprehensive definition of health is provided by the:
   a. Biomedical model.
   b. Hippocratic model.
   c. World Health Organization.
   d. Population Health model.
   e. International Classification of Functioning.

2. Which of the following is the primary focus of health psychology?
   a. health promotion, maintenance and recovery

b. etiology and correlates of health and illness
c. revising the health care system
d. finding the cure for diseases like HIV and cancer
e. studying patient-practitioner interactions

3. _____ refers to the number of cases of a disease that exist at some given point in time. _____ refers to the number of deaths due to particular causes.
   a. Morbidity; Mortality
   b. Mortality; Morbidity
   c. Epidemiology; Pathogenesis
   d. Etiology; Epidemiology
   e. Morbidity; Etiology

4. The Greek physician best known for dissections and providing us with anatomy data was:
   a. Plato.
   b. Galen.
   c. Hippocrates.
   d. Descartes.
   e. Aginostophenes.

5. The most common definition of health across cultures is health as:
   a. The absence of disease.
   b. Spiritual happiness.
   c. Communion with God.
   d. A state of balance.

6. One of the first organizations to combine medicine with psychology, started by Dunbar and Alexander was:
   a. Health Psychology.
   b. Society for Behavioral Medicine.
   c. Psychosomatic Medicine.

d. Mind-Body Institute.
e. National Institute of Mental Health (NIMH).

7. Culture is best defined as:
   a. A set of beliefs shared by a group.
   b. Race and ethnicity.
   c. Religion, family values, and race.
   d. The values of our parents and family members.

8. One of the most powerful predictors of health disparities in North America is:
   a. Sex.
   b. Socioeconomic status.
   c. Race.
   d. Ethnicity.

9. In studying about cultural differences in health, we should remember that:
   a. In-group differences are often larger than between-group differences.
   b. Between-group differences are often larger than in-group differences.
   c. Racial differences outweigh all other cultural differences.
   d. Most cultural differences are insignificant from a global level.

10. Studies where one group gets an experimental drug and another gets a placebo are called:
    a. Randomized clinical trials.
    b. Correlational studies.
    c. Quasi-experimental studies.
    d. Longitudinal studies.

WEB RESOURCES

Visit the companion website at **www.cengage.com/ psychology/gurung**, where you will find online resources for this book, including chapter-by-chapter quizzes, Web links, and more!

World Health Organization
http://www.who.int/en

Explore the different pages of the main menu for health initiatives around the world.

Health Psychology
http://www.health-psych.org

Webpage of Division 38: Health Psychology of the American Psychological Association. Check out the education and training page for information on careers and the "What's New" section for hot topics in the field.

American Psychosomatic Society
http://www.psychosomatic.org

The educational resources link has a number of interesting reports, white papers, and some interesting PowerPoint presentations.

Society for Behavioral Medicine
http://www.sbm.org

This is another great education, training, and career development link with a frequently updated listing of news and research findings.

KEY TERMS, CONCEPTS, AND PEOPLE

absolute risk, 28

Alexander, Franz, 20

analyses of variance (ANOVAs), 26

APA Division 38, 23

ayurveda, 7

behavioral medicine, 21

biomedical approach, 6

biopsychosocial approach, 17

clinical health psychology, 24

context, 11

correlation coefficient, 25

correlational studies, 27

cross-sectional, 28

culture, 11

dependent variable, 27

Descartes, René, 18

direct correlations, 25

Dunbar, Helen Flanders, 20

epidemiology, 22

evidence-based treatments, 24

experimental designs, 27

Freud, Sigmund, 20

Galen, 19

health psychology, 23

health, 5

Hippocrates, 18

incidence rates, 28

independent variable, 27

James, William, 20

level of analysis, 11

logistic regression, 26

longitudinal, 28

morbidity, 22

mortality, 22

multivariate analyses of variance (MANOVAs), 26

odds ratio, 26

partial correlations, 25

placebo, 27

prevalence rates, 28

prospective, 28

psychosomatic medicine, 20

quasi-experimental designs, 27

randomized, controlled, or clinical trials (RCTs), 27

regression analyses, 26

relative risk, 28

retrospective, 28

sex, 14

socioeconomic status, 12

traditional Chinese medicine, 6

WHO, 5

ESSENTIAL READINGS

Baum, A., & Posluszny, D. M. (1999). Health psychology: Mapping biobehavioral contributions to health and illness. *Annual Review of Psychology*, 50, 137–163.

Matarazzo, J. D. (1980). Behavioral health and behavioral medicine: Frontiers for a new health psychology. *American Psychologist*, 35(9), 807–817.

Suls, J., & Rothman, A. (2004). Evolution of the biopsychosocial model: Prospects and challenges for health psychology. *Health Psychology*, 23(2), 119–126.

Taylor, S. E. (1990). Health psychology: The science and the field. *American Psychologist*, 45(1), 40–50.

Cultural Approaches to Health

You are probably not aware of the number of things that you take for granted. There are many facts that you probably accept easily: The earth is round. It revolves around the sun. These you know. You also may believe you know why some things happen the way they do. If you stay outside in the cold rain without a raincoat, you believe you will catch a cold (at least that is what your mom always told you). If you eat too much fatty food, you know you will put on weight. Every culture has its own beliefs. Many Southeast Asian mothers place a black spot on their babies' heads to ward away the "evil eye" that could cause their babies harm. Kabala-following celebrities, such as Madonna, wear red bracelets for the same reason. Some religious groups, such as the Christian Scientists, believe that the use of excessive medication is against God's will. All of us grow up with understandings of how various illnesses are caused. These understandings come from the cultural groups of which we are a part. However, we are not always aware that our understandings of the causes of our good health and of the treatment of sicknesses are culturally dependent. If we believe a virus or bacteria caused an infection, we will be willing to use antibiotic medications to treat it. What if you believed that an infection was caused by the looks of a jealous neighbor or because you had angered the spirits of the wind?

In most of the countries around the globe, health is understood using either the Western evidence-based medical approach or traditional indigenous approaches (Prasadarao, 2009). In traditional systems, wide ranges of practitioners provide help. For example, in Sub-Saharan Africa, there are four types of traditional healers who provide health care: traditional birth attendants (TBAs); faith healers; diviners and spiritualists; and herbalists. The TBAs focus on pregnancy-related problems and offer treatment to women. Faith healers, mostly men, use religious scriptures, prayers, and holy water in their treatment approach. Diviners, mostly women, seriously ill themselves prior to becoming healers, specialize in diagnosing illness through divination. They act as mediums between people and their ancestors and Gods. Spiritualists use supernatural forces in diagnosis and treatment. Herbalists, mostly men, apply herbal medicines in their healing approach (Stekelenburg et al., 2005).

Even in the United States, health beliefs and health behaviors vary by cultural groups (Landrine, & Klonoff, 1992; 2001). The majority of the population of the United States is of European origin, with the largest ancestral roots being traceable to Germany (15%), Ireland (11%), the United Kingdom (9%), and Italy (6%). Major racial and national minority groups include Hispanics, African American (either of U.S., African, or Caribbean parentage), Chinese, Filipinos, and Japanese (U.S. Census Bureau, 2004). According to the 2000 Census, it was estimated that European Americans comprised

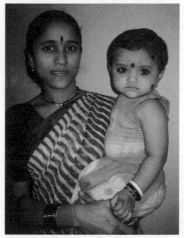

Courtesy of Regan Gurung

The Evil Eye

In cultures around the world, the evil eye is the name for a sickness transmitted—usually without intention—by someone who is envious, jealous, or covetous. Latino and Asian Indian mothers try to make sure their children do not get the "evil eye" by placing large black dots on their children's foreheads.

75.1 percent of the population; Hispanics, 12.5 percent; African Americans, 12.3 percent; Asians and Pacific Islanders, 3.7 percent; and Native Americans (American Indians, Eskimos, and Aleuts), 0.9 percent. Italian Americans in New York may have different traditional ways of approaching illness than do Polish Americans in Milwaukee. Women in New Mexico and men in Chicago may have the same physical problem, but their doctors must take into account the existing differences in their patients' social systems (differences in culture, beliefs, family structure, and economic class) and their patients' expectations of health care and health care workers to cure them. This chapter describes the major philosophical approaches followed by Americans of different cultural backgrounds. These different approaches can explain variances in health behaviors. Remember that an effective health psychologist has to be ready to deal with the diversity of people and their beliefs. To help a person stay healthy and recover when sick, you must understand what his or her specific understanding of health and sickness is. Once you understand, you can use variations on the basic tools and theories to intervene and help. I will describe some of America's diverse ethnic and religious beliefs as they relate to health, focusing on contemporary views of the Chinese Taoist and East Indian Ayurvedic approaches to health, Latino folk medicine (curanderismo), and American Indian spiritualism. Be aware that the majority of the beliefs and practices we will discuss have not passed the critical eye of Western scientific inquiry (e.g., spirits cause illness). However, as all good psychologists know, if someone believes something strongly enough, then those beliefs can influence that person's behavior and reactions. Thus, it is important to know what different people believe. Even if you do not believe it yourself, shared understanding facilitates communication and successful health and healing.

VARIETIES OF WORLD MEDICINE

Different cultures have different definitions of health. Each culture evolves with a unique understanding of the creation of human beings and our purpose in life. According to archaeological evidence, our ancestors probably believed that our bodies worked because of magic. Potions, rings, charms, and bracelets were devised to rid the body of the harmful demons and spirits that brought illness and suffering. Some of these ancient beliefs often find their way into popular literature and underlie our enchantment with heady fare such as the *Lord of the Rings* trilogy, the *Chronicles of Narnia*, and even the light and fanciful *Harry Potter* series. A person's eyes in particular were believed to be the sites of power and magic, whereas animal eyes routinely were used in a range of treatments (Monte, 1993).

Globally, health beliefs and practices are closely tied to religion and nationality, which are components of culture not given much attention in Western medicine. In predominantly Hindu countries such as India, for example, modern medical practitioners are complemented by traditional healers who offer treatment for physical and mental illness in rural villages. There are three types of these healers: Vaids, who are healers practicing indigenous systems of medicine; Mantarwadis, who are healers using astrology and charms for cure; and Patris, who are healers acting as mediums for spirits and demons (Kapur, 1979). The Vaids practice **Ayurveda**—the traditional Indian medicine system—and they offer treatment predominantly by administering medications. These Vaids believe that the illness is caused by "an imbalance between the natural elements" brought forth by environmental factors, certain diets, uninhibited sexual indulgence, and the influence of demons. These factors cause "excess heat, cold, bile, wind, or fluid secretions" leading to the development of physical and mental illness (Kapur, 1979). In Muslim countries such as Pakistan, traditional healers include khalifs, gadinashins, imams, hakims, and others who practice magic and sorcery (Karim, Saeed, Rana, Mubbasher, & Jenkins, 2004). Farooqi (2006) studied the nature of traditional healing consultation in 87 Muslim psychiatric patients treated at public hospitals in Pakistan. This study revealed that 55 percent to 73 percent of patients with various psychiatric disorders sought help from one or more traditional healers.

Although still changing, our understanding of the body crystallized about 5,000 years ago when the Chinese, Indians, Greeks, and Egyptians began to study the body extensively. Table 2.1 shows the evolution of different medical systems. The medical traditions and different approaches to health held by most Americans today derive from these early systems.

SYNTHESIZE, EVALUATE, APPLY	• What are your main beliefs about the causes and cures of illnesses? • From where do your beliefs come? What evidence do you need to support your beliefs?

TABLE **2.1**

Key Figures and Medical Events in World History: Many of these key figures and events are mentioned in this chapter and throughout the text. However, the history of health psychology is rich, and you may find it worthwhile to research other key figures and events on your own. See the notes at the end of the chapter for suggested readings.

Western Medicine	Chinese Traditional Medicine	American Indian	Mexican/Mexican American Curanderismo	Other World Cultures and Medicine
Greeks—Hippocrates (400 B.C.)	The Yellow Emperor's Classic of Internal Medicine (approximately 100 B.C.)	Europeans first witness native rituals and traditions (approximately A.D. 1500)	Aztec, Mayan influences— (dates unknown)	Mesopotamia (4000 B.C.)
Galen (100 B.C.)			15th-century Spanish-Moorish medicine	Indian Ayurveda (4000 B.C.)
Avicenna (A.D. 1000)				Egypt (3000 B.C.),
Da Vinci (1500s)		Folk medicine passed on orally for centuries	Folk medicine passed on orally for centuries	Iti (2500 B.C.),
Vesalius (1600s)				Imhotep (2700 B.C.)
Harvey (1600s)				Unani (A.D. 900)
Pasteur (1800s)				
Roentgen (1800s)				
Fleming (Penicillin) (1928)				

WESTERN BIOMEDICINE

The most common approach to medicine, Western biomedicine, is derived from the work of Greek physicians, such as Hippocrates and Galen. Western biomedicine is the practice of medicine that most Americans support. American medical schools, hospitals, and emergency rooms all use this Western approach. Egocentrically, most Americans refer to any other approach to health and wellness as **complementary and alternative medicine**. Chinese acupuncture is perhaps the most commonly known "alternative" medicine, but millions of Americans also practice other means to improve their health (e.g., the use of herbal supplements). Other traditional beliefs and practices will be discussed later in this chapter.

Let's start with the most common reference point, Western biomedicine. Also referred to as modern medicine, conventional medicine, or **allopathy**, Western biomedicine is one of the most dominant forms of health care in the world today. Hallmarks of this approach are an increasing reliance on technology and the use of complex scientific procedures for the diagnosis and treatment of illness. Treatments using this approach are designed to cause the opposite effect as that created by the disease. If you have a fever, you are prescribed medication to reduce the temperature. Western biomedicine views the body as a biochemical machine with distinct parts. Often called **reductionist,** Western biomedicine searches for the single smallest unit responsible for the illness. Western doctors try to localize the cause of an illness to the parts directly surrounding the original point of the problem.

Greek Roots

Western biomedicine often claims the fourth-century B.C. Greek, Hippocrates, as its "father," primarily because he was the first to separate medicine from religion and myth and to bring scientific and analytical reasoning to health care. There were physicians before Hippocrates. In the third millennium B.C., physicians in ancient Mesopotamia (modern Iraq) developed an official medical system based on a diagnostic framework that derived from sources as varied as omens and divination techniques and the inspection of livers of sacrificed animals (Porter, 2002). Treatments were coordinated by a lead physician and combined religious rites and empirical treatments such as the use of drugs and practice of surgery. Similarly, in Egypt, the Pharaohs also had a line of physicians. There was Iri, Keeper of the Royal Rectum (the Pharaoh's enema expert), and the most famous, Imhotep, chief physician to the Pharaoh Zozer, both of whom used large amounts of religious rituals to aid their curing (Udwadia, 2000). Essentially, secular medicine only appeared in the Greek-speaking world as practiced by the fifth-century B.C. Hippocratic doctors.

Personality psychologists often recount Hippocrates's humoral theory of what made people different. He argued that our personalities were a function of the level of certain bodily fluids or humors. If you had a lot of black bile, you would be sad or melancholic. If you had a lot of blood, you would be cheerful or sanguine. Because there were very few explicit cures back then, the etiology of disease had not yet been sufficiently mapped out; one of the main roles of the physician was as support provider. Beyond this supportive element of the medical practitioner, biomedical doctors use few of Hippocrates's healing methods today. A few centuries later, Galen, the "emperor" of medicine under the Roman Empire, and much later the Italian artist Leonardo da Vinci (in the fifteenth to sixteenth centuries) and the Flemish physician Andreas Vesalius (sixteenth century), greatly advanced Western biomedicine with their studies of human anatomy. William Harvey, an English physician, first described the circulation of blood and the functioning of the heart in 1628. Biomedicine had its first major boost with the discovery of the high-power microscope. The Dutch naturalist Antonius van Leeuwenhoek ground lenses to magnify objects 300 times. Compare this magnification to that of the electron microscope, invented in 1932, which magnifies specimens to a power of 5 million. Here is a *trivia question*: What was one of the first specimens observed under the lens? (Answer: Human sperm. Leeuwenhoek was careful to establish that the specimen was a "residue after conjugal coitus" and not a product of "sinfully defiling" himself, Leeuwenhoek, 1677, in Roach, 2006).

Technological Innovations

Western biomedicine has strong ties to technology. Once the microscope became widely used, blood, saliva, and other bodily fluids were closely examined, leading to a better understanding of the structures and functions of a wide variety of cells. Louis Pasteur really took the next big leap for medicine. As one of the most significant events in the nineteenth century, Pasteur proved that viruses and bacteria could cause disease. In 1878, Pasteur presented his germ theory to the French Academy of Medicine (Udwadia, 2000). Just a few years later in 1885, the German scientist Wilhelm Roentgen discovered X-rays. Roentgen discovered that passing highly charged waves of energy through the body and then onto a sensitive photographic plate created accurate images of the body's interior. This technological advance enabled doctors to look into the body to see what was causing illnesses or problems and together with the microscope took the diagnosis of illness to new heights. More advances in the twentieth century, such as magnetic resonance imaging (MRI) and computerized axial tomography (CAT) scans, led to closer examinations of the body and bodily functions, especially the brain. Technology, by introducing the study of the cellular level, fueled the drive of Western medicine to find the answers to the causes of illnesses and death. Similar to the behavioral psychologist, Western medicinal practitioners primarily focus on what can be observed. The presence of observable factors (e.g., cancerous cells or bacteria) thereby explains any move away from positive health.

Cures and treatment, especially modern pharmacology, developed to attack ailments in the body. Medicines, using a biomedical approach can be defined as essentially concentrated purified chemical substances that target a particular aspect of the disease process. The chemical composition of some drugs (e.g., **opioids**) mirrors that of naturally occurring substances (e.g., **opiates**). For example, morphine, an opioid that was first extracted in 1805, is identical to chemicals produced by opiates in our body, as there are receptors that accept morphine in our brains. Other milestones in the development of drugs include the discovery of antibacterial sulfonamides in 1935 and the production of antibiotics such as penicillin in the 1940s (although it was first discovered in 1928). Many thousands of different drugs are available today for nearly every ache, pain, or irritation you may have.

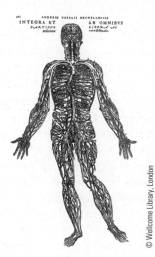

© Wellcome Library, London

© Wellcome Library, London

Early Drawings of Anatomy

Some of the earliest drawings of anatomy were done by the Flemish physician Andreas Vesalius.

The other main element of Western biomedicine is surgery. First practiced by early Egyptians and Peruvians 6,000 years ago, surgery has evolved into an art. If an X-ray reveals a problem or a miniscule camera detects a problem in a vein, artery, or one of the many ducts and tubes that we have (e.g., gastric tract or pulmonary tract), skilled surgeons open up the body and attempt to remedy the problem. The first coronary bypass was performed in 1951 and the first heart transplant was performed in 1967. While major surgical milestones are relatively recent, today, there are few operations still deemed medically impossible. The reliance on technology and the evolution of pharmacology and surgery signal the main approach of Western biomedicine to healing. If you visit a medical doctor with a problem, the routine is straightforward. Your answers to the doctor's questions guide what tests, X-ray studies, or scans you will need. Subsequent test results help the doctor identify the disease-causing agents and medicines or surgical method needed to cure the problem. Health, according to this model, is the absence of disease. The Western doctor starts with a symptom, searches for the underlying mechanisms or causes, and attempts to fight the disease with drugs or surgery. Most Americans believe that germs cause disease and expect to take some sort of pill to treat the disease. This main belief of Western medicine is very different from the beliefs and approaches of other cultural groups.

SYNTHESIZE, EVALUATE, APPLY	• Identify the two most significant events in medical history. Rationalize your choice. • What evidence would you need to see before you tried a new treatment? • Why would medical inventions and innovation make folk medicine use less likely?

TRADITIONAL CHINESE MEDICINE

Traditional Chinese Medicine (TCM) is probably used to treat more people than any other form of medicine (largely because China is the most populated country in the world). However, even in North America, there are a large number of TCM schools and practitioners. In fact, acupuncture, one form of TCM, is covered by most health insurance policies (acupuncture will be discussed in the Focus section at the end of this chapter). Feng shui is not a part of TCM, but if you have heard of this Chinese art of arranging your living space to "optimize energy flow," you will have some feel for this very different approach to life. In fact, you will see that you may have been exposed to many aspects of the beliefs underlying TCM.

In TCM, the body is treated as a whole. Each part of the body is intrinsically connected to other parts of the body and to what is happening around the person. Critical elements of a healthy life include a person's food choices, relationships, and emotional life. In TCM, everyone is a part of a larger creation and lives and flourishes in unison with it. In stark contrast to reductionist Western biomedicine that focuses on a cellular microscopic level of diagnosis, TCM is macroscopic. In TCM, humankind is viewed in relation to nature and the physical laws that govern it. Some interesting paradoxes are seen when we compare Western medicine with TCM. Although TCM does not have the concept of a nervous system nor does it recognize the endocrine system, TCM still treats problems the West calls endocrine and neurological disorders. TCM also uses terminology that may appear bizarre to a Westerner. For example, diseases are thought to be caused by imbalances in yin and yang or by too much "heat" or "wind."

Sources of Illness

Two main systems categorize the forces identified in TCM that influence health and well-being: yin and yang (Figure 2.1) and the five phases. According to one Chinese philosophy, all life and the entire universe originated from a single unified source called **Tao** (pronounced "dow," like the stock market index, *Dow* Jones). The main ideas about the Tao are encompassed in a 5,000-word poem called the *Tao Te Ching* written about 2,500 years ago that describes a way of life from the reign of the "Yellow Emperor" Huang Ti (Reid, 1989). In fact, Chinese medicine is based on *The Yellow Emperor's Classic of Internal Medicine* (approximately 100 B.C.). The Tao is an integrated and undifferentiated whole with two opposing forces—the *yin* and the *yang*—that combine to create everything in the universe.

Yin and yang are mutually interdependent, constantly interactive, and potentially interchangeable forces. As you can see in Figure 2.1, each yin and yang contains the seed of the other (the little dot in the center of each comma-shaped component). The circle represents the supreme source, or Tao. Yin translates to "shady side of a hill" whereas yang translates to "sunny side of the hill." Yin is traditionally thought of as darkness, the moon, cold, and female, whereas yang is thought of as light, the sun, hot, and male. In TCM, 10 vital organs are divided into five pairs, each consisting of one "solid" yin organ and one "hollow" yang organ. TCM practitioners believe that the yin organs—the heart, liver, pancreas, kidney, and lungs—are more vital than the yang organs, and dysfunctions of yin organs cause the greatest health problems. The paired yang organs are the gallbladder, small intestine, large intestine, and bladder. A healthy individual has a balanced amount of yin and yang. If a person is sick, his or her forces are out of balance. Specific symptoms relate to an excess of either yin or yang. For example, if you are flushed, have a fever, are constipated, and have high blood pressure, you have too much yang.

FIGURE **2.1** The Chinese Symbol for Yin and Yang
The two halves represent the complementary nature of all energy in the universe.

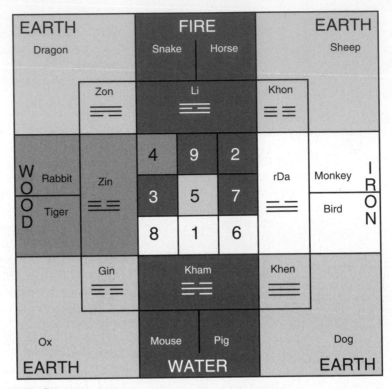

FIGURE **2.2** The Five Elements with Related Numerals and Animals

The five elements are in effect the five energies that, according to Taoist cosmology, comprise the energy matrix of the universe. In Traditional Chinese Medicine theory, these five dynamic bodies (fire, water, wood, earth, and metal) balance the internal organs of the human body.

The five phases or elemental activities refer to specific active forces and illustrate the intricate associations that the ancient Chinese saw between human beings and nature (Figure 2.2). Energy, or **qi** (pronounced "chee"), another critical aspect of TCM, moves within the body in the same pattern as it does in nature with each season and with different foods helping to optimize energy flow within the body. The five elements of wood, fire, earth, metal, and water each link to a season of the year, a specific organ, and a specific food (Table 2.2). Each element has specific characteristics, is generated by one of the other forces, and is suppressed by another. For example, wood generates fire that turns things to earth that forms metals. The heart is ruled by fire, the liver by wood, and the kidneys by water. Fire provides qi to the heart and then passes on qi to the earth element and correspondingly to the stomach, the spleen, and pancreas. Figure 2.3 illustrates how the different elements, seasons, organs, and foods interact.

Figure 2.3 also illustrates how one system depends on another. TCM doctors utilize such diagrams to treat patients. Let's say that a person eats too much salt, which causes kidney disorders. The kidney and bladder (the

TABLE **2.2**
The Chinese Elements and Associations

Elements	Wood	Fire	Earth	Metal	Water
Colors	Blue/green	Red	Yellow	White	Black
Symbols	Dragon	Phoenix	Caldron	Tiger	Tortoise
Seasons	Spring	Summer	Between	Autumn	Winter
Months	1–2	4–5	3, 6, 9, 12	7–8	10–11
Conditions	Rain	Heat	Wind	Clear	Cold
Directions	East	South	Center	West	North
Planets	Jupiter	Mars	Saturn	Venus	Mercury
Days	Thursday	Tuesday	Saturday	Friday	Wednesday
Animals	Scaled	Winged	Naked	Furred	Shelled
Actions	Countenance	Sight	Thought	Speech	Listening
Senses	Sight	Taste	Touch	Smell	Hearing
Sounds	Calling	Laughing	Singing	Lamenting	Moaning
Tastes	Sour	Bitter	Sweet	Acrid/spicy	Salty
Smells	Goatish	Burning	Fragrant	Rank	Rotten
Organs	Liver	Heart	Spleen	Lungs	Kidneys

Source: Kaptchuk (2000).

water element) control the heart and small intestine (fire). Consequently, kidney disorders cause heart disorders and high blood pressure. To treat the condition, the TCM doctor treats the controlling element, water, by reducing the intake of salt, oils, and fats (which influences body water levels) and increasing mild aerobic exercise (fire).

Treatment

In TCM, optimal health consists of balancing yin and yang and optimizing the smooth flow of qi through the body by the coordination of the five elements. Qi flows through the body in 12 precise, orderly patterns called meridians. Meridians translate from the Chinese term *jing-luo* to mean "to go through something that connects or attaches." In Chinese meridian theory, meridian channels are unseen but embody a form of informational network (Kaptchuk, 2000). The 12 meridians are associated with organs in the body. Two additional meridians unify different systems (Figure 2.4). Blocked meridians can cause illness by bringing about hyperactivity of certain organs and underactivity of others. Without the right amount of qi, the organs, tissues, and cells no longer eliminate waste and therefore, with the accumulation of such toxins, harbor more disease. Thus, many symptoms of diseases are interpreted as the body's efforts to cure itself. The runny nose and sweating of a cold and fever are the body's ways of eliminating the underlying

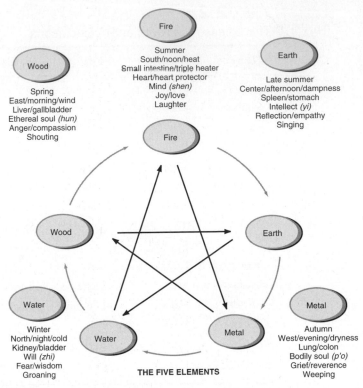

FIGURE **2.3** Balance between Seasons and Organs

The Five-element theory provides us with an understanding of how our bodies are linked to the seasons, elements, and emotions.

conditions that cause the disease. The meridians can be cleared and qi recharged with acupuncture and specific diets.

The trained TCM physician focuses on both the physiology and the psychology of the individual. Yes, this is similar to the way health psychologists function but with different tools and underlying assumptions. All relevant information, including the symptoms and patients' general life characteristics, such as whether they are happy with their jobs and what they are eating, are all woven together into a "pattern of disharmony." Instead of asking, what is *causing* what? the doctor asks, what is *related to* what? The aim of treatment is to settle the imbalance. The TCM practitioner prescribes massage, acupuncture or acupressure, herbs, dietary changes, and exercises such as *qi gong* as primary treatments. Qi gong combines movement, meditation, and the regulation of breathing to enhance the flow of qi in the body to improve blood circulation and to promote immune function.

For some North Americans, the preceding sections may read like Greek (or Chinese!). Meridians? Qi? Yin? Yang? Does any of this work? TCM has been the subject of considerable study for more than 50 years (Kaptchuk, 2000). The Chinese have performed many experimental analyses of traditional medicine, and the results have been positive enough to give TCM and Western

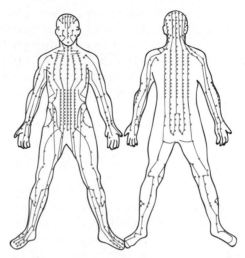

FIGURE **2.4** Meridians

Meridians are the passageways of qi and blood flow through the body. Meridians consist of channels and branches reaching every part of the body. Meridians act as the important route for circulating qi.

biomedicine an equal place in modern Chinese hospitals. Not only do many doctors in China provide patients with a prescription for pharmacological drugs as they would receive here in America, but they also provide a prescription for TCM cures (e.g., herbs or ointments). In many Chinese hospitals, the two dispensaries sit side by side. Most patients in China as well as in America have the choice of which method to use. Western medicine is used more often for acute problems (by Chinese and Chinese Americans), and TCM is used more often for chronic problems.

There is a growing body of research being conducted on different TCMs. Some empirical studies suggest that TCMs are no more effective than Western medicines. For example, 620 cocaine-dependent patients took part in a randomized clinical trial where one third of the participants received acupuncture. The acupuncture group did not show significant reduction in drug use (Margolin et al., 2002. There is a larger body of work supporting TCMs, though much of the research validating TCM was done without the use of robust Western scientific methodology. Part of the problem is that testing TCMs have special challenges (Margolin, Avants, & Kleber, 1998; Nahin & Straus, 2001). How do you provide a comparative control condition or placebo when you are testing acupuncture? Comparative alternatives to having fine needles being inserted into your skin are difficult to find. Western doctors and scientists do not accept the majority of the Chinese findings. The Chinese are beginning to use better research methodologies, and research results have begun to satisfy Western doctors. For example, a Western medical examination showed patients to have peptic ulcers, and a Chinese examination of the same patients yielded a diagnosis based on the five elements previously described. Doctors treated these patients with herbs based on TCM, and the patients showed significant recovery 2 months later (Zhou, Hu, & Pi, 1991). Treatment of patients with heart disease provides similar success stories (Zhang, Liang, & Ye, 1995). Much of the research conducted on TCM in America analyzes the constituents of herbs used in treatment, and many such studies show that the active ingredients of the herbs facilitate cures (Chang, Chang, Kuo, & Chang, 1997; Hon, et al., 2007; Stickel, Egerer, & Seitz, 2000; Way & Chen, 1999). The growing evidence notwithstanding, it will be some time before TCM is accepted widely, but its time may be sooner than we think.

AYURVEDA: TRADITIONAL INDIAN MEDICINE

You may be more familiar with Ayurveda, or traditional Indian medicine, than you realize. This is not American Indian medicine (which will be discussed later) but the approach to health that came from the Indian subcontinent. Yoga is a part of Ayurvedic practices. Many herbal supplements in use today came into prominence because of ancient Ayurvedic writings, and various health care products on the market that tout natural bases (e.g., Aveda products) have roots in Ayurveda. Although you do not see as much explicit evidence of this form of medicine in North America (i.e., you may not find Ayurveda shops in the "Little India" sections of American cities, but certainly may find Chinese herb shops in American "Chinatowns"), many Americans practice forms of Ayurveda. Ayurveda originated more than 6,000 years ago and was considered a medicine of the masses. In fact, the basic ideology underlying Ayurveda still influences how the billion inhabitants of India today view health. Many Indian Americans even use the prescriptions of Ayurveda in daily life (e.g., swallowing raw garlic is good for you and chewing on cloves helps toothaches), and many European Americans are using Ayurvedic practices such as yoga and natural supplements. The first two major Ayurvedic texts, the *Charaka Samhita* and the *Sushruta Samhita*, have been dated to 1000 B.C., although Ayurvedic practices are also referred to in the Vedas (3000 to 2000 B.C.), ancient Indian texts containing the wisdom of sages and sacrificial rituals. The *Charaka Samhita* has 120 chapters covering diverse areas such as the general principles of Ayurveda, the causes and symptoms of disease, physiology and medical ethics, prognosis, therapy, and pharmacy (Svoboda, 1992).

Approximately 2,000 years ago, Charaka, an Indian sage, developed Ayurveda, a traditional Indian holistic system of medicine (Lyssenko, 2004; Singh, 2007). Charaka described four causative factors in mental illness: a) diet (incompatible, vitiated, and unclean food); b) disrespect to Gods, elders, and teachers; c) mental shock due to emotions such as excessive fear and joy; and d) faulty bodily activity. Thus, Ayurveda considers a biopsychosocial approach in formulating causative factors in mental disorders (Prasadarao & Sudhir, 2001). Charaka, while emphasizing the need for harmony between body, mind, and soul, focused on preventive, curative, and promotive aspects of mental health. Ancient Indian court physicians further developed Ayurvedic practices and were given vast resources because the health of the king was considered equivalent to the health of the state (Svoboda, 1992). Ayurvedic medicine was well developed by the time of the Buddha (500 B.C.) and the rise of Buddhism. Jivaka, the royal physician to the Buddha, was so well known that people actually became Buddhists so he could treat them. When Alexander the Great invaded India in 326 B.C., he took Ayurvedic physicians back to Greece with him—one of the first times people of the two cultures were exposed to each other. The use of Ayurveda flourished until A.D. 900 when Muslim invaders came into India and created a new form of medicine called Unani, a combination of Greek and Ayurvedic medicine with Arabic medicine (Udwadia, 2000). Ayurveda continued in different forms even after European forces invaded India around A.D. 1500, bringing Western medicine with them.

The basic core of Ayurvedic medicine parallels the way members of most Asian American cultures view life. A healthy system is made up of healthy units working together in a symbiotic relationship with the well-being of the individual being indivisible from the well-being of the community, the land, the supernatural world, or the universe. This collectivistic orientation automatically influences perceptions of social support, as well as how people react when they are sick or stressed. This book elaborates on this subject in later chapters.

Sources of Illness

TCM and Ayurveda share many similarities. Ayurvedic science also uses the notion of basic elements: five great elements form the basis of the universe. Earth represents the solid state, water the liquid state, air the gaseous state, fire the power to change the state of any substance, and ether, simultaneously the source of all matter and the space in which it exists (Svoboda, 1992). Each of these elements can either nourish the body, balance the body serving to heal, or imbalance the body serving as a poison. Achieving the right balance of these elements in the body is critical to maintaining a healthy state. These elements also combine to form three major forces that influence physiological functions critical to healthy living. Ether and air combine to form the *Vata dosha*, fire and water combine to form the *Pitta dosha*, and water and earth elements combine to form the *Kapha dosha*. Vata directs nerve impulses, circulation, respiration, and elimination. Pitta is responsible for metabolism in the organ and tissue systems as well as cellular metabolism. Kapha is responsible for growth and protection. We are all made up of unique proportions of Vata, Pitta, and Kapha that cause disease when they go out of balance. These three doshas are also referred to as humors or bodily fluids and correspond to the Greek humors of phlegm (Kapha) and choler (Pitta). There is no equivalent to the Greek humor blood, nor is Vata or "wind" represented in the Greek system (Udwadia, 2000). Similar to the meridians in TCM, the existence of these forces is demonstrated more by inference and results of their hypothesized effects than by physical observation. Vata, Pitta, and Kapha are also associated with specific body type characteristics as shown in Table 2.3.

In addition to diseases caused by the imbalances of the doshas, Ayurveda identifies diseases as having six other key causes. Some diseases are recognized as being due to natural changes in the body, genetic predispositions, trauma, gods or demons, due to the season, or due to deformities present at birth. Again, similar to the Chinese, Ayurvedic sages also evoke the importance of balancing hot and cold. Heat, even the fever of desire for certain foods, is also thought to be an important source of illness.

TABLE **2.3**

The Major Constitutions of the Body in Ayurvedic Medicine

Characteristic	Vata	Pitta	Kapha
Body frame	Thin, irregular	Medium	Heavy
Weight	Easy to lose Hard to gain	Easy to lose Easy to gain	Hard to lose Easy to gain
Skin	Dark, tans deeply	Light, burns easily	Medium
Sweat	Scanty	Profuse	Moderate
Hair	Dry, coarse, curly Often dark	Fine, straight Light	Oily, thick Brown
Appetite	Variable	Intense	Regular
Climate	Prefers warm	Prefers cool	Prefers change of season
Stamina	Poor	Medium	Good
Speech	Talkative	Purposeful	Cautious
Sex drive	Variable	Intense	Steady
Emotion	Fearful	Angry	Avoids confrontation
Memory	Learns quickly Forgets quickly	Learns quickly Forgets slowly	Learns slowly Forgets slowly

Source: Svoboda (1992).

In general, Ayurvedic practitioners believe that health is a natural state and one maintained by keeping the body clear of toxins and the mind relaxed and stress free. The accumulation of toxins can occur when we are stressed and when waste is not effectively eliminated from the body. Consequently, some of the major Ayurvedic treatments involve detoxification and effective waste removal.

Treatment

The Ayurvedic physician uses different methods to diagnose a disease. First, there is a complete inspection of the patient. This involves looking for abnormalities in the body (e.g., discoloration of the skin), listening for abnormal sounds (e.g., irregular breathing), and even smelling the patient because imbalances in diet and the body are thought to result in characteristic odors (especially in the urine). The physician also uses palpitation of the body to feel for problems and often thoroughly interrogates the patient to assess for any changes in lifestyle or routine. After a diagnosis is made, a number of treatments are prescribed.

There are many forms of treatment in the Ayurvedic system of medicine, and many of them have made inroads into the Western consciousness. Some of these treatments exist on the fringe of Western biomedicine as complementary therapies (these are discussed in more detail later in this chapter). Others, such as yoga, are now common in even the smaller cities and towns of this continent (yoga is addressed in Chapter 11). "New age" spiritualists, who probably encountered treatments having origins in Ayurveda on travels through Southeast Asia, also practice many of them. Because imbalance is a source of illness, Ayurvedic medicine employs a number of techniques to reestablish balance. These include purification, surgery, drugs, diet, herbs, minerals, massage, color and gem therapy, homeopathy, acupressure, music, yoga, aromatherapy, and meditation. These treatments can be divided into therapies involving dietary changes and changes of activities at the level of the physical body and in tune with the seasons and climate, therapies aimed to clear the mind, and therapies involving spiritual rituals. Although not labeled "Ayurvedic," you will encounter many of these (especially the last few) in health clinics in North America today.

Perhaps one of the most commonly seen forms of Ayurvedic treatments in North America (in alternative medicine circles, spas, and clinics nationwide and especially in California, New Mexico, and New York) is the *Panchakarma* or "five actions." Similar to ancient Egyptian methods to purify the body, Ayurvedic medicine recommends five ways that the body should be purged of toxins: vomiting, laxatives, enemas, nasal medication, and bloodletting. Some of these may sound primitive and you should definitely not try any of them at home, but each is considered critical in a return to health. Other distinctive treatments involve the ingestion of oily and fatty foods as a form of internal purification and making the patient sweat, the latter being a therapy also common to American Indian medicine, as we shall discuss shortly.

The use of plants and herbal remedies plays a major part in Ayurvedic medicine. About 600 different medicinal plants are mentioned in the core Ayurvedic texts. A note of caution: just knowing the name of the plant is not enough. The texts even prescribe how the plant should be grown (e.g., type of soil and water) and where it should be grown. The use of plants to cure is perhaps one of the key areas in which you will see Ayurveda used in North America. Western drug companies have used a number of plants originally used in India to cure diseases. For example, psyllium seed is used for bowel problems, and other plants are used to reduce blood pressure, control diarrhea, and lessen the risk of liver or heart problems. A substance called forskolin, isolated from the *Coleus forskohlii* plant, has been used in Ayurveda for treating heart disease, and its use has now been empirically validated by Western biomedicine (Ding & Staudinger, 2005).

CURANDERISMO AND SPIRITUALISM

The year 2003 signaled a major change in the cultural face of the United States of America. For the first time in the history of the United States, Americans of Latino descent became the largest minority group, narrowly edging out African Americans (U.S. Census Bureau, 2003). Latinos are present in every state in the United States, with large concentrations in California, Texas, and Arizona. Latinos are a very diverse group of people. There are Latinos from Mexico, Puerto Rico, Cuba, the Dominican Republic, and, of course, from Spain (as suggested by the term *Hispanic*). The health beliefs of this large part of the North American population correspondingly become important to consider. We will focus on the beliefs of the largest subgroup of Latinos, Mexican Americans.

Curanderismo is the Mexican American folk healing system that often coexists side by side with Western biomedicine. Coming from the Spanish verb *curar* meaning "to heal," curanderos are full-time healers. The curandero's office is in the community, often in the healer's own home. There are no appointments, forms, or fees, and you pay whatever you believe the healer deserves. This form of healing relies heavily on the patient's faith and belief systems and uses everyday herbs, fruits, eggs, and oils. In studies beginning as early as 1959, researchers (Clark, 1959; Torrey, 1969) first focused on "Mexican American cultural illnesses," such as *mal de ojo* (sickness from admiring a baby too much). More recent work (Trotter & Chavira, 1997) focuses on the healers themselves, their beliefs, training processes, and processes for treatment. Surveys of Mexican Americans show that even among highly assimilated Mexican Americans, traditional and indigenous practices still persist (Lopez, 2005; Miller, Safranski, & Heur, 2004).

Sources of Illness

The Mexican American cultural framework acknowledges the existence of two sources of illness, one natural and one supernatural. When the natural and supernatural worlds exist in harmony, optimal health is achieved. Disharmony between these realms breeds illness (Madsen, 1968). Beyond this supernatural balance component, the curandero's concept of the cause of illness parallels that of Western biomedicine. Like biomedical practitioners, curanderos believe that germs and other natural factors can cause illness. However, curanderos also believe that there are supernatural causes to illness in addition to natural factors. If an evil spirit, a witch, or a sorcerer causes an illness, then only a supernatural solution will be sufficient for a cure. Illness can also be caused if a

Curandera Maria de Lourdez Gonzales Avila of Mexico City performing an incense cleansing ritual on her students during a workshop in Albuquerque, New Mexico

person's energy field is weakened or disrupted. Whether diabetes, alcoholism, or cancer, if a spirit caused it, supernatural intervention is the only thing that can cure it. Although curanderos seem to give the devil his due, they often are realistic in their searches for a cause. Trotter and Chavira (1997) conducted extensive interviews with curanderos and reported that some identify more supernatural causes than others do. For example, a student once asked the authors to take him to a curandero. The student, let's call him Hector, felt hexed by a former girlfriend (he admitted he had treated her badly). Now Hector was feeling sick and exhausted and was performing badly in school. The curandero examined Hector with his magical training and then asked him a series of questions concerning his health behaviors and habits. He determined that instead of a hex, Hector's symptoms developed from too much partying, too much drinking, and not enough studying!

Unlike Western biomedicine and TCM, the practices of curanderismo are based on Judeo-Christian beliefs and customs. The Bible has influenced curanderismo through references made to the specific healing properties of natural substances such as plants (see Luke 10:34). Curanderos's healing and cures are influenced by the Bible's proclamation that belief in God can and does heal directly and that people with a gift from God can heal in his name. The concept of the soul, central to Christianity, also provides support for the existence of saints (good souls) and devils (bad souls). The bad souls can cause illness and the good souls, harnessed by the shamanism and sorcery of the curanderismo, can cure.

Treatment

Curanderos use three levels of treatment depending on the source of the illness: material, spiritual, and mental (Trotter & Chavira, 1997). Working on the material level, curanderos use things found in any house (eggs, lemons, garlic, and ribbons) and religious symbols (a crucifix, water, oils, and incense). These material things often are designed to either emit or absorb vibrating energy that repairs the energy field around a person. Ceremonies include prayers, ritual sweepings, or cleansings (Torres & Sawyer, 2005). The spiritual level of treatment often includes the curandero entering a trance, leaving his or her body, and playing the role of a medium. This spiritual treatment allows a spirit to commandeer the curandero's body, facilitating a cure in the patient. On some occasions, the spirit will prescribe simple herbal remedies (via the curandero). On other occasions, the spirit will perform further rituals. The mental level of treatment relies on the power held by the individual curandero, rather than on spirits or materials. Some illnesses (e.g., physical) often are treated by herbs alone (DeStefano, 2001), and psychological problems may be treated by a combination of all these types of treatments.

In a manner akin to that of health psychologists, curanderos explicitly focus on social, psychological, and biological problems (Trotter & Chavira, 1997). The difference is that they add a focus on spiritual problems as well. From a social perspective, the community where the curanderos work recognizes and accepts what the curandero is trying to achieve. The social world is important to the curanderos who evaluate the patient's direct and extended support system. The patient's moods and feelings are weighed together with any physical symptoms. Finally, there is always a ritual petition to God and other spiritual beings to help with the healing process.

Curanderos each have their own set of specializations. For example, midwives (*parteras*) help with births, masseuses (*sobaderos*) treat muscle sprains, and herbalists (*yerberos*) prescribe different plants (Avila & Parker, 2000). For most Mexican Americans, the choice between curanderismo and Western biomedicine is an either/or proposition. Some individuals use both systems, and some stay completely away from Western hospitals as much as they can (sometimes because they do not have enough money to use them). Acculturated and higher social class Mexican Americans tend to rely exclusively on Western biomedicine. The existence of this strong cultural and historical folk medicine and the large numbers of its adherents make this approach to illness an important alternative style for us to consider in our study of the psychology of health.

There are limited empirical studies of the effects of curanderismo, though there are many different accounts of the practices available in health and medical journals (Healy, 2000; Trotter, 2001). More and more medical journals are publishing articles on this form of healing (e.g., Bearison, Minian, & Granowetter, 2002, on asthma; Miller, Safranski, & Heur, 2004, on the treatment of diabetes; Ortiz & Torres, 2007, on the treatment of alcoholism) but little has been found in mainstream health psychology. The uses of curanderismo have been associated with negative health outcomes that are more often seen in print. For example, DeBollonia et al. (2008) report a case of a young child who had to be hospitalized for isopropyl alcohol toxicity due to the use of a curanderismo treatment of "espanto" (evil spirits).

AMERICAN INDIAN MEDICINE

Many elements of the American Indian belief system and the approach to health are somewhat consistent with elements of curanderismo and TCM and provide a strong contrast to Western biomedicine. American Indians comprise about 1 percent of the population of the United States today. Although approximately 500 nations of American Indians live in the United States, the main beliefs are relatively consistent across the groups. We will provide a generalized introduction in this section, but note that different tribes have different variations on the basic beliefs (e.g., Crow, 2001, for the Muskogee; Howard and Willie, 1984, for the Oklahoma Seminoles; Lewis, 1990, for the Oglala Sioux; Looks for Buffalo Hand, 1998, for Oglala Lakota practices; Mayes & Lacy, 1989, for the Navajo). Four practices are common to most (Cohen, 2003; Kavasch & Baar, 1999): the use of herbal remedies, the employment of ritual purification or purging, the use of symbolic rituals and ceremonies, and the involvement of healers, also referred to as medicine men, medicine women, or **shamans** (though the latter is primarily used for the healers of northern Europe, Eliade, 1964). Native Americans have utilized and benefited from these practices for at least 10,000 years and possibly much longer.

A brief aside: You may wonder what the politically correct way to refer to American Indians, Native Americans, or First Nations Peoples is. Today, as was the case historically, First Nations People identify themselves by family, community (or band), clan, and nation. The terms "nation" and "tribe" are often used interchangeably though the term "nation" is generally more appropriate (Cohen, 2003). If you are not going to use the family-band-clan-nation nomenclature, using First Nations People, Native American, or American Indian is kosher.

Sources of Illness

Similar to the ancient Chinese, American Indians believed that human beings and the natural world are closely intertwined. The fate of humankind and the fate of the trees, the mountains, the sky, and the oceans are all linked. The Navajos call this "walking in beauty," a worldview in which everything in life is connected and influences everything else. In this system, sickness is a result of things falling out of balance and of losing one's way in the path of beauty (Alvord & Van Pelt, 2000). Animals are sacred, the winds are sacred, and trees and plants, bugs, and rocks are sacred. Every human and every object corresponds to a presence in the spirit world, and these spirits promote health or cause illness. Spiritual rejuvenation and the achievement of a general sense of physical, emotional, and communal harmony are at the heart of American Indian medicine. Shamans coordinate American Indian medicine and inherit the ability to communicate with spirits in much the same way that Mexican American curanderos do. Shamans spend much of their day listening to their patients, asking about their family and their behaviors and beliefs and making connections between the patient's life and their illness. Shamans do not treat spirits as metaphors or prayers as a way to trick a body into healing. Shamans treat spirits as real entities, respecting them as they would any other intelligent being or living person.

Treatment

Ritual and ceremony play a major role in American Indian medicine. One of the most potent and frequent ceremonies is the sweat lodge (Mehl-Medrona, 1998). Medicine men hold lodges or "sweats" for different reasons. Sometimes a sweat

© Robert Harding Picture Library Ltd./Alamy Limited

An American Indian Shaman in a Trance

purifies the people present; at other times, a sweat is dedicated to someone with cancer or another terminal illness. Before each sweat, attendees tie prayer strings and pouches, little bags of red, black, yellow, or white cloth (Bruchac, 1993). Each color represents a direction and type of spirit, and the choice of color depends on the ceremony to be performed. Each pouch contains sacred tobacco, the burning of which is believed to please the spirits. The sweat leader, often a shaman, decides on the number of prayer bags depending on why the sweat is needed. The ceremony takes place in a sweat lodge, which looks like a half dome of rocks and sticks covered with blankets and furs to keep the air locked in and the light out. The lodge symbolizes the world and the womb of Mother Earth. Even though the structure is only a half dome, participants believe that the rest of the sphere continues down inside the earth below it. Heated rocks are placed in a pit in the middle of the half dome. A short distance away from the lodge, a "firekeeper" heats rocks in a wood fire, often for hours before the event. The rocks are called *elders* because the rocks of the earth are seen as ancient observers. The number of rocks used also depends on the type of ceremony and is decided on by the lodge leader. The firekeeper builds a fire, prays over it and with it, and then places the stones in the fire, building the wood up around the rocks. He then keeps the rocks covered until it is time for them to be brought into the lodge (carried in with a pitchfork or shovel). Participants in the sweat sing sacred songs in separate rounds during the ceremony. After each round, the firekeeper brings in another set of hot rocks, and more songs are sung or prayers said. The sequence of prayers, chants, and singing following the addition of hot rocks continues until all the rocks are brought in. The hot stones raise the temperature inside the lodge, leading to profuse perspiration, which is thought to detoxify the body. Because of the darkness and the heat, participants often experience hallucinations that connect to spirit guides or provide insight into personal conditions.

Other ceremonies are also used. For example, the Lakota and Navajo use the medicine wheel, the sacred hoop, and the *sing*, which is a community healing ceremony lasting from two to nine days and guided by a highly

An American Indian Sweat Lodge
A fire pit outside the door is where the "elders" or rocks are heated.

skilled specialist called a *singer*. Many healers also employ dancing, sand painting, chanting, drumming (which places a person's spirit into alignment with the heartbeat of Mother Earth), and feathers and rattles to remove blockages and stagnations of energy that may be contributing to ill health. Sometimes sacred stones are rubbed over the part of the person's body suspected to be diseased. Although many American Indians prefer to consult a conventional medical doctor for conditions that require antibiotics or surgery, herbal remedies continue to play a substantial role in treatment of various physical, emotional, and spiritual ailments. The herbs prescribed vary from tribe to tribe, depending upon the ailment and what herbs are available in a particular area. Some shamans suggest that the herbs be eaten directly. Others suggest taking them mixed with water (like an herbal tea) or even with food. Healers burn herbs such as sage, sweet grass, or cedar (called a *smudge*) in almost every ceremony, and let the restorative smoke drift over the patient.

Today most American Indians use a blend of Western biomedicine and American Indian spiritualism. Most reservations usually have both spiritual healers and Western doctors, but frequently traditional American Indians are wary of the doctors and first seek out medicine men.

AFRICAN AMERICAN BELIEFS

In addition to these four basic approaches to health, there is also a wealth of other belief systems to learn. A full description of all of the different folk medicines existing in the world today is beyond the scope of this book, but remember that there are additional belief systems both in Northern America and around the globe that remain for your further explorations. One example is the African American culture. For many members of this cultural group, health beliefs reflect cultural roots that include elements of African healing, medicine of the Civil War South, European medical and anatomical folklore, West Indies voodoo religion, fundamentalist Christianity, and other belief systems.

African American communities have become very diverse, especially with the recent arrival of people from Haiti and other Caribbean countries and Africa. Similar to the American Indians, many people of African descent also hold a strong connection to nature and rely on *inyangas* (traditional herbalists). Even today in Africa, hospitals and modern medicines are invariably the last resort in illness. The traditional African seeks relief in the herbal lore of the ancestors and consults the *inyanga*, who is in charge of the physical health of the people (Bradford, 2005). When bewitchment is suspected, which happens frequently among the traditional people of Africa, or there is a personal family crisis or love or financial problem, the patient is taken to a *sangoma* (spiritual diviner or spiritual/traditional healer), who is believed to have spiritual powers and is able to work with the ancestral spirits or spirit guides (Bradford, 2005). The sangoma uses various methods such as "throwing the bones" (*amathambo*, also known by other names depending on the cultural group) or going into a spiritual trance to consult the ancestral spirits or spirit guides to find the diagnosis or cure for the problem, be it bewitchment, love, or another problem. Depending on the response from the higher source, a decision will be made on what herbs and mixes (*intelezis*) should be used and in what manner (e.g., orally, burning). If more powerful medicine is needed, numerous "magical rites" can or will be performed according to rituals handed down from sangoma to sangoma (Bradford, 2005). In South Africa, there are more than 70,000 sangomas or spiritual healers who dispense herbal medicines and even issue medical certificates to employees for purposes of sick leave.

Even though you may have had some awareness of the Greek roots of Western medicine (e.g., the Hippocratic oath taken by doctors) or Chinese medicine (e.g., acupuncture) or even Indian traditional medicine (e.g., the Ayurvedic practice of yoga), other cultural ways of healing such as the sangoma are not as well known and, worse, are often ridiculed by the mass media. For example, many visitors to the city of New Orleans take voodoo tours around the city and joke about sticking pins in dolls made up to look like their bosses or enemies. The story is that a pin in the arm of the doll should cause pain in the arm of the person it is meant to represent. There is a rich history and tradition to voodoo that goes well beyond such parodied anecdotes. Many African Americans believe in a form of folk medicine that incorporates and mirrors aspects of voodoo (really spelled v-o-d-o-u), which is a type of religion derived from some of the world's oldest known religions that have been present in Africa since the beginning of human civilization (Heaven & Booth, 2003). When Africans were brought to the Americas (historians estimate that approximately 250,000 slaves were imported), religious persecution forced them to practice voodoo in secret. To allow voodoo to survive, its followers adopted many elements of Christianity. Today, voodoo is a legitimate religion in a number of areas of the world, including Brazil, where it is called *Candomblé*, and the English-speaking Caribbean, where it is called *Obeah*. In most of the United States, however, White slavers were successful in stripping slaves of their voodoo traditions and beliefs (Heaven & Booth, 2003). In some parts of the United States, the remnants are stronger than in others. Some African American communities in isolated areas such as the coast and islands of North Carolina survived intact well into the twentieth century. Here, "Gullah" culture involving the belief in herbalism, spiritualism, and black magic, thrived (Pinckney, 2003). What was called voodoo in other parts of the country was called "the root" (meaning charm). A number of other cultures, such as the American Indians described earlier and Hmong Americans, still believe that shamans and medicine men can influence health. Although shamanistic rituals and voodoo rites may seem to be ineffectual ways to cure according to Western science, the rituals have meaning to those who believe in them and should not be ignored or ridiculed.

SYNTHESIZE, EVALUATE, APPLY	• What are the main causes of illness in Traditional Chinese Medicine? To American Indians? In curanderismo? • Compare and contrast the different treatments used in the different approaches. • How should the field of health psychology best use information about diverse approaches to health? • Identify the critical biopsychosocial factors underlying each diverse approach to health.

ARE COMPLEMENTARY AND ALTERNATIVE APPROACHES VALID?

Most of the non-Western approaches to medicine described in this chapter are commonly referred to as complementary or alternative approaches to medicine (CAMs). Voodoo and shamanistic rites do not fall under the CAM umbrella; although, the term *complementary and alternative medicine* generally describes any healing philosophies and therapies that mainstream Western (conventional) medicine does not commonly use. Table 2.4 describes the main CAMs.

TABLE **2.4**

Major Complementary and Alternative Medicines

Acupuncture is a method of healing developed in China at least 2,000 years ago. Procedures involve stimulation of anatomical points on the body by a variety of techniques.

Aromatherapy involves the use of essential oils (extracts or essences) from flowers, herbs, and trees to promote health and well-being.

Ayurveda is a medical system that has been practiced primarily in the Indian subcontinent for 5,000 years. Ayurveda includes diet and herbal remedies and emphasizes the use of body, mind, and spirit in disease prevention and treatment.

Chiropractic focuses on the relationship between bodily structure (primarily that of the spine) and function, and how that relationship affects the preservation and restoration of health. Chiropractors use manipulative therapy as an integral treatment tool.

Dietary supplements are products (other than tobacco) taken by mouth that contain a "dietary ingredient" intended to supplement the diet. Dietary ingredients may include vitamins, minerals, herbs or other botanicals, amino acids, and substances such as enzymes, organ tissues, and metabolites.

Electromagnetic fields (EMFs, also called electric and magnetic fields) are invisible lines of force that surround all electrical devices. Earth also produces EMFs; electric fields are produced when there is thunderstorm activity, and magnetic fields are believed to be produced by electric currents flowing at Earth's core.

Homeopathic medicine is an alternative medical system. In homeopathic medicine, there is a belief that "like cures like," meaning that small, highly diluted quantities of medicinal substances are given to cure symptoms, when the same substances given at higher or more concentrated doses would actually cause those symptoms.

Massage therapists manipulate muscle and connective tissue to enhance the function of those tissues and promote relaxation and well-being.

Naturopathic medicine proposes that there is a healing power in the body that establishes, maintains, and restores health. Practitioners work with the patient with a goal of supporting this power, through treatments such as nutrition and lifestyle counseling, dietary supplements, medicinal plants, exercise, homeopathy, and treatments from Traditional Chinese Medicine.

Qi gong is a component of Traditional Chinese Medicine that combines movement, meditation, and regulation of breathing to enhance the flow of *qi* in the body, improve blood circulation, and enhance immune function.

Reiki is a Japanese word representing universal life energy. Reiki is based on the belief that when spiritual energy is channeled through a Reiki practitioner, the patient's spirit is healed, which in turn heals the physical body.

Therapeutic touch is derived from an ancient technique called laying-on of hands. It is based on the premise that the healing force of the therapist affects the patient's recovery; healing is promoted when the body's energies are in balance; and, by passing their hands over the patient, healers can identify energy imbalances.

Source: National Center for Complementary and Alternative Medicine (2005).

Earlier, we described how Western medicine started. Spurred on by technological innovations and inquiring minds, Western biomedicine became what we know today. How did different non-Western people discover their methods? The most plausible answer and one supported by contemporary adherents of non-Western treatments is by trial and error. When a person was sick, he or she ate the bark or leaves of a number of different herbs. Most of the herbs may not have had any effect, and the person either suffered or died. Some herbs may have produced an immediate cure. Automatically then, that herb would be known to help with that certain ailment. Of course, many practitioners of traditional medicine do not offer the trial and error explanation. The ancient Chinese text, *The Yellow Emperor's Classic of Internal Medicine*, which is the basis for Traditional Chinese Medicine, suggests that communications with the heavens account for traditional medical practices. Similarly, American Indian shamans and Latino curanderos derive their healing powers from communications with spirits (Trotter & Chavira, 1997). The different origins of traditional beliefs notwithstanding, the fact is that many different cultures (ethnic, racial, religious, and others) have different beliefs about health and illness. Are these valid beliefs? Do the different methods work? This is a question that modern science is beginning to tackle. Given the growing diversity in the composition of North America, a major way to increase the utilization of health services is to learn more about the different cultural approaches to health. The major treatments used by each are summarized in Table 2.5.

If you are not already surprised by the different aspects of Chinese medicine, curanderismo, and American Indian spiritualism, you may be when you look at what some other peoples in North America actually do to cure themselves. You have heard of special diets (e.g., Atkins, Ornish, and Weil), but there is also a category of treatments called orthomolecular therapies in which patients eat substances such as magnesium, melatonin, and megadoses of vitamins. Some biological therapies use laetrile (iron and aluminum oxide), shark cartilage, and bee pollen to treat autoimmune and inflammatory diseases. In other CAMs, the body is manipulated. For example, chiropractors

TABLE **2.5**
Treatment Differences Summarized

	Major Treatments
Western biomedicine	Medication, surgery
Traditional Chinese medicine	Herbs, acupuncture, qi-gong
Ayurveda	Herbs, yoga, *Panchakarma* (purification), meditation, aromatherapy, massage
Curanderismo	Material, spiritual, and mental
American Indian medicine	Sweat lodges, prayer, herbs, medicine wheel
African American beliefs	Herbs, magical rites

and osteopathic manipulators work with the musculoskeletal system. There are separate categories of "energy therapies" such as Reiki. Practitioners channel energy from their spirit to heal the patient's body. Other energy treatments use magnetic and electrical fields to alleviate pain and cure sickness. There is a wide spectrum of therapeutic modalities covered by the CAM umbrella (Jones, 2005). Approximately 36 percent of people in North America use some form of complementary medicine according to the National Center for Complementary and Alternative Medicine (Arias, 2004; Barnes, Powell-Griner, McFann, & Nahin, 2004). When prayer and the use of megavitamins are included, that number climbs to 62 percent and the findings are relatively consistent across ethnic groups. People of all backgrounds use CAMs but some people are more likely than others to use CAM. Overall, CAM use is greater by women, people with higher educational levels, people who have been hospitalized in the past year, and former smokers (compared with current smokers or those who have never smoked, NCCAM, 2007). The *Journal of the American Medical Association* reported that the most popular therapies were herbal medicines, massage, megavitamins, self-help groups, folk remedies, energy healing, and homeopathy (Astin, Marie, Pelletier, Hansen, & Haskell, 1998).

Given the growing exposure of the Western world to non-Western medicines, it is important to ask whether the different approaches meet the rigorous tests of the scientific method before adopting alternate styles of behavior or different cures. The U.S. government recognizes the importance of different approaches to health. In 1998, Congress established the National Center for Complementary and Alternative Medicine (NCCAM) to stimulate, develop, and support research on CAMs for public benefit. In addition to the techniques used by the main approaches described earlier, the NCCAM also studies the effectiveness of other CAMs such as aromatherapy, meditation, acupuncture/acupressure, hypnosis, dance, music and art therapy, and even prayer. Empirical reports of effectiveness trials of CAMs should be ready in the near future.

The critical point to realize about these varying beliefs is that health psychologists must be aware of a person's beliefs in order to treat the person comprehensively. Followers of Western medicine arrive at their beliefs about the values of Western medicine in the same way that the believers of other cultures come to their beliefs about their medical practices. People learn their beliefs from their parents or other people around them. Your mother telling you that your cold is due to a virus establishes a belief system just as someone else's mother telling him or her that his or her cold is due to the evil looks of a neighbor also establishes a belief system. In both cases, the listening child may believe the story. What people believe influences what they do to remedy the situation. Giving antibiotics to someone who believes his or her cold is due to evil eyes may not yield the same effects as giving antibiotics to someone who believes his or her cold is due to a germ. Belief is a strong tool in the arsenal of the healer and an important element for the health psychologist to consider when attempting to maintain health and prevent illness. Often people educated in the West will express contempt for non-Western ways of looking at health. What do you mean spirits and evil eyes can cause illness? How can the weather and winds

A Chinese Herbalist Store with Different Drawers for the Different Herbs

make a difference? Why do you have to keep the spirits happy to be healthy? Ideas such as these make some snicker and others roll their eyes in disbelief. Although many non-Western beliefs have not been tested by the scientific method, for many of their practitioners, there is no need to have this proof. A long tradition of believing in a medical practice is enough for many who hold non-Western beliefs. To some extent, this is comparable to Christians who have faith in the words of the Bible or Hindus who believe in the Upanishads or the Bhagavad Gita (ancient Hindu scriptures). Scientific evidence is not needed when you have faith. To successfully treat and influence people with different beliefs we have to know first what they believe.

SYNTHESIZE, EVALUATE, APPLY	• What do the different approaches to health have in common? • Using an empirical scientific approach, evaluate each different approach to health. • What are the psychological processes by which a health belief can influence recovery? • Compare and contrast the different philosophical approaches to health.

FOCUS ON APPLICATIONS

Acupuncture

"Needles, needles, big long needles, poking into me. A human pin cushion." This is a common response when people are asked what the word acupuncture brings to mind. Yes, needles are involved. Yes, they are poked into the patient. Yes, the patient often look likes a pincushion. However, you should also know that the needles are minute, thin, flexible wires, barely a few millimeters thick. The procedure is so painless that if you close your eyes when the needles are being placed, you will not even feel them (believe me; I have tried it many times).

(continues)

FOCUS ON APPLICATIONS *(continued)*

Acupuncture is one of the most scientifically validated forms of alternate medicine and is gaining popularity in hospitals nationwide. In 1993, the Food and Drug Administration estimated that Americans made nearly 12 million visits per year to acupuncture practitioners, spending more than one-half billion dollars. The 2002 National Health Interview Survey estimated that 8.2 million Americans had used acupuncture and 2.1 million had used it the previous year (Burke, Upchurch, Dye, & Chu, 2006). The practice of acupuncture in North America only began in the 1970s (as stated earlier, acupuncture has been a part of Chinese traditional medicine for thousands of years). When President Nixon first opened the door to the Far East, journalists who accompanied him on his tour of China witnessed surgeries performed on animals and humans for which no anesthesia was used. Instead, Chinese surgeons used acupuncture with slender needles piercing into predetermined points of the body.

Practitioners of Traditional Chinese Medicine determined that there are as many as 2,000 acupuncture points on the human body connected by 20 pathways (12 main and 8 secondary) called meridians. These meridians conduct energy, or qi, between the surface of the body and its internal organs. Each acupuncture point has a different effect on the qi that passes through it. Acupuncture keeps the balance between yin and yang, thus allowing for the normal flow of qi throughout the body and restoring health to the mind and body.

Several theories have been presented to explain exactly how acupuncture works. One theory suggests that pain impulses are blocked from reaching the spinal cord or brain at various "gates" to these areas. Because a majority of acupuncture points are either connected to (or are located near) neural structures, it is possible that acupuncture stimulates the nervous system. Another theory hypothesizes that acupuncture stimulates the body to produce endorphins, which reduce pain. Other studies have found that opioids (also pain relievers) may be released into the body during acupuncture treatment.

In the late 1970s, the World Health Organization recognized the ability of acupuncture and Traditional Chinese Medicine to treat nearly four dozen common ailments, including neuro-musculoskeletal conditions (such as arthritis, neuralgia, insomnia, dizziness, and neck/shoulder pain); emotional and psychological disorders (such as depression and anxiety); circulatory disorders (such as hypertension, angina pectoris, arteriosclerosis, and anemia); addictions to alcohol, nicotine, and other drugs; respiratory disorders (such as emphysema, sinusitis, allergies, and bronchitis); and gastrointestinal conditions (such as food allergies, ulcers, chronic diarrhea, constipation, indigestion, intestinal weakness, anorexia, and gastritis). In 1997, a summary statement released by the National Institutes of Health declared that acupuncture could be useful by itself or in combination with other therapies to treat addiction, headaches, menstrual cramps, tennis elbow, fibromyalgia, myofascial pain, osteoarthritis, lower back pain, carpal tunnel syndrome, and asthma. Other studies have demonstrated that acupuncture may help in the rehabilitation of stroke patients and can relieve nausea in patients recovering from surgery.

Many Western medicine practitioners in North America are actively incorporating acupuncture into mainstream medicine. Some doctors belong to the American Academy of Medical Acupuncture, an organization founded in 1987 by a group of physicians who graduated from an acupuncture training program at the UCLA School of Medicine. Schools for acupuncture training also have been established all across America. Several councils provide structure for the various training schools (e.g., the Council of Colleges of Acupuncture and Oriental Medicine), and accreditation boards (e.g., the Accreditation Commission for Acupuncture and Oriental Medicine [ACAOM]) have brought more acceptance and oversight to the practice of acupuncture in the United States.

SUMMARY

- Different cultures have varied ideas about what constitutes being healthy and what behaviors are healthy. Such beliefs vary by sex, religion, ethnicity, and nationality, to name a few. Writings about health and illness go as far back as 3000 B.C. to the times of the Mesopotamians and Egyptians.

- Western medicine has its roots in the writings of the Greek physicians Hippocrates and Galen. Also called allopathy, this approach focuses on causing the opposite effect from that created by the disease and is driven to rid the body of illness. Clear ideas of anatomy and circulation were some of the early contributions of Greek research to health.
- Western medicine advanced with improvements in technology, specifically the discovery of the microscope and the X-ray and innovations in surgery. Pasteur's work on germ theory showing that germs and bacteria caused illness greatly solidified the focus of Western medicine on physical sources of illness.
- Curanderismo is the Mexican American folk healing system that often coexists with Western medicine. This healing system uses herbs, fruits, eggs, and oils and places emphasis on spiritual causes of illness. An imbalance between the spiritual and natural world is seen to be the cause of illness.
- Curanderos treat patients on material, spiritual, and mental levels, depending on where the illness is thought to have begun. Spiritual treatments may involve the healer going into a trance and playing the role of a medium. Material treatments involve household items and religious symbols, and mental treatments rely on the power held by the healer.
- Traditional Chinese Medicine (TCM) treats the body as a whole in which every single part is intrinsically linked to other parts and to what is happening around the person. According to TCM, food, relationships, and spiritual harmony are all conducive to health. Diseases are thought to be caused by imbalances in yin and yang.
- Yin and yang are mutually interdependent, interchangeable forces that make up the entire universe. The Tao, or energy force, of the universe is influenced by the balance of yin and yang and needs to be fostered for optimal health. Main treatments include acupuncture and herbal therapy.
- American Indian medicine also focuses on spiritual balance and living in harmony with nature. The most common practices involve the use of herbal remedies, ritual purification or purging, symbolic rituals and ceremonies, and the involvement of shamans.

TEST YOURSELF

Check your understanding of the topics in this chapter by answering the following questions. Answers appear in the Appendix.

1. Complementary and alternative medicine is the name given to a category of medical atreatments:
   a. designed to add to Western medicine.
   b. practiced by Chinese and Indians.
   c. that is non-Western in origin.
   d. that does not involve biomedical drugs or procedures.
2. Western biomedicine is also referred to as:
   a. Allopathy.
   b. Homeopathy.
   c. Hellenistic.
   d. Physiopathy.
3. The earliest known diagnostic system of medicine involving physicians and combining religious rites and empirical treatments was seen in:
   a. Mesopotamia.
   b. Greece.
   c. Pakistan.
   d. Japan.

4. Each of the following directly contributed to our knowledge of human anatomy except:
   a. William Harvey.
   b. Galen.
   c. Leonardo Da Vinci.
   d. Andreas Vesalius.
5. According to the most recent census data the largest minority group in the United States is:
   a. African American.
   b. Latino
   c. Asian American
   d. American Indian
6. The Mexican American folk healing system is referred to as:
   a. Mal de ojo
   b. Machismo
   c. Curanderismo
   d. Elchupacabra
7. Which of the following cultural belief systems of medicine is heavily based on Christian beliefs and practices?
   a. Western biomedicine
   b. curanderismo
   c. Chinese Traditional Medicine
   d. American Indian medicine

8. One folk remedy common to American Indian, Mexican American, and Traditional Chinese medicine is:
   a. Plants
   b. Needles
   c. Saunas
   d. Prayer
9. Which of the following assumptions of Traditional Chinese Medicine is NOT correct?
   a. Meridian channels guide energy through the body.
   b. The nervous system is linked to the meridian system.
   c. Health is a balance of mind and body.
   d. Health is best dealt within a macroscopic fashion.
10. Which of the following is NOT something a shaman would do:
   a. Listen to patients and task about family, behaviors, and beliefs
   b. Treat spirits as metaphors
   c. Chant and pray in a trance
   d. Attempt to connect illness to a patient's life

WEB RESOURCES

Visit the companion website at **www.cengage.com/psychology/gurung**, where you will find online resources for this book, including chapter-by-chapter quizzes, Web links, and more!

Various Cultural Histories of Medicine
http://www.mic.ki.se/History.html

A site hosted by the Karolinska Institute, one of the leading medical universities in Europe. It provides extensive information on ancient medical practices (Mesopotamian, Egyptian, Chinese, Indian, Islamic, Western) and a history of disease.

National Center for Complementary and Alternative Medicine
http://nccam.nih.gov

A comprehensive site detailing varieties of CAM with health information on popular alternate medicinal practices, ongoing clinical trials, and research findings.

Understanding Race
http://www.understandingrace.org/home.html

Home of the RACE Project, which explains differences among people and reveals the reality – and unreality – of race. The story of race is complex and may challenge how we think about race and human variation, about the differences and similarities among people.

The Cross-Cultural Health Care Program
http://www.xculture.org/

A good example of an organization dedicated to preventing cultural clashes in the health care system. The CCHCP serves as a bridge between communities and health care institutions to ensure full access to quality health care that is culturally and linguistically appropriate.

The Center for Research on Ethnicity, Culture, and Health (CRECH)
http://www.crech.org/

CRECH develops new approaches to research and research training relevant to the description and understanding of racial and ethnic health disparities.

KEY TERMS, CONCEPTS, AND PEOPLE

allopathy, 37
ayurveda, 36
complementary and alternative medicine, 37
curanderismo, 50
Da Vinci, Leonardo, 38

Galen, 37
Harvey, William, 38
Hippocrates, 37
opiates and opioids, 39
Pasteur, Louis, 39
qi, 42

reductionist, 37
Shamans, 53
Tao, 41
traditional Chinese medicine, 40

van Leeuwenhoek, Antonius, 38
Vesalius, Andreas, 38
Western biomedicine, 37

ESSENTIAL READINGS

Cohen, K. (2003). *Honoring the medicine: The essential guide to Native American healing.* New York: Ballantine Books.

Kaptchuk, T. J. (2000). *The web that has no weaver: Understanding Chinese medicine.* Chicago: Contemporary Books.

Landrine, H., & Klonoff, E. A. (2001). Cultural diversity and health psychology. In A. Baum, T. A. Revenson, & J. E. Singer (Eds.), *Handbook of health psychology.* Mahwah, NJ: Erlbaum.

Trotter, R. T., & Chavira, J. A. (1997). *Curanderismo: Mexican American folk healing.* Athens: University of Georgia Press.

Essential Physiology

Essentially, our biology determines our longevity and how comfortably we live. Our biological systems—our brain, heart, lungs, nervous system, circulatory system—keep us alive, but can be damaged or compromised when we are sick or when we practice unhealthy behaviors. Smoking and drinking can clog arteries just as much as a poor diet can (and sometimes even more). A premise of health psychology is that our minds (e.g., how we think), our personalities, and our behaviors influence our bodies and our biology. Thusly, a firm understanding of the basic physiological systems is critical to comprehending how the different components of the biopsychosocial model come together and influence behavior. For some readers of this book, a chapter dedicated to biology presents an onerous task (maybe you took a psychology course hoping to get away from biology and thought that the biology chapter in your introductory psychology textbook was peculiar). The good news is that understanding biology often makes many psychological phenomena clearer. For example, why do we have trouble remembering facts we have studied when we are stressed during an exam? Answer: Because the memory part of the brain (the hippocampus) and the emotion part (the amygdala) are right next to each other. To comprehend health psychology, understanding basic physiology is critical (and worth the extra effort). This chapter covers the pertinent material; many more biological details exist that are relevant to health.

This chapter details the most essential components that are important in understanding the biopsychosocial model and the health psychological research, theories, and processes described in this book.

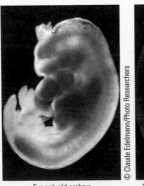 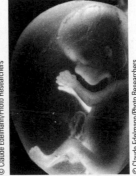

5 week old embryo   14 week old fetus

The Developing Human Being: Different Stages of Prenatal Growth

Courtesy of Regan Gurung

Mother-Infant Bonding

Each of the following sections corresponds to different chapters in the book (e.g., the nervous system is necessary to understanding stress processes described in Chapter 4). You can choose to read each corresponding section as needed. The following section on biological development provides a strong foundation.

BIOLOGICAL DEVELOPMENT

Our first challenge is to understand how our bodies develop. This will set the stage for us to discuss how our psychology and society can influence this biological development and subsequently our health (and the field of health psychology).

The Prenatal Period

The infant is born with predispositions and a genetic inheritance that shape many future developments. For the baby to have a chance to grow and develop, it first has to be born. Although that may sound like an odd thing to say (or at least extremely obvious), not all pregnancies end with a successful labor and delivery (Dunkel-Schetter, Gurung, Lobel, & Wadhwa, 2001; Wadhwa, Dunkel-Schetter, Chicz-DeMet, Porto, & Sandman, 1996). Furthermore, many things can happen in the time *before* a baby is born (the **prenatal period**), and the less time that the baby has in the womb, or in utero, the less time it will have to grow and develop normally. In fact, the length of **gestation** (time in womb) is one of the most important health psychological outcome variables used to study pregnancy. **Preterm births** (delivery before 37 weeks of gestation) are the most direct causes of **low birth weight** (LBW) babies, who have a higher risk for developmental and mental complications (Newnham, 1998). Extreme preterm and LBW babies have a substantially higher risk of infant mortality (McCormick, 1985). Surprisingly, the United States has an exceedingly high rate of LBW babies relative to other industrialized nations, and the rate has been climbing over the past 10 years (David & Collins, 1997). For example, the percentage of LBW infants born in the

United States is estimated to be 8 percent compared with only 4 percent for Sweden (UNICEF & WHO, 2004).

As another good example of the usefulness of the biopsychosocial model, the biological development of the fetus can be seriously influenced by the psychological state of the mother—her moods, her feelings, and her thoughts (the *psycho* part)—as well as the networks she has and the social situation in which she is living (the *social* part). In fact, the quality of the social environment the mother lives in may prove to be one of the main factors in the influence psychosocial aspects have on healthy biological functioning (Siegrist & Marmot, 2004; Taylor, Repetti, & Seeman, 1997). The biopsychosocial model also provides comprehensive predictions of complications in pregnancy, pregnancy length, and fetal growth (Smilkstein, Helsper-Lucas, Ashworth, Montano, & Pagel, 1984; St-Laurent et al., 2008).

During the nine months before delivery, many clear-cut physiological changes take place. A woman may not even know that she is pregnant until approximately two weeks after conception, when she is unlikely to menstruate (although some women do have what looks like a menstrual flow even when pregnant). However, there are clues. Her breasts may swell and become tender, and some women may become nauseous. Once the sperm and ova fuse to form a fertilized egg (the zygote), the zygote implants itself in the uterine wall and begins to grow, and cells differentiate into various internal structures. By the end of the second week, the organism is called an embryo. At the ninth week of gestation, the embryo is called a fetus, and the time until delivery is called the fetal period (Table 3.1). Of all the senses, only hearing is developed before birth and the fetus shows a preference for the mother's voice. Some mothers believe that playing classical music will improve fetal development. Similarly, you may have heard of the Mozart effect (Rauscher, Shaw, & Ky, 1993), the finding that the cadences and tempo of the classical composer's music can improve performance in certain areas (spatial-temporal tasks such as jigsaw puzzles and some forms of reasoning). However, here is some bad news for classical music fans—the validity of the Mozart effect is questionable (Fudin & Lembessis, 2004).

The developing embryo and fetus are particularly sensitive to teratogens, factors such as environmental toxins, and drugs, capable of causing developmental abnormalities. A key focus for the health psychologist is to ensure that expectant mothers refrain from the use of alcohol, caffeine, nicotine, and other drugs or medications (Calhoun & Alforque, 1996; Zimmer & Zimmer, 1998). Behaviors such as smoking, bad diet, and insufficient medical treatments all negatively affect fetal growth and infant health (McCormick et al., 1990). Some bad habits such as alcohol consumption during pregnancy can even influence the child when it grows to adolescence (Carmichael et al., 1997). Any alcohol misuse can harm the development of the baby's organs. Fetal exposure to teratogens is higher for ethnic minority populations (Dunkel-Schetter et al., 2001). Stress is particularly dangerous to the prenatal infant and the more stress a mother experiences, the more she risks delivery of a preterm or LBW baby (Wadhwa, Sandman, Porto, Dunkel-Schetter, & Garite, 1993). However, let's not forget about the baby's father. Secondhand smoke from the baby's father, for example, as well as stress in the form of

TABLE **3.1**
Critical Milestones in Prenatal Development

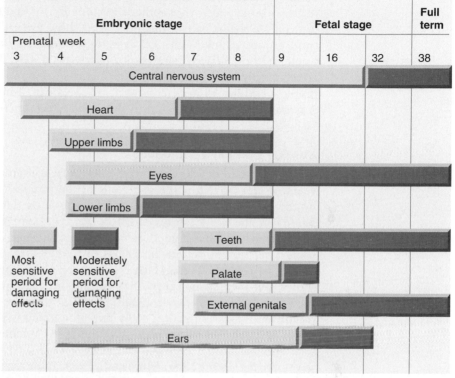

Adapted from Weiten (2005).

emotional or physical abuse, can also interfere with the baby's and mother's health (Dunkel-Schetter et al., 2001).

Two other aspects of pregnancy have strong psychological components: miscarriage and labor/delivery. A miscarriage (medically referred to as a spontaneous abortion) occurs when the zygote, embryo, or fetus is released from the uterus before it is ready to survive on its own. Although not usually discussed publicly, miscarriages occur often. Nearly 20 percent of pregnancies end in miscarriage, and 33 percent of women have a miscarriage at some point during their reproductive years (DeFrain, Millspaugh, & Xiao-lin, 1996). This can be a traumatizing experience and expecting couples often seek counseling and other types of support to better cope with the stress. Some personality types can manage better such trauma than others (more on this in Chapters 4 and Chapter 5), but the amount of social support provided to the couple, and the way they process their feelings and cope with this event, can have major implications for their mental and physical health (Swanson, 2000). Often discussing the problem versus ignoring it eases the emotional pain. Having friends and family express their love and care for the couple at this point is also especially helpful.

Another period when social support can play a major role in pregnancy is during labor and delivery. Childbirth is a stressful event, especially because it involves risk to both the mother's and the infant's lives. Complications arising during this time are the fifth-highest causes of infant mortality in the United States (National Center for Health Statistics, 2003). Psychosocial factors (e.g., social support, the mother's personality, or the presence of a companion) play a major role at this point and show great differences between cultural groups (Dunkel-Schetter, Sagrestano, Feldman, & Killingsworth, 1996; Keinan, 1997; Shiao, Andrews, & Helmreich, 2005). For example, the family is reportedly the most important source of support for African American mothers (Miller, 1992), followed by Mexican Americans and European Americans (Sagrestano, Feldman, Rini, Woo, & Dunkel-Schetter, 1999).

Infancy and Early Childhood

The growth and development of the newborn is dramatic during the first two years of life. Driven by the secretions of the pituitary gland and coordinated by the hypothalamus, hormones pulse through the body, stimulating growth. Based on the work of investigators such as Gesell (1928) and Meredith (1973), we now have a good picture of what normal development for a child should be. As can be seen on charts in the doctors' office or in the parents' home, babies grow irregularly. There are long intervals between growth spikes and they do not grow in a continuous pattern with the same growth every week (Vander Zanden, 2002). The nervous system develops the most rapidly in the early months. How parents interact with their babies is a key factor in infant development. Greater physical contact between the caregiver and child has always been associated with more successful social and physical development (Stern, 1995; Winnicott, 1965), although there is mixed support for this hypothesis. For example, Field (1998) demonstrated that the more a baby is touched and stroked, the faster it develops. However, a review of the research suggested that, although massage for preterm infants influences clinical outcome measures such as medical complications or length of stay and caregiver or parental satisfaction, the evidence of benefits for developmental outcomes is weak (Vickers, Ohlsson, Lacy, & Horsley, 2002). Touch has other important influences, such as playing a role in stress and coping, as we shall discuss in the next chapter (Taylor, Klein, Lewis, Gruenwald, Gurung, & Updegraff, 2000).

During early childhood (ages 2 to 6), the child tends to become more active. Food plays a critical role in muscle growth and the height of the child. This is an important time for parents to watch how much a child eats and when he or she eats. Strength, coordination, and range of motion all continue to increase. Some interesting cultural differences are seen in these early years of development. African American children tend to mature more quickly (as measured by bone growth, percent fat, and number of baby teeth) than European American children (Vander Zanden, 2002). Asian American children show some of the slowest rates of physical change (Keats, 2000).

After early childhood, physical growth slows down in general and children become more skilled in controlling their bodies. Middle childhood (age 7 to adolescence) is the stage during which children tend to be the healthiest and experience significant changes in cognitive development.

Adolescence

Adolescence (ages 12 to 17) can be perhaps one of the most turbulent periods in an individual's life. A flurry of biological activity morphs the child into a young adult and sometimes the grown-up exterior surges ahead of the still underdeveloped interior or cognitive development. This mismatch between biological and psychological factors often has dire health consequences. Adolescence is another critical juncture during which health psychology's biopsychosocial approach nicely reminds us on which different factors we need to focus.

The key biological milestone in adolescence is **puberty**. At puberty, a genetic timing mechanism activates the pituitary gland and an increasing level of growth hormone is produced in the body. The activation of the pituitary stimulates the manufacture of estrogen and progesterone in girls and testosterone in boys. The increase in sex hormones triggers the growth of secondary sex characteristics, leading to the development of breasts and the beginning of menstruation in women and the deepening of the voice and the growth of facial hair in men. Of direct importance to our study of how different health behaviors may develop is research that shows that boys with lower levels of testosterone are more likely to show behavioral problems such as rebelliousness that can catalyze initiating smoking and experimentation with illicit substances (Schaal, Tremblay, Soussignan, & Susman, 1996). In the brain, white matter increases with the growth of fibers that establish connections between brain regions, and the prefrontal cortex, corpus callosum, and temporal lobes increase in size (Paus, 1999).

The age at which puberty occurs has been shifting forward in time, demonstrating the possible interaction between our biology and our psychology and society. For example, at the beginning of the twentieth century, the average age for the onset of menstruation was 15 or 16. Less than 100 years later, the average age was just older than 12 (Brumberg, 1997). Why is this the case? The best guesses are increases in stress and higher levels of environmental toxins in contemporary society, but there is no answer yet. Environmental factors combine to make this physiological milestone a great equalizer of ethnic differences. When girls of Jewish, African, Italian, and Japanese descent are raised under the same living conditions, they all begin to menstruate at the same early age (Huffman, 1981). Furthermore, after years of immigration, regardless of ethnicity, girls menstruate earlier in North America than in their countries of origin (Brumberg, 1997). Both boys and girls experience a growth spurt, although this tends to happen for girls almost two years before it happens for boys. This spurt continues until around the age of 18. Young adults increase between 7 and 8 inches in height.

Adulthood and Aging

The college years, 18 to 21, are often referred to as the young adult years with adulthood stretching up to at least 65 years of age after which point adults are often referred to as older adults (though there are many 67-year-olds who would take offense to this label). Limited changes in physical development occur after the adolescent years. The body does not appear to have any other specific timed changes occurring for at least another 10 to 30 years after puberty and the adolescent growth spurt. Yet, during this period, our health behaviors are perhaps most important in determining how pain free we live our lives and how long our later years will be. Some changes do happen. The hair tends to thin and turn gray, and many men experience receding hairlines. The storage of body fat also increases and the distribution of fat changes. For example, our bodies store more fat on our waists, causing an increased waist-to-hip ratio (WHR). Higher WHRs are warning signs for coronary heart disease and a signal of excessive wear and tear on the body (Seeman, Singer, Horwitz, & McEwen, 1997). Overall, our bodies tend to put on weight until our mid-50s. Constant physical activity is necessary to compensate during these years. We then start to lose weight and slowly our height decreases (after approximately age 60) and our bones shrink (from our body using up the calcium stored in them). Some other clear physiological markers of aging are also present. Hearing and vision degrade first, which can have a severe impact on the quality of day-to-day life by interfering with activities such as driving and walking. Other age-related changes including hormonal functioning are seen, most notably in women.

Menopause, or the ending of the menstrual period, typically occurs in the early 50s. Simultaneously, secretion of a number of female sex hormones decreases, and these changes may be associated with a variety of mood problems and even risks for various diseases (Matthews et al., 1997). Psychology can play a role in this as well. Reactions to menopause vary greatly, depending on the expectations that women have (Matthews, 1992), and many women experience few emotional problems (Dennerstein, 1996). Expecting to experience mood swings and depression can make mood swings and depression more likely to be experienced. The bigger issue on the table is whether women should start taking hormone pills to replace the natural cycle. Hormone replacement therapy was a common practice for many years until 2002 when the intervention arm of the Women's Health Initiative study testing the effects of hormone replacement was halted because women receiving the drug were found to have a higher risk for certain cancers (Rossouw et al., 2002). Some evidence suggests that some forms of hormone replacement may be safe (Bond, Hirota, Fortin, & Col, 2002), but researchers have not reached a consensus yet.

Although we often stereotype older adults as being weak and forgetful, the natural breakdown of muscles and the loss of memory do not start until much later in life. In a longitudinal study begun in 1956, Schaie (1993) demonstrated that the majority of participants showed no significant decline in most mental abilities until the age of 81. The common saying, "Use it or lose it," is very pertinent (Sandborn, 2000). Maintaining a constant routine of physical activity can prolong good health and activity and ensure that an aging adult can continue to perform comfortably the activities of daily living into their 70s and 80s. Marinelli and Plummer (1999) had members of different community groups participate in regular physical activity. This activity led to an increase in the participants' physical, social, emotional, and intellectual health. Similarly, older adults who have new experiences to occupy their minds, experience less memory loss over time (Ball et al., 2002).

© Anderson-Ross/Jupiter Images

Being Mentally and Physically Active Has Few Age Limits

Although there are some natural physiological changes as we age, the greater cause of loss of muscle tone is not using them enough.

SYNTHESIZE, EVALUATE, APPLY	• Given what you know about physical development, what recommendations do you have for parents? • What are the psychosocial implications of the different physical milestones of development (e.g., puberty, menstruation, menopause)? • What are the most different ways that psychosocial factors can hinder prenatal development?

THE NERVOUS SYSTEM

Understanding the physiological bases of stress provides us with a better understanding of how psychology can make a difference. The nervous system is the most critical physiological player. Its functioning also influences the endocrine system together with which it modulates the functioning of the cardiovascular system, the respiratory system, the digestive system, and the reproductive system.

The nervous system can be divided into two main parts: the central nervous system (CNS) (consisting of the brain and spinal cord), and the peripheral nervous system (consisting of all the nervous tissue and cells outside the brain and spinal cord).

The Central Nervous System

The primary function of the Central Nervous System (CNS) is to process and coordinate information that it receives from the peripheral nervous system. In essence, the CNS is the command center of the body with the brain as the main coordinator. The brain coordinates every aspect of the stress response. In addition, the "psychological" part of health psychology has its physiological basis in different parts of the brain (Figure 3.1).

The vertebrate brain can be divided into three main parts. The hindbrain or rhombencephalon is located at the back of the brain and consists of the

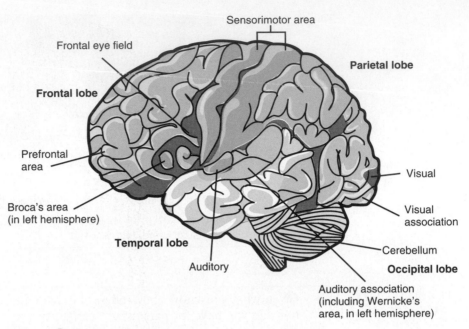

FIGURE **3.1** The Human Brain
Most of what we see is the forebrain with its four main lobes.

medulla, pons, and cerebellum. The medulla controls life-support functions (e.g., breathing), the pons relays information from the spinal cord to the higher brain areas, and the cerebellum controls motor coordination and movement in response to sensory stimuli. The midbrain or mesencephalon consists of structures that process visual information (superior colliculus) and auditory information (inferior colliculus) and those that play a key role in attention, pain control, and emotions (tegmentum, periaqueductal gray, and substantia nigra). The reticular formation plays a key role in the stress response handling emergency responses. It is a group of neurons that takes up a large portion of the midbrain but runs from the hindbrain to the forebrain.

The forebrain, or prosencephalon, is the part of the brain that you most likely associate with the word *brain*, that bean-shaped structure with grooves and fissures. This is the area where all that makes us human resides. Thinking, consciousnesses, talking, eating, and creating are all functions housed in the forebrain. Most of what you see or picture is only the cerebral cortex, the surface lobes of the brain. The cortex consists of four lobes. The frontal lobe contains the motor cortex and key command centers for the body. The parietal lobe processes sensory data from the body. The temporal lobe processes auditory, smell, and taste information. The occipital lobe processes visual information.

Under the cerebral cortex are other key forebrain structures. Perhaps the single most influential part of the brain is located in the forebrain. The hypothalamus directly controls the activity of the pituitary gland, which releases hormones and correspondingly regulates all of our motivated behaviors. Just above

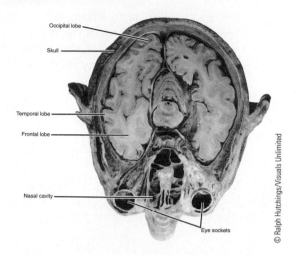

Occipital lobe

Skull

Temporal lobe

Frontal lobe

Nasal cavity

Eye sockets

© Ralph Hutchings/Visuals Unlimited

Physiology of the Brain

A cross-sectional slice of a real human brain showing the compartments of the skull and brain matter.

---

the hypothalamus (*hypo* means *below*, *hyper* means *above* or *over*—just like a *hyper* friend is *over*active) lies the thalamus, which relays information from the brain stem to the entire cerebral cortex. The temporal lobe houses the hippocampus and amygdala, two structures making up what is called the limbic system. The hippocampus plays a pivotal role in emotions and memory, and the amygdala produces fear, escape, rage, and aggression. Many of these structures will feature prominently in the first major stress theory we discuss.

The spinal cord extends from the base of the skull to the tailbone and in cross-section resembles a gray "X." The gray matter consists of cell bodies of neurons and is surrounded by bundles of white axons. Bundles of axons are referred to as tracts (in the CNS) and nerves (in the peripheral nervous system). Bundles of cell bodies are referred to as nuclei (in the CNS) and ganglia (in the peripheral nervous system). Sensory information from the peripheral nervous system travels up the tracts in the CNS to the brain.

The Peripheral Nervous System

The peripheral nervous system transmits information to the entire body with 12 pairs of cranial nerves and 31 pairs of spinal nerves (one pair leaving the spinal cord at each of the vertebra in our spines). The two nerves comprising a pair serve each side of the body. The peripheral nervous system has two main divisions, the somatic nervous system and the autonomic nervous system. The somatic nervous system controls the skeletal muscles and is under conscious control. You can decide to move your arm to prop this book up higher, and then you can do it. The autonomic nervous system coordinates muscles not under your voluntary control and acts automatically in response to signals from the CNS. Your heart muscles, for example, are under autonomic control. One signal from the hypothalamus can lead to your heart rate jumping up. Another signal can make it slow down. An arm of the autonomic system called the sympathetic nervous system (SNS) produces the speeding up responses. Another arm of the system known as the parasympathetic nervous system (PNS) produces the slowing down responses. We discuss further these two arms of the autonomic system in the context of stress in the next chapter.

SYNTHESIZE, EVALUATE, APPLY	• What are the major parts of the nervous system? • What different parts of the brain are most active when you are dancing to music? • Defend the statement "the nervous system is the most important system of the body." • What nervous system physiological mechanisms could explain how psychological and societal factors interact with biological ones?

THE ENDOCRINE SYSTEM

Why should you care about the endocrine system? One word: diabetes. There was a time (probably before your time) when type 2 diabetes (the most common form) occurred mainly in the elderly. Today, even children as young as 13 are diagnosed with it (CDC, 2008) and approximately 21 million North Americans have diabetes (National Diabetes Information Clearinghouse, NDIC, 2008). Both forms of diabetes (more on this later in this section) are a result of the body's cells not taking in enough **insulin**, a hormone produced in the pancreas that regulates glucose uptake. Insulin and a host of other hormones regulate a number of the body's activities and are secreted by the endocrine glands.

It was originally thought that the nervous system with its network of neurons spreading throughout the body was the main way the body's functions were regulated. In the 1900s, researchers studying the triggers of pancreatic juices blocked the action of neurons in the intestines and found that the pancreas was still able to respond. They assumed that the gland itself was secreting an active substance (creatively called *secretin*) that worked on food. This substance was later called a "hormone" from the Greek *hormon*, meaning to set in motion. Correspondingly, the discovery of a separate system from the nervous system led to its being called the **endocrine system** from the Greek *endon* meaning 'within', and *krinein* meaning 'separate' (Starr & McMillan, 2006).

Key Components and Mechanics

The key players in the endocrine system are the hormones and the ductless glands that produce them (which are summarized in Figure 3.2). The major glands (with examples of the hormones they secrete) are the pituitary gland (oxytocin), pineal (melatonin), thyroid (thyroxine), parathyroid (parathyroid hormone), thymus (thymosins), pancreas (insulin), adrenal (cortisol and catecholamines), ovaries (estrogen), and testes (androgens). The ovaries and testes, collectively referred to as the **gonads,** are also our primarily reproductive organs.

The major functions of each of these hormones are also summarized in Figure 3.2. Hormones often interact and have different functions (Starr & McMillan, 2006). The effect of one hormone can counteract the effect of

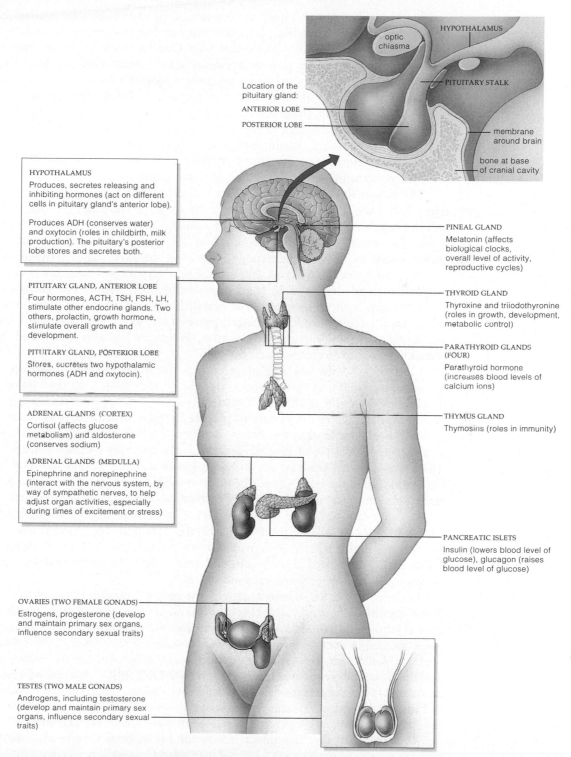

Location of the pituitary gland:

optic chiasma

HYPOTHALAMUS

PITUITARY STALK

ANTERIOR LOBE

POSTERIOR LOBE

membrane around brain

bone at base of cranial cavity

HYPOTHALAMUS

Produces, secretes releasing and inhibiting hormones (act on different cells in pituitary gland's anterior lobe).

Produces ADH (conserves water) and oxytocin (roles in childbirth, milk production). The pituitary's posterior lobe stores and secretes both.

PITUITARY GLAND, ANTERIOR LOBE

Four hormones, ACTH, TSH, FSH, LH, stimulate other endocrine glands. Two others, prolactin, growth hormone, stimulate overall growth and development.

PITUITARY GLAND, POSTERIOR LOBE

Stores, secretes two hypothalamic hormones (ADH and oxytocin).

ADRENAL GLANDS (CORTEX)

Cortisol (affects glucose metabolism) and aldosterone (conserves sodium)

ADRENAL GLANDS (MEDULLA)

Epinephrine and norepinephrine (interact with the nervous system, by way of sympathetic nerves, to help adjust organ activities, especially during times of excitement or stress)

OVARIES (TWO FEMALE GONADS)

Estrogens, progesterone (develop and maintain primary sex organs, influence secondary sexual traits)

TESTES (TWO MALE GONADS)

Androgens, including testosterone (develop and maintain primary sex organs, influence secondary sexual traits)

PINEAL GLAND

Melatonin (affects biological clocks, overall level of activity, reproductive cycles)

THYROID GLAND

Thyroxine and triiodothyronine (roles in growth, development, metabolic control)

PARATHYROID GLANDS (FOUR)

Parathyroid hormone (increases blood levels of calcium ions)

THYMUS GLAND

Thymosins (roles in immunity)

PANCREATIC ISLETS

Insulin (lowers blood level of glucose), glucagon (raises blood level of glucose)

FIGURE **3.2** The Endocrine System

another (e.g., glucagon and insulin). Sometimes, two hormones are needed to interact to cause an effect (e.g., lactation from prolactin, oxytocin, and estrogen). There is even a warm-up act function: One hormone serves to start a process that is finished by another hormone (e.g., implantation of a fertilized egg after the uterus is exposed to estrogen then progesterone).

The hormones are divided into two major categories: steroids such as estrogens, testosterone, progesterone, aldosterone, and cortisol; and nonsteroids such as the amines (e.g., norepinephrine and epinephrine), peptides (e.g., oxytocin), proteins (e.g., insulin and prolactin), and glycoproteins (e.g., follicle stimulating hormone). The steroid hormones are synthesized from cholesterol whereas the nonsteroids are derived from amino acids.

The hypothalamus and the pituitary gland (described in the nervous system section) are the major controllers of the different endocrine glands. You will see a specific detailed case of these players in action in Chapter 4 on stress. In general, the hypothalamus and the pituitary gland interact to control secretion of hormones, nicely illustrating the partnership between the nervous and endocrine systems. In fact, the two systems are often referred to as one neuroendocrine system (e.g., Brannon & Feist, 2007). The glands of the endocrine system secrete hormones directly into the bloodstream by which they are circulated to different parts of the body. Just like the lock and key mechanisms of neurotransmitters, hormones are also specialized to connect to unique receptors on target cells.

In addition to the key role played by the endocrine system in the stress response, the functions of hormones are also directly tied in to the etiology of diabetes, a common chronic illness. When we eat, the pancreas secretes insulin that stimulates the update of glucose by muscles and fat cells. Insulin lowers the glucose level in the blood. Between meals our body's cells use up glucose and as the blood glucose decreases, the pancreas secretes *glucagon*, which breaks down amino acids and glycogen to increase the glucose level in the blood. When the body cannot produce enough insulin or when the insulin target cells cannot react to it, **diabetes mellitus** (diabetes for short) develops.

Diabetes can be of two forms. In type 1 or 'insulin dependent' diabetes (10% of diabetics), insulin producing cells are destroyed. This form is seen at an early age and is treated with insulin injections (American Diabetes Association, 2008). In type 2 diabetes, insulin levels are close to normal but the receptor cells cannot properly respond to insulin.

Diabetes is a classic example of why the biopsychosocial model in health psychology is so important and shows the relevance of culture. Biology interacts with psychological moods and health behaviors such as eating, which in turn are influenced by societal norms. After adjusting for population age differences, Mexican Americans, the largest Hispanic/Latino subgroup, are 1.7 times as likely to have diabetes as non-Hispanic whites (NDIC, 2008). The age-adjusted prevalence rates for diabetes show that whereas close to 20 percent of American Indians, 15 percent of African Americans, and 14 percent of Hispanic Americans have diabetes, only 8 percent of European Americans have diabetes.

Though a bad diet is a direct risk factor for diabetes (Hu et al., 2001), research now suggests that smoking is a major factor as well. A recent literature review of studies including 1.2 million participants showed that on average, tobacco users have a 44 percent higher chance of developing type 2 diabetes (Willi, Bodenmann, Ghali, Faris, & Cornuz, 2007). The risk of diabetes was greater for heavy smokers (20 or more cigarettes/day) than for lighter smokers, and lower for former smokers compared with active smokers.

In addition to diabetes, another hormone that has implications for mental and physical health is **melatonin**. Produced by the pineal gland, melatonin affects the reproductive cycle and how we sleep. Not receiving enough sunlight can cause seasonal affective disorder (SAD), which can be alleviated by controlling levels of melatonin (Lewy, Lefler, Emens, & Bauer, 2006). We shall hear more about diabetes and the risks of trying to get more sun in Chapter 7 on health behaviors.

THE CIRCULATORY SYSTEM

The circulatory system had many people guessing for centuries. Today we understand the mechanisms that provide every cell in our body with life-giving oxygen, but this was not always the case. At first, it was believed that life was maintained not by the constituents of blood, but by a vital spirit, or *pneuma*. The Greek Empedocles of Agrigentum, who lived around 500 to 430 B.C., was the first to postulate that the heart was the center of the circulatory system, although he believed it to be the seat of life-giving pneuma. This pneumatic theory held a long time. Later Greeks added to our knowledge of circulation, but pneumaticism still reigned. For example, Erasistratus (around 300 B.C.) identified the role played by veins and arteries and even traced them down to the limits of his vision, to the fine branches that later came to be called capillaries. The greatest early contributor to our understanding was Galen (around 150 B.C.; see Chapters 1 and 2) who through his animal dissections clarified the functions of the arteries and veins. His only mistake, apart from also accepting the pneumatic theory, was in believing the heart was a form of heater that warmed the blood instead of recognizing it as a pump. He believed blood flowed because of the pulsing of the arteries and moved back and forth like the tides (not in a circular fashion). It was not until the work of English physician William Harvey in 1628 that we got a complete understanding of the circulatory system. The Italian Marcello Malphighi discovered capillaries in 1689, the only component that Harvey could not see but about which he had correctly hypothesized.

Key Components

The circulatory system is so named because the blood flows in a circle (from the Latin, *circus*—the next time the circus is in town notice that it plays in the middle of a big circle as well). The heart, arteries, veins, and capillaries are the key components of the system.

The human heart with its muscular myocardium walls is about the size of a clenched fist, sits just beneath our breastbone, and is protected by a fibrous sac called the pericardium. The heart has two main halves. The right half receives blood low in oxygen from all over the body and pumps it to the lungs. The left half receives blood rich in oxygen from the lungs and pumps it back all over the body. Each half of the heart is further divided into

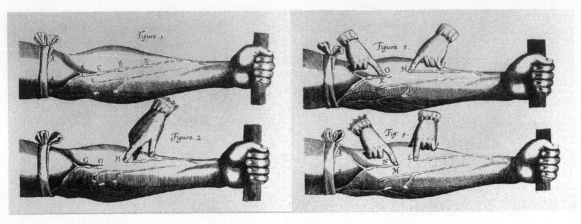

Illustration of William Harvey's Experiments in his *On the Circulation of the Blood* (1628)

Venal valves had already been discovered, but here Harvey shows that venal blood flows only toward the heart. He put a ligature on an arm to make the veins and their valves obvious and then pressed blood away from the heart and showed that the vein would remain empty because it was blocked by the valve.

two chambers. The upper and thinner-walled chambers on each side are called the **atria**; the lower, thicker-walled chambers on each side are called **ventricles**.

Blood vessels that carry blood away from the heart are called arteries, and the vessels that carry blood to the heart are called veins. Two large veins, the superior (from the upper parts of the body) and the inferior (from the lower parts of the body) venae cavae, carry deoxygenated blood into the heart. A large artery carries oxygenated blood to the rest of the body. Two other vessels carry blood between the heart and the lungs. The **pulmonary artery** carries deoxygenated blood from the heart to the lungs, and the **pulmonary vein** carries blood from the lungs to the heart. What keeps everything separate? Its valves. A system of valves ensures that the blood flows in one direction only (a nice idea that would work great to keep backwash to a minimum when one is sipping from a can or bottle). Each valve consists of flaps of connective tissue and the actual sound of a heartbeat is the sound of the valves closing. The first "buh" is when the valves between the atria and ventricles close. The second "bub" is when the valves between the ventricles and the arteries shut. The heart, the valves, and its main vessels and chambers are shown in Figure 3.3.

The Mechanics of Circulation

As Harvey first clearly showed, humans have what is called double circuit circulation. Deoxygenated blood from all over the body flows into the heart, from where it is pumped to the lungs. In the lungs, the carbon dioxide in the blood is removed and oxygen flows into the blood in the tissues and air sacs of the lungs. The blood then flows back to the heart and is pumped to the rest of the body. The circuit between the heart and the lungs is called pulmonary circulation (*pulmo* is Latin for "lung"). The circuit around the rest of the body is called systemic circulation. As the arteries leave the heart, they get

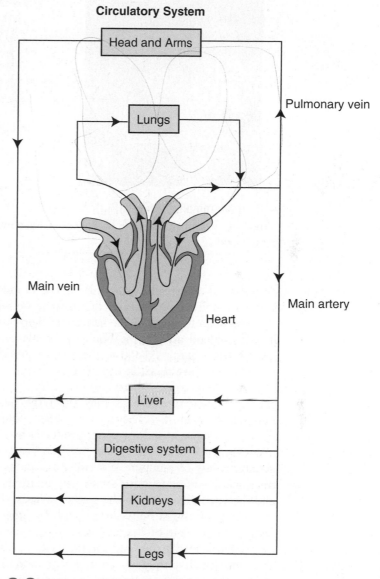

Circulatory System

FIGURE **3.3** The Circulatory System

narrower and branch out many times into smaller vessels called arterioles. They then narrow into even finer vessels called **capillaries**. Veins similarly branch into smaller vessels, called venules, and into even smaller vessels also called capillaries. Is this the same word? Yes, it is, and the same location too. Because the blood vessels all form one giant circle, they must meet somewhere, and that place is the capillaries. Like a neighborhood recycling center where metal cans are turned in and the material is reused, oxygen slips out of the capillaries and into the surrounding cells and tissues, and carbon

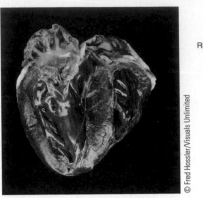

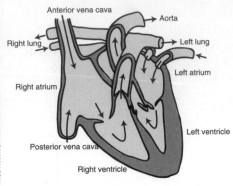

Anterior vena cava

Aorta

Right lung

Left lung

Left atrium

Right atrium

Left ventricle

Posterior vena cava

Right ventricle

© Fred Hossler/Visuals Unlimited

A Real Mammalian Heart (Pig)

Notice the thick muscular lining of the walls. These muscles contract and expand to pump blood.

dioxide and other cell wastes slip in. The blood then moves from the capillaries into the veins and back to the heart to be rejuvenated.

The main function of the heart is to help put oxygen into the blood and to push the blood around the body to the places where it is needed. When the heart beats, it pumps blood to the arteries. Because the diameters of the vessels near the heart are much larger than the diameters of the arteries that the blood is being pumped into, there is pressure in the arteries. The arteries also influence this blood pressure as they resist the blood flow. Healthy arteries are muscular and elastic. They stretch when your heart pumps blood through them, with more stretching being produced by stronger pumping. The pressure rises with each beat and falls in between beats as the heart muscles relax. The actual process of pumping is a two-stage process consisting of a cycle of contractions by different parts of the heart. In the first stage, the atria contract and the ventricles relax. In the second stage, the reverse takes place.

The heart beats between 55 and 85 times per minute when you are at rest, but the rate of beating can change dramatically with each different move. Break into a run, and the rate will increase to get oxygen to the organs and muscles that need it. Take a nap, and it will slow down. It can even change from minute to minute, depending on what you are thinking. If you are watching a movie and a scary part comes on, your heart will speed up (or even "skip a beat," which really reflects an irregular beat and not really a skipped beat). Blood pressure is described using two numbers, the **systolic** pressure (when the heart is beating) and the **diastolic** pressure (when the heart is resting) and is measured in millimeters of mercury (mm Hg), which is the height in millimeters of mercury that the pressure could support. A healthy adult's blood pressure should be less than 120/80 mm Hg.

A Biological Primer

You may have noticed that medical journals tend to be filled with a lot of big words. Those of you in premedical programs or in medical school or those working toward degrees in occupational or physical therapy have probably already had your encounters with medical terminology (it pays to know some Latin, doesn't it?). If you are truly term phobic, then skip the next paragraph (and lose the chance to impress your friends with your erudition and M.D.-like medical knowledge). In discussing CVDs and reading the medical literature, you will probably encounter many technical terms with which you need to be familiar. **Angina pectoris** (chest pain) is a common symptom of heart attacks, or **myocardial infarctions** (cardiac arrest/CHD/CAD). The myocardium is the medical term for the muscle of the heart. You may also read about **ischemia,** a term for the condition in which blood flow is limited in a certain part of the body. Heart attacks are called myocardial ischemias, although more specifically, heart attacks result from ischemias to the cardiac region. Many millions of Americans have ischemias without even knowing it; these are called silent ischemias. Because silent ischemias are not accompanied by angina, individuals who have them may also have a heart attack without warning (American Heart Association, 2004).

THE DIGESTIVE SYSTEM

What you eat can have serious implications for your health (see Chapter 7 for details on what a healthy diet is). Your diet also is linked to your likelihood of being diabetic, developing coronary heart disease, and can influence how you cope with cancer (see Chapter 12 and Chapter 13). A diet high in fat and cholesterol is a major contributor to obesity. Therefore, it helps to know a little about the digestive process.

Key Components and Mechanics

The digestive system is essentially a tube with two openings (sorry, facts are facts). We take in food through our mouths and, well, you know how we excrete it. The entire span from mouth to anus is referred to as the **gastrointestinal tract (GI).** Food moves from the mouth through the throat and pharynx into the esophagus and then into the stomach. The stomach can stretch to take food in and is often the site of invasive surgery to curb eating (more on this later). From the stomach, the food moves into the small intestines (the duodenum, the jejunum, and the ileum), which totals almost 20 feet in length and is all wound up in our body cavity. The last part of the GI tract is the large intestine, or colon, which terminates in the rectum and anus. A little known fact: Colon cancer is the third leading form of cancer for both men and women and results from small clumps of cells called **polyps** that turn cancerous (see Chapter 13). Figure 3.4 summarizes the main parts of the digestive system and indicates what agents act on the food at each site.

Chewing and salivary enzymes begin breaking down food in the mouth. In the stomach, gastric fluids start digesting proteins. Secretions from the liver, gallbladder, and pancreas act on food in the small intestine where nutrients are absorbed. The entire inner length of the small intestine is comprised of many circular folds that greatly increase its surface area to optimize nutrient absorption. The large intestine stores undigested matter for excretion (Starr & McMillan, 2006).

Major Components:

MOUTH (ORAL CAVITY)
Entrance to system; food is moistened and chewed; polysaccharide digestion starts.

PHARYNX
Entrance to tubular part of system (and to respiratory system); moves food forward by contracting sequentially.

ESOPHAGUS
Muscular, saliva-moistened tube that moves food from pharynx to stomach.

STOMACH
Muscular sac; stretches to store food taken in. Gastric fluid mixes with food and kills many pathogens; protein digestion starts.

SMALL INTESTINE
First part (duodenum, C-shaped, about 10 inches long) receives secretions from liver, gallbladder, and pancreas.

In second part (jejunum, about 8 feet long), most nutrients are digested and absorbed.

Third part (ileum, 11–12 feet long) absorbs some nutrients; delivers unabsorbed material to large intestine.

LARGE INTESTINE (COLON)
Concentrates and stores undigested matter by absorbing mineral ions, water; about 5 feet long: divided into ascending, transverse, and descending portions.

RECTUM
Distension stimulates expulsion of feces.

ANUS
End of system; terminal opening through which feces are expelled.

Accessory Structures:

SALIVARY GLANDS
Glands (three main pairs, many minor ones) that secrete saliva, a fluid with polysaccharide-digesting enzymes, buffers, and mucus (which moistens and lubricates food).

LIVER
Secretes bile (for emulsifying fat); roles in carbohydrate, fat, and protein metabolism.

GALLBLADDER
Stores and concentrates bile that the liver secretes.

PANCREAS
Secretes enzymes that break down all major food molecules; secretes buffers against HCl from the stomach.

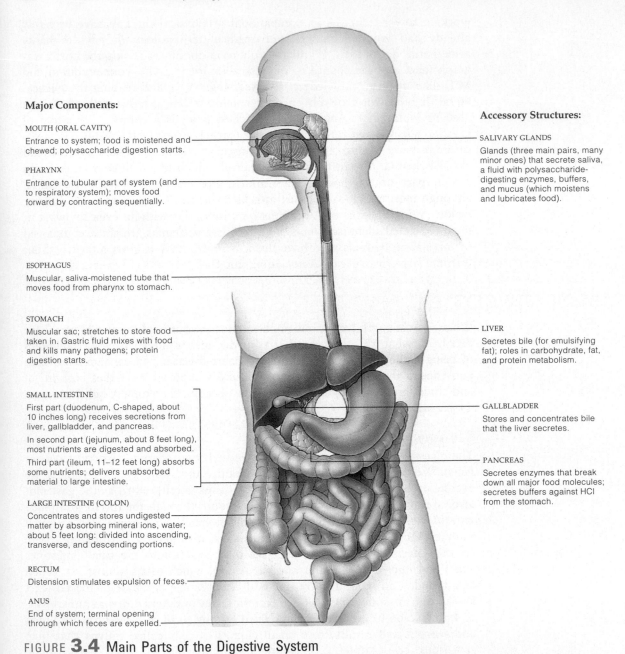

FIGURE **3.4** Main Parts of the Digestive System

In addition to obesity, other major health problems related to the digestive system are gastroenteritis (an inflammation of the lining of the stomach and small intestine), diarrhea (frequent watery bowel movements), dysentery (diarrhea plus blood, pus, and mucus), hemorrhoids (condition in which the veins around the anus or lower rectum are swollen and inflamed), gallstones (pebble-like substances that develop in the gallbladder that block bile flow), and irritable bowel syndrome (disorder characterized commonly by cramping, abdominal pain, bloating, constipation, and diarrhea). Ulcerative colitis is a disease that causes inflammation and sores, called ulcers, in the lining of the rectum and colon (National Digestive Diseases Information Clearinghouse, NDDIC, 2008). Sixty to 70 million people are affected by digestive diseases (Adams, Hendershot, & Marano, 1999).

One digestive system health problem that is of special relevance to the study of health behaviors is alcoholism. Alcohol is processed through the liver and excessive alcohol use can damage the liver, which is why alcoholics often develop liver disease. Liver cirrhosis (see Chapter 7 for more detail) is one of the ten leading causes of death in the United States (CDC, 2008).

Regarding health behavior, (and in the face of the rise of obesity rates in North America), you may be curious about **bariatric**, or weight loss, surgery. **Bariatric surgery** is becoming more popular (Santry, Gillen, & Lauderdale, 2005). The most common type is gastric bypass surgery, which is the stapling of the stomach to create a smaller pouch. A section of the small intestine is then cut out. This "bypass" of sections of the intestine cuts down on how many nutrients are absorbed. Another bariatric technique is "Lap-Band" surgery, where an adjustable silicone band is attached to the stomach to make it smaller and to cut down on eating. Inflating the band squeezes more of the stomach shut. It is important to note that these techniques are not for everybody. It is only recommended for obese individuals who have severe weight-related medical problems. Even though these procedures are an effective treatment for severe obesity, there is risk of early death following bariatric surgery (Flum, Salem, Elrod, Dellinger, Cheadle, & Chan, 2005; Livingston, 2007).

A Note on the Renal/Urinary System

The digestive system does not handle metabolism and excretion of wastes on its own. Every time you feel your bladder pressure you to search for the nearest bathroom you are experiencing the effects of the renal or urinary system. Isn't it the worst when it happens during the really good part of a film?

The major components of the renal system are the kidneys, ureters, urinary bladder, and urethra (see Figure 3.5). Each kidney contains blood vessels and tubes called nephrons. The nephrons filter water and substances such as urea and sodium out of the blood, and produce urine. Each day more blood flows through your kidneys than through any other organ except the lungs (Starr & McMillan, 2006).

The contents of your urine provide important insights into your health. If you are stressed, your urine will show high levels of cortisol and other stress hormones. The body maintains a balance between acidity and alkalinity with the aid of the renal system. If the blood stream is too acidic, the urine will be acidic. If you are diabetic, your urine will have high levels of glucose. In fact, Greek physicians reportedly tasted their patient's urine to confirm a diagnosis of diabetes (Adler, 2004), and the technical name for diabetes, *diabetes mellitus*, reflects the sweeter urine phenomenon (mellitus means honey).

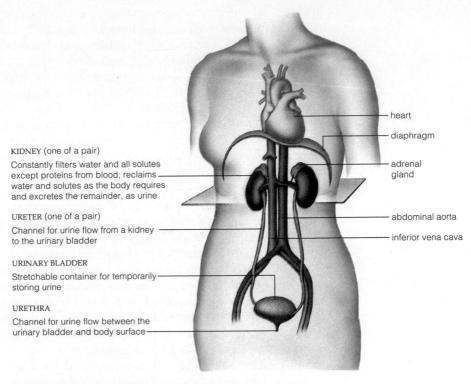

KIDNEY (one of a pair)
Constantly filters water and all solutes except proteins from blood; reclaims water and solutes as the body requires and excretes the remainder, as urine

URETER (one of a pair)
Channel for urine flow from a kidney to the urinary bladder

URINARY BLADDER
Stretchable container for temporarily storing urine

URETHRA
Channel for urine flow between the urinary bladder and body surface

heart

diaphragm

adrenal gland

abdominal aorta

inferior vena cava

FIGURE **3.5** Renal System Main Parts

SYNTHESIZE, EVALUATE, APPLY

- What are the ways the digestive, endocrine, and circulatory systems interact?
- What are the main parts of each system and what function do they serve?
- How could different health behaviors influence the workings of each of the systems described above?

THE PHYSIOLOGY OF IMMUNITY

The **immune system** is the component of our bodies that protects us from threats, mostly in the form of bacteria and germs. The components of the immune system serve two main functions: (1) to discriminate what constitutes our bodies from what are foreign substances, and (2) to destroy and clear those foreign substances and infected cells. We shall give you first an overview of the main components of the system, and then we will take a closer look at exactly how immunity works.

The immune system is composed of a collection of cells and organs. Similar to the circulatory and nervous systems, the immune system has a network of capillaries, the **lymphatic system**, and small oval bodies called lymph nodes (Figure 3.6). The lymphatic capillaries lie along blood vessels and

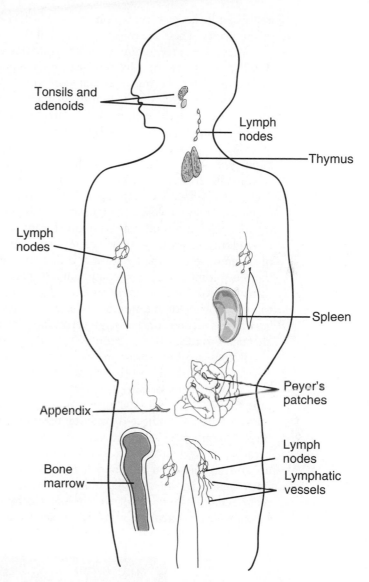

Tonsils and
adenoids

Lymph
nodes

Thymus

Lymph
nodes

Spleen

Peyer's
patches

Appendix

Lymph
nodes

Bone
marrow

Lymphatic
vessels

FIGURE **3.6** The Main Components of the Immune System

carry a colorless fluid called lymph that is composed of fats, proteins, and water and holds the key cells of the immune system, white blood cells (WBCs), or **leukocytes**. Lymph nodes serve as a filtering system and are packed with leukocytes. Leukocytes filter microorganisms and other particles from the lymph and greatly reduce our risks of infection. There are three main types of leukocytes. The most common (comprising between 50 percent and 70 percent of leukocytes) are polymorphonuclear granulocytes. While common, polymorphonuclear granulocytes play a minor role in psychoneuroimmunology and have proven difficult to study. Therefore, we do not discuss them in detail in this book. The most important leukocytes are lymphocytes, which comprise 20 percent to 40 percent of leukocytes. These are the true fighters of the immune system.

There are three main types of lymphocytes, two of which, **T cells** and **B cells**, are further subdivided into more types. T cells and B cells are both formed in the bone marrow, but each one is conveniently named based on where they mature. T cells mature in the thymus gland, an organ situated at the base of the neck. Although you rarely hear much about the thymus (unlike the liver, kidneys, or heart), it is the main site for T-cell development. It is prominent when we are young but shrinks after we reach puberty. There are three main types of T cells. The workhorses are the T cytotoxic cells, or T_C cells. These cells are responsible for killing virally infected cells. A second kind of T cell is the helper T cell, or T_H cell. These cells enhance the functioning of other T cells and play a role in the maturation of B cells. They serve as sentinels, prowling through our bloodstreams looking for invaders. When they encounter foreign cells, germs, or bacteria, they secrete chemical messengers that draw other types of immune cells to the location and destroy the invaders. T_H cells are some of the most common T cells, comprising 30 percent to 60 percent of T cells. The third kind of T cell is the suppressor T cell, or T_S cell. These cells slow down the functioning of the immune system and prevent the body from damaging itself. In particular, once foreign germs have been eliminated, the T_S cells secrete chemicals to turn off the action of T_C and T_H cells.

B cells are both born in and mature in the bone marrow. One type of B cell, the antibody-producing B cell, forms specific substances earmarked for specific germs or **antigens** (*anti*body *gen*erators, more on this later). The other form of B cell, the memory B cell, is the one that explains why so many of us are subjected to immunizations and vaccinations during childhood. Memory B cells are cells that form a template or identification for invading antigens. Memory B cells circulate in the body for many years after an antigen has been eliminated, ready to identify it if it were to invade the body again. By having this indicator of the antigen, illness is less likely to recur because the moment we are infected by the antigen, the memory B cells recognize it and activate our bodies' defenses.

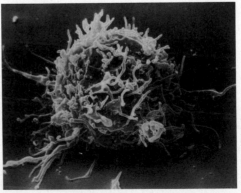

© Nibsc/Photo Researchers

A T Cell

The third kind of lymphocyte is the **natural killer (NK) cell**. These cells circulate in the body, playing a role in different immune responses and especially in destroying diseased cells by injecting them with toxic chemicals. Table 3.2 shows a summary of the different components of the immune system.

There are other hard-working immune cells as well. The foot soldiers of the effort, and often those at the forefront of defenses, are monocytes (circulating in the lymphatic system) and macrophages (a type of monocyte found in the tissue). These cells are the first to attack germs or foreign invaders, destroying them by engulfing and devouring them. In fact, if you want to joke with a friend of yours who eats a lot, you can call him or her a "macrophage" because the word translates literally from its Greek origins to mean "large eater" (yes, this is somewhat nerdy humor but fun nonetheless). Other important immune system components are the chemical messengers, especially interleukin-1 and -2, and interferon, a chemical that prevents viral infections from spreading. Another component of the immune system is the spleen, a ductless organ in the upper left of our abdomen, which serves as a filter for blood. The least common cells are the monocytes and macrophages. Last and perhaps least important (given that many people have them removed) are the tonsils. The tonsils are oval tissue masses in the mouth (open up and say "ah" and you can see them). Their primary function is the storage of lymphocytes.

TABLE **3.2**

Main Cells of the Immune System

Key components

1. Bone marrow (origin of white blood cells [WBCs]) or leukocytes (three types)
    i.   50 percent to 70 percent polymorphonuclear granulocytes (PMNs)—hard to study, minor role in psychoneuroimmunology
    ii. 20 percent to 40 percent lymphocytes
         T (mature in thymus)
         T cytotoxic (TC) (CD8): kill virally infected cells
             T helper (TH): enhance functioning; moderate maturation of B cells (30%–60% of T cells)
             T suppressor (TS): slow down the immune system
         B (mature in bone marrow)
             B antigen-producing
             B memory
         Natural killer (NK)
    iii. 2 percent to 8 percent monocytes (circulating)/macrophages (in tissue)
         Their chemical messengers are interleukin-1 and -2; interferon

2. Lymph vessels (lie along blood vessels) and lymph node—filtering system (packed with WBCs)
    thymus (T-cell school where T cells differentiate)
    spleen (filter for blood)

THE PROCESS OF DEFENSE

Our primary foes are microorganisms such as bacteria and viruses. As mentioned at the start of this chapter, germs surround us. The doorknobs you touch, the chairs you sit on, and the air that you breathe are all filled with germs. Sometimes germ transmission is more direct; for example, when people with a cold hand something to you after blowing their nose, they are probably passing on the cold virus. Most directly, you can be infected by the bite of another living creature that carries the virus (e.g., an insect, animal, or fellow human being).

The main lines of entry for foreign invaders are the skin and the different openings of the body: the nasal passage and mouth (the upper respiratory system), the walls of the stomach and intestine (the gastrointestinal tract), and the sexual and excretory organs (urogenital tract). We have a number of basic processes that protect us at each of these points. We secrete mucus (e.g., in the lining of the nose) that serves to trap germs and prevent their entry. We cough to get germs out of our lungs. Our skin also has a number of glands that secrete a mild oily substance called sebum that also serves to prevent microorganisms from breaking the skin barrier or from growing on the skin. Most microorganisms do not get past the barrier of the thick pile of cell layers that make up the epidermis. As shown in Figure 3.7, the outer layer consists of nondividing cells, many of which are dead or dying, that protect the dividing skin cells beneath. Even when germs do enter the body on particles of food or dust, they usually die due to exposure to lysozyme,

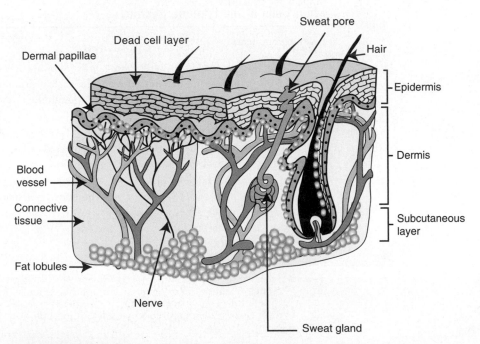

FIGURE **3.7** Cross-Section of the Skin Showing the Different Layers That Serve as Our Body's First Line of Defense

an enzyme found in saliva and tears, which digests the cell walls of many microorganisms. These barriers do not rely on the cells of the immune system and are referred to as **nonimmunologic defenses**.

Nonspecific or Natural Immunity

In addition to these defenses on the body's surface, we also have internal processes that similarly do not differentiate between different types of invaders. These **nonspecific immune** defenses work on a wide variety of disease-causing microorganisms. In the body, macrophages, described above, circulate in the immune system on the lookout for external cells not recognized as being the body's own. When such cells are identified, the body may respond with inflamation and swelling. You may notice this if you fall and skin your knee. The area around the injury swells from an increase in blood flow to the area. The immune cells stream into the damaged site to destroy and inactivate germs potentially present in the dirt or dust you have in the wound. The secretion of chemicals such as **histamine** instigates the swelling or **inflammatory response**. If you have allergies, you are probably familiar with the effect of histamines, which can cause the itching in the eyes, nose, and throat that accompanies the swelling. When the pollen count is too high or you find your allergies being active, your immune system is essentially reacting to all the substances in the air (as taken in through your nasal passage and mouth) and secreting histamine. The inflammation is accompanied often by a fever, indicating that your body is combating the germs (bacteria cannot survive in high temperatures). The actual destruction is accomplished by macrophages that engulf the antigens by **phagocytosis** (the name given to the engulfing process). NK cells and T_C cells may also join the fray. This form of immunity is also referred to as natural or innate immunity.

Acquired Immunity

Do you wonder why we give babies a large number of injections? Those immunizations function as a proactive step to prevent future infection. How does that work? We have another form of immunity, which is referred to as **acquired immunity** and is a form of a specific immune response. This immunity involves the activation of a unique group of cells, the lymphocytes, which are designed to respond to specific microorganisms that the body has encountered before. Acquired immunity is distinguished from nonspecific or natural immunity by five characteristics (Kusnecov, 2002):

1. *Specificity*. Each foreign particle generates only one specific immune response. In this form of immunity, the body is only responding to specific antigens that it has encountered before.
2. *Diversity*. Different immune cells recognize different antigens.
3. *Memory*. Each lymphocyte that bonds to a specific antigen the first time it invades the body will recognize the same antigen if it returns. In subsequent attacks of the same antigen, its matching lymphocyte will be higher in intensity and faster.
4. *Self-Limitation*. After an antigen is destroyed, the responding cells will be turned off or suppressed (T_S cells).

5. *Self/Nonself-Discrimination.* An essential capability of the lymphocytes of the immune system is their ability to discriminate cells from within our own body from those that originated outside our body.

Acquired immunity takes place either in the blood or in cells. The form of immunity orchestrated by immune cells circulating in the blood is also referred to as **humoral-mediated immunity.**

Here is how humoral-mediated immunity works (Figure 3.8). When a bacterial or viral cell enters the bloodstream, the macrophages identify the antigens on the cell's surface and bind to the cell. This bond causes the macrophage to release the chemical transmitter interleukin-1 that alerts T_H cells. The T_H cells proliferate or multiply and release a second chemical messenger, B-cell growth factor. This chemical causes B cells to proliferate. The B cells form structures named antibodies that are designed to bond to the specific invader, hence immobilizing it and targeting it for destruction. Different B cells produce different antibodies, depending on the type of antigen with which they are faced. Every antigen contains one or more epitopes, a specific shape and charge distribution recognized by antibodies. Epitopes are small parts of molecules on each antigen, and it is estimated that the immune system can make antibodies to recognize more than 100 million different epitopes. In addition, memory B cells save a copy of the antibody and remain circulating in the blood after the attack has been completed. These memory B cells have a print, as it were, of the invader and, therefore, are ready to sound the alarm if they encounter the same invader again. When we are immunized as babies, our body produces a large number of memory B cells in response to a small amount of the injected germ (e.g., smallpox), hence protecting us from getting that same sickness later in life. Of course, we also acquire this form of immunity when we actually have (not just been vaccinated for) certain illnesses. For example, if you had chickenpox as a child, you are not likely to get it again because you have circulating B memory cells for chickenpox.

Humoral-mediated immunity is one form of specific immunity. Another form takes place at the level of the cell. **Cell-mediated immunity** involves

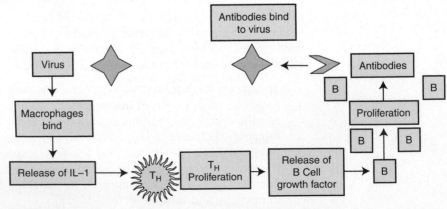

FIGURE **3.8** Humoral-Mediated Immunity

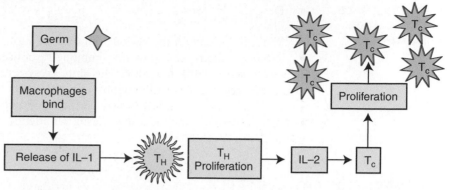

FIGURE **3.9** Cell-Mediated Immunity

T cells although the first few stages are similar to the process for humoral-mediated immunity. In this case, the antigen is first recognized by macrophages, which activate T_H cells. T_H cells then release interleukin-1, which stimulates the proliferation of more T_H cells. The multiplying T cells now release interleukin-2, which leads to T_C cell proliferation. The T_C cells then attack and destroy the antigens. Figure 3.9 shows both forms of immune responses.

Measures of Immune Response

How do you know how active your immune system is? Well, we could make you sick and see how quickly you recover, but there are easier ways to find out. Researchers measure immunity by using blood or saliva samples. A common technique is that an antigen (germ) is added to the sample and then cell activity is measured. First, you can look for **differentiation**, or how much the immune cells divide into the different types of cells (e.g., T_C or T_H or T_S). You can also look for **proliferation** or the extent to which the immune cells multiply. A strong immune response is characterized by great differentiation and proliferation. Immune functioning can also be measured by the extent or levels of chemical messengers (e.g., interferon) present in the sample in response to the antigen. Finally, and perhaps most directly, you can measure **cytotoxicity** or the extent to which the antigens are killed or destroyed. If there are no antigens left in the sample shortly after they are introduced, the person probably has a strong immune system.

Although seemingly straightforward, assessing immune functioning is associated with many problems. First, no single test is available, and it is hard to compare reports from different tests. There is also a lot of variability among assays; results vary from laboratory to laboratory, depending on the technician performing the tests and the serum used. The time of the day and the season can also influence results. Paradoxically, it is not always clear what a "good direction" of immune functioning is. Sometimes a lot of differentiation may suggest strong immunity (the body is reacting); at other times a lot of differentiation may suggest low immunity (the first lines of defense are inadequate). Finally, tests of immunity are available only for blood and not lymph, making a good measurement difficult.

- Describe the pros and cons of the body's way of protecting itself from illness.
- What functions do the various cell differentiations serve?
- What are the basic nonspecific immune responses?
- Given what you know about the immune system, what health behaviors would you recommend maintain optimal health?
- How are cell and humeral mediated immunity different?
- Why do people start sniffling during an allergic reaction?

THE RESPIRATORY SYSTEM

To run, walk, bike, mountain climb, or live in general, you need oxygen, as the cells in our body rely on **aerobic respiration,** a metabolic pathway (means of getting energy) that requires oxygen and produces carbon dioxide. The respiratory system is what facilitates this gas exchange.

Key Components and Mechanics

Figure 3.10 shows the key structures that are part of the respiratory system. You know the basic drill. We breathe in through our nose and mouth and the air moves into the throat, past the larynx, through the trachea, or windpipe, into the lungs. The nose has some first lines of immune defenses: nose hairs that keep out dust and other particulate debris, and mucus, which traps bacteria. The windpipe branches into two airways, one leading into each lung. The lungs are elastic organs protected by the ribcage and separated by our heart. Each soft, spongy lung is covered in a thin membrane.

Inside each lung, the airways (bronchi) branch into smaller and smaller bronchioles. The bronchioles end in little sacs known as **alveoli** clusters. Each lung has approximately 150 million alveoli (Starr & McMillan, 2006). The alveoli are the point at which the cardiovascular system takes over (see Figure 3.3) and where the main gas transfer takes place.

For our purposes, the respiratory system is important in a number of ways. First, poor health behaviors such as smoking wreak havoc on the lungs (see the accompanying photographs of lungs). Second, lung capacity is an important measure of cardiovascular fitness (see Chapter 7). In addition, asthma, one of the most common chronic illnesses, is an incurable respiratory condition.

Asthma is a chronic illness that requires a lot of coping, but it is not always thought of as being in the same category as CVDs, stroke, and diabetes, because it is rarely fatal by itself. Deaths from asthma range from 1.4 per 100,000 for European Americans to 3.4 per 100,000 for African Americans (National Center for Health Statistics, 2003). Asthma affects approximately 15 million Americans, including approximately 10 percent to 12 percent of children younger than age 18. Asthma may occur at any age, although onset is more common in individuals younger than age 40. During 1980 to 1999, asthma prevalence, morbidity, and mortality increased among North American adults. These annual rates were higher among certain ethnic groups. For example, 11.6 percent of American Indians and 9.3 percent of African Americans

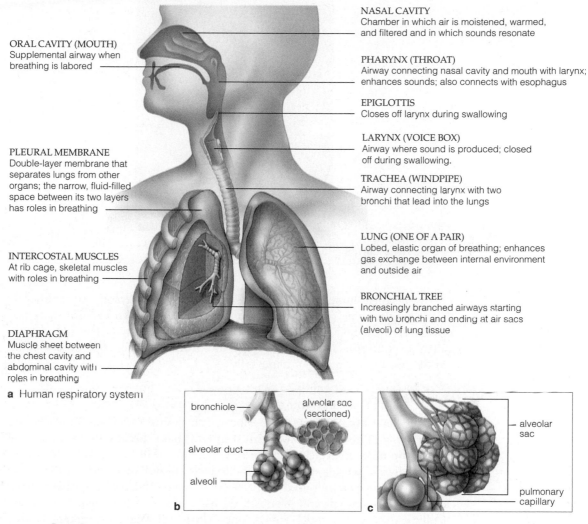

ORAL CAVITY (MOUTH)
Supplemental airway when
breathing is labored

NASAL CAVITY
Chamber in which air is moistened, warmed,
and filtered and in which sounds resonate

PHARYNX (THROAT)
Airway connecting nasal cavity and mouth with larynx;
enhances sounds; also connects with esophagus

EPIGLOTTIS
Closes off larynx during swallowing

LARYNX (VOICE BOX)
Airway where sound is produced; closed
off during swallowing.

PLEURAL MEMBRANE
Double-layer membrane that
separates lungs from other
organs; the narrow, fluid-filled
space between its two layers
has roles in breathing

TRACHEA (WINDPIPE)
Airway connecting larynx with two
bronchi that lead into the lungs

LUNG (ONE OF A PAIR)
Lobed, elastic organ of breathing; enhances
gas exchange between internal environment
and outside air

INTERCOSTAL MUSCLES
At rib cage, skeletal muscles
with roles in breathing

BRONCHIAL TREE
Increasingly branched airways starting
with two bronchi and ending at air sacs
(alveoli) of lung tissue

DIAPHRAGM
Muscle sheet between
the chest cavity and
abdominal cavity with
roles in breathing

a Human respiratory system

bronchiole

alveolar sac
(sectioned)

alveolar duct

alveoli

b

alveolar
sac

pulmonary
capillary

c

FIGURE **3.10** Respiratory System

versus 7.6 percent of European Americans reported cases of asthma. Some
ethnic groups have significantly low levels of asthma (e.g., 2.9% of Asian
Americans). In addition, racial/ethnic minority populations reported higher
use of emergency departments and doctors' offices for asthma treatment
than European Americans (CDC, 2002). Slight geographical variations are
seen. Within the United States, current asthma prevalence is 7.5 percent,
ranging from 5.8 percent in South Carolina to 10.0 percent in Maine.

Asthma is a disease of the airways of the lungs, characterized by tightening
of these airways. If you have asthma, you may cough or wheeze (a whistling
sort of breathing), feel out of breath, and have chest pains. The tightening of
the airways and inflammation, referred to as an asthma attack or episode, can
be triggered by tobacco smoke, excessive exercise, allergies, some weather

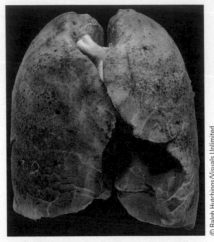

© Ralph Hutchings/Visuals Unlimited

A Smoker's Lungs Show Disease

conditions (high humidity or cold air), and even extreme emotional experiences. For example, some people with asthma have been known to have an episode during very exciting movies. However, coping with asthma has not received much attention in health psychology literature because of asthma's significantly lower association with mortality.

WHAT ABOUT CULTURE?

You may have noticed that there has been little discussion of cultural differences in our study of human physiological systems. That is because there are few differences in physiology across cultures. Unlike different humanoid cultures that inhabit diverse worlds in a science fiction film—some with two heads, others who have evolved to not need nostrils—all humans have the same physiological systems. Different cultural groups even have near identical genetic make-ups (Collins, 2007). The more critical question is whether the different cultural approaches to health (described in Chapter 2) also utilize knowledge of the physiological systems as Western biomedicine does. Unlike the theoretical meridians of Traditional Chinese Medicine (TCM), the existence of the physiological systems are not in doubt (though remember the Chinese do not doubt meridians exist). Not all cultures use them the same way.

TCM recognizes a number of important organs but focus on the activity and functions of the organs instead of on the fixed somatic structure that performs the activity (Kaptchuk, 2000). In this sense, the Chinese do not use a comparable system of anatomy as described in this chapter. Whereas the Chinese recognize organs such as the liver, what is meant by the "liver" is not the same as what Western medicine refers to as the liver. Similarly, some organs recognized by the Chinese, such as the Triple Burner, are not recognized by Western medicine. As mentioned in Chapter 2, TCM organizes the organs by Yin (heart, lungs, spleen, liver, and kidneys) and Yang (gall bladder, stomach, small intestine, large intestine, bladder, and triple burner). Each set has different categories of

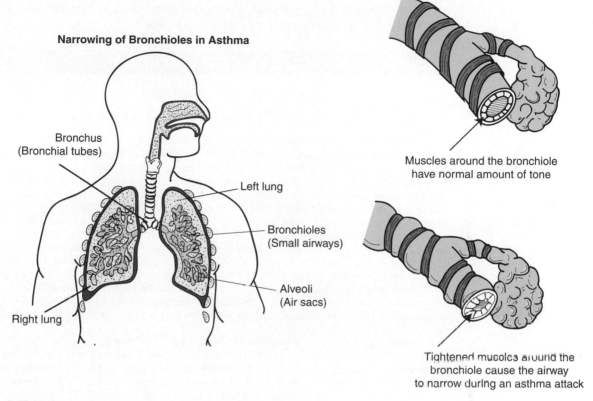

Narrowing of Bronchioles in Asthma

Bronchus
(Bronchial tubes)

Left lung

Bronchioles
(Small airways)

Alveoli
(Air sacs)

Right lung

Muscles around the bronchiole
have normal amount of tone

Tightened muscles around the
bronchiole cause the airway
to narrow during an asthma attack

Asthma

Asthma is also a chronic illness. The diagram shows the main physiological problems causing asthma.

functions. Instead of focusing on physiology, TCM focuses on symptoms displayed by the patient to arrive at a diagnosis.

Ayurveda, similar to TCM, also describes uniquely human physiology. Unlike TCM, Ayurvedic writings more explicitly detail anatomy, and there is a complex set of terms and descriptions for the different physiological components and processes (see Chapter 2). For example, the substances called *doshas* discussed in the previous chapter enable the spiritual and mental planes of existence to express themselves through the physical body (Svoboda, 1993). There are counterparts to the circulation system, such as *srotas* that channel nutrients and waste. There are also structures similar to the nerve plexuses of Western biomedicine (e.g., the solar plexus), the *chakras*, although again the form and function of these nodes is somewhat different from that described by Western science. According to ayurvedic science, there are six chakras arranged along the spinal cord that serve to channel *prana*, or life-force.

Curanderismo, as a blend of Western biomedicine and spiritualism, uses a similar understanding of the physiological systems as Western science, but utilizes a wealth of additional alternative treatments to influence the same systems. With American Indian medicine and African American medicine, comparable anatomy and physiological systems are not explicit or integral parts of the understanding and treatment of health and illness.

FOCUS ON APPLICATIONS

The Games We Play
(Can Have Physiological Implications)

Every holiday season brings a new gaming console to the market—those of you who were children in the 1970s and 1980s may remember Atari, Commodore 64, and Donkey Kong. If a Nintendo Wii was your first gaming platform (or a Playstation like the PS3), you probably think Atari is a relic from a museum (hey it was fun and all we had in those good ole days). Video/computer games were once either "shoot-em-up" or fantasy and involved little more than moving your fingers/thumbs/joystick. We've come a long way baby! The Wii has onscreen players that mimic your every kinesthetic move (e.g., golf, tennis, or yoga). You swing your arm, your player on the screen swings its arm. Games now come in greater varieties than ever before. Some can be played online with partners across the planet. Graphics are getting better. The action is better. The links to aggression are getting stronger too (Carnagey, Anderson, & Bushman, 2007; Konijjjn, BBBijvank, & Bushman, 2007). Yes, some video games have been shown to increase violence in the children, adolescents, and adults playing them. This translates into physiological reactivity and the activity of the nervous and endocrine systems. If video games can be evil, can they also be used for good? Perhaps.

There is a product on the market called "Wild Divine." It is billed as providing "multimedia solution to promote self-care and wellness" (www.wilddivine.com). The Web site has calming imagery and phrases such as "Breathe, meditate, relax" and features well-known names in health and healing such as Dr. Dean Ornish, Dr. Deepak Chopra, and Dr. Andrew Weil. There are a number of packages that feature computer games designed to make you relax using biofeedback. The game comes with little sensors you clasp onto your fingers, which connect you to the computer (Star Trek fans, if any remain, think of Borg). As you relax, images, structures, and forms on the screen change as they are manipulated by your changing heart rate. For example, one exercise involves juggling. The more you relax, the more colored balls on-screen (amid a fantastical setting) rise in the air and jump somersaults. However, could what was essentially a videogame actually relate to physiological changes in the endocrine and nervous system activity? Roethel and Gurung (2007) decided to find out.

There is little empirical evidence to prove that stress management techniques reduce anxiety and the psychological symptoms of stress. Roethel and Gurung (2007) tested the effectiveness of the guided biofeedback provided by the game by collecting self-reported and physiological measures of stress (see more on the stress response in the next chapter). Salivary cortisol samples were taken pre- and post- intervention in each condition. Subjects obtained the saliva samples themselves by using a disposable pipette, which was inserted below the tongue, and samples were transferred to small plastic vials. The samples were then immediately transferred to a laboratory refrigerator, and soon after transferred to a laboratory freezer. The saliva samples were analyzed using high-sensitivity salivary cortisol ELISA assay kits.

Subjects were instructed to refrain from consuming alcohol six hours prior to participation in the study, and to refrain from smoking, high-intensity physical activity, eating, and consuming caffeine one hour prior to their appointment to control for error in cortisol levels. Additionally, the experiment was scheduled in the morning hours (9:00–11:00 a.m.) to control for the diurnal rhythm of cortisol. In true biopsychosocial fashion, we measured both physiological and psychological measures.

Subjects were assigned to one of two conditions to learn and practice a stress management technique in the lab: the game or a control condition. Subjects in the

(continues)

FOCUS ON APPLICATIONS *(continued)*

biofeedback condition learned and practiced the Healing Rhythms by the Wild Divine Project, which is marketed as a new-age innovative relaxation technique. In this game, subjects practiced breathing techniques, regulated their heart rate, and increased their level of concentration, with devices that recorded the physiological responses to these exercises. The biofeedback sensors detect galvanic skin conductance (GSR), or the activity of the subject's sweat glands, and heart rate variability (HRV), the variation in the beat-to-beat interval of the pumping heart. Subjects were instructed to complete six specified biofeedback challenges, each lasting approximately five minutes. Directions were given for each challenge through the interface with the game. The biofeedback challenges were successfully navigated by controlling physiological responses with respect to proper breathing, concentration, and general level of arousal.

Subjects in the control condition worked on homework for 30 minutes, the same amount of time as in the other conditions, and later were given the opportunity to participate in one of the stress management programs.

There were two in-lab training sessions (interventions). The interventions included one-on-one guided training and practice of the assigned stress management technique early in the spring semester, which we expected would be a time of low stress. The participants were also asked to practice the same intervention in the lab just prior to finals week of the same semester, which we expected would be a more stressful time for the students.

Playing the game actually resulted in both physiological and psychological changes. Within the Guided Biofeedback condition, significant differences in measures of mood states were observed, as well as a decrease in psychological symptoms. Specifically, there were significant decreases in measures of anger and hostility, depression, and fatigue. Analysis of salivary cortisol showed a significant decrease in cortisol, a major stress hormone, for the guided biofeedback condition.

Not bad for a videogame. Now to go test the Nintendo Wii.

SUMMARY

- The prenatal stage of human development is critical to the formation of a healthy physiological system, and the health behaviors of the mother, influenced by her culture, can strongly influence the development of the baby.
- The nervous system is divided into the central and peripheral systems. The central nervous system is comprised of the brain and spinal cord. The peripheral nervous system is comprised of the somatic and autonomic nervous systems.
- The nervous and endocrine systems regulate the functioning of the body by secreting different neurotransmitters and hormones.
- The digestive and renal systems are responsible for the metabolic activity in the body and excrete waste. The liver is a major organ debilitated by excessive alcohol consumption. Diabetes is a major chronic illness caused by the body's inability to use insulin.
- The heart is made up of four chambers: two atria and two ventricles. Arteries carry oxygenated blood away from the heart and veins carry deoxygenated blood to the heart. Blood pressure is described as systolic and diastolic pressures for when the heart is beating and resting, respectively.
- The immune system comprises our body's protection system. The cells and organs of this system filter out bacteria and viruses that infiltrate our bodies and break down infected cells.

- The main components of the immune system are the lymph nodes, lymph fluid, and leukocytes or white blood cells. Lymphocytes are T cells and B cells, the primary defensive cells of the system along with macrophages. There are many types of lymphocytes, each with specific immune functions. The strength of an immune response can be determined by measuring cell differentiation, proliferation, or cytotoxicity.
- Natural immunity is brought about by circulating macrophages and the secretion of histamines, which instigate inflammatory responses. Macrophages engulf antigens or invading germs by phagocytosis. Acquired immunity is the response of lymphocytes to specific microorganisms and takes place in the blood or in the cells and tissue.

TEST YOURSELF

Check your understanding of the topics in this chapter by answering the following questions. Answers appear in the Appendix.

1. One of the facts of physical development and aging is that we tend to lose certain functions (e.g., muscle fitness and memory) faster if:
   a. Our cognitive development is faster.
   b. We misuse them.
   c. We get older faster.
   d. We do not use them.
2. Pregnant mothers should watch out for _____, environmental toxins that can cause developmental abnormalities.
   a. teratogens
   b. cytoclines
   c. carcinoxides
   d. butalamenes
3. The group of neurons that runs from the hindbrain to the forebrain and plays a key role in handling emergency responses during stress is:
   a. Basil ganglia.
   b. Reticular formation.
   c. Suprachiasmatic nucleus.
   d. Inferior colliculus.
4. The superior colliculus, inferior colliculus, tegmentum, periaqeductal gray, and substania nigra are all structures in the:
   a. Forebrain.
   b. Midbrain.
   c. Hindbrain.
   d. Hypothalamus.
5. The endocrine hormone most related to the metabolism of food, especially glucose, is:

   a. Oxytocin.
   b. Prolactin.
   c. Gastrin.
   d. Insulin.
6. Problems due to limited blood flow in certain parts of the body are referred to as:
   a. Ischemias.
   b. Arteriosclerosis.
   c. Cardiac arrhythmias.
   d. Angina pectoris.
7. Excessive obesity can be cured by _____ but is a risky procedure.
   a. isometric exercise
   b. barometric surgery
   c. laproscopic surgery
   d. cardiac surgery
8. One of the main functions of the immune system is to:
   a. Minimize the pain from illness and infection.
   b. Destroy foreign substances and infected cells.
   c. Rebuild cells after illness.
   d. Reduce stress at the cellular level.
9. The most important cells of the immune system are the:
   a. Leukocytes.
   b. Macrophages.
   c. Microphages.
   d. Red blood cells.

10. An important organ in the immune system that filters the blood is the:
    a. Heart.
    b. Lungs.
    c. Spleen.
    d. Kidneys.

WEB RESOURCES

Visit the companion Web site at **www.cengage.com/psychology/gurung**, where you will find online resources for this book, including chapter-by-chapter quizzes, Web links, and more!

Get Body Smart
http://www.getbodysmart.com/

GetBodySmart is Scott Sheffield's creation of a fully animated and interactive eBook about human anatomy and physiology. It's a great learning tool.

The Brain
http://www.brain.com/

A great compilation of sites with different imagery of the brain. Try the Neuroscience Gateway for the latest research, news, and events in neuroscience. Click on the Brain Atlas sites for cross-sections and MRI images and for images of a diseased brain.

Web Human
http://placid.skidmore.edu/human/index.php

Web-HUMAN is a systems physiology teaching simulation that presents educators and students with full Web access to Tom Coleman's classic physiology simulation program HUMAN.

KEY TERMS, CONCEPTS, AND PEOPLE

acquired immunity, 91
adolescence, 71
aerobic respiration, 94
alveoli, 94
angina pectoris, 83
antigens, 88
asthma, 94
atria, 80
B cells, 88
bariatric surgery, 85
bariatric, 85
capillaries, 81
cell-mediated immunity, 92

cytotoxicity, 93
diabetes mellitus, 78
diastolic, 82
differentiation, 93
dolescence, 71
endocrine system, 76
gastrointestinal tract (GI), 83
gestation, 67
gonads, 76
histamine, 91
humoral-mediated immunity, 92
immune system, 86

inflammatory response, 91
insulin, 76
ischemia, 83
leukocytes, 87
low birth weight, 67
lymphatic system, 86
melatonin, 79
menopause, 72
myocardial infarctions, 83
natural killer (NK) cell, 89
nonimmunologic defenses, 91

nonspecific immunity, 91
phagocytosis, 91
polyps, 83
prenatal period, 67
preterm births, 67
proliferation, 93
puberty, 71
pulmonary artery, 80
pulmonary vein, 80
systolic, 82
T cells, 88
ventricles, 80

ESSENTIAL READINGS

Blass, E. M. (Ed.) (2001). *Developmental psychobiology*. Boston: Springer Press.

Campbell, N. A., & Reece, J. B. (2004). *Biology*. Boston: Pearson.

Starr, C., & McMillan, B. (2006). *Human biology*. Pacific Grove, CA: Brooks/Cole.

Stress Across Cultures

D on't you just hate those times when you have to introduce yourself to a large group of strangers? Most of us do. Maybe it is a first day of class, and the instructor has everyone say something about themselves. Maybe it is a meeting where everybody has to share opinions. Your heart starts to beat a little faster as your turn approaches. You run over what you want to say in your head, while thoughts about how others will perceive you intrude on your planning ("How will this make me look?"). You barely notice what other people say before your turn. Your palms may become moist, and your face may turn red. The moment arrives when you must speak, and the drumbeat of your heart hammers away in a frenzied crescendo. Suddenly, when you finish, the world is a whole different place, and the birds start singing in the trees again.

Stress is a term that everybody uses freely and that we all seem to understand naturally. "Don't stress out" is often used interchangeably with other soothing advice, such as "Don't freak out," all slang phrases related to those dreaded times when everything seems to go wrong or there is too much to do and too little time. There are many such stressful times in life. For example, when you have not started even on the large paper that is due the next day, or you have reached Sunday night after having wasted the entire weekend when you should have been studying for a test on Monday. How about having your car break down and getting sick and having a close family member have a major accident (all at the same time)? Almost everyone can recall a number of times when they have felt "stressed." However, stress has many meanings that we often do not acknowledge. There are many intriguing aspects to stress and how we experience it. Some things that caused you stress at one time (e.g., making sure you had the right clothes for a very important date, or giving a five-minute presentation in a class) may amuse you today. Some things that are stressful for some people (such as getting up to sing at a Karaoke machine) are actually enjoyable for others. At its most extreme, stress can kill, severely hamper health, or drive someone to behave in risky, unhealthy ways.

WHAT IS STRESS?

What exactly is **stress**? Why do different people and cultures experience stress differently? What can we do to reduce stress? These are some of the questions that we will answer in this chapter. We begin by defining the term and looking at how health psychologists study stress. You will notice that the factors that cause stress for people have varied historically. These varying factors map onto the main psychological theories that attempt to explain stress. Finally, we will look at how we can measure stress in an effort to control and manage it. In contrast to some early theories of stress, we will focus on the role of psychological processes, specifically thinking and behavior. We will also examine how different types of stress are associated with different

A Variety of Stressors Are Present in Everyday Life

cultures (e.g., socioeconomic status, age, and ethnicity), reviewing how different cultural beliefs influence the experience of stress.

Stress can be defined in many different ways. It has been studied using different approaches, and everyone has a different notion of what is stressful to them (Table 4.1). It is important that a definition of stress can be applied to many different people (and animals too). All negative events need not be stressful, and all positive events are not automatically free from stress. For example, losing your job may sound initially like a stressful event, but it may be a happy event if you hated your job and if this now opens up new opportunities for you. Similarly, although finding a romantic partner after a long period of being single sounds like a very positive event, you may worry about how to make sure the relationship lasts or whether your partner likes you or not. These worries could make this positive event stressful. As you can see, stress is subjective. What then is a convenient way to measure stress?

Most researchers argue that the best way to know when a person is stressed is to look at how his or her body responds to a situation. If the sympathetic nervous system activates in response to an event, then the person is under stress. This activation results in elevated heart rate, respiration, and circulation (this is a good time to look over the section on the nervous system in Chapter 3). Many early definitions of stress relied heavily on biological activity. Cannon (1929) viewed stress as the biological mobilization of the body for action, involving sympathetic activation and endocrine activity. Selye (1956) similarly saw stress as the activation of a host of physiological systems. Later theorists added more psychological components to the process of stress (e.g., Lazarus, 1966). Psychological theories defined stress as being caused when the perceived demands on the organism exceeded the resources to meet those demands (e.g., Frankenhaeuser et al., 1989). Although these different definitions have all been well supported, the easiest way to define stress is as "the upsetting of homeostasis" (Cannon, 1929). Each of our bodies has an optimal level of functioning for blood glucose level, body temperature, rate of circulation, and breathing. **Homeostasis** is the ideal level of bodily functions (Starr & McMillan, 2006). Similar to the thermostat in homes, our

TABLE **4.1**
Definitions of Stress

A substantial imbalance between environmental demand and the response capability of the focal organism (p. 17)	McGrath (1970)
The response to the actual loss, threat of loss, or lack of gain of resources that all individuals actively seek to gain and maintain	Hobfoll (1989)
A condition or feeling experienced when a person perceives that demands exceed the personal and social resources the individual is able to mobilize	Lazarus (1966)
Psychosocial stress reflects the subject's inability to forestall or diminish perception, recall, anticipation, or imagination of disvalued circumstances, those that in reality or fantasy signify great and/or increased distance from desirable (valued) experiential states, and consequently, evoke a need to approximate the valued states (p. 196)	Kaplan (1983)
A perceptual phenomenon arising from a comparison between the demand on the person and his or her ability to cope. An imbalance in this mechanism, when coping is important, gives rise to the experience of stress, and to the stress response	Cox (1978)
The upsetting of homeostasis	Cannon (1929)

body is designed to maintain its optimal level in all areas of functioning. We set our thermostats and if the temperature drops below the set level, the furnace starts. In this way a constant temperature is maintained. The hypothalamus in our brains similarly maintains set levels. Stress to our systems can thus be seen as something that upsets our ideal balance. This simple but effective definition of stress harkens back to the origins of the word stress.

Physicists have long studied the effects of large forces on solid structures, and stress was originally used to describe the force exerted on a body, which results in deformation or strain. Stress has similar effects on our body. A **stressor** is *anything* that disrupts the body's homeostatic balance. The **stress response** is what is done to reestablish the homeostatic balance. This definition allows for subjectivity because stressors can vary among individuals (Guenole, Chernyshenko, Stark, McGregor, & Ganesh, 2008). If an event does not activate your stress response or disrupt your system, it is just another event. If an event disrupts you, it is a stressor. One person's event can be another person's stressor. Likewise, even if talking in public is not stressful for you, remember it could be very stressful for someone else.

Stress over Time

Stressors today differ from what was perceived as stressful in the past. A list of common stressors can be seen in Table 4.2. If you review the list you will see that most of the examples are psychological in nature. They are not

TABLE **4.2**

Some of the Major Stressors As Assessed by the Hassles Scales

1.	Death of a close family member	100
2.	Death of a close friend	73
3.	Divorce between parents	65
4.	Jail term	63
5.	Major personal injury	63
6.	Marriage	58
7.	Fired from job	50
8.	Failed important course	47
9.	Change in health of a family member	45
10.	Pregnancy	44
11.	Sex problems	44
12.	Serious argument with family member	40
13.	Change in financial status	39
14.	Change of major	39
15.	Trouble with parents	39
16.	New girlfriend or boyfriend	38
17.	Increased workload at school	37
18.	Outstanding personal achievement	36
19.	First semester in college	35
20.	Change in living conditions	31
21.	Serious argument with instructor	30
22.	Lower grades than expected	29
23.	Change in sleeping habits	29
24.	Change in social habits	29
25.	Change in eating habits	28
26.	Chronic car trouble	26
27.	Change in number of family get-togethers	26
28.	Too many missed classes	25
29.	Change of college	24
30.	Dropped more than one class	23
31.	Minor traffic violations	20

On the scale, you can determine your "stress score" by adding up the number of points corresponding to the events that you have experienced in the past six months or expect to experience in the coming six months.
Source: Hales (2000)

tangible threats such as impending invasion by a powerful army or being mauled by a wildcat, but are things that we worry about or "stress over." There is also a range of stressful events that are tangible. Living in a loud neighborhood or a very cold environment can be stressful too.

Our current stress response is hypothesized to have developed in response to the stressors faced by primitive humans. Both early theorists such as Cannon (1929) and recent researchers such as Sapolsky (2004) suggested that the physiological responses to stress evolved many hundreds, even thousands, of years ago. Consider the early days of civilization before humans lived in cities and towns. Archaeological evidence suggests that humans as we know them today first flourished on the African continent (see Diamond, 2005, for a review of the archaeological evidence). Many wild animals roamed the African savannahs, including saber-toothed tigers, mammoths, and a host of other predators. Most of the early stressors were physical in nature and short term or **acute**. Imagine the early human going out of his or her cave looking for some fresh cactus flowers for lunch. Suddenly the roar of a nearby pack of lions looking for their lunch changes the stroll into an all out sprint for survival. The body had to be able to get ready to mobilize for sudden action in this fashion. Other than predatory animals, our ancestors probably also had to deal with marauding tribes who launched sneak attacks to steal food or mates. Again, the body had to be ready to fight at a moment's notice. Early stressors were most likely acute physical stressors.

With an acute physical stressor, your stress response either worked—you escaped the beast or defeated the ravaging tribes—or that was the end of your story. Those humans with better stress responses lived to reproduce. As civilization proceeded, humans started to live longer and experience more long-term, or **chronic**, stressors. Once agriculture flourished and humans traded nomadic lifestyles for village and town living, the types of stressors changed. Sometimes crops failed, and people would go hungry for long periods. At other times, weather conditions such as drought made food scarce. As the domestication of animals increased, germs from them probably caused large numbers of illnesses. All of these stressors could cause prolonged illnesses, but again the stressors were physical in nature. For much of human history, especially through the Middle Ages when thousands of people died of bubonic plague, the main stressors and causes of death were physical in nature. As described in Chapter 1, medicine was not a successful cure of disease until the last hundred years, and diseases such as pneumonia, tuberculosis, and influenza caused great physical stress and death.

Today, stressors are very different. Yes, people in some countries still die of diseases due to viruses and bacteria. People who live in countries with lots of political strife and civil war (e.g., large parts of Africa, India, and the Far East) or those living in high-crime neighborhoods (some North American inner cities) may actually worry about physical threats to their bodies. But the main physical killers in the United States, such as heart disease, are caused and made worse by the slow accumulation of psychological damage. Much of this damage is related to stress. Today, the major stressors in North America are psychological in nature. Our thoughts and the pressures we apply to ourselves generate stress (*anticipatory* stress, Sapolsky, 2004). Few physical stressors exist here today. Instead, the bulk of our stress is self-generated and related to the pressures, frustrations, and changes of everyday modern life.

Yet the bottom line is that stress, whether physical or psychological in nature, leads to a variety of poor health outcomes (e.g., Segerstrom & Miller, 2004).

MAIN THEORIES OF STRESS

Cannon's Fight-or-Flight Theory

Walter Cannon applied the concept of homeostasis to the study of human interactions with the environment (Cannon, 1914). Specifically, he studied how stressors affect the sympathetic nervous system (SNS). His basic idea is intuitive and can be remembered by a simple example. Imagine going to a Saturday night movie. You drove to the cinema by yourself and the only parking spot you found was far away from the theater doors. After the movie, you walk back to your car alone because the friends you met had closer parking spots. As you reach your car, you hear a crunching sound in the dark behind you. You stop. The crunching stops. You start walking faster, and the crunching speeds up. You scramble for your keys and in the reflection of your car window you see a hulking thug draw up behind you. He is masked and carries a very big stick. You can probably guess what your body is doing. Your heart pumps faster, your blood pressure rises, you breathe faster, you may be a little flushed, and your palms may be sweaty. And there you have it. All these reactions are caused by the SNS that prepares our body for action as described in Figure 4.1. Activation of the SNS increases circulation, respiration, and metabolism, all factors that fuel your body to ready it either to fight the hoodlum or flee, escaping as fast as you can (those who run away live to fight another day). The higher respiration rate gets more oxygen into your lungs, the increased heart rate and blood pressure get the oxygenated blood to the muscles, and the increased metabolism breaks down energy for use by the fighting/fleeing muscles. The SNS also turns off certain systems in response to stress. Faced by a threatening mugger, you are probably not in a mood for two things: food and sex. Your body cannot be wasting resources and energy on these things. The SNS down-regulates (turns off) the digestive system and the reproductive system in times of stress.

The complete reversal of this process (the activating of some systems and the deactivating of others) is what helps your body recover from a stressor and is managed by the parasympathetic nervous system (PNS). The PNS decreases circulation and respiration and increases digestion and reproduction. Correspondingly, most stress management techniques work to activate your PNS and slow down breathing and heart rate. The PNS and SNS are both parts of the autonomic nervous system and are coordinated by higher brain structures such as the hypothalamus.

Cannon (1914) was the first to sketch this pattern of responding to stress and to map out the full level of physiological activation. Cannon argued that when faced with a stressor, the SNS is activated (as just described), and in turn it activates the adrenal glands that secrete a class of hormones called

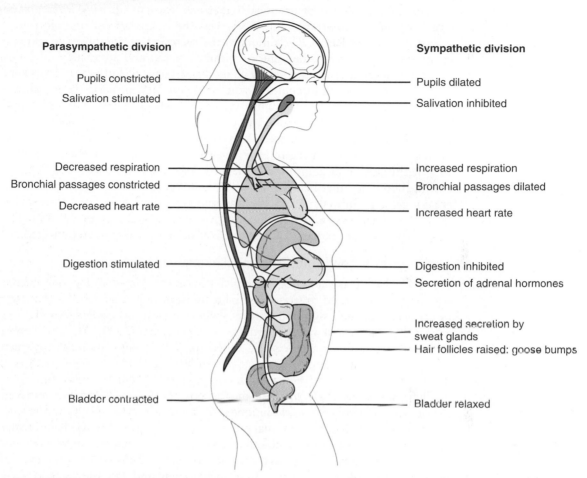

FIGURE **4.1** Major Components of the Autonomic Nervous System Involved in the Stress Response

catecholamines. The two major catecholamines are epinephrine and norepinephrine. Although these two names may seem strange to you, you may already know the main stress hormone. Epinephrine is also known as adrenalin (the British name). You have probably heard the phrase "my adrenalin was flowing" to suggest that someone was stressed or ready for action (the British hard rock band Def Leppard even titled one of their albums *Adrenalize* to signify how "pumped up" they were). The inner part of the adrenal glands, an area called the medulla, produces both these hormones. Consequently, Cannon's **fight-or-flight theory** of stress describes stress as leading to **sympathetic-adrenal-medullary (SAM) activation**. This fight-or-flight system has eight clear-cut effects (Guyton, 1977). Blood pressure, blood flow to large muscles, total energy consumption, blood glucose concentration, energy release in the muscles, muscular strength, mental activity, and the rate of blood coagulation all increase.

An intricate dance of chemical secretions leads to all these events. The hypothalamus orchestrates the SNS via the secretion of corticotropin-releasing factor (CRF). CRF stimulates the secretion of adrenocorticotrophic hormone (ACTH) from the anterior pituitary gland and stimulates the locus coeruleus (located in the pons area of the brain stem) to increase the levels of norepinephrine (or noradrenalin if you are in England or a Def Leppard fan) in the system. Epinephrine is what increases both the heart rate and blood pressure. With prolonged stress, there is a circular reaction and higher levels of epinephrine increase the secretions of ACTH. Research during the past 30 years has shown that the relative levels of epinephrine and norepinephrine vary with the type of emotion experienced with one being more of a "flight" chemical and the other being more of a "fight" chemical. Epinephrine is present in greater amounts when we are scared; norepinephrine is present in greater amounts when we are angry (Ax, 1953; Ward et al., 1983). The different physiological parts of SAM activation are heavily interconnected.

Taylor et al.'s Tend-and-Befriend Theory

For years health psychologists assumed Canon's model was the only major way both sexes reacted to stress. Then a team from UCLA launched a challenge to conventional thinking about stress. Shelley Taylor and colleagues (Taylor, Klein, Lewis, Gruenewald, Gurung, & Updegraff, 2000; Taylor, Lewis, Gruenewald, Gurung, Updegraff, & Klein, 2002) suggested that women **tend-and-befriend** in addition to fighting or fleeing.

Diverse findings in the stress literature just do not fit with the fight-or-flight model. The fight or flight model assumes that men and women faced the same challenges in our evolutionary history. However, this was not true. Females have always been primary caregivers of infants due to their greater investment in giving birth (a minimum investment of 9 months for women versus minutes for men). Men have easily been able to fight or flee, but women often had to look after infants. If women fought and lost they would leave their infant defenseless. If women ran they would either have to leave their infant behind or the weight of the infant would surely slow them down and lead to capture. Instead, Taylor et al. (2000) argued that women developed additional stress responses aimed to protect, calm, and quiet the child, to remove it from harm's way (i.e., tending), and to marshal resources to help. Essentially, women create social networks to provide resources and protection for themselves and their infants (i.e., befriending). The tend-and-befriend response, thus, provides more reasonable stress responses for females than the basic fight or flight theory. This new theory builds on the brain's attachment/caregiving system, which counteracts the metabolic activity associated with the traditional fight-or-flight stress response—increased heart rate, blood pressure and cortisol levels—and leads to nurturing and affiliative behavior.

Existing evidence from research with nonhuman animals, neuroendocrine studies, and human-based social psychology supports this new theory. Neuro-endocrine research shows that although women show the same immediate hormonal and sympathetic nervous system response to acute stress, other factors intervene to make fight-or-flight less likely in females. In terms of the fight response, while male aggression appears to be driven by hormones such as testosterone, female aggression is not. In fact, a major female hormone, oxytocin, actually counteracts the effects of stress chemicals such as cortisol and the catecholamines. Oxytocin inhibits flight and enhances relaxation, reduces fearfulness and decreases the other stress responses typical to the fight-or-flight response. Strong evidence suggests oxytocin underlies both the tending and the befriending parts of the theory. Supporting the role of oxytocin in befriending, blocking oxytocin in women actually makes them spend less time with their friends (Jamner, Alberts, Leigh, & Klein, 1998).

In terms of tending, oxytocin plays a key role in maternal bonding. Although extensively studied in animals, the tending role of oxytocin in humans has only newly been illustrated. Feldman, Weller, Zagoory-Sharon and Levine (2007) measured the oxytocin levels in pregnant women twice during their pregnancy and once after they had given birth. Women with higher levels of oxytocin bonded better with their babies and behaved in ways to form better bonds (e.g., feeding in special ways). More oxytocin in early life is also related to later tending and befriending in both animals (Bales, van Westerhuyzen, Lewis-Reese, Grotte, Lanter, & Carter, 2007) and humans (Fries, Ziegler, Kurian, Jacoris, & Pollak, 2005; Taylor, 2006).

Tending is observed in animal studies when rat pups are removed from their nest for brief periods—a stressful situation for pups and mothers—and then returned. The mothers immediately move to soothe their pups by licking, grooming, and nursing them (Meaney, 2001). Similar behaviors are seen in sheep (Kendrick et al., 1997) and monkeys (Martel et al. 1993). In humans, breastfeeding mothers are found to be calmer (Ulvas-Moberg, 1996), and touch has been shown to soothe both the mother and infant (Field, 1996). In clear support of the theory Repetti and Wood (1997) showed on the one hand, that after a stressful day on the job, men want to be left alone and often fight with their spouses and kids. Women, on the other hand, actually tended when stressed, spending more time with their kids and having more physical contact with them.

Selye's General Adaptation Syndrome

Hans Selye was a young assistant professor in search of direction when a colleague gave him some ovarian extracts. Selye set out to determine the role played by these extracts and, quite by chance, discovered another major explanation for the stress response. In his early experiments, he injected rats with the ovarian extract and observed them for changes. After months of study, he found that the rats had developed ulcers. Before running naked through town screaming excitedly (like Archimedes the Greek on discovering how to measure density) and as a good scientist, he decided to replicate his findings. He recreated the study and added a control group—a group of rats who got a placebo injection instead of the extract. Lo and behold, he found that his control group developed ulcers as well. What did this mean?

Well, Selye was not an established animal handler, and he had a lot of trouble weighing, injecting, and studying his rats. Through different forms of (unintended) mistreatment, he actually stressed both the experimental and control groups, resulting in both groups developing ulcers. The rats also had other physiological problems such as shrunken adrenal glands and deformed lymph nodes (Selye, 1956). On realizing the actual true cause of the ulcers, Selye exposed rats to a variety of stressors such as extreme heat and cold, sounds, and rain. He found that in every case, the rats developed physiological problems similar to those in his first groups of rats. Selye concluded that organisms must have a general, nonspecific response to a variety of stressful events. Specifically, he hypothesized that no matter what the stressor, the body would react in the same way and theorized that these responses were driven by the **hypothalamic-pituitary-adrenal (HPA) axis.** HPA AXIS

The first part of the HPA axis sequence of activation resembles the characteristics of SAM activation. The hypothalamus activates the pituitary gland that then activates the adrenal gland. The difference in Selye's theory is that a different part of the adrenal gland, the cortex, gets activated. The cortex is the outer part of the adrenal gland (the medulla in SAM activation is the inner part) and secretes a class of hormones called corticosteroids. The major hormone in this class is cortisol (hydrocortisone). Cortisol generates energy to deal with the stressor by converting stored glycogen into glucose, a process called gluconeogenesis. Gluconeogenesis aids in breaking down protein, the mobilization of fat, and the stabilization of lysosomes. See Figures 4.2A and B for a summary of the basic physiological reactions to stress.

Selye argued that organisms have a general way of responding to all stressors, what he called a **general adaptation syndrome** (Figure 4.3). When faced with a stressor, whether a wild animal, a threatening mugger, or intense cold, the body first goes into a state of alarm. HPA axis activation takes place, and the body attempts to cope with the stressor during a period of resistance. If the stressor persists for too long, the body breaks down in a state of exhaustion. Many acute or short-term stressors can be successfully

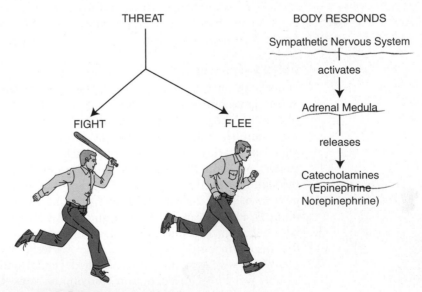

FIGURE **4.2A** The Basic Fight-or-Flight Response
Our body secretes hormones to prepare our body to deal with a stressor.

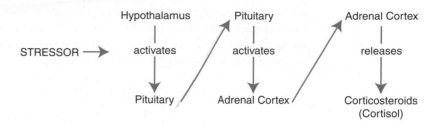

FIGURE **4.2B** The Main Physiological Pathway in Hans Selye's General Adaptation System

dealt with in the resistance stage. Chronic or long-term stressors drive us to exhaustion. Chronic stressors can exert true physiological and psychological damage on human bodies.

Cannon (1914) and Selye (1956) were the earliest theorists to offer physiological bases for stress. In summary, combining their models suggests that our SNS and the hypothalamus coordinate a physiological stress response that involves the pituitary and adrenal glands and the secretion of catecholamines and corticosteroids. Later stress researchers expanded and modified the early ideas. For example, in contrast to Selye's theory of a general adaptation, Mason (1971) argued that stress responses are based on the type of stressor that we are dealing with. In all of these three theories, psychological aspects did not play major roles. Cannon suggested that organisms had threshold levels and that if stressors were below these limits, the fight-or-flight response

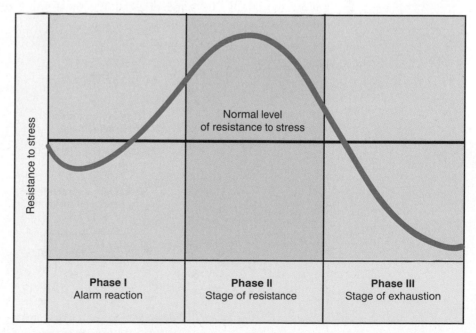

FIGURE **4.3** Main Stages in Hans Selye's General Adaptation System

did not activate. He also discussed emotional stressors, suggesting that mental processes played some role. Likewise, both Cannon and Selye believed that events had to be recognized as threatening to activate the response. However, neither scientist explained how this happened.

Lazarus' Cognitive Appraisal Model

Richard Lazarus (1966) devised the first psychological model of stress. Lazarus saw stress as the imbalance between the demands placed on the individual and that individual's resources to cope (Figure 4.4). He argued that the experience of stress differed significantly across individuals, depending on how they interpreted the event and the outcome of a specific sequence of thinking patterns called **appraisals**.

All of us are faced with demands. In school, you have papers to write and exams to take. At work, you may have projects and production deadlines to meet or a certain number of sales to make. Even in our personal lives, our family and friends rely on us and expect us to do various things. These different expectations, deadlines, and situations are all potential stressors. However, according to Lazarus, these expectations, deadlines, and situations are just events until we deem them to be stressful. The main cognitive process at work here is making appraisals. On the *Antiques Road Show*, an informative and fairly entertaining program on PBS, people bring in artifacts or possessions that often look like junk taken from their attics. Experts appraise the articles for how much they are worth, sometimes surprising the owners ("Did you know the table you bought at a garage sale for $50.00 is a colonial handmade collectable worth $15,000?"). When we appraise events, we follow essentially the same process. We set a value or judge the nature or quality of a situation or event.

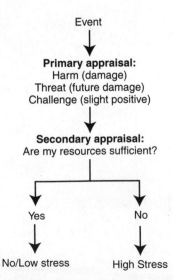

FIGURE **4.4** Main Stages of Lazarus' Cognitive Appraisal Model

Lazarus suggested that we make two major types of appraisals when we face any potentially stressful event. During **primary appraisals,** we ascertain whether the event is positive, negative, or neutral, and if negative, if it is harmful, threatening, or challenging. A harm (or harm-loss) appraisal is made when we expect to lose or actually lose something of great personal significance. For example, when we break up a close relationship we lose a confidante. The event can involve psychological aspects such as loss of support from the ex-partner or love of a parent who is dying, harm to one's self-esteem with the loss of a job, or even physical harm and loss from the diagnosis of a terminal illness. Threat appraisals are made when we believe the event will be extremely demanding and will put us at risk for damage. If you think that your bad performance on an upcoming project can severely ruin your reputation, or that taking part in a certain race will hurt your body, you are seeing the project or race as a threat. Challenge appraisals occur in situations when we believe that we can grow from dealing with the event and may even look at the positive ways that we can benefit from an event. For example, you can view an exam as harmful to your self-esteem and a threat if you expect to do badly or as a challenge to your intelligence and how much you have studied. A primary appraisal can be heavily influenced by the stake we have in the outcome of the event (Lazarus, 1991).

After we make a primary appraisal, we assess whether or not we have the necessary resources to cope with the event. During **secondary appraisal** we essentially determine whether we can deal with the event and how we can cope. We may think about the social support we have, who can help us, and what exactly can be done. We are asking ourselves the question, "Do I have what it takes to cope?" The answer is critical. If the answer is "no," and we appraised the event as being harmful and threatening and determined that we do not have the resources to cope, then the event is a stressor. If we appraised the event as a challenge and feel that we have the resources to deal with it, the event remains just that, an event. All along this process there is often cognitive reappraisal taking place during which we can change how we view the situation. As Shakespeare said in Hamlet, "There is nothing either good or bad, but thinking makes it so."

SYNTHESIZE, EVALUATE, APPLY	• What are the different factors that make it difficult to define stress? • What are the pros and cons of the different theories of stress? • How can you merge the different theories of stress?

FACTORS INFLUENCING OUR APPRAISALS

Many factors contribute to appraisals of events (Table 4.3). The duration of an event can play an important role in the process. Acute or short-term events may be appraised differently from chronic or long-term events. For example, you may not worry too much if you know that you will have houseguests for a weekend. You know that even though your routine is going to be disrupted, it will not be for too long. You will have an entirely different reaction if, on the other hand, you hear that your in-laws will be staying with you for

TABLE **4.3**
Main Dimensions of Stress

Duration: Acute vs. chronic	**Predictability:** Predictable vs. unpredictable
Valence: Negative vs. positive	**Definition:** Ambiguous vs. clear cut
Control: Having control leads to longevity	**Centrality:** Proximity to cause

3 months (something in-laws of some ethnic groups in North America will often do). Similarly, acute physical threats, such as taking a wrong turn and driving through a dangerous part of town, can have very different effects from chronic physical threats, such as living in a high-crime neighborhood.

Events can have either a positive or negative **valence**. This dimension of stress is more straightforward. Some events are automatically more threatening on the surface, such as having to speak in front of 500 people or being shot at by trigger-happy delinquents. Others can be positive on the surface, such as getting married. However, these positive events can involve a lot of demands on your mind and body such as planning and coordinating the event. The valence of an event often is colored by our emotional memories of similar events. We store emotional memories with other details of the event (Anderson, 1990), and these can influence future appraisals. A negative experience of public speaking in the past can influence our appraisal of doing it again in the future.

Control is another important feature in stress. When we believe that we have control over a situation, the situation is less likely to be stressful. Knowing that you are capable of changing the event is less stressful than not having any control over it. In a study demonstrating the positive effects of control, researchers gave 91 nursing home residents extra control over their day-to-day activities, their menus, and a little plant (they were told that they were completely responsible for the care of the plant). They were told that they were also responsible for themselves, and their day-to-day lives. In contrast, a similar group of residents was given a communication emphasizing that staff members were responsible for them and planned their activities. The comparison group had no control over aspects of their lives such as their menus. After 6 months, the group with control was significantly better off (Langer & Rodin, 1976).

Control can make a difference in how we cope with diseases, such as type 2 diabetes and coronary heart disease. New research shows that physical activity and healthy diets can reverse the effects of these potentially fatal diseases (Ornish et al., 1998). If you monitor what you eat and how much exercise you get, you reduce your chances of having a heart attack. Knowing that you can control the course of these diseases (based on your lifestyle choices) makes the diagnosis of coronary heart disease and diabetes less stressful.

Predictability is related to control. Think about sitting in a dentist's chair. If the dentist needs to use the drill but you have no idea how long the drilling is going to last, you will be stressed. Being able to predict how long a drill is going to be used reduces stress. Research from the first Gulf War showed that when Israel was bombed, the citizens' ability to predict what the missiles held greatly reduced their stress. When the bombing first began, many people were hospitalized *just from the trauma*. They did not know whether the warheads contained chemical weapons or not (Wolfe & Proctor, 1996). When a signal preceded an oncoming missile attack in a similar wartime study, this predictability of stress led to a reduction in the number of stress-related problems reported (Rosenhan & Seligman, 1989).

Not having all the details about an event or not having the mental resources to understand fully what needs to be done in a certain case may make the outcome of the event unpredictable and stressful. For example, patients did not perceive scheduled medical examinations in a veterans' hospital to be stressful when information about the medical procedures that were going to be used or needed was provided (Mischel, 1984). Hence the **definition** of the event is also important. Ambiguous events are a lot more stressful than are clear-cut ones.

SYNTHESIZE, EVALUATE, APPLY	• What are the key dimensions in which stress can vary? • How do you think the dimensions of stress can influence how you cope with stress? • Does an event have to be consciously experienced to be stressful? Why or why not?

THE ROLE OF CULTURE IN APPRAISAL

Culture influences both the appraisal of stress and the experience of stress. Given the central role of appraisal to the process of stress, anything that influences your appraisals correspondingly can influence how much stress you experience. One major influence on appraisals is culture. Different cultural groups have different expectations for various aspects of life, and these different expectations can make a low-threat event to one cultural group be a high-threat event to another group. For example, European Americans customarily look one another in the eye when speaking. This same behavior is considered rude among many Asian Americans. This difference between ethnicities also holds between different sexes. In many Asian cultures it is impolite for a woman to look a man directly in the eyes and converse or even to have the most basic physical contact. Cultural differences can lead to many stressful situations especially in the context of health care. Imagine a female European American doctor directly looking at a male Asian American. Interactions such as these between doctors and patients of different cultures (and sexes) can sometimes be strained, as we will discuss in more detail in Chapter 8.

Culture also influences the experience of stress. Not everyone in the United States is treated in the same way. Therefore, members of some cultural groups may experience more stress than others (Contrada et al., 2000). For example, many businesses are male dominated: oftentimes men are in higher positions of power and authority. It can be stressful for a female manager working around a group of all male managers. Age often interacts with gender to differentially influence how much stress someone experiences. Adolescent girls, for example, experience some of the highest levels of stress among children (Rudolph & Hammen, 1999).

Together with age and gender cultural differences, some of the most critical differences in the experience of stress are due to race and ethnicity. It may be stressful for a white European American to live in a predominantly African American neighborhood or for an African American to live in a predominantly white European American neighborhood. Many minority groups experience high levels of stress because of their ethnicity, race, or religious beliefs. Many cities in America are enclaves for certain ethnic groups that may make outsiders feel unwelcome. For example, driving through a Chinatown in New York, Toronto, or San Francisco and not being Chinese or strolling through little Havana in Miami and not being Cuban or through little Italy in Boston and not being Italian can be stressful to many. Of course, a large part of the stress may be in the appraisal and the mind of the perceiver (the Chinese Americans of Chinatown are not trying to stress you out), but as we know, real or not, a perception of stress is bad enough for our bodies.

Cultural differences in appraisal and in exposure to situations have led to the formulation of multicultural models of the stress process. Hobfoll (1998) points our attention to how the appraisal process can be biased by a range of conscious and nonconscious processes, such as cultural and familial norms. If your family has raised you to fear a certain group, pulling you out of the path of an approaching person of color, you are going to be conditioned to fear persons of that group. In a similar vein, Slavin, Rainer, McCreary, and Gowda (1991) expanded Lazarus and Folkman's (1984) **cognitive appraisal model** of stress to include a number of culture-specific dimensions (Figure 4.5). Slavin et al. (1991) argued that the occurrence of potentially stressful events can vary based on minority status, discrimination, or specific cultural customs. Furthermore, the primary appraisal of the occurring event can be biased by how the culture interprets the event. Similarly, the secondary appraisal, coping efforts, and final outcomes can be modified by the culture of the individual. For example, some cultural groups (e.g., Mexican and African Americans) have closer family ties and more active social support networks that could influence secondary appraisals. These cultural differences can even be seen at the level of the family (influenced by, but not necessarily completely due to, race or ethnicity). Some family cultural environments, based on the way parents raise their children, can be a lot more stressful than others. Families in which both parents are always fighting or low socioeconomic levels lead to hardships can be stressful (Repetti, Taylor, & Seeman, 2002).

STRESS AND PSYCHOPATHOLOGY: THE DIATHESIS-STRESS MODEL

The relationship between stress and psychopathology has been well documented in children and adolescents (see Compas et al, 2001, Lewinsohn, Joiner, & Rohde, 2001) and in adults (Mazure, 1998; Segrin, 1999; Hammen, 2003).

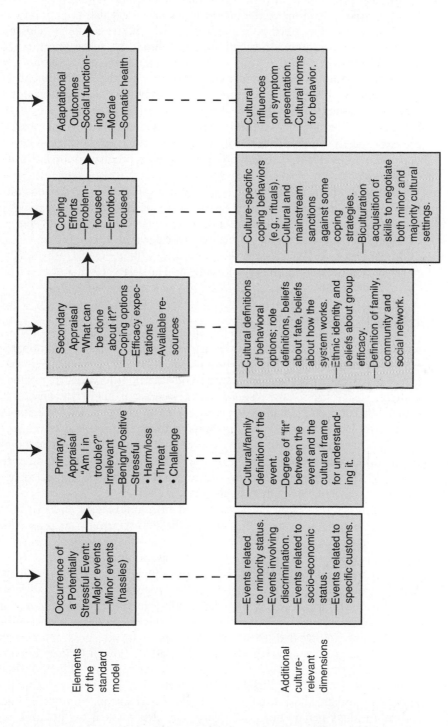

FIGURE **4.5** A Cultural Model of the Stress Response

Source: Adapted from Slavin, L. A., Rainer, K. L., McCreary, M. L., & Gowda, K. K. (1991). Toward a multicultural model of the stress process. *Journal of Counseling & Development.* Special Multiculturalism as a fourth force in counseling, 70(1), 156–163.

Yet, not everyone who experiences stressful life events and chronic stress develops psychological disorders (Gurung & Roethel, in press).

To explain this, one of the main frameworks in which the etiology of psychopathology is described is through the diathesis-stress model. This multidimensional model, first described in the context of schizophrenia (Bleuler, 1963; Rosenthal, 1970) involves a relationship between vulnerable predispositions (diathesis) and stress as contributors to the development of psychopathology. The theory posits that stress may serve as an activator of the diathesis, leading to the development and manifestation of psychopathology (Monroe & Simons, 1991). Individuals with a diathesis (a vulnerability) who are exposed to significant stress may be more likely to develop mental disorders than individuals who do not have similar predispositions (Monroe & Simons, 1991).

For individuals suffering from a mental disorder, the occurrence of stressful life events may act to further sensitize the individual to subsequent stressful life events and may initiate future episodes or relapses of the mental disorder, as seen with major depressive disorder (Harkness, Bruce, & Lumley, 2006; Mazure, 1998; Monroe & Harkness, 2005; Post, 1992) and schizophrenia (Ventura, Nuechterlein, Lukoff, & Hardesty, 1989).

CULTURE AS A CRITICAL STRESSOR

Culture may act as a stressor in the diathesis-stress model of psychopathology, activating certain vulnerabilities and predispositions that may lead to the emergence of psychopathology. In a study comparing differences in psychological distress, social stress, and resources in a sample of culturally diverse adolescents, Hispanic and Asian Americans reported higher levels of social stress, were more likely to experience psychological distress, and had lower scores on resources in the context of family, coping, self-esteem, and socioeconomic status than European Americans. Furthermore, compared to European Americans, Hispanic and African Americans had an increased likelihood of experiencing social stress (Choi, Meininger, & Roberts, 2006).

The interaction between physical and mental stressors and mental health issues are clearly seen in studies of specific ethnic groups such as American Indians. American Indians have a high risk of developing mental health disorders and have higher numbers of this population in need of mental health services (Harris, Edlund, & Larson, 2005; Nelson, McCoy, Stetter, & Vanderwagen, 1992). Two major studies document the magnitude of this problem. Data from the National Health Interview Survey indicated that American Indians were significantly more likely to report experiencing recent "serious psychological distress" and feelings of helplessness compared to all other ethnic groups surveyed (Barnes, Adams, & Powell-Griner, 2005). Data from the Behavioral Risk Factor Surveillance System (BRFSS) regarding health-related quality of life show that during the years 2000 through 2004, American Indians had experienced the greatest mean number of mentally unhealthy days per month (4.8). They also experienced the greatest percentage of frequent mental distress, defined as 14 or more unhealthy days in a month (15.1%), compared to all the other ethnic groups in the nationwide sample (Centers for Disease Control and Prevention, 2005). As a general survey of the mental health prevalence in American Indian populations living on or near a reservation in the Northern Plains and the Southwest area of the United States, Beals et al. (2005) found that diagnoses of alcohol dependence, post-traumatic stress disorder, and depression were the most prevalent DSM-IV diagnoses. American Indians in both tribes had a higher prevalence of PTSD, a higher prevalence of substance abuse, and a lower prevalence of depression, as compared to a nationally representative survey documenting the prevalence of mental health disorders.

Perceived Discrimination

One of the biggest cultural chronic stressors that has serious implications for the development and treatment of mental illness is perceived discrimination. The current emphasis of research in race-based discrimination spans disciplines such as sociology, psychology, and neuroscience. For example, Mays, Cochran, and Barnes (2007) describe and review current perspectives in a comprehensive approach for understanding the mediating and moderating variables in the relationship between race-based discrimination and health disparities. Specifically, these perspectives are social spaces and environments, family environments and development, and physiological approaches. In a nationally representative study of discrimination viewed in the context of "major discrimination" and "day-to-day perceived discrimination," it was found that for all races, "major discrimination" was significantly correlated with psychological distress and major depression, while "day-to-day perceived discrimination" was significantly associated with the development of emotional problems and mental disorders such as psychological distress, depression, and generalized anxiety disorder (Kessler et al., 1999).

The link between perceived discrimination and depression is common and has been found in a number of ethnic groups (Moradi & Risco, 2006). In a study examining the relationship between perceived discrimination and depression and moderating variables of coping, acculturation, and ethnic social support in a sample of Korean immigrants living in Canada, Noh and Kaspar (2003) found a significant association between perceived discrimination and depression. The utilization of ethnic social support moderated the relationship between perceived discrimination, emotion-focused coping, and depressive symptoms (for more on coping and moderation see Chapter 5). Individuals who used emotion-focused coping frequently and had more ethnic social support had fewer depressive symptoms, as compared to others who had less ethnic social support and more depressive symptoms (Noh et al., 1999; Noh & Kaspar, 2003).

A significant association between perceived discrimination and depressive symptoms was also seen in a sample of Mexican immigrants and U.S.-born individuals of Mexican descent in California. Mexican immigrants who were highly acculturated were the most likely to have experienced perceived discrimination, followed by less-acculturated immigrants, and U.S.-born individuals of Mexican descent who were the least likely to have experienced perceived discrimination (Finch, Kolody, & Vega, 2000). Perceived discrimination was also associated with depressive symptoms in a sample of American Indians in the upper Midwest (Whitbeck et al, 2002). However, involvement in traditional practices such as participation in traditional activities such as powwows and knowledge and use of tribal languages (reflecting measures of cultural identification) decreased the association between discrimination and depression (Whitbeck et al, 2002).

There is some evidence that the effects of discrimination stress can have a stronger effect on men. Utsey, Payne, Jackson, and Jones (2002) found gender differences in the relationships among race-related stress, quality of life, and life satisfaction in a sample of elderly African Americans. Males in this sample had significantly higher scores than females for race-related stress in the context of institutional racism and collective racism. Data also indicated a significant relationship between institutional racism as a predictor of quality of life and life satisfaction; higher ratings of race-related stress attributed to institutional racism predicted a lower rating of quality of life and life satisfaction.

The negative effects of discrimination go beyond the ethnic and racial aspects of culture. Individuals in sexual minority groups may be at increased risk for suffering from mental disorders. Studies have shown that there is a higher prevalence of mental health disorders among lesbian, gay, and bisexual populations. Explanations for the increased prevalence may include sources of minority stress such as prejudice, stigmatization, and discrimination (see Meyer, 2003). A study by Diaz et al. (2001) found that social discrimination was a strong predictor of mental health symptoms and psychological stress in a sample of gay and bisexual men in three large U.S. cities. Furthermore, social isolation and low self-esteem were two sources of stress identified that may be viewed in the context of stemming from social discrimination.

Other stressors can compromise mental health such as socioeconomic status. A study by Rosen et al. (2003) examined the prevalence of psychiatric disorders and substance abuse in a sample of Caucasian and African American single mothers and found that being White and on welfare increased the risk of developing mental health problems. Very often low SES participants live in high crime neighborhoods that can be also a source of stress as it contributes to mental health outcomes. Neighborhoods that have areas of concentrated poverty, disorder, and low cohesion may be associated with negative mental health outcomes and increased risky behaviors (for review, see Sampson, Morenoff, & Gannon-Rowley, 2002).

| **SYNTHESIZE, EVALUATE, APPLY** | <ul><li>What are the key ways that culture can influence the experience of stress?</li><li>Why may some cultural differences be more pertinent to the study of stress than others?</li><li>Which of the different varieties of stress are most susceptible to cultural differences?</li><li>What are the sociopolitical benefits and hazards of taking a cultural approach to stress?</li></ul> |

MEASURING STRESS

A variety of tools can assess the different psychological and physiological aspects of stress. The easiest way to measure whether someone is stressed is to ask. If your colleague at work seems stressed, a simple question may confirm your observation. To make a valid and reliable measure of stress, health psychologists have devised a number of different forms of measurement. Most measures take the form of questionnaire checklists for which test subjects are given a number of different events (e.g., getting fired, having a fight with a romantic partner, or getting in trouble with the law). They are asked to indicate which of the events happened to them in a given period of time (e.g., the last 6 months). Adding the number of events that the person experienced provides an estimate of the demands placed on the individual and hence his or her level of stress. Examples of such questionnaires are the Life Experiences Survey (Sarason, Johnson, & Seigel, 1978) and the Social Readjustment Rating Scale (Holmes & Rahe , 1967), as shown in Table 4.4.

Early stress research was focused primarily on major events in peoples' lives or **life events** (Brown & Harris, 1978; Coddington, 1972; Holmes & Rahe, 1967; Sarason et al., 1978). For example, the Social Readjustment Rating Scale (SRRS) (Holmes & Rahe, 1967) consists of 43 items, each with a different value called a Life Change Unit or LCU (a revised and updated version can be seen in Table 4.2). The association between life events, increased physical disease and injury, and psychological distress has varied. Correlations have been strong (Dohrenwand & Dohrenwand, 1974; Holmes & Rahe, 1967; Thoits, 1983), moderate (Ross & Mirowsky, 1979) or minimal (Schroeder & Costa, 1984). Although the SRRS is one of the critical landmarks in the measurement of stress, it has been heavily criticized and is not as widely used today. Sometimes the occurrence of an event does not make it stressful. A number of more recent questionnaire measures of stress ask both if an event happened *and* how much distress it caused. Respondents are often asked to use a scale (e.g., ranging from 1 "happened but not distressing" to 6 "caused a lot of personal distress" to indicate just how much the event influenced them. In the Life Experiences Survey, participants rate each event on a 7-point scale, ranging from extremely negative (23) to extremely positive (13). This form of measure compensates for the subjective aspect of stress and the fact that people's appraisals can vary by letting different individuals indicate how much each event influenced their well-being.

Together with major life events, you probably know that small hassles can add up: the neighbor who is always noisy in the mornings, being stuck in traffic, or having too many things to do. There is a scale to measure even these little things. The Hassles and Uplifts Scale (Kanner, Coyne, Schaefer, & Lazarus, 1981) consists of 117 events. Small hassles have been shown to negatively affect health and aggravate the damage done by major life events (Weinberger, Hiner, & Tierney, 1987).

Although many of these measures tap into acute one-time events and daily hassles, other questionnaires assess major chronic stressors (Lepore, 1997). For example, Gurung, Taylor, Kemeny, and Myers (2004) demonstrated the utility of measuring chronic stress to predict depression in an

TABLE **4.4**
The Life Experiences Scale

Listed below are a number of events that sometimes bring about change in the lives of those who experience them and that necessitate social readjustment. *Please check those events that you have experienced in the recent past and indicate the time period during which you have experienced each event.* Be sure that all check marks are directly across from the items to which they correspond.

　　Also, for each item checked below, please indicate the extent to which you viewed the event as having either a positive or a negative impact on your life at the time the event occurred. That is, indicate the type and extent of impact that the event had. A rating of –3 would indicate an extremely negative impact. A rating of 0 suggests no impact (neither positive nor negative). A rating of +3 would indicate an extremely positive impact.

	0 to 6 mo	7 mo to 1 yr	extremely negative	moderately negative	somewhat negative	no impact	slightly positive	moderately positive	extremely positive
Section 1									
1. Marriage			–3	–2	–1	0	+1	+2	+3
2. Detention in jail or comparable institution			–3	–2	–1	0	+1	+2	+3
3. Death of spouse			–3	–2	–1	0	+1	+2	+3
4. Major change in sleeping habits (much more or much less sleep)			–3	–2	–1	0	+1	+2	+3
5. Death of close family member:									
a. mother			–3	–2	–1	0	+1	+2	+3
b. father			–3	–2	–1	0	+1	+2	+3
c. brother			–3	–2	–1	0	+1	+2	+3
d. sister			–3	–2	–1	0	+1	+2	+3
e. grandmother			–3	–2	–1	0	+1	+2	+3
f. grandfather			–3	–2	–1	0	+1	+2	+3
6. Major change in eating habits (much more or much less food intake)			–3	–2	–1	0	+1	+2	+3
7. Foreclosure on mortgage or loan			–3	–2	–1	0	+1	+2	+3
8. Death of close friend			–3	–2	–1	0	+1	+2	+3
9. Outstanding personal achievement			–3	–2	–1	0	+1	+2	+3
10. Minor law violations (traffic tickets, disturbing the peace, etc.)			–3	–2	–1	0	+1	+2	+3
11. *Male*: Wife/girlfriend's pregnancy			–3	–2	–1	0	+1	+2	+3
12. *Female*: Pregnancy			–3	–2	–1	0	+1	+2	+3
13. Changed work situation (different work responsibility, major change in working conditions, working hours, etc.)			–3	–2	–1	0	+1	+2	+3

(continues)

TABLE **4.4** (*continued*)
The Life Experiences Scale

		0 to 6 mo	7 mo to 1 yr	extremely negative	moderately negative	somewhat negative	no impact	slightly positive	moderately positive	extremely positive
14.	New job			−3	−2	−1	0	+1	+2	+3
15.	Serious illness or injury of close family member:									
	a. father			−3	−2	−1	0	+1	+2	+3
	b. mother			−3	−2	−1	0	+1	+2	+3
	c. sister			−3	−2	−1	0	+1	+2	+3
	d. brother			−3	−2	−1	0	+1	+2	+3
	e. grandfather			−3	−2	−1	0	+1	+2	+3
	f. grandmother			−3	−2	−1	0	+1	+2	+3
	g. spouse			−3	−2	−1	0	+1	+2	+3
	h. other (specify)			−3	−2	−1	0	+1	+2	+3
16.	Sexual difficulties			−3	−2	−1	0	+1	+2	+3
17.	Trouble with employer (in danger of losing job, being suspended, demoted, etc.)			−3	−2	−1	0	+1	+2	+3
18.	Trouble with in-laws			−3	−2	−1	0	+1	+2	+3
19.	Major change in financial status (a lot better off or a lot worse off)			−3	−2	−1	0	+1	+2	+3
20.	Major change in closeness of family members (increased or decreased closeness)			−3	−2	−1	0	+1	+2	+3
21.	Gaining a new family member (through birth, adoption, family member moving in, etc.)			−3	−2	−1	0	+1	+2	+3
22.	Change of residence			−3	−2	−1	0	+1	+2	+3
23.	Marital separation from mate (due to conflict)			−3	−2	−1	0	+1	+2	+3
24.	Major change in church activities (increased or decreased attendance)			−3	−2	−1	0	+1	+2	+3
25.	Marital reconciliation with mate			−3	−2	−1	0	+1	+2	+3
26.	Major change in number of arguments with spouse (a lot more or a lot less arguments)			−3	−2	−1	0	+1	+2	+3
27.	*Married male*: Change in wife's work outside the home (beginning work, ceasing work, changing to a new job, etc.)			−3	−2	−1	0	+1	+2	+3
28.	*Married female*: Change in husband's work (loss of job, beginning new job, retirement, etc.)			−3	−2	−1	0	+1	+2	+3

TABLE **4.4** (*continued*)
The Life Experiences Scale

		0 to 6 mo	7 mo to 1 yr	extremely negative	moderately negative	somewhat negative	no impact	slightly positive	moderately positive	extremely positive
29.	Major change in usual type and/or amount of recreation			−3	−2	−1	0	+1	+2	+3
30.	Borrowing more than $10,000 (buying home, business, etc.)			−3	−2	−1	0	+1	+2	+3
31.	Borrowing less than $10,000 (buying car, TV, getting school loan, etc.)			−3	−2	−1	0	+1	+2	+3
32.	Being fired from job			−3	−2	−1	0	+1	+2	+3
33.	*Male*: Wife/girlfriend having abortion			−3	−2	−1	0	+1	+2	+3
34.	*Female*: Having abortion			−3	−2	−1	0	+1	+2	+3
35.	Major personal illness or injury			−3	−2	−1	0	+1	+2	+3
36.	Major change in social activities, e.g., parties, movies, visiting (increased or decreased participation)			−3	−2	−1	0	+1	+2	+3
37.	Major change in living conditions of family (building new home, remodeling, deterioration of home, neighborhood, etc.)			−3	−2	−1	0	+1	+2	+3
38.	Divorce			−3	−2	−1	0	+1	+2	+3
39.	Serious injury or illness of close friend			−3	−2	−1	0	+1	+2	+3
40.	Retirement from work			−3	−2	−1	0	+1	+2	+3
41.	Son or daughter leaving home (due to marriage, college, etc.)			−3	−2	−1	0	+1	+2	+3
42.	Ending of formal schooling			−3	−2	−1	0	+1	+2	+3
43.	Separation from spouse (due to work, travel, etc.)			−3	−2	−1	0	+1	+2	+3
44.	Engagement			−3	−2	−1	0	+1	+2	+3
45.	Breaking up with boyfriend/girlfriend			−3	−2	−1	0	+1	+2	+3
46.	Leaving home for the first time			−3	−2	−1	0	+1	+2	+3
47.	Reconciliation with boyfriend/girlfriend			−3	−2	−1	0	+1	+2	+3
Other recent experiences that have had an impact on your life. List and rate.										
48.	_____			−3	−2	−1	0	+1	+2	+3
49.	_____			−3	−2	−1	0	+1	+2	+3
50.	_____			−3	−2	−1	0	+1	+2	+3

(continues)

TABLE **4.4** (continued)
The Life Experiences Scale

	0 to 6 mo	7 mo to 1 yr	extremely negative	moderately negative	somewhat negative	no impact	slightly positive	moderately positive	extremely positive
Section 2: Student Only									
51. Beginning a new school experience at a higher academic level (college, graduate school, professional school, etc.)			−3	−2	−1	0	+1	+2	+3
52. Changing to a new school at same academic level (undergraduate, graduate, etc.)			−3	−2	−1	0	+1	+2	+3
53. Academic probation			−3	−2	−1	0	+1	+2	+3
54. Being dismissed from dormitory or other residence			−3	−2	−1	0	+1	+2	+3
55. Failing an important exam			−3	−2	−1	0	+1	+2	+3
56. Changing a major			−3	−2	−1	0	+1	+2	+3
57. Failing a course			−3	−2	−1	0	+1	+2	+3
58. Dropping a course			−3	−2	−1	0	+1	+2	+3
59. Joining a fraternity/sorority			−3	−2	−1	0	+1	+2	+3
60. Financial problems concerning school (in danger of not having sufficient money to continue)			−3	−2	−1	0	+1	+2	+3

To Score LES

Negative Events

Add all scores for which subject has indicated a negative sign. Then use absolute value.

Positive Events

Add all scores for which subject has indicated a positive sign. Then use absolute value.

Total Events

Add absolute scores (i.e., disregarding sign) for positive and negative events together:

e.g., Positive = x, Negative = y, Total = $x + y$

(disregarding sign)

Source: Sarason, Johnson, and Seigal (1978).

ethnically diverse sample of low-income women at risk for contracting AIDS. Chronic stress or burden and low socioeconomic status were significant predictors of changes in depression for African American women and Latina women, respectively. Gurung et al. (2004) measured chronic burden using a 21-item scale developed from focus groups in which HIV-positive women discussed the life stresses that they faced. The researchers compiled a list of the most commonly mentioned stressors from the focus groups. Then participants in the study indicated whether or not they had experienced each stressor during the previous six months and the extent to which each stressor was a problem for them using a four-point scale ranging from one "Not a problem for me in the last six months" to four "A major problem for me in the last six months." The final list, shown in Table 4.5, included financial difficulties, transportation problems, housing problems, childcare or caregiving difficulties, difficulties in personal relationships, work-related difficulties, exposure to accident or injury, immigration or citizenship problems, and exposure to crime and discrimination. This new measure of chronic stress promises to add to our ability to predict the effects of long-term stressors.

TABLE **4.5**
The Chronic Burden Scale

1. Not having enough money to cover the basic needs of life (food, clothing, housing)
2. Not having any savings to meet problems that come up
3. No reliable source of transportation (such as car that works or reliable bus service)
4. Housing problems (uncertainty about housing, problems with landlord)
5. Problems arranging child care
6. Being a caregiver for someone (taking care of someone sick, elderly, or infirm)
7. Divorce or separation from partner
8. Long-term, unresolved conflict with someone very important (child, parent, lover/partner, sibling, or friend)
9. Being fired or laid off
10. Trouble with your employer (in danger of losing job or being suspended/demoted)
11. Having work hours or responsibilities change for the worse
12. Partner's work hours or responsibilities change for the worse
13. Serious accident, injury, or new illness happening to you or a close family member/spouse/partner/close friend
14. You or a close family member/spouse/partner/close friend being the victim of a crime or physical assault
15. Chronic pain or restriction of movements due to injury or illness
16. Long-term medical problems
17. Either you or someone you are close to and depend on having immigration or citizenship problems
18. You or a close family member/spouse/partner/close friend being arrested or sent to jail
19. Living in a high-crime area
20. Losing the help of someone you depend on (person moved, got sick, or otherwise was unavailable)
21. Being discriminated against because of your race, nationality, gender, or sexual orientation

Source: Gurung, Taylor, Kemeny, and Myers (2004).

Most of the measures of stress discussed so far ask whether certain specific events actually took place or not. Whether hassles or life events, the assumption is that if you experienced one of these, then you are likely to experience stress. A different type of assessment focuses on perceived stress. As the term suggests, this approach relies on what the individual feels. Cohen, Kamarck, and Mermelstein (1985) developed the Perceived Stress Scale that asks respondents how often they felt certain thoughts or feelings in the preceding month. One question asks how often the person was upset because of something that happened unexpectedly. Another asks how often the person felt angry because of uncontrollable things. Responses to the perceived stress scale reliably predict a range of health issues such as coronary heart disease (Strodl, Kenardy, & Aroney, 2003) and immune responses to vaccinations (Burns, Drayson, Ring, & Carroll, 2002).

Asking if someone is stressed can give us a good indicator of how stressed they really are. However, our perceptions of stress are not always accurate. Sometimes we may not be completely honest about our experiences (both to ourselves or to researchers who want to know). To compensate for these inaccuracies, a vast array of physiological measures can be used. It is difficult to trick your physiology. If you look back to the physiological effects of stress, you can see how you can get a measure of stress without asking questions. You can measure a person's blood pressure (systolic and diastolic), take his or her temperature, or measure his or her heart rate. When we become stressed, sympathetic activation increases all these physiological measures. Most laboratory studies of stress, especially experimental studies in which a person is stressed on purpose, use physiological measures. Some use galvanic skin responses, a measure of how our skin conducts electricity. We sweat more when we get stressed and even a minute increase in perspiration at the skin's surface increases the rate at which our skin conducts electricity. Measuring devices pick up this increase in conductance.

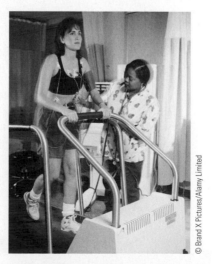

© Brand X Pictures/Alamy Limited

A Modern Measure of Physiological Reactions to Stress: The Stress Test

In many studies blood samples are taken for assessment of the levels of different chemical markers. The levels of stress chemicals in the blood, such as cortisol, epinephrine, and norepinephrine, increase when we are stressed. The number and types of different immune system cells vary when we become stressed. A small sample of blood, even a few tablespoons, helps researchers assess stress levels. For example, Janice Keicolt-Glaser and colleagues watch married couples fight and then use blood samples from them to assess how stressed the argument made them (Kiecolt-Glaser, Bane, Glaser, & Malarkey, 2003, more in the relationship stress section below). A note of warning: many other activities besides stressful ones can also instigate some of these physiological responses so measures need to be interpreted with caution.

DIFFERENT VARIETIES OF STRESSORS

Many different areas of life can be stressful. In today's world and in the health psychological literature on stress, we tend to focus on three main areas of stress that encompass the majority of life: relationships, work, and the environment. In addition, a number of physical stressors also are present in today's world. Millions of people around the world do not have enough food to eat or have insufficient shelter. Most of us in North America do not experience these stressors but often create our own stressful worlds in our heads as we negotiate our situations of relationships and work.

Relationship Stress

At every stage of life, interacting with others can be potentially stressful. The adolescence period in particular is a transitional period during which the importance of the peer group increases as the importance of the family decreases (Larson & Asmussen, 1991). Levels of conflict with parents and

© Amy Etra/PhotoEdit

Conflictual Relationships Can Cause Wear and Tear on the Mind and Body hence interpersonal stress rise (Laursen, 1996). The large number of divorces in North America also reflects the level of relationship conflict in adulthood. A number of health psychologists are actively studying the effects of marital conflict and divorce as stressors and their effects on health.

An unhealthy close relationship can be particularly problematic not just for your mental state of mind but for your physiology as well. Kiecolt-Glaser, Bane, Glaser, and Malarkey (2003) collected physiological measures from 90 couples during their first year of marriage (time 1) and found that these measures related to breakups and marital satisfaction 10 years later (time 2). Compared with those who remained together, the stress hormone levels (e.g., epinephrine) of divorced couples were 34 percent higher during conflict discussions and 22 percent higher throughout the day, and both epinephrine and norepinephrine levels were 16 percent higher at night. Couples whose marriages were troubled at time 2 produced 34 percent more norepinephrine during conflict, 24 percent more norepinephrine during the daytime, and 17 percent more during nighttime hours at time 1 than the couples with untroubled marriages.

The family is another area of focus in the context of stress and relationships. The family cycle has distinct phases—partner selection, marital adjustment, raising and caring for children, having children leave, and retirement—each of which can be associated with stressors (Aldwin, 1994; Elkin, 1994; Patterson, 2002). The ways parents deal with stress can serve as critical models for how children deal with stress and can influence the children's own health as well (Kilmer, Cowen, & Wyman, 2001). Events such as the death of a parent, divorce, the departure of a child to college or to the military, the loss of income, hospitalization, or a long-term chronic illness of a family member or even imprisonment, can be stressful and need to be adjusted to (McCubbin & Patterson, 1983). A number of stress theories have been devised, especially to focus on family dynamics and stress (e.g., Hill, 1949; Patterson & Garwick, 1994), that closely parallel Lazarus' (1991) cognitive appraisal model described before.

Abuse is one family stressor receiving great attention today. There is growing evidence of spouse and child abuse (e.g., National Council on Child Abuse and Family Violence, 2008) and growing literature on violence during pregnancy (e.g., Ballard et al., 1998; Dunkel-Schetter, Gurung, Lobel, & Wadhwa, 2001). In fact, family violence may be a more common problem for pregnant women than some conditions for which they are routinely screened and evaluated.

Work Stress

A 2007 APA poll reported that 74 percent of North Americans felt work was their top stressor (APA, 2007). Job stress can produce physical health problems, psychological distress, and behavioral changes. On a physical level, there are many thousands of deaths on the job every year. For example, 5,840 fatal workplace injuries were reported in 2006 (U.S. Department of Labor, 2008). Day-to-day stress can make a person more likely to develop physical problems later.

Occupational stress even has an entry in the *Diagnostic and Statistical Manual of Mental Disorders* (DSM-IV) (American Psychiatric Association, 1994),

Workload Can Be a Major Form of Stress

the main tool used to diagnose clinical disorders. Some symptoms of work stress include feelings of frustration, anger, and resentment, lowered self-esteem, boredom, job dissatisfaction, mental fatigue, loss of concentration, loss of spontaneity and creativity, and emotional hyperactivity. Know anyone experiencing any of these? Maybe this person should look at how happy he or she is at work. Psychologically speaking, work stress can arise from a number of factors:

1. Cognitive overload: having too much to do.
2. Role conflict: being unsure of one's job description.
3. Ambiguity: not knowing what one is supposed to be doing.
4. Discrimination: job ceilings that prevent one from rising in the ranks.
5. Not getting promoted, because of sexism, ageism, or other prejudices.
6. Poor social networks preventing outlets to process job stress.
7. Lack of control over what one is doing and when it is done.
8. Multiple roles that need to be balanced.
9. Not being challenged enough.

At first glance it may seem like the last item should not be a problem. Why would someone not want a comfortable, easy job? Everly and Girdano (1980) described and documented deprivational stress, a form of stress resulting from a job that fails to maintain the worker's interest and attention. The National Institute for Occupational Safety and Health even described assembly-line hysteria, a condition in which workers with boring repetitive jobs display symptoms of nausea, muscle weakness, headaches, and blurry vision, without any physical basis. These symptoms are more likely a psychological consequence of boredom because of this lack of physical cause.

If a person is unhappy or stressed at work there are consequences for both the individual and for people close to the individual. Work stress has been shown to spill over into family life and personal interactions (Perry-Jenkins, Repetti, & Crouter, 2002; Wang, Leineweber, Kirkeeide, Svane, Schenck-Gustafsson, Theorell, & Orth-Gomér, 2007). For example, Doumas, Margolin, and John (2003) had 49 husbands and wives separately complete daily diaries addressing questions about work experiences, health-promoting behaviors, and marital interactions over 42 consecutive days. The researchers found that spouses reported more positive marital interactions on days when they worked less.

Many different theories demonstrate the interconnectedness of the work and home spheres. This interconnectedness is referred to as a **stress contagion effect** (Edwards & Rothbard, 2000; Voydanoff, 2002). Bolger, DeLongis, Kessler, and Wethington (1989) first recognized and defined two specific types of stress contagion: spillover and crossover. **Spillover** refers to the intra-individual transmission of stress, when stress occurring in one domain of an individual's life affects other domains of life (Westman & Etizon, 1995). In comparison, **crossover** is the transmission of stress *between* individuals. Crossover occurs when stress or strain experienced by an individual affects the stress or strain of another individual (Westman & Vinokur, 1998). Crossover can occur between workers at a worksite or between an employee and his or her family.

The majority of studies on work stress have been cross-sectional, focusing on the crossover from the husband to the wife. Most studies show positive correlations between occupational stressors and spouse's stress or strain (Jones & Fletcher, 1993; Westman, 2001). Of note, crossover studies examining crossover from wives to husbands have not produced any consistent findings (Westman, 2001), and the literature suggests that wives are more vulnerable to their husband's stress than husbands to their wives' stress.

The work stress contagion findings are explained by a combination of ecological theory and role theory. Ecological theory (Bronfenbrenner, 1977) identifies different levels or systems in which the individual acts. Work and home domains are examples of **microsystems**. A microsystem includes the activities and roles the individual takes on in a particular setting. A **mesosystem** contains the relationships and interactions between microsystems at a specific point in time. Bronfenbrenner's concept of **reciprocity** recognizes that systems are not independent of one another but are in constant interaction. Consequently, elements of the work domain affect elements of the home domain and vice versa.

According to the **role theory** of Kahn, Wolfe, Quinn, Snoek, and Rosenthal (1964) stress contagion from work to home rises as a person's roles increase and if those roles lack definition. A role is the set of behaviors to be performed and is determined by one's own perceptions and the expectations of others. As an individual accumulates roles, the quantity and incompatibility of role demands increase. An individual experiences role strain that results in increased role conflict and ambiguity (Voydanoff, 2002). **Role ambiguity** is the degree to which required information regarding role expectations are available, clear, and communicated to the focal person. When companies establish new positions, the expectation for what someone in that position has to do is often undefined. Someone in this new position or in any position for which the job description is inadequate can experience role ambiguity. **Role conflict** is the incompatibility of expectations for a given role and between different roles. Sometimes a job may require a person to evaluate a member of his or her own work team when the evaluation also contributes to his or her own raise or bonus. In this case you have a conflict between making an accurate assessment and potentially hurting your own pay.

Environmental Stress

Working and living in a noisy environment can lead to many problems. Noise can even retard learning in children (Bronzaft & McCarthy, 1975). Children living close to an airport where constant roars of jet engines interrupt their daily lives were found to have higher levels of stress and more learning difficulties than students not living close to an airport (Cohen, Evans, Krantz, & Stokols, 1980). In a similar study, Cohen, Glass, and Singer (1973) showed that children living in noisy homes near busy roadways had greater difficulties with reading tasks than did children who lived in quiet homes. In a classic series of studies on the effects of noise, Glass and Singer (1972) had students work on different tasks and then exposed them to bursts of sound. Unpredictable bursts of sound hindered their performance the most, but those students who faced consistent background sounds during early tasks performed badly on later tasks. Noise can play a large role in how stressed we feel and is often implicitly influencing our well-being.

Just as noise can be a problem, crowding can also be stressful. If you grew up in a nice quiet city or town with a population of between 30,000 and 100,000 or less, your experiences with crowding are very different from mine. I grew up in Mumbai (previously Bombay), a city with a population tilting the scales at 20,000,000 (yes, 20 million). Overcrowding can often produce negative moods for men (Freedman, 1975; not so much for women in support of the Tend and Befriend theory), physiological arousal (e.g., higher blood pressure), increased illness, more aggression, and a host of other stressful outcomes. Even if you do not live in a big city, you can see the effects of crowding at large gatherings. Large rock concerts, state fairs, or amusement parks during holiday weekends can become overcrowded, making people feel stressed and frustrated.

Environmental stressors can be divided into three main categories: background stressors, natural disaster stressors, and techno-political stressors. **Background stressors** include crowding and noise, together with air pollution and chemical pollution (Fisher, Bell, & Baum, 1984). All of these can be long-term stressors and affect a large number of people. A second major category of environmental stressors is **natural disaster stressors**. These are short-term

© AFP/Getty Images

Natural Events Are a Form of Environmental Stress
Hurricane Katrina wiped out 80% of New Orleans

stressors and are often more severe than long-term stressors. For example, natural disasters such as flooding, earthquakes, and hurricanes can kill thousands of people and survivors often experience severe psychological consequences lasting a lifetime (Leach, 1995; Norris, Byrne, & Diaz, 2002). Take Hurricane Katrina. It hit New Orleans in 2005 and damaged 80 percent of the city. Almost the entire city was evacuated, and close to 1,500 died (Louisiana Department of Health and Hospitals, 2006). Not surprisingly, this major disaster had stressful effects resulting in mental illness, suicidality and post-traumatic stress disorder (PTSD), a specific form of mental illness related to the experience of severe stress, that influenced thousands (Dalton, Scheeringa, & Zeanah, 2008; Galea, et al. 2007). Two years after Katrina, the rate of PTSD was 10 times higher in New Orleans than in the general public (Yost-Hammer & Hammer, in press).

The third category of stressors can be called **techno-political stressors**. Although these types of stressors can be unpredictable and uncontrollable like natural disasters, they are directly linked to technological or political causes. Some examples are nuclear reactor accidents (e.g., Three Mile Island in Pennsylvania and Chernobyl in Russia), chemical plant accidents (e.g., the Union Carbide accident in Bhopal, India), and dam-related flooding (e.g., Buffalo Creek in West Virginia). Political tragedies, such as wars and acts of terrorism, are also extremely stressful. In a longitudinal study of over 2,000 adults, it was found that stress-responses to the 9/11 attacks predicted increased heart problems even three years after the attacks (Holman et al., 2008).

A number of other factors are stressful even though at first they do not appear to be. Many of us wish we had less to do and become stressed trying to complete everything that we have to do. However, not having enough to do can also be stressful. Bexton, Heron, and Scott (1954) paid students to just lie in bed and sleep. This seems pretty easy, right? Well, the twist was that they had to lie in a cubicle with their hands and arms padded and with glasses on that blocked their vision. They could not hear any outside sounds. No subject could do it for more than 3 days, and all reported extreme boredom, restlessness, and growing levels of stress, thus proving that boredom and low levels of sensory stimulation can be stressful too.

CONSEQUENCES OF STRESS

In a nutshell, stress can make a person sick. Stress can have a variety of direct physiological effects on the body: damage to the heart (Johnston, Tuomisto, & Patching, 2008); suppression of the immune system and neuronal damage (Segerstrom, 2007); an increase in GI symptoms (Blanchard et al., 2008); and Irritable Bowel Syndrome (Levenson, 2007). Stress can also have direct cognitive and behavioral effects such as distraction and memory loss (Wilson et al., 2007), though stress can also improve memory for emotional aspects of events (Buchanan & Tranel, 2008). Stress also can have secondary effects such as exacerbating illnesses and delaying recovery (see Dougall & Baum, 2002). Figure 4.6 illustrates some of the stress-related illnesses.

Most of the early major theories of stress (e.g., Selye and Cannon) paid a lot of attention to the physiological changes in the body that accompany the

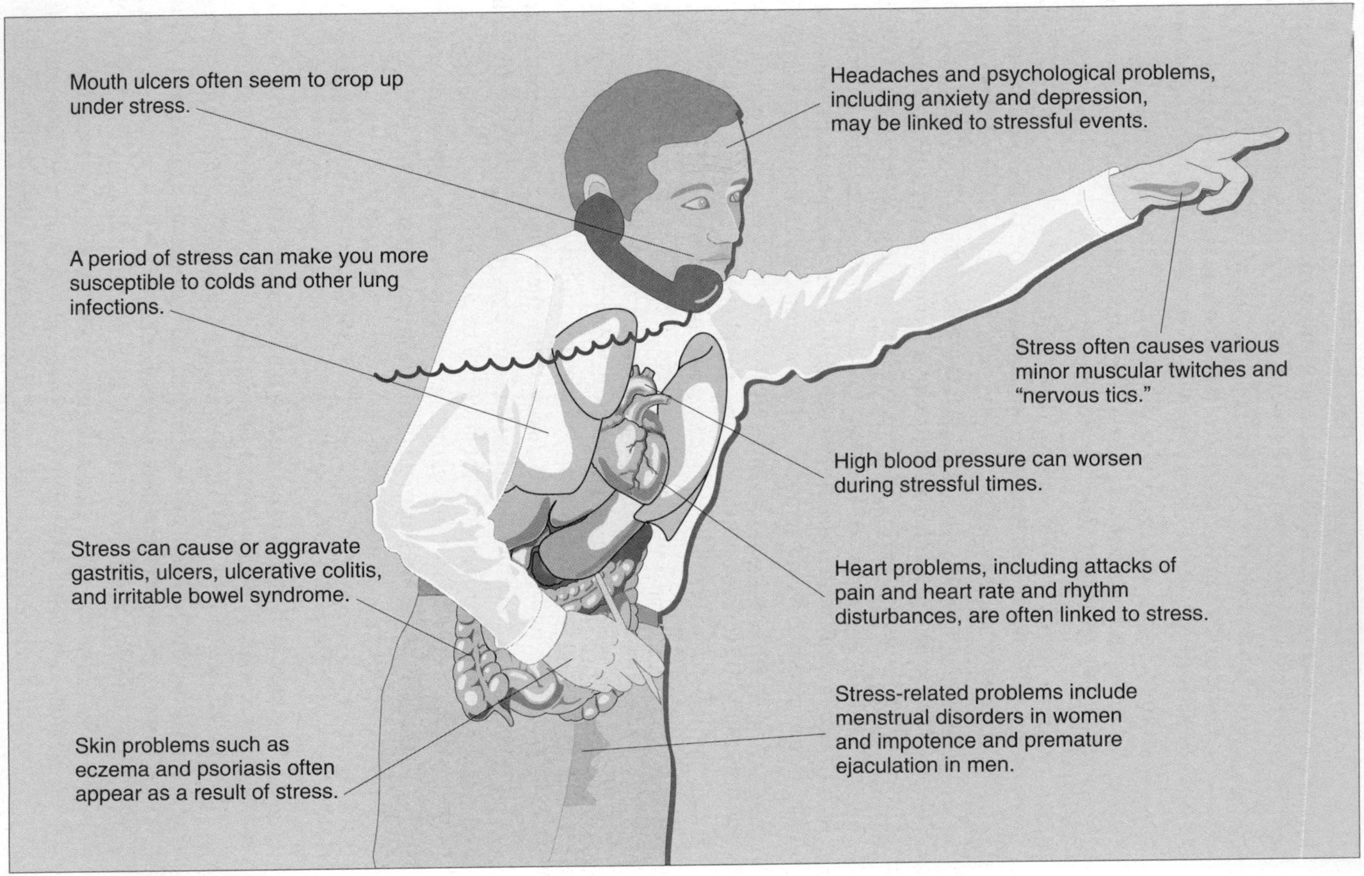

FIGURE **4.6** Stress-Induced Illness

Source: Diane Hales (2000). *An Invitation to Health.* San Francisco: Wadsworth.

experience of stress. There is a good reason for that. A lot happens in our body when we get stressed. For example, the sympathetic nervous system has connections all over the body (nerves project all over the body from the brain and spinal cord) from sweat gland to muscles and hair follicles, all of which are stimulated to some extent during stress. We have also discussed the two main systems that are activated: the HPA axis releasing corticosteroids and SAM activation releasing norepinephrine and epinephrine. From a practical standpoint the activation of these systems is important and critical. They prepare our bodies to deal with stressors. A problem arises when we experience stress for a long time. Chronic, long-term stressors cause wear and tear on body systems, leading to tissue damage and irregular responding, hypertension, and ulcers (Levenson, 2007). How long is too long? The answer to that question depends on the individual. Let us not forget that the potentially stressful event can be acute or chronic, a person's appraisal and awareness of the stressor can be acute or chronic, and the actual mental and physiological consequences can be acute or chronic (Baum, O'Keefe, & Davidson, 1990).

Chronic stress can lead to other physiological consequences. Some people develop heart problems or loss of appetite. Others have sexual problems (e.g., men are unable to have or maintain an erection) or develop skin problems (e.g., rashes) or nervous ticks (e.g., uncontrollable jerky movements or winking). Chronic stress is a problem for many people and can be either objective (living in a noisy neighborhood) or subjective (overworking week after week and month after month). Health psychologists who focus directly on *allostatic load,* or the effects of chronic stress, have unearthed some disturbing findings (McEwen, 1998).

Allostasis is defined as the ability to achieve stability through change (Korte, Koolhaas, Wingfield, & McEwen, 2005). Our environments keep changing, putting our body systems through various fluctuations to adjust to them. The different forces that shake our homeostatic balance stretch our systems to act like rubber bands. It is critical to our survival that our systems go back to their original shape and function like a taut rubber band does when it is released. With chronic stress, wear and tear on the body result from chronic overactivity or underactivity of allostatic systems (i.e., a load). Being under an allostatic load can have three main consequences.

Look at Figure 4.7. The first line represents normal responses to stress (a). For most acute stressors, our sympathetic system is activated before and during the event (say you have to make an oral presentation), and we adapt afterwards. Even if this acute stressor is repeated a few times (you have to give a number of talks in a month), the healthy stress response shows an activation followed by a return to baseline functioning. In the case of chronic stress (say living in a risky neighborhood where there are frequent stressors), allostatic load is seen when the post-stress adaptation or the normal lessening of the response for repeat stressors is not seen (b). You still respond, but it is a lower activation each time. Correspondingly, there is a prolonged exposure to the different stress hormones. This extra exposure can lead to a host of problems such as coronary heart disease. Another result of allostatic load takes place when our body is unable to shut off the stress response after the stressor stops. This again leads to extended exposure to stress hormones.

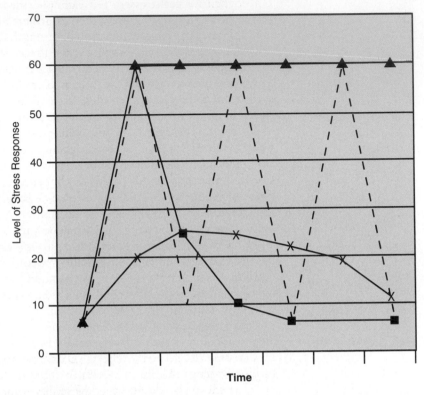

Consequences of Allostatic Load
1. Frequent stress: Lack of adaptation (see b).
2. Inability to shut off responses after stress stops (see c).
3. Inadequate response: One system does not work, other overcompensates (see d).

FIGURE **4.7** Main Effects of Allostatic Load

The final case is system malfunctions in the response to stress. One system may not work, and other systems overcompensate. This also leads to extended exposure to stress hormones.

Bruce McEwen and colleagues have identified many markers of allostatic load (McEwen & Wingfield, 2003). Major markers include hypertension (high blood pressure), atherosclerosis (calcium deposits on arteries), fat staying in the system longer, higher waist-to-hip ratios (when fat goes to the waist not the hips), and sleep disruption. Extended stress also interferes with the immune system (more on this in Chapter 13) and interferes with memory. Long-term stress actually destroys neurons in the hippocampus (they grow back if the stress is short term). Long-term stress and allostatic load as well as short-term stressors also have negative effects on our behavior, our thoughts or cognition, and our feelings. Going beyond physiology, stress makes us act, feel, and think differently.

Stress affects one's mood, behavior, problem solving, motivations, and goals and can cause distraction, memory lapses, and a host of other psychological consequences (Dougall & Baum, 2002). You are more likely to get depressed and be fearful when you are stressed, angry, or aggravated. People under stress often lose their tempers and are not as patient as they normally would be. In an interesting study about the effects of stress on memory, Cahill, Prins, Weber, & McGaugh (1994) told two groups of students a story. The experimental group heard about a boy who had an accident, lost his legs, and had them reattached (a very stressful situation). The control group heard a neutral version of the story in which the boy watched what was happening in a hospital. Half the participants in each group received a drug that blocked the action of norepinephrine, thereby reducing stress; the other half got a placebo. A week later all participants were asked to recall as many elements of the story as they could. The participants in the stress condition who received the placebo (and hence felt the effects of stress) remembered the least amount of information.

Stress also influences our behaviors. When we are stressed, we often are busy thinking about the cause of the stress, which allows our attention to other tasks to suffer. Paying bills on time, remembering appointments, taking medicines, watering plants, or caring for a pet can all be negatively affected (Baba, Jamal, & Tourigny, 1998; Kompier & DiMartino, 1995; McNally, 1997). Obviously, the quality of work and the nature of interactions with friends and colleagues can also suffer. In some cases, people may not be able to sleep and may experience changes in their eating and drinking behavior (Conway, Vickers, Weid, & Rahe, 1981; Mellman, 1997).

POST-TRAUMATIC STRESS DISORDER

Post-traumatic stress disorder (PTSD) is a psychological disorder that is a possible consequence of a major stressful event. The PTSD diagnosis includes a prerequisite traumatic event, three subsets of symptom types (e.g., flashbacks), a requisite duration of symptoms beyond one month after the associated event, and a significant decrease in functioning (Helsley, 2008). Recently, psychologists have argued that PTSD can occur even if the event is not experienced directly (i.e., the event is seen on television). Evidence surrounding 9/11 supports this perspective (Marshall et al., 2007). There have been many controversies surrounding this disorder such as the recent broadening of the definition of the traumatic event that is required to meet a diagnosis for PTSD and the political climate surrounding its conception (Yeomans & Forman, 2009).

In one of the biggest reviews of studies on PTSD, Ozer, Best, Lipsey, and Weiss (2003) reviewed 2,647 studies of PTSD and found that psychological processes at the time of or around the trauma (i.e., peritraumatic), not prior characteristics (e.g. family history, prior trauma, and prior adjustment), are the strongest predictors of PTSD. Ozer et al., (2003) also noted that for a long period of time, the study of extreme responses to stress centered around war but have since expanded to other stressors such as environmental stress (see above) and sexual assault (Campbell, Greeson, Bybee, & Raja, 2008).

There is considerable cultural variability in PTSD prevalence. For example, differences in traumatic stress across gender have been observed in both the United States and Mexico after landfall of comparable hurricanes (Norris, Perilla, Ibanez, & Murphy, 2001). Al-Saffar, Borga, Edman, and Hallstrom (2003) sampled foreign nationals (Turkey, Iran, Saudia Arabia) who had immigrated to Sweden at least four years prior to the study. All participants had previous

TABLE **4.6**

Major Theories Compared

Name	Key Author	Main Concept
Fight-or-Flight	Walter Cannon	Sympathetic Adrenal Medulla activation prepares the body to fight or flee. Release of Catecholamines (epinephrine and norepinephrine).
Tend-and-Befriend	Shelley Taylor et al.	Females have additional responses to stress: Tend to and safeguard infants and befriend other females. Driven by oxytocin.
Cognitive Appraisal	Richard Lazarus	When faced with a novel event we first appraise it as either harmful, damaging, or challenging (Primary appraisal), and then examine our resources to see if we can cope with the stressor (Secondary appraisal).
General Adaptation Syndrome	Hans Selye	Organisms have a common response to a variety of stressors and proceed through stages of alarm, resistance, and exhaustion.

trauma exposure, yet response across ethnic differences was highly variable. The study found the presence of PTSD in 69 percent of the Iranians, 59 percent of the Saudis, 53 percent of the Turks, and only 29 percent of the Swedes.

A growing number of international epidemiological studies conclude that PTSD is found across cultures particularly in samples exposed to violence (Marsella & Christopher, 2004: Yeomans & Forman, 2009). Nonetheless, the sole application of the PTSD model may not be the most useful model around which to focus prevention and treatment services across cultures. De Jong (2005), despite having researched PTSD prevalence rates around the globe, articulates the need to put more attention on other mental health issues that remain under investigated, such as mood disorders, somatoform disorder, dissociative disorders, and other anxiety disorders. PTSD may not always be the best diagnosis, covering other problems. For example, Laban et al. (2005) found that among Iraqi asylum seekers postmigration challenges in their daily life were the best predictors of psychopathology, even more so than traumatic events themselves.

Stress has many different causes, can be studied in different ways, and has many different effects. In the next chapter we shall examine the different ways to cope.

SYNTHESIZE, EVALUATE, APPLY	<ul><li>How can your knowledge of Lazarus' theory reduce relationship stress?</li><li>What strategies and structures can employers use to keep work stress at a minimum?</li><li>How can the results of spillover and contagion studies be applied to improving family life?</li><li>What do you think are the most potent consequences of stress?</li></ul>

FOCUS ON CURRENT ISSUES

Stress Really Can Kill: The Baskerville Effect, Culture, & Stress

Many crime and mystery buffs regard the classic Sherlock Holmes' tale, *The Hounds of the Baskervilles*, as one of the best ways to be introduced to Sir Arthur Conan Doyle's legendary detective. (Spoiler alert: If you have not read it yet but are tempted, skip this section as it will reveal a major plot element). In the novel, the fictional Charles Baskerville dies as a result of the stress of running into the fierce hound of the book's title. The book has all the elements of a good read: family curses, *Monk*-esque detective smarts, and rich descriptions of the English moors. Key point: man dies of fright. Does this literary case study have real-life parallels? There are tales of Australian Aborigines dying if they are cursed: a healthy person on one day can keel over and die the next if he or she is told that they are cursed. The sociologist David Phillips and colleagues provide some provocative data (Phillips, Liu, Kwok, Jarvinen, Zhang, & Abramson et al., 2001). Also, the University of California San Diego team showed that heart attacks actually increase on psychologically stressful "unlucky" days.

Phillips et al. (2001) compared the death certificates of over 200,000 Chinese and Japanese Americans with 47,000 European Americans. The researchers matched deaths by cause, patient status, sex, age, and marital status and controlled for seasonal differences. The findings were astounding. For the Chinese and Japanese Americans, deaths peaked on the fourth day of the month. On such days, there was a 13 percent increase in deaths. No such pattern existed for the European Americans.

For many Chinese and Japanese, the number four is considered unlucky. In fact, in Mandarin, Cantonese, and Japanese, the number is pronounced the same as the word "death" (Milne, 2002). Throughout China and Japan, the number is not used in numbering floors or rooms in hospitals. In North America, we associate similar attributes to the number 13 (not to be confused with the suspense film *The Number 23* with Jim Carey, although there was also some death and stress involved there). The bottom line is that superstition can be stressful. If you believe bad things will happen on a certain day, there is a chance they will. This phenomenon, referred to by social psychologists as a self-fulfilling prophecy (Merton, 1948; see Chapters 8 and 9), has only recently been found to also result in powerful behavior changes (Madon, Guyll, Buller, Scherr, Willard, & Spoth, 2008 for self-fulfilling prophecy and drinking behavior). The suggestion from the Phillips et al. (2001) data is that the stress of an unlucky day may be strong enough to cause physiological damage. This takes the self-fulfilling prophecy to a whole new level.

The Baskerville effect, as it has come to be called, could not be explained in any other way. The ethnic groups who fear the number 4 seem more likely to die of cardiac arrest on the fourth of the month. This finding has some major implications for health psychologists and health care practitioners. It highlights the need to take into account beliefs and superstitions. If an American Indian or Hindu patient comes into a hospital room with a black or red thread tied around his or her wrist and the doctors or nurses have it cut off, the patient's health could be at stake. American Indians (see Chapter 3) and Hindus both use sacred threads. Sometimes the threads are part of healing ceremonies such as sweat lodges. The person wearing the thread may believe that their health is dependent on the string and cutting it off may prove to be a psychological affront that could tip the balance between fighting the good fight and throwing in the towel. The Baskerville effect certainty seems to suggest that this may be the case. Different cultural groups are superstitious or fear different things. Being sensitive to these differences and helping people cope better with even stressors that may seem silly to others can clearly be very important. Chapter 5 tells the full story of coping and resilience.

SUMMARY

- Stress is the physiological and psychological experience of disruption to our homeostatic balance. We are stressed any time excessive demands are placed on our body and mind. Stressors are factors that disrupt our homeostasis. Early stressors were acute and more physical in nature. Today stressors are long term and more psychological in nature.

- Stress activates the nervous system, especially the sympathetic nervous system, which in turn mobilizes the body for action. The parasympathetic system restores the body to rest after the stressor ends. The physiological stress response is characterized by the activation of different physiological pathways and the release of stress hormones.

- There are three major theories of stress. Cannon described the fight-or-flight response, which involves sympathetic adrenal medulla activation and the release of catecholamines. Selye described the general adaptation syndrome involving hypothalamic-pituitary-adrenal axis activation and the release of cortisol. Lazarus described a cognitive appraisal model of stress with primary and secondary appraisals of events as determining stress.

- Many factors influence stress appraisal such as the duration, severity, valence, controllability, predictability, and ambiguity of the stressor.

- Stress can by measured by questionnaire and using physiological measures such as blood pressure, galvanic skin response, and analysis of stress chemicals in saliva and urine.

- Different cultural groups experience different stressors by how they appraise stress and by how they are treated (e.g., low socioeconomic status individuals experience higher stress levels). Different cultural models of stress exist to incorporate such factors.

- Research is conducted on three main varieties of stressors: work stressors, environmental stressors, and relationship stressors.

- Stress has serious physiological and psychological consequences on the body. Allostatic load, or the effects of chronic stress, can cause heart and memory problems.

- Recently, researchers have postulated a new theory of stress, the tend-and-befriend model, which suggests that men and women have evolved different stress mechanisms.

TEST YOURSELF

Check your understanding of the topics in this chapter by answering the following questions. Answers appear in the Appendix.

1. Stress is best defined as:
   a. Negative events that tax the body.
   b. Challenges to the body systems.
   c. The perception of strain.
   d. Upsetting of homeostasis.

2. The earliest theory of stress suggests our current response is a remnant of our evolutionary past and was developed by:
   a. Walter Cannon.
   b. Hans Selye.

c. Richard Lazarus.

d. Rene Descartes.

3. During the fight or flight response, epinephrine does which of the following:

a. Increases heart rate and blood pressure.

b. Energizes the muscles.

c. Converts fat into energy.

d. Gets oxygen into the bloodstream.

4. According to Hans Selye, the _____ phase of the stress response is responsible for the physiological damage related to stress.

a. Alarm

b. Resistance

c. Threat

d. Exhaustion

5. According to Lazarus' cognitive appraisal model, in primary appraisal, people assess whether an event involves each of the following except:

a. Fear.

b. Harm.

c. Threat.

d. Challenge.

6. When a close friend is undergoing a lot of stress, we tend to feel stressed as well. We are not as affected by events taking place in far off lands and to strangers. The main dimension of stress varying in this example is:

a. Duration

b. Valence

c. Definition

d. Centrality

7. Not having money to cover basic needs, divorce, living in a high crime area, being fired, having housing problems and long-term medical problems are all examples of which of the following:

a. Environmental stressors

b. Chronic burden

c. Acute stressors

d. Unpredictable stressors

8. As someone gets stressed, heart rate increases and there will be a slight increase in perspiration. This can be seen best by measuring:

a. Galvanic skin response.

b. Temperature.

c. Blood pressure.

d. Electroencephalograms.

9. Workers with boring repetitive jobs sometimes show symptoms of nausea, headaches, muscle weakness, and blurry vision without any physical basis. This is known as:

a. Deprivational stress

b. Assembly-line hysteria

c. Cognitive load

d. Ambiguity disorder

10. Chronic stress over time can cause wear and tear on the body. This can have serious physical and psychological consequences and is called:

a. Exhaustion.

b. Allostasis.

c. Contagion.

d. Fatigue.

WEB RESOURCES

Visit the companion website at **www.cengage.com/ psychology/gurung**, where you will find online resources for this book, including chapter-by-chapter quizzes, Web links, and more!

Stressed At Work?
http://www.cdc.gov/niosh/stresswk.html

Here you will find a publication of the National Institute for Occupational Safety and Health. The site provides additional knowledge about the causes of stress at work and outlines steps that can be taken to prevent job stress.

Handling Stress without Smoking
cis.nci.nih.gov/fact/10_3.htm

Many smokers report using nicotine to help them deal with stress and report increases in stress when they try to quit smoking. This National Cancer Institute site provides important information on how to handle stress without smoking.

Relieving Trauma
www.nimh.nih.gov/publicat/reliving.cfm

Post-Traumatic Stress Disorder (PTSD) is a mental illness that affects millions of Americans who have experienced stressful events. This National Institute of Mental Health site provides valuable information on what PTSD is and how to cope with it.

KEY TERMS, CONCEPTS, AND PEOPLE

acute, 107

allostasis, 137

appraisals, 114

background stressors, 134

Cannon, Walter, 108

catecholamines, 109

chronic, 107

cognitive appraisal model, 118

control, 116

crossover, 133

definition, 117

ecological theory, 133

fight-or-flight theory, 109

general adaptation syndrome, 112

Holmes and Rahe, 123

homeostasis, 104

hypothalamic-pituitary-adrenal (HPA) axis, 112

Keicolt-Glaser, Janice, 130

Lazarus, Richard, 114

life events, 123

McEwen, Bruce, 138

mesosystem, 133

microsystems, 133

natural disaster stressors, 134

predictability, 116

primary appraisal, 115

reciprocity, 133

role ambiguity, 133

role conflict, 133

role theory, 133

secondary appraisal, 115

Selye, Hans, 111

spillover, 133

stress contagion effect, 133

stress response, 105

stress, 103

stressor, 105

sympathetic-adrenal-medullary (SAM) activation, 109

Taylor, Shelley, 110

techno-political stressors, 135

tend-and-befriend, 110

valence, 116

ESSENTIAL READINGS

Cannon, W. B. (1963). *Bodily changes in pain, hunger, fear and rage*. Oxford, England: Harper & Row.

Cohen, S. (1980). Aftereffects of stress on human performance and social behavior: A review of research and theory. *Psychological Bulletin, 88*, 82–108.

Kemeny, M. E. (2003). The psychobiology of stress. *Current Directions in Psychological Science, 12*(4), 124–129.

Lazarus, R. S., & Folkman, S. (1984). *Stress, appraisal, and coping*. New York: Springer.

Taylor, S. E., Klein, L. C., Lewis, B., Gruenewald, T., Gurung, R. A. R., & Updegraff, J. (2000). The female stress response: Tend and befriend not fight or flight. *Psychological Review, 107*, 411–429.

Coping and Social Support

You do not have to look far for examples of how to cope. Even popular music through the ages provides us with examples of what we should do when we are stressed. Perhaps the most helpful chorus of all and one supported by substantial psychological research is by The Beatles, who illustrated the positive aspects of social support, showing we can "get by with a little help from our friends." Jump forward to the 1980s (and then to 2007 when they reunited for a world tour) when The Police suggested that, "when the world is running down, you make the best of what's still around." In another musical example of good coping, the band REM suggested that even when it may seem like "it's the end of the world as we know it," you can still feel fine. Apart from reflecting life, music also provides a wonderful way to cope with stress. I know many people who listen to a number of specific songs when they feel unhappy or anxious. Of course, listening to music is just one way to cope, but these songs illustrate two major categories of coping with stress. First, you can cope by virtue of things you do as an individual that will vary with your personality and coping style (e.g., be optimistic or make the best of the situation). Second, you can cope by drawing on social networks for what you need to help you through the stressful situation (e.g., ask a friend to help you).

WHAT IS COPING?

In this chapter, we review the major ways to cope. **Coping** is defined as individual efforts made to manage distressing problems and emotions that affect the physical and psychological outcomes of stress (Somerfield & McCrae, 2000). If stress is a disturbance in homeostasis, coping is whatever we do to reestablish our homeostatic balances. Different factors can influence the severity of a stressor (i.e., moderators and mediators of stress) and influence coping as well. We will briefly summarize the most common ways of coping and discuss different styles of coping across cultures. Given the central role of social support, we will spend some time getting a good feel for this powerful construct, highlighting how it varies across cultures.

Stress and coping research is one of the most exciting and most active areas in health psychology. We have already discussed the many different types of stress in Chapter 4. As psychologists reached a better understanding of stress, research correspondingly studied how people coped with the stress. Given the impact stress can have on the mind and body, finding successful ways to cope is imperative. Unfortunately, finding the best ways to cope is not as easy as it may sound. Yes, you can observe people coping with various stressors and see which people get sick and which people do not. You can see who shows grace under pressure and who cracks. Finally, you figure out why the successful people did not get sick or did not crack and there you have your answer. Oh, if only it were so simple.

There are two key issues. First, remember that people and situations vary a lot. What may work for one person may not work for another. Similarly, what works in one situation may not work well in another. If that is not enough variability, what works for one person in one situation may not work for another person in the same situation. Second, as human beings, we are tempted to look for direct causes of events. For example, we tend to think in very straightforward ways and believe that some factor, say personality, will directly lead to a certain outcome. If you are optimistic, you will cope better and be less stressed. If you do not have a lot of social support, you will be more stressed and cope worse than if you had high social support. Although these statements are true in general, they greatly simplify the actual process of coping. A lot can influence what happens when you are stressed and what the result of your coping with the stressor will be.

To compensate for these two issues, that people and situations vary and that coping is a complex process, health psychologists consider a variety of factors surrounding stressful events. They measure different aspects of the person or organism coping to best account for individual differences in coping, and they also attempt to identify the different factors that influence the **coping process**, the process of reacting to a stressor and resulting in either a favorable (health and well-being) or unfavorable (sickness and unhappiness) outcome. These individual differences and the different factors that influence the process are referred to as moderators and mediators. As you will see, coping both moderates and mediates the relationship between stress and how you feel because of it. Getting a good feel for what these terms mean and how they are different from each other can be a challenge (nice primary appraisal), but we know you have the skills to do it (nice secondary appraisal).

MODERATORS VERSUS MEDIATORS

There are many different ways coping can influence a health outcome. Although health psychologists originally focused on studying the direct relationships between stressors (e.g., public speaking) and outcomes (e.g., blood pressure), today researchers are paying more and more attention to the underlying causal mechanisms and processes by which psychological factors influence health (MacKinnon & Luecken, 2008). Asking questions about specific effects (e.g., how, when, for whom, under what conditions, does public speaking lead to increased blood pressure?) requires moving beyond the examination of direct relationships to focus on additional factors that can explain how two variables are related. *Mediation* and *moderation* are two common examples of the type of processes now studied in detail across the field of health psychology (Kraemer, Kiernan, Essex, & Kupfer, 2008).

In life you will see that people who have a lot of a certain characteristic (are "high" on that variable) tend to behave and react differently than people who have a little of that characteristic (are "low" on that variable). The rich tend to be healthier than the poor are. Older people tend to be more health conscious than younger people are. People high in social support tend to

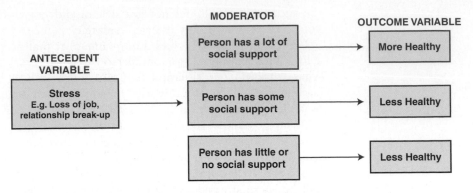

FIGURE **5.1** Moderation

People high in support show fewer negative effects when stressed than people low in support.

cope better than people low in social support do. In each of these cases the variables—income, age, and social support—are called moderators. A **moderator** is a variable that changes the *magnitude* (and sometimes the direction) of the relationship between an antecedent variable and an outcome variable (Aiken & West, 1991). This is easier to understand in a picture. Look at Figure 5.1. In the example of social support, the number of stressors can be the antecedent variable and well-being is the outcome. A simple **direct effect** would be that people with more stressors are more unhappy (a positive correlation). However, as I said earlier, things are more complex than that. In any group of people, some people will have more social support than others will. Let's measure social support and divide the people into a high support and a low support group. We would find that people with more support are happier than people with less social support are. Social support has moderated or buffered the relationship between stress and well-being. Such moderating effects of support are now well established and seen in a variety of life examples (e.g., divorced fathers' parenting, DeGarmo, Patras, & Eap, 2008). Being high or low on some factor often moderates how we react to stress.

Coping is often what you do when you are stressed. What you do can either help or hurt. The response to a stressor and the factors that follow a stressor influence what the outcome is going to be. These responses and factors between the stressor and the outcome are called mediators. A **mediator** is the intervening process (variable) through which an antecedent variable influences an outcome variable. Mediation can be described as a relationship where an independent variable changes a mediating variable, which then changes a dependent variable (MacKinnon, 2008). Coping behaviors in general and specific health behaviors are common mediators. Look at Figure 5.2. Instead of stress directly making you feel good or bad, it may influence your health behaviors (e.g., you drink alcohol or eat more) that *in turn* influence whether you feel good or bad. Here, health behaviors have mediated the relationship.

A large body of literature in health psychology concerns interventions aimed at improving well-being by enhancing coping, based on the assumption that

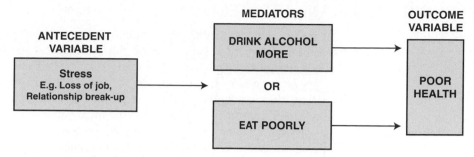

FIGURE **5.2** Mediation

Stress often leads people to make poor health choices, which then influences their health. In this case, poor health behaviors are playing the role of mediator.

effective coping is a mediator (Coyne & Racioppo, 2000; Franko, Thompson, Affenito, Barton, & Striegel-Moore, 2008; Moos, 2008;). There are a number of statistical procedures to test for mediation (Kraemer et al., 2008). It is easy to see whether mediation is taking place by comparing the correlation between the antecedent and outcome variables before and after the potential mediator is entered into the statistical analysis. If the variable you are studying is a mediator, the relationship between the antecedent and outcome variable significantly changes (gets lower) once the mediator is in the analysis. If you are stressed and you take a nap, you will probably wake up feeling better. If you are stressed and you do not take a nap, you may feel worse. In this example, sleep is said to mediate the relationship between your stress level and how you feel. This chapter will discuss many other mediators and moderators (e.g., moderating effects of hostility; Vella, Kamarck & Shiffman, 2008).

Think about the different biopsychosocial variables we have discussed so far and see whether you can tell the difference between moderators and mediators. Most variables health psychologists study (e.g., coping styles and social support) can be both mediators and moderators. The role of the variable depends on the study (e.g., a cross-sectional study versus a prospective study), the statistical analyses used to test the variable, the situation, or the variable under study. As a rule, mediators are changed by the stressor and correspondingly change the outcome. If more stress leads to you asking for more social support, which leads to you feeling better, social support is a mediator. If a longitudinal study shows that those with more stress exercise more and this makes them feel better, then exercise is a mediator. If a correlational study shows that the group of people who exercise more are less distressed than a similar group of stressed individuals who exercise less, then exercise is moderator. In the first case (mediation), exercise follows the stressor, changing in level and influencing the outcome. In the second case (moderation), we are looking at two separate groups of exercisers. The only variables that cannot be both mediators and moderators are those that cannot change as a function of the stressor or antecedent variable. Age, ethnicity, and race are examples of moderators that cannot be mediators (e.g., being more stressed cannot change your race).

COPING STYLES AND STRATEGIES

Coping includes anything people do to manage problems or emotional responses, whether successful or not (Carver & Scheier, 1994; Lazarus & Folkman, 1984; Pearlin & Schooler, 1978). We have both coping styles and coping strategies. **Coping styles** are general predispositions to dealing with stress; they are tools a person tends to use repeatedly. The two most basic styles are **approach coping** and **avoidant coping**. An individual can approach a stressor and make active efforts to resolve it, or he can try to avoid the problem (Moos & Schaefer, 1993). Many terms are used in studies of these two basic styles as shown in Table 5.1.

Coping strategies refer to the specific behavioral and psychological efforts that people use to master, tolerate, reduce, or minimize stressful events (Lazarus & Launier, 1978). Even though coping can refer to many different behaviors, it is easy to identify some main types of coping. Either you can do something about the problem or you can ignore it. Researchers have particularly distinguished between problem-focused or emotion-focused coping strategies.

Problem-focused coping involves directly facing the stressful situation and working hard to resolve it. For example, if you have a demanding, aggressive boss at work, you may experience a lot of stress at your job. If you report the issue to your human resources department or have a direct conversation with your boss, you are taking concrete action to deal with the situation and following a problem-focused approach.

Sometimes the first thing you do is deal with the emotions surrounding the stressor. A person finding out that he or she is HIV positive or has test results showing cancer may experience a surge of fear and anxiety and is driven to cope with these feelings. The person may deny the test results or not want to talk about them for some time. This strategy of coping is referred to as **emotion-focused coping** because you use either mental or behavioral methods to deal with the feelings resulting from the stress. More often than not, problem-focused and emotion-focused styles are pitted against each other. Although conceptually distinct, both strategies are interdependent and work together, with one supplementing the other in the overall coping process (Lazarus, 2000; Tennen, Affleck, Armeli, & Carney, 2000).

A recent study of changes in glycosylated hemoglobin (HbA1c), a key clinical indicator of glycemic control and a critical part of diabetes care, nicely

TABLE **5.1**
Coping Styles

Approach	Avoidance	Reference
Monitoring	Blunting	Miller (1987)
Vigilance	Cognitive avoidance	Krohne (1993)
Problem-focused	Emotion-focused + Appraisal-focused	Billings and Moos (1984)

illustrates the effect of coping strategies. Tsenkova, Love, Singer, and Ryff (2008) conducted a two-year longitudinal study (see Chapter 1 for research designs) on 97 older women (aged between 61 and 91). Tsenkova et al. measured coping strategies, medical history, positive emotions, health behaviors, and HbA1c levels. Higher levels of problem-focused coping predicted lower levels of HbA1c (a direct effect and a good thing). This relationship was moderated by positive mood—women who reported low levels of positive mood were worse off than those with high levels of positive mood (i.e., showed more negative effects of low problem-focused coping on changes in HbA1c).

SYNTHESIZE, EVALUATE, APPLY	• What are some biopsychosocial mediators and moderators of stress and coping? • What are the major drawbacks to current coping research? • What are the main coping styles? Generate situations in which each would be optimal. • How do the different ways of coping apply to the different theories of stress?

What Is the Best Way to Cope?

One of these styles looks better than the other. In general, people who rely primarily on *approach coping* adapt better to life stressors and experience less negative affect than those who make use of *avoidant coping* (Aspinwall & Taylor, 1992; Folkman, Lazarus, Gruen, & DeLongis, 1986). A large body of work demonstrates the deleterious emotional impact of avoidant coping in a variety of populations (e.g., Aldwin & Revenson, 1987; Fleishman & Fogel, 1994; Stanton & Snider, 1993). Avoiding paying taxes can only cause more stress as you rush to complete the form at the last moment or face the consequences of being late. Waiting until the last moment to study actually makes those last moments even more stressful. Sure, not thinking about taxes until April 14 or about the exam until the night before may seem like you are gaining some carefree days, but your avoidance has only accentuated your stress. Furthermore, the benefits from avoidance may be fewer than you think. In some samples, avoidance may exacerbate emotional distress. Ironically, people often become preoccupied with the thoughts that they attempt to suppress, and the inhibition of thoughts, feelings, and behaviors can cause physiological arousal (cf. Lobel, Yali, Zhu, & DeVincent, 1998). Also, the use of avoidant coping requires sustained effort to screen out stressor-relevant thoughts. If you do not want to think of the test that you have not studied for or the work assignment that you have not started on, a part of your cognitive processes are making sure that you are not thinking of the troubling aspect. You are using some mental energy just to make sure you do not think about something that troubles you.

It sounds like avoidant, emotion-focused coping may not be the best style; so, is approach-problem-solving coping the best? There is no real "best in show." The situation is an important consideration. The best coping style to use depends on the severity, duration, controllability, and emotionality of the situation (Aldwin, 1994; Auerbach, 1989). Even when you consider the type of situation, it is critical to be specific about it. People may want to know the best way to cope with breast cancer or diabetes. You may want to know the best way to cope with the loss of a loved one. Just referring to breast cancer or diabetes in general may not be as helpful as discussing coping with different stages of breast cancer or different problem areas of diabetes such as managing episodes of hypoglycemia (Maes, Leventhal, & de Ridder, 1996).

There is over-reliance on the "problem-focused coping is good; emotion-focused coping is bad" dichotomy. This can be dangerous because sometimes using the seemingly better problem-focused coping style can be associated with poorer psychological outcomes (Bolger, 1990; Coyne & Gottlieb, 1996). There is the additional consideration that it is sometimes hard to define which style of coping a certain behavior is. Coyne and Racioppo (2000) use the example of "seeking social support." Seeking social support can be either problem- or emotion-focused coping, and its success depends on the timing and circumstances of the seeking, how, what, and from whom the support is sought, and the actions to which support seeking refers. For example, wanting your doctor to spend more time with you to tell you about a diagnosis is a form of seeking support that gives you emotional support and information on how to deal with the issue.

It is essentially best to match the type of coping you use with the situation and with your comfort level. For example, if you work in a hospital and you are stressed by how many hours you work and how many patients you see, you have some control over the situation. Finding a way to be scheduled for better hours is a problem-focused way to cope. By way of contrast, avoidant, emotion-focused coping may be beneficial in the short term because this coping style gives your body time to recover from the physiological responses to and shock of the stressor. If you were diagnosed with cancer and you are so anxious that you cannot function, it may be better to be emotion-focused and first cope with your emotions and ignore the issue because it stresses you. At some point, however, you must face the problem, get more information about it, and learn what you should do to deal with it.

WHO COPES WELL?

Some people cope with stress by buying and consuming a pint (or a gallon!) of their favorite ice cream. Others go for a fast run. Still others sleep extra hours and do not eat. You may have some friends or coworkers who are not fazed even when everything seems to be going wrong. Other individuals fall apart and get "freaked out" by the most minor negative events. As you read in Chapter 4, how a person appraises an event can determine the extent to which that person thinks it is stressful. According to Lazarus and Folkman's (1984) framework, cognitive appraisals and coping are two critical mediators of responses to stressful events. A person's subjective perception of stress will depend on the objective features of the situation (e.g., potentially stressful life events) and the way that person appraises the events. Your feeling of stress depends both on how many things you really have due and on how serious or demanding you think the assignments or deadlines are. Even if you do not really have too much to do, just believing that you have too much to do or

© K. Beebee/Custom Medical Stock

Indulgence

One way of coping is to indulge in something that you know is not great for you. Too much snack food and watching television all night is bad for your health, but it seems so soothing when we are stressed.

that what you have to do is very difficult can be stressful. A person experiences distress when primary appraisals of threat exceed secondary appraisals of coping ability (Folkman, Lazarus, Gruen, & DeLongis, 1986). One's secondary appraisal will depend in large part on the personal resources a person brings to the situation, such as personality factors (e.g., optimism) and perceived resources for coping with the situation. Many factors influence how someone appraises a situation and correspondingly copes with stress. In this section, we will examine some of the factors that influence appraisals and coping and will determine what makes the difference between weathering the storm and falling to pieces.

PERSONALITY AND COPING

A person's personality characteristics provide some of the best clues as to how they will cope with a stressor (Cosway, Endler, Sadler, & Deary, 2000; Penley & Tomaka, 2002). **Personality** is defined as an individual's unique set of consistent behavioral traits, where traits are durable dispositions to behave in a particular way in a variety of situations. When you described yourself in the "Who am I?" task in Chapter 1, you probably used a number of trait terms to describe yourself (e.g., honest, dependable, funny, or social). One of the earliest personality psychologists, Gordon Allport (1961), scoured an unabridged dictionary and collected more than 4,500 descriptors used to describe personality. Later personality theorists such as Cattell (1966) used statistical analyses to measure correlations between these different descriptors. Cattell found that all 4,500 descriptors could be encompassed by just 16 terms. It gets better. McCrae and Costa (1987) further narrowed these 16 terms down to a core of only five as part of their five-factor model of personality. Often referred to as the "Big Five," a wealth of research suggests that personality can be sufficiently measured by assessing how conscientious, agreeable, neurotic, open to experience, and extraverted a person is (John & Srivastava, 1999; Wiggins & Trapnell, 1997). For an easy way to remember them, we like to use the acronym CANOE or try OCEAN if you live on the coast. Clear definitions and examples of each trait are listed in Table 5.2.

In addition to the Big 5 traits, a number of other personality characteristics, sometimes grouped into patterns, influence health. For example, you have probably heard about Type A personalities. The Type A behavior pattern was perhaps the first and most controversial aspect of personality that was thought to relate to stress and coping. The cardiologists Friedman and Rosenman (1959, 1974) identified the **Type A coronary-prone behavior pattern** based on their observations of heart patients who showed a sense of time urgency (always doing more than one thing at the same time), competitiveness, and hostility in their interactions with other people. People with this constellation of personality characteristics were found to have a higher risk for coronary heart disease and stress. Early interventions helped such individuals cope better. There were problems replicating Friedman and Rosenman's hypothesized link between cardiovascular disease and Type A personality, and it later became clear that the critical personality risk factor was hostility (Dembrowski, MacDougall, Williams, Haney, & Blumenthal, 1985). Hostility was the component that reliably predicted heart attacks. Having a sense of time urgency and being competitive is all right, but being hostile is most dangerous to your health. Remember that the next time you feel like snapping at someone or giving in to traffic road rage.

Hostility also provides us with another good example of how personality characteristics can be moderators of the relationship between psychological factors and stressful outcomes. Vella, Kamarck, and Shiffman (2008) tested the role of hostility in moderating the effects of positive social interactions on ambulatory blood pressure (ABP). The researchers monitored the ABP of 341 adults for 6 days (readings taken every 45 minutes while participants were awake). Participants also kept a diary and recorded mood and social interactions at the time of each ABP measurement. Sure enough, low-hostile participants experiencing supportive interactions showed reductions

TABLE **5.2**
The Big Five Personality Traits

Trait	Characteristics
Conscientiousness	Ethical, dependable, productive, purposeful
Agreeableness	Sympathetic, warm, trusting, cooperative
Neuroticism	Anxious, insecure, guilt-prone, self-conscious
Openness to experience	Daring, nonconforming, imaginative
Extraversion	Talkative, sociable, fun-loving, affectionate

in ABP. This was not the case for high-hostile participants (remember moderation = differences between participants high and low on a variable). The researchers concluded that hostile individuals may find offers of support stressful and may fail to benefit from intimacy during everyday life (Vella et al., 2008).

Does it follow then that people with different personalities will use different methods to cope with stress? For the most part this is true. It is probably no surprise that some personality types use different coping styles than others, and empirical tests mostly confirm this assumption. For example, in a study of 298 outpatients with depression, those patients with less-adaptive coping strategies (i.e., emotion-focused coping) had less-adaptive personality traits (i.e., neuroticism) and were more depressed. The reverse was found for adaptive problem-focused coping strategies (McWilliams, Cox, & Enns, 2003). In another study, neuroticism was highly related to avoidant coping, agreeableness was negatively related to problem-focused coping, and conscientiousness was positively related to problem-focused coping and negatively related to avoidant coping (McCormick, Dowd, Quirk, & Zegarra, 1998). Clearly, personality styles can predict what coping style a person is likely to use, but there is not always a direct relationship.

One thing to keep in mind is that coping styles are not merely reflections of personality but mediate the relationship between personality and well-being. Therefore, although having a high level of optimism or a low level of neuroticism is associated with feeling less stressed in general, people with these personality characteristics are more likely to use more adaptive coping styles and hence decrease their stress. A study of college students illustrates this process. The students completed measures of perceived stress, social support, optimism, and coping in their first semester of college. The optimists had smaller increases in stress and depression over the course of the first semester of college, but mediational analyses showed that the optimists were more likely to use adaptive coping styles, such as positive reinterpretation and growth (Brissette, Scheier, & Carver, 2002). Therefore, the personality style led to the favoring of a specific coping style, which then influenced well-being; the personality style did not directly influence the outcome. Similarly, knowing the coping styles of heart failure patients in addition to just knowing their personalities enabled researchers to predict better their depression (Murberg, Bru, & Stephens, 2002). Again, coping style mediated the relationship between personality and well-being.

Beyond these core aspects of personality, people vary on a number of other characteristics that can influence their coping. For example, health psychologists suggest that we pay close attention to the concepts of optimism, mastery, hardiness, and resilience.

Optimism refers to generalized outcome expectancies that good things, rather than bad things, will happen (Carver & Scheier, 1999; Carver, Scheier, & Weintraub, 1989). Optimists are the people who can always find the positive aspects of any situation and always seem to look on the bright side of life no matter how bad things are. This personality trait is associated with a number of health-related factors. Optimists tend to cope better with stress and practice better health behaviors (Scheier et al., 1989; Taylor et al., 1992).

Optimism is strongly and positively correlated with problem-focused coping strategies and strongly negatively correlated with avoidant coping strategies (Scheier, Weintraub, & Carver, 1986). Optimists, in general, show good psychological well-being (Armor & Taylor, 1998), suggesting that optimism may moderate depression. Optimism relates to the presence of active potent natural killer cells during stress (Segerstrom, Taylor, Kemeny, & Fahey, 1998), and serves as protection against HIV exposure by decreasing intentions to engage in unsafe sex (Carvajal, Garner, & Evans, 1998). Measures of AIDS-related optimism have been related to a slower disease course (Taylor, Kemeny, Reed, Bower, & Gruenewald, 2000). Optimists differ significantly from pessimists in secondary (but not primary) appraisal, coping, and adjustment. In addition, knowing a person's level of optimism adds significantly to predictions of that person's adjustment, beyond what was accounted for by knowing about how the person makes appraisals and copes (Chang, 1998).

Mastery is a relatively stable tendency of an individual and another variable that can influence the appraisal of stress and help people cope (Dweck & Sorich, 1999). Mastery is defined as the extent to which one regards one's life chances as being under one's own control (Pearlin & Schooler, 1978, p. 5). Someone with a high level of mastery believes that he or she has the capability to succeed at whatever task is at hand. Conceptually similar to perceived control, locus of control, and self-efficacy, mastery has been found to be a moderator in many studies of stress and appraisal (Aldwin, Sutton, & Lachman, 1996; Cox & Ferguson, 1991; Frone, Russell, & Cooper, 1995; Herman-Stahl & Petersen, 1996; Pearlin & Skaff, 1995; Skaff, Pearlin, & Mullan, 1996; Wallston, 1992). For example, Hemenover and Dienstbier (1996) showed that mastery predicted stress appraisals for an intellectual task in a group of college students in various situations, including academic stressors. Students with high levels of mastery reported lower levels of stress. Mausbach et al., (2008) showed that for people high in mastery, negative life events were not related to increases in plasma PAI-1 antigen levels (an antigen, see Chapter 3, related to cardiovascular disease). This was not the case for people low in mastery. In the realm of parent-child interactions, feelings of mastery among parents improves their coping with stressful events and has indirect beneficial effects on their children, teaching them to develop a sense of control by striving to confront stressful events actively (Rogers, Parcel, & Menaghan, 1991). The effects of mastery also vary by age. Ben-Zur (2002) measured the coping styles and mastery levels of 168 young and old community residents and found that older people with elevated feelings of mastery used more efficient coping strategies.

Two other personality characteristics that moderate the effects of stress and aid coping are *hardiness* and *resilience*. People who are strongly committed to their lives, enjoy challenges, and have a high level of control over their lives are high on the trait of **hardiness** (Maddi & Kobasa, 1991). In general, being hardy is related to better adjustment to a range of health issues (Kobasa, Maddi, & Kahn, 1982; Pollack, 1986).

Resilience closely relates to hardiness. If you see a person who has encountered a tremendous number of stressful events but always seems to bounce back into action and still do fine, he or she is said to be **resilient** (Fredrickson,

Tugade, Waugh, & Larkin, 2003). Like hardiness, resiliency accompanies adaptive coping strategies that lead to better mental and physical health. A number of psychological factors are linked to resiliency such as finding/having a purpose in life (Wang, Lightsey, Pietruszka, Uruk, & Wells, 2007), experiencing positive emotions (Burns, at al., 2008; Fredrickson et al., 2003; Tugade, Fredrickson, & Barrett, 2004), and quality relationships (Gilligan, 2008), especially coming from a cohesive family (McClure, Chavez, Agars, Peacock, & Matosian, 2008). Although early studies of this concept were conducted with children, there is now a wealth of research on resilience across the life course (see Ryff & Singer, 2003a, 2003b, for reviews).

Resilience can also be studied at a group level (e.g., the family resilience studies of Ortega, Beauchemin, & Kaniskan, 2008) and varies by cultural group (Harvey & Tummala-Narra, 2007; Xu, 2007). Prominent factors of resilient families include positive outlook, spirituality, family member accord, flexibility, family communication, financial management, family time, shared recreation, routines and rituals, and support networks (Black & Lobo, 2008). There has also been an increase in research exploring how culture and resilience interact. In a review of how adversity and resilience influence the development of youth from diverse cultural backgrounds, Clauss-Ehlers (2008) found that cultural factors were related to measures of five aspects of resilience: childhood stressors, global coping, adaptive coping, maladaptive coping, and sociocultural support. Childhood stressors were experienced differentially by individuals from different racial/ethnic and social class status backgrounds, supporting proposals that ecological aspects, notably cultural background and experiences, influence the development of resilience. In another example, African American college students who received racial socialization messages and perceived that they had social support were more resilient (Brown, 2008).

COPING AND CULTURE

Although culture brings its own unique set of problems to accentuate stress and accordingly mental illness (see Chapter 4), culture also has its strengths. It is also important to consider cultural variation in coping methods and strategies when individuals are dealing with stress.

Coping styles vary across cultures; in fact, culture can be a factor that mediates specific coping styles and strategies (see Chun, Moos, & Cronkite, 2006). Terms such as individualistic and collectivistic are often used to describe the general orientation of other cultures, and can be extended to describe individuals' coping styles in these cultures. For example, many East Asian cultures are collectivistic. These cultures emphasize interdependence on others in many roles and functions. The orientation of the United States and European countries, by contrast, is individualistic. They emphasize independence and reliance on the self (Markus & Kitayama, 1991; Oyserman, Coon, & Kemmelmeier, 2002). These cultural orientations, in turn, may influence how individuals in these cultures cope with stress (Chun, Moos, & Cronkite, 2006; Yeh & Inose, 2002). Specific coping methods within the collectivistic orientation included individualistic coping (coping alone through participation in solitary activities); seeking social support from family, members of their ethnic groups, or individuals who had gone through similar loss; forbearance (emotion-based coping); religiosity; and traditional healing practices. Coping strategies typically associated with individualistic cultures are approach-based, while avoidance-based coping strategies are often associated with collectivistic cultures (Chun, Moos, & Cronkite, 2006). In an example of these styles, Yeh, Inman, Kim, & Okubo (2006) found that in a sample of Asian American families who had lost a family member in the September 11 attacks, the subjects used collectivistic coping methods to deal with the stress caused by their losses.

In another example of how culture mediates coping styles, Bailey and Dua (1999) showed that some immigrant groups cope differently from others, and coping style can vary with acculturation and ethnic identity (discussed next). Asian students moving to Australia showed high levels of perceived stress and tended to employ collectivist coping strategies more than any other group during their first six months away from home. Anglo Australians were lowest on measures of perceived stress and tended to use individualist coping styles. However, an interesting thing happened. As the Asians became more Australian, they started using coping styles that were more similar to those of the other non-Asian Australians (Bailey & Dua, 1999).

Ethnic Identity

One of the major mediators of the stress-mental health relationship is ethnic identity. Dubow, Pargament, Boxer, and Tarakeshwar (2000) found that ethnic identity was positively correlated with ethnic-related stressors and coping strategies in Jewish adolescents. That is, the Jewish adolescents in the study reported experiencing stressors related to religious and social practices, yet they were able to rely on coping strategies and resources unique to their ethnic group for better outcomes. In another example, Mossakowski (2007) assessed the relationship of perceived discrimination, ethnic identity, and mental health outcomes in a sample of Filipino Americans. Higher ratings of ethnic identity were associated with low rates of depression and depressive symptoms. Conversely, Gamnst et al. (2002) found that in a sample of Latinos, individuals who had low levels of ethnic identity were more likely to have poorer mental health outcomes, as assessed by declining global assessment of functioning (GAF) scores during a three-month period of community mental health treatment.

Mental health outcomes may be better for immigrants to the United States, as opposed to people from the same cultural group born in the United States. For example, Landale, Oropesa, Llanes, and Gorman (1999) found that Puerto Rican immigrant women, compared to Puerto Rican women born in the United States, reported fewer stressful life events and fewer adverse health behaviors during pregnancy. Similarly, Vega et al. (2004) compared 12-month prevalence rates of mood, anxiety, and substance use disorders of Mexican American immigrants and U.S.-born citizens of Mexican descent, finding that the prevalence rates of these disorders were significantly less in the immigrant population than in the U.S.-born population. Another study on the same ethnic group found Mexican Americans to have better mental health ratings than Mexican citizens and non-Hispanic European Americans, while Mexican citizens reported higher ratings of physical health than Mexican Americans and non-Hispanic Whites (Farley et al., 2005).

Being an immigrant can sometimes make things worse. For example, for immigrants, the rates of psychiatric disorders may increase with duration of time living in the United States. While Vega et al. (2004) found lower rates of mood, anxiety, and substance use disorders in Mexican American immigrants, results also indicated that immigrants who had lived in the United States for 13 years or less had 12-month prevalence rates of 9.2 percent, increasing to 18.4 percent for residents residing for greater than 13 years. In comparison, U.S.-born Mexican Americans had prevalence rates of 27.4 percent for any psychiatric disorder within the past 12 months.

Other studies have looked at the impact of generational status on rates of mental health disorders for immigrants to the United States. Williams et al. (2006) found that in a sample of black Caribbean immigrants and African Americans, ethnicity, gender, and generational status variables moderated the risk of 12-month prevalence of psychiatric disorders. For instance, Caribbean Black women had lower rates of psychiatric disorders than African American women did, while Caribbean Black men had higher rates of psychiatric disorders than African American men did in the past 12 months. Furthermore, the prevalence of psychiatric disorders varied by generational status, such that 3rd generation immigrants had the highest rates of psychiatric disorders, while 1st generation immigrants had the highest rates of psychiatric disorders in the past 12 months.

Acculturation

Ethnic identity formation is more of an issue for non-European Americans, as they are often made very aware of their not being White. For non-White children, the stress of forming one's ethnic identity is compounded by the fact that often parents are experiencing their own problems with the culture that surrounds them (Berrol, 1995). Immigrants, for example, often single-handedly enter a culture different from their own, leaving their families behind in their home cultures (Saran, 1985). They differ in the extent to which they acculturate, and while some remain steadfast in retaining the values and norms with which they were raised, some subtly adapt to the different world around them (Helweg & Helweg, 1990). Acculturation is correspondingly an important variable. Being acculturated may mean different things to different people, and there have been many approaches to studying acculturation (Berry, Phinney, Sam, & Vedder, 2006). Roland (1990), who has studied and compared various cultures, sees the acculturation process as primarily entailing the adoption of one culture at the expense of the other. In contrast, Berry, Trimble, & Olmedo (1986) define four models of acculturation that directly pertain to the issues we have raised here. A strong identification with both groups is indicative of integration or biculturalism; a strong identification with only the dominant culture reflects assimilation; with only the ethnic group, separation; with neither group, marginalization.

Acculturation and ethnic identity formation are both factors that are critical aspects of human development that are of much more significance to non-European Americans and can influence health and health behaviors. Attending to acculturation and ethnic identity takes us beyond the basic cultural differences in health and can be seen in both mental and physical health. For example, African Americans have been found to have higher rates of mental disorders compared with European Americans and Mexican Americans, but these findings vary with acculturation level (Robins, Locke, & Regier, 1991; Ying, 1995). In many cases, greater acculturation is associated with better mental health (e.g., Balls Organista, Organista, & Kurasaki, 2002), although this is not the case for all ethnic groups or with physical health. Higher acculturated Mexican Americans, for example, have been found to be more depressed than recent immigrants with lower acculturation scores (Vega et al., 1998).

The acculturation-physical health link is just as fascinating. In general, recent immigrants are healthier than better-acculturated nonimmigrants (Myers & Rodriguez, 2002; Popkin & Udry, 1998). Cancer, diabetes, and risky sexual behavior are higher among most acculturated non-Europeans (Fujimoto, 1992; Hines, Snowden, & Graves, 1998; Harmon, Castro, & Coe, 1996), and there are only a few exceptions: acculturation is related to lower rates of diabetes among Mexican Americans (Hazuda, Haffner, Stern, & Eifler, 1988). The positive relationship can be seen across many cultural groups, although as you can guess, the relationship is sometimes very complex when you add sex differences to the mix. More acculturated Mexican Americans are more likely to have high blood pressure than less acculturated Mexican Americans (Espino & Maldonado, 1990). Still, whereas less acculturated Latino American men drink more and are more likely to engage in risky sexual behavior, it is the more acculturated Latina women who drink more (Hines & Caetano, 1998).

Given that culture can be broadly defined as encompassing other factors such as religion, it is important to remember that acculturation may take place when any two or more cultural groups come into contact, and that there is a lot of variance within each cultural group. When a Catholic dates or marries a Lutheran or someone from the South dates or marries someone from the North, acculturative pressure can influence both relationships, and the children of both couples can have problems forming their identities, which could affect their health and health behaviors.

SYNTHESIZE, EVALUATE, APPLY	<ul><li>How do different personality styles/traits relate to coping?</li><li>What are the key cultural factors involved in coping?</li><li>How would you evaluate your own coping mechanisms?</li><li>Do you cope in ways not discussed in this chapter?</li></ul>

SOCIAL SUPPORT

How we cope with stress often is influenced by how much support we receive from others around us. Even more importantly, just the perception that support would be available if we need it can greatly enhance our coping strategies and health (e.g., Lett, 2007). Not surprisingly then, social support is one of the most important factors in the study of stress and coping.

The sociologist Durkheim (1897, 1951) first provided empirical evidence of the importance of social support and showed that a lack of social relationships increased the probability of a person committing suicide. The connections of social support to health were strengthened by the work of Cassel (1976) and Cobb (1976) who demonstrated that the "presence of other members of the same species" was a critical ingredient to good health. This social support to health connection was supported later by the now classic 9-year epidemiological study done in Alameda County, California, where men and women who were socially integrated lived longer (Berkman, 1985; Berkman & Syme, 1979). In fact, the age-adjusted relative risk for mortality for the men and women with weak social connections (e.g., marriage, contact with family members and close friends, and memberships in religious and volunteer organizations) was almost twice as high as the risk for the participants with strong social connections.

The evidence showing the usefulness of social support is astounding. **Social support**, generally defined as emotional, informational, or instrumental assistance from others (Dunkel-Schetter & Bennett, 1990), has been tied to better health, more rapid recovery from illness, and a lower risk for mortality (Gallicchio, Hoffman, & Helzlsouer, 2007; House, Umberson, & Landis, 1988; O'Donovan, A., & Hughes, 2008; Sarason, Sarason, & Gurung, 2001; Uchino, Cacioppo, & Kiecolt-Glaser, 1996). Social support also reduces psychological distress during stress (Cohen & Wills, 1985; Ditzen, Schmidt, Strauss, Nater, Ehlert, & Heinrichs, 2008; Gallagher, Phillips, Ferraro, Drayson, & Carroll, 2008). Epidemiological studies document increased risk for depression among people who lack social support (Stanfeld, Rael, Head, Shipley, & Marmot, 1997; Yuh et al., 2008). Studies of people with HIV infection suggest that social support from peers is critical for emotional well-being and, in periods of crisis, family support may become an especially important determinant of emotional well-being (Crystal & Kersting, 1998; Miller & Cole, 1998).

© Mary Kate Denny/PhotoEdit

Support Network
Our social networks, friends, and colleagues can be a major source of social support.

Types of Social Support

Beware of loose definitions! The statement, "social support is helpful," is really too general to be practical. Social support undoubtedly is an effective aid to health and coping with stress. However, the majority of research findings available mask an important fact: there are many different types of social support. Table 5.3 provides an overview of the main ways in which social support can differ. The most basic division is between **network measures** and **functional measures**. The earliest research looked at a person's networks (e.g., Berkman, 1985), asking whether the person was married or not or asking how many people the person saw on a weekly basis. The measurement of networks also varied. Some researchers just asked for the number of people in a network whereas others also assessed the relationship of the support provider to the support recipient.

Even greater variety exists in the functional measures of support. Functional support is assessed in two main ways. You can measure the social support the person reports was provided to him or her, called **received support**, or the social support the person believes to be available to him or her, called **perceived support**. These two forms of support vary further in the function that they serve. If you think about when you are stressed, the type of support that you get and that will be helpful will depend largely on the type of stress you are experiencing. If you are stressed because you have a big assignment due at school, but you do not even know how to begin, any information

TABLE **5.3**

Main Forms of Social Support and How It Can Be Measured

I. Networks	Structure and existence of social relationships
	Frequency contacts; composition (who-friend, family, coworker)?
	Perceived: If something happens you will get help (if needed it will be there)
	Are you loved, valued and esteemed?
	Satisfaction: Was what you got enough?
	Received: When something happened, how much did you get?
II. Sources	Relationship partner, family, friends, fellow workers, doctors, nurses.
III. Types	*Emotional*: Empathy, caring, concern.
	Esteem: Confidence building, encouragement.
	Instrumental/Tangible: Direct assistance, cash, etc.
	Informational: Advice, directions, feedback.
IV. Specificity	*Global*: (for stressor and source, e.g., all stressors or from everyone?).
	Specific: (for this event *or* in this relationship?).
	Time: Over last year, last month, last week.

that you obtain about how to do it will be helpful. If you are stressed because your car broke down and you do not know how you will go to work, then someone giving you a ride will best help you cope. If someone close to you passes away or you have trouble in a close relationship, people who show you that you are esteemed, loved, and cared for will be the most supportive. These are the three main types of received support, and each has its counterpart form of perceived support. Received or perceived support can be (1) instrumental (also called tangible or material support, e.g., the loan of the car), (2) informational (or advice, e.g., how to do your assignment), and (3) emotional (e.g., being told that people care for you).

Other distinctions become important in the measurement of support and are essential to maximizing its predictor power. For example, you can measure global support—a person's sense of support from people in general, or specific support—support from a specific person or relationship. The recipient or perceiver's satisfaction with social support can be studied. Finally, you can create categories by focusing on who is providing the support and the source of support (e.g., spouse, family, friends, doctors, or medical staff). These different categories can fit into a hierarchy with the general approach (received or perceived) as the primary dimension (Table 5.3). Within each of these, the source of support can be distinguished, and finally, different types or functions of support can be embedded within each source (Schwarzer, Dunkel-Schetter, & Kemeny, 1994). The most effective and theoretically compelling model combines **received and perceived support** measures but separates them by source (Dunkel-Schetter, Gurung, Lobel, & Wadhwa, 2001).

A study of social support provided during pregnancy provides an example of how different forms of social support can be studied. The major comparison is between support transactions at the level of a couple or dyad (e.g., support provided to the baby's mother from the baby's father) versus at the level of a network or group (e.g., support provided by friends and family). Another set of studies focused on the impact of support from professional sources (e.g., nurses and doctors) (Blondel, 1998). How do the effects of support from these three different sources compare? In a study designed to answer this question, Gurung, Dunkel-Schetter, Colins, Rini, & Hobel (2005) compared the support a woman received from her baby's father with the support received from her friends and family. The ethnically diverse sample consisted of 480 women (African American, Latin American, and non-Hispanic European Americans). Various types of support measures were assessed at multiple time points before the birth, together with standard measures of depression and anxiety. Different sources of support were associated with different outcomes. Specifically, social support from the baby's father predicted significantly less anxiety but not significant differences in depressed mood. Support from the mother's friends and family was a significant predictor of the mother's depressed mood but did not predict her anxiety (cf. Kalil, Gruber, Conley, & Sytniac, 1993). Social support from the baby's father predicted maternal changes in anxiety independent of sociodemographic variables such as age, ethnicity, and socioeconomic status and individual difference measures such as mastery and coping. This difference in support effects by source is consistent with the theory and some results in the social support literature showing that support is most effective when the type of support a person needs matches the type of support provided (e.g., Cutrona, 1990). Others discuss the existence of an optimal support provider for different specific needs (Cantor, 1979; Litwak, 1985).

CULTURAL VARIABLES IN SOCIAL SUPPORT

Culture shapes beliefs about health and illness and provides the context by which an individual evaluates his or her situation and decides whether he or she needs social support and how much. Not surprisingly, strong cultural differences exist in social support (Burleson & Mortenson, 2003; Norris, Murphy, Kaniasty, Perilla, & Ortis, 2001; Goodwin & Giles, 2003; Hyun et al., 2002; Taylor et al., 2004). Findings from three studies by Taylor et al. indicate that Asians and Asian Americans were less likely to rely on social support for coping with stress than European Americans. Additionally, the data indicate that these cultural differences in seeking social support may be due to concerns with violating relationship norms. In the collectivist Asian cultures, the emphasis is to maintain group harmony and cohesion, putting the needs of others before the self. Therefore, relying on others for social support was seen as disrupting this balance (Taylor et al., 2004).

Gender is one of the most robust predictors of use of social support (Taylor et al., 2000; Unger, McAvay, Bruce, Berkman, & Seeman, 1999). Women receive and give more support over the life course (e.g., Rook & Schuster, 1996), and women experience greater benefits from social network interactions (see Antonucci & Akiyama, 1987; Berkman, Vaccarino, & Seeman, 1993; Flaherty & Richman, 1989; Shumaker & Hill, 1991, for reviews). Some studies have shown that for men, friendships and nonfamily activities decline with age, whereas women's friendships outside the home do not change (Field, 1999).

Strong gender differences exist in social support. Luckow, Reifman, and McIntosh (1998) analyzed gender differences in coping and found that the

Social Support among Women
Women often turn to other women for social support and to share their emotions.

largest difference arose in seeking and using social support. Of the 26 studies that tested for gender differences, one study showed no differences and 25 favored women. None of the studies favored men (Luckow et al., 1998). Indeed, so reliable is this gender effect that, following the early studies on affiliation in response to stress by Schachter (1959), most subsequent research on affiliation under stress used only female participants.

Across the entire life cycle, females are more likely to mobilize social support, especially from other females, in times of stress. They seek it out more, they receive more support, and they are more satisfied with the support they receive. Adolescent girls report more informal sources of support than do boys, and girls are more likely to turn to their same-sex peers for support than are boys (e.g., Copeland & Hess, 1995; see Belle, 1989, for a review). Female college students report having more available helpers and receiving more support than males do (e.g., Ptacek, Smith, & Zanas, 1992; see Belle, 1989, for a review). Adult women maintain more same-sex close relationships, mobilize more social support in times of stress, rely less heavily on their spouses for social support, and turn to female friends more often (Belle, 1989; McDonald & Korabik, 1991; Ogus, Greenglass, & Burke, 1990). They also report more benefits from contact with their female friends and relatives (although they are also more vulnerable to network events as a cause of psychological distress), and provide more frequent and more effective social support to others than men (Taylor et al., 2000). Although females give help to both males and females in their support networks, they are more likely to seek help and social support from other female relatives and female friends than from males (Belle, 1989; Wethington, McLeod, & Kessler, 1987).

Women are also more engaged in their social networks. They are significantly better at sharing what is going on in their networks than men. For example, a woman is more likely to discuss the major illnesses of her children with others and is more likely to report being involved if there is a crisis event in the network (Wethington et al., 1987). In an extensive study of social networks, Veroff, Kulka, and Douvan (1981) reported that women were 30 percent more likely than men to have provided some type of support in response to network stressors, including economic and work-related difficulties, interpersonal problems, death, and negative health events. Gender also affects social support receipt: Men receive emotional support primarily from their spouses, whereas women draw more heavily on their friends, relatives, and children for emotional support (Gurung, Taylor, & Seeman, 2003).

So consistent and strong are these findings that theorists have argued for basic gender differences in orientation toward others, with women maintaining a collectivist orientation (Markus & Kitayama, 1991) or connectedness (Clancy & Dollinger, 1993; Niedenthal & Beike, 1997; Kashima et al., 1995), and men maintaining a more individualistic orientation (Cross & Madson, 1997). These findings appear to generalize across cultures. In their study of six cultures, Whiting and Whiting (1975) found that women and girls seek more help from others and give more help to others than men do, and Edwards (1993) found similar sex differences across 12 cultures.

Let's go back to social support in pregnancy to highlight some more specific cultural differences. Studies of ethnic minority groups in the United States show that for some groups (e.g., African Americans and Latinas), the family, particularly female relatives, are a critical source of support in pregnancy (Knouse, 1991; Zuniga, 1992). Mexican American families tend to live in close units with tight bonds to other family units and with the extended family serving as the primary source of support (Campos, Dunkel-Schetter, Abdou, Hobel, Glynn, & Sandman, 2008; Chilman, 1993). Similarly, the family is the most important source of support to African Americans (Cauce, Felner, & Primavera, 1982; Miller, 1992). In one of the most cited studies of ethnic differences in support, Norbeck and Anderson (1989) measured life stress, social support, anxiety state, and substance use at mid- and late pregnancy in Hispanic, European American, and African American low-income women. This study found that none of the social support measures was a significant predictor of gestational age, birth weight, or gestation and labor complications when the sample was analyzed as a whole. However, for African American women, lack of social support from the woman's partner or mother was a significant predictor of gestational complications and of the likelihood of prolonged labor and cesarean section complications. For European Americans, social support was significantly related to length of labor and to drug use. None of the support measures was a statistically significant predictor of complications or birth outcomes for the Hispanics. Analyzing ethnic groups separately, none just statistically controlling for ethnicity, has yielded similar differences in social support in a number of other studies (e.g., Gurung, Dunkel-Schetter, Collins, Rini, & Hobol, 2005; Gurung, Taylor, Kemeny, & Myers, 2004).

In a direct test of ethnic differences in social support, Sagrestano, Feldman, Rini, Woo, and Dunkel-Schetter (2000) analyzed data from two multiethnic prospective studies of African American, Latina, and non-Hispanic White pregnant women and found strong ethnic differences in support from family and friends. African American women reported receiving the most support from family. Latinas and European American women reported receiving support from the next levels. However, White women reported more family members in their social networks than did Latinas. Furthermore, Latinas reported higher-quality interactions with family. In another study, Campos et al. (2008) examined the association of **familialism**, a cultural value that emphasizes close family relationships, with social support, stress, pregnancy anxiety, and infant birth weight. Latinas scored higher on familialism than European Americans. Familialism was positively correlated with social support and negatively correlated with stress and pregnancy anxiety in the overall sample. The associations of familialism with social support and stress were significantly stronger among Latinas than European Americans. Moreover, higher social support was associated with higher infant birth weight among foreign-born Latinas only.

THEORIES OF SOCIAL SUPPORT CHANGE

How do our social networks change over time? Are you still friends with the people you were friends with when you were in grade school? Do you call the same people for help today as you did 10 years ago? There are two main theories of how our networks change (Gurung & Von Dras, 2007). The **social convoy model** (Antonucci, 1991) provides a conceptual framework for

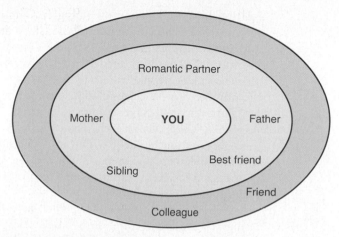

FIGURE **5.3** A Social Convoy

You are in the center, the people closest to you are in the first circle, and the people not as close are in the outer circles. As we age we should maintain our convoy to keep emotionally healthy.

studying age-related changes in structural and compositional characteristics of social networks (Figure 5.3). This model suggests that people are motivated to maintain their social network sizes as they themselves age, despite changes in the composition of the networks. Individuals construct and maintain social relationships while becoming increasingly aware of specific strengths and weaknesses of particular members. This knowledge allows them to select different network members for different functions (e.g., certain people are relied on for emotional support and others for instrumental support) and possibly avoid members who are not supportive. Empirical support for the model (Kahn & Antonucci, 1984; Müller, Nordt, Lauber, & Rössler, 2007) clearly identifies the importance of simultaneously looking at different sources when studying changes in age-related social support. Although specific nonsupportive network members may drop out over time, the social convoy model suggests that general levels of support will be constant or even increase, given that social support is coordinated to optimize support receipt. We work to make sure we get the most out of our networks and that our networks contain those who will give us what we need.

Socioemotional selectivity theory (Carstensen, 1987; Carstensen & Fisher, 1991) proposes that people prune their social networks to maintain a desired emotional state depending on the extent to which time is perceived as limited. Basic functions of social interaction, such as maintaining a good mood, differ in respect to their relative importance for determining social preferences across the lifespan. When we get older, we believe that we have less time and want to maximize the time we have. We do not want to waste time on people or things that are not worth it. Emphasis in old age is placed on achieving short-term emotional goals. Correspondingly, whereas older adults' social networks may be smaller than those of younger adults, the numbers of close relationships are comparable (Lang & Carstensen, 1998). Lang and Carstensen (1994) examined the interrelationships among age, network composition, and social support in a representative sample of 156 community-dwelling and institutionalized adults aged 70 to 104 years. They found that the social networks of older people were only half as large as those of younger people, but the number of very close relationships did not differ across age groups.

Both theories have empirical evidence supporting them (Antonucci & Akiyama, 1995; Carstensen, Isaacowitz, & Charles, 1999; Lansford, Sherman, & Antonucci, 1998). The evidence indicates that it is not necessarily the size, membership, or particular structure of the network, but the quality of transactions (i.e., perceived and received social support) that is critical to mental and physical health.

Is there clear evidence of whether support increases or decreases in time? Using longitudinal, community-based data from the MacArthur Studies of Successful Aging, Gurung et al. (2003) examined determinants of changes in social support receipt among 439 married older adults. Men and women in the sample were surveyed over a period of 6 years, and support received was assessed at the beginning and end of the study. In general, social support increased over time, especially for those with many preexisting social ties, but those experiencing more psychological distress and cognitive dysfunction reported more negative encounters with others.

One last point on social support. At the start of this chapter, we mentioned that there are many individual differences in coping. This is true for social support as well. We are active managers of our social networks and play a role in determining how much support we get. In addition to experiencing changes in who we have in our networks due to nonelective events such as death of network members, people differ in their propensity to prune or augment their own networks and in their likelihood of being pruned from or added to others' networks. Referred to in the support literature as "evocative qualities," personal characteristics may be critical determinants of whether support transactions increase or decrease over time (Pierce, Lakey, Sarason, & Sarason, 1997).

COMMON MEASURES OF COPING

Can specific styles of coping be identified across individuals and settings? Although there are not necessarily a "big five" of coping as there are for personality, people cope in some clear-cut ways. Each of the two main styles discussed previously, problem-focused and emotion-focused coping, have many separate subcomponents, each of which can be assessed by questionnaires. Two of the most commonly used measures are the Ways of Coping Questionnaire (WCQ) (Folkman & Lazarus, 1988) and the COPE (Carver et al., 1989).

Ways of Coping Questionnaire

The WCQ first started as the Ways of Coping Checklist (WCC) (Aldwin, Folkman, Schaefer, Coyne, & Lazarus, 1980). Devised from a pool of 68 items with a yes-no response format, the original checklist yielded two main factors with the majority (40) of the items forming a problem-solving subscale and the rest an emotion-focused subscale. Over time, the use of the scale with different populations yielded varying numbers of major factors. The current version of the WCQ consists of 50 items with 16 filler items and has a 4-point Likert rating scale for responses. Scientists ask participants to think of a real-life stressor (e.g., a conflict at work) and respond to each question. The WCQ has eight different subscales reflecting problem-focused and emotion-focused coping:

1. Confrontive Coping (e.g., I stood my ground and fought for what I wanted)
2. Distancing (e.g., I went on as if nothing had happened)
3. Self-Controlling (e.g., I tried to keep my feelings to myself)
4. Seeking Social Support (e.g., I talked to someone to find out more about the situation)
5. Accepting Responsibility (e.g., I criticized or lectured myself)
6. Escape Avoidance (e.g., I hoped a miracle would happen)
7. Planful Problem Solving (e.g., I made a plan of action and followed it)
8. Positive Reappraisal (e.g., I changed or grew as a person in a good way).

As you can tell, using one of these coping styles (e.g., seeking support) can automatically involve using another one (e.g., problem solving). This is not something theoretically controlled for with this measure and has been cited as one of its major problems (Schwarzer & Schwarzer, 1996). Different researchers have adapted the WCQ to correspond directly to specific stressors. For example, Dunkel-Schetter, Feinstein, Taylor, and Falke (1992) rewrote the WCQ to measure how patients coped with cancer.

The COPE

In contrast to the WCQ whose subscales were devised using primarily empirical methods (e.g., factor analysis), Carver et al. (1989) used a rational scale construction procedure. They first created different subscales (versus using statistical procedures to determine the subscales) and tested them on a sample of 978 undergraduates. Furthermore, instead of asking for coping responses to a specific stressor, the students were asked what they usually do when they are experiencing considerable stress. This procedure yielded the **COPE** inventory (Carver et al., 1989) containing 13 scales with four items each. The main subscales representing different forms of problem-focused and emotion-focused coping are the following:

1. Active Coping (e.g., I do what has to be done, one step at a time)
2. Planning (e.g., I make a plan of action)
3. Suppression of Competing Activities (e.g., I put aside other activities to concentrate on this)
4. Restraint Coping (e.g., I force myself to wait for the right time to do something)
5. Seeking Social Support for Instrumental Reasons (e.g., I talk to someone to find out more about the situation)
6. Seeking Social Support for Emotional Reasons (e.g., I talk to someone about how I feel)
7. Positive Reinterpretation and Growth (e.g., I learn something from the experience)

8. Acceptance (e.g., I learn to live with it)
9. Turning to Religion (e.g., I put my trust in God)
10. Focus and Venting of Emotions (e.g., I let my feelings out)
11. Denial (e.g., I refuse to believe that it has happened)
12. Behavioral Disengagement (e.g., I just give up trying to reach my goal)
13. Mental Disengagement (e.g., I daydream about things other than this)

Later versions included additional items relating to the use of humor and alcohol as coping mechanisms. The COPE has separate subscales for the different types of social support seeking: problem-focused and emotion-focused support seeking.

Other measures of coping, including scales by Amirkhan (1990) and McCrae (1984), are variations on the WCQ and the COPE. Many of these scales are targeted for special populations, such as the Life Events and Coping Inventory for Children (Dise-Lewis, 1988), the Adolescent Coping Orientation for Problem Experiences Inventory (Patterson & McCubbin, 1987), and the Life Situations Inventory (Feifel & Strack, 1989), which is aimed at assessing coping with real-life circumstances in middle-aged and elderly men.

Be warned, some researchers lament the overuse of coping instruments (e.g., Coyne & Racioppo, 2000), and others report few consistent positive associations between the use of any particular coping style and positive outcomes (Coyne & Gottlieb, 1996; Watson & Hubbard, 1996). The main problem seems to be that some of the questions are too general, and researchers tend to utilize one standard measure across many different situations, thereby ignoring the unique aspects of different stressors. In addition, the summary scores achieved by adding together the responses to the different questions on the scales dilute and omit important information such as timing, sequencing, and appropriateness of a specific behavior (Coyne & Racioppo, 2000). Finally, many of the coping styles are closely related to personality characteristics and correlate strongly with distress, both variables that serve to confound coping results. These problems notwithstanding, the coping scales allow health psychologists to study large numbers of people using limited time and money and allow for a quantification of the coping process (Lazarus, 2000). To compensate for some of the problems of scale measures, most contemporary coping researchers also include detailed interviews and observations to assess coping (Folkman & Moskowitz, 2000).

SYNTHESIZE, EVALUATE, APPLY	• What are the main types of social support? • Which dimensions/types are more related to distress? • What are some factors to bear in mind to provide effective social support? • What would you rate as the most effective measure of coping?

KEYS TO COPING WITH STRESS

Suggesting you "just relax" may sound trite, but if you can successfully relax, you can bring about psychological and physiological changes that will help you deal well with stress. Even though it may seem easy, relaxing well requires some practice and some knowledge. Health psychological research has identified two major types of strategies that are useful to help people cope better and relax. The first broad category is called relaxation-based approaches and includes methods such as mindfulness, meditation, yoga, biofeedback, hypnosis, and the relaxation response. The second major category is cognitive-behavioral approaches and includes the use of learning theory (i.e., classical and operant conditioning) and other means designed to help a person label the problem, discuss the emotions associated with it, and find a way to solve it.

Relaxation-Based Approaches

In relaxation-based approaches, the goals are to reduce the cognitive load or number of thoughts a person is experiencing and to activate the parasympathetic nervous system to help the body recover from the activation of the sympathetic system. Most stressors that we experience today are stressors related to thinking. It is our worrying about problems and anticipating threats that cause the most havoc. We can sit around and think ourselves into a frenzy. Right now, you can let your mind wander to how much money you owe, to all the different things that you have to do, to a performance you have to give, or to the kids you have to pick up or feed, and so on. The generation and fixation on all these thoughts can activate the stress response (mediated by the specific primary and secondary appraisals we make, of course). Relaxation-based approaches stop or at least reduce our fixation on these different stressful thoughts, thereby automatically lessening the stress response.

Most relaxation-based techniques ask a person to focus on a specific thought, word, image, or phrase. By focusing on just one item and giving it complete attention, the person is not thinking about all the things that are stressful. Together with the focus on a single object comes a slowing down of the breathing and a lowering of heart rate, respiration, circulation, and

Relaxation

There are many forms of meditation that can be very relaxing. Here a person reads a magazine and tries to relax.

essentially all the functions of the body supervised by the parasympathetic nervous system. Most importantly, the different stress chemicals (catecholamines and cortisol) are no longer released. Most practices such as mindfulness, meditation, and yoga use this slowing down of the breath and clearing of the thoughts to bring about stress relief. Mindfulness, in particular, involves intentionally bringing one's attention to the internal and external experiences occurring in the present moment and is often taught through a variety of meditation exercises. It has been empirically demonstrated to result in increased immune activity (Davidson et al., 2003), stress reduction (Carlson, Speca, Patel, & Goodey, 2003; Schure, Christopher, & Christopher, 2008), and a host of other positive health outcomes (Baer, 2003; Kabat-Zinn, 2003).

Sometimes guided imagery, imagining different peaceful scenarios, or aromatherapy, the use of calming smells and scents, can also aid in relaxation. Table 5.4 gives you something you can try at home. Similarly, progressive muscle relaxation, in which you focus your attention on specific muscle groups and alternately tighten and relax them (Lolak, Connors, Sheridan, & Wise, 2008) can be beneficial.

TABLE **5.4**

Guided Imagery Instructions: Have a friend read these out to you slowly. Find a comfortable position and listen to the words and try to picture what is being said.

Picture yourself right now in a log cabin somewhere high up in the mountains…. It's wintertime, but even though it is very cold outside, you can enjoy the comfort of being in that cabin … for inside of the cabin is a large fireplace with a brightly blazing fire providing plenty of heat and warmth … and now you can go up to one of the windows and notice the frost on the windowpane … you can even put your warm hand on the cold, hard glass of the windowpane feeling the heat from your hand and fingers melting the frost … And then to get a view of the outside, you can begin to open the window, feeling it give way against the pressure of your hand; as the window opens, you take a big breath of that pure, fresh, cool mountain air and feel so good. Looking outside you can see the snow on the ground and lots of tall evergreen trees. And then looking off in the distance and seeing a wonderful view … perhaps of a valley down below or other mountain peaks far, far in the distance…. And now you can close the window and walk over to the fire feeling its warmth as you get closer…. Go ahead and sit back in a comfortable chair facing the fire … or if you wish, you can lie down next to the fire on a soft bearskin rug … feeling the soothing warmth of the fire against your skin … letting your body absorb the warmth bringing deep relaxation and comfort…. You can also enjoy looking at the fire, seeing the burning logs, hearing the crackling of the logs and hissing sound from the sap encountering the fire … smelling the fragrant smoke from the burning logs. You can even look around noticing the room as it is illuminated by the light from the fire … noticing the flickering shadows on the walls … noticing the furniture and any other objects in the room … just look around and take it all in … all the sights and sounds and smells … feeling so peaceful in this place …. so calm and completely tranquil. And you can be reminded that even though the cold wind is howling outside, you can feel so warm and comfortable inside … letting that comfort spread to all parts of your mind. And in this place you have absolutely nothing to worry about … for all that really matters is that you just allow yourself to enjoy the peacefulness, enjoy the deep comfort of being in this place right now … as a relaxed, drowsy feeling comes over you … and all the sights and sounds and smells gradually fade far away … while you drift … and float and dream in that cabin far off in the mountains. (Pause) And now, whenever you are ready, you can bring yourself back to a normal, alert, and wide-awake state by counting slowly from 1 to 3, so that when you reach the number 3 you will open your eyes feeling completely refreshed and comfortable.

Biofeedback involves the use of an electronic monitoring device that tracks physiological processes (e.g., pulse) and provides feedback regarding changes. If you are stressed, your high pulse is indicated by either a sound (e.g., pinging) or an image on a screen (e.g., a large circle). The goal is to make your pulse slow down (hence making the pinging slow or the image on the screen smaller). By trying different methods, such as slowing down your breathing, you see the results directly on the machine. The machine reinforces your attempts to calm down by producing less pinging. You are more likely to do whatever it was you did to reduce the pinging, and operant conditioning helps you develop a way to cope. Biofeedback is often used in conjunction with cognitive-behavioral therapy to help people cope with stress (Yahav & Cohen, 2008).

Another form of conditioning, classical conditioning, lies between relaxation and behavioral therapy. **Systematic desensitization** is a form of classical conditioning in which stressful thoughts or events are paired with relaxation (e.g., Duff, Levine, Beatty, Woolbright, & Park, 2007). According to classical conditioning, whenever two events are linked enough times, responses that came naturally in response to one event now are found to occur in response to the second event. Let's say that you are scared to speak in public. Your first step is to create a hierarchy of the things about public speaking that scare you with the scariest thing at the top of the list (e.g., the moment just before you start and are facing 50 strangers) and the least scary aspect at the bottom (e.g., a month before you have to speak). Then, while thinking about the thing at the bottom of your list you practice relaxing. You do this until you can think about the speech a month away and still feel the conditioned response, relaxation. You now pick the next scary event in your hierarchy and pair that one with relaxation. In this way, you move up your list until you can think about being in front of people and still feel relaxed. Once this link between the thought and the relaxation has been strengthened, the next time you are in front of a group of people you should feel the relaxation that you conditioned (Figure 5.4).

Courtesy of Regan Gurung

Biofeedback
Biofeedback helps you monitor your heart rate and use your mind to slow it down.

An Anxiety Hierarchy for Systematic Desensitization	
Degree of fear	
5	I'm standing on the balcony of the top floor of an apartment tower.
10	I'm standing on a stepladder in the kitchen to change a light bulb.
15	I'm walking on a ridge. The edge is hidden by shrubs and treetops.
20	I'm sitting on the slope of a mountain, looking out over the horizon.
25	I'm crossing a bridge 6 feet above a creek. The bridge consists of an 18-inch-wide board with a handrail on one side.
30	I'm riding a ski lift 8 feet above the ground.
35	I'm crossing a shallow, wide creek on an 18-inch-wide board, 3 feet above the water level.
40	I'm climbing a ladder outside the house to reach a second-story window.
45	I'm pulling myself up a 30-degree wet, slippery slope on a steel cable.
50	I'm scrambling up a rock, 8 feet high.
55	I'm walking 10 feet on a resilient, 18-inch-wide board, which spans an 8-foot-deep gulch.
60	I'm walking on a wide plateau, 2 feet from the edge of a cliff.
65	I'm skiing an intermediate hill. The snow is packed.
70	I'm walking over a railway trestle.
75	I'm walking on the side of an embankment. The path slopes to the outside.
80	I'm riding a chair lift 15 feet above the ground.
85	I'm walking up a long, steep slope.
90	I'm walking up (or down) a 15-degree slope on a 3-foot-wide trail. On one side of the trail the terrain drops down sharply; on the other side is a steep upward slope.
95	I'm walking on a 3-foot-wide ridge. The slopes on both sides are long and more than 25 degrees steep.
100	I'm walking on a 3-foot-wide ridge. The trail slopes on one side. The drop on either side of the trail is more than 25 degrees.

FIGURE **5.4** A Stress Hierarchy

The most stressful event is at the bottom. You pair relaxation with the first event and then move down until you can imagine your most stressful event and be relaxed.

Cognitive-Behavioral Approaches

Cognitive-behavioral therapies that treat clinical disorders can easily be adapted to cope with stress. For example, **cognitive restructuring** can be used to replace stress-provoking thoughts (e.g., "everyone is going to be looking at how I perform") with realistic, unthreatening thoughts (e.g., "everyone is too busy to see what I am doing"). Similarly, Ellis' (1987) rational-emotional therapy is often used to identify and change irrational beliefs that a person may have that can cause stress. In a similar fashion, Beck's (1976) cognitive therapy involves the identification and change of maladaptive thought patterns that can often be automatic and cause stress (e.g., you always assume that people do not believe you). Another cognitive approach, Meichenbaum and Cameron's (1983) stress-inoculation training provides people with skills for reducing stress such as having the person (1) learn more about the nature of the stressor and how people react to it, (2) learn and practice things to do when they do get stressed (separately referred to as proactive coping by Aspinwall & Taylor, 1997), and (3) practice the new skills in response to a real or imagined stressor.

Emotional expression is one of the most widely researched forms of cognitive-behavioral therapies in recent history (Niederhoffer & Pennebaker, 2002; Smyth & Pennebaker, 2001), as shown in Table 5.5. Although most therapies involve the sharing and discussion of a troubling issue, emotional expression involves disclosure in writing. A number of studies have shown that just writing out your feelings can lead to a range of positive outcomes. The basic procedure is simple. Participants write about extremely important emotional issues, exploring their deepest emotions and thoughts. They are asked to include their relationships with others (parents, lovers, and friends), their past, present, and future, and their goals and plans. All their writing remains completely confidential, and they are asked not to worry about spelling or grammar.

The only rule is that once they begin writing they are to continue until the time (often 15 minutes) is up. People following this simple exercise are less likely to get sick (Greenberg & Stone, 1992; Pennebaker & Beall, 1986; Richards, Pennebaker, & Beall, 1995) and they report reduced levels of stress, less negative moods, and less depression (Kline, Fekete, & Sears, 2008; Murray & Segal, 1994; Rime, 1995).

Another way to cope with stress is to increase your physical activity (Brown, 1991; Chafin, Christenfeld, & Gerin, 2008; Johansson, Hassmén, &

TABLE **5.5**
Key Examples of Emotional Expression Studies

Author/Date	Sample	Duration	Result
Francis and Pennebaker (1992)	University employees	1/week 4 weeks	Lower absenteeism
Pennebaker et al. (1991)	College students	3/week	Better grades
Spera et al. (1994)	Unemployed professionals		Quicker reemployment
Pennebaker et al. (1988)	College students		Improved immune functioning
Langens & Schuler (2007)	College students	Study 1–3 days (20 minutes each) Study 2–4 days (20 minutes each)	Reduction of emotional impact of upsetting event (Study 1) and in physical symptoms (Study 2)
Petrie et al. (2004)	HIV-infected patients	4 days (30 minutes each)	Increased lymphocyte count
Ullrich and Lutgendorf (2002)	College students	1 month	Increased meaning finding
Zakowski et al. (2004)	Cancer patients	3 days (20 minutes each)	Reduced stress

Exercising

Exercising can prove to be a great stress reliever.

Jouper, 2008). People who exercise on a regular basis tend to be less depressed and less stressed (Norlander, Bood, & Archer, 2002; Salmon, 2001). If you are wondering if this is just a correlation and guessing that people who are less stressed may exercise more (notice how many people skip their workouts when they have a lot of things due?), fear not. In addition to correlational studies, a number of experimental manipulations have established that exercise helps individuals cope with stress (Babyak et al., 2000; Kerr & Kuk, 2001). For example, Johansson et al. measured anxiety and depression in 59 regular qigong (a Traditional Chinese exercise, see Chapter 2) exercisers. Depression, anger, fatigue, and anxiety scores decreased significantly in the qigong group but not in the control group. Exercise helps mainly by influencing the release and metabolism of stress hormones and varying the way that the sympathetic nervous system reacts to stress (Forcier et al., 2006). For example, 53 members of the Austin Fire Department were randomly assigned to an exercise or no exercise condition and then stressed with a fire drill. Before training, the groups did not differ in their cardiovascular response to the fire drill. Significant group differences were observed after training. Exercise-trained participants reacted with significantly lower pulse and mean arterial pressure than their counterparts in the control condition (Throne, Bartholomew, Craig, & Farrar, 2000). The next time you feel stressed with work, it may be worth the effort to exercise even if you only take a quick-paced walk outside.

How do you know when coping works? You feel better, your heart rate, pulse, and breathing are normal, your thinking is clearer, and your general sense of well-being improves. Consistent with the emerging movement in psychology to focus on the positive outcomes in life, referred to as the **positive psychology** movement (Seligman & Csikszentmihalyi, 2000; more on this in Chapter 14), health psychologists have begun to investigate a wide range of positive outcomes (for a review see Somerfield & McCrae, 2000).

- How would you design a stress management program for people at a local company using what you know about coping?
- What are the coping styles inherent to emotional expression interventions?
- How can religion be just another form of social support?
- How are the different physiological components of stress counteracted by the different coping methods?

FOCUS ON CURRENT ISSUES

May God Help You

Millions of people around the world turn in the same direction when they are stressed. It is not a point on the compass; it is toward God. It may not be the same God, but for many people religion and religious institutions provide a major way to cope with stress. After being neglected in the field of psychology for many years, religion and prayer have received a lot of attention in the last decade. Does believing in God cure diseases and help you live longer? We review the empirical literature in health psychology on this topic in Chapter 10.

To some extent, world events forced religion onto center stage. The September 11, 2001, attacks by Islamic terrorists in the United States, the clashes between Palestinians and Israelis in the Middle East and Hindu and Muslims in India, and the sex abuse scandals in the Catholic Church are just some examples. More importantly, religion is a focus of study because most people who are stressed or who face seemingly insurmountable problems pray. In fact, religious beliefs and practices appear to be especially important in stressful situations that push people to the limits of their resources (Pargament, 2002; Wachholtz, Pearce, Koenig, 2007). Religious coping has been found to help people deal with a range of problems such as living in stressful neighborhoods (Krause, 1998) and dealing with lack of sexual gratification (Wallin & Clark, 1964). Religion is more helpful in some situations than others. For example, the degree and recency of loss (Mattlin, Wethington, & Kessler, 1990; Maton, 1989) make a difference (religion moderated high-loss situations and recent loss of a child).

Are you religious? To some, the answer is as simple as saying whether they believe in God or not. To others and to the researchers who study it, **religiosity** is measured by looking at the frequency of temple/church/mosque/synagogue attendance, the average frequency of prayer, and the commitment to religious rituals. Many people classify themselves as followers of a certain denomination but rush to add that they are not "practicing." Such people may identify themselves as being of a certain religion (e.g., Hindu), but still not stick to the rules of that religion (e.g., being vegetarian). No matter what your religious background, you probably use some form of religious coping at some time or the other. Different world religions such as Christianity, Islam, and Hinduism include different beliefs, rituals, practices, and standards, but they all share the idea that we have entities or higher powers who created us and who are in some way involved in our lives. Turning to the higher powers in times of stress is as natural as a young child turning to his or her parent when she is scared or threatened.

An interesting example of the use of religion and faith as a coping mechanism can be seen in a movie called *Signs*. In it, hunky actor Australian Mel Gibson plays a former priest named Graham Hess who lost his faith after his wife was killed in an accident. Strange crop circles turn up on his Pennsylvania farm and around the world. Suddenly, aliens invade the earth (the circles are the signs of contact). People are terrified. Graham's brother in the movie needs reassurance, and Graham replies that there are two kinds of people. Some people see scary things like the aliens and recognize them as signs from God. These are the people who believe in miracles and have faith. They see these signs as evidence that God exists, trust that God will save them, and are calm. The other kind of people are nonbelievers and, seeing the invasion, realize that they have no one to turn to or no one to watch out for them and are terrified. Which type you are

(continues)

FOCUS ON CURRENT ISSUES *(continued)*

determines how you cope. Although not scientifically tested (this is a Hollywood production after all) that basic dichotomy is at the heart of the role of religion in coping.

As you read in our discussion of coping styles, the COPE does have a subscale to assess the use of religion, but the study of religious coping has been much more intensive than that. Pargament (1997), in his book on religion and psychology, documents an array of cases in which religion is used as a coping mechanism and notes that our tendency to turn to God intensifies as situations become more critical. Of course, people use religion in different ways. You can turn everything over to God (deferring religious coping— "whatever happens is God's will, what will be will be"), you can engage God's help and work with what God has provided (self-directed religious coping—"God helps those who help themselves"), or you can work with God (collaborative religious coping—"with God on my side, how can I lose?"). This is no big surprise, because, similar to the emotion-focused strategies discussed earlier in the chapter, deferring religious coping is not optimal (Schaefer & Gorsuch, 1991).

In addition to these three styles, Pargament, Smith, Koenig, and Perez (1998) identified two major dimensions of religious coping: positive and negative religious coping. Positive religious coping methods (e.g., seeking spiritual support from God and using collaborative coping) have helped a wide range of people including refugees (Ai, Peterson, & Huang, 2003), victims of natural disasters (Smith, Pargament, Brant, & Oliver, 2000), older hospitalized patients (Koenig, Pargament, & Nielsen, 1998), and students (Pargament, Koenig, & Perez, 2000). Negative religious coping methods (e.g., questioning the power of God and expressing anger toward God) have been related to poorer adjustment among many groups such as medical rehabilitation patients (Fitchett, Rybarczyk, DeMarco, & Nicholas, 1999), students (Exline, Yali, & Lobel, 1999), and victims of natural disasters (Pargament et al., 1998).

Religious coping in general can be such a great aid that the lack of it can be problematic for some. For example, Strawbridge, Shema, Cohen, Roberts, and Kaplan (1998) found that although personal and organizational religiosity buffered the effects of stressors, such as financial problems, poor health, and disability or depression, the lack of personal religiousness amplified the effects of child problems and the lack of organizational religiousness amplified the effects of marital problems and abuse.

SUMMARY

- Coping is defined as individual efforts to manage distressing problems and emotions that affect the physical and psychological outcomes of stress. A coping response may be anything we do to reestablish our homeostatic balance.
- Many different cultural factors buffer or moderate and mediate the effects of stress and influence coping. Our age, sex, socioeconomic status, religion, and ethnicity are some of the key cultural buffers.
- The two primary coping styles are problem-focused or approach coping and emotion-focused or avoidant coping. The efficacy of each depends on the nature of the stressor, especially its duration and controllability.
- A variety of personality traits is associated with more effective coping. People high in self-esteem, who are conscientious, low in neuroticism, optimistic, hardy, and resilient and have a sense of mastery, cope better with stress.
- Social support is one of the most important factors influencing coping. Commonly defined as emotional, information, or instrumental assistance from others, social support has been associated with a variety of positive health outcomes.

- Social support can be received or perceived, global or specific, or vary in function. It can be emotional, informational, or tangible. Support works best when it matches the needs of the individual.
- Some cultural groups have higher levels of support than others, depending on the context. African Americans tend to derive more support from their families than do other ethnic groups. Individuals with strong religious ties perceive having more support than those with weak religious ties. Women also give and receive more social support than men.
- Coping is commonly measured by questionnaire and is divided into many categories. Major types of coping are confrontative, distancing, self-controlling, accepting responsibility, seeking social support, escape avoidance, positive reappraisal, suppression, planning, turning to religion, venting of emotions, denial, and the use of humor.
- Two major categories of coping are relaxation-based (meditation, yoga, biofeedback, hypnosis, guided imagery, and progressive muscle relaxation) and cognitive-behavioral (using learning theory, systematic desensitization, psychoanalysis, and emotional expression).

TEST YOURSELF

Check your understanding of the topics in this chapter by answering the following questions. Answers appear in the Appendix.

1. Coping is best defined as:
   a. individual efforts made to manage the outcomes of stress.
   b. processes designed to increase relaxation.
   c. ways to prevent stressful events from occurring.
   d. techniques to reduce the impact of stress.
2. Life is complex and few variables directly influence each other. Moderating variables:
   a. are those that directly influence stress and coping.
   b. change the relationship between variables.
   c. are more powerful than mediator variables.
   d. are more important for predicting Western coping styles.
3. Most of the following variables can be mediators and moderators except for:
   a. happiness.
   b. optimism.
   c. social support.
   d. sex.
4. The theory of social support change that proposes that people prune their networks to maintain a desired emotional state depending on the extent to which time is perceived as limited is:
   a. socioemotional selectivity theory.
   b. gain-loss theory.
   c. social convoy theory.
   d. optimization theory.
5. One of the most commonly studied mediators in health psychology is/are:
   a. sex.
   b. social support.
   c. health behaviors.
   d. stress.
6. The two most basic styles of coping are:
   a. positive and negative.
   b. acute and chronic.
   c. approach and avoidant.
   d. primary and secondary.
7. Each of the following is considered one of the "Big Five" factors in personality except:
   a. extraversion.
   b. neuroticism.
   c. agreeableness.
   d. optimism.

8. In contrast to early research on the Type A personality, current views hold that the most unhealthy component of the Type A profile is:
   a. being competitive.
   b. showing a sense of time urgency.
   c. being hostile.
   d. being hardy.
9. People who enjoy challenges, have a high level of control, and are committed to their lives are high in:
   a. optimism.
   b. hardiness.
   c. extraversion.
   d. mastery.
10. The empirical evidence suggests that the following cultural group receives the most social support from its members during stressors such as pregnancy.
    a. European American
    b. Chinese American
    c. Japanese American
    d. Mexican American

WEB RESOURCES

Visit the companion website at **www.cengage.com/ psychology/gurung**, where you will find online resources for this book, including chapter-by-chapter quizzes, Web links, and more!

Wild Divine-The Biofeedback Program
www.wilddivine.com

This is a good example of a commercial product designed to help coping using biofeedback. This is an interesting and fun way to relax.

Guide to Grieving and Bereavement
http://www.helpguide.org/mental/grief_loss.htm

This is a helpful online guide managed by a non-profit site providing tips on how to cope with grief and loss.

APA Help Center
http://apahelpcenter.org/featuredtopics/feature.php? id=6

This is the American Psychological Association's guide to resiliency featuring tips to build resiliency and a further review of the literature on resiliency.

KEY TERMS, CONCEPTS, AND PEOPLE

ESSENTIAL READINGS

Lazarus, R. S. (2000). Toward better research on stress and coping. *American Psychologist, 55*(6), 665–673.

Skinner, E. A., Edge, K., Altman, J., & Sherwood, H. (2003). Searching for the structure of coping: A review and critique of category systems for classifying ways of coping. *Psychological Bulletin, 129*(2), 216–269.

Somerfield, M. R., & McCrae, R. R. (2000). Stress and coping research: Methodological challenges, theoretical advances, and clinical applications. *American Psychologist, 55*(6), 620–625.

Uchino, B. N., Cacioppo, J. T., & Kiecolt-Glaser, J. K. (1996). The relationship between social support and physiological processes: A review with emphasis on underlying mechanisms and implications for health. *Psychological Bulletin, 119*(3), 488–531.

Models of Behavior Change

What are five health behaviors that you could improve on? Do you know the extent to which doing them or not doing them influences your risk of an early death? Most of us know what it takes to live a long and healthy life—at least we think we know. Eat well. Don't drink too much alcohol. Don't smoke. Get some exercise. These are some of the most common actions considered to make someone healthy. You can also hope that you do not inherit any dangerous conditions from your parents. However, it is not that easy. You may want to eat well, but what exactly does "eating well" mean? You may think you know, but research and the media suggest that the "right" things to eat are always changing. One day, eating a lot of meat is thought to be bad for you; the next day not eating enough meat is bad. Even if you do figure out what is good for you through all the mixed messages in the media, it is still one thing to know what the good thing to do is, and a completely different thing to actually do it. Likewise, you may know that exercise is important, but do you manage to exercise as often as you should? Do you plan on exercising but don't because you are too tired or you do not have enough time? Join the club, and we don't mean the YMCA or your local health club (just being a member of a health club does not always mean you will exercise more anyway). Millions of people would like to exercise, and plan on exercising more than they do currently, but just do not manage to do it.

In this chapter, we will show you how health psychologists explain why we don't do all that we should and why we do some of what we should not. Even though people know that it is important to get physical activity, why do some people not exercise? If smokers know the risks of tobacco addiction, why do they still smoke? What are the different stages that people go through as they consider changing a behavior and then try to do it? Health psychologists have devised many theories to explain the performance of health behaviors and ways to institute change (Michie, Rothman, & Sheeran, 2007; Noar, 2006; Rothman, Hertel, Baldwin, & Bartels, 2008; Schwarzer, 2008). We will summarize first the key theories on health behavior performance and change and then describe how psychologists intervene to change behaviors.

WHAT ARE HEALTHY BEHAVIORS?

Healthy behaviors are defined as any specific behaviors that maintain and enhance health. These can range from the mundane (e.g., brushing your teeth and flossing) to the critical (e.g., not practicing unsafe sex with multiple partners). Many of our daily behaviors can influence our health and how long and how happily we live. Do you wear your seatbelt when you drive? You should.

A majority of road fatalities are due to the drivers or passengers not wearing seatbelts (de Lapparent, 2008; National Highway Traffic Safety Administration, 2008). Wearing a seatbelt is a health behavior. Many of the most common health problems that plague us today are worsened, and in some cases even caused, by unhealthy behaviors. For example, eating a lot of fatty foods and not getting enough physical activity increases the likelihood of developing type 2 diabetes and coronary heart disease (Daubenmier et al., 2007). One specific unhealthy behavior, smoking, can be tied to a range of negative health outcomes such as lung cancer and heart disease (Joseph et al., 2008). In fact, tobacco use, unhealthy diet, and lack of physical activity accounted for approximately 71 percent of the more than 1 million preventable deaths in the year 2000 (Mokdad, Marks, Stroup, & Gerberding, 2004, 2005).

Before health psychology was a field of study in its own right, health educators stressed the relevance of political, economical, and social factors as determinants of health (Derryberry, 1960; Glanz, Rimer, & Viswanath, 2008; Nyswander, 1966). In the 1970s, the emphasis shifted to urging health educators to focus on the institutions and social conditions that impede or facilitate individuals reaching optimal health instead of focusing on just individuals and their families (Griffiths, 1972). Correspondingly, policy, advocacy, and organizational change have been the central activities of public health and health education (Glanz, Rimer, & Marcus-Lewis, 2002). **Health education** attempts to close the gap between what is known about optimal health practices and what is actually done (Griffiths). The goal of health education is to teach people to limit behaviors detrimental to their health and increase behaviors that are conducive to health (Green, Kreuter, Partridge, & Deeds, 1980; Simonds, 1976). Closely paralleling the biopsychosocial approach, health educators pay attention to a range of factors including the individual, interpersonal relationships, institutions, community, and public policy (Smedley & Syme, 2000). Health

© IT Stock Free/Jupiter Images

Physical Activity

Being physically active is one of the most beneficial health behaviors you can perform. Most individuals use gyms or clubs to get their work-outs, but even walking and climbing stairs at work can burn enough energy to keep you healthy.

psychologists essentially follow the same agenda but with more focus on individual factors such as attitudes, beliefs, and personality traits.

The Healthy People Programs

Different health behaviors are important for different people. Nonsmoking and fit, but very overworked, nurses may need to change their sleeping habits. On the other hand, healthy college students practicing unsafe sex may have sexual behavior as their key change behavior. The most important health behaviors are outlined as **Leading Health Indicators** established by the U.S. Department of Health and Human Services' **Healthy People 2010** Program. As a group, the Leading Health Indicators reflect the major health concerns in the United States at the beginning of the twenty-first century (Healthy People 2010, 2003). The Leading Health Indicators are physical activity, overweight and obesity, tobacco use, substance abuse, responsible sexual behavior, mental health, injury and violence, environmental quality, immunization, and access to health care. Correspondingly, physical activity, eating well, smoking, alcohol and drug use, and sexual behavior are some of the health behaviors studied most by health psychologists. The objectives for the next program, Healthy People 2020, are still in development. Table 6.1 lists the main objectives for the 2010 program.

The Healthy People series of programs are science-based, 10-year national objectives for promoting health and preventing disease. It consists of a statement of national health objectives designed to identify the most significant

TABLE **6.1**
Healthy People 2010: Goals and Main Areas of Focus

Overarching goals
1. Increase quality and years of healthy life
2. Eliminate health disparities

Focus areas

1. Access to Quality Health Services	14. Immunization and Infectious Diseases
2. Arthritis, Osteoporosis, and Chronic Back Conditions	15. Injury and Violence Prevention
	16. Maternal, Infant, and Child Health
3. Cancer	17. Medical Produce Safety
4. Chronic Kidney Disease	18. Mental Health and Mental Disorders
5. Diabetes	19. Nutrition and Overweight
6. Disability and Secondary Conditions	20. Occupational Safety and Health
7. Educational and Community-Based Programs	21. Oral Health
	22. Physical Activity and Fitness
8. Environmental Health	23. Public Health Infrastructure
9. Family Planning	24. Respiratory Diseases
10. Food Safety	25. Sexually Transmitted Diseases
11. Health Communication	26. Substance Abuse
12. Heart Disease and Stroke	27. Tobacco Use
13. HIV	28. Vision and Hearing

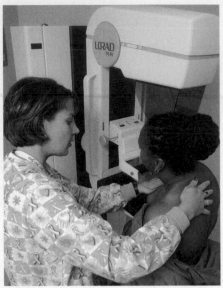

© Robin Nelson/PhotoEdit

Mammogram Machine

Women being tested place their breasts between the plates, which then are clamped down to squeeze the breast tissue. Although playing a key role in the prevention of breast cancer, mammograms can be painful and cause discomfort. Tests for testicular cancer do not involve any such machine squeezing.

preventable threats to the health of Americans as well as national goals to reduce these threats. Currently, Healthy People 2010 is guiding a national improvement effort to increase quality of life and to eliminate health disparities (U.S. Department of Health & Human Services, 2008). Healthy People 2020 will be the next health prevention agenda for the United States (released in early 2009).

The Healthy People Consortium, an alliance of more than 350 national membership organizations and 250 state health, mental health, substance abuse, and environmental agencies, developed the current Healthy People 2010 program. Additionally, through a series of regional and national meetings and an interactive Web site, more than 11,000 public comments on the draft objectives were received. This provided the American public with a say and provided input from all levels of society. The Leading Health Indicators will and are being used to measure the health of people in the United States between the years 2000 and 2010.

Living a healthy life entails more than just doing the right things on a personal level. Many health behaviors necessitate the help of medical institutions and trained professionals. For example, although you control what you buy and eat, whether or not you exercise or smoke, and how much you drink, it is also important to have medical check-ups. Cancers, such as breast cancer and testicular cancer, begin as tiny lumps. Whereas personal self-examinations catch many lumps in their early stages, it is important for both men and women to schedule regular check-ups for a thorough examination. Scheduled check-ups for prostate or breast cancers are more important for older men and women, respectively, but even young children need to visit medical institutions for vaccinations and immunizations.

Health psychologists aim to get people to improve personal health behaviors and to remember to get the various check-ups that their cultural demographics (i.e., age, sex, and ethnicity) may require. Health psychologists use **interventions**—specific programs designed to assess levels of behaviors, introduce ways to change them, measure whether change has occurred, and assess the impact of the change. The ultimate goal of health psychological interventions is to decrease the number of deaths due to preventable diseases, delay the time of death, and improve quality of life (especially for the elderly). Increasing the numbers of positive health behaviors practiced also saves money. When more money is spent on increasing healthy behaviors, the nation (via health care costs) and employers spend less money (Andersen, Rice, & Kominski, 2007). An ounce of prevention really is worth a pound of cure.

WHAT DETERMINES HEALTH BEHAVIORS?

Our developmental history—comprising both our physiological and psychological make-up—plays a major role in the health behaviors we practice. If you smoke, why? Why don't you get enough exercise? Do you eat well? An examination of our developmental history and our cultural backgrounds using the biopsychosocial perspective can answer all these questions (Figure 6.1).

Biological Factors

Biologically, we are born with many predispositions that can influence the types of health behaviors that we practice. For example, if both your parents are very overweight, there is a good chance that you will be overweight or have a propensity to put on weight. From our parents we inherit metabolic

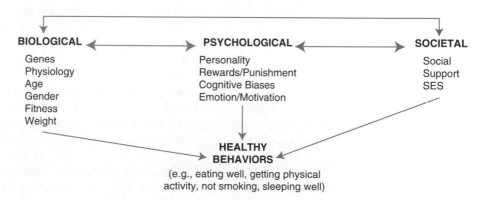

FIGURE **6.1** Healthy Behaviors

There are biological, psychological, and social factors that determine healthy behaviors. These are just some of the many ingredients that contribute to good health.

rates, which determine how we break down and process what we eat. We also inherit the type of muscle definition we can have. For example, if you have always wanted a flat stomach with each separate muscle block clearly defined ("the six-pack"), you must watch what you eat and do many sit-ups. Unfortunately, that is not the end of the story. Some of us will not be able to achieve well-defined "washboard abs" no matter how many sit-ups we do because we may not have the specific muscle type for this. Yes, having the right muscle type in the abdominal region is determined by your biology and genetic inheritance. Similarly, the likelihood of becoming addicted to smoking or drinking also has been shown to have a biological basis. For example, the dopamine D_2 receptor gene plays a role in alcoholism. People (and animals) who have more copies of this gene show a higher likelihood of becoming addicted to alcohol (Finckh, 2001).

Psychological Factors

In examining the psychological predictors of health behaviors, we see many of the usual suspects again. Similar to our discussion of stress in Chapter 4, personality traits and characteristics play a large role in determining health behaviors (Friedman, 2000; Park, & Gaffey, 2007; Salovey, Rothman, & Rodin, 1998; Wasylkiw & Fekken, 2002; Williams et al., 2008). The Big Five personality traits (discussed in Chapter 5) are good indicators of a person's likelihood to practice specific health behaviors (Jerram & Coleman, 1999) and can even predict children's health behaviors. For example, one study showed that girls' higher in neuroticism, introversion, and disagreeableness perform more risky behaviors. Boys higher in extraversion and disagreeableness take more risks (Markey, Markey, Ericksen, & Tinsley, 2006).

Conscientiousness and agreeableness are particularly noteworthy predictors of health behaviors and cognitive attitudes and tendencies (Bogg & Roberts, 2004; Hagger-Johnson, & Whiteman, 2007). However, because associations are evident for each of the personality traits, all of the Big Five personality traits should be included in research on health behaviors to investigate their relevance for clinical practice. It is also important to note that positive traits are not always associated with positive health behaviors. For example, extraverts are more likely to participate in risky behaviors such as drinking (Hampson, Goldberg, Vogt, & Dubanoski, 2007, Theakston, Stewart, Dawson, Knowlden-Loewen, & Lehman, 2004).

In a demonstration of the long-term impact of personality, Hampson, Goldberg, Vogt, and Dubanoski (2007) studied 1,054 participants in the Hawaii Personality and Health study. This population-based longitudinal study of personality and health spanned 40 years from childhood to midlife. The study found that childhood agreeableness and conscientiousness influenced adult health status mediated by healthy eating habits, and smoking. Similarly, Caspi et al. (1997) followed babies until they were 21 years old. Results showed that a constellation of adolescent personality traits (with developmental origins in childhood) did link to different health-risk behaviors at 21. The study also determined that associations between personality and different health-risk behaviors were not seen simply because the same people engaged in different health-risk behaviors. Instead, the associations implicated the same personality type in different but related behaviors. Therefore, in planning campaigns, perhaps health professionals need to design programs that appeal to the unique psychological makeup of persons most at risk for particular behaviors (Caspi et al.).

Social Factors

The "social" part of the biopsychosocial model is very important as well. Think back to when you were young. Did your parents ever hassle you about what you watched on television, which movies you went to, or (depending on how old you are) which Web sites you surfed on the Internet? If you complained about the restrictions they placed on what you were exposed to, here is something to think about. The media messages we are exposed to have a strong impact on the types of health behaviors we perform. The culture we live in and what we are surrounded by give us a lot of information about what is acceptable and what is not. As we grow and look out at the communicators of culture (e.g., magazines, movies, or television), what we see can influence what we do. This sounds feasible, right?

To prove this association Sargent, Dalton, Heatherton, and Beach (2003) first counted the occurrences of smoking in each of 600 popular movies. They gave teens a list of 50 recent popular films selected randomly from a pool of 600 recent popular films that they had analyzed for tobacco depictions. Based on the films each student reported seeing from the list of 50, the researchers tallied the total number of times that a teen would have been exposed to smoking or other tobacco use. More than 31 percent of teenagers who saw 150 or more instances of actors smoking on film tried smoking themselves, compared with about 5 percent of teens who saw 50 or fewer tobacco-related scenes. The prevalence of susceptibility to smoking increased with higher categories of exposure: 16 percent among students who viewed 0 to 50 movie tobacco occurrences; 21 percent among students who viewed 51 to 100 occurrences; 28 percent among students who viewed 101 to 150 occurrences; and 36 percent among students who viewed more than 150 occurrences. The association remained statistically significant after controlling for gender; grade in school; school performance; school; friend, sibling, and parent smoking; sensation-seeking; rebelliousness; and self-esteem (Sargent et al., 2002). Similar relationships between movie watching and drinking have also been found (Dalton et al., 2002).

Psychological and social factors also interact. Jessor, Turbin, and Costa (1998) tested the role of psychosocial factors on a wide range of adolescent health-enhancing behaviors—healthy diet, regular exercise, adequate sleep, good dental hygiene, and seatbelt use. The researchers assessed the perceived effects of health-compromising behavior, the presence of parents or friends who model health behavior, involvement in prosocial activities, and church attendance among 1,493 Hispanic, White, and Black high school students in a large, urban school district. Both individual difference factors and social factors (e.g., church attendance and behaviors of social networks) predicted adolescent health behavior.

- Pick a healthy behavior that you do not perform sufficiently. Use each of the three main theories of health behavior change to explain why.
- What are the pros and cons of the Healthy People 2010 approach to changing health behaviors (look at www.healthypeople.gov for more details)?
- What are the main biopsychosocial factors determining why you get the physical activity that you do?
- Given how personality traits influence a number of different behaviors, how can you best use knowledge of someone's personality to predict his or her likelihood of performing health behaviors?

KEY THEORIES OF HEALTH BEHAVIOR CHANGE

Health psychologists' approaches to understanding and changing the extent to which health behaviors are practiced nicely illustrate the scientific method. Look at a real world problem, devise a theory of why it occurs, design research to test it, and then apply successful theory to help intervene and solve the problem. There have been and continue to be a number of different theories to explain why we practice some behaviors and fail to practice others (Noar, 2005; Rothman, Hertel, Baldwin, & Bartels, 2008; Schwarzer, 2008). The next section of this chapter introduces you to the major health psychological theories of behavior change.

THE HEALTH BELIEF MODEL

The **Health Belief Model** (HBM) represents one of the first theoretical approaches to studying why we behave the way that we do. The basic contention of the HBM is that our beliefs relating to the **effectiveness**, ease, and **consequences** of doing (or not doing) a certain behavior will determine whether we do (or do not do) that behavior. It is one of the most widely used frameworks and has been used for both behavior change and maintenance. It was developed when a group of social psychologists were brought together at the U.S. Public Health Service to try to explain why people did not participate in programs to prevent or detect disease (Hochbaum, 1958; Rosenstock, 1960). The HBM was then extended to explain people's responses to illness symptoms (Kirscht, 1971) and also to explain what influences whether someone will adhere to his or her prescribed treatments (Becker, 1974).

The formulation of the HBM provides a good illustration of how social psychology and cognitive and behaviorist views influenced health psychology. For example, learning theorists such as Skinner (1938) believed that we learned to do a certain behavior if it was followed by a positive outcome (a reinforcement). Therefore, if exercising made us feel healthy we would be more likely to exercise. Cognitive theorists added a focus on the value of an outcome (e.g., health) and the expectation that a particular action (e.g., exercise) will achieve that outcome. The HBM is a value-expectancy theory in which the values and expectations were reformulated from abstract concepts

Smoking in the Movies

One of the major social factors influencing adolescent smoking is the movies. In the early days of filmmaking (e.g., Jimmy Stewart left) actors were often sent cartons of 'smokes' so they would smoke on screen. Later, movie companies were paid to show cigarettes on screen.

into health-related behaviors and concepts. A big issue in the 1950s was that a large number of eligible adults did not undergo screening for tuberculosis (TB) although TB was a big health problem and the screenings were free. Beginning in 1952, Hochbaum (1958) conducted surveys of more than 1,200 adults to understand why this was the case. He found that 82 percent of the people who believed they were susceptible and who believed early detection worked had at least one voluntary chest X-ray. Only 21 percent of the people who had neither belief had an X-ray.

How does the HBM explain health behavior? The model, built on Hochbaum's surveys, suggests that individuals will perform healthy behaviors if they believe they are susceptible to the health issue, if they believe it will have severe consequences, if they believe that their behavior will be beneficial in reducing the severity or susceptibility, and if they believe that the anticipated benefits of the behavior outweigh its costs (or barriers). The main components are described in Figure 6.2.

Another factor that was added to the model with great success was the concept of **self-efficacy**. Self-efficacy is defined as the conviction that one can successfully execute the behavior required to produce the outcome (Bandura, 1977) and was added to the HBM by Rosenstock, Strecher, and Becker (1988). This suggests that it is not enough just to know what behaviors *will* efficiently reduce severity and susceptibility, but one has to be confident that one can actually do that behavior.

Is one more component more important than the others you may ask? There is a problem with answering that question. The measurement of HBM components has been inconsistent and a majority of studies conducted with it

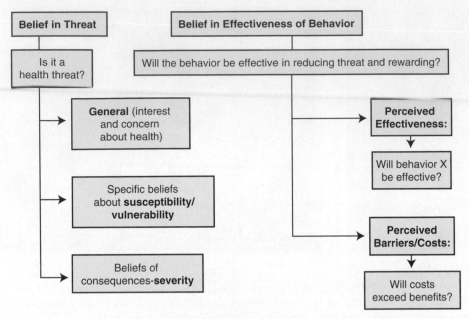

FIGURE **6.2** Main Components of the Health Belief Model

did not use reliable or valid measures of constructs. Part of the reason is that researchers fail to adequately control for the relationship between different components. Another reason is that health beliefs and health behaviors have often been measured simultaneously, contaminating the findings. If I first ask you whether you believe drinking is dangerous and then immediately ask you if you drink, your answers may not be the same as if I asked you each question at a different time. There are good examples of HBM measures when you look at specific actions for certain illnesses such as cancer screening (Champion, 1999; Rawl, Champion, Menon, & Foster, 2000).

Here is an example of how you can take a theory and put it into action. An intervention study targeting the susceptibility, benefits, and barriers components of the HBM may be performed as follows:

Champion, Ray, Heilman, and Springston (2000) had counselors speak to more than 300 low-income African American women. Counselors (1) clarified misconceptions and provided information to (2) increase the perceptions of benefits, (3) increase perceptions of susceptibility, and (4) reduce the perceptions of barriers of getting mammograms. For example, many women were scared of the procedure (it involves the breast tissue being squeezed between the steel plates of a machine). The most frequently mentioned barriers were the fear of finding something wrong, the fear of pain, and the fear of what the radiation used by the machine could do. Almost half the women in the experimental group who previously did not get a mammogram got one. Only 18 percent of the women in the control group got one. Even phone counseling targeting HBM components had similar effects (Duan, Fox, Derose, & Carson, 2000).

In general, a number of empirical studies have established the utility of the HBM (Becker, 1974; Janz & Becker, 1984). Perceived barriers are the most powerful component of the model across studies. Although perceived susceptibility and benefits are both important, knowing how susceptible one feels is a better predictor of that person's health prevention behavior and knowing the person's perceptions of benefits is a better predictor of his or her sick-role behaviors (Janz, Champion, & Strecher, 2002).

Culture and the Health Belief Model

The HBM has also been used in different cultural settings. Together with scales and interventions being designed for specific populations such as the African American women mentioned above, numerous studies have investigated the usefulness of the HBM in multicultural settings. Fulton, Rakowski, and Jones (1995) compared Latina, non-Latina Black, and non-Latina White women and found that Latina women were less likely than others to perceive themselves as susceptible to breast cancer and less likely to perceive breast cancer as curable. Similarly, Byrd, Mullen, Selwyn, and Lorimor (1996) found that Latina women were more likely to have the following barriers to getting prenatal care in the later stages of pregnancy: embarrassment with the physical examination, long waiting times for the doctor, and poor patient-practitioner interactions. Lee (2000) also found embarrassment to be a significant barrier for Korean American women seeking cervical cancer screenings. Research has even found differences between age groups within ethnicity (i.e., between young and old Chinese Americans; Tang, Solomon, & McCracken, 2000), and provides us with ways to adopt health care delivery to best suit different populations. For example, one study found that American Indian women were reluctant to talk openly about their personal health to physicians (a barrier) and so lay health educators were used to present a screening education program (Dignan et al, 1995).

THEORY OF PLANNED BEHAVIOR

Another way to try to predict whether someone is going to do something is to see if he or she *intends* to do something. Let's say we go to dinner together at a restaurant that has great desserts. If you want to predict whether or not I am going to get some dessert, all you have to do is ask. If my intentions are to get some dessert, I will probably get some (I love dessert). Behavioral intentions play a major role in many models of health behavior change such as the Theory of Reasoned Action (Fishbein & Ajzen, 1975), the Theory of Planned Behavior (TPB) (Ajzen, 1988), the Protection Motivation Theory (Rogers, 1983), and the previously mentioned concept of self-efficacy (Bandura, 1977).

So what is an **intention**? Fishbein and Ajzen (1975) defined an intention as a person's subjective probability that he or she will perform the behavior in question. It is essentially an estimate of the probability of your doing something. If you ask me if I want dessert at the start of a meal when I am hungry, the probability that I will say "yes" will be higher than after a meal when I have stuffed myself. Thus, to get a good measure of intentions, they need to be measured with a high degree of specificity regarding the attitude toward the exact action (e.g., eating dessert), the target (e.g., chocolate cake), the context (e.g., on that day), and the time (e.g., right after the meal). The TPB, an extension and updating of the Theory of Reasoned Action, assumes that people decide to behave a certain way on the basis of their intentions, which are dependent on their attitude toward the behavior, and their perceptions of the social norms regarding the behavior.

Similar to the HBM, attitudes toward the behavior are based on what the person believes are the consequences of the behavior and how important these consequences are (both costs and benefits). Will eating dessert make me put on weight? One of the most useful components is the one assessing perceived norms. This assesses what *you* think others think about the behavior or the **normative beliefs**. Do the people you know support eating sweet things? If you believe that everyone around you thinks that eating dessert is an acceptable thing, you are more likely to want to do it. Of course, you also may not care what people around you think. Your **motivation to comply** with others' preferences is also part of the perception of social norms. If you care about the people around you *and* they support dessert eating, you are more likely to eat dessert. The full model with its components is shown in Figure 6.3.

Culture and the Theory of Planned Behavior

The TPB has been used in many different settings. For example, Montano, Kasprzyk, von Haeften, and Fishbein (2001) used questionnaire data to identify TPB measures that best predicted condom use among African American, Latina, and European American women. They recruited participants from the Seattle area and interviewed them at two time points 3 months apart. Participants were asked about their condom use, their beliefs about the consequences of the condom use, their intentions to use condoms, and their attitudes toward condom use. The researchers also measured the participants' perceptions of the subjective norms about condom use. Specifically, Montano et al. (2001) had participants rate whether 15 different friends and relatives thought they should use condoms. The researchers also assessed the participants' motivation to comply with what their friends said. There was a strong significant correlation between intending to use a condom and actually using

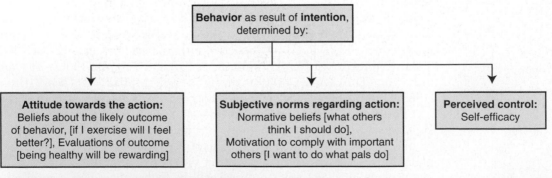

FIGURE **6.3** Major Components of the Theory of Planned Behavior

one, as measured by self-report. Similarly, in support of the TPB model, subjective norms and attitudes toward condom use and perceived behavioral control were also significant predictors of the behavior.

Although tested in multiethnic samples (Montano et al., 2001), it is becoming clear that models such as the TPB do not apply in the same way across cultural groups. For example, ethnic differences are seen in the relative effects of peers and parents on adolescents' substance use. Peers exert a stronger influence on cigarette use among Whites and Latinos than among African Americans (Gottfredson & Koper, 1996). On the other hand, parents have a greater impact on the use of alcohol among African American children than among White children (Clark, Scarisbrick-Hauser, Gautam, & Wirk, 1999). Thus, although the TPB might predict tobacco use among both African American and White children, the relative contribution of the key components (especially of the subjective norm factor) differs among cultural groups. The TPB and Theory of Reasoned Action have both been used to predict adolescent smoking in other cultures such as China (Guo et al., 2007).

TRANSTHEORETICAL MODEL

Every December, as the New Year approaches, it is New Year's resolution time. Men and women around the nation vow to do more of this or less of that. The newspapers provide tips on how best to make and keep resolutions. You often see extensive mention of the **Transtheoretical Model** (TTM) (Prochaska & DiClemente, 1983) of behavior change. It was developed to identify common themes across different intervention theories (hence *Transtheoretical*) and notes that we process through different stages as we think about, attempt to, and finally change any specific behavior.

College-Based Interventions

A number of college-based interventions have used the Theory of Planned Behavior Model to increase the use of sun screen and reduce skin cancer. This poster uses credible, attractive role models to make sun protection more normative.

Different psychological traditions had different processes to account for why people changed their behaviors: the behaviorists argued that people changed to manipulate the contingency of reward and punishment; the humanists believed that helping relationships spurred change; and the psychodynamic theorists suggested that change came about due to consciousness raising. DiClemente and Prochaska (1982) assessed whether a group of smokers who were trying to quit used any of these processes. The researchers found that smokers used different processes at different times in their quest to quit smoking and first identified that behavior change unfolds in a series of stages. From smoking, the stage model was extended to study a variety of behaviors with health consequences including alcohol and substance abuse, delinquency, eating disorders and obesity, consumption of high-fat diets, unsafe sex with the risk of HIV/AIDS, and sun exposure (Prochaska, Redding, & Evers, 2002).

The TTM sees change as a process occurring through a series of six stages. The main stages are summarized in Table 6.2. If you know what stage a person is in, you will need to tailor your intervention to fit the state of mind that the stage describes. When people are not aware that they are practicing a behavior that is unhealthy or do not intend to take any action to change a behavior (especially not in the next six months), they are said to be in the **precontemplation** stage. People could have tried to change before, failed, and become demoralized to change, or they may just be misinformed about the actual consequences of their behavior. Some teenage smokers are so confident about their own health that they do not believe smoking is a problem for them and have no intention of quitting. People in this stage

TABLE **6.2**

Stages of Change: The Transtheoretical Model

1. **Precontemplation**

    —Not aware of behavior, no intention to change

2. **Contemplation**

    —Aware that problem exists, thinking about change

    —Weighing pros and cons

3. **Preparation**

    —Intend to change, modified but not committed

4. **Action**

    —Modified and commitment to time and energy

5. **Maintenance**

    Working to prevent relapse

6. **Termination Phase**

avoid reading, thinking, or talking about their unhealthy behaviors. Health promotion programs are often wasted on them because they either do not know they have a problem or do not really care.

When people recognize they may be doing something unhealthy and then intend to change (within the next month), they are said to be in the **contemplation** stage. Here they are more aware of the benefits of changing and are also very cognizant of the problems that changing may involve. For the dieter, it may be avoiding the foods that he or she has grown to love. For the smoker, it may mean not spending time with the buddies he or she always used to smoke with. The ambivalence associated with knowing the pros and cons of the behavior change often keeps people in this stage for a long time and calls for unique interventions.

Preparation is the stage in which the person is ready to take action to change the behavior. He or she generates a plan and has specific ideas of how to change. Someone who wants to lose weight may go out and buy new workout clothes and a gym membership. Someone who wants to drink less may give away all the alcohol in his or her house or have a talk with his or her doctor to get help. In essence, these people make a commitment to spend time and money on changing their behaviors. As you can guess, this is the stage people should be in if an intervention is going to have any effect.

Once people are actually changing their behavior, they are in the **action** stage. The change has to have taken place over the last six months and should involve active efforts to change the behavior. For example, frequent trips to the gym characterize someone who is in the action stage of trying to lose weight. Does any attempt to change behavior no matter how small count as being in the action stage? No, it does not. People must reach a criterion that health professionals can agree is sufficient to reduce the risk for disease (Prochaska et al., 2002), for example, losing enough weight to no longer be classified as obese or abstaining from smoking for a significant period of time.

Maintenance is the stage in which people try to not fall back into performing their unhealthy behaviors or relapsing. They may still be changing their behaviors and performing new behaviors, but they are not doing them as often as someone in the action stage. In this stage, the temptation to relapse is reduced, and there is often confidence that the new behavior changes can be continued for a period of time. For example, maintenance of abstinence from smoking can last from six months to five years (U.S. Department of Health and Human Services, 2000).

Finally, people may reach a stage in which they are no longer tempted by the unhealthy behavior they have changed. The ex-smoker who no longer craves a cigarette, the ex-fast food addict who now no longer feels like eating a burger and fries, and the once-couch potato who cannot think of not getting regular physical activity. If a person reaches this point, he or she is in the **termination** stage. Can this stage be achieved? Snow, Prochaska, and Rossi (1992) found that less than 20 percent of former smokers and alcoholics reached this zero-temptation stage. For the most part, this part of the model has been loosely interpreted as representing a lifetime of maintenance.

The most helpful contribution of the TTM is that it clearly identifies how interventions can be successful. Interventions need to be tailored according to the stage of change that a person is in. The most common application involves the tailoring of communications to match the needs of the individual. For example, individuals who are in the precontemplation stage could be given information that would make changing their behavior more of a pro and hence move themselves into the contemplation stage (Kreuter, Strecher, & Glassman, 1999). Of course, just knowing what stage a person is in is not enough. Abrams, Herzog, Emmons, and Linnan (2000) tested whether knowing a smoker's TTM stage or knowing the extent of addiction would better predict cessation over 12 to 24 months. They found that addiction-related variables such as number of cigarettes smoked and the duration of prior quit attempts were better predictors than the TTM.

SYNTHESIZE, EVALUATE, APPLY

- Compare and contrast each of the main models of health behavior change.
- Are there any factors that need to be added to the models of behavior change?
- How would you use the Transtheoretical Model to refine interventions to decrease smoking?
- Let us say you want to get all your friends to eat better. You have read about the Health Beliefs Model in class and think that is an interesting model to use. Write one question that you would ask your friends to assess each component of the model.

ADDITIONAL THEORIES OF HEALTH BEHAVIOR CHANGE

In addition to the three major theories discussed above, there are many additional theories used to explain and predict health behaviors. A host of relatively new theories/models are garnering attention. For example, the Precaution Adoption Process Model (PAPM) identifies seven stages along the path from lack of awareness to action (Weinstein & Sandman, 1992).

Another theory, Social Cognitive Theory (SCT; Bandura, 1986) is a comprehensive theory of behavior change that posits that health behaviors must be understood in the context of reciprocal determinism, or the idea that characteristics of a person, one's environment, and the behavior itself all interact and determine whether a behavior is performed. This model considers attitudes, beliefs, and the surroundings in examining behavior. SCT suggests, however, that the most central determinant of health behavior change is self-efficacy, a concept discussed above that is now included in numerous theories of health behavior (Noar, 2005; Noar & Zimmerman, 2005). The SCT was originally considered too comprehensive; some also believed it lacked predictive specificity. However, it now has been reworked explicitly for use in the context of health behaviors (Bandura, 1998).

A last theory, Schwarzer's (1992) Health Action Process Approach (HAPA), rectifies many of the shortcomings of other models. The HAPA distinguishes between two main phases: when a decision to act is made, and when the action is carried out. During the initial phase of the HAPA, people

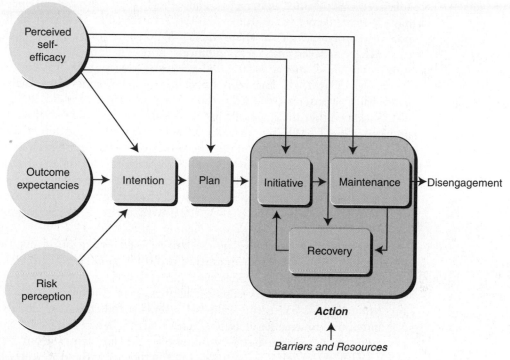

FIGURE **6.4** The Health Action Process Approach

develop an intention to act based on beliefs about the risk and outcomes and their self-efficacy. After a goal has been established within this phase, people enter a volition phase in which they plan the details of action, initiate action, and cope with the difficulties of successfully completing the action. The main components are seen in Figure 6.4. The HAPA has been found to be applicable to a wide variety of health behaviors such as exercise, breast self-exams, seat belt use, dieting, and dental flossing (Schwarzer, 2008).

COMPARING THE MODELS AND THEIR LIMITATIONS

The HBM, TPM, and TTM are the most widely cited models of health behavior change in health psychology (Glanz, Rimer, & Lewis, 2002; Glanz, Rimer, & Viswanath, 2008). They have each received strong support but they (and the studies used to test them) also have some limitations (Ogden, 2003; Schwarzer, 2008; Weinstein, 2007).

In general, the models discussed do not explicitly factor in changes in mindsets over time (Schwarzer, 2008), and do not address how exactly beliefs or intentions are translated into action, the "intention-behavior" gap (Sheeran, 2002). There are other limitations. For example, the HBM has not been as rigorously quantified as the TPB, but its components have received considerable empirical support (Mullen, Hersey, & Iverson, 1987). Some of its components still need to be better understood and others, such as beliefs about severity, have low predictive value (Rimer, 2002). Similarly, the TPB and the TTM do not necessarily include all the elements responsible for behavior change and can each be supplemented with additional concepts. The TPB does not recognize emotional elements such as the perceived susceptibility to illness as does the HBM. The TTM has been criticized for suggesting individuals cannot move back or progress forward without skipping steps (Bandura, 2000). Sutton (2005) argued that the stages are arbitrary subdivisions of a continuous process and hence the TTM is circular and flawed. Furthermore, different studies use different time frames (e.g., six months versus one year) in operationally defining a stage. Based on these issues, some researchers call for greater precision in articulating the processes through which theories are refined, in specifying the mediating variables and processes of change, and in describing techniques to change behavior and their links with theory (Michie, Rothman, & Sheeran, 2007).

Few studies have pitted more than one theory against another (c.f., Weinstein, 1993). Noar and Zimmerman (2005) found that of 2,901 articles reviewed, only 16 percent mentioned more than one theory. Only 19 (1%) were true empirical comparisons of theories. In a notable exception, Garcia and Mann (2003) tested the ability of several social-cognitive models to predict intentions to engage in two different health behaviors (resisting dieting and performing a breast self-examination). All constructs from the HBM (with and without self-efficacy), the TPB (with and without perceived behavioral control), and the motivational process of the HAPA (Schwarzer, 1992) were measured simultaneously in two samples. The authors hypothesized that models that included self-efficacy (or the related construct of perceived behavioral control) would be more effective than the models that did not include it. Their results supported this prediction. The HAPA was the best predictor of intentions to engage in both behaviors. Additional comparative research will continue to provide health psychologists with practical theories.

CHANGING BEHAVIORS: INTERVENTIONS

Understanding why we do or do not do something is important because it provides us with a way to change and make a difference in our health. Armed with the knowledge about what determines behavior, health psychologists attempt to intervene to change behaviors. As you can see from the preceding discussion, our behavior is determined by the attitudes, beliefs, and intentions we have toward it and on the stage that we are in.

Health psychologists have tried different techniques to get people to do what is healthy. In the 1950s, the most common advertisements to change behavior tried to scare the viewer into changing. To some extent you still see some fear appeals today. Many high schools use posters of blackened lungs or rotten teeth to get students not to smoke. Together with using scary visuals, early interventions also tried to provide information about different health hazards. The theory was that if you knew more about the dangers of doing a certain behavior, you may be more likely to not do it. With the advances in television and technology in the 1970s and 1980s, these fear and

Billboards

Billboards like these two sponsored by the California antismoking campaign are a form of intervention that reaches many thousands of people.

information appeals were broadcast via mass media. Most mass media appeals have the benefits of reaching a large number of people relatively easily. Together with alerting people to health risks, these forms of interventions can have a cumulative effect over time and can also reinforce other change techniques.

Different interventions focus on different antecedents of behavior. Some health psychologists choose to change a person's attitudes to change his or her behavior; others attempt to change his or her beliefs or intentions. The way an intervention is designed can depend on the specific behavior that needs to be changed (e.g. obesity, Stice, Shaw, & Marti, 2006), the funding available for the behavior change, and the number of people that the intervention has to reach. To put all these different factors into order, let's look at some of the basic principles of intervention design. Some additional suggestions from a review summarizing effective interventions (Rotheram-Borus & Duan, 2003) are shown in Table 6.3.

Top Ten Prescriptions

1. **Interventions Should Be Based on Theory**. Having a theory is important for many reasons. First, it helps focus attention on the most important factors that need to be addressed for the behavior change at hand. For example, the application of the TPB to change specific behaviors involves identifying underlying beliefs that determine one's attitude, subjective norms, and perceived behavioral control, and having the intervention address these components. Theories also help target special cultural groups (e.g., low socioeconomic status individuals). For example, there is substantial evidence that richer people tend to be in more advanced stages of change than poorer people are (Adams & White, 2007). Far too often researchers try to address as many different aspects of behavior as they can in an intervention. They fill posters with arguments and information that tackle these different aspects. If such interventions do result in changing behavior, it is hard to identify what catalyzed the change because the contents of the intervention were not based on a theory. Thus, it is hard to replicate the findings and difficult to focus on and identify what actually worked. This "throw in everything including the kitchen sink" approach to

TABLE **6.3**

Additional Success Strategies for Interventions

1. Use private enterprise models of product development to increase the dissemination of the intervention to the general public.
2. Initiate interventions by teams committed to a specific problem.
3. Provide investigators with training in management.
4. Establish the acceptability of the program's design features to consumers, providers, and funding agencies before the development and evaluation of the program.
5. Use data from national marketing surveys to tailor intervention designs and delivery formats for different subgroups.
6. Identify essential ingredients of the intervention to facilitate adaptation of the program.
7. Implement the program with a goal to maintain change over extended periods of time.
8. The implementation plan should include program evolution over time, rather than replication with fidelity.
9. The intervention should be branded and certified by a credible agency.

Source: From Rotheram-Borus, M. J., & Duan, N. (2003). Next generation of preventive interventions. *Journal of the American Academy of Child and Adolescent Psychiatry, 42(5)*, 518–526.

interventions can lead to change but more often than not involves the use of money without the promise of successful replication of the behavior or prolonged success. Interventions based on theory have a better chance of being useful over the long run. Many interventions also combine a number of theories to be as effective as possible (e.g., increasing physical behavior, Michie, Hardeman, Fanshawe, Prevost, Taylor, & Kinmonth, 2008).

2. **Intervene at the Appropriate Level.** When designing an intervention, the researcher has to decide what the best unit of intervention is. You can design an advertising campaign to target an entire city, state, or part of the country. You can also decide to target areas of a city or town, neighborhood, or community (Campbell, Hudson, Resnicow, Blakeney, Paxton, & Baskin, 2007). You can get even more specific and target couples, families, or specific individuals in a family. Research overwhelmingly suggests that if one member of a relationship practices healthy behaviors, the other will be more likely to practice healthy behaviors as well (Meyler, Stimpson, & Peek, 2007).

The level at which you intervene should be appropriate to the problem at hand. If the issue is something like obesity, and people in specific states are more at risk than others, a statewide campaign may be better. If the issue is something like smoking and only members of a specific cultural group, say high school students, are at risk, then targeting that group is critical. Interventions can also target policy makers; changing the superstructure of government and policies toward specific health behaviors can also result in behavior change. Many state governments have raised the tax on cigarettes and have seen a corresponding drop in cigarette purchases among young adults (Campaign for Tobacco-Free Kids, 2008).

3. **Size Matters.** The size of the intervention closely relates to the extent of behavior change seen in response to it. Size can refer to the duration of the intervention and to the intensity of the intervention. Sustained interventions are more likely to lead to sustained behavior change. Furthermore, in many studies, rates of high-risk behavior increase when interventions are withdrawn. Having an intervention continue over a long period of time, even if it is not too involving, can still ensure that the unhealthy behavior is kept at bay. For example, if you want to have a group exercise more, having them complete weekly exercise logs that are turned in (increasing accountability and involvement) is likely to make them be active. More intense interventions are more likely to result in greater risk reduction. For example, Rotheram-Borus and colleagues (2003) designed a successful intervention called Street Smart for runaway children. Street Smart provided these children with access to health care and condoms and delivered a 10-session skill-focused prevention program based on social learning theory. The more sessions conducted, the better the success rate was. Finally, the effect size of an intervention is another good indicator of success. Effect size is a statistical measure of the power of any experimental manipulation. Even if there is a small sample, looking at the effect size can provide a useful estimate of the effectiveness of the intervention.

4. **Interventions Should Target People at Risk.** When researchers do not take pains to intervene at the appropriate level, large numbers of people are exposed to the intervention with the hope that those who need it are included in the exposed group. This shotgun approach can waste a lot of time and money. In some cases, it may be difficult to find out who is most in need of the intervention, but attempting to do so can lead to better, more directed interventions. Investigators can find out who is at risk by identifying risk factors. For interventions to increase the use of mammograms, investigators can identify groups of women who have high rates of breast cancer and find measures to identify them. Culture comes in handy here. There may be people in a specific part of the country, a specific ethnic group, a religious group, or an age group who are more likely to perform an unhealthy behavior or be at risk for a specific disease. Identifying that group, finding out where they are located, and going to them are effective ways to intervene. The more an intervention is tailored to fit individuals at risk the more likely it will work (Noar, Benac, & Harris, 2007).

5. **Interventions Should Be Appropriate for the Risk Group/Risk Factor.** Once a risk group is identified, the intervention should be designed to be appropriate for that group. If you are targeting a specific age group, sex, ethnic group, or member of a specific sexual orientation, format the intervention in a way that appeals to and is understandable by the target group. If you want to target bad eating behaviors of seventh-grade students, the language of the intervention should not be set at the level of college freshmen. If the intervention is to appeal to a certain ethnic or religious group, it should use terminology, images, or styles familiar to that group. In addition, it is important to remember that not everyone speaks English. Interventions aimed to change the behaviors of people from different ethnic groups in which different languages are spoken should be designed in the language of the target population.

6. Be Sure Your Intervention Does Only What You Want It to Do. Sometimes an intervention can have unintended effects. Interventions to curb eating disorders provide a sad example. Prevention programs for eating disorders attempt to simultaneously prevent new occurrences (primary prevention) and encourage students who already have symptoms to seek early treatment (secondary prevention), even though ideal strategies for these two types of prevention may be incompatible with each other. In a study to assess the effectiveness of such programs, Mann et al. (1997) evaluated an eating disorder prevention program. In the intervention, classmates who had recovered from eating disorders described their experiences and provided information about eating disorders. Paradoxically, at follow-up, intervention participants had slightly more symptoms of eating disorders than did control subjects instead of fewer symptoms. Mann et al. hypothesized that the program may have been ineffective in preventing eating disorders because by reducing the stigma of these disorders (to encourage students with problems to seek help), the program may have inadvertently normalized them. Similarly, researchers should be sure that their control group is not receiving anything special. If an intervention consists of providing social support over the phone but the control group also receives phone calls (for information gathering), control group participants may still rate the calls as being supportive.

7. Preventing Dropouts Should Be a Priority. Not everyone in a longitudinal research study stays in the study until the end. Similarly, not everyone who enrolls in an intervention study attends all the sessions. Although dropouts are an unpleasant fact for most longitudinal research studies, they can be especially problematic for interventions. First, the participant is not getting the entire treatment. Second, the presence of dropouts hinders a thorough assessment of the intervention. This is akin to having a cold and being prescribed a course of antibiotics only to stop taking the medicine once you start feeling better. Just like colds, unhealthy behaviors can return once the intervention/treatment has been stopped. Researchers need to devote resources to preventing attrition and simultaneously collect data to be sure they can assess the effects of attrition.

8. Be Ethical. Although interventions are designed to get people to perform healthy behaviors and reduce unhealthy behaviors, these notable ends do not justify unethical means. It is important for the researchers to respect participants' rights and refrain from using deception or making false claims about the ills of unhealthy behaviors or the virtues of healthy ones. There are enough facts about most health behaviors so that researchers should not be tempted to exaggerate details for a stronger effect. In interventions that include a control group and an intervention group, it is critical that members of the control group participate in the intervention after the study is over. This way they too can get the benefits of the intervention. Health professionals should also be thinking of what will happen once the intervention is removed. Will the behavior go back to what it was before the intervention? Will an unhealthy behavior get worse because the intervention is seen as a crutch, the removal of which is detrimental?

9. Be Culturally Sensitive. Some models of health behavior change are automatically culturally sensitive, but most theories are designed to apply to any cultural group. Researchers must pay close attention to the symbols and language used because the same symbol may mean different things to different cultures. A great example is the swastika, a cross made up of four Ls. For centuries it was a good luck emblem (and is still considered a good luck emblem by Hindus), but its meaning was corrupted when it became the symbol of Hitler's Nazi Germany. Thus, its use for good luck by some cultures (e.g., Hindus) may offend others (e.g., Jews). Similarly, researchers cannot assume that everyone speaks English, and language differences should be kept in mind. Interventions that apply at the community level often take cultural differences into account. For example, the Community Organization and Development model for health promotion in communities of color involves community-controlled coalitions that undertake their own community assessment and design culturally relevant interventions (Braithewaite, Bianchi, & Taylor, 1994). In other cases, general theories are revised for use with culturally diverse populations. Gilliland and colleagues (1998) tweaked Social Learning theory ideas into an intervention especially designed to reduce the incidence of type 2 diabetes among American Indians and Native Hawaiians. Their programs use problem-solving approaches and involve family and social networks to fit the different circumstances and values of each cultural group. Such culturally based interventions have increased movement along stages of change for fat intake and physical activity (Mau et al., 2001). Some researchers do not believe that a general, one-size-fits-all-cultures theory is valid and suggest that new culturally sensitive models need to be developed and used (Oomen, Owen, & Suggs, 1999). Given the increase in cultural diversity in North America today, much more research needs to be applied to designing and assessing culturally valid interventions.

In a recent example, Fisher, Burnet, Huang, Chin, and Cagney (2007) reviewed culturally sensitive interventions aimed at narrowing racial disparities in health care. Thirty-eight interventions of three types were identified: interventions that modified the health behaviors of ethnic minority patients, that increased access to health care, and that modified the health care system to better serve minority patients. Individual-level interventions (see points 2 and 3 above) typically tapped community members' expertise to shape programs. Access interventions largely involved screening programs, incorporating patient navigators and lay educators. Health care interventions focused on the roles of nurses, counselors, and community health workers to deliver culturally tailored health information. These interventions increased patients' knowledge for self-care, decreased barriers to access, and improved providers' cultural competence. The researchers concluded that interventions explicitly factoring in using culture show tremendous promise in reducing health disparities, but more research is needed to understand their health effects in combination with other interventions.

10. **Prevent Relapse.** Sometimes it is not enough to intervene to change behavior, see the behavior change, and then walk away. One of the biggest problems in health behavior change involves fostering maintenance of the new behavior (Marlatt & George, 1990). Be aware that smoking a single cigarette after quitting, eating one slice of pizza if you are on a diet, or skipping one day of exercise may not constitute relapse. Yet, the person's failure to

change can be demoralizing and can sometimes lead to increased levels of the original unhealthy behavior. Relapse occurs when the behavior that was changed reoccurs on a consistent basis. Good interventions should strive to ensure that relapse does not occur by providing participants with the cognitive and behavioral skills to maintain the behavior change.

Together with these main points, health professionals designing interventions should strive to compensate for individual differences as much as possible. A smoking intervention that works on one campus may not necessarily work in exactly the same way on another campus even if it is in the same state. People's personalities vary as well, and not everyone in an intervention is going to react in the same way. A good way for you to assess how well you understand the 10 key aspects is to use them. Pick a health issue—e.g., secondhand smoke in the workplace or binge drinking on campus—and see if you can design an intervention using these 10 principles. Fine-tune your intervention according to the demographics of your location. You know your peers best, and your intervention can be as powerful (if not more powerful) than those designed by the experts. In the next chapter I will discuss some of the main health behaviors that interventions attempt to influence and give you some examples of interventions to compare yours with.

SYNTHESIZE, EVALUATE, APPLY	• Can you think of any additional factors to optimize the delivery of interventions? • What are the major weaknesses of a "shotgun" approach to interventions? • Design a study that would incorporate the best aspects of all the models of health behavior change. • What biopsychosocial factors do you think can predict relapse?

CHANGING PERSONAL BEHAVIOR

On an individual level you can change health behaviors as well. If reading this book has highlighted some of the health behaviors you would like to change, then there are some easy things you can do. First, take a week or two and closely monitor the behavior that you want to change. If you would like to eat better, write down everything you eat or drink for a week (including times, places, and hunger). If you want to stop smoking, similarly write down every time you smoke (the urge, the company, and so on). Self-observation or self-monitoring is the first and most important step. Then use what you have learned from this chapter and other parts of the book (e.g., Chapter 5 for help to cope with stress, something that thwarts most attempts to stop smoking). List the barriers that are preventing you from changing the unhealthy behavior, or adding the healthy behavior. Think about your susceptibility and vulnerability to the consequences of not changing. Think about the severity of the health problem that could result if you do not change. Also, assess what stage you are in. Using this information, you can develop a plan to change in an organized manner. Use principles of operant conditioning (reinforcement and punishment) to make sure you keep on track and set achievable goals. By paying close attention to the different biopsychosocial correlates of health

TABLE **6.4**
Major Theories Compared

Theory	Main Components/Ideas
Health Belief Model (HBM)	Beliefs in threat (severity, susceptibility) and effectiveness of health change behaviors
Theory of Planned Behavior (TPB)	Intention to change; attitudes toward action; subjective norms regarding action; self-efficacy
Transtheoretical Model (TTM)	Six stages that a person proceeds through: precontemplation, contemplation, preparation, action, maintenance, termination
Social Cognitive Theory (SCT)	Health behaviors must be understood in the context of reciprocal determinism, or the idea that characteristics of a person, one's environment, and the behavior itself all interact and determine whether a behavior is performed
Precaution Adoption Process Model (PAPM)	Person moves from being unaware of issue, to unengaged by issue, to deciding not to act, to planning to act but not yet acting, to acting, to maintenance
Health Action Process Approach (HAPA)	Two main phases: factors influencing intention to act and the processes that take place after the intention leading up to the behavior

behaviors as discussed here, you should be able to develop the behavioral and cognitive skills to change any behavior you desire.

FOCUS ON APPLICATIONS

You Know You Want To …: Reducing Smoking in College

Interventions to reduce smoking in college students have focused on the use of antismoking advertising campaigns and educational material (Freeman, Hennessy, & Marzullo 2001; Greenberg & Pollack, 1981). Even when the message that smoking is harmful is broadcast loud and clear, many college students still choose to smoke. Some interventions have attempted to change behavior by changing campus smoking policies. Results indicate that campus-wide policy changes may result in a decrease in the number of cigarettes smoked, at least on campus (Apel, Klein, McDermott, & Westhoff, 1997).

Research consistently shows that teenagers and college students misperceive and overestimate their peers' use of tobacco (Perkins, Meilman, Leichliter, Cashin, & Presley, 1999). Changing high school and middle school children's' misperceptions might be a beneficial strategy (Sussman, 1998; Hansen, 1993), though until recently there have been few published studies related to correcting tobacco use misperceptions (see Perkins, 2003, for a review). Let us tell you about one way some researchers are trying to change this.

Researchers at the University of Wisconsin in Oshkosh, Wisconsin, began their research by studying the different psychological reasons for why people smoked. They noticed that one of the biggest reasons students started smoking was that students thought that it was actually a pretty normal thing to do. Students believed that many of their peers were smoking.

(continues)

FOCUS ON APPLICATIONS *(continued)*

The researchers knew that this was not the case. The researchers realized that if the college could show that this was not really the case, students may decrease their smoking behavior. This approach is called a Social Norms Approach.

Social norming research has shown that college students often believe that those engaging in healthy behavior are in the minority when, in fact, they are not. Health psychologists acknowledge that norms are important predictors of health behaviors. For example, the theory of planned behaviors discussed previously holds that health behaviors directly result from behavioral intentions that are composed of attitudes toward the specific action, perceived behavioral control, and subjective norms regarding the action. If people who smoke believe that smoking is normative, or if they believe that their friends do not believe that not smoking is the norm, these people are less likely to change their behavior. An inaccurate perception of the norms could also get non-smokers to try smoking. If impressionable students believe that most students their age smoke, these distorted perceptions of group behavior and attitudes may lead them to comply with an inaccurate peer pressure (Grube, McGree, & Morgan, 1986).

So what did the research team do? They assessed the actual and perceived behaviors and attitudes of the students and developed a social marketing campaign to modify misperceptions.

(continues)

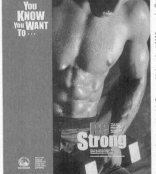

Courtesy Student Health Center, University of Wisconsin Oshkosh

Posters

Posters are often a cheap way to convey a message, whether in workplaces or across college campuses. This series of posters was designed to curb college smoking by highlighting all the different rewards of not smoking. By quitting, people can save money, are more kissable, and do not have to go out in the cold in the winter to smoke (more on this specific series in the next chapter).

FOCUS ON APPLICATIONS *(continued)*

The multimedia campaign used posters (as shown), an "art car" (a car painted with anti-smoking information), television and radio ads, a mannequin (covered with messages about the dangers of smoking), information tables, varsity sport promotions, and other promotional items (e.g., plastic piggy banks) to convey the message collected from the campus wide surveys. The primary message was that few students smoked and those that did wanted to quit smoking. The "You know you want to…" theme shown in the posters tested well with students and captured the power of positive norming. "You know you want to…" promoted cessation services and directed smokers and nonsmokers toward resources to learn more about the healthy benefits of being smoke free. For example, one poster "You know you want to… get out of the cold" included the statistics of quitting and the finding that nearly three out of four students wanted to help a friend quit smoking (and get out from the cold where smokers who cannot smoke indoors have to go). A marketing survey completed three months after the introduction of the campaign showed that 91 percent of students reported seeing the "You know you want to…" posters.

Did the Social Norms Approach work? The intervention was a resounding success (Gurung & Abhold, 2004). At the start of the intervention, 34 percent of students on campus smoked. When the students were surveyed a year after the media campaign, the number of smokers dropped down to 27 percent. Twisting the old adage—what you don't know can't hurt you—well, what you *think* you know can (especially when it is inaccurate).

SUMMARY

- Health behaviors are specific behaviors that maintain and enhance health. The most important are getting physical activity, limiting the consumption of alcohol, not smoking, and eating well, all described as Leading Health Indicators. Health educators close the gap between what is known as optimal health practices and what is actually done. Interventions are specific programs designed to assess levels of behaviors, introduce ways to change them, measure whether change has occurred, and assess the impact of the change.
- There are biopsychosocial determinants of health behaviors. Biologically we have genetic predispositions that can influence the types of health behaviors we practice and our metabolic rates or risk of addiction. Psychologically, personality traits, self-esteem, and social support are some key factors influencing health behaviors. Social aspects such as the culture we are raised in also predict healthy behaviors.
- Three major theories predict the extent to which we perform health behaviors. The Health Belief Model suggests that our beliefs relating to the effectiveness, ease, and consequences of performing or not performing a behavior will influence whether or not we do or do not do it. Our perception of susceptibility, the consequences of the illness, and the extent to which we believe behavior change is effective and worthwhile all contribute to the likelihood of performing the behavior.
- The Theory of Planned Behavior suggests that our intentions to perform a behavior are the most important predictors of whether we do it and are influenced by our attitudes toward the behavior and the perceptions of the social norms regarding the behavior.
- The Transtheoretical Model of behavior change suggests that we pass through key phases in regard to a behavior. We move from not thinking

about changing or precontemplation to contemplating change, to preparing to change, to changing (action stage), and then to maintenance of the change.
- There are several prescriptions to keep in mind when one is designing interventions to change behavior. Interventions should be based on theory, be at the appropriate level, be at the right level of severity, target people at risk, be appropriate for the risk group, only do what they are designed to do, be ethical, be culturally sensitive, and be designed to minimize dropouts and relapse.

TEST YOURSELF

Check your understanding of the topics in this chapter by answering the following questions. Answers appear in the Appendix.

1. According to the demographic factors discussed in class and the text, which of the following individuals is most likely to practice good health behaviors?
   a. Joan, a 45-year-old high school dropout who works two jobs to support her family
   b. Janet, a 30–year-old high school graduate who is a file clerk in a small store and will be married next month
   c. Doug, a divorced 50-year-old corporate attorney
   d. David, a 35-year-old assistant professor who has just celebrated his 8th wedding anniversary
2. The specific field that stresses the relevance of political, economic, and social factors in health is:
   a. health psychology.
   b. medical sociology.
   c. epidemiology.
   d. health education.
3. Personality plays a big role in health. For example, people high in the trait of _____ report more medical problems and more visits to the doctor.
   a. conscientiousness
   b. open to experience
   c. extraversion
   d. neuroticism
4. According to the Health Beliefs Model, health behaviors are strongly linked to:
   a. beliefs in threat.
   b. stages of change.

c. social norms.
d. age and sex.
5. Which of the following is not a major component of the Health Beliefs Model? Belief in:
   a. susceptibility
   b. consequences
   c. effectiveness
   d. social norms
6. The theory of planned behavior focuses on a person's:
   a. attitudes toward health.
   b. intentions to the behavior.
   c. beliefs about the behavior.
   d. plans to change behavior.
7. It is not enough to only know a person's perceptions of what the social norms are to predict if they will change their health behavior. You must also assess their:
   a. motivation to comply.
   b. self-efficacy.
   c. age and sex.
   d. perception of vulnerability.
8. As we think about changing our health behaviors, we progress through different stages. The best health psychological model to get at this is the:
   a. Health Beliefs Model.
   b. Theory of Planned Behavior.
   c. Transtheoretical Model.
   d. Health Action Process Approach.

9. Relapsing, or falling back into performing unhealthy behaviors is the biggest problem in which stage of the Transtheoretical Model?
   a. Termination stage
   b. Contemplation stage
   c. Action stage
   d. Maintenance stage

10. To change a behavior, the very first thing a person should do is spend a week or so and use:
    a. self-monitoring.
    b. operant conditioning.
    c. classical conditioning.
    d. self-control.

WEB RESOURCES

Visit the companion Web site at **www.cengage.com/ psychology/gurung**, where you will find online resources for this book, including chapter-by-chapter quizzes, Web links, and more!

President's Challenge:
http://www.presidentschallenge.org/

This is an online site with great tips on how to get 30 minutes of exercise a day. The National President's Challenge is a six-week physical activity challenge designed to get America up and moving 30 minutes a day, five days a week. The Challenge aims to encourage people of all ages and abilities to find activities they love and to live a healthier lifestyle.

National Institute of Health:
http://health.nih.gov/

This is a great hub site that has up-to-date information on a variety of health behaviors and research being done to improve health (see the Healthy Lifestyles and Research in Action links).

KEY TERMS, CONCEPTS, AND PEOPLE

action, 197

Bandura, 191

consequences, 191

contemplation, 197

effectiveness, 191

Fishbein and Ajzen, 193

Health Belief Model, 191

health education, 184

healthy behaviors, 183

Healthy People 2010, 185

intention, 193

interventions, 187

Leading Health Indicators, 185

maintenance, 197

motivation to comply, 194

normative beliefs, 194

precontemplation, 196

preparation, 197

Prochaska and DiClemente, 195

Rosenstock and Hochbaum, 191

self-efficacy, 191

termination, 197

Transtheoretical Model, 195

ESSENTIAL READINGS

Bellg, A. J., Borrelli, B., Resnick, B., Hecht, J., Minicucci, D., Ory, M., et al. (2004). Enhancing treatment fidelity in health behavior change studies: Best practices and recommendations for the NIH behavior change consortium. *Health Psychology, 23*(5), 443–451.

Noar, S. M. (2005). A health educator's guide to theories of health behavior. *International Quarterly of Community Health Education, 24,* 75–92.

Schwarzer, R. (2008). Modeling health behavior change: How to predict and modify the adoption and maintenance of health behaviors. *Applied Psychology: An International Review, 57,* 1–29.

Shah, J. Y., & Gardner, W. L. (Eds.). (2008). *Handbook of motivation science*. New York: Guilford Press.

CHAPTER 7

Health Behaviors: Eating, Physical Activity, Smoking and Drinking

"**E**at, drink, and be merry!" sounds like a simple plan for being content. Of course, we need to eat and drink to survive; however, recent studies link happiness to longer life as well (Moskowitz, Epel, & Acree, 2008). Unfortunately, being "merry" is associated too often with eating too much (or eating unhealthy foods), drinking too much, smoking, and a host of other unhealthy activities. The extent to which people perform each of the main health behaviors can vary dramatically. Some people eat too much, while others eat too little. Some people rarely move from the couch, whereas others spend too much time working out. While many people have never smoked a cigarette in their lives (puffing but not inhaling still counts as smoking), it is estimated that more than one-fifth of the people in the United States smoke regularly. There are even trends and fads within each of these behaviors. At the turn of the twenty-first century, yoga centers became popular as millions of Americans began trying this form of physical activity. Simultaneously, many thousands of people experimented with the contemporary specialized diets, such as cutting out all carbohydrates from their diets as suggested in the Atkins and South Beach programs. What is healthy eating? How much physical activity is appropriate? When does substance use become substance *abuse*

© Banana Stock/Jupiter Images

Behaviors That Can Influence Our Health

Eating can be a lot of fun, but one should not eat too much, too little, or the wrong variety of food. If you eat too much and do not get the physical activity to burn off the extra calories, you have even more problems. Do you drink alcohol with your meals? Do you smoke? All these behaviors have serious health consequences.

leading to unhealthy consequences? In this chapter, we explore the different behaviors that can influence our health.

Every health behavior (particularly what and how much we eat and how much exercise we get) is strongly influenced by a range of sociocultural factors. Health problems relating to poor eating habits and limited exercise are more prevalent in some cultures than in other cultures. For example, many African Americans experience high rates of hypertension, and many American Indians experience high rates of diabetes. Let's determine why these cultural differences exist and what can be done about them. In the previous chapter, we explored a few of the main psychological theories that can predict the performance of health behaviors and the theories of behavior change. This chapter focuses on three major categories of health behaviors: eating; physical activity; and smoking and drinking. Here, we will describe the factors influencing each behavior and how they vary across cultures. We will focus on the developmental precedents of unhealthy behaviors and discuss the unhealthy consequences related to each behavior.

EATING

According to the National Center for Health Statistics, nearly 33 percent of adult Americans will be considered obese by the mid-twenty-first century (National Center for Health Statistics, 2006). That is nearly one-third of the adults in America! Just as shocking are the projected obesity prevalence rates for children. These statistics show that obesity among children age 6 to 11 could be as much as 15.3 percent and the rate among children age 12 to 19 as much as 15.5 percent. While recent statistics show that obesity rates were somewhat consistent between the years 1999 and 2006, just 15 years earlier in the 1980s, only 13 percent of adult Americans were considered obese (Ogden, Carroll, & Flegal, 2008). That is a significant difference. When we factor in people considered to be "overweight," the number rises to 66 percent! It is imperative that we grasp healthy eating behaviors and proper nutrition in order to turn this dangerous trend around.

What percentage of your daily diet is carbohydrates? What percentage is protein? What about fat? How much do you eat? Are you eating a balanced diet? What *is* a balanced diet? These are some of the most common questions asked about food and eating. The answers to these questions are decisive in determining your health. However, with new research coming out weekly and the influence that media coverage has on health-related issues and trends, some of these answers seem to change weekly! The following section provides facts relating to all of these questions and issues. It also provides a behavioral background for why we eat what we eat, when we choose to eat, and how much we choose to eat. In the following section, we will also discuss the main health problems that arise when we do not eat well and the most common types of eating disorders.

Eating is something we all must do. However, did you know that most of us do not pay enough attention to what and how we eat? Many of us do other activities while we eat such as watch television, read newspapers or

Obesity

Obesity is one of America's greatest health concerns today. Even children are getting larger, and the health consequences of being overweight are increasing.

---

magazines, or drive (not a good idea). Assess your consumption. Think about the last few days. How many times did you ingest something yesterday? What did you eat? How much did you eat? What determined what and how much you consumed? Why did you pick what you ate? Use Table 7.1 and list every thing that you have eaten in the past 24 hours. Try to identify why you ate what you did. Your list will provide a reference point to think about while reading the remaining material in this chapter.

What Should We Be Eating?

The U.S. Department of Agriculture's (USDA) earliest attempts to inform consumers about how much protein, fats, and carbohydrates to consume date back to the early 1900s. The first food guide was published in 1916 and consisted of five major food groups (e.g., fats, carbohydrates; Welsh, Davis, & Shaw, 1993). The economic problems of the Depression in the 1930s greatly influenced American families' food purchasing and consumption habits as they were forced to balance price and nutrition. Affordable foods were often low in nutritional value. To alleviate this situation, the USDA released buying guides with 12 food groups in the 1930s. The USDA changed these guides several times over the next several decades with the determined number of food groups fluctuating from seven in the 1940s to five in the 1970s with the introduction of the "Hassle-Free" Foundation diet. The **Food Guide Pyramid**, which was introduced in 1984 and used six food groups as a guide, was printed on such products as bread packages and cereal boxes and was used until early-2005. This guide was revised once in the early 1990s based on the U.S. Department of Health and Human Services' (DHHS) Surgeon General's Report on Nutrition and Health. This report included the recommendations

TABLE **7.1**

Examine the factors that affect your eating habits: Choose one day of the week that is typical of your eating pattern. In the table below, list all the foods and drinks that you consumed on that day. Then list the other requested information. Use these symbols: taste (T), convenience (C), emotion (E), availability (A), advertising (AD), weight control (WT), hunger (H), family values (FV), peers (P), nutritional value (NV), cost ($), and health (HT) as reasons for choice. You may be surprised by what you see.

Eating Habits Survey

Time of Day	Minutes Spent Eating	Meal/ Snack	Degree of Hunger (0–5)	Activity While Eating	Food and Quantity	Others Present?	Reason for Food Choice

of a panel of nutritional experts selected by the USDA and the DHHS. The Food Guide Pyramid established the basic principles of a balanced diet designed to help people maintain or improve their general health and reduce the risk of diet-related diseases. This guide, while easily recognized, was neither well used nor well understood (Escobar, 1999). Given the problems with understanding the structure of the pyramid and the cultural variations needed for it to apply to all Americans—not to mention the continuously updated nutritional research involved—the Food Guide Pyramid was no longer used by the year 2005.

In January of that year, the DHHS released an updated set of nutritional guidelines for Americans complete with a new pictorial guide revamping the pyramid and was named MyPyramid (DHHS, 2005; Haven, Burns, Britten, & Davis, 2006). A modified version for older adults was released in January 2008 (Lichtenstein, Rasmussen, Yu, Epstein, & Russell, 2008). Key changes include emphasizing the consumption of more whole grains, a variety of fruits and vegetables, and an increase in physical activity. As you can see in Figure 7.1, MyPyramid has a staircase on one side to remind Americans that exercise is an important complement to good eating. Instead of the horizontal bands of the old pyramid, there are now rainbow-colored bands streaming down. Food groups are represented by six different colors: orange representing grains, green representing vegetables, red representing fruits, yellow representing oils, blue representing milk products, and purple representing meat and beans. The

GRAINS	VEGETABLES	FRUITS	MILK	MEAT & BEANS
Eat 6 oz. every day	Eat 2$^1/_2$ cups every day	Eat 2 cups every day	Get 3 cups every day for kids aged 2 to 8, It's 2	Eat 5$^1/_2$ oz. every day

FIGURE **7.1** The USDA MyPyramid

Oils are also included (the narrow band between fruits and milk).

bands are wider for grains, vegetables, fruit, and milk products to remind people to consume more of these foods. One pyramid no longer fits all people. There are 12 individually tailored models for different age groups as well as different models for men and women in these age groups.

The food guides show foods typically eaten by North Americans to illustrate the USDA and DHHS recommendations. The pyramid suggests the types and amount of foods to eat each day. Four factors were considered in establishing the serving sizes: typical portion sizes from food consumption surveys, ease of use, nutrient content, and traditional uses of foods (Herring, Britten, Davis, & Tuepker, 2000). Although a single serving of one type of fruit may have more calories than a single serving of another (i.e., apple versus orange), the number of different serving sizes was kept to a minimum to make the pyramid easy to use. Did the phrase "traditional uses of food" make you think? Do different cultural groups have different traditional foods? Absolutely they do! To compensate for this, Oldways Preservation and Exchange Trust of Cambridge, Massachusetts, developed food pyramids for different cultural groups. Mediterranean, Asian, and Latino Diet Pyramids as seen in Figure 7.2 incorporate habits of various cultural groups in the United States. There is even an American Indian food pyramid. The main difference between

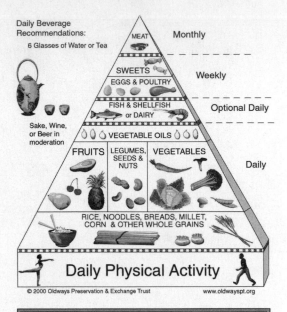

The Traditional Healthy
Asian Diet Pyramid

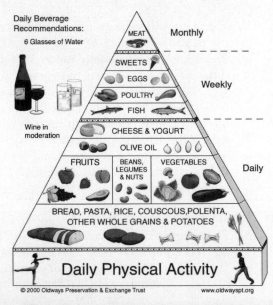

The Traditional Healthy
Mediterranean Diet Pyramid

FIGURE **7.2** Food Pyramids for Different Cultural Groups

Source: *Copyright © 2000 Oldways Preservation & Exchange Trust. Reprinted by permission.*

these pyramids and the standard USDA pyramid is that the culturally diverse pyramids illustrate proportions of food to be consumed and not exact serving sizes. Furthermore, the Oldways pyramids show foods specific to the different cultures and suggest consumption amounts over a period of two to three days, several weeks, or even months, in contrast to the USDA guide.

These different guides highlight the fact that what we eat often is deeply tied to our cultural backgrounds. Throughout history, many cultures have ascribed health-promoting powers to certain foods, and many religions have followed specific dietary practices. Chinese "herbs of immortality" were a popular fad among the ancient Chinese. These herbs have a modern manifestation in Chinese herbs marketed to bodybuilders in health food stores. Different cultures have different beliefs about what foods to consume. As described in Chapter 1 and Chapter 2, many cultures, including the Chinese culture, believe that some foods are "hot" and others are "cold." This belief refers to a food's influence on health and well-being, not to the temperature or spiciness of foods. Cold foods include most vegetables, tropical fruits, dairy products, and inexpensive cuts of meat (e.g., rump roast). Hot foods include chili peppers, garlic, onion, most grains, expensive cuts of meat, oils, and alcohol. Just as the USDA Food Guidesbalance nutritional value, cultures such as the Chinese and the ancient Indians suggested eating foods to balance energy levels. Most non-Western cultures believe that the type of food eaten needs to balance the type or condition of the person. For example, pregnancy is considered a "hot" condition during which many Latinos typically avoid hot foods, believing this will prevent the infant from contracting a "hot" illness, such as a skin rash. In contrast to the Hispanic beliefs, the Chinese believe that pregnancy is a "cold" condition during which the expectant mother should consume hot foods to keep in balance and remain healthy.

Development of Food Preferences

Have you wondered why you like certain foods and dislike others? A part of our **food preferences** are biologically programmed into us (Adler, Hoon, Mueller, Chandrasekar, Ryba, & Zuker, 2000; Bartoshuk, 1993). There are two completely innate preferences. Humans innately prefer sweet and salty tastes and are adverse to sour tastes. In general, our experiences and exposure to food determine the bulk of our preferences. If the context in which you were given broccoli was positive, you probably will develop a preference for broccoli. If you always were forced to eat your beans, you probably will develop an aversion to beans. If you were raised near a cheese factory, you probably will develop a preference for cheese. Basic reward and punishment and sociocultural factors also play a large role in the development of our food preferences (Cooke, 2007; Finlayson, King, & Blundell, 2008; Richards, & Smith, 2007). Children growing up in families who eat together often develop healthier eating habits—and are healthier adults too—(Franko, Thomson, Affenito, Barton, & Striegel-Moore, 2008). Foods used as rewards (e.g., clean your room and you get your ice cream) or paired with fun social events or holidays (e.g., Mom's spice cake at Christmas) automatically become preferred. A recent study of over a 1,000 children showed that the ethnicity of the parents and correspondingly ethnic food preferences also influenced what children ate (Bruss, Applegate, Quitugua, Palacios, & Morris, 2007).

Obesity

You often hear about the weight problem in the United States and the alarming level of obese and overweight children and adults (e.g., Ogden, Carroll, Curtin, McDowell, Tabak, & Flegal, 2006). Over half of the people in the United States are either overweight or obese (Center for Disease Control, 2008). What exactly do the terms obese and overweight mean? There are established norms for body weight. As seen in Table 7.2, research has established the weight range for healthy living for people of different heights. If a person weighs more than his or her normal range, he or she is referred to as being overweight. **Obesity** is defined as having a **body mass index** (BMI) of 30 or greater. A BMI of between 25 and 29.9 qualifies a person as overweight. To calculate your BMI, multiply your weight by 703 and divide it by the square of your height measured in inches [BMI = (Wt × 703)/(Ht × Ht)].

Although the BMI score is commonly used, there is an important caveat in its use and it should not be used as the only indicator of a person's healthy weight. It misrepresents weight in different cultural groups (Bates, Acevedo-Garcia, Alegría, & Krieger, 2008). This misrepresentation also helps explain some inconsistencies in the eating behavior literature by demonstrating the impact of controlling for BMI when BMI and eating behaviors are compared in individuals from different racial/ethnic backgrounds. Gluck and Geliebter (2002) demonstrated this in a study of European, African, and Asian American women who completed an Eating Habits Questionnaire (EHQ) and other measures of body image and eating. European Americans had greater body dissatisfaction (as measured by a higher difference between current and ideal image) than Asian Americans and higher EHQ scores than both Asian Americans and African Americans. African American women chose a larger body size as their ideal than the other groups. The caveat with BMI is this: Asian American women had a significantly lower BMI than both other groups. However, after controlling (i.e., statistically adjusting) for BMI, ideal body size differences were minimized. Also after controlling for BMI, both European Americans and Asian American had greater body discrepancy and EHQ scores than African Americans (Gluck & Geliebter, 2002).

The bottom line is that similar to many of the health behaviors discussed in this chapter, obesity varies significantly by ethnicity and socioeconomic status (Delva, Johnston, & O'Malley, 2007). In a large national study, a sizable proportion of European American, African American, and Hispanic participants were overweight (60% to 85%) and obese (30% to 50%), while fewer Chinese American participants were overweight (33%) or obese (5%) (Burke et al., 2008).

Here is some bad news. Our weight increases (not counting the weight gain with pregnancy) as a natural part of the aging process (Figure 7.3). The weight of infants usually doubles in the first 6 months, and older adults gain weight as their metabolic system naturally slows with age. For important reasons, pregnant women add 30 to 35 pounds of weight on average to sustain a pregnancy. Obesity, however, is more than a normal addition of weight

TABLE **7.2**
Body Mass Index

	Normal						Overweight					Obese						
BMI	19	20	21	22	23	24	25	26	27	28	29	30	31	32	33	34	35	36
Height (feet & inches)								Body Weight (pounds)										
4'10"	91	96	100	105	110	115	119	124	129	134	138	143	148	153	158	162	167	172
4'11"	94	99	104	109	114	119	124	128	133	138	143	148	153	158	163	168	173	178
5'	97	102	107	112	118	123	128	133	138	143	148	153	158	163	168	174	179	184
5'1"	100	106	111	116	122	127	132	137	143	148	153	158	164	169	174	180	185	190
5'2"	104	109	115	120	126	131	136	142	147	153	158	164	169	175	180	186	191	196
5'3"	107	113	118	124	130	135	141	146	152	158	163	169	175	180	186	191	197	203
5'4"	110	116	122	128	134	140	145	151	157	163	169	174	180	186	192	197	204	209
5'5"	114	120	126	132	138	144	150	156	162	168	174	180	186	192	198	204	210	216
5'6"	118	124	130	136	142	148	155	161	167	173	179	186	192	198	204	210	216	223
5'7"	121	127	134	140	146	153	159	166	172	178	185	191	198	204	211	217	223	230
5'8"	125	131	138	144	151	158	164	171	177	184	190	197	203	210	216	223	230	236
5'9"	128	135	142	149	155	162	169	176	182	189	196	203	209	216	223	230	236	243
5'10"	132	139	146	153	160	167	174	181	188	195	202	209	216	222	229	236	243	250
5'11"	136	143	150	157	165	172	179	186	193	200	208	215	222	229	236	243	250	257
6'	140	147	154	162	169	177	184	191	199	206	213	221	228	235	242	250	258	265
6'1"	144	151	159	166	174	182	189	197	204	212	219	227	235	242	250	257	265	272
6'2"	148	155	163	171	179	186	194	202	210	218	225	233	241	249	256	264	272	280
6'3"	152	160	168	176	184	192	200	208	216	224	232	240	248	256	264	272	279	287
6'4"	156	164	172	180	189	197	205	213	221	230	238	246	254	263	271	279	287	295

(continued)

TABLE **7.2** *(continued)*
Body Mass Index

BMI Height (feet & inches)	Obese									Extreme Obesity								
	37	38	39	40	41	42	43	44	45	46	47	48	49	50	51	52	53	54
									Body Weight (pounds)									
4'10"	177	181	186	191	196	201	205	210	215	220	225	229	234	239	244	248	253	258
4'11"	183	188	193	198	203	208	212	217	222	227	232	237	242	247	252	257	262	267
5'	189	194	199	204	209	215	220	225	230	235	240	245	250	255	261	266	271	276
5'1"	195	201	206	211	217	222	227	232	238	243	248	254	259	264	269	275	280	285
5'2"	202	207	213	218	224	229	235	240	246	251	256	262	267	273	278	284	289	295
5'3"	208	214	220	225	231	237	242	248	254	259	265	270	278	282	287	293	299	304
5'4"	215	221	227	232	238	244	250	256	262	267	273	279	285	291	296	302	308	314
5'5"	222	228	324	240	246	252	258	264	270	276	282	288	294	300	306	312	318	324
5'6"	229	235	241	247	253	260	266	272	278	284	291	297	303	309	315	322	328	334
5'7"	236	242	249	255	261	268	274	280	287	293	299	306	312	319	325	331	338	344
5'8"	243	249	256	262	269	276	282	289	295	302	308	315	322	328	335	341	348	354
5'9"	250	257	263	270	277	284	291	297	304	311	318	324	331	338	345	351	358	365
5'10"	257	264	271	278	285	292	299	306	313	320	327	334	341	348	355	362	369	376
5'11"	265	272	279	286	293	301	308	315	322	329	338	343	351	358	365	372	379	386
6'	272	279	287	294	302	309	316	324	331	338	346	353	361	368	375	383	390	397
6'1"	280	288	295	302	310	318	325	333	340	348	355	363	371	378	386	393	401	408
6'2"	287	295	303	311	319	326	334	342	350	358	365	373	381	389	396	404	412	420
6'3"	295	303	311	319	327	335	343	351	359	367	375	383	391	399	407	415	423	431
6'4"	304	312	320	328	336	344	353	361	369	377	385	394	402	410	418	426	435	443

Source: National Heart, Lung and Blood Institute.

The BMI score is valid for both men and women but it does have some limits: It may *overestimate* body fat in athletes and others who have a muscular build; and it may *underestimate* body fat in older persons and others who have lost muscle mass.

needed for growth or health. The chance of being obese increases with age, and obesity occurs more commonly in women than in men, especially among non-European American women. Approximately 55 percent to 60 percent of African American and Mexican American women 40 to 60 years of age are overweight (Wing & Polley, 2002).

Being obese means more that just having and unhealthy appearance. Obesity increases the chances of having a chronic disease, exacerbates conditions such as coronary heart disease, and correspondingly shortens life (Adams et al., 2006). Those who are obese know it, suggesting that interventions focusing only on health risks of *obesity* may provide minimal new information and induce little new weight loss (Finkelstein, Brown, & Evans, 2008). As the number of overweight and obese people increases, the prevalence of problems such as type 2 diabetes, gallbladder disease, coronary heart disease, high blood cholesterol levels, high blood pressure, and osteoarthritis also increases. The chance of having two or more health conditions increases with weight in all racial and ethnic subgroups (DHHS, 2005). Gaining extra weight in adulthood even increases the risk of heart attacks (Willett & Singer, 1995). In the Second National Health and Nutrition Examination Survey (NHANES II), overweight adults were three times more likely to develop diabetes and high blood pressure (Van Itallie, 1985). In fact, there is almost a direct negative correlation between BMI and mortality. The higher your BMI, the sooner you may die. One study, the Nurses' Health Study, followed 115,000 women age 30 to 55 for 16 years (Manson et al., 1995). Women with BMIs of 19 to 21 showed the lowest mortality rates. Women with a BMI of 32 or greater were almost four times more likely to die from cardiovascular disease and twice as likely to die from cancer compared with women who had BMIs less than 19. There is currently a controversy regarding the exact levels of BMI that are unhealthy. It is possible that being a little overweight (e.g., BMI between 25 and 30) may serve a protective function, but it is clear that being obese, especially BMIs over 35, is very unhealthy (Flegal et al., 2005; Katzmarzyk, 2001). In case you were wondering, you CAN be too thin! Research also shows that BMIs under 18 put a person at risk for health problems (Flegal et al., 2005).

Obesity is caused by a complex blend of biology, psychology, and social factors (Berthoud & Morrison, 2008). A person may be obese or have excess body fat for a number of reasons. The significant reason is a combination of bad eating habits (eating too much or too many high-calorie foods) with lack of enough physical activity. In addition, if calorie intake is greater than calorie output, you are going to gain weight. Both genetic and environmental factors also are at work. Clearly, genetics plays a role in obesity (Bouchard, 1995). Twin studies show that identical twins when overfed are both likely to gain similar amounts of weight, whereas fraternal twins do not show this relationship (Bouchard et al., 1990). There are even specific genes linked to obesity. The *ob* gene, which codes for the protein leptin, has been linked to obesity (Campfield, Smith, & Burn, 1996). Leptin signals satiety and people with mutated *ob* genes do not have as much leptin, which possibly leads to overeating. Of course, dramatic increases in obesity are not necessarily due to dramatic mutations of the *ob* gene. A person's environment factors in as well.

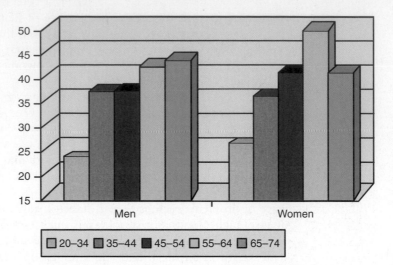

FIGURE **7.3** Being Overweight Increases with Age

The percentage of overweight people increases with age. As you get older, you are at risk for gaining weight. As the body's metabolic rate slows down, you need to increase your physical activity level and pay more attention to what you eat to ensure that you do not add pounds.

Changes in food marketing and availability are the most recent and blatant environmental factors influencing eating (Hawkes, 2007; Linn, & Novosat, 2008). The fast food industry has been "supersizing" its offerings. For a small increase in cost, fast-food chains generate a large profit from the public, many of whom like to get large servings. The influence of larger servings in restaurants is seen as one component of a Western way of life because it tends to be localized to developed countries. As proof of the ills of "Western living," Ravussin, Valencia, Esparza, Bennett, and Schulz (1994) compared Pima Indians in the United States with Pima Indians living in a rural part of Mexico. The U.S. Pima Indians had a mean BMI of 35.5. The Mexican Pima Indians had an average BMI of 25.1. Similarly, Alvord and Van Pelt (2000) have also documented rising cases of gallbladder infection and other diet-related problems in the Navajo Indians of New Mexico. How much food does a person really need? The actual amount of food in a recommended serving may surprise you (Figure 7.4).

Most overweight people eat more than normal weight people eat and often do not even realize the quantities they consume (Lichtman et al., 1992). That said, overweight people do not just eat more of anything. Taste and quality are particularly important. One study suggests that overweight individuals actually prefer (and eat) more fat than normal weight people (Rolls & Shide, 1992). Be warned though, most people eat more if they are given larger servings (Wansink, van Ittersum, & Painter, 2006). Furthermore, a greater variety of foods presented leads to greater quantities consumed by individual eaters (Temple, Giacomelli, Roemmich, & Epstein, 2008; Wansink & Sobal, 2007). Hetherington and Rolls (1996) showed that if only one type of food is available at a meal, people eat a moderate amount of it. If a second

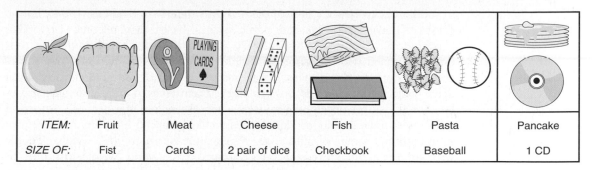

ITEM:	Fruit	Meat	Cheese	Fish	Pasta	Pancake
SIZE OF:	Fist	Cards	2 pair of dice	Checkbook	Baseball	1 CD

FIGURE **7.4** A Handy Guide to Serving Sizes

Lay your fist next to your food (e.g., your pasta or potatoes or vegetables) to see how much you need. How much is a serving size? Use your hands: most adult fists = 1 cup (single serving). Your easy guide to serving sizes: Serving sizes are smaller than most people think.

food is then introduced, the amount of the new food eaten will be more than if it was presented by itself. This phenomenon is called **sensory specific satiety**. Even thinking that there is more variety can make you eat more. Kahn and Wansink (2005) showed that people will eat more jellybeans when they are mixed up (and there seems to be more variety) than when a number of varieties are served separately. Simply changing the cost of foods makes a difference too (Faith, Fontaine, Baskin, & Allison, 2007). The cheaper the food is, the more people will eat, which even applies to healthy items such as fruits (Jeffery, French, Raether, & Baxter, 1994). Therefore, a variety of social and psychological factors influence how much we eat and when we eat it (Stroebe, 2008). For example, we also eat more when we are stressed or hassled (O'Conner, Jones, Conner, McMillan, & Ferguson, 2008).

A review of obesity prevention programs showed that the most successful programs targeted children, adolescents, and females; were relatively brief; solely targeted weight control versus other health behaviors (e.g., smoking); were evaluated in pilot trials; and were trials in which participants must have volunteered to participate (Stice, Shaw, & Marti, 2006).

Eating Disorders

The defining characteristic of all eating disorders is a severe disturbance in eating behaviors (Diagnostic and Statistical Manual of Mental Disorders, Fourth Edition, Text Revision, DSM-IV-TR; American Psychiatric Association, 2000). Diagnostic criteria are currently provided for two eating disorders, *anorexia nervosa* and *bulimia nervosa*, and a third general category, *eating disorder not otherwise specified*. It is important to note that dieting by itself has not been linked to increased eating disorder symptoms (Williamson et al., 2008).

Many people have psychological problems, such as low self-esteem, that contribute to an unhealthy relationship with food. For others, being overweight leads to disorderly eating. For example, obesity has been associated with binge eating disorder, in which obese individuals consume large quantities of food and experience a lack of control over their lives (Marcus, 1993). Eating disorders have biological and psychological bases (Monteleone, Tortorella, Castaldo, Di Filippo, & Maj, 2007; Stice, 2002). Problems with low self-esteem coupled with pressures to be like slim models or actresses and actors on television, in the movies, or in magazines, and bad role models often drive some young girls and boys to starve themselves. Young girls, in particular, are at risk for developing anorexia nervosa or bulimia nervosa. Anorexia involves an intense fear of gaining weight, a disturbed body image, a refusal to maintain normal weight, and extreme measures to lose weight. People with anorexia often exercise 2 to 3 hours a day, take weight-loss pills or appetite suppressants, abuse laxatives, and skip meals. No matter how thin they get, anorexics are only happy when they lose more weight. This condition can sometimes be fatal. Bulimia involves habitually overeating followed by self-induced vomiting, fasting, and excessive exercise. The eating is usually done in secret and is then accompanied by intense guilt and weight gain concerns. Given the strong psychological and social components to eating disorders and possible genetic predispositions, the biopsychosocial approach of health psychologists to illness can be a great aid in preventing eating disorders and helping individuals who already suffer from one or more of them.

Culture and Eating Disorders

The cross cultural study, diagnosis, assessment, and treatment of eating disorders is in its infancy; although, a review of the literature shows that eating disorders are clearly influenced by culture (Markey, Vander Wal, & Gibbons, 2009).

There are some significant cultural differences in eating disorders and with the body image problems that cause them. Cultures vary in their concepts of ideal body shape, and sociocultural models of body image suggest that the prevalence of eating disorders and body image disturbance in Western countries is partially attributable to cultural ideals of beauty that value thinness. Furthermore, most assessment tools have been validated only on samples of European Americans, lack specificity in defining cultural groups, and show biases in detecting and reporting eating disorders in women of color (Gilbert, 2003).

Eating disorders are not just a European American problem. For example, Edman and Yates (2004) found no cultural differences in eating disorder symptoms or self-dissatisfaction or body dissatisfaction scores between Asian American and European American women. Furthermore, eating disorders have been reported in nearly every area of the world (Anderson-Fye & Becker, 2004). Prevalence rates of eating disorders outside North America, especially in Japan, Singapore, Korea, the Middle East, and Africa have been found to be comparable to those in Western countries.

Rates of eating disorders do vary by ethnicity within the United States and no ethnic group is completely immune. Some cultural groups may have higher rates of eating disorders than others. Caballero, Sunday, and Halmi (2004) compared Latino and European American patients with anorexia nervosa or bulimia on severity and types of preoccupations and rituals related to eating disorders and the motivation to change. Patients were interviewed with the Yale-Brown-Cornell Eating Disorder Scale (YBC-EDS). All YBC-EDS scores were higher for the Latino group who also had more preoccupations and rituals. Latinos were also more likely to have rituals in many measured categories. Exactly how culture contributes to eating disorders is still unclear, but researchers are beginning to explicitly look at the role of culture in the development of eating behaviors and the formation of body image (Markey, 2004).

When compared with European American women, African American women tend to have lower rates of anorexia nervosa but similar rates of binge eating, and Latina women may have slightly higher rates of eating disorders than both of these ethnic groups (Markey, Vander Wal, & Gibbons, 2009). Asian American women have the lowest rates of eating disorders among the major ethnic groups in the United States, while Native American women have the highest rates.

Having contact with or being influenced by Western culture significantly increases the prevalence of eating disorders, especially in the case of bulimia nervosa (Keel & Klump, 2003). In an unsettling example, Becker, Burwell, Gilman, Herzog, and Hamburg (2002) showed that exposure to Western media (introduction of television) in Fiji was associated with an increase in symptoms of eating disorders and self-induced vomiting to lose weight. Rapid modernization has also been found to result in difficulties with disordered eating and body dissatisfaction in Asian and Caribbean countries (Katzman, Hermans, Van Hoeken, & Hoek, 2004).

SYNTHESIZE, EVALUATE, APPLY	• How do your physical activity and dietary patterns compare with prescribed levels for good health? • What are the main reasons for people not eating a balanced diet? • What are the differences between the cultural food pyramids? • What are the pros and cons of having different pyramids? • What are the biggest factors influencing the development of food preferences? • Apply what you know about food and exercise to develop a plan for optimal health.

PHYSICAL ACTIVITY

Most people know that exercise is good for their health. Unfortunately, few people manage to successfully adopt and maintain an exercise habit (Marcus et al., 2000; Shields, Spink, Chad, Muhajarine, Humbert, & Odnokon, 2008). There are many physical and psychological benefits of physical exercise, including lowered blood pressure, weight loss, stress reduction, and increased self-confidence (Brownson, Chang, Davis, & Smith, 1991; Calvo, Szabo, & Capafons, 1996; Fontane, 1996; Taylor, Doust, & Webborn, 1998; U.S. Department of Health and Human Services, 2000). **Physical activity** is any bodily movement produced by contraction of the skeletal muscles that results in energy expenditure (Caspersen, Powell, & Christenson, 1985). How physically active are you? Do you exercise regularly? Do you take an elevator when you could use the stairs?

Physical Activity

You do not have to go to a gym to get your daily requirement of physical activity. Even walking can burn energy. A brisk 20-minute daily walk has been found to be enough to prevent weight gain.

How much physical activity is needed? In 1995 the American College of Sports Medicine and the Centers for Disease Control and Prevention published national guidelines on Physical Activity and Public Health (Pate et al., 1995). The authors suggested that each adult should accumulate at least 30 minutes of moderate-intensity physical activity on most, preferably all, days of the week. These guidelines were updated in 2003 to suggest that at least 60 minutes of physical activity per day is optimal for a healthy life (Porter, 2003). This information was particularly depressing for people who had trouble exercising even 20 minutes a few times a week. The most recent prescription is that all healthy adults age 18 to 65 years need moderate aerobic physical activity for a minimum of 30 minutes five days each week or vigorous aerobic physical activity for a minimum of 20 minutes three days each week (Haskell et al., 2007). An hour each day may be optimal, but even 30 minutes is healthy. (Eden, Orleans, Mulrow, Pender, & Teutsch, 2002).

We have discussed how much exercise you need, but how much exercise should you do? It is important to remember that there are numerous ways that you can expend energy and be physically active. When people think about the recommendations for physical activity they often picture going to a gym, running, biking, or lifting weights. About 50 percent to 70 percent of the total amount of energy we burn relates to the working of our different cells and organ systems, referred to as our *basal metabolic rate*. Another 7 percent to 10 percent of energy is used to break down the food we eat, called the *thermic effect of food* (Ravussin & Rising, 1992). The rest of the energy we burn is physical activity, including the things we have to do every day, such as bathing, grooming, or moving around the house or office, and the things that we choose to do, such as playing sports, dancing, or walking as a leisure-,time activity. The more physical activities we choose to do, the more energy we expend. The amount of energy used in different daily activities is shown in Table 7.3.

TABLE **7.3**

Energy Used in Various Physical Activities

Activity	Calories Burned in 5 Minutes (Typically*)	
	Woman	Man
Walking fast	20	30
Washing a car	20	30
Having sex	20	30
Doing yard work	20	30
Painting	20	30
Mowing the lawn	25	35
Biking to work	30	40
Walking up stairs	35	45
Running up stairs	75	100

*Calories estimated for a 132-pound woman and a 176-pound man. Adjust proportionally to your weight if needed.

Exercise is defined as activity planned with the goal of improving one or more aspects of physical fitness (Caspersen et al., 1985). Exercise contributes to our level of fitness, defined as the ability to perform daily tasks with vigor and alertness without undue fatigue, enjoy leisure time activities, and meet unforeseen challenges (Phillips, Kiernan, & King, 2002). Are you fit? Several different components can assess whether you are fit or not. Cardiovascular endurance, often referred to as aerobic fitness, refers to the body's capacity to take in, transport, and utilize oxygen. A common measure of aerobic fitness is the volume of oxygen (VO_2) a person uses during different tasks. Muscular strength, muscular endurance, muscular power, speed, flexibility, agility, balance, good reaction times, and a low percentage of body fat are other components used to assess fitness (Phillips et al., 2002). Generally, most national studies of health behaviors use "physical activity" rather than "exercise levels" to assess health, although both are important components of a healthy lifestyle.

Most commonly used measures of physical activity assess leisure time activities that require energy use above the level of daily living. This type of measurement works well in countries such as the United States and in the study of other populations with high socioeconomic status (SES) because most jobs in these economic environments do not require expending too much energy. Sitting at a desk or standing in one spot in a production line does not use as much energy as working in a field. In developing countries and among population with lower SES, a lot more energy is spent on the job (Pereira et al., 1998). In the United States, ethnic minority groups have lower levels of leisure-time physical activity (LTPA) than do European Americans but it is unclear how much of this is explained by differences in socioeconomic status and health (Xiaoxing, & Baker, 2007). Leisure-time physical activity was lower for African Americans and Latinos compared with European Americans, and LTPA steadily declined with lower levels of education.

Cultural Variations in Physical Activity

Ethnic, socioeconomic, age, and sex differences all account for cultural differences in physical activity (Byrd-Williams, Kelly, Davis, Spruijt-Metz, Goran, 2007; Cerin, E., Vandelanotte, Leslie, & Merom, 2008; Swartz, Strath, Parker, Miller, & Cieslik, 2007). Statistics show that minority groups in the United States consistently have relatively lower physical activity levels than majority group members (Cassetta, Boden-Albala, Sciacca, & Giardina, 2007; Kriska, 2000). Minority women are among the least active subgroups in American society (Brownson et al., 2000; Lee, 2005). A cross-sectional study conducted in 1996 and 1997 among 2,912 African American, American Indian, Alaskan Native, Latina, and European Americanwomen age 40 years and older showed that physical activity was lowest among African Americans, American Indians, and Alaskan Natives (Brownson et al., 2000). In three national surveys, the **National Health Interview Survey** (NHIS, 1991), the **Third National Health and Nutritional Examination Survey** (NHANES III, 1988–1991), and the **Surgeon General's Report** (DHHS, 1996), physical activity was found to be lowest among people with low incomes and lower levels of education.

In general, people are more active when they are younger. For example, 64 percent of students in grades 9 to 12 engaged in vigorous physical activity three or more days per week for at least 20 minutes versus only 16 percent of people age 18 and older (CDC, 2003). Age and ethnicity also have an effect. Pima Indian, Latino, African American, and Asian American children are less active than European American children (Aron, 1993; Stevens, 1996). A school-based survey of 551 girls showed that more minority girls reported getting less than one hour of strenuous activity per week than nonminority girls. Minority girls also watched television on average five hours longer per week than nonminority girls (Wolf, 1993). Having a television in your bedroom is even worse. Adolescents with a bedroom television reported more television viewing time, less physical activity, poorer dietary habits, fewer family meals, and poorer school performance (Barr-Anderson, van den Berg, Neumark-Sztainer, & Story, 2008). Sex, ethnicity, socioeconomic status, and age were also associated with the presence of a bedroom television.

Physical Consequences of Physical Activity

Being physically active and exercising daily are good for physical health. As mentioned earlier, there is some debate about how much exercise is needed, but no debate about whether or not it is needed. Clearly, it is required for well-being. As early as the mid-twentieth century, physically active individuals were shown to be less likely to develop coronary heart disease (Kahn, 1963; Morris, Heady, Raffle, Roberts, & Parks, 1953). Physical activity not only reduces mortality from different diseases (Bouchard, 2001; Kohl, 2001) but also increases life expectancy (Blair, Kohl, Gordon, & Paffenbarger, 1992; Lee & Skerrett, 2001; Paffenbarger, Hyde, Wing, & Hsieh, 1986) and improves cardiovascular recovery from stress (Chafin, Christenfeld, & Gerin, 2008). In particular, physical activity (controlling for the ill effects of a bad diet or smoking) has been identified as an independent risk factor in development of diseases such as cardiovascular disease (Berlin & Colditz, 1990; Pate, 1995). Evidence is accumulating that shows connections between physical activity and cancers (Thune & Furberg, 2001). In general, higher levels of both occupational and leisure-time physical activity relate to lower levels of prostate, lung, testicular, colon, rectal, and breast cancers, although evidence in some of these cases is inconsistent. In addition, being physically active relates to lower incidence of type 2 diabetes (Hu et al., 2001; Manson, Shore, Baron, Ackerson, & Neligh, 1992; Wannamethee, Shaper, & Alberti, 2000), osteoporosis or loss of bone density (Greendale, Barrett-Conner, Edelstein, Ingles, & Halle, 1995; Mussolino, Looker, & Orwoll, 2001), strokes (Wannamethee & Shaper, 1992), and hypertension (Reaven, Barrett-Conner, & Edelstein, 1991).

Psychological Consequences of Physical Activity

Being physically active is probably beneficial for psychological health as well. Why do we mention only "probably?" At this point, few methodologically sound longitudinal studies have been performed to test the causal relationship between physical activity and mental health (Morgan, 1997; Phillips et al., 2002). Nevertheless, a strong body of correlation work suggests that there is a link. Furthermore, a growing number of studies support the idea that **physical** exercise is a lifestyle factor that might lead to increased **physical** and **mental health** throughout life (Hillman, Erickson, & Kramer, 2008). In Chapter 4, you read that exercising can be a great stress reliever. This is just one of the many positive associations between physical activity and mental health. Numerous epidemiological studies and reviews of research link higher levels of physical activity with reduced symptoms of depression (Dunn, Trivedi, & O'Neal, 2001; Farmer et al., 1988; Paffenbarger, Lee, & Leung, 1994). Physical activity also reduces anxiety (Bhui & Fletcher, 2000; Raglin, 1997) and increases self-esteem (Sonstoem, 1997). Covey and Feltz (1991) highlighted the role of physical activity in development, concluding that physically active high school girls report significantly healthier self-image and coping characteristics than physically inactive girls. Similarly, Wankel and Berger (1990) showed that physical activity is significantly related to personal growth, social integration, and positive social change. However, these associations may not hold for elderly persons (Brown, 1992) and interventions to increase physical activity among the elderly show limited success (Baker et al., 2007). Evidence does exist showing physical exercise may reduce depression in the short term among the elderly (Sjösten, & Kivelä, 2006).

To some extent, finding links between physical activity and mental health can be frustrating. The link appears to make sense. You may notice that you feel better after a run, walk, or bicycle ride, but robust demonstrations of this association are difficult to find. Physical activity could lead to better mental health because activity increases monoamines such as norepinephrine, epinephrine, dopamine, and serotonin, and it releases endorphins. Unfortunately, evidence for each of these possibilities is spotty (Phillips et al., 2002). What can we be sure of? Physical activity prevents excessive weight gain (the dangers of which are described above) and is linked clearly to physical well-being.

- Evaluate the literature on the psychological effects of exercise. Design an empirical study to resolve the ambiguities.
- Describe how eating and physical activity can interact with each other.
- Apply your knowledge to design an intervention to increase physical activity among your peers.

SMOKING AND DRINKING

Both smoking and drinking are commonly considered to be vices. Although tobacco and alcohol are both potentially addictive substances, the body metabolizes alcohol and nicotine differently. Alcohol is a liquid, absorbed in the stomach, from where it then travels to the heart, the lungs, and finally to the brain. The active elements of tobacco, such as nicotine, are usually inhaled, resulting in a rapid transmission to the brain. Smoking has quick effects. Whereas a drinker may consume alcohol several times a week or a day, a pack-a-day smoker experiences about 200 puffs a day or "behavioral reinforcers" in a wide variety of social settings. The majority of regular smokers are addicted, although many people can use alcohol socially and not become addicted (Russell, 1990). This difference in social use and the amount of **behavioral cueing** explains, in part, why the relapse rates for tobacco addiction is higher than those for alcohol **addiction**. Many alcoholics can quit drinking but have more difficulty quitting smoking then also quitting smoking. People who always smoke at a bar are tempted to smoke when they are at a bar.

Our society has social and cultural differences in how we treat the use of each substance. Tobacco use is legal for the vast majority of college-age students, whereas alcohol use is illegal for those younger than 21. Alcohol use is also prohibited during work hours and has been relegated to certain "social" events (except for alcoholics who drink regardless) which usually occur in the evening. Tobacco use, on the other hand, is a more accepted daily behavior and can occur at any time of the day in a variety of settings. Circumstances may make smoking appear more common than it actually is. Because of current trends in indoor air policies, smokers are forced to stand outside building entrances, which further increases their visibility and fuels misperceptions of the prevalence of smoking.

SMOKING

In 2006, one-fifth of all North Americans admitted to regularly putting a flame to little paper-covered cylinders of dry leaves, and sucking the bitter smoke into their lungs (i.e., smokingU.S. Department of Health and Human Services, 2007). Tobacco contains roughly 500 chemicals, and tobacco smoke contains about 4,000 chemicals (Dube & Green, 1982). With these statistics and this knowledge of cigarettes containing this many chemicals, not to mention cancer-causing black tar and an addictive substance called nicotine, one may wonder why smokers persist. Many smokers who know the same information wonder why they persist as well, and many try to quit.

Who smokes more? If you have followed the trends in prevalence of smoking in North America, you know there is good news and bad news. The numbers of smokers substantially decreased between 1993 and 2006 for all age groups, except those between age 18 and 24 (U.S. Department of Health and Human Services, 2007). Between 2003 and 2005, the percentage of high school students who reported smoking cigarettes in the past month remained stable at 22 percent to 23 percent, which is a drop from 36 percent in 1997. The reduction of smoking or the cessation of tobacco use among college students is a critical public health priority. Within the last 10 years, college student smoking prevalence has dropped from nearly 30 percent (Rigotti, Lee, & Wechsler, 2000; Wechsler, Kelley, Seibring, Kuo, & Rigotti, 2001) to slightly less than 20 percent (Harris, Schwartz, & Thompson, 2008; Thompson et al., 2007).

Tobacco use is the leading cause of preventable morbidity and mortality in the United States (DHHS, 2002; Mokdad et al., 2005). Yet, smoking continues in the broader culture as well as on high school and college campuses (Hilts, 1996; Glantz et al., 1996). Longitudinal data from the Monitoring the Future Studies (Johnston, O'Malley, & Bachman, 2001) indicate that although past month use by high school seniors fell in the late 1970s and stabilized in the 1980s, it rose steadily in the 1990s. One may be tempted to believe that this lack of change and increase in smoking can be attributed to students not having enough information about tobacco or demographic issues, but this is not the case. At the college level, no significant differences are found among smokers and nonsmokers and the year in college, sex, age, race, or having attended public or private high schools (DeBernardo et al., 1999). DeBernardo et al. also showed that whereas 98 percent of those who responded felt that they understood the harmful effects of smoking on their health, just 39.1 percent of smokers seriously considered stopping and even 11.5 percent of nonsmokers intended to start smoking! These data prove that knowledge alone is insufficient to change behavior.

Cultural Variations in Smoking

When looking at the general population, we see some clear-cut cultural differences in who smokes. Men smoke more than women (DHHS, 2007). People earning less and who are not well educated smoke more than people higher on the socioeconomic ladder (Aekplakorn, Hogan, Tiptaradol, Wibulpolprasert, Punyaratabandhu, & Lim, 2008; DHHS, 2007). In fact, people in more deprived neighborhoods that have higher crime rates and less access to health care are more likely to smoke (Duncan, Jones, & Moon, 1999). Studies also show that military people with lower ranks smoke more than higher-ranked officers (Cunradi, Moore, & Ames, 2008). Geography also accounts for differences in smoking rates. In 2003, Kentucky had the highest number of smokers in the United States. Table 7.4 shows smoking rates for different states, while Table 7.5 shows smoking rates for different countries.

The most pronounced differences in smoking are racial and ethnic (Figure 7.5). The American Lung Association reports that American Indians have the highest rates of smoking (36%), followed by African Americans (26%), European Americans (24%), and then Asian and Pacific Islanders (17%).

Smoking and culture have some interesting interactions. African Americans who are more traditional are more likely to smoke than African

TABLE **7.4**

Estimated Prevalence of Current Cigarette Smoking[1] Among Adults, by Area and Sex—Behavioral Risk Factor Surveillance System, United States, 2006

State/Area	Men %	Men (95% CI[2])	Women %	Women (95% CI)	Total %	Total (95% CI)
Alabama	26.3	(22.6–30.0)	20.6	(18.5–22.7)	23.3	(21.2–25.4)
Alaska	25.3	(21.2–29.4)	22.9	(19.4–26.4)	24.2	(21.5–26.9)
Arizona	21.7	(17.7–25.7)	14.7	(12.3–17.1)	18.1	(15.8–20.4)
Arkansas	25.9	(23.5–28.3)	21.7	(20.0–23.4)	23.7	(22.2–25.2)
California	18.5	(16.3–20.7)	11.4	(10.1–12.7)	14.9	(13.6–16.2)
Colorado	19.3	(17.2–21.4)	16.4	(14.9–17.9)	17.9	(16.6–19.2)
Connecticut	18.9	(17.0–20.8)	15.3	(14.0–16.6)	17.0	(15.9–18.1)
Delaware	23.3	(20.2–26.4)	20.2	(17.6–22.8)	21.7	(19.7–23.7)
District of Columbia	21.4	(18.4–24.4)	14.9	(13.1–16.7)	17.9	(16.2–19.6)
Florida	23.6	(21.5–25.7)	18.7	(17.3–20.1)	21.0	(19.7–22.3)
Georgia	22.4	(20.1–24.7)	17.7	(16.2–19.2)	20.0	(18.7–21.3)
Hawaii	19.2	(17.1–21.3)	16.0	(14.3–17.7)	17.5	(16.2–18.8)
Idaho	18.7	(16.4–21.0)	15.0	(13.4–16.6)	16.8	(15.4–18.2)
Illinois	24.2	(21.6–26.8)	17.0	(15.3–18.7)	20.5	(18.9–22.1)
Indiana	26.3	(24.0–28.6)	21.9	(20.2–23.6)	24.1	(22.7–25.5)
Iowa	23.2	(20.9–25.5)	19.9	(18.2–21.6)	21.5	(20.1–22.9)
Kansas	22.2	(20.2–24.2)	18.0	(16.7–19.3)	20.0	(18.8–21.2)
Kentucky	29.1	(26.1–32.1)	28.1	(26.0–30.2)	28.6	(26.8–30.4)
Louisiana	26.6	(24.3–28.9)	20.5	(19.0–22.0)	23.4	(22.0–24.8)
Maine	21.8	(19.2–24.4)	20.0	(18.0–22.0)	20.9	(19.3–22.5)
Maryland	19.1	(17.0–21.2)	16.7	(15.0–17.8)	17.8	(16.6–19.0)
Massachusetts	19.4	(17.5–21.3)	16.4	(15.0–17.8)	17.8	(16.6–19.0)
Michigan	24.8	(22.3–27.3)	20.1	(18.4–21.8)	22.4	(20.9–23.9)
Minnesota	18.5	(16.1–20.9)	18.2	(16.3–20.1)	18.3	(16.8–19.8)
Mississippi	27.9	(25.2–30.6)	22.5	(20.8–24.2)	25.1	(23.5–26.7)
Missouri	24.7	(21.6–27.8)	22.1	(19.9–24.3)	23.3	(21.4–25.2)
Montana	18.5	(16.3–20.7)	19.6	(17.9–21.3)	19.0	(17.6–20.4)
Nebraska	19.6	(17.5–21.7)	17.7	(16.1–19.3)	18.6	(17.3–19.9)
Nevada	22.9	(19.7–26.1)	21.4	(18.5–24.3)	22.2	(20.0–24.4)
New Hampshire	19.3	(17.2–21.4)	18.2	(16.6–19.8)	18.7	(17.4–20.0)
New jersey	20.8	(19.1–22.5)	15.6	(14.5–16.7)	18.1	(17.1–19.1)
New Mexico	22.6	(20.3–24.9)	17.8	(16.2–19.4)	20.2	(18.8–21.6)
New York	19.0	(16.8–21.2)	17.6	(15.9–19.3)	18.3	(16.9–19.7)

(continued)

TABLE **7.4** *(continued)*

Estimated Prevalence of Current Cigarette Smoking[1] Among Adults, by Area and Sex—Behavioral Risk Factor Surveillance System, United States, 2006

State/Area	Men %	Men (95% CI[2])	Women %	Women (95% CI)	Total %	Total (95% CI)
North Carolina	25.3	(23.7–26.9)	19.0	(17.9–20.1)	22.1	(21.1–23.1)
North Dakota	21.0	(18.4–23.6)	18.1	(16.1–20.1)	19.6	(18.0–21.2)
Ohio	24.9	(21.0–28.8)	20.2	(17.6–22.8)	22.5	(20.2–24.8)
Oklahoma	27.9	(25.7–30.1)	22.5	(21.0–24.0)	25.1	(23.7–26.5)
Oregon	19.7	(17.3–22.1)	17.2	(15.5–18.9)	18.5	(17.0–20.0)
Pennsylvania	22.3	(19.9–24.7)	20.8	(19.1–22.5)	21.5	(20.0–23.0)
Rhode Island	19.7	(16.9–22.5)	18.9	(16.8–21.0)	19.3	(17.6–21.0)
South Carolina	25.7	(23.6–27.8)	19.2	(17.8–20.6)	22.3	(21.1–23.5)
South Dakota	21.6	(19.2–24.0)	19.2	(17.4–21.0)	20.4	(18.9–21.9)
Tennessee	23.8	(20.7–26.9)	21.5	(19.3–23.7)	22.6	(20.7–24.5)
Texas	20.6	(17.8–23.4)	15.6	(13.7–17.5)	18.1	(16.4–19.8)
Utah	10.4	(8.6–12.2)	9.2	(7.8–10.6)	9.8	(8.7–10.9)
Vermont	19.4	(17.5–23.3)	16.7	(15.2–18.2)	18.0	(16.8–19.2)
Virginia	20.1	(17.6–22.6)	18.5	(16.3–20.7)	19.3	(17.7–20.9)
Washington	18.9	(17.7–20.1)	15.3	(14.5–16.1)	17.1	(16.4–17.8)
West Virginia	25.4	(22.7–28.1)	26.0	(23.7–28.3)	25.7	(23.9–27.5)
Wisconsin	23.4	(20.8–26.0)	18.3	(16.4–20.2)	20.8	(19.2–22.4)
Wyoming	23.8	(21.4–26.2)	19.4	(17.6–21.2)	21.6	(20.1–23.1)
Median	22.2	–	18.5	–	20.2	–
Puerto Rico	17.4	(15.1–19.7)	8.2	(7.0–9.4)	12.5	(11.2–13.8)
U.S. Virgin Islands	12.1	(9.8–14.4)	6.4	(5.2–7.6)	9.1	(7.8–10.4)

Source: http://www.cdc.gov/mmwr/preview/mmwrhtml/mm5638a2.html]

[1]Persons aged ≥ 18 years who reported having smoked ≥ 100 cigarettes during their lifetime and who currently smoke every day or same days.
[2]Confidence interval.

Americans acculturated to mainstream European American ways (Klonoff & Landrine, 2001). In contrast, some Asian Americans and Latinos are less likely to smoke if they are more traditional in their ways (Lafferty, Heaney, & Chen, 1999). In another interaction of smoking and ethnicity, Llabre, Klein, Saab, McCalla, and Schneiderman (1998) found that when African Americans are exposed to stress (demonstrated in an experimental setting), they show greater changes in the functioning of their blood vessels than in the functioning of their heart muscles. This has implications for the development of cerebrovascular disease for African Americans who are smokers.

TABLE **7.5**

Percentage Regular Daily Smokers by Country, Adults Aged 15 Years and Over, Latest Year Between 1997 and 2005, Selected European Countries

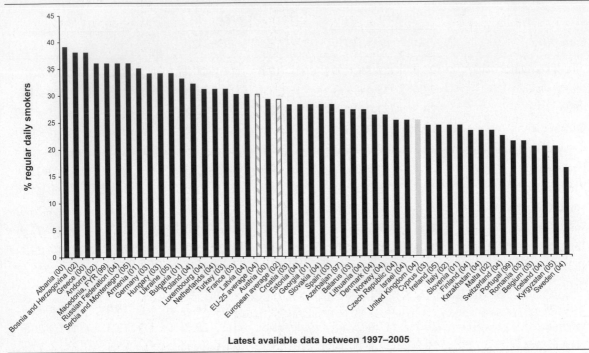

Latest available data between 1997–2005

Source: World Health Organization (2006) European Health for All statistical database. http://www.euro.who.int/hfadb. Office for National Statistics (2005) Living in Britain: Results from the 2004 General Household Survey. The Stationery Office: London.

Why Do People Smoke?

In keeping with the biopsychosocial approach of health psychology, biological, psychological, and social factors contribute to the initiation of smoking. Biologically, nicotine has some pleasing effects on the brain and body, and it works extremely fast. The moment a smoker puffs a cigarette, the nicotine is absorbed through the fine inner lining of the cheek and reaches the brain within 15 seconds. In general, nicotine causes good moods, reduced feelings of hunger, and increased alertness and attention (Grunberg, Faraday, & Rahman, 2002).

In addition to these biological effects, there are some clear genetic components to smoking (Pomerleau & Kardia, 1999). If one member of an identical twin set chooses to smoke, the other will probably smoke as well. Is a specific gene involved? Lerman et al. (1999) showed that versions of the dopamine transporter gene *SLC6A3* and the dopamine receptor gene *DRD2* are associated with the likelihood of smoking. People who had specific versions of these genes were more likely to start smoking before age 16 than those individuals who did not have them. The genotype most related to addictive behavior, *DRD2-A1*, was most commonly found in African Americans, the ethnic group with high smoking rates. Another clue to the physiological reasons for smoking

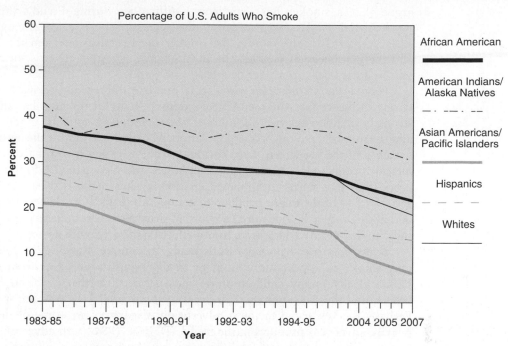

FIGURE **7.5** Percentage of U.S. Adults Who Smoke
There are significant differences in smoking rates across cultural groups.
Source: National Health Interview Survey.
Source: *National Center for Health Statistics, Centers for Disease Control and Prevention, 1978–1995. Health, United States (2004).*

comes from studies showing how people are addicted to nicotine. Smokers may not even be conscious of the extent of their physiological addiction. For example, when unknowing smokers were given cigarettes that had lower levels of nicotine, they automatically puffed longer and took more puffs (Schachter, 1980). Consequently, they smoked more low-nicotine cigarettes to get amounts of the nicotine comparable to those that they were used to.

Psychological Causes of Addiction

People start smoking for many psychological reasons. Some personality types, such as individuals with low self-esteem who can be easily influenced or extroverts who savor the stimulation of nicotine, are more likely to smoke. Extroverts find the nicotine arousal rewarding and smoke to increase this arousal. Some of the developmental theories discussed in Chapter 3 also help to explain initiation. For example, Erikson's theory of human social development suggests that the struggle both to overcome inferiority and establish an identity can make a person more likely to smoke. Others have extended Erikson's theory to explain adolescent deviant behavior. Turbin, Jessor, and Costa (2000) see problem behaviors such as smoking as special cases of the transition process experienced by all adolescents. Although difficult to measure and not conclusively linked to smoking, some theorists and many advertisers have used psychoanalytical theory to explain smoking. These groups argue that a smoker has experienced difficulties during Freud's theorized psychosocial oral stage. Because the pleasure-causing erogenous zone (see Chapter 3) is the mouth, the smoker derives pleasure from the mouth and the placement of the cigarette in it. Many suggestive advertisements also use Freudian ideas to attract people to smoking.

People start smoking for many social and cultural reasons. Movies can be a strong influence (see Chapter 6). An extensive body of research has shown a strong correlation between the number of people shown smoking in the movies and the number smoking in the population. Many people imitate the heroes and heroines of the big screen. Even cartoons are not off limits to tobacco companies for product placements. Goldstein, Sobel, and Newman (1999) found that more than two thirds of animated children's films made between 1937 and 1997 by five of the major production companies (e.g., Walt Disney, Universal, and 20th Century Fox) featured tobacco in story plots without clear verbal messages of any negative long-term health effects associated with its use.

Sometimes social pressure leads people to smoke. Rebellious adolescents may smoke to appear more adult or to distinguish themselves from others. Paradoxically, many children start smoking because they want to be like others, and thus they imitate their peers or family members who are smoking. Perhaps the key social factor is advertising. Cigarettes are some of the most heavily advertised products in the media (DHHS, 1994) with advertising budgets reaching more than $1 billion per year. Until recently, younger children were the key targets. Camel cigarettes had a cartoon character named Joe Camel that was recognized second to only Mickey Mouse among North American children (Grunberg, Brown, & Klein, 1997). It is suggested that the use of the cartoon character and the subsequent higher familiarity of the Camel brand accounts for why close to 40 percent of adolescent smokers began smoking with Camels or Camel Lights.

Physiological Consequences of Smoking

There is no doubt that smoking can kill. A smoker has a significantly greater chance of dying earlier than a nonsmoker, if all other variables are held constant. The chance increases with the amount smoked, the length of time one has smoked, and the tar and nicotine contents of the cigarettes (Grunberg et al., 1997). The longer one smokes, the greater the risk of dying prematurely. The overall risk of dying also increases for smokers who inhale smoke versus those who only puff it in and out. Smokers are most likely to die prematurely from coronary heart disease, related cardiovascular diseases, or a range of cancers of the respiratory tract. Common smoking-related cancers are cancers of the lung, larynx, oral cavity, pancreas, and esophagus. Cigarette smoke is by far the most common cause of emphysema, a progressive lung disease (Carpenter et al., 2007). Table 7.6 shows how the rates of cancer vary for men and women and how the risks are lower for nonsmokers.

Smoking has a **synergistic effect** on many health issues. Women who use oral contraceptives and who smoke have an increased risk of dying from ovarian, cervical, or uterine cancers (Vessey, Painter, & Yeates, 2003). Teenage girls who smoke have an increased risk of developing breast cancer before they reach menopause (Band, Le, Fang, & Deschamps, 2002). Similarly,

Smoking

Early media campaigns (before media advertising was regulated by the Surgeon General) used celebrities to get people to smoke. Here the then Hollywood actor and later President Ronald Reagan and President Roosevelt appear in ads and press photos with cigarettes lit.

people who have coronary heart disease and who smoke are more likely to die from a heart attack than are nonsmokers with coronary heart disease (Goldenberg et al., 2003). Howard et al. (1998) found that cigarette smoking increases plaque formation around arteries by as much as 50 percent in a three-year period. This atherosclerosis can increase blood pressure and hasten the occurrence of a stroke or cardiac arrest. Among women undergoing treatment for early breast cancer, those who smoke are more than twice as likely to die from the cancer as are nonsmoking women. In a study examining the effect of smoking on long-term outcomes of breast cancer patients treated with conservative surgery and radiation, researchers found that women who continue to smoke during therapy are 2.5 times more likely to die from the cancer than are women with no history of smoking (American Cancer Society, 2005). The study examined 1,039 nonsmokers and 861 smokers who underwent conservative therapy for breast cancer from March 1970 to December 2002. In addition, smoking correlates with increased occurrences of numerous diseases from sexual impotence to vision and hearing problems and ovarian cysts to multiple sclerosis and even the common cold (American Cancer Society, 2005).

Although still debatable because of conflicting studies, the evidence weighs in against **secondhand smoke** or **environmental tobacco smoke** (ETS). ETS is

TABLE **7.6**

Smoking and Cancer Mortality Table. Not all Cancers are Equally
Influenced by Smoking. Notice the Differences in Relative Risk from
Smoking for the Different Types of Cancers and the Sex Differences

Type of Cancer	Gender	Relative Risk Among Smokers	Relative Risk Among Smokers	Mortality Attributable to Smoking	Mortality Attributable to Smoking
		Current	Former	Percent	Number
Lung	Male	22.4	9.4	90	82,800
	Female	11.9	4.7	79	40,300
Larynx	Male	10.5	5.2	81	24,000
	Female	17.8	11.9	87	700
Oral Cavity	Male	27.5	8.8	92	4,900
	Female	5.6	2.9	61	1,800
Esophagus	Male	7.6	5.8	78	5,700
	Female	10.3	3.2	75	1,900
Pancreas	Male	2.1	1.1	29	3,500
	Female	2.3	1.8	34	4,500
Bladder	Male	2.9	1.9	47	3,000
	Female	2.6	1.9	37	1,200
Kidney	Male	3.0	2.0	48	3,000
	Female	1.4	1.2	12	500
Stomach	Male	1.5	?	17	1,400
	Female	1.5	?	25	1,300
Leukemia	Male	2.0	?	20	2,000
	Female	2.0	?	20	1,600
Cervix	Female	2.1	1.9	31	1,400
Endometrial	Female	0.7	1.0	—	—

Source: Center for Disease Control. Annual smoking-attributable mortality, years of potential life lost, and productivity losses—United States, 1997–2001. MMWR 2005;54:625–628.

the tobacco smoke inhaled by nonsmokers who are in the presence of smokers. This passive smoking is linked to lung cancer (Kreuzer, Krauss, Kreienbrock, Jockel, & Wichmann, 2000) and cardiovascular disease (He et al., 1999; Kawachi et al., 1997). Infants and children are probably most at risk from ETS. Early exposure to ETS has been linked to an increased risk of asthma (Larsson, Frisk, Hallstrom, Kiviloog, & Lundback, 2001). All in all, it is clear that any amount of tobacco use is detrimental to health.

DRINKING

When health psychologists refer to drinking as a health behavior, they are referring to alcohol consumption. Drinking water seems to be good for youalthough the "drink 8 glasses of water a day" prescription was recently found to have no scientific basis (Negoianu & Goldfarb, 2008)—everybody promotes the prescription, but nobody is sure where it came from). In contrast, alcohol consumption is responsible for 100,000 deaths each year, the third-leading cause of death after tobacco and insufficient physical activity and poor diet (McGinnis & Foege, 1993; Mokdad et al., 2005). Be aware that whether drinking alcohol is a good thing or a bad thing has probably stimulated more spirited conversations than any other health behavior topic. Smoking is dangerous, no question, but is drinking? The government recommendation is that men can consume "safely" two drinks per day and that women can safely consume one drink per day (USDA, 2000). You have also probably had friends justify their drinking by citing research concluding that a drink per day is actually *better* than no drinks at all. Is this true? How much alcohol, if any at all, is healthy? First, let's get familiar with usage.

Who Drinks, How Much, and Why?

Patterns for drinking and causes for initiation of drinking are similar to those for smoking. This chapter outlines some of the major differences. In 2006, 67 percent of men and 56 percent of women were classified as drinkers (DHHS, 2007). Alcohol is the drug of choice among high school youth with

© Art Resource, Inc.

Drinking and Addiction

The British painter William Hogarth had some strong opinions of what could happen if people drank too much strong liquor. In Gin Lane (1751) he represents the horror of what could happen if people became addicted to gin.

51 percent of high school seniors having used alcohol in the past 30 days (NIDA, 2000). While many sources suggest that some drinking is all right, it is important to distinguish between use and misuse. **Alcohol abuse** is characterized by one or more of the following as a result of alcohol use: (1) failure to fulfill major role obligations; (2) recurrent physically hazardous use; (3) recurrent alcohol-related legal problems; or (4) continued use despite persistent alcohol-related social or interpersonal problems (Wood, Vinson, & Sher, 2002). At most colleges, alcohol abuse is evident. Nearly half of college students are **binge drinkers**—men who have consumed five or more drinks in a row and women who have consumed four or more drinks in a row at least once during the previous 2 weeks (Wechler, Moeykens, Davenport, Castillo, & Hansen, 2000). Alcohol has also been linked to severity of aggression, especially at bars and parties for college students (Tremblay, Graham, & Wells, 2008). In the general population, approximately 13.8 million people abuse alcohol or are dependent on it (Grant et al., 1994). Alcohol abuse is 2.5 to 5 times higher in men than in women, but this sex difference is least pronounced in people age 18 to 24 (Grant et al., 1991). Like smoking, many cultural differences are manifested in drinking, especially across ethnic, SES, religious, and geographical lines. Beer is the most commonly consumed of alcohol (57% of drinkers) followed by hard liquor (e.g., gin, rum, and vodka, 29%) and wine (13%) (Williams, Stinson, Sanchez, & Dufour, 1998).

As with many other health behaviors, it is important to take a biopsychosocial approach to understanding why people drink. Biologicallye, there are some genetic predictors of alcoholism (Johnson-Greene, & Denning, 2008). Alcohol misuse tends to run in families (Merikangas, 1990), and identical twins have a much higher concordance of both alcohol use and misuse than fraternal twins (Ball & Murray, 1994; McGue, 1999). This shows that there are genetic predispositions to starting to drink. Research has even identified different markers at the genetic level. For example, people with certain genes, such as the beta-subunit of alcohol dehydrogenase, are more sensitive to alcohol (Johnson-Greene, & Denning, 2008). The presence of this gene varies across ethnic groups (McGue, 1999; NIAAA, 1993). Earlier research was misleading. For example, from the early 1990s, researchers were certain that the dopamine DRD2 receptor gene was one of the best markers for severe alcoholism (Blum et al., 1990). Later research showed this not to be the case (Gelernter, Goldman, & Risch, 1992). However, there is considerable optimism that we are close to identifying the key genes that place a person at risk for alcoholism (McGue, 1999). Some significant nongenetic biological markers of vulnerability to alcoholism are known. Children of alcoholics, a vulnerable group, have different brain wave activity (reduced P3 waves) in response to the presentation of alcohol-related stimuli material (Polich, Pollock, & Bloom, 1994). They show also lower activity levels of the enzyme monoamine oxidase (von Knorring, Oreland, & von Knorring, 1987) and are less sensitive to the subjective intoxicating effects of alcohol (Schucklit, 1994). The lower sensitivity to alcohol (i.e., they do not feel as "buzzed" as a more sensitive person after drinking) may lead them to drink greater amounts.

Psychologically, three broad personality characteristics are linked to alcoholism. People who are high in neuroticism, who are impulsive, and who are extroverted are more likely to become alcoholic (Sher & Trull, 1994). Given the many behaviors with which these traits are associated, they are seen more as mediators or moderating variables within larger psychosocial etiological models of alcoholism (Wood et al., 2002). They are not direct causes of alcoholism. Research has also identified patterns of thinking that could put a person at risk for alcoholism. Maisto, Carey, and Bradizza (1999) reviewed the ways that social learning theories have been applied to alcohol use. This review showed that there are a number of specific beliefs that people have about the behavioral, cognitive, and emotional effects of drinking (alcohol outcome expectancies), which can predict their likelihood of drinking (see also Goldman, DelBoca, & Darkes, 1999). For example, if young adults have a positive alcohol outcome expectancy (they expect good effects from drinking) before the first time they drink, then they are more likely to drink more subsequently (Smith, Goldman, Greenbaum, & Christiansen, 1995).

Blending biological and psychological causes of drinking, alcohol also seems to be used to reduce stress (Cappell & Greeley, 1987). The consumption of alcohol serves as a reinforcement: the positive feelings after alcohol consumption increase the behavior of drinking, and drinking is associated with a decrease in stress. For example, students in a study were told that they were taking part in a taste test to obscure the true intent of the researchers (to test effects of alcohol). These students drank more when they were stressed by the experimentersthan when they were not (Statsiewicz & Lisman, 1989). Alcohol, stress, and smoking all go together: In a study of African American women, Webb and Cary (2008) found that the odds of smoking were greater for older women who had less education, lower income, greater perceived stress, and more frequent heavy alcohol use.

With whom people spend their time makes a difference in how much they drink. From a psychosocial standpoint, children of alcoholics are more likely to drink (Chassin, Rogosch, & Barrera, 1991), as are people with friends who drink (Wills & Cleary, 1999). Curran, Stice, and Chassin (1997) also showed that drinkers do not just pick friends who drink, but drinkers can make nondrinkers start drinking. Sometimes, just believing that it is normal to drink can make a person drink even if this perceived norm is completely inaccurate. Baer, Stacy, and Larimer (1991) found that college students nearly always perceived that their close friends consumed alcohol more frequently than they did. Accuracy does matter (and not in a way you would expect). At campuses where students have more accurate perceptions of alcohol use, students are likely to drink on more days throughout the year than at campuses where students have greater misperceptions of alcohol use (Licciardone, 2003).

Finally, as with smoking, the media and advertising also play a large part in getting people to start drinking (Grube & Wallack, 1994). In a study of over 1,000 sixth, seventh, and eighth graders, researchers found the following: 29 percent of those who never drank alcohol either owned or wanted to use an alcohol branded promotional item; 12 percent of students could name the brand of their favorite alcohol ad; and, 59 percent were not receptive to alcohol marketing (Henriksen, Feighery, Schleicher, & Fortmann, 2008). During a follow-up study one year later, approximately 29 percent of the adolescents reported having drunk alcohol, and 13 percent reported drinking at least one or two days in the past month. Those who had never had alcohol at the time of the initial study, but who had reported high receptivity to alcohol marketing, were 77 percent more likely to have started drinking by the follow-up study than those who had not been receptive to the alcohol advertising.

Consequences of Alcohol Abuse

Drinking too much has been shown to negatively impact most organ systems and to be a major cause of injuries, many of them fatal (NIAAA, 1997). For many of the injuries, age is a critical factor because consequences of drinking are different across the lifespan. Prenatal infants often suffer the consequences of alcohol. Of course, they are not doing the drinking. Mothers who drink during pregnancy can influence the development of their fetuses. Fetal alcohol syndrome, described in Chapter 3, results in developmental abnormalities and is a major result of mothers drinking (NIAAA, 1997; Streissguth et al., 1994). Alcohol-related motor accidents are the leading consequence of drinking for underage drinkers. The 21-year age limit is more than an arbitrary line drawn by the government (although it may have originally been one). A report compiling several studies on brain damage and alcohol concluded that underage drinkers face a greater risk of damage to the prefrontal regions of their brains. Double the amount of alcohol is required to do the same damage to someone older than 21. The development of the frontal lobes continues until age 16, after which the brain maintains a high rate of energy expenditure that does not decrease until age 20 (Hoover, 2002). Consequently, underage drinking does retard brain cell growth.

Liver disease is one of the most common consequences of drinking excessively for older drinkers (Crabb, 1993). Problems range from excess fat in the liver to a swelling of the liver or to permanent and progressive scarring, referred to as cirrhosis of the liver. The risks of developing cirrhosis vary by sex; women are more likely to develop the problem (Lieber, 1994). Drinking too much—more than six drinks per day (less for some)—also increases the risk of cardiovascular problems (Richardson, Wodak, Atkinson, Saunders, & Jewitt, 1986) and stroke (NIAAA, 1997). Drinking three to four drinks per day and drinking frequently have both been linked to hypertension (Marmot et al., 1994; Russel, Cooper, Frone, & Welte, 1991; Thadhani et al., 2002). Other health consequences include problems with the pancreas (Steinberg & Tenner, 1994), blackouts (Vinson, 1989), memory loss (Parsons, 1994), and chronic brain disease (Victor, 1993).

Together with its interactions with other health behaviors, alcohol use also relates to many different psychological problems and negative social behaviors. Families in which the parents abuse alcohol are often uncomfortable environments for a child. More fighting and conflict, less cohesion and expressiveness, and more child injuries are reported in alcoholic families (Bijur, Kurzon, Overpeck, & Scheidt, 1992; Sher, 1991). People who abuse alcohol are also more likely to partake in risky sex (Leigh & Stall, 1993), drive dangerously (Yi, Stinson, Williams, & Bertolucci, 1998), and be involved in crimes such as assault (Murdoch, Pihl, & Ross, 1990) and especially sexual assault (Cole, 2006; Roizen, 1997). People who drink too much alcohol or drink too often are also more at risk for a range of psychological disorders, such as anxiety and mood disorders (Kessler et al., 1997). Note, however, that in many of these cases, it is hard to establish causal links because of the many other factors that may have been involved.

The possibility of the benefits of some alcohol consumption has received a lot of media attention in the last few years. Some reports show evidence of health benefits for small or moderate amounts of alcohol consumption (Albert et al., 1999; Friedman, Armstrong, Kipp, & Klatsky, 2001). In fact, current research is showing that people who consume two standard drinks per day have a 20 percent lower risk for coronary heart disease than those who do not drink (Corrao, Bagnardi, Vittadini, & Favilli, 2000). What is a **standard drink?** The medical field agrees that a 12-ounce serving of beer (a standard bottle or can), a 5-ounce glass of wine, or 1.5-ounces of gin, vodka, rum, or scotch, is a standard serving.

Some hypothesize moderate alcohol consumption to be the answer to the **French paradox**—the fact that most people in France have a diet that is high in fat, yet still have lower rates of heart disease. For example, Renaud, Gueguen, Siest, and Salamon (1999) studied 36,250 healthy French men between 1978 and 1983 and found that both those who drank beer (28% of the sample) and those who drank wine (61%) had less risk of cardiovascular diseases. The reduction in mortality risk varies depending on what one consumes. People who drink a glass of wine each day show a lower risk for mortality than those who drink spirits or beer (Gronbaek at al., 1995; Renaud et al., 1999). Still, this lowered risk may be due to other positive health behaviors that wine drinkers perform, or to healthy elements in their environment (Mortensen, Jensen, Sanders, & Reinisch, 2001; Wannamethee & Shaper, 1999). For instance, wine drinkers may be better off economically, may eat better, and may exercise more. Yet, there are actual benefits to moderate alcohol consumption, which are tied to the ability of alcohol to reduce the risk for coronary heart disease by raising the drinker's levels of high-density lipoprotein (HDL) cholesterol. Higher levels of HDL cholesterol help to keep the arteries free of blockage. So should nondrinkers older than 21 now start drinking? The answer is "no" still (Bau, Bau, Rosito, Manfroi, & Fuchs, 2007; Fuchs, & Chambless, 2007). There is simply not enough clinical and epidemiological evidence for science to recommend the consumption of alcohol to those who abstain. Remember, other health behaviors can lower the risk of coronary heart disease, and moderate drinkers face the risk of becoming heavy drinkers, which would truly be detrimental to their health. Furthermore, the French eat smaller serving sizes than Americans, which could partially explain the paradox (so wine may not be your answer to overeating).

SYNTHESIZE, EVALUATE, APPLY	<ul><li>What are the common elements underlying the performance of health behaviors?</li><li>How would high levels of stress influence each of these behaviors and why?</li><li>What are possible causes for the cultural differences seen in the performance of each behavior?</li><li>What should the priorities for future research on health behaviors be?</li><li>What aspects of twenty-first-century society accentuate the performance of unhealthy behaviors?</li></ul>

FOCUS ON APPLICATIONS

The Truth about the "Freshman Fifteen"

Almost every college first year student has been warned to watch out for the dreaded "Freshman Fifteen." Stories of this mythical beast, the supposed 15 pound weight gain that takes place during the first year of college, has echoed around college dorms and hallways for decades. Parents warn their sons and daugthers to be careful, and friends and classmates at school are on the lookout for the impending additional pounds. Similar to the "drink eight glasses of water a day" rule (debunked by Negoianu & Goldfarb, 2008), the facts on this issue are still unclear. Given the severe health consequences of being overweight, and that millions of college students could be at risk if this phenomenon is valid, is the Freshman 15 is a great topicto explore. The "freshman 15" is a good example of how our biology, our psychology, and societal factors interact. Our discussion of the topic also provides us with another opportunity to explore health psychology. Besides, scrutinizing data (if any) of folklore is fun!

The good news is that there is some solid research on the topic (Butler, Black, Blue, Gretebeck, 2004; Holm-Denoma, Joiner, Vohs, & Heatherton, 2008; Morrow, Heesch, Dinger, Hull, Kneehans, & Fields, 2006). The bad news is that if you only listened to the spin the media put on the research without reading actual articles from the research, you may wind up misinformed or underinformed. It is imperative to good research and study to read original research (you should be looking up articles cited in this book on the topics that interest you). Even research that does not completely support the freshman 15 idea (e.g., Levitsky, Halbmaier, Mrdjenovic, 2004) is spun to sound like it does. In order for you to better understand this (and how it can be misinterpreted), we will discuss three studies on college student weight gain.

Firstly, it is easy to see why the freshman 15 idea is intuitively believable. You do not need to be a first-year student to know that some students gain weight in school. Professors often notice the difference in students' appearances even from fall to spring sessions!" Going to college, away from the routine of home and home-cooked food, can change certainly dietary patterns. Most college food is not considered especially low in fat or healthy. College students are continuously exposed to unhealthy food options like low-cost food and fast food. Due to late-night studying, they can experience drastic shifts in sleep-wake cycles and associated snacking, and many skip breakfast and make other unhealthy food-related choices. In 2004, the media exposed a study that seemed to support the freshman 15 idea. Levitsky et al., (2004) studied 60 first-year students from Cornell University recruited from two large introductory courses. The students were weighed at the beginning and end of their first 12 weeks of college. The students, on average, gained about 0.3 pound per week, which is almost 11 times more than the weekly weight gain expected in 17 and 18 year olds and almost 20 times more than the average weight gain of an American adult. However, the results showed that the mean weight gain of the first-year students was a little over four pounds. Four pounds. Not fifteen. The study showed that the two main influences for the weight gain were eating in the "all-you-can-eat" dining halls and snacking and eating high-fat "junk food." More than likely, the media picked up only the statistics that showed some students in the study gaining as much as 18 pounds. However, by reading the original article, you will learn that some of the students even *lost* 13 pounds!

The low mean in the Levitsky et al. (2004) study is not an anomaly. Morrow, et al. (2006), studied 137 first-year women students during the 2004 to 2005 academic year. A baseline measurement occurred within the first six weeks of the fall semester, with the follow-up visit occurring during the last six weeks of the following spring semester. At each visit, the researchers measured height, weight, BMI, waist and hip circumferences, and body composition. Morrow et al. (2006) found significant increases on all measures except waist-to-hip ratio. The mean weight gain was only 2.2. pounds.

A different study by Holm-Denoma et al. (2008) used a larger sample size (607 students) with both men and women participating. The study was robust. They studied

(continues)

FOCUS ON APPLICATIONS *(continued)*

students during their last year of high school (not first year of college) through the first nine months of their first college term. They not only recorded the students' weight and height, but measured self-esteem, eating habits, interpersonal relationships, exercise patterns, and disordered eating behaviors throughout the study. The results showed that both men and women gained a significant amount of weight (3.5 and 4.0 pounds, respectively). Weight gain occurred before the end of the fall semester and was maintained as the year progressed. Similar to Levitsky et al., (2004) students in this sample also gained weight at a much higher rate than that of average American adults. For men (and somewhat paradoxically), frequently engaging in exercise predicted weight gain as did (not so paradoxically) having troublesome relationships with parents. For women, having positive relationships with parents predicted weight gain.

SUMMARY

- Obesity is one of America's greatest health threats. Few Americans eat a balanced diet or get a sufficient amount of nutrients. Obesity increases the chances of developing a chronic disease and increases the chances of developing coronary heart disease. Obesity can be caused by both genetic and environmental influences. MyPyramid illustrates the USDA recommendations for a healthy diet and has been modified for different cultural groups.
- Food preferences develop at an early age and are strongly influenced by the ways parents feed infants and children. There are innate preferences, but the majority of our tastes come about because of exposure to various foods as we grow.
- Physical activity is any bodily movement that results in energy expenditure. People should get at least 30 minutes of physical activity five times per week to maintain a healthy lifestyle. Ethnic, socioeconomic, age, and sex differences all account for cultural differences in physical activity. Physically active individuals are less likely to develop coronary heart disease and are more likely to live longer. Physical activity has also been associated with better mental health.
- Smoking is most common among college-aged individuals. Rates of smoking are dropping across most age groups (except the 18 to 24 year range). The most pronounced differences are ethnic and racial, followed by socioeconomic status. Evidence is building to support a genetic component to smoking, whereas a number of different personality traits, such as low self-esteem and extroversion, are associated with increased addiction to smoking. The media and movies are also linked to rates of smoking.
- Smokers are much more likely to die prematurely from coronary heart disease and numerous cancers than nonsmokers are and there are significant sex differences in rates of cancer due to smoking.
- Alcohol consumption is responsible for more than 100,000 deaths each year although some research suggests that drinking moderate levels of alcohol can actually have health benefits. Like smoking, there are genetic and environmental reasons for alcohol abuse. People who are extroverted, neurotic, and impulsive are most likely to abuse alcohol. Drinking too much has been shown to negatively impact most organ systems and to be a major cause of injuries.

TEST YOURSELF

Check your understanding of the topics in this chapter by answering the following questions. Answers appear in the Appendix.

1. The most current guide to eating, MyPyramid, was published in:
   a. 1930.
   b. 1984.
   c. 1990.
   d. 2005.

2. According to Chinese and Indian cultures, garlic, onions, most grains, alcohol, and oils are all considered:
   a. cold foods.
   b. hot foods.
   c. energy foods.
   d. Qi foods.

3. Westernization has often been blamed for problems with obesity. Strong evidence comes from the study of Pima Indians (Ravussin et al., 1994). Which of the following results is correct?
   a. acculturated Pima Indians had the highest BMIs
   b. unacculturated Pima Indians had the highest BMIs
   c. U.S. Pima Indians had the highest BMIs
   d. Mexican Pima Indians had the highest BMIs

4. Having more varieties of food present often leads to the consumption of more food. This phenomenon is referred to as:
   a. lipid overload theory.
   b. sensory specific satiety.
   c. hypersatiation.
   d. hyper sensory saturation.

5. Which of the following statements about culture and eating disorders is NOT TRUE?
   a. Most body image research has focused on European Americans.
   b. Cultures vary in ideal body shape perceptions.
   c. Eating disorders are primarily a problem associated with European Americans.
   d. Research has found no differences between Asian and European American women.

6. Which of the following is the primary carcinogenic component of smoking?
   a. nicotine
   b. tar
   c. damage to air sacs/alveoli
   d. higher lung carbon monoxide

7. The standard definition of "overweight" according to U.S. medical institutions is a BMI rate that is:
   a. closer to 1.00.
   b. above 20.
   c. between 25 and 29.
   d. over 30.

8. One of the paradoxical synergistic effects of smoking relates to stress. New data show that:
   a. stress can actually make a nonsmoker start to smoke.
   b. stress could make someone likely to drink more, and therefore possibly start smoking.
   c. smoking and stress are actually not related at all.
   d. smoking and nicotine addiction could actually make someone more stressed.

9. The ethnic group with the highest smoking rate is:
   a. African American.
   b. Asian American.
   c. Latino.
   d. European American.

10. People high in the personality traits of _____ are more at risk of becoming alcoholic.
    a. neuroticism and conscientiousness
    b. neuroticism and extraversion
    c. extraversion and pessimism
    d. pessimism and self-esteem

WEB RESOURCES

Visit the companion Web site at **www.cengage.com/psychology/gurung**, where you will find online resources for this book, including chapter-by-chapter quizzes, Web links, and more!

MyPyramid
www.MyPyramid.gov

This site will allow you to take a closer look at the food pyramid and what choices are right for you. The site includes detailed information on what and how much you should be eating.

Center for Disease Control
http://www.cdc.ov/tobacco/

This site has a tobacco information page and a variety of resources including recent research on the topic.

National Jewish
http://nationaljewish.org/justquit/justquit.html

This site offers excellent resources to help people quit smoking.

Canadian Smokefree
http://www.smoke-free.ca/default.htm

This site is a great way to check how many toxins you are exposed to from secondhand smoke.

KEY TERMS, CONCEPTS, AND PEOPLE

addiction, 232
alcohol abuse, 242
behavioral cueing, 232
binge drinkers, 242
body mass index, 220
exercise, 229
Food Guide Pyramid, 215
food preferences, 219
French paradox, 245
mental health, 231
National Health Interview Survey, 230
obesity, 220
physical activity, 227
secondhand smoke/environmental tobacco smoke, 239
sensory specific satiety, 225
standard drink, 245
Surgeon General's Report, 230
synergistic effect, 238
Third National Health and Nutritional Examination Survey, 230

ESSENTIAL READINGS

Dubbert, P. M. (2002). Physical activity and exercise: Recent advances and current challenges. *Journal of Consulting and Clinical Psychology*, 70(3), 526–536.

Marlatt, G. A., & Witkiewitz, K. (2002). Harm reduction approaches to alcohol use: Health promotion, prevention, and treatment. *Addictive Behaviors*, 27(6), 867–886.

Niaura, R., & Abrams, D. B. (2002). Smoking cessation: Progress, priorities, and prospectus. *Journal of Consulting and Clinical Psychology*, 70(3), 494–509.

Wadden, T. A.Brownell, K. D., & Foster, G. D. (2002). Obesity: Responding to the global epidemic. *Journal of Consulting and Clinical Psychology*, 70(3), 510–525.

Factors Surrounding Illness

W hat do you do if you have a headache? Most of us wait some time to see if it goes away and then take a pill if it does not. What if you sprain your ankle or pull a muscle? Most of us have heard that you first apply a cold pack, then apply a hot pack, and then wrap the ankle and rest. However, more complex remedies may be required for other types of aches or pains. What if you develop a rash or your skin turns different colors? What if you have a deep throbbing pain in your stomach that does not go away? What if you find a lump under your skin? Do you go to your doctor immediately? Do you use a homemade family remedy and see if the problem goes away? Would you have a local shaman sacrifice a chicken for you? Physical, mental, emotional, and spiritual health are all positive contributions to well-being; however, we all can face adversity at some point in our lives. Different cultures have different ways of coping and reacting to symptoms of illness. This chapter describes what we do when we do not feel well. We will focus primarily on physical health and describe what we do if and when we get sick (for a complete description of the role of culture in mental health, refer to Eshun & Gurung, 2009). Figure 8.1 shows an overview of the main stages in the process of feeling better and the major accompanying factors. If you are seriously considering a career in the health care profession, especially as a doctor or nurse, this chapter is especially important for you to read.

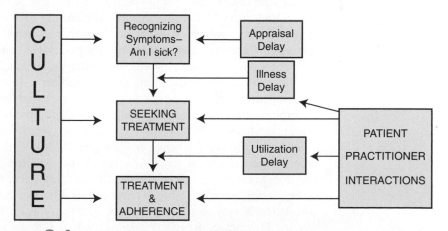

FIGURE **8.1** Overview of the Main Stages of an Illness and Some of the Critical Delays in Seeking Treatment

CULTURE AND ILLNESS BEHAVIORS

Many factors surround illness, and culture influences every one of them (Galanti, 2004; Loue, Lane, Lloyd, & Loh, 1999). Before we are treated, we have to recognize that we have a problem. We then seek treatment. Once we get a diagnosis, we have to adhere to the course of treatment prescribed for us. Recognition, seeking treatment, and adhering to treatment—collectively referred to as illness behaviors—are three main stages influenced by our cultural backgrounds. **Illness behaviors** are the varying ways individuals respond to physiological symptoms, monitor internal states, define and interpret symptoms, make attributions, take remedial actions, and utilize various forms of informal and formal care (Mechanic, 1995). A number of sociodemographic variables such as age, sex, ethnicity, and socioeconomic status can influence peoples' illness behaviors. For example, African Americans' mistrust of the health care system is often cited as a cause of racial disparities in health (Bediako, Lavender, & Yasin, 2007). This has even led to the development of a questionnaire measure, the Cultural Mistrust Inventory (Moseley, Freed, Bullard, & Goold, 2007). In addition, Latinos do not utilize inpatient mental health services as much as other ethnic groups (Escobar, Randolph, & Hill, 1986). Even when there may be few superficial differences, a closer analysis reveals some of the complexity of culture. For example, Berkanovic and Telesky (1985) found few differences between African, European, and Mexican Americans in terms of reporting illnesses, but they did find that African Americans were less likely to define short-term physical sensations as illnesses and were more likely to consult physicians if it was easy to do so and if they felt a particularly high risk for illness. African Americans were also less likely than Mexican Americans and European Americans to consult others in deciding whether to go to the doctor. Even age and where you live are important. Chowdhury, Islam, Gulshan, and Chakraborty (2007) found that younger mothers were significantly less likely to seek professional health care at the time of birth. Similarly, the odds for rural women seeking health care services from a doctor, nurse or midwife were half those of urban women.

Other variables also influence utilization of health services: There is a marked underutilization of mental health resources by many non-European American groups, suggesting an increased focus on the availability of and preference for alternative medicine (Balls Organista, Organista, & Kurasaki, 2002; Sue, Nakamura, Chung, &Yee-Bradbury, 1994). Nearly 75 percent of Asian Americans in a recent large study reported using at least one type of complementary or alternative medicine (CAM) in the past 12 months, which was significantly higher than the national prevalence rate (Hsiao, Wong, Goldstein, Becerra, Cheng, & Wenger, 2006). Chinese Americans had the highest prevalence of any CAM use. Thus, traditional medicine continues to be important regardless of the significant increase in the use of Western medicine among minority patients, and many minority groups report the use of a dual health system (Chung & Lin, 1994; Chan & Chang, 1976; Higginbotham, Trevino, & Ray, 1990; Lin & Lin, 1978; also see Chapter 2). Ayurvedic medicine, an ancient Indian tradition rooted in the humoral theory of health in which the proper balance of bodily humors indicates health, is especially popular among Indians (Ramakrishna & Wiess, 1992). Acculturation and ethnic identity (discussed in more detail in Chapter 3) can play an important part in the use of Western mental health resources and health services as well. For example, African Americans who strongly identified with their ethnicity and who had experienced discrimination reported a lower probability of health care utilization in comparison with those with weaker ethnic identities (Richman, Kohn-Wood, & Williams, 2007). Folsom, et al., (2007) found that for Latino Americans, having a provider who spoke the same language as the patient (indicating less acculturation) was a better predictor of mental health service use than having a provider of the same ethnicity. Spanish-speaking Latinos differed from both English-speaking Latinos and Caucasians on most measures of health care use. Acculturation is generally linked to greater use of Western medicine. In a sample of Chinese patients, the number of years individuals spent in America was negatively correlated to the use of Chinese medicine (Chan & Chang, 1976). The correlation of acculturation and treatment use is different for other alternative medicines. Su, Li, and Pagán (2008) found that as immigrants stay longer in the United States, or as their use of English becomes more proficient, the likelihood that they use CAM increases.

Whereas this is good to know in itself, the acculturation and ethnic identity of the health providers may be even more important, given the way the American health system is set up (Pacquiao, 2007). Doctors are seen as credible people in powerful positions whose advice can have an important impact on the health behaviors of their patients. This perception suggests that it is important to look at the ethnic identity and acculturation of doctors and, more importantly, their beliefs and preferences, since these factors may influence their referrals and their prescriptions. Minority doctors with strong ethnic identities who are well assimilated or integrated may be more likely to be comfortable prescribing alternative medicine or serving minority patients (Cookley, 2007; Gurung & Mehta, 2001). Yet evidence suggests that the underutilization of medical resources by some ethnic groups, such as Asian Americans for example, is due to under-referral by their health practitioners (Ahmed, Bestall, Ahmedzai, Payne, Clark, & Noble, 2007; Sue et al., 1994).

Before getting more deeply into how culture intersects with illness behaviors, let's understand some basic processes at work. Key social psychological theories influence interpersonal interactions and are important in understanding illness behaviors. These theories mostly hold across cultures. We will first discuss these theories and then extend them to demonstrate how different cultural beliefs can influence the use and utility of health care services.

RECOGNIZING SYMPTOMS

With physical problems, it is often clear when you need to see a doctor. A serious car or bike accident immediately brings medics to the scene. Other physical accidents such as those from sports-related activities (like sprains or breaks) are also taken care of immediately. The limited movement caused by a sprain or the pain from a potential broken bone leads people to go to a hospital for an X-ray or to have the injury examined by a doctor. With other injuries, if symptoms at first do not seem to be life threatening, people may ignore them or delay going to a doctor. Why is this the case? Many psychological factors help us understand some of these reasons.

The Confirmation Bias

Once we believe something is true, we often change the way we interpret new information and the way we look at the world because of it. We tend to try to confirm our belief and have a bias in how we process information. This is a **confirmation bias**. Social psychologists have shown that if there is any ambiguity in a person's behavior, people are likely to interpret what they see in a way that is consistent with their bias (Olson, Roese, & Zanna, 1996). If we believe that a change in our bodies is not a symptom of illness, we will probably look for information to support that belief and find it. For example, if you have spent too much time in the sun and have pale skin there is a chance that you may develop some form of skin cancer (Stack, 2003). The first signs are often discolorations of the skin that are round in nature (i.e., without irregular outlines). You could look at one of these developing spots and believe that it is a blemish or a growing pimple or that it was always there. You may now look at your skin and try to draw attention to parts that look great, ignoring the developing skin spots. You confirm your bias that you are right and cancer free by thinking that you have always had those spots off and on and they never meant anything before. You may even think that you have actually been feeling especially great recently so the spots could not be the beginning of a problem.

This confirmation bias can lead to misperceptions of the social world and an accentuation of symptoms that do get attention. If you believe that you do not need to go to a doctor to seek treatment for flu-like symptoms or a cold, and you have managed without seeing a doctor on past occasions, or if you see others who do not seem to go when they have symptoms, you may begin to overestimate how successful you can be by not going to a doctor. One of the areas that the confirmation bias seems to appear is in the case of Attention Deficit Disorder (ADD). Hall, Ashley, Bramlett, Dielmann, and Murphy (2005) examined the effect of hearing about negative symptoms versus positive symptoms and then looking to find them. They checked to see if looking for one sort of symptom would relate to the assessment and subsequent classification of ADD in children in public schools. Overall, when looking for the negatively phrased symptoms, study participants found more children fitting an ADD diagnosis. The pattern of differences between how the symptoms were described suggested a confirmation bias was taking place.

We not only find confirmation for what we expect to see, but we also tend to overestimate how often we are right (Shavitt, Sanbonmatsu, Smittipatana, & Posavac, 1999). The belief that our expectations have been correct more often than they actually have been is referred to as an **illusory correlation**. A partial explanation for why confirmation biases occur is that we ignore disconfirmations of our biases and selectively remember information to support our biases (Fiske, 1998).

© PYTHON PICTURES/EMI/Picture Desk

Misattributions

Some wounds are hard to misattribute. This knight from *Monty Python and the Holy Grail* clearly needs medical attention as he has just lost both an arm and a leg. In the movie, however, the knight says "It's just a flesh wound." We often misattribute certain symptoms and avoid getting medical attention.

Attributions and Misattributions

Another social psychological process that can influence the recognition of symptoms is related to how we determine the cause of events. The cognitive process of assigning meaning to a symptom or behavior is referred to as making **attributions** (Jones et al., 1972). Many factors influence our attributions (Miller & Diefenbach, 1998). If your stomach hurts, you may attribute the pain to what you just ate. If you have not eaten anything different recently, you are more likely to worry about a stomach pain than if you have just tried something that is very different (spicier or oilier than you are used to). How you attribute a pain in your chest may depend on physical factors such as your age or psychological factors such as beliefs that you hold about illness in general. A teenager may be likely to think of a chest pain as gas or a cramp of sorts. An older person may worry about a heart attack. The cause to which you attribute your symptoms can influence whether you seek treatment for them or not.

Attributions vary across cultures and are influenced by culture as well. Mexican American children may consider hearing voices to be evidence of a religious experience (Padilla & Ruiz, 1973), whereas most European Americans may consider it a sign of mental imbalance. Hmong Americans consider epilepsy the mark of a shaman (Fadiman, 1997). Beliefs about the cause of a disease will directly correspond to how it will be dealt with. If the spirits mean that you should have a certain pain, then it would be angering them and risking further pain if you tried to do something to alleviate it. A study of the role of cultural context of psychological illness among elder immigrants from the former Soviet Union showed that cultural stigma influenced the attribution of cause, physical expression of symptoms, and attitudes toward seeking professional help (Polyakova, & Pacquiao, 2006).

Sometimes, we mistakenly label our physiological experiences based on external factors (Schachter & Singer, 1962). If you feel tired and there are several people at work with colds, you are likely to **misattribute** your tiredness to your developing a cold, when it could be due to your not getting enough sleep. This misattribution can increase your anxiety and in combination with a confirmation bias (that you have caught a cold), you may soon find yourself accumulating more evidence to support your theory. Your belief that you are getting sick will, in fact, make you sick (a **self-fulfilling prophecy**). Such self-fulfilling prophecies can contribute to the continual use of folk medicines and treatments. If you are biased against Western biomedicine, you will probably not try to get better after a visit to a doctor. If you are biased toward shamanism, you are probably going to feel a lot better after a shamanistic ritual is performed over you (Chapter 2). Sometimes your doctor does not even have to support your attribution to help you feel better. Snell (1967) found that African Americans who believed they have been "hexed" could be treated effectively by a psychiatrist using hypnosis, even when the psychiatrist did not believe in hexing.

Yet physicians can fall prey to misattribution problems as well. Evidence suggests that biases against the mentally ill lead physicians to commonly misattribute physical illness signs and symptoms as being due to concurrent mental disorders (Thornicroft, Rose, & Kassam, 2007). This can lead to underdiagnosis and mistreatment of the physical conditions.

Personality

Before we look at cultural levels of difference, let's look at key individual factors. Perhaps the most common individual factor that influences the recognition of symptoms and the seeking of treatment is personality. As described in Chapter 5, personality is what defines each one of us. We have a unique and stable set of characteristics that relate to consistent patterns of behavior across situations. In general, different personality styles are related to a number of health outcomes (Contrada & Guyll, 2001), but there are many personality characteristics that relate to seeking treatment.

Studies have shown that people who are relatively high in anxiety tend to report more symptoms of illness than others do (Feldman, Cohen, Gwaltney, Doyle, & Skoner, 1999; Leventhal, Hansell, Diefenbach, Leventhal, & Glass, 1996). Neuroticism is another key personality trait in this regard. People who are high in neuroticism experience higher levels of anxiety and tend to be "high-strung." This characteristic often translates into oversensitivity to symptoms and to more complaining about ill health (Brown & Moskowitz, 1997). In fact, a thorough review of the personality and health literature suggested that people with chronic negative affect show a disease-prone personality (Friedman & Booth-Kewley, 1987).

Some people's personality types make them more attentive to bodily sensations, and they report more symptoms than others (Barsky, 1988). People who monitor their symptoms to an extreme may be **hypochondriacs**. Hypochondriasis, or hypochondria, is a psychological disorder characterized by excessive preoccupation with one's health and constant worry about developing physical illnesses. Hypochondriacs believe that any minor change in their condition could be a sign of a major problem. They are constantly going to their physicians to be checked. Even when they are told they are all right, they do not believe the diagnosis and may change doctors (Holder-Perkins & Wise, 2001). In a study of symptom reporting among patients with different psychological problems, hypochondriacs reported suffering more often from abdominal pain, and they reported a higher intolerance of bodily complaints (Bleichhardt, Timmer, & Rief, 2005).

Other personality traits such as optimism and self-esteem normally buffer us against stress and illness but may delay us from seeking treatment. For example, look at people with high self-esteem. They believe that they are very healthy and are optimistic in their outlook. They may also believe that their bodies can fight off infections or heal without any specific medical treatment. These people may wait to see if they get better. Low self-esteem individuals have been found to report more health problems (Stinson et al., 2008).

Other specific individual differences influence how patients fare in the health care process. Patients vary in how much they want to be involved in their treatment and how much information they want. **Behavioral involvement** includes the patient's attitude toward self-care, specifically an active involvement in treatment. **Informational involvement** measures how much the patient wants to know about his or her illness and specific details of its treatment. Each form of involvement has different implications in the health care setting (Auerbach, 2000; Christensen, Smith, Turner, Holman, & Gregory, 1990). For example, it may be important to match a patient with a certain preference for information (high in informational involvement) with a practitioner who is accepting of such a preference (a "preference-match"). A large-scale review of the literature on the preference-match strategy in physician patient communication showed varying degrees of support for the positive effects of matching patients' preferred levels of information, decisional control, and consultative interpersonal behavior (Kiesler, & Auerbach, 2006). In a college health care center setting, the degree of match between students' desired and actual level of involvement in their care was associated with greater satisfaction (Campbell, Auerbach, & Kiesler, 2007). Mahler and Kulik (1991) measured these two variables with male coronary bypass patients. The researchers found that patients who had a high desire for behavioral involvement compared with those who had a low desire for behavioral involvement experienced less ambulation dysfunction, fewer social interaction problems, and less emotional upset immediately after release from the hospital. Patients who had a high desire for information involvement compared with those who had a low desire for information involvement experienced more social interaction and emotional problems during this period. At final follow up, these involvement group differences disappeared, and no differences in cardiac health were found (Mahler & Kulik, 1991). Nonetheless, these results suggest these variables should be taken into account to improve patient recovery in the period right after surgery.

Some individuals are more sensitive to their health states than others (Arntz & de Jong, 1993). Referred to as **private body consciousness**, this increased vigilance over the body may also cause the patient to feel more discomfort than the patient with low vigilance. Differences in vigilance may underlie a major sex difference in symptom reporting. Women both perceive and report more physical symptoms than men do (Goldberg, DePue, Kazura, & Niaura, 1998), which could be due to women being higher in private body consciousness. A recent study designed to investigate how symptom reporting varies by time of day, day of the week, gender and generation, found that women report more symptoms throughout the day (in general, symptoms are reported most in the mornings and evenings, Michel, 2007).

Keep in mind that factors influencing symptom reporting (or lack thereof) will vary with the illness. For example, participants in a study of factors influencing delay in reporting symptoms of lung cancer reported lack of symptom experience, lack of knowledge, and fear as key issues (Tod, Craven, & Allmark, 2008). Blame and stigma because of smoking were also prevalent influences, as well as cultural factors, irregular patterns of health care utilization and underlying attitudes of indifference. Families played a critical role in overcoming delay. For some illnesses, the previously mentioned sex differences are not seen (for example, post-traumatic stress disorder, Chung, & Breslau, 2008).

SYNTHESIZE, EVALUATE, APPLY	<ul><li>What are the cultural factors that influence your use of health care?</li><li>Develop a personality profile of the person most likely to seek treatment at the optimal time.</li><li>What are the main psychological processes that underlie the recognizing and reporting of symptoms?</li><li>How could the different approaches to health described in Chapter 2 influence symptom recognition and the health care process described in this chapter?</li></ul>

SEEKING TREATMENT

Once you recognize you have a problem, you have to decide to seek treatment. DiMatteo (1991) has identified a number of different reasons why people do not seek treatment. She suggests that (1) people often misinterpret and underestimate the significance of their symptoms, (2) they worry about how they will look if the symptoms turn out to be nothing, (3) they are concerned about troubling their physicians, (4) they do not want to change their social plans by having to see a doctor, and (5) they tend to waste time on unimportant things, such as getting their personal belongings together, before going to the hospital.

Understanding Delays

A substantial area of health psychology examines why people delay seeking treatment (e.g., Tullmann, Haugh, Dracup, & Bourguignon, 2007). There are three main components of delay. People sometimes take a lot of time to recognize they have symptoms; this is **appraisal delay**, and many psychological factors discussed previously can prevent symptom recognition. Appraisal delay can lead to **illness delay**, the time between the recognition that one is ill and the decision to seek care. Finally, there are often **utilization delays** between the decision to seek care and the actual behaviors to obtain medical health care. Beyond the absence of the main triggers described above, a host of other psychological reasons explains why people delay. Sometimes the delay in seeking treatment results from the symptoms of a problem being misattributed. For example, many heart attack patients do not immediately call 911 for assistance because they believe the pains they are experiencing may be due to other, less serious problems such as indigestion or the flu, which are not potentially fatal (Scherck, 1997).

The different psychosocial barriers to recognizing symptoms and reporting them notwithstanding (Table 8.1), some factors increase the likelihood that a person will seek treatment (Figure 8.2). Health psychologists refer to these as **triggers** (Verbrugge, 1985). There are five triggers that will increase the likelihood that a person will seek treatment (Zola, 1964). First, the degree to which you are frightened by symptoms is critical. If the symptoms are out of view, like located on your back, or if they do not cause too much pain, they may be easy to ignore. You may tell yourself that you will do something about the problem if it gets worse but not otherwise. If your symptoms do cause a lot of pain or are noticeable or if you believe they may indicate a serious illness, you may worry about them, and your anxiety will increase, possibly prompting you to go to a doctor. Correspondingly, the second trigger is the nature and quality of symptoms. The more symptoms you have and the worse they are, the more likely you are to go to a doctor. Sometimes symptoms get so severe that your interactions with your romantic partner, spouse, friends, and family may suffer. If you are in too much pain to attend social events or have had low energy for some time and your symptoms interfere with relationships, this interpersonal crisis is likely to trigger a visit to the doctor. This interference with life can go beyond your personal relationships and extend to your job or to plans that you have made. Social interference—when your occupation or vacation is threatened by symptoms—is the fourth trigger. Finally, even if you do not want to seek treatment, your employer could pressure you to get treatment or return to work. Many businesses have noticed that their insurance rates are much higher for smokers. To cut health insurance costs, employees are provided with incentives to get treatment to quit smoking and in many cases face implicit and explicit pressure to quit smoking. **Social sanctioning** such as this can also trigger a visit to the doctor.

TABLE **8.1**

Major Reasons for Delays in Seeking Treatment

Misinterpretation of symptoms

Fear of false alarms

Concerns with troubling health care professionals

Interference with social plans

Packing and rescheduling before going to the hospital

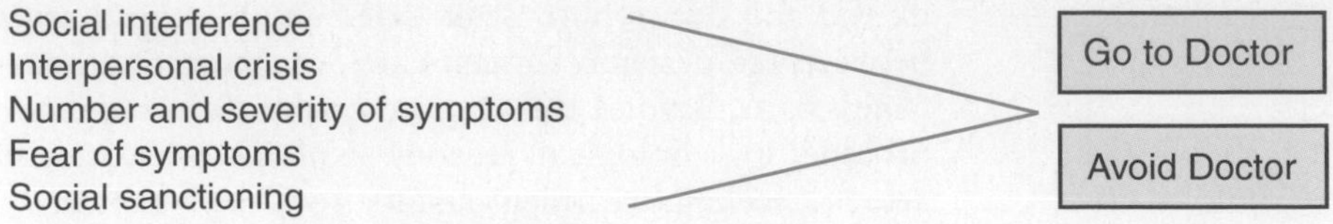

Social interference
Interpersonal crisis
Number and severity of symptoms
Fear of symptoms
Social sanctioning

Go to Doctor

Avoid Doctor

FIGURE **8.2** Main Triggers in Seeking Treatment

In addition to the various psychosocial factors influencing treatment seeking, a number of explicit cultural variables play a role. To begin, there are consistent age and sex differences. Women and elderly persons use health services at a significantly higher rate than do men and younger individuals (Cockerham, 1997; Fuller, Edwards, Sermsri, & Vorakitphokatron, 1993; National Center for Health Statistics, 2004). Part of this difference is because these two groups have more specific issues that need care such as pregnancy and childbirth for women, and chronic and terminal illnesses among elderly persons. In addition, women have been shown to be more sensitive to changes in their bodies than men are (Leventhal, Diefenbach, & Leventhal, 1992) and may find it more socially acceptable to report symptoms than men. Men may not report symptoms or pains as much so as not to appear weak ("boys don't cry").

Treatment seeking varies by ethnicity as well. In one of the most systematic studies of ethnic differences, Suchman (1965) studied ethnic groups in New York and found that many non-European Americans tended to form close, exclusive relationships with friends, family, and members of their ethnic group and to show skepticism of medical care. These groups were more likely to rely on a **lay-referral system**—nonprofessionals such as family, friends, and neighbors—in coping with illness symptoms instead of seeking biomedical treatment. Beyond relying on a lay-referral system, some ethnic groups refrain from seeking treatment from biomedically trained physicians in hospitals, relying instead on folk medicine (as discussed in Chapter 2). Although there are few recent studies on the treatment-seeking behavior of different ethnic groups, older studies of groups such as Mexican Americans show them as being reluctant to visit physicians (Andersen, Lewis, Giachello, Aday, & Chiu, 1981). Having close-knit networks or having strong religious beliefs does not always prevent someone from seeking treatment. In contrast to Suchman's data, Geertsen, Kane, Klauber, Rindflesh, and Gray (1975) showed that members of the close-knit Mormon community in Salt Lake City were actually more likely to seek treatment than members of loosely knit communities.

Perhaps the biggest cultural factor predicting the seeking of treatment is socioeconomic status (SES). In fact, many conditions that may at first appear to be a function of ethnicity may actually be due to poverty. Early sociological studies describe a culture of poverty in which poverty over time influences the development of psychological traits and behaviors including the utilization of health services (Koos, 1954; Rundall & Wheeler, 1979). This lack of utilization is directly correlated with financial barriers to medical care as demonstrated by the increase in utilization of health care by low-income groups after the introduction of national insurance programs such as Medicaid and Medicare in the 1960s. SES may also influence the type of care sought. Kleinman (1980) showed that only upper middle-class families treated all illnesses with Western biomedicine and only lower-class families treated all illnesses at home. Still, the opposite pattern was seen with wealthier Puerto Ricans in New York who were more likely to consult spiritual healers than were poorer individuals (Garrison, 1977).

The Hospital Setting

Once people decide to utilize medical services, they have to face the bureaucracies of a hospital. There are both for-profit and nonprofit hospitals, and cities with many hospitals find each hospital competing for patients. Sometimes this can benefit the patient as hospitals offer discounts and special services to be more appealing. Many hospital administrators view health care primarily as a business (Knox, 1998). Unfortunately, this attitude contributes to patient dissatisfaction with the process of getting treatment. Even for most emergencies, people still have to provide evidence of ability to pay the bill. This may take the form of health insurance from a job or may sometimes be personal insurance. Many millions of American citizens do not have health insurance of any form, a factor that can prevent them from going to the hospital except for the extreme situations. Most hospital visits begin with filling out forms and gathering information and are often accompanied by long waiting periods. For these two reasons and a host of others, most people dread having to go to a hospital.

The majority of the tedium of going to a hospital is hard to avoid. Medical visits have to follow a certain pattern. A health care professional, usually a physician's assistant or a nurse practitioner, first gathers basic information from the patient (e.g., medical history and main symptoms). Then a medical examination of the relevant areas of the body is conducted. Further medical tests are recommended or a diagnosis is made, followed by the prescription of a treatment regimen. The physician may only spend a very brief time with each patient, and this is often one of the major causes of dissatisfaction with the treatment-seeking process (Chung, Hamill, Kim, Walter, & Wilkins, 1999). Doctors would like

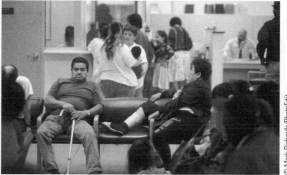

Going to the Hospital

Hospitals can be intimidating places. There is much activity, and a lot of equipment often is involved.

to spend more time with their patients (Probst, Greenhouse, & Selassie, 1997), but they cannot because most have a quota (set by the hospital resulting from a complex interplay of health maintenance organization and insurance billing requirements) of patients that they need to see in a day (Waitzkin, 1985).

In clear recognition of the fact that hospitals are stressful for patients, more attention is being paid to ways that the physical environment of the hospital can be altered (Rashid, & Zimring, 2008). In many cases, indoor environments may set in motion processes that cause stress by affecting individual and workplace dynamics. Ulrich (2004) reviewed over 600 studies documenting the impact of a range of design features like improved lighting that can help reduce stress and pain and increase other outcomes. For example, lower noise levels were linked with reduced work demands by staff, increased workplace social support, and improved quality of care for patients (Blomkvist, Eriksen, Theorell, Ulrich, & Rasmanis, 2005). A conceptually similar study looked at the effects of the hospital environment on stress during blood donations. Ulrich, Simons, and Miles (2003) found that stress was lowest when there was no television playing in the rooms and when videotapes of nature scenes were playing. An important clinical implication of the findings is that the common practice of playing uncontrollable daytime television in healthcare waiting areas where stress is a problem may actually have stressful, not stress-reducing, influences on many patients.

Staff Relations

Health psychologists have begun to pay attention to another level of interaction in hospitals. Going beyond the interaction between a doctor and a patient (discussed in more detail in the last section of this chapter), the diversity within hospital staff compels a look at staff relationships as well. Not only are patients culturally diverse, but hospital staffs are also. In addition to European American staff, hospitals frequently have large numbers of doctors of East Indian, Chinese, and Middle Eastern descent and nurses from Mexico, the Philippines, and other non-White ethnicities (Galanti, 2004). Different cultures have different expectations of the roles played by the different levels of hospital staff. For example, some East Indian male physicians tend to be sexist and are not as respectful of European American nurses (Gurung & Mehta, 2001). The doctor-nurse relationship can be strongly influenced by the culture of each person. Some cultures are more respectful of authority than others, and have a greater desire to maintain harmony and avoid conflict. Nurses of Asian or Latino backgrounds are sometimes reticent to stand up to questionable behavior by European American doctors.

Gender and culture also influence interdoctor and internurse relationships. Some East Indian female physicians often feel intimidated by their male counterparts. Male nurses sometimes have discordant interactions with their female counterparts. Medicine is a hierarchical profession in which orders are followed by rank and not sex, but this hierarchy can often cause problems for men from male-dominant cultures. Medical staff members also face conflicts between their roles as health care providers and their own religious beliefs. Galanti (2004) recounted a case study in which a nurse who was a Jehovah's

Staff Diversity

Doctors and nurses often come from many different cultural backgrounds.

Witness refused to aid in a blood transfer in an emergency room because blood transfusions were against her faith. In another case, a devout Catholic nurse refused to participate in an abortion. An interesting side note is that the Hippocratic Oath sworn by doctors actually directly addresses abortion—doctors have to swear not to do it (see Chapter 1 for the Oath).

SYNTHESIZE, EVALUATE, APPLY	<ul><li>How do the different psychological processes interact to delay the seeking of treatment?</li><li>What recommendations do you have to make the hospital environment more patient friendly?</li><li>How can triggers be utilized to ensure all who need treatment get it?</li><li>When do you know when to go to a doctor? What are your triggers?</li></ul>

ADHERENCE TO TREATMENT

Once the patient and practitioner interact and a diagnosis is made, the patient has to follow the doctor's prescription and recommendations. The extent to which a patient's behavior matches with his or her practitioner's advice is referred to as **adherence** (Kaplan & Simon, 1990). Nonadherence can cause morbidity and influence clinical diagnosis of treatment plans, the cost-effectiveness of health care, and the effectiveness of clinical trials (Shearer & Evans, 2001). In the biomedical arena, adherence is focused more on medication compliance and refers to the degree or extent of conformity to the recommendations about day-to-day treatment by the provider with respect to the timing, dosage, and frequency (Cramer, et al., 2008). Such medication complication/adherence is especially critical for patients with Acquired Immunodeficiency Syndrome (AIDS) for whom non-adherence can be fatal. Consequently, a large body of research focuses especially on increasing adherence among AIDS patients (e.g., Atkinson, Schönnesson, Williams, & Timpson, 2008; Koenig, Pals, Bush, Pratt Palmore, Stratford, & Ellerbrock, 2008).

Studies suggest that adherence in general ranges from 15 percent to 93 percent (Haynes, McKibbon, & Kanani, 1996). Recent work suggests that treatment adherence can be increased by simply having the physician pay closer attention to the patient after diagnosis (more monitoring and follow ups, Llorca, 2008). Regardless, a large number of patients do not completely adhere to medical treatment (Myers & Midence, 1998; Rand & Weeks, 1998). Various psychosocial factors, including many cultural forces, influence the extent to which ill patients adhere to treatments.

There are many practical concerns that influence adherence. As you can guess, adherence rates vary according to the type of treatment prescribed and to the disease or illness a patient has. Rapoff (1999) showed that about 33 percent of patients do not adhere to prescriptions for acute illnesses, whereas around 55 percent of patients do not adhere to treatments for chronic illnesses (Erlen, & Caruthers, 2007). Some treatments are easier to adhere to than others are. You are much more likely to not do something that you dislike (it is easy to avoid eating Brussels sprouts if you did not like them before) than to stop doing something that you do like (avoid sweets). Some treatments are long term and complex, severely interfere with life, and affect desirable behaviors. Such treatments automatically are associated with low levels of adherence. Patients' intentions to adhere, their understanding of the treatment, and their satisfaction with their practitioners can also influence how likely they are to adhere. In fact, many of the health behavior change models, such as the Health Belief Model described in Chapter 6, also help predict which patients will adhere to their treatments.

There are new imaginative ways to increase adherence. Brendryen and Kraft (2008) tested the effectiveness of a 54-week fully automated digital multi-media smoking cessation intervention. The treatment group received 400 contacts by Internet and phone resulting in improved adherence to free nicotine replacement therapy (NRT) and a higher level of post-cessation self-efficacy. In similar support of the benefits of monitoring, Modi, A. C., Marciel, Slater, Drotar, and Quittner, (2008) found that preadolescents and adolescents who spent more of their treatment time supervised by parents, particularly mothers, had better adherence. Nonadherence can take many different forms. Ryan (1998) showed that villagers in Cameroon did not directly follow their doctor's advice, but they did make still an effort to do things that would improve their health. For example, they chose treatments that were less expensive and easier to perform than what the doctor ordered. Other individuals may go overboard. Reis (1993) found that patients with asthma used their sprays for relief more often than prescribed. Sometimes patients indirectly disobey their doctors' orders. Referred to as **creative nonadherence**, patients sometimes modify and supplement their treatment plans. For example, patients may save a dose for later or skip or discontinue a course of medicine if they are feeling well. Nonadherence and intentions to adhere are particularly important to watch for when patients start a new medication for a chronic illness (Clifford, Barber, & Horne, 2008). In such cases, intentional nonadherers, compared with adherers, have lower perceptions of the necessity of their new medication and higher levels of concerns about taking it. Conversely, unintentional nonadherers are not significantly different from adherers.

In addition to the psychological reasons that explain nonadherence, culture, by itself, can also be a major explanatory force. As described in Chapter 2, different cultural groups have different beliefs. Ethnic groups, racial groups, people from different geographical regions, and even men and women—all of these members of different cultures—may have beliefs that are barriers to adherence. For example, most European American women quickly go back to work after the births of their babies. In contrast, many Asian American women believe that a week or a month resting period ('lying-in') is needed during which the mother spends time in bed to recover. Anderson (1993) suggested that the health care system might be organized to favor the majority culture. Thus, social, political, and economic barriers can prevent minority group members from complying with their practitioner's prescriptions.

One large area in which cultural beliefs interfere with adherence to treatment involves dietary practices. Many treatments involve either food restrictions or prescriptions to eat certain foods. These prescriptions may not fit with some cultural beliefs. For example, Muslims are forbidden to eat from sunrise to sunset during the month of Ramadan, an important Muslim festival. Orthodox Jews follow kosher dietary laws that forbid eating pork, shellfish, and nonkosher red meat and poultry, or mixing meat and dairy products (no cheeseburgers allowed). Hindus do not eat beef. Many Catholics do not eat meat on Fridays during the season of Lent. There are many documented cases in which hospital staffs unknowingly attempt to feed patients certain foods that are against the patients' cultural beliefs (Galanti, 2004).

The three main stages in the health-illness process (recognizing symptoms, seeking treatment, and adherence to treatment) are all related to patient-practitioner interactions.

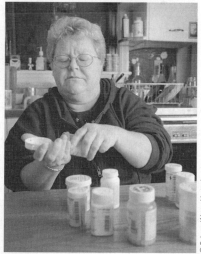

© Enigma/Alamy Limited

Nonadherence
Complex treatments and having to take many medications often cause nonadherence.

PATIENT-PRACTITIONER INTERACTIONS

When a patient has recognized that he or she has symptoms of an illness and has sought treatment from a health care professional, it is only the beginning of the journey toward recovery. Many things occur as the patient interacts with the health care system: negotiating the paperwork of insurance and registration at the hospital to begin, and then actually seeing a doctor and getting a diagnosis. When you do see a doctor, the quality of your interaction with him or her can play a big role in how you feel and in the extent to which you adhere to the prescribed treatment.

Patient-practitioner interactions can vary around some basic themes (Ballard-Reisch, 1990; Roter & Hall, 1992). Szasz and Hollender (1956) describe three major models of interaction. In the active-passive model, the doctor plays a pivotal role, making the majority of the decisions because the patient is unable to do so (because of his or her medical condition). Here the patient has little to no say in what is done. In the guidance-cooperation model, the doctor still takes the primary role in diagnosis and treatment, but the patient plays a part by answering questions, although he or she does not take part in decision making regarding treatment. In the mutual cooperation model, the doctor and patient work together at every stage, consulting each other on the planning of tests for diagnosis and in decisions regarding treatment. Obviously, the optimal model of interaction, the mutual cooperation model, is characterized by effective patient-practitioner communication and an open exchange of ideas and concerns. Good communication is perhaps one of the most critical ingredients in successful patient-practitioner interactions. Let's take a closer look at factors that influence these interactions.

Communication

Conversations between doctors and their patients can range from being narrowly biomedical, in which the doctor uses a lot of medical jargon and limits conversation using closed-ended questions, to consumerist, in which the patient is primarily the one doing the talking and getting answers to his or her questions (Roter et al., 1997). The extent to which doctors discuss psychological or social issues varies greatly, especially across cultures. Many factors influence the quality of communication between doctors and patients (Clark, et al., 2008; Ong, DeHaes, Hoos, & Lammes, 1995).

Different cultures have different expectations for communication. In the West, it is very common for people to use small talk, for example, "How are you doing?" It is rare that the speaker really wants to know the answers to rhetorical questions such as this. Non-Western cultures rarely engage in small talk to the same extent (Triandis, 1996). Sometimes it may seem like doctors are from Venus and patients are from Mars (to borrow the analogy from a pop psychologist's attempt to characterize male and female interactional patterns). It is not uncommon to see a patient looking confused at a doctor while the doctor is trying to explain a procedure or diagnosis using technical terms, with the patient understanding only a fraction of the conversation.

© LWA/Larry Williams/Blend Images/Jupiter Images

Patient/Practitioner Communication

Good communication between doctor and patient is integral to patient adherence to a treatment plan. Unfortunately, many doctors must rush to meet a certain number of patients in a day, necessitating quick patient/doctor interaction.

Psychologists have identified many key ways that communication can go wrong. One of the major cultural dimensions influencing patient-practitioner communication is individualism and collectivism. As described in Chapter 2, people in different cultures vary in the level to which they are self-focused or independent/individualistic or other/group-focused or collectivistic. When it comes to communication between the doctor and patient, a patient's level of collectivism can be a key factor. Collectivists tend to communicate all but the most important piece of information, which the doctor is supposed to supply to make the whole message comprehensible (Triandis, 1996). This strategy has the advantage of allowing a collectivist to monitor another's feelings and avoid disrupting harmony (Armstrong & Swartzman, 2001). The individualist on the other hand, who is not as concerned with maintaining social harmony, is more likely to get straight to the point. Combine an individualist doctor and a collectivistic patient and you have a recipe for frustration because the doctor wants the point and the patient is offended by the doctor's drive for the point.

Doctors have been found to do many things that inhibit communication. Some doctors may not listen to everything the patient says (Probst et al., 1997), often talking too much. A look at the statistics makes some doctors almost seem rude. Beckman and Frankel found in 1984 that on average, doctors cut off their patients after only 18 seconds. Happily, things have gotten better since this study (Roter & Hall, 2006). Still, in talking to patients, doctors may use too much medical jargon that the patient does not understand (Cormier, Cormier, & Weisser, 1984). Given the Latin roots of many disease classifications and the technical terms used to describe many procedures and even different parts of the body, it is not surprising that a layperson may be confused by medical jargon. Although providing a common language for doctors to communicate with each other and being valid ways to describe aspects of illness, the inappropriate use of medical terminology can confuse, frustrate, and even anger patients (Frankel, 1995). Phillips (1996) found that patients are particularly dissatisfied with treatment when doctors appear to deliberately use jargon even when it does not seem to be needed. Conversely, some doctors "dumb down" the message or talk down to patients, assuming that they do not understand.

Patients contribute to communication problems with doctors as well. Patients are often very anxious when they go to a doctor (Graugaard & Finset, 2000). This anxiety may make them not describe all their symptoms or have difficulty concentrating on the doctor's questions. Sometimes patients from lower socioeconomic backgrounds or those who speak a different language may not understand what is being asked of them. Language problems can even occur between people who speak English. This author was raised in Bombay, India, where the English spoken is British English (the "Queen's English"). In India and Britain, a *rubber* is an eraser. In America, a rubber is a condom. In college, I quickly learned that difference (much to my embarrassment) after the first time I made a mistake on an exam and needed to erase it. In a health care setting, simple word usage can play a big role in the context of conversations about birth control. Another example is the word *positive*. In most everyday contexts, positive connotes a good thing. In the context of an HIV test, however, having positive test results is not a good thing at all. To make matters worse, the same English word may mean different things in other languages. If someone told you that he or she got a stomachache from eating a puto, the language the person speaks makes a big difference. The word *puto* means "rice cake" in the Philippines but "male prostitute" in Spanish. Similarly, to *douche* is to shower in Dutch, but it has a very different meaning in English (feminine hygiene).

Additionally, different symptoms may mean different things in different cultures, making some patients hesitant to describe a symptom that they believe relates to a very personal or private bodily function.

There is one more element of communication that stands apart from the previous discussion—communicating uncertainty. There is a growing trend toward shared decision making in medicine (Moumjid, Gafni, Bremond, & Carrere, 2007) that brings with it a need for patients to be able to interpret large amounts of medical information. Much of this information, such as outcomes, risks, and benefits, is often uncertain. Patients are faced with probabilities and relative risk formats (see research section of Chapter 1) that are difficult to understand (Covey, 2007). This is particularly important when conveying information about health risks (Lipkus, 2007) and benefits and risks of different drugs (Schwartz, Woloshin, & Welch, 2007). This problem is compounded by cultural differences such as language mismatches. Research on the best ways to communicate uncertainty (Politi, Han, & Col, 2007) and the development of decision aids (McCaffery, Irwig, & Bossuyt, 2007) are currently underway.

Cultural Stereotyping

We all hold various stereotypes. For example, you may believe that Asians are good at math, or women are bad at math. **Stereotypes** are widely held

© Jose Luis Pelaez/Getty Images

Sex Biases in Medicine

It is important that doctors do not stereotype based on any cultural factor, including the gender of a patient. Research shows considerable sexism/gender biases in how patients are treated.

beliefs that people have certain characteristics because of their membership in a particular group. Many stereotypes may have a kernel of truth to them, but human beings treat stereotypes as if they are always accurate for all members of the group. Social psychologists have argued that we use stereotypes as a shortcut. When we do not have the cognitive time or energy to find out more about somebody, we fall back on what we have heard about the cultural group that he or she belongs to.

Stereotypes of doctors or patients based on their sex, ethnicity, or religion are one of the biggest factors influencing the quality of patient-practitioner communication and interactions. In the limited time that doctors and nurses have to interact with patients, their behavior may often be influenced by their stereotypes of their patients instead of realities. Many such stereotypes exist and play a role in the hospital setting. For example, Americans of Middle Eastern and Indian descent are often believed to be demanding and to express their pain freely and loudly (Galanti, 2004). Mexican Americans stereotypically have large families. Asian American men and women are stereotypically very quiet and stoic. If doctors see older patients or female patients, they may make assumptions about how the patients will behave or about their pain tolerance or behaviors based on ageist or sexist stereotypes (Hall, Epstein, DeCiantis, & McNeil, 1993; Haug & Ory, 1987). It is important to remember, as discussed in Chapter 1, that even though there may be some individuals who fit a certain cultural stereotype, there is a lot of variance within cultures. Generalizations based on stereotypes can be inaccurate, may be offensive, and can sometimes result in malpractice claims. Sadly, there is empirical evidence showing that some cultural groups like African Americans, Latinos, or low SES individuals are given less information and are treated worse than other groups (Hooper, Comstock, Goodwin, & Goodwin, 1982). An extreme case of the problems with cultural stereotyping is discussed in the focus on clinical application section at the end of this chapter.

In addition to stereotyping of race and ethnicity, there is also evidence for differential treatment by sex. Women are treated differently from the way men are treated (Curtis, Al-Khatib, Shea, Hammill, Hernandez, & Schulman, 2007). Some forms of implantable heart devices are used two to three times more in men than in women with similar symptoms, even though heart disease is the leading cause of death among women. The device is also used more in white men than black men. It gets worse for older women. When compared to men of the same age group, women over 50 are less likely to be admitted to hospital intensive care units, have shorter stays in ICU if admitted, receive fewer emergency medical treatments, and are more at risk of dying in intensive care and in hospital (Fowler et al., 2007). This sex bias is also seen concerning knee surgery. Physicians are more likely to recommend knee surgery to a male patient than to a female patient. In one study, the odds of an orthopedic surgeon recommending total knee arthroplasty to a male patient was 22 times that for a female patient. (Borkhoff, Hawker, Kreder, Glazier, Mahomed, & Wright, 2008).

Cultural Competency

Related to stereotyping is the concept of **cultural competency** (Sue, 2006). A health care provider's understanding of patients' cultural characteristics, values, and traditions can contribute to the quality of treatment delivered. Poor cultural competency can negatively impact the communication between doctors and patients and consequently lead to poorer care (Perloff, Bonder, Ray, Ray, & Siminoff, 2006). Overreliance on stereotypes can lead to poor competency. Given the importance of this concept, researchers have developed measures of health care provider cultural competence that nicely tap into patients' perceptions of their doctors and nurses. Lucas, Michalopoulou, Falzarano, Menon, & Cunningham (2008) developed a theoretically grounded, generally applicable measure comprised of patient judgments of their physician's cultural knowledge, awareness, and skill. Testing the scale with predominantly African American patients, the researchers showed perceptions of cultural competency correlated with measures of trust, satisfaction, and discrimination.

© AP Photo

Hmong American Women in Traditional Festive Clothes
Seeing someone in non-western outfits can enhance how they are stereotyped.

If health care providers are not culturally competent and tend to stereotype, patients may feel discrimination. Perceived discrimination has also been studied in the relationship with health service utilization. Spencer and Chen (2004) found that discrimination played a role in informal help-seeking in a population of Chinese Americans. Sources of informal services for emotional problems could be considered as primarily help from friends and relatives (ethnic social support) or from traditional practitioners or physicians. In this study, subjects who reported experiencing language-based discrimination (poor treatment due to language barriers) were more likely to use informal support services for emotional problems. Additionally, there were significant gender differences. Females in the sample were more likely than males to seek informal services and help. As you can see, many different steps are involved in the process of getting sick and recovering. Many individual difference factors and major cultural differences can influence the extent to which patients recognize their symptoms, report them, seek treatment, and adhere to their treatments. Understanding and incorporating these differences are critical to optimizing the success of a health care system.

SYNTHESIZE, EVALUATE, APPLY

- What recommendations do you have to make the hospital environment more patient friendly?
- Given the time constraints faced by hospital staff, what can be done to improve patient treatment?
- Summarize how cultural differences create conflict between patients and practitioners and between staff members. What are key solutions?
- What can be done to prevent cultural stereotyping?

FOCUS ON APPLICATIONS

When the Spirit Catches You, Cultures Clash

BAAAM!!! When a door slams hard, you may jump back, startled at the sound. Your ears may ring and you may even direct a harsh stare in the direction of the person who did it. Would you worry about what the slamming could mean for your soul? Most probably you would not, yet that is exactly what Foua Lee worried about when her elder daughter Yer Lee slammed the front door of the family apartment. Within seconds, Foua's youngest daughter and Yer's younger sister, Lia, fainted. The Lees had little doubt about what happened. The sound of the slamming door had been so alarming that little Lia Lee's soul had fled her body and become lost. What followed as the Lee family struggled to cure Lia is a tragic story of how the clash of two sets of cultural beliefs, in this case those of Western biomedicine and Hmong folk beliefs, can have fatal consequences. Cultural differences led to innumerable complications, deplorable patient-practitioner interactions, and delays in the recognition, reporting, and adequate treatment of Lia Lee's epilepsy or *quag dab peg*, literally translated from the Hmong language to mean "the spirit catches you and you fall down" (Fadiman, 1997).

The Hmong people originally lived in the hills of Laos in Southeast Asia (right next to Vietnam). In 1975, Laos fell to Communist forces, and 150,000 Hmong fled to refugee camps in Thailand and then to America. In fact, the American government promised the Hmong asylum in exchange for their help in fighting the Vietnam War. Correspondingly, thousands of Hmong men, women, and children immigrated to America and settled primarily in California, Minnesota, and Wisconsin. Most of the Hmong immigrants do not speak English, and all the

(continues)

FOCUS ON APPLICATIONS *(continued)*

Hmong hold a belief system very different from that of Western culture. The Hmong believe that illness can be caused by a variety of different factors such as eating the wrong food, having sinful ancestors, being cursed, having one's blood sucked by a spirit or *dab*, touching a newborn mouse, and having bird dropping fall on one's head. The most common cause of illness is soul loss. When Lia Lee convulsed and collapsed, the family automatically thought that her soul was lost. And that's not all. The seizures were paradoxically seen as a mixed blessing. To the Hmong, *quag dab peg* is a special illness and often the sign of a shaman. You can guess how that belief was received when they took Lia to the local hospital.

In the hospital, almost all of the issues described in this chapter became factors. Initially, none of the doctors or nurses could really understand what had happened to the little girl because none of the health practitioners spoke Hmong, the Lee family spoke very little English, and there were no interpreters on hand. Lia had stopped convulsing by the time she had reached the hospital so the only symptoms she showed were a cough and a congested chest. The resident on duty did what he could with the limited information, and Lia was sent home after her parents signed a paper acknowledging the receipt of instructions for care. However, the Lees could not read. The prescription was not followed. To accentuate the dangers of nonadherence, the Lee family decided to use their own treatment for the soul loss based on their own cultural beliefs. Lia Lee was soon back in the emergency room a second and then a third time. On the third arrival, the consulting physician deemed her to have meningitis and ordered a spinal tap, but Lia's parents resisted only to be finally convinced.

Lia had repeated seizures over the next few years, and there were problems with every step of her treatment. When she was checked into the hospital, her father and many other members of the family stayed with her, often ignoring the posted visiting hours and interfering with the treatment. At one time, the nurses had used restraints on Lia to prevent her from hurting herself when she had a seizure. Lia's father could not understand why this was being done to his daughter, and no one could speak Hmong to tell him. When the nurses were out of the room he untied Lia's restraints and placed her on the floor, much to the disapproval of the hospital staff who had to restrain her again. Most of the time the Lee parents were uncertain of what medicines to give Lia, and in another form of nonadherence, they just skipped giving her medications when the drug regimen became too complex, substituting folk remedies instead.

The Lee family sacrificed a cow, cut the heads off chickens, and attempted a number of different shamanistic remedies, but none worked. Still the family worked hard to keep Lia happy, even opting to keep her at home and take care of her instead of having her be in the hospital. Unfortunately, although many Hmong see epilepsy as a sign of divinity and are content to just care for the person with it without necessarily trying for a cure, this approach is not approved by Western society, and a family services agency removed Lia Lee from her loving parents and placed her in a foster home. The Lees got their daughter back, but it was not the end of Lia's problems. Sadly, the plot thickened. After a further series of miscommunications between the Western doctors and this Hmong family, Lia Lee went into a coma and never regained consciousness.

What started out as a straightforward case of epilepsy spiraled out of control. Were the Lees to blame? Yes, they did not give Lia the medicines they were supposed to, but this nonadherence was a combination of their not understanding why and what they had to do and not wanting to do it because of their own beliefs. Was the Western medical system to blame? Yes, many assumptions and guesses were made about what the problem was and often the Lees were stereotyped and mistreated because of it. The language barrier was also a large part of the problem and, as in many cases throughout our nation, the health practitioners did not have the time or the necessary cultural education to know better. Although this is an extreme case, the travesty of Lia's vegetative state resulting from the collision of these two cultures is, nonetheless, an important reminder of how important cultural differences are to the patient-practitioner interaction and the seeking and delivery of medical treatment.

SUMMARY

- Illness behaviors are the varying ways individuals respond to physiological symptoms, monitor internal states, define and interpret symptoms, and essentially work toward getting better. The first step in coping with an illness is to identify the symptoms. Then we need to report them and adhere to treatment prescriptions. Delays can occur at each of these steps.
- Many psychological factors such as confirmation biases, personality styles, and attributional problems compounded by cultural differences interfere with accurate symptom recognition. Delays in appraising illness can lead to delays in seeking help and utilizing health care. A number of different triggers increase the likelihood that people will seek treatment. Socioeconomic status is perhaps the largest cultural factor that predicts the seeking of treatment. People living in poverty are less likely to have sufficient health care or utilize it effectively.
- The bureaucracies of the hospital setting sometimes make it difficult for patients to have their illnesses treated. A variety of factors influence staff relationships with patients. Staff often stereotype patients based on SES, sex, age, and ethnicity. In particular, stereotyping and prejudice, language barriers, use of jargon, and time pressure influence communication between patient and practitioners.
- Adherence to treatment varies based on the complexity of the treatment, the extent to which the treatment interferes with social functioning, and the duration and severity of the treatment. A large number of patients do not fully adhere to doctor's prescriptions. Nonadherence is compounded by different cultural factors.

TEST YOURSELF

Check your understanding of the topics in this chapter by answering the following questions. Answers appear in the Appendix.

1. The varying ways that individuals respond to physiological symptoms, monitor internal states, recognize symptoms, and utilize health care are all considered:
   a. health behaviors.
   b. illness behaviors.
   c. proactive coping.
   d. reactivity measures.

2. The first and most important step that the patient has to negotiate successfully in the transition from health to illness is the:
   a. acceptance of sickness.
   b. recognition of symptoms.
   c. reporting of symptoms.
   d. preparation for sickness.

3. Research assessing the utilization of health care and services routinely finds that _____ do not utilize health care as much as others do.
   a. high SES individuals
   b. high self esteem individuals
   c. women
   d. minority group members

4. Many social psychological processes help explain illness behaviors (or their absence). If you do not think you are sick, you are likely to ignore symptoms of the sickness and only look for evidence that you are healthy. This is called:
   a. a self-fulfilling prophecy.
   b. selective attention.

    c. A confirmation bias.

    d. impression management.

5. An example of how assigning meaning to a symptom can vary across cultures can be seen in how:

    a. Mexican American children consider hearing voices to be a religious experience.

    b. Hmong Americans consider epilepsy to be purely a physical defect.

    c. American Indians consider cancer a 'White man's disease."

    d. Chinese Americans use acupuncture to realign energy flow.

6. A patient's attitude to health care and the extent to which they want to be a part of their treatment is referred to as the level of:

    a. self-control.

    b. self-efficacy.

    c. behavioral involvement.

    d. patient-practitioner coherence

7. Which of the following is NOT a major reason why people do not seek treatment?

    a. People underestimate the significance of symptoms.

    b. People assume the symptoms will turn out to be nothing.

    c. People do not want to bother their doctors.

    d. People overestimate the significance of their symptoms.

8. There are many cultural reasons that explain why people do not recognize that they have symptoms of an illness. Often, a long time passes from a symptom occurrence to the recognition that it is a problem. This can be harmful and is referred to as:

    a. appraisal delay.

    b. illness delay.

    c. utilization delay.

    d. cultural delay.

9. Which of the following is not one of the five triggers (Zola, 1964) that increase the likelihood of a person seeking treatment?

    a. degree to which the symptoms frighten you

    b. the nature and quality of symptoms

    c. whether you have experienced the symptom before

    d. if the symptoms interfere with work or personal relationships

10. The _____ form of patient-practitioner communication involves the patient doing the bulk of the talking and getting answers to their questions.

    a. mutual cooperative

    b. active-passive

    c. patient-focused

    d. Consumerist

WEB RESOURCES

Visit the companion website at **www.cengage.com/psychology/gurung**, where you will find online resources for this book, including chapter-by-chapter quizzes, Web links, and more!

Transcultural Nursing
http://www.culturediversity.org/index.html

This is a site for increasing cultural awareness in health care. It offers great profiles of different cultural groups and resources to learn more about cultural differences in hospitals.

AMSA
http://www.amsa.org/programs/gpit/cultural.cfm

This is a descriptive site for increasing cultural competency in medicine, and includes examples of questions relating to culture that practitioners can ask patients as well as discussion questions to test your understanding.

The Provider's Guide
http://erc.msh.org/mainpage.cfm?file=1.0.
htm&module=provider&language=English:

This is a provider's guide to quality and culture. It is a Web site designed to assist health care

organizations to provide culturally competent care to diverse populations. There are audio and video files on the main topics discussed in this chapter (and more).

KEY TERMS, CONCEPTS, AND PEOPLE

adherence, 263

appraisal delay, 258

attributions, 255

behavioral involvement, 257

confirmation bias, 254

creative nonadherence, 264

cultural competency, 270

hypochondriacs, 256

illness behaviors, 252

illness delay, 258

illusory correlation, 254

informational involvement, 257

lay-referral system, 260

misattribute, 256

private body consciousness, 257

self-fulfilling prophecy, 256

social sanctioning, 259

stereotypes, 269

triggers, 259

utilization delays, 259

ESSENTIAL READINGS

DiMatteo, M. R. (2004). Social support and patient adherence to medical treatment: A meta-analysis. *Health Psychology*, 23(2), 207–218.

Galanti, G. (2004). *Caring for patients from different cultures: Case studies from American hospitals.* Philadelphia: University of Pennsylvania Press.

Kleinman, A., Eisenberg, L., & Good, B. (1978). Culture, illness, and cure: Clinical lessons from anthropologic and cross-cultural research. *Annals of Internal Medicine*, 88, 250–258.

Nilchaikovit, T., Hill, J. M., & Holland, J. C. (1993). The effects of culture on illness behavior and medical care: Asian and American differences. *General Hospital Psychiatry*, 15, 41–50.

Ong, L. M. L., DeHaes, J. C. J. M., Hoos, A. M., & Lammes, F. B. (1995). Doctor-patient communication: A review of the literature. *Social Science and Medicine*, 40(7), 903–918.

Pain

The world seems like such a different place when we are in pain. Whether it is a mild headache from a stressful day, the ache of a twisted ankle from a misstep, a stomachache from spoiled food, or the skinned knee from a fall during basketball, pain is uncomfortable and is something we want to avoid. In the midst of a painful experience, we long for the time when the pain will be gone. We try anything we can to escape pain. For common pains such as headaches, we may reach for aspirin or may take a nap, hoping that the pain will be gone once the pill takes effect or when we wake up. There are many cultural differences in how we cope with pain, and many cultural explanations for why we feel pain. What is pain? Why do we experience it? How is it caused? Maybe the most important question of all is, what are the ways to relieve it? In this chapter, we describe the phenomenon of pain and answer each of these questions. First, we discuss the different types of pain and look at how pain has been explained over the centuries. We then discuss some of the major ways we can cope with pain, making the distinction between short-term and long-term pain management. Lastly, this chapter highlights some the ways different cultures cope with pain.

What exactly is pain? At the most basic level, pain can be referred to as **nociception,** the activation of specialized nerve fibers that signal the occurrence of tissue damage. Nociception is often accompanied by cognitive, behavioral, and affective states. Your thoughts are influenced by pain, your behaviors change when you are in pain, and your feelings are influenced by pain. Of

© Ruth Fremson/The New York Times/Redux

Expressions and Causes of Pain Vary Significantly Across Cultures

Many of the world's poor suffer in pain. Zainabu Sesay, at her home in Sierra Leone, receive hospice care, but no morphine is available to ease the pain of breast cancer.

course, pain can also be purely emotional in nature, without nociception, and is often described as suffering. Pain is a phenomenon that clearly exemplifies how important taking a biopsychosocial approach can be. Whereas pain can have direct biological causes—for example, if you get punched on your arm you will more than likely feel pain—the experience of pain is strongly influenced by psychological and cultural factors.

As signified by the technical definition of nociception, pain is essential to survival. Some cultures interpret pain differently and may have different ways to cope with it, but in all cases pain serves the same purpose. Pain warns us of bodily danger and provides feedback of bodily functions. If you are hiking up a hill and you place your foot on a rock in the wrong way, your foot may hurt before you put all your weight on it. You automatically place it down in the right way. If you break your arm, the pain in the limb is a reminder to you to refrain from using it to give it time to heal. When you get too close to a fire, the pain from the heat reminds you to keep a safe distance from the fire. When you experience pain you are more likely to go to a doctor. Unfortunately, the opposite is also true. Finnegan et al. (1995) found that heart attack victims who did not experience too much pain delayed seeking care for their symptoms.

CULTURAL VARIATIONS IN THE EXPERIENCE OF PAIN

Many cultural factors influence the perception and experience of pain, but two of these stand out: sex and ethnicity. In large part, the cultural variations are due to differences in socialization and expectations across different cultural groups. Boys are socialized to not express themselves when experiencing pain and girls are socialized to express pain when they need to. If a man cries in pain, he is seen as less masculine, but it is perfectly acceptable for a woman to cry because of pain. There are also different expectations for pain tolerance across ethnicities and races. Middle Eastern women are more likely to scream during delivery than are Japanese women.

Sex Differences

A growing body of research suggests that there are sex differences at every level—biological, psychological, and social—in the experience of persistent pain (Bernardes, Keogh, & Lima, 2008; Fillingim, 2003; Greenspan et al., 2007; Johnson, 2008; Komiyama, Kawara, & De Laat, 2007; Lynch, Kashikar-Zuck, Goldschneider, & Jones, 2007; O'Brien, Atchison, Gremillion, Waxenberg, & Robinson, 2008; Rollman, 2003). There is so much evidence for this difference that in September 2006, members of the Sex, Gender and Pain Special Interest Group of the International Association for the Study of Pain gathered to summarize what is known about sex and gender differences in pain, collect the "best practice" guidelines for pain research with respect to sex and gender, and set a research agenda for this area of study (Greenspan et al., 2007).

Some of the differences include the finding that for experimentally delivered stimuli to the body, females have lower thresholds, greater ability to discriminate, higher pain ratings, and less tolerance of noxious stimuli than males (Berkley, 1997). Of note, these differences only existed for some forms of painful stimulations and varied based on situational factors such as the experimental setting. For internal pains, Berkley (1997) found that women report more multiple pains in more areas of the body than men do. Similar to studies of depression and anxiety, women are more likely to report pain to a doctor and to experience more frequent episodes of pain (Muellersdorf & Soederback, 2000). Men report less pain, cope better with pain, and respond to treatment for pain differently from women (Walker & Carmody, 1998), although there are perhaps more within-group differences than between-group differences. Some painful diseases are more prevalent among females and others among males, and, for many diseases, symptoms differ between females and males (Barsky, Peekna, & Borus, 2001). In terms of types of pain, the only significant sex differences relate to headaches (including migraine), facial, and back pain (Breslau & Rasmussen, 2001).

Ethnic Differences

Members of different ethnic groups, similar to members of the two sexes, give very different meanings to the experience of pain. These differences take the form of when pain should be expressed, how the pain should be expressed (e.g., verbally and behaviorally), what the expression of the pain signifies about the individual, and how long the pain should be expressed (Bates, Edwards, & Anderson, 1993; Bates, Rankin-Hill, & Sanchez-Ayendez, 1997; Mailis-Cagnon et al., 2007).

The clinical literature on ethnicity and pain has been focused primarily on two ethnic groups, African Americans and European Americans (e.g., Campbell, France, Robinson, Logan, Geffken, & Fillingim, 2008; Fuentes, Hart-Johnson, & Green, 2007), and the differences are clear. For example, Edwards, Fillingim, and Keefe (2001) reviewed the pain literature and found that studies show greater sensitivity to experimental pain stimuli among African Americans compared with European Americans. Clinical studies of acute and persistent pain also showed higher levels among African American patients compared with European Americans. Similarly, Riley et al. (2002) tested for ethnic differences in the processing of chronic pain in 1,557 European American and African American chronic pain patients. Results showed that after controls for pain duration and education were applied, African Americans reported significantly higher levels of pain unpleasantness, emotional response to pain, and pain behavior but not pain intensity than did European Americans. African Americans with chronic pain report significantly more pain and sleep disturbance as well as more symptoms consistent with post-traumatic stress disorder and depression than White Americans (Green, Baker, Sato, Washington, & Smith, 2003).

There is now a growing literature that includes Latin American populations (Reyes-Gibby, Aday, Todd, Cleeland, Anderson, 2007). In one large community sample study, non-Latino African Americans and Latin Americans had higher risk for severe pain compared with non-Latino European Americans (Reyes-Gibby et al., 2007). Of note, some of these ethnic differences between African American, Latin American, and European Americans may be due to ethnic identity, which serves as a mediator (see Chapter 5) of the differences (Rahim-Williams, Riley, Herrera, Campbell, Hastie, & Fillingim, 2007).

Other ethnic groups show differences as well. Studies have documented differences among different groups in America (Faucett, Gordon, & Levine, 1994; Lipton & Marbach, 1984) as well as across different nationalities (Komiyama, Kawara, & De Laat, 2007; Mailis-Cagnon et al., 2007; Sanders et al., 1992). In an experimental design (the researchers actually manipulated how much pain participants felt), Lawlis, Achterberg, Kenner, and Kopetz (1984) studied the experience of chronic back pain in Mexican Americans, European Americans, and African Americans. They induced pain in participants and collected reports of how much pain could be tolerated and when the induced pain matched the chronic pain. The authors also collected observer ratings of pain behavior to match self-reports. In a clear demonstration of how culture can cover up differences, Mexican Americans reported the highest level of pain when the induced pain matched the chronic pain, but they were judged as not showing an "exaggerated" pain response. European Americans reported less chronic pain but had a lower pain tolerance than Mexican Americans, and the African American group did not differ from either of the other groups on any measures of pain.

Moving to a larger scale, interesting differences in pain perception are seen when geographical areas are compared. Bates et al. (1997) compared participants living in New England with those living in Puerto Rico. Participants were European American and Latino in New England and Puerto Rican in Puerto Rico. New Englanders held Western biomedical beliefs and felt high levels of control of their pain. Both New England patients and practitioners shared this view, but these patients experienced high treatment-related stress. The Puerto Ricans with more holistic beliefs preferred biopsychosocial approaches to the treatment of pain. Interestingly, here too patients and practitioners shared the same values, but the patients experienced less treatment-related stress.

Other cultural factors are important in the context of pain. Some ethnic groups may have language barriers that influence the success with which the patients convey their level of pain or understand the doctor's instructions. Many ethnic groups experience disproportional levels of stress due to acculturation or lower socioeconomic status. Prolonged experiences of stress could result from unemployment or family issues relating to changes in roles or the process of acculturating to a new dominant society. For example, Latinos are the fastest growing ethnic group in North America but have experienced decreasing economic and educational levels and are underrepresented in those who have health insurance (Betancourt & Fuentes, 2001). All these factors represent significant psychological factors for Latinos and those in other cultural groups coping with chronic pain.

Before you assume that if someone is from a different culture he or she has to experience pain differently, remember that there are also big individual differences within cultures. In addition, a number of studies have failed to find significant cultural differences in pain perceptions (Flannery, Sos, & McGovern, 1981; Pfefferbaum, Adams, & Aceves, 1990). The different studies compared different ethnic groups *and* different measures of pain, making it tougher to understand the basic phenomenon. The samples are often not heterogeneous and are not always chosen by random sampling (Korol & Craig, 2001). Future health psychological research should aim to have bigger groups for comparison

Members of some cultural groups seem to be able to endure firewalking without pain. In fact, firewalking can be explained by the laws of physics rather than cultural beliefs. Here Brian, a U.S. college student, walks across coals as part of a leadership training program.

to produce a more thorough understanding of cultural differences. Still, an increased focus on cultural influences in pain can already be seen in some areas of health care. For example, home care clinicians have been urged to be aware of the impact of various ethnic and even religions backgrounds on the perception of pain and subsequent acceptance of treatment regimens (Callister, 2003). Reviews of home care procedures suggest that when the clinician deals with different cultures, a continuum of characteristics is seen ranging from stoicism, denial, and a reluctance to accept treatment to loud exclamations of pain (Ondeck, 2003). There is a particular need for a better understanding of some of the cultural healing techniques used for pain.

Sex and ethnic differences also interact, and this interaction changes as we grow older. As we age our pain thresholds increase, but we get less and less tolerant of pain and tend to report it more (Lautenbacher & Strian, 1991; Skevington, 1995). Pain also tends to increase in frequency as we age (Mottram, Peat, Thomas, Wilkie, & Croft, 2008).

SYNTHESIZE, EVALUATE, APPLY	• What cultural factors influence your experience of pain? • How would people with different approaches to health (as described in Chapter 2) experience pain differently? Given what you know about different cultures, what other differences in the experience of pain would you think exist?

TYPOLOGIES AND BIOLOGY OF PAIN

Think about how you describe your sensations of pain. After running into a wall or a corner of the table, you may experience a numbing pain. A headache throbs. A tooth aches. A burn smarts. There are many different causes for the sensation we refer to as pain. In addition, many different words can be used to describe pain. Pain has been classified in many different ways: it can be short term, referred to as **acute** pain, or it can be experienced for a long period of time, termed **chronic** pain. If the chronic pain is associated with a disease such as cancer, it is referred to as chronic malignant pain. If it is not associated with a malignant state, such as lower back pain, it is referred to as chronic noncancer pain (Turk, 2001). Acute pain can last for minutes, hours, or even days or weeks. Chronic pain often persists for months or even years. Pain can be limited to a small area, say your lower back, or spread out over a large area, for example, your entire body when you have the flu.

In addition to terms based on the duration of the pain (e.g., acute and chronic), pain can be described based on its origins. For example, purely psychological pain without a physiological basis is referred to as **psychogenic pain**. Pure nociception without significant psychological pain is referred to as **neuropathic pain**. Similarly, physiological pain without specific tissue damage is referred to as **somatic pain** (Turk, 2001).

There are four distinct physiological processes critical to understanding pain: transduction, transmission, modulation, and perception (Fields, 1987). **Transduction** takes place at the level of the receptors where chemical (e.g., caustic fumes), mechanical (e.g., a pinprick), or thermal (e.g., a flame) energy is converted in electrochemical nerve impulses. This electrochemical energy is then transmitted or relayed from the sensory receptors to the central nervous system. Substance P is a neurotransmitter that plays a role in transmission. The sensory nerve fibers transmitting signals from the receptors to the spinal cord are called **afferent fibers** and are part of the peripheral nervous system. The spinal cord neurons that relay the signal up to the brain are part of the central nervous system and ascend to the brainstem. In the brain, neurons transmit impulses between the thalamus and the various parts of the cortex. **Modulation** refers to the neural activity leading to the control of pain transmissions between the various parts of the brain. The main parts of the nervous system involved in modulation are the frontal cortex, hypothalamus, periaqueductal gray matter, reticular formation, and medulla in the brain and the areas of the spinal cord to be described shortly. The end result of these three processes is perception of pain when the neural activity of transmission and modulation results in a subjective experience (Figure 9.1).

MEASURING PAIN

Given the multifaceted nature of pain, it is particularly difficult to measure. Can we objectively measure tissue damage? No, we really cannot. Furthermore, the same physical problem may cause different amounts of pain to different people. A broken limb may hurt Nikhil much more than the same break may hurt Nathan. Given the number of words that one can use to describe pain, we also encounter major language issues when we try to ask someone if he or she is in pain or what sort of pain he or she is experiencing. These issues make measuring pain difficult.

Most hospitals in North America now consider pain to be a **vital sign**, one of five basic measures that doctors get from patients (temperature, pulse,

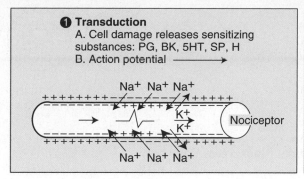

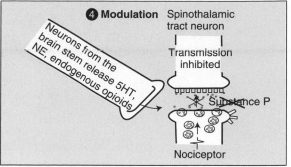

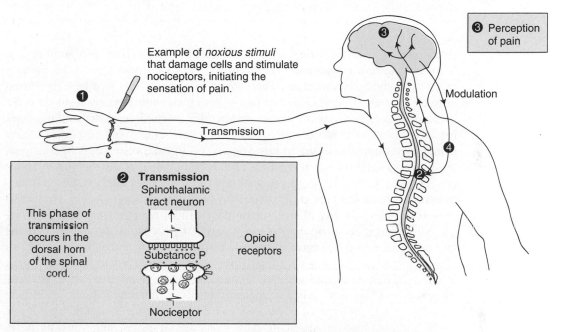

FIGURE **9.1** Four Basic Processes Involved in Understanding Pain

The location where each process takes place is shown with the corresponding numbers on the diagram.

Source: *From McCaffery and Pasero*, Pain: Clinical Manual, *p. 21. Copyright © 1999 Mosby, Inc. Reprinted by permission of Elsevier.*

blood pressure, and respiration are the other four). Given that pain has to be measured right away, how do you do it if the patient does not speak English and no interpreter is available? How do you do it if the patient is a young child who cannot comprehend the question?

Basic Pain Measures

Hospitals have a variety of simple ways to assess pain that can be used across cultures. Regardless of the race, ethnicity, or age of the patient, illustrations of different levels of pain can help in pain assessment (Jensen & Karoly, 2001). A sample pictorial measure of pain is shown in Figure 9.2. The young patient is shown a

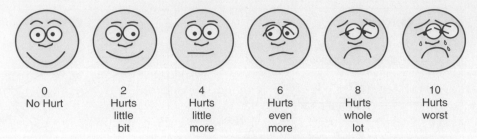

FIGURE **9.2** Sample Pictorial Measure of Pain
A pictorial measure of pain can be used by young children and people from different cultures (labels are translated to different languages).

series of 6 to 10 descriptive faces. At one end of the spectrum is a smiling face (representing no or low pain). At the other end of the spectrum is a frowning face (representing lots of pain). The patient indicates which face best represents how he or she is feeling. This measure is also used with patients from different cultural backgrounds with simple instructions printed in different languages beneath it (McGrath & Gillespie, 2001). For example, in many hospitals ranging from Green Bay, Wisconsin, to Los Angeles, California, color clipboards or posters with the scale shown in Figure 9.2 are accompanied by instructions in Spanish. Together with this simple pictorial measure, hospitals also use a continuous measure of pain. Patients are instructed to pick how much pain they are feeling on a scale of 0 to 10 with 0 meaning no pain and 10 signifying extreme pain.

Even simple measures can reveal important procedural problems. Patients and physicians often disagree in their assessment of pain intensity. Staton et al. (2007) explored the impact of patient factors on underestimation of pain intensity. Physicians underestimated pain intensity relative to their patients 39 percent of the time. Forty-six percent agreed with their patients' pain perception, and 15 percent of physicians overestimated their patients' pain levels by ≥2 points. Racism raised its ugly head again: physicians were twice as likely to underestimate pain in the African American patients compared to all other ethnicities combined.

The McGill Pain Questionnaire (MPQ)

A number of validated pain questionnaires are used in addition to the preceding simple measures of pain. The MPQ is one of the earliest and most frequently used questionnaires and draws on the fact that we use words to describe pain (Melzack, 1975). It consists of three main dimensions, sensory, affective, and evaluative, with each tapping into different aspects of pain. The sensory aspect captures the frequency, location, and sensory quality of pain, such as spreading, burning, pulsing, or crushing. The affective aspect captures more emotional qualities like annoying, terrifying, exhausting, or sickening. The evaluative aspect captures the experience of pain (for example, agonizing or excruciating). In addition, patients can indicate where exactly they feel pain on two outlines of the human body as shown in Figure 9.3.

ST. VINCENT HOSPITAL
GREEN BAY, WISCONSIN
www.stvincenthospital.org
PAIN ASSESSMENT FORM

Date:_____
Patient's Goal_____
Age____

1. Current Intensity:

—10 Worst pain imaginable
— 9
— 8
— 7
— 6
— 5
— 4
— 3
— 2
— 1
— 0

2. How and when did pain begin? Did something trigger your pain?
_____
_____

3. Where is the pain located? I = Internal, E = external. Use drawing.

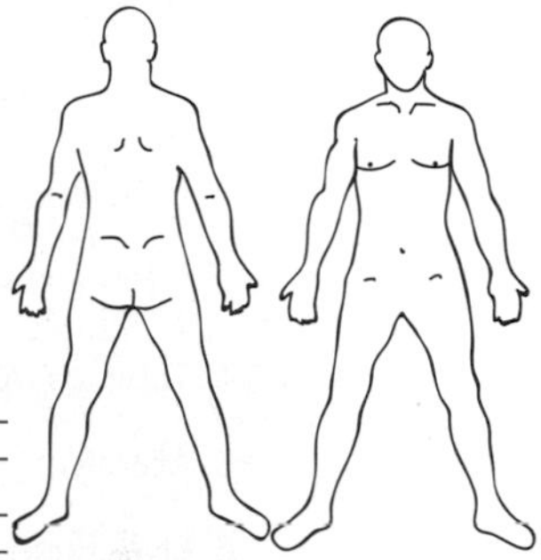

4. Is pain:
Continuous Intermittent
Describe patterns/changes:
_____
_____
_____
_____
_____

5. Describe in your own words what your pain feels like. _____
_____
6. What makes the pain better/what has helped in the past? _____
_____
7. What makes the pain worse/what has not helped in the past?_____
_____
8. What other symptoms accompany your pain?_____
9. How does pain affect your:

Sleep _____
Appetite _____
Physial Activity _____
Concentration _____
Emotions (Anxiety Factor) _____
Social Relationships_____
What would you like to do that you are not able to now? _____
10. What do you think is causing your pain? _____
11. Current analgesics and nonpharmacologic regimes: _____
12. Plan/comments: _____
_____
_____
_____
_____Signature/Date_____

FIGURE **9.3** A Hospital Measure of Pain

Notice the many different aspects of the phenomenon of pain that are assessed.
Copyright © 2005 St. Vincent Hospital. Used by permission of the author.

(continues)

1. Medical History
   Diabetes   Depression   Peptic Ulcer   Gout
   Liver Disease   Renal Disease   Osteoarthritis   Cardiac Disease
   Fibromyalgia   Rheumatoid Arthritis   Neuromuscular Disease   HTN
   Migraines   Wounds   Spondylolisthesis   Other_____

2. Previous Treatments
   Pain Clinic Injections   Chronic Pain Clinic   Spiritual Consult   Guided Imagery
   Massage Therapy   Herbal Treatment   Psychotherapy   Body Mechanics
   Vocational Rehab   Aquatic Therapy   Physical Therapy   Other_____
   Occupational Therapy   Dietary Consult   Relaxation

3. Other Physician Consults:
   Chiropractic   Neurosurgeon   Addictionologist
   Rehab Physiatrist   Orthopod   Pain Physician
   Rheumatologist   Neurologist   Other_____

4. Tobacco, Alcohol, Nonprescription meds. Explain _____

5. Allergies:_____

6. Liver Function: _____AST _____ALT _____Alk. Phos.

7. Renal Function:_____Creat. _____BUN

8. Other medications: _____
   _____

9. Side effects of analgesics/adjuvants:
   Constipation   Xerostomia   Drowsiness   Twitching   Other_____

10. History of accidents:_____
    _____

11. History of previous surgeries:_____
    _____

12. Results of scans, x-rays, cultures, etc. _____
    _____

13. Other consultants and their recommendations:_____
    _____
    _____

14. Follow-up visits and recommendations:
    Date   Comments   Signature
    _____
    _____
    _____

FIGURE **9.3** (*continued*)
A Hospital Measure of Pain

The Multidimensional Pain Inventory (MPI)

The MPI is a longer measure consisting of 52 questions and divided into three main sections (Kerns, Turk, & Rudy, 1985). Using a more biopsychosocial approach, the first section assesses the intensity of pain, the patient's view of his or her own functioning with pain and other aspects such as the extent to which pain interferes with the patient's life. The second section measures the patient's views of how those with close relationships respond to him or her. The third section assesses the extent to which the pain prevents the patient from taking part in daily life by measuring how often the patient partakes in 30 different daily activities. This form of measurement of the patient's perceptions and behaviors is seen in other pain measures as well. For example, the Multiaxial Assessment of Pain (MAP) (Turk & Rudy, 1986) measures both psychological and behavioral aspects of pain.

The Short Form with 36 Questions (SF-36)

Some general measures of health include measures of pain. Ware, Snow, Kosinski, and Gandek (1993) developed the (pedestrian, but precisely named) SF-36, a health status questionnaire with eight scales assessing most of the important dimensions of health status. Together with measuring aspects such as physical and social functioning, the SF-36 also has a measure of Bodily Pain. The Bodily Pain scale has a range of 0 to 100 and has been suggested as a good tool for busy primary care clinicians because its use facilitates and focuses listening, and the result can be viewed as a vital sign (Wetzler, Lum, & Bush, 2000).

Other Measures

Other psychological tests such as the Minnesota Multiphasic Personality Inventory (MMPI) and the Beck Depression Inventory (Beck, Ward, Mendelson, Mock, & Erbaugh, 1961) are also used to get a sense of a person's pain. For example, patients who are likely to experience chronic pain are also likely to score high on the MMPI subscales of hypochondriasis, depression, and hysteria (referred to as the neurotic triad) (Bradley & Van der Heide, 1984). More recently, Mason, Skevington, and Osborn (2008) developed a pain and discomfort module (PDM) designed to assess the full impact of quality of life (QoL, more on this in the next chapter) relating to chronic pain. The PDM is a self-administered, multidimensional subjective assessment of pain-related QoL, with potential to evaluate pain-relieving interventions, and identify sufferer's needs.

In addition to paper and pencil measures and interviews, you can also assess the extent to which people are in pain by just observing their behaviors. Even for something as mundane as sleeping in an odd way and getting a crook in your neck, your behaviors change. You walk with a slightly different step because of the pain in your neck, and you may grimace as you turn your head. For patients with chronic pain, the pain can impact many aspects of their lives. They may moan and groan in pain, walk with trouble, and even avoid doing things that they have to do, such as picking up a bag of groceries. Likewise, even if patients report not feeling a lot of pain, a doctor can get a sense of their pain levels by watching how they sit, stand, move, and talk (Fordyce, 1990).

The use of objective pain measures is also important when treating patients who cannot speak (such as patients in intensive care units). Objective measures vary in applicability based on the types of patients they are used with (see Li, Puntillo, & Miaskowski, 2008, for a review). Although the physiological measures such as electroencephalography, electromyography (EMG), and skin conductance are often used to assess pain (Blanchard & Andrasik, 1985), they have not always been found to be very helpful (Flor, 2001).

THEORIES OF PAIN

Early Physiological and Psychological Approaches

So how did humankind explain pain in the first place? Healers, shamans, and physicians throughout history encountered people with pain and were driven to help them get rid of it. To treat pain, one must have a sense of how it is caused. There have been many explanations for pain over the last 3,000 or so years. Table 9.1 summarizes the main theories of pain. Going back as far as we can to the Greeks, we find that pain was considered an experience subject to rational thinking just like any other experience or behavior. Centuries later, Descartes (1664) provided one of the first theories of how we experience pain. He argued that pain is the result of specific stimuli acting on the body: the stronger the stimuli, the stronger the pain. Descartes hypothesized the existence of long nerves that extended through the body from the brain to the sense organs. Sensations at the skin's surface, for example, the bite of a dog, would be relayed to the brain, which would then coordinate a response (pulling your hand away).

This unidimensional model of pain used a **specificity** concept, later made explicit by Von Frey (1894). Pain was thought to be a specific independent sensation such as heat or touch, with specialized receptors responding to specific stimuli. Specialized centers in the brain would then stimulate actions

TABLE **9.1**

Main Theories of Pain from an Historical Perspective

3000 B.C.	Evil spirits
1000 B.C.	God's will
500 B.C.	Irrational thinking—Greeks
1664 A.D.	Specific stimuli—Descartes
1886	Pattern theory
1884	Specificity theory
1959	Pain-prone personality—Engel
1965	Gate control theory—Melzack and Wall
1974	Cognitive-behavioral model—Brewer
1990	Diathesis-stress theory of pain (Turk et al.)
1999	Neuromatrix theory of pain—Melzack

to avoid further harm. Concurrent with the formulation of the specificity theory, Goldschneider (1886) suggested that pain results from a combination of impulses from nerve endings. According to this **pattern theory**, different patterns of stimulations caused different types of pain. No separate pain system was needed and instead of the intensity of the stimulus, strong, mild, and medium levels of pain resulted in how impulses were integrated in the dorsal horn of the spinal cord.

Although prevalent for many years, neither model explained some basic observations. For example, patients with similar objectively determined injuries vary greatly in their reports of pain severity (Turk, 2001a). Similarly, patients experiencing the same reports of pain who are treated in similar ways do not experience similar relief. Furthermore, surgery designed to alleviate pain by severing the neurological pathways responsible for it often does not work (Turk & Nash, 1996).

In contrast to both these physiological theories (neither of which had any place for psychological influences on pain), Engel (1959) proposed one of the first models to allow for the role of emotions and perceptions. Having a **pain-prone personality** was thought to predispose a person to experience persistent pain. Expanded on by Blumer and Heilbronn (1984), the pain-prone person tends to deny emotional and interpersonal problems, is unable to cope with anger and hostility, and has a family history of depression, alcoholism, and chronic pain. Not only was there little empirical support for this theory (Turk & Salovey, 1984), but it did not account for how pain itself can produce changes in personality. Nonetheless, there is something intuitively satisfying about individual differences in pain perception. In recognition of the fact that psychological factors can predispose one to pain, the American Psychiatric Association created two psychiatric diagnoses: pain associated with psychological factors either with or without a diagnosed medical condition (Turk, 2001b).

Biopsychological Theories of Pain

So far, the different theories we have discussed were primarily physiological or psychological in nature. In lieu of purely psychological predispositions to pain, many researchers attempted to link these two aspects (e.g., Pilowsky & Spence, 1975; Waddell, Main, Morris, DiPaola, & Gray, 1984). One of the earlier models, the cognitive-behavioral model (e.g., Brewer, 1974; Turk, Meichenbaum, & Genest, 1983) suggested that people get conditioned to experience pain on the basis of learned expectations. For example, you hear that dentist office visits can be painful and you condition yourself to fear going to the dentist and then experience more pain when you do go. People with pain are thought to have negative expectations about their own ability to function normally without experiencing pain and believe they have limited ability to control pain. Similar to the cognitive-behavioral model, and as a variation on the pain-prone personality idea, theorists proposed that some individuals may have physiological predispositions to pain that interact with psychological factors to cause pain. Referred to as the **diathesis-stress model**, Flor, Birbaumer, and Turk (1990) proposed that predisposing factors, such as a reduced threshold of nociception, precipitating stimuli, such as an injury,

© National Library of Medicine

Descartes' (1664) Model of Pain and Suffering

According to Descartes, there was a specific system for pain that was responsible for the sensation of the stimulus and the experience of the pain.

and maintaining processes, such as the expectation that the pain will persist, are all important in explaining pain. Although this theory provides a compelling model for the etiology of many forms of pain, the most widely accepted theory of pain is one first published in 1965.

The Gate Control Theory of Pain

The most effective biopsychosocial theory of pain comes from Melzack and colleagues (Melzack & Casey, 1968; Melzack & Wall, 1965). Referred to as the **gate control theory** (GCT) of pain, this model proposed that the bulk of the action takes place in the dorsal horn substantia gelatinosa of the spinal cord and is influenced by the brain. The diagram in Figure 9.4 shows the key components of this model.

Some basic features of the GCT are consistent with older theories of pain. For example, we start with pain receptors located throughout the body. Some are on the surface just under the skin. These receptors inform us when we are poked, scratched, cut, or scraped. Other receptors are deeper in the muscles and among the glands and organs, telling us about muscular strains and pulls and changes in normal functions. In partial support of specificity theory, some receptors only convey pain information. Others also report on general sensations such as contact and temperature. All of these receptors send nerve projections to the spinal cord to the aforementioned dorsal horn. Now here is where the GCT was innovative. Instead of these nerves from the receptors sending impulses directly to the brain, the GCT proposed that the neural impulses from the peripheral nervous system are modulated by a "gate-like" mechanism in the dorsal horn before they flow into the central nervous system up to the brain. What exactly is going on in the dorsal horn?

Three main types of nerve fibers are involved: A fibers, C fibers, and the "gate" interneurons (see Figure 9.4). Melzack and Wall (1965) found that the

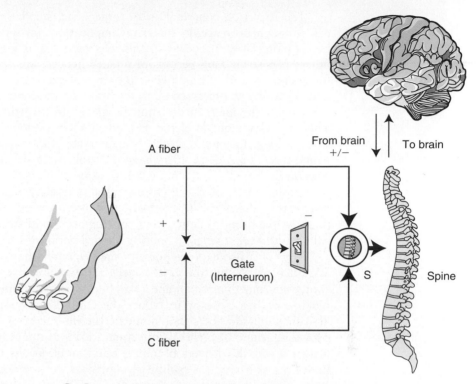

FIGURE **9.4** Key Components of the Gate Control Theory

Pain receptors on the surface of our bodies (e.g., on our feet) are connected to the brain via A and C fibers, interneurons, and the spinal cord.
Positive sign (ı) signify activation.
Negative sign (–) signify deactivation.

diameters of the fibers of the peripheral nervous system varied in size. A-beta fibers have a large diameter and are myelinated (insulated with a protein sheath), resulting in quick transmission of impulses. C fibers are smaller in diameter and are not myelinated, resulting in slower transmission of impulses. A-delta fibers, another form of A fiber, are also small in diameter and have a function similar to that of C fibers. Each of the different fibers (A-beta, A-delta, and C) synapse on both the interneuron and on to the central nervous system neurons going up to the brain (see I and S in Figure 9.4). The interneurons are hypothetical gates that are located in the spinal cord and do not allow pain sensations to be relayed up to the brain if they are stimulated by the A-beta fibers (meaning that they close the gate). If they are not stimulated or if they are inhibited by the action of the C fibers or A-delta fibers, they allow pain sensations to be sent up to the brain (i.e., the gate remains open). The interneuron is thus an inhibitory neuron. The status of the gate depends on the balance of activity between small diameter (A-delta and C) and large diameter (A-beta) fibers.

The theorized combination of large fiber, small fiber, interneuron, and descending neuron activity has many implications for when and how we experience pain. First, it nicely explains why some pains are short lived whereas others persist for long periods of time. Whenever we experience sharp pains for a short period of time (we step on a nail), the A-beta fibers are activated and (1) send a fast message up to the brain via the central nervous system and (2) activate the interneuron, shut the gate, and turn the pain experience off. This is why we only feel the pain for a short period. When we experience slow, aching, burning pains with greater motivational and affective components, the C or A-delta fibers have probably been stimulated. They not only pass on the impulse to the brain, but they also inhibit the firing of the interneuron closing the gate. Some chronic conditions may cause long-term pain by deactivating the A-beta fibers. Herniated discs, tumors, and some injuries may decrease the firing of large fibers, making even mild stimuli that are not typically painful cause severe pain for extended periods of time (Turk, 2001a).

The GTC also explains some of the behaviors that we use to relieve pain. We often try to shut the gate ourselves. If we have a sharp pain in a certain spot, even something small like a bug bite, we often scratch around the pain or pinch ourselves close by to reduce the pain. This **counterirritation** serves to activate the large fibers that stimulate the interneuron, shutting the gate and providing temporary relief (Zimmerman, 1979). Counterirritation is sometimes achieved with the delivery of minute bursts of electricity to nerve endings right under the skin near the painful area or near the spinal cord near the painful area (Nashold, Somjen, & Friedman, 1972). This transcutaneous electrical nerve stimulation has been found to produce relief for a variety of diverse pains (Kim & Dellon, 2001). Together with psychological ways to activate the descending **efferent pathways** and close the gate described above, researchers have found that electrically stimulating the brain can also reduce pain (Reynolds, 1969), a process referred to as **stimulation-produced analgesia**.

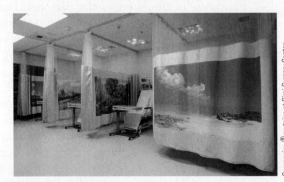

Sereneview® curtains at Simi Surgery Center.
© 2008 Catalina Curtain Company, Inc.

Room with a View

Based on the finding that a good view can help patients cope with pain, you can now buy curtains with scenic views on them. Now even if a patient does not get a room with a view or if the hospital does not have a good location to provide views, patients can still reap some of the benefits of natural vistas.

SYNTHESIZE, EVALUATE, APPLY	<ul><li>Combine the different measures of pain to generate an optimal measure of pain.</li><li>Compare and contrast the main theories of pain.</li><li>Are there any types of pain that the gate control theory would not be able to explain?</li></ul>

THE PSYCHOLOGY OF PAIN

In one of the earliest studies of how psychological factors influence pain, Beecher (1955) compared World War II soldiers' experiences of pain on the battlefield with the pain experienced by civilians. He found that for injuries of similar severity, approximately 80 percent of the civilians requested pain-killers whereas only 33 percent of the soldiers did. Even the self-reports were different. Whereas only 42 percent of the soldiers reported that their pain was in the severe to medium range, 75 percent of civilians reported their pain to be in this range. The stress of battle and possibly the realization that their injuries meant they were returning home seemed to lessen the soldiers' pain. In another fascinating example, patients recovering from gallbladder surgery whose windows faced greenery and trees requested significantly fewer painkillers than patients who did not have a view (Ulrich, 1984)! Consider that next time you have to recuperate from an illness.

The difference having a good view can have on pain tolerance and health has spawned numerous studies investigating the link between environments and health (see Chapter 8 for hospital design work). More medical environments include computer generated nature scenes or art images projected on the walls of patients' hospital rooms, often combined with background music of the patient's choice. Tse, Ng, Chung, and Wong (2002) measured study participants' pain thresholds while wearing light-weight eyeglasses that projected a feeling of watching a 52-inch television screen at 6 1/2 feet in distance. One group watched a silent nature video. The control group watched a blank screen. Participants watching the nature scene tolerated more pain. Studies such as these suggest that even simulating natural environments is tied to increased pain control and decreased patient suffering (Malenbaum, Keefe, de C. Williams, Ulrich, R., & Somers, 2008).

Even virtual reality is coming into play. Immersive **virtual reality** (VR) has proved to be potentially valuable as a pain control technique (Hoffman, Patterson, Carrougher, & Sharar, 2001; Hoffman, Patterson, Seibel, Soltani, Jewett-Leahy, & Sharar, 2008). In virtual reality environments, patients see realistic images without distractions. A common methodology involves patients wearing a High-Tech-VR helmet with a 60-degree field-of-view head-mounted display. The technology allows users to interact at many levels with the virtual environment, using many of their senses, and encouraging them to completely enter the virtual world they are experiencing. The distraction from being in a virtual world apparently leads to lower experiences of pain and discomfort (Garcia-Palacios, Hoffman, Richards, Seibel, & Sharar, 2007). Wondering if playing videogames also has the same effect on pain? Apparently they do (Wiederhold, & Wiederhold, 2007; Windich-Biermeier, Sjoberg, Dale, Eshelman, & Guzzetta, 2007).

Where does psychological control fit in with the biological models discussed above? Melzack and Wall (1965) also proposed that descending pathways from the brain also modulate activity at the level of the dorsal horn. In addition to the afferent transmissions to the spinal cord from the receptors in the periphery, efferent (from the brain via the spinal cord to the receptors) activity also influences pain sensations. Different psychological states such as anxiety or fear can increase the levels of pain experienced. In such scenarios, the descending pathway activates the C fibers that turn the interneuron off and increase the pain sensations making their way up to the brain. On the other hand, when someone is happy or optimistic, these positive affective states also influence the transmission of pain because the descending pathways now activate the interneurons and shut the gate, lessening the pain sensation. For this reason, a football player may not feel the pain of a violent tackle if it is in the middle of an important game, and he is excited or focused on winning. Similarly, if a person is bleeding from a cut but has not noticed she was hurt, she may not feel any pain. A lot depends on how we appraise an event. Similar to Lazarus' cognitive appraisal theory of stress (see Chapter 4), if we appraise a wound or illness to be severe, descending pathways from the brain to the dorsal horn can accentuate the level of pain experienced.

In addition to appraisal, many other psychological factors can modulate the experience of pain via the descending efferent pathway. Bandura (1969) first highlighted the role of observational or social learning in many areas of human life. Social learning can even influence pain. If a young child sees her mother receive an injection without a reaction, the child will probably not react as much to receiving an injection herself. If the same child sees her mom scream and yell in pain when receiving an injection, this child may expect to feel a lot of pain as well. A number of studies have documented the role of social learning (e.g., Craig, 1988). Pain and pain behaviors can be modified by other basic learning and behaviorist theories as well. Psychological pain can be operantly conditioned. For example, if complaining a lot when one is in pain results in getting a lot of attention, the pain behavior can be reinforced and strengthened. Flor, Kerns, and Turk (1987) found that chronic pain patients reported more pain when they had spouses who were considerate and caring.

Pain can also be classically conditioned. If every visit to the dentist's office is accompanied by pain, like that occurred sometimes with a lot of drilling, one is likely to experience fear at just the thought of going to the dentist. This classically conditioned fear can predispose a person to experience more pain when he or she actually goes to the dentist. Even if you have not experienced pain at a dentist's office, just believing a visit can be painful can be enough to activate those descending pathways and increase your experience of pain. A large body of research documents the fact that patients' beliefs about pain, their attitudes, the context in which the pain is experienced, expectancies, and perceptions all affect their reports of pain (Jensen, Turner, & Romano, 1994; Meagher, Arnau, & Rhudy, 2001; Slater, Hall, Atkinson, & Garfin, 1991; Turk, 2001a).

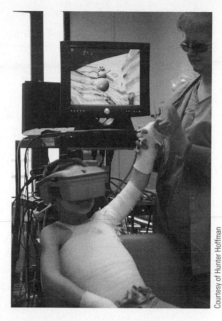

Courtesy of Hunter Hoffman

Virtual Reality (VR) and Pain

New techniques developed by key researchers such as Hunter Hoffman at the University of Washington use VR helmets to help alleviate pain. Here a patient is led through an exercise.

SYNTHESIZE, EVALUATE, APPLY	• What are other possible reasons to explain the results of Beecher's study with soldiers and Ulrich's study of patients with a view? • What aspects of the hospital setting (described in Chapter 8) can negatively influence the experience of pain? • How does the cognitive appraisal model of stress relate to pain perception?

PAIN MANAGEMENT TECHNIQUES

There are three main categories of pain management techniques. The entire list is summarized in Table 9.2. The use of each of these will depend on the duration of the pain, the tolerance levels of individuals, and their pain thresholds. Some of us have high **thresholds** for pain. This means it takes a lot of painful stimuli for us to perceive something as being painful. Even if we have a low threshold for pain and perceive pain easily, we may still have a high **tolerance** level. Tolerance is the amount beyond which pain becomes unbearable, and we cannot accept any more. The main cultural differences that I discussed previously relate more to pain tolerance than to pain threshold. Men and women or members of different ethnicities tend to have different tolerance levels based on their expectations and cultural backgrounds.

TABLE **9.2**
Major Pain Management Techniques

Chemical—Aspirin, acetaminophen, ibuprofen	Hypnosis
Chemical—Morphine	Biofeedback
Stimulation-produced analgesia	Relaxation
Acupuncture	Guided imagery
Surgical—Transcutaneous electrical nerve stimulation	Meditation
Distraction	Long-term self-management programs

We will examine some primarily physiological ways to reduce pain and also a wide variety of psychological techniques. Methods in each of these two categories can be used to cope with either acute or chronic pain although they are all used primarily for short-term treatment. The discussion of the third category of techniques will focus specifically on chronic pain and will include self-management programs. Our goal is to understand analgesia or pain relief.

Physiological Treatments

Chemical

For most common pains, such as twisted ankles, headaches, bruises, and body aches from colds or flu, most individuals turn to over-the counter medications. In most countries around the world, a number of tablets are available to alleviate pain. You have probably taken an aspirin, a Tylenol, or a Motrin at some point (or many) in your life. The use of these quick-shot pain relievers is so common that you can even buy pills with the active chemical ingredients (e.g., aspirin, acetaminophen, or ibuprofen) in bulk packages of 500 to 1,000 pills. These medications act locally, often at the site of the pain. There are three major categories of physiological pain relievers: Non-opioids such as acetaminophen, Opioids such as oxycodone and morphine, and Adjuvants such as benzodiazepines (valium), corticosteroids, antidepressants, and local anesthetics.

For pain associated with surgery and for chronic pains, patients are often given stronger medications like narcotics such as morphine. Morphine binds to receptors in the periaqueductal gray area of the midbrain and produces pronounced analgesia and pleasant moods. Because of its effectiveness, there is a tendency for patients to want to use it regularly. This can lead to tolerance, drug dependence, and addiction (Julien, 2001). Morphine is part of a class of chemicals referred to as opiates, drugs made from plants that regulate pain in the body by mimicking the effects of opioids, chemicals made by the body that regulate pain. First discovered by Akil, Mayer, and Liebeskind (1976), opioids (more technically, endogenous opioid peptides) can be divided into three main classes: beta-endorphins, proenkephalin, and prodynorphin. Each class exerts its pain-relieving effects in different parts of the body.

Opioid therapy for chronic noncancer pain is controversial due to concerns regarding its long-term effectiveness and the possibility of addiction. A systematic review of the clinical evidence on patients treated with opioids showed little evidence of addiction (Noble, Tregear, Treadwell, & Schoelles, 2008). Signs of opioid addiction were reported in only 0.05% (1/2,042) of patients and abuse in only 0.43% (3/685). The study did show that many patients withdrew from the clinical trials due to adverse effects or due to not getting sufficient pain relief. The controversy exists because there is also some evidence for addiction. Another study showed addiction in 50 percent of chronic non-malignant pain patients and up to 7.7 percent for cancer patients (Hojsted & Sjogren, 2007).

Interestingly enough, there are some clear cultural differences in who is given opioids. Pletcher, Kertesz, Kohn, & Gonzales (2008) looked at pain-related visits to U.S. emergency departments using "reason-for-visit" and physician diagnosis codes from 13 years (1993–2005) of the National Hospital Ambulatory Medical Care Survey. The authors found that pain-related visits accounted for 42 percent of emergency department visits. Of note, European American patients with pain were more likely to receive an opioid (31%) than African American (23%), Latin American (24%), or Asian American patients (28%).

Our body sometimes releases opioids when we are stressed, a state that can be induced by motor activity such as physical activity. You have probably heard of a phenomenon known as the "runner's high," referring to a positive mood state achieved by approximately 20 minutes of physical activity such as running (Heitkamp, Schulz, Rocker, & Dickhuth, 1998). This is a form of stress-induced analgesia (SIA) and has also been documented in a variety of experimental settings (Helmstetter & Bellgowan, 1994). For example, rats who are stressed by repeated immersions in cold water show SIA and higher pain tolerance when their tails are placed on a hot plate (no, this is not a pretty picture). Research now suggests that in addition to physical activity, even meditation can release beta-endorphins (Harte, Eifert, & Smith, 1995). The occurrence of SIA is not definite though. There is some controversy about what exactly causes SIA because some studies have not replicated the effect (e.g., Kraemer, Dzewaltowski, Blair, Rinehardt, & Castracane, 1990).

Acupuncture

This Chinese traditional medicine treatment, discussed in Chapter 2, is often used to relieve pain (Goldman et al., 2008; Lee, Pittler, Shin, Kong, & Ernst, 2008; Wang, & Audette, 2008). The acupuncturist inserts fine metal needles into the skin at predetermined points. These points, charted from the work of Chinese physicians over centuries, are thought to stimulate energy flow. Disruptions in energy flow can cause pain. Western biomedicine interprets the effectiveness of acupuncture as being due to the needles stimulating large fibers that close the gate. Acupuncture can produce such high levels of analgesia that even entire surgical procedures in China have been performed without the use of anesthetics. Not only has acupuncture been empirically shown to reduce pain, but also it does so without the side effects of many other medications (Berman et al., 1999; Leng, 1999). Although some studies suggest that acupuncture works because of a placebo effect (e.g., White & Ernst, 1999), it has been found to produce endorphins because the injection of naloxone, an endorphin blocker, also reduces the effectiveness of acupuncture. Furthermore, if the location of the needle is moved by even millimeters from where it is supposed to be, there is no analgesic effect, supporting a valid physiological basis for this treatment.

Another treatment from Chinese Traditional Medicine—qigong (see Chapter 2)—is also showing promise in pain management. A recent review of 141 studies including randomized clinical trials (see Chapter 1) demonstrated greater pain reductions in the qigong groups compared with control groups (Lee, Pittler, & Ernst, 2007). There was a significant effect of qigong compared with general care for treating chronic pain.

Surgical

Sometimes pain can be so intense that a person may just want to cut out that part of his or her body to get rid of the pain. Some version of this macabre scenario did take place hundreds of years ago when surgeons cut off infected limbs for which there was no cure, but this is not something considered today. Yet, given our understanding of the physiological pathways of pain, some treatments for pain do involve the severing of nerves that transmit pain or lesioning of sections of the brain responsible for pain perceptions. Unfortunately, although this method sounds great in theory, practical usage is limited because pain relief from surgery tends to be short lived as nerve pathways grow back and reconnect.

Other Physiology-Related Methods

There are now medical devices that offer patients nonsurgical treatment options for treating some pains such as chronic lower back pain. These methods involve computerized decompression systems that have been clinically tested to be effective (Macario, Richmond, Auster, & Pergolizzi, 2008).

There are also some physiological treatments that do not involve medication. Many hospitals use heat, cold, and vibrations to alleviate pain. Heat, for example, may be applied over or around the painful area or on the opposite side of the body from where the pain is (contralaterally) and it helps relieve the pain. Hot packs and rubber hot water bottles are most commonly used. Plastic bags with ice or ice water, ice packs, and cloths soaked in cold water are used to deliver cold. Some of the pains that benefit from cold include

© Columbus Instruments

Studying Stress-Induced Analgesia in a Rat Using Excessive Exercise arthritis and other musculoskeletal pain, bleeding, episiotomy, skin damage, swelling, acute arthritis pain, and headaches (Triest-Robertson, 2008). Heat tends to decrease sensitivity to pain while cold numbs. Both help with muscle spasms. Neither is used for more than 20–30 minutes and is discontinued if there is skin irritation. Vibration (using handheld, cordless vibrators) and light massage are also used for muscle spasm pain, neck and back pain, tension headaches, and tooth pains.

Psychological Treatments

A wide variety of psychological methods can be used to reduce pain. As discussed in the previous chapter and earlier in this chapter, our expectations of hospitals, injuries, or treatments can influence our experience of pain and discomfort. If you think a certain wound or procedure is going to be painful, you will probably experience more pain. You can use this same psychological angle to your advantage. If you expect a certain method of pain relief to work, it probably will. This power of expectation is often referred to as a placebo effect. Beyond expectations influencing pain, our psychology can influence our experience of pain in a variety of other ways.

Psychological States and Cognitive Styles

Given those descending pathways from the brain, our moods can influence our pain. As discussed in the section on the GCT, if we are anxious, depressed, tense, fearful, or sad, we are likely to experience more pain. Often these negative mood states can lead to biased forms of thinking. These cognitive biases can accentuate the feelings of pain and need to be modified. For example, people often exaggerate the extent of an injury (catastrophize), believe the pain will last forever (stable attributional style), believe they have no control over the pain (external locus of control), or just give up and fail to try to alleviate their pain (learned helplessness). Other pain patients feel victimized by the situation and cannot get past the fact that the pain is happening to them. They often blame themselves and feel worthless, sometimes excessively dwelling on the pain. Changing these detrimental cognitions can aid pain relief.

Distraction

Another way to vary psychological states to lessen pain is to distract the person from the pain (Eccleston, 1995). If you have a headache or a stomachache and are not doing anything but sitting and thinking about how bad you are feeling, chances are you will not feel much better anytime soon. Instead, if you distract yourself from the pain by reading, watching television or a movie, or even surfing on the Internet, you can alleviate some of the pain. Cognitive distraction can also take the form of guided imagery in which patients immerse themselves in an involving and pleasing scenario (Fors, Sexton, & Gotestam, 2002; Sheikh, 2003) or the use of music (MacDonald et al., 2003; Magill, 2001).

Hypnosis

One method that combines distraction with relaxation and a self-fulfilling prophecy is hypnosis (from the Greek word for sleep). It was first popularized by the Austrian Mesmer who hypnotized patients (this treatment later became known as mesmerization) to effect cures in eighteenth century Europe and then later was practiced by the Scottish physician Braid who used it as anesthesia for surgery and then by Freud in his treatment of psychopathology. Under hypnosis, some patients have been found to be able to withstand treatments that would otherwise cause considerable pain (Patterson, Adcock, & Bombardier, 1997). In hypnosis, a patient is induced into a relaxed state, often by being told to focus on an object or the calming voice of the doctor, and is then given a suggestion (e.g., the pain is fading) that is recalled when the patient comes out of the "hypnotic trance" (Hilgard, 1978). Although the exact mechanism by which hypnotism works is still unclear, hypnosis can influence both affective and sensory components of pain (Lang et al., 2000; Rainville, Carrier, Hofbauer, Bushnell, & Duncan 1999; Sellick & Zaza, 1998).

General Cognitive Methods

Other cognitive methods to treat pain are similar to those used to cope with stress. As described in chapter 5, biofeedback, relaxation, guided imagery, and meditation are all forms of cognitive therapy that can alleviate pain. Biofeedback allows a person to get more control over his or her autonomic activity and together with relaxation and meditation helps to reduce anxiety and muscle tension. This facilitates the redirection of blood flow away from the painful areas. Even meditation by itself has been found to be very effective for pain relief (Morone, Greco, & Weiner, 2008).

It bears repeating that different health problems have different challenges for pain management. For example, one specific difficulty relating to effective pain control in patients with chronic kidney disease is that pain killers are underprescribed in patients on dialysis in end-stage kidney disease (Williams & Manias, 2008). Furthermore, most painkillers are excreted in the urine or by the liver, and the avoidance of simple painkillers like **acetaminophen, or Tylenol,** is advised. Pain management also varies by who is being treated. In a review of 1469 published articles on interventions for acute pain in hospitalized children, Stinson, Yamada, Dickson, Lamba, and Stevens (2008) found distraction and hypnosis to be the two leading treatment methods. Other methods may work better for other patients (see the section at the end of the chapter).

© National Library of Medicine

Franz Anton Mesmer Hypnotizing a Patient

SYNTHESIZE, EVALUATE, APPLY	<ul><li>What are the biopsychosocial bases of the different pain management techniques?</li><li>What guidelines would you recommend for the use of morphine, a potentially addictive pain reliever?</li><li>Describe a technique to use both classical and operant conditioning to alleviate pain.</li><li>Evaluate the pros and cons of each of the different pain management techniques.</li></ul>

SELF-MANAGEMENT OF CHRONIC PAIN

Many of the methods discussed in the preceding section are used extensively to treat acute pain. Some of them, such as imagery and hypnosis, are used with chronic pain as well. Still, chronic pain is different and calls for unique strategies. One category of pain relief therapy differs from the straightforward medical model in terms of its goals for change and in terms of who is responsible for change. **Self-management** programs (e.g., Hanson & Gerber, 1990; Kroenke et al., 2007; Nolte, Elsworth, Sinclair, Osborne, 2007) make the patient with chronic pain the one with the major responsibility for making the change rather than the doctor or the health professional staff. These programs have fewer side effects because psychological change—ways of thinking and behaving—are emphasized over the use of medications. In most cases, physicians refer patients to such programs only after medications have been tried. Correspondingly, there is less use of physical procedures and medication and more use of cognitive-behavioral change.

These programs focus on many different elements of the pain experience: the emotional, cognitive, and sensory experiences of pain; the behaviors and actions influenced by pain; and the social consequences of pain, such as the balance of work and play, daily physical activity, and interactions with the social environment. The patient is trained to attend to and modify many of the cognitive processes that can influence pain perception as discussed earlier, for example: the focus of attention, memories of previous experiences with pain and events related to the pain condition, perceived coping alternatives, expectations regarding impact of chronic pain on well-being, and attitudes and beliefs regarding oneself and others. The main goals of such programs are to:

1. Provide skill training to divert attention away from pain;
2. Improve physical condition (via physical reconditioning);
3. Increase daily physical activity;
4. Provide ways to cope more effectively with episodes of intense pain (without medication);
5. Provide skills to manage depression, anger, and aggression; and,
6. Decrease tension, anxiety, stressful life demands, and interpersonal conflict.

After an intensive interview, staff evaluate pain and pain behaviors and take a medical history. The medical staff then assesses the patient's functional status, such as his or her actual physical, emotional, and mental status. The patient and staff together develop program goals, and the patient signs a contract agreeing to work toward the goals. The specific components include some medication but are primarily geared toward patient education. The patient gets skills training, learns relaxation, and learns how to change maladaptive cognitions and maladaptive behaviors (like poor nutritional habits). Finally, the program includes relapse prevention and follow up.

Pain is something that we all will experience at some point in our lives. There are a number of different ways that we can cope with pain, and our cultural backgrounds may favor some over others. Given the complexity and the potential severity of the pain experience, the more ways that you know about how to cope with pain, the better off you will be.

FOCUS ON APPLICATIONS

A Hospital Case Study

Pain assessment is a growing focus in hospitals around America. In this chapter we discussed many physiological and psychological ways that pain is managed, but what do patients actually use? This section will give you a view from the ground up and will discuss a clinical assessment of patient satisfaction with pain management and the varying preferences for different types of pain management.

Many hospitals pay close attention to how successful they are in helping patients cope with pain. In Green Bay, Wisconsin, there are three major nonprofit hospitals in town, and representatives from each hospital gather once a month to evaluate how pain is being treated. This Pain and Comfort Team (PACT) reviews the latest research on pain management and holds training sessions for health care professionals to pass on new information. PACT also periodically assesses patient satisfaction with pain treatment (Triest-Robertson, 2008). This description of one of their studies provides a rich picture of what patients go through in a hospital (Triest-Robertson, Gurung, Brosig, Whitfield, & Pfutzenreuter, 2001).

Patients in short-term stay, postsurgery wards, and a cancer ward completed a short one-page questionnaire either before leaving the hospital or at home. All together 445 patients participated in the study. The questionnaire asked what their worst pain experience was, how often this pain was experienced, and which of a number of pain relief methods was used to cope with the pain. Patients were also asked how satisfied they were with the health care professionals they interacted with.

The worst pain experienced by patients on a standard 10-point scale was 6.28. Of great pragmatic significance, location of completion of the questionnaires was a significant factor: satisfaction with pain management was significantly higher when forms were completed in the hospital. Once patients went home, it is likely that their recollection of their experiences was not as fresh as when they were still in the hospital. Of course, the reason for the pain also made a difference. As you may expect, satisfaction with pain relief significantly differed by floor. Patients who were in short-term stay were the most satisfied with their pain management. The differences were significant even when controls were added for severity of pain (i.e., worst pain) and the number of times worst pain was experienced (both of these variables were significant factors).

So how do patients cope with pain? People use many different ways to cope with pain. The study found that although medication was the most commonly chosen pain relief method, with 50 percent of the respondents saying they used pills or morphine when they felt pain, a significant number of different methods were also used. Close to 20 percent of the patients also used prayer and relaxation, 14 percent used breathing techniques and other forms of

(continues)

FOCUS ON APPLICATIONS *(continued)*

distraction, and 8 percent used music. Which of these was the most effective? Although medications again came out a clear winner (8.9 on a 9-point scale with 9 being most relief), other forms of pain management were very effective as well. Relaxation and prayer were both rated 6.8, and breathing and distraction rated in the high 5s. Music was only rated a little more than 1.

The predictors of satisfaction with pain management also varied by floor. The most significant predictors of satisfaction were the number of times worst pain was experienced, how often patients were asked what their acceptable level of pain was, and how much control they perceived they had. Assessment studies such as this can provide hospitals with clear-cut ways to improve the services they provide and to decrease their patients' experiences of pain.

SUMMARY

- Pain has physiological and psychological components and behavioral, cognitive, and affective states. Two of the largest cultural variations in pain are due to ethnicity and sex, both influenced by socialization. Females have lower thresholds and less tolerance for pain than males. When and how pain should be expressed varies among ethnic groups.

- Pain can be acute or chronic and can get worse with time or stay stable. It is measured by simple pictorial measures or by questionnaire. One of the most common questionnaire measures, the McGill Pain Questionnaire, assesses sensory, affective, and evaluative aspects of pain.

- Early theories of pain attributed causes to spiritual sources. Various models of pain have been formulated, ranging from the unidimensional specificity theory hypothesizing specialized receptors for pain to the heavily psychological pain-prone personality idea, which suggested that certain personality types were more likely to experience pain. The most commonly used theory is the gate control theory, which posits that pain can be modulated at the level of the spinal cord and can also be influenced by impulses coming from the brain.

- Four basic physiological processes critical to the experience of pain are transduction, transmission, modulation, and perception. Psychologically, classical conditioning, operant conditioning, and observational learning can influence pain.

- Some ways to relieve pain include counterirritation, transcutaneous electrical nerve stimulation, and stimulation-produced analgesia. A range of physiological and psychological treatments are available. Physiological treatments include the use of medication, acupuncture, and surgery. Psychological treatments include distraction, hypnosis, biofeedback, relaxation, guided imagery, and progressive muscle relaxation.

- The management of chronic pain often calls for additional techniques. The most common are self-management programs for pain in which patients are empowered to control their experiences to alleviate their pain.

TEST YOURSELF

Check your understanding of the topics in this chapter by answering the following questions. Answers appear in the Appendix.

1. Pain or nociception can best be defined as the:
   a. activation of nerve fibers signaling tissue damage.
   b. the activation of specific sensory areas of the brain.
   c. being hurt in body or spirit.
   d. experiencing severe physical or psychological discomfort.

2. There are many cultural variations in the experience of pain. These differences are primarily due to _____.
   a. genetics
   b. age
   c. socialization
   d. tolerance

3. There is evidence for sex differences at _____ level of the experience of pain.
   a. the biological
   b. the psychological
   c. the social
   d. every

4. The bulk of the clinical research done on ethnic differences in pain has compared:
   a. Asian Americans with African Americans.
   b. Asian Americans with European Americans.
   c. Latinos with European Americans.
   d. African Americans with European Americans.

5. As we grow older:
   a. our threshold for pain decreases.
   b. our threshold for pain increases.
   c. our tolerance increases.
   d. we report pain less.

6. Pain experienced with diseases such as cancer is classified as:
   a. acute.
   b. chronic malignant.
   c. chronic sensory.
   d. acute malignant.

7. There are many distinct processes critical to the process of experiencing pain. _____ takes place at the level of the receptors where the nerve impulses are stimulated.
   a. Transmission
   b. Transduction
   c. Modulation
   d. Perception

8. One of the pain questionnaire measures is the:
   a. Rosenberg Pain scale.
   b. Melzack and Wall self diagnosis scale.
   c. Turk Pain Report.
   d. McGill Pain Questionnaire.

9. One of the novel features of Gate Control theory is the presence of a(n) _____ that modulates the experience of pain at the level of the spinal cord.
   a. neurochemical
   b. interneuron
   c. hormone
   d. trigger gland

10. Activities such as prolonged physical activity and even meditation have been shown to release _____ into our system, which are accompanied by pain relief.
    a. opiates
    b. opioids
    c. oeretonin
    d. cortisol

WEB RESOURCES

Visit the companion Web site at **www.cengage.com/ psychology/gurung**, where you will find online resources for this book, including chapter-by-chapter quizzes, web links, and more!

American Pain Society
http://ampainsoc.org

> This is the Web site of the American Pain Society, a multidisciplinary community consisting of health professionals in different disciplines working to increase the knowledge of pain.

The American Pain Foundation
http://www.painfoundation.org

> The American Pain Foundation hosts a library of information on pain accessible online. It also has a large list of pain-related links.

City of Hope: Beckman Research Institute
http://www.cityofhope.org/prc/

> This lists good resources for pain management managed by the Beckman research institute. It has another vast list of resources focusing on health care, quality of life, and coping with pain in hospital settings.

Self-Management Programs: Stanford University
http://patienteducation.stanford.edu/programs/

> This site shows examples of Self Management Programs for pain from the Stanford University School of Medicine.

Camp Pain Retreat
www.painretreat.net

> A public service, Camp Pain Retreat is an interactive Web site for families with children who experience functional abdominal pain and headaches. Camp Pain Retreat provides psychoeducational materials to help parents better understand their child's pain and cognitive-behavioral strategies for parents to help their children cope more effectively. For children, there are audio podcasts at the different areas in Camp Pain Retreat that can be downloaded and listened to on an iPod or mp3 player with relaxation training and guided imagery. The website also includes printable materials and access to an on-line forum.

KEY TERMS, CONCEPTS, AND PEOPLE

acute, 282	Melzack, Ronald, 284	psychogenic pain, 282	thresholds, 295
chronic, 282	Melzack and Wall, 291	Self-management, 301	tolerance, 295
counterirritation, 292	Modulation, 282	somatic pain, 282	Transduction, 282
diathesis-stress model, 289	neuropathic pain, 282	specificity, 288	Turk, Dennis, 288
gate control theory, 290	nociception, 277	stimulation-produced analgesia, 292	vital sign, 282
McGill Pain Questionnaire, 284	pain-prone personality, 289	stress-induced analgesia, 297	
	pattern theory, 289		

ESSENTIAL READINGS

Audette, J. F., & Bailey, A. (Eds.) (2008). *Integrative pain medicine: The science and practice of complementary and alternative medicine in pain management. Contemporary pain medicine.* Totowa, NJ: Humana Press.

Fordyce, W. E. (1988). Pain and suffering: A reappraisal. *American Psychologist*, 43(4), 276–282.

Gatchel, R. J. (2005). *Clinical essentials of pain management.* Washington, DC: American Psychological Association.

Melzack, R., & Wall, P. D. (1965). Pain mechanisms: A new theory. *Science*, 150(3699), 971–979.

Turk, D. C., & Okifuji, A. (2002). Psychological factors in chronic pain: Evolution and revolution. *Journal of Consulting and Clinical Psychology*, 70(3), 678–690.

Chronic Illness, Terminal Illness, and Death

Colds, body aches, headaches, and fevers are temporary ailments that most of us suffer occasionally and none of us looks forward to (even when it gets us out of a workday or school day!). Unfortunately, not all illnesses are temporary, or acute. **Chronic illnesses** are illnesses or diseases that have long duration or frequent recurrence. Back pain may be acute or chronic; arthritis is usually chronic. Some chronic diseases may even be terminal, such as cancer, diabetes, cardiovascular disease (CVD), and coronary heart disease (CHD). There are over 162 million cases of chronic disease in America (DeVol et al., 2007) and they have an annual economic impact of $1.3 trillion.

Some chronic illnesses occur early in life, such as asthma (see Chapter 3 for more on asthma), and last for a lifetime. Others, such as cancers, may strike at any age. Most chronic illnesses are accompanied by some physiological, psychological, and social changes for the individual and culture influences the ways of coping with these illnesses. There are differences in how men and women cope, the old and the young cope, and in how different ethnic and religious groups cope. In this chapter, we focus on some of the common topics surrounding chronic illnesses. How do you react when you find out you have a chronic illness? What does having a chronic illness do to your life? What can you do to cope? How do different people cope?

Though often referred to collectively, there is great variation within each type of chronic disease. For example, there are many different types of cancer, such as lung, breast, and prostate cancer, and the biological and psychological correlates of one type may not be the same for another. Chronic illnesses also vary in other ways. It may be a **progressive illness**—an illness that

© Digital Vision/Getty Images

Back pain is one of the most commonly reported chronic pains.

becomes worse with time, or a **remitting illness**—one that diminishes with time and ends. Treatments can vary in duration and invasiveness and to the extent to which they interrupt daily life. Some treatments may require hospital admittance, while others may simply require self-administered medications. Prognoses vary and more and more chronic diseases previously incurable are now curable. The pain from a chronic disease and the side effects of treatment often vary tremendously from illness to illness and even from person to person (with the same illness). Consequently, the clinician needs to consider many different biopsychosocial factors when trying to understand how people cope with and adjust to chronic illnesses.

PREVALENCE RATES OF CHRONIC ILLNESSES

What are the most common chronic illnesses? Historically, people died relatively young. Archaeological evidence suggests that men and women lived only until their early twenties in prehistory and the main causes of death were predation by animals and other hostile humans. There were few, if any, chronic illnesses. Most illnesses resulting from viruses or bacteria were short-lived simply because there were few cures for them—if you got sick, you died. During the Roman Empire (around A.D. 100), **life expectancy** was between 22 and 25 years. Current estimates, shown in Table 10.1, suggest that women born in 2006 will live about 81 years and men will live about 76 years (National vital statistics reports, 2008). This is a big change even when compared to only 100 years ago: women born in 1900 lived on average 48.3 years and men lived 46.3 years. This change in life expectancy is largely due to the immense improvements in medicine that can postpone death. However, we do not all have the same life expectancy: Table 10.1 shows dramatic cultural differences in life expectancies both by sex and by ethnicity throughout the years. African American and European American men and women life expectancies changed over time and both groups have different life expectancies today. There is also a significant sex difference—women live on average five years longer than men. Science has yet to prove why this is true. The reasons may be that women give and receive more social support, may be biologically fitter, and perform fewer risky behaviors.

Today, the major causes of death are CVDs, cancer, lower respiratory diseases, diabetes, influenza, and pneumonia. There are surprising statistics: close to 50 percent of Americans have a chronic illness; more than 64 million Americans have a CVD (the total population of the United States is 301 million); 50 million Americans have high blood pressure; nearly 5 million Americans have had strokes (American Heart Association, 2008), and 1.5 million men and women have some type of cancer (American Cancer Society, 2008). Diabetes, an illness that can hasten the onset of CVDs, is a common chronic illness with more than 18 million Americans estimated to have either type 1 or type 2 diabetes. In fact, heart disease and stroke account for approximately 65 percent of deaths due to diabetes (Center for Disease Control, 2008). The prognosis is dim. Figure 10.1 shows the projected levels of major chronic diseases by the year 2023.

TABLE **10.1**

Life Expectancy across Age, Race, and Sex, Selected Years 1900–2006, United States

Specified age and year	All races		White		Black or African American	
	Male	Female	Male	Female	Male	Female
At birth						
1900..........	46.3	48.3	46.6	48.7	32.5	33.5
1950............	65.6	71.1	66.5	72.2	59.1	62.9
1960............	66.6	73.1	67.4	74.1	61.1	66.3
1970............	67.1	74.7	68.0	75.6	60.0	68.3
1980............	70.0	77.4	70.7	78.1	63.8	72.5
1990............	71.8	78.8	72.7	79.4	64.5	73.6
2000............	74.3	79.7	74.9	80.1	68.3	75.2
2006............	75.4	80.7	76.0	81.0	70.0	76.9
At 65 years	Remaining life expectancy in years					
1950[3]............	12.8	15.0	12.8	15.1	12.9	14.9
1960[3]............	12.8	15.8	12.9	15.9	12.7	15.1
1970............	13.1	17.0	13.1	17.1	12.5	15.7
1980............	14.1	18.3	14.2	18.4	13.0	16.8
2000............	16.2	19.3	16.3	19.4	14.2	17.7
2006............	17.4	20.3	17.5	20.3	15.5	19.1
At 75 years	Remaining life expectancy in years					
1980............	8.8	11.5	8.8	11.5	8.3	10.7
1990............	9.4	12.0	9.4	12.0	8.6	11.2
2000............	10.1	12.3	10.1	12.3	9.2	11.6
2006............	10.9	13.0	10.9	13.0	10.2	12.6

Adapted from Table 27. Life expectancy at birth, at 65 years of age, and at 75 years of age, by race and sex: United States, selected years 1900–2005; http://www.cdc.gov/nchs/data/hus/hus07.pdf#027. Page 192, and Table 1. Deaths and death rates by age, sex, race, and Hispanic origin, and age-adjusted death rates by sex, race, and Hispanic origin: United States, final 2005 and preliminary 2006—Con; http://www.cdc.gov/nchs/data/nvsr/nvsr56/nvsr56_16.pdf. Page 10.

SYNTHESIZE, EVALUATE, APPLY

- What are the most common chronic illnesses?
- What sociocultural factors explain the most common causes of death and chronic illness? How do chronic illnesses vary?

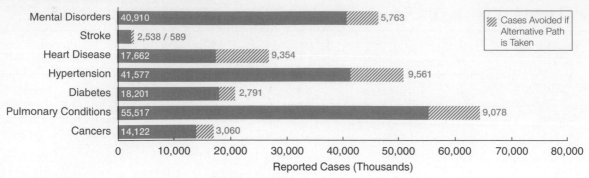

FIGURE **10.1** Projected Levels of Major Chronic Diseases by the Year 2023

Source: Milken Institute

COPING WITH CHRONIC ILLNESSES

Improving one's diet, not smoking, and consuming minimal alcoholic beverages (see Chapter 7) may help prevent chronic illnesses, but do not guarantee avoiding these illnesses.

Goals of Treatment

Before we discuss how one can cope with having a chronic illness, it is important to consider some goals for treatment. Science has made many advances in the treatment of cancer and HIV infection, and some research suggests that illnesses such as CHD and diabetes can be reversed (e.g., Kapur, 2007; Ornish et al., 1998); however, we still cannot cure these illnesses. Therefore, helping people cope with having these illnesses becomes very important. Health psychologists have studied different forms of adjustment to chronic illness. Five major forms of adjustment are the successful performance of daily tasks, the absence of psychological disorders, low levels of negative affect and high levels of positive affect, good functional status, and the experience of satisfaction in different areas of life (Stanton, Collins, & Sworowski, 2001). Of all of these, the most common psychological outcome studied is the quality of life.

Quality of Life

The most commonly used measure of how someone is coping with a chronic illness is a measure of his or her **quality of life** (QOL). Important for planning further treatment, QOL was originally a measure made by the physician, purely by whether the disease was present or absent. If the disease presence was strong, it was assumed that QOL would be low. It is now clear that patients are the best judges of their own QOL. Asking patients how much pain they are experiencing and how they feel (e.g., assessing depression and anxiety) is a valuable way to determine how well they are coping. Quality of life includes several components. Similar to measures of adjustment, QOL includes a measure of physical status and functioning, psychological status, social functioning, and the presence of the disease- or treatment-related symptoms. Using a patient's subjective view can be relative and, therefore, problematic (Sprangers, 1996). For example, a patient may compare their treatment progress and corresponding quality of life to another patient's and become discouraged. Nonetheless, QOL is still the primary measure of adjustment to chronic illnesses.

Quality of life and predicting it vary by culture, especially by socioeconomic status (SES) and age. Conceptualizations of QOL are different for adult populations as they are for younger adults for whom developmental stage and peer group and family are more important (Taylor & Gibson, 2008). A common measure of QOL is shown in Table 10.2.

There are also some counter-intuitive findings of which to be aware. Many people with chronic illnesses report unexpectedly high QOL. For example, many people with paraplegia report mood levels approaching those of healthy people (Dijkers, 2005). It is possible that patients with chronic illnesses adapt to their illness over time and perhaps even become stronger because of it (Damschroder, Zikmund-Fisher, & Ubel, 2008). Let's take a look at the different biological, psychological, and sociocultural factors that can influence QOL and adjustment.

BIOPSYCHOSOCIAL COMPONENTS OF ADJUSTMENT

Many of us will contract a chronic illness at some point in our lives. However, it is clear that changing health behaviors can greatly reduce the chance of contracting some chronic illnesses (DeVol, 2007; Nicassio, Meyerowitz, & Kerns, 2004; Smith, Orleans, & Jenkins, 2004). For example, Blanchard et al. (2004) asked cancer survivors to complete a survey that included lifestyle behavior questions and a measure of health status. The survivors who practiced more than one of the recommended levels of lifestyle behaviors had a significantly better QOL than those who only met one recommendation (Blanchard et al., 2004). Furthermore, any psychological strategies can help one cope with chronic illness. For example, Wright, Barlow, Turner, and Bancroft (2003) studied the efficacy of self-management skill training for patients with chronic illnesses. Adjusting for baseline values and sex, significant increases were found on cognitive symptom management, self-efficacy in fighting the disease and its symptoms, and communication with doctors. Similar significant decreases were found on fatigue, anxiety, and depression, although there were no changes in the use of health care resources or on self-reported exercise behavior (Wright et al., 2003).

Adjustment to chronic illnesses has many different components. Patients need to cope with not only their own affect, behaviors, and cognitions concerning the illness, they need to revise also their lifestyles to accommodate the treatment and cope with how others in their social networks respond to them because of their illness (Whittemore, & Dixon, 2008). They may experience many different feelings including anxiety, depression, and frustration and may not be able to perform common functions such as going to work or even shopping for their own groceries. It is critical for patients to integrate the illness into their life. However, it is easy for patients to be stressed by the illness. Daily

TABLE **10.2**

The World Health Organization Quality of Life Brief Measure (Commonly administered in an interview)

The following questions ask how you feel about your quality of life, health, or other areas of your life. I will read out each question to you, along with the response options. **Please choose the answer that appears most appropriate.** If you are unsure about which response to give to a question, the first response you think of is often the best one.

Please keep in mind your standards, hopes, pleasures and concerns. We ask that you think about your life **in the last four weeks.**

	Very poor	Poor	Neither poor nor good	Good	Very good
1. How would you rate your quality of life?	1	2	3	4	5

	Very dissatisfied	dissatisfied	Neither satisfied nor dissatisfied	Satisfied	Very satisfied
2. How satisfied are you with your health?	1	2	3	4	5

The following questions ask about **how much** you have experienced certain things in the last four weeks.

	Not at all	A little	A moderate amount	Very much	An extreme amount
3. To what extent do you feel that physical pain prevents you from doing what you need to do?	5	4	3	2	1
4. How much do you need any medical treatment to function in your daily life?	5	4	3	2	1
5. How much do you enjoy life?	1	2	3	4	5
6. To what extent do you feel your life to be meaningful?	1	2	3	4	5

The following questions ask about how much you have experienced certain things **in the last four weeks.**

	Not at all	A little	A moderate amount	Very much	Extremely
7. How well are you able to concentrate?	1	2	3	4	5
8. How safe do you feel in your daily life?	1	2	3	4	5
9. How healthy is your physical environment?	1	2	3	4	5

(continued)

TABLE **10.2** (*continued*)

The World Health Organization Quality of Life Brief Measure (Commonly administered in an interview)

The following questions ask about how completely you experienced or were able to do certain things in the last four weeks.

	Not at all	A little	Moderately	Mostly	Completely
10. Do you have enough energy for everyday life?	1	2	3	4	5
11. Are you able to accept your bodily appearance?	1	2	3	4	5
12. Have you enough money to meet your needs?	1	2	3	4	5
13. How available to you is the information that you need in your day-to-day life?	1	2	3	4	5
14. To what extent do you have the opportunity for leisure activities?	1	2	3	4	5

	Very poor	Poor	Neither poor nor good	Good	Very good
15. How well are you able to get around?	1	2	3	4	5

	Very dissatisfied	Dissatisfied	Neither satisfied nor dissatisfied	Satisfied	Very satisfied
16. How satisfied are you with your sleep?	1	2	3	4	5
17. How satisfied are you with your ability to perform your daily living activities?	1	2	3	4	5
18. How satisfied are you with your capacity for work?	1	2	3	4	5
19. How satisfied are you with yourself?	1	2	3	4	5
20. How satisfied are you with your personal relationships?	1	2	3	4	5
21. How satisfied are you with your sex life?	1	2	3	4	5
22. How satisfied are you with the support you get from your friends?	1	2	3	4	5

TABLE **10.2** (*continued*)
The World Health Organization Quality of Life Brief Measure (Commonly administered in an interview)

The following questions ask about how completely you experienced or were able to do certain things in the last four weeks.

	Very dissatisfied	Dissatisfied	Neither satisfied nor dissatisfied	Satisfied	Very satisfied
23. How satisfied are you with the conditions of your living place?	1	2	3	4	5
24. How satisfied are you with your access to health services?	1	2	3	4	5
25. How satisfied are you with your transport?	1	2	3	4	5

The following question refers to how often you have felt or experienced certain things in the last four weeks.

	Never	Seldom	Quite often	Very often	Always
26. How often do you have negative feelings such as blue mood, despair, anxiety, depression?	1	2	3	4	5

Do you have any comments about the assessment?

[The following table should be completed after the interview is finished]

Equations for computing domain scores	Raw score	Transformed scores* 4–20	Transformed scores* 0–100
27. **Domain 1** (6–Q3) + (6–Q4) + Q10 + Q15 + Q16 + Q17 + Q18 □ + □ + □ + □ + □ + □ + □	a=	b:	c:
28. **Domain 2** Q5 + Q6 + Q7 + Q11 + Q19 + (6–Q26) □ + □ + □ + □ + □ + □	a=	b:	c:
29. **Domain 3** Q20 + Q21 + Q22 □ + □ + □	a=	b:	c:
30. **Domain 4** Q8 + Q9 + Q12 + Q13 + Q14 + Q23 + Q24 + Q25 □ + □ + □ + □ + □ + □ + □ + □	a=	b:	c:

*See Procedures Manual, pages 13–15.

tasks, changing symptoms, and fluctuating emotions can be overwhelming (Whittemore & Dixon, 2008). There are numerous challenges to the process of integration and successful self-management with psychosocial, vocational, and existential support is critical. Next, we will discuss some of the different components of adjustment using the major approaches in health psychology.

Biological Issues

Biologically, different chronic illnesses will have different courses. For example, cancer and CHD (the two leading causes of death for Americans) inflict significant changes in the body. Cancer causes cells to grow uncontrollably, harming surrounding tissue and limiting normal function. In CHD, the blood vessels around the heart are clogged with plaque and fat, changing blood flow and possibly leading to a heart attack. Other chronic illnesses such as diabetes and asthma similarly have physiological correlates, such as changes in insulin sensitivity and the blocking of breathing channels. People with overactive bladders (OAD) worry they will not be able to control their bladders (Nicolson, Kopp, Chapple, & Kelleher, 2008). The slow physiological changes limit functioning in many areas and are often accompanied by pain. Consequently, physical rehabilitation is a big component of any treatment of chronic illnesses. The loss of function and increase in pain also have major consequences for how the patient views the world and psychological issues need to be considered as well.

Psychological Issues

Psychological Aspects of Coping

There has been growing interest in the role of psychological factors in adjustment to chronic illnesses (Samson & Siam, 2008). In a review of both theoretical and empirical literature on adjusting to chronic illnesses, Stanton, Collins, and Sworowski (2001) identified two key multidimensional psychological aspects. First, the individual has to go through an adjustment, which includes cognitive aspects such as intrusive thoughts and changing views of the self, emotional aspects such as depression and anxiety, and behavioral and physical aspects such as dealing with pain or not being able to perform daily activities. Second, the sick person must make interpersonal adjustments, negotiating personal relationships with friends and family as well as professional relationships with health care providers.

Perhaps one of the most effective psychological resources that a person with a chronic illness has is his or her mental approach to the situation and **appraisals** (Maes, Leventhal, & de Ridder, 1996; see Chapter 4, Lazarus & Folkman, 1984). Patients' primary and secondary appraisals of the illness can correspondingly influence how they fare. If the illness is seen as a challenge (primary appraisal) and they believe they have a lot of social support to cope with it (secondary appraisal), they will probably have a higher QOL (Gatchel & Oordt, 2003b). A number of health psychologists have modified the theory from its original context (i.e., stress) and have adapted it to help explain coping with chronic illnesses such as arthritis (Smith & Wallston, 1992), breast cancer (Stanton & Snider, 1993), and AIDS (Pakenham, Dadds, & Terry, 1994). In a recent study of women with HIV, Bova, Burwick, and Quinones (2008) tested the effectiveness of a positive life skills (PLS) workshop. Positive life skills were based on the cognitive appraisal model of stress and coping. Small group sessions (6 to 15 women) met weekly for ten consecutive weeks to identify and dialogue about personal and group learning needs. Women explored the power of art, science, and alternative

Physical therapy is an important part of coping with the biological aspects of chronic illnesses, but mobility can influence the psychosocial aspects as well.

therapies as venues for reframing the meaning of HIV in their lives. The six-year longitudinal study showed that the PLS workshop was effective at increasing antiretroviral adherence, improving mental well-being, and reducing stress (Bova et al., 2008).

Psychological Responses to Chronic Illness

There are some common psychological responses to chronic illnesses. **Denial** is one of the psychological reactions first felt the moment a person is informed that he or she has a chronic illness. The person may feel unbalanced and consciously or unconsciously attempt to block out reality and the implications of the test. Denial may be beneficial for a very short period early in the process because it reduces anxiety, but it is harmful in the long term because it decreases adherence to treatment and is associated with delays in reporting and seeking treatment. Another common psychological reaction to a positive test result or even experiencing symptoms of a chronic illness is **anxiety**. Anxiety interferes with healthy functioning, causing a person to cope poorly and delay the recognition and reporting of symptoms. Anxiety is often high when the patient is waiting for test results, receiving a diagnosis, and awaiting invasive medical procedures. Not knowing about the course of the illness or not having enough information about what the illness entails is especially anxiety provoking. Such lack of information-induced anxiety is more pronounced in populations of lower socioeconomic status and in some ethnic groups.

The most common negative reaction to a chronic illness tends to be **depression** (DeVellis, 1995; Kessing, Harhoff, & Andersen, 2008; Payman, George, & Ryburn, 2008; van't Spijker, Trijsburg, & Duivenvoorden, 1997). Depression can be either biological or psychological in nature and can go undiagnosed often because its symptoms are shadowed by the symptoms of the chronic illness. Unlike anxiety, depression tends to a long-term reaction and increases as pain and disability increase. When patients get depressed, they are less motivated to cope actively with the illness, tend to interpret any bodily change negatively, and sometimes are even commit or attempt suicide.

The form of psychological reaction varies also depending on the illness and varies considerably across individuals with the same illness. Personality factors, the amount of social support one receives or perceives to have, and cultural beliefs surrounding the illness can all influence coping with the illness and can alleviate depression and anxiety. Chapter 5 included details about the ways different personalities influence coping. The same relationships that link stress and coping link chronic illnesses and coping. The Big 5 personality variables (conscientiousness, agreeableness, neuroticism, openness, and extraversion; see Chapter 5) have been linked to coping in general (Bolger, 1990) and coping with chronic illnesses in particular (Affleck, Tennen, Urrows, & Higgins, 1992; Friedman et al., 1995; Smith, Wallston, & Dwyer, 1995). Similarly, being high in positive affect is also a good thing for those with chronic illnesses. Positive affect was significantly associated with having a lower risk of dying from any cause (all—cause mortality) in people with diabetes (Moskowitz, Epel, & Acree, 2008).

Optimism is another powerful personality characteristic in coping with chronic illnesses (Affleck, Tennen, & Apter, 2001; Fournier, de Ridder, & Bensing, 2003). Carver et al. (1993) first demonstrated convincingly the role of optimism in women coping with breast cancer. When measured before surgery, the optimistic women were those using more active coping and facing the disease, and those with less distress. This pattern held for three further assessments at 3, 6, and 12 months after the surgery. Optimism is also helpful in coping with diabetes mellitus, rheumatoid arthritis, and multiple sclerosis (Fournier, de Ridder, & Bensing, 2002a, 2000b), coronary bypass surgery (Scheier et al., 2003), and HIV infection (Lutgendorf, Klimas, Antoni, Brickman, & Fletcher, 1995). Building optimism can go a long way. For example, falling, common in older chronically ill adults, predicts poorer physical health and greater negative emotions among the group (Ruthig, Chipperfield, Newall, Perry, & Hall, 2007). Falling also causes drops in optimism, which mediates the effects of falling on health and well-being. Recovery from falling can be enhanced by bolstering optimism (Ruthig et al., 2007). In general, different personality characteristics can greatly help coping (Cervone, Shadel, Smith, & Fiori, 2006; Oxlad & Wade, 2008).

Another important component of psychological coping is related to how patients compare themselves with others with the disease and how much meaning they derive from the illness. For example, studies on upward and downward social comparison show that people can sometimes compare themselves with those better-off than they are ("Boy, my coworker has the same problem, and he is doing so much better than I am") or worse-off than themselves ("Oh, at least I am doing better than my neighbor who has the same illness"). Women who cope better with breast cancer make comparisons with people who are inferior or less fortunate than they are to enhance their self-esteem (Wood, Taylor, & Lichtman, 1985). Chinese women facing breast cancer were also found to "make the best of it." The essences of Chinese women's experiences were that they faced the reality of the cancer diagnosis, took an active part in the cancer treatment, sustained an optimistic spirit, sustained physical activity, and reflected and moved on (Fu, Xu, Liu, & Haber, 2008).

Finding meaning in your illness can often be beneficial, but in some cases it can be detrimental to well-being as well. Originally, research documented that finding meaning in your experience can lead to positive well-being and better adjustment to the disease (Taylor, 1983). There are some important qualifications to this early finding. Tomich and Helgeson (2004) examined the consequences of finding meaning (they called it "benefit finding") on QOL in 364 women diagnosed with stage I, II, or III breast cancer. Benefit finding and QOL were measured four months postdiagnosis (T1), three months after T1 (T2), and six months after T2 (T3). Women with lower socioeconomic status, minority women, and those with more severe levels of the disease perceived more benefits at baseline. Benefit finding was associated with more negative affect at baseline and also interacted with the stage of disease, such that negative relationships to QOL across time were limited to those with more severe disease. Findings suggest that there are qualifiers as to whether "finding something good in the bad" is, in itself, good or bad (Tomich & Helgeson, 2004). We discuss this further in Chapter 12.

SYNTHESIZE, EVALUATE, APPLY	• Evaluate the main goals of treatment. Should there be more? • Why is it important to have a valid and reliable measure of quality of life? • How do the main biopsychosocial components of adjustment to chronic illness compare with the factors for adjustment to stress? Identify the similarities and differences. • How do you think different personality characteristics (e.g., optimism) will change how one reacts to a chronic illness?

CULTURE AND CHRONIC ILLNESS

A person's sociocultural environment has many implications for how he or she copes with chronic illnesses. José, who lives with a large extended Mexican American family, is going to cope with a diagnosis of cancer differently than from Joshua, who lives alone and far away from his European American family. Jessica, a devout Catholic, may face breast cancer very differently from Carmel, an agnostic. Friends, family, and society can make a big difference in how one copes. If you get a chronic illness that is disdained in society, you are likely to be discriminated against for having the disease, and this discrimination can negatively influence your ability to cope with it.

Family and Neighborhoods

The environment in which you live can accentuate a disease or help control it (Gurung, Taylor, Kemeny, & Myers, 2004; Holahan, Moos, Holahan, & Brennan, 1997). Stressful events influence anxiety levels, thereby influencing adjustment to the disease (Evers, Kraaimaat, Geenen, & Bijlsma, 1997; Lepore & Evans, 1996). In a major review of the ways that sociocultural factors can affect a patient, Taylor, Repetti, and Seeman (1997) traced the different ways that unhealthy environments—stressful work or family situations, living in a neighborhood with a high crime rate, being unemployed, or having multiple chronic burdens—can reduce social support and hurt adaptation to illness. As shown in Figure 10.2, each of these different elements plays a role in influencing perceptions and the availability of coping resources.

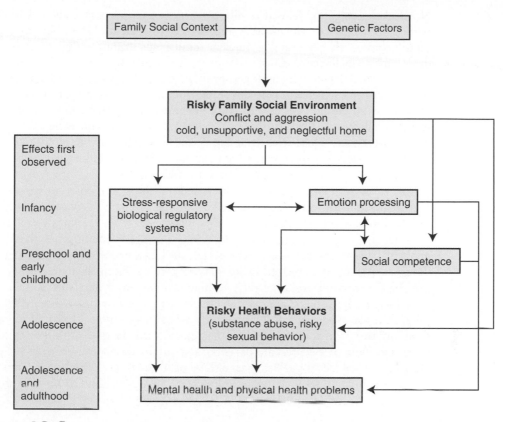

FIGURE **10.2** Various Aspects of the Environments We Live in Can Influence How We Cope With Chronic Illnesses

The importance of social factors such as the family and community structures increases when the person with the chronic illness is a child (Brown, Wiener, & Kupst, 2008; Lauver, 2008; Obeidallah, Hauser, & Jacobson, 2001). For example, the family dynamics can change significantly when a child is diagnosed with diabetes. Some families become more protective and controlling when an adolescent has diabetes (if you thought an early curfew was bad when you were young, imagine your parents wanting complete control over what you eat and drink). In such situations, families may get overtaxed and summon help from the extended family, neighbors, or the community (Stack & Burton, 1993). A supportive community is proven to be advantageous. Statistics show that adolescents living in dangerous neighborhoods are more susceptible to engaging in risky behaviors, hence accentuating the course of their chronic illnesses (Obeidallah et al., 2001).

The composition of a family can vary. Each form of family described below relates to a different family environment and can influence coping with chronic illnesses of the family members. The **nuclear family** consists of a mother (female), a father (male), and unmarried children. Nuclear families account for approximately 25 percent of the different types of families in

North America. The **blended family** consists of two parents, either or both of whom may have been previously married, with their children. The **extended family** consists of a blended or nuclear family plus grandparents or grandchildren, aunts, uncles, and other relatives. Some ethnic groups are more likely to have extended families living together than others. For example, 31 percent of African American families are extended versus 20 percent of other ethnic groups. Some ethnic groups and some religions also include *fictive kin* in the basic family unit. Many Catholic Mexican Americans (and other Catholics) have godparents—close friends of the family who serve as the children's additional caregivers. You may also hear about "**broken families,**" consisting of divorced and/or single parents living with their kids.

Families that argue and in which relationships are cold, unsupportive, and neglectful, are referred to as **risky families** (Repetti, Taylor, & Seeman, 2002). Biology and social environments interact as negative family characteristics (such as abuse, aggression, or conflict), create vulnerabilities that interact with genetically based vulnerabilities, and can negatively impact chronic illnesses. Again, SES and ethnicity play key roles. Families living below the poverty line are more likely to live in high-crime areas where the risks to children increase and the accessibility to health care services decreases (Mayer & Jencks, 1989). Some psychologists study whether one type of family is better than another. Particular attention has been paid to gay families (children with two male or two female parents) and single-parent families. At present, no clear evidence suggests that either of these two types of families is unhealthy for children (Patterson, Fulcher, & Wainright, 2002; Weinraub, Horvath, & Gringlas, 2002).

Culture and Ethnicity

Your cultural environment is important as well. The experience and outcomes of illness are shaped by cultural factors that influence how it is perceived, labeled, and explained and how the experience is valued. For example, African Americans with chronic illness have poorer outcomes than European Americans in the United States (Lederer et al., 2008). Therefore, we actually learn ways of being ill that depend on our cultural backgrounds (see Chapter 2). Someone coming from a self-reliant farm family may be taught to downplay illness and put up a brave face and keep on working. Someone else who grew up in a city may be more likely to follow the complete bedrest prescriptions of a doctor. Both the patients' and the providers' cultural approaches to the source of disease and illness affect patients' care-seeking behavior and treatment opinions, choices, and compliance (Turner, 1996). In the last few years, practitioners have been sensitized to the role of cultural factors, especially acculturation, in rates of life-threatening chronic illnesses. For example, when treating migrants, practitioners are now more aware of casual factors of illnesses such as having to deal with changing diets and stress from their new environment, stressors that often lead to certain diseases like obesity and prostate cancer (Jasso et al., 2004). There is also extensive research on the role of linguistic competency (e.g., Ngo-Metzger et al. 2003) and ethnic match of patient and practitioner in coping with chronic illnesses (e.g., Tarn et al. 2005; see Chapter 8 for more on this topic).

Some cultural groups react to chronic illnesses differently from others (Galanti, 2004; Gurung et al., 2004). Many collectivist groups see chronic illnesses as something that an entire family or community, not just the individual, has to cope with. In the last section of Chapter 8, we discussed how the Hmong family rallied around the sick child with epilepsy and endured personal hardships to take care of her. There are similar cultural patterns across different religious and ethnic groups. For example, many church groups have organized programs to take care of chronically ill worshippers.

Are there cultural differences in how ethnic groups cope with specific illnesses? Research in this area is growing. For example, Culver, Arena, Wimberly, Antoni, and Carver (2004) tested for differences in coping responses in middle-class African American, Latinas, and European American women with early stage breast cancer. They found only two differences in coping (controlling for medical variables, education, and distress). Compared with European American women, the other two groups both reported using humor-based coping less and religion-based coping more. There was one difference in how coping related to distress. Venting related more strongly to elevated distress among Latinas than among non-Latinas (Culver et al., 2004).

Religion (as seen in coping with breast cancer) plays a key role in understanding cultural differences in coping with chronic illnesses. Spirituality in particular, plays an especially strong role in the self-management of chronic illness among older women (Harvey, 2008). In a study directly testing the role of religion in coping with pain and psychological adjustment, Abraido-Lanza, Vasquez, and Echeverria (2004) found that Latinos with arthritis reported using high levels of religious coping. Further analysis indicated that religious coping was correlated with active but not passive coping and directly related to psychological well-being. Passive coping was associated with greater pain and worse adjustment. Findings such as this, together with similar work in other ethnic groups, such as African American (Farran, Paun, & Elliot, 2003), suggest that interventions and community-based outreach approaches should embrace an appreciation for expressions and experiences of spirituality for both patients and caregivers.

The cultural group's beliefs about health and illness are important as well. For many chronic medical problems, a patient's coping behaviors and adherence to treatment will depend on the quality of the patient-practitioner interaction (see Chapter 8). Some earlier studies suggests that patients whose beliefs favor folk medicine are healthier when they seek treatment from folk healers rather than biomedical doctors (Kleinman, Eisenberg, & Good, 1978; Mehl-Medrona, 1998; also see Chapter 2). This could be because of the corresponding belief systems as well as the relative closeness in social class between patient and practitioner. In other cases, it may be because the doctor's own cultural identity may influence how he or she treats a patient from a similar culture (Gurung & Mehta, 2001). In many folk and traditional medical systems, a greater emphasis is also placed on communication, which can increase patient satisfaction and adherence to treatment.

Prejudice and discrimination account for many negative outcomes for certain cultural groups. Lederer et al. (2008) conducted a retrospective cohort study of 280 non-Hispanic African American and 5,272 non-Hispanic

© Courtesy of Regan Gurung

Chapels in Hospitals

Many hospitals have chapels such as the one shown here. Caregivers can come and pray for their loved ones and even patients who are too sick to go to church can go say a prayer.

European American adults age 40 years and older with chronic obstructive pulmonary disease (COPD). The patients were listed for lung transplantation in the United States between 1995 and 2004. African Americans in the study were more likely to have pulmonary hypertension, to be obese and diabetic, to lack private health insurance, and to live in poorer neighborhoods. After listing for lung transplantation, these patients were less likely to undergo transplantation and more likely to die or to be removed from the list compared with the non-Hispanic European American patients. Unequal access to care may have contributed to these differences.

Social Support

The most research conducted in sociocultural factors of chronically ill patients is in social support (Stanton et al., 2001). Empirical studies and reviews show that people with more social support have more positive adjustment to chronic illnesses. Illnesses studied ranged from cancer (Blanchard, Albrecht, Ruckdeschel, Grant, & Hemmick, 1996) and CVD (Shumaker & Czajlowski, 1994) to rheumatic diseases (DeVellis, Revenson, & Blalock, 1997). Having a socially supportive environment often makes the patient more actively cope with the illness and less likely to disengage and get worse (Schreurs & de Ridder, 1997). In the case of a chronic illness such as coronary heart disease, social network size and having a stressed partner can influence morbidity and mortality by influencing whether patients attend rehabilitation (Molloy, Perkins-Porras, Strike, & Steptoe, 2008). Social networks also help maintain quality of life.

There are some important cultural differences in how social support is used (Taylor, Welch, Kim, Sherman, 2007; also see Chapter 5). For example, a recent review of studies on culture and social support shows that Asians and Asian Americans are more reluctant to explicitly ask for support from others than are European Americans (Kim, Sherman, & Taylor, 2008). This is likely due to their concern about the potentially negative relational consequences of such behaviors. Asians and Asian Americans are more likely to use and benefit from forms of support that do not involve explicit disclosure of personal stressful events and feelings of distress. We will discuss more about the role of culture and social support in chronic illnesses later in this book.

INTERVENTIONS

Health psychologists are invaluable in providing important interventions and guidance to help primary care physicians with chronically ill patients (Gatchel & Oordt, 2003a). Interventions to help patients with chronic illnesses serve to alleviate the different biopsychosocial problems they may experience. I will provide a brief overview of different treatments for chronic illnesses here. Each treatment will be covered in greater detail in Chapters 11 to 13.

Physicians prescribe treatment as each illness dictates. Illnesses such as CHD often require surgery of some form if the blockages to the arteries are too severe. CVD patients are often given medications such as statins to reduce their cholesterol levels and slow down the clogging of their arteries. Illnesses such as cancer and HIV infection often require medications designed to slow down the growth of the cancerous cells or viral activity. In many cases, patients are also given pharmacological agents to help with psychological problems such as depression and anxiety or to reduce pain to increase motor activity.

Motivational interviewing (MI) is a type of counseling that helps patients to change coping behaviors (Rollnick, William, & Butler, 2008). Motivational interviewing is a directive, patient-centered counseling style for eliciting behavior change by helping patients to explore and resolve ambivalence. A well validated approach used to work with people who are not ready to or who do not believe they can change their behaviors, MI builds on a patient's internal motivation to change without telling him or her what to do. The approach uses a combination of empathic listening, exploring ambivalence, and eliciting and strengthening change talk. Psychological interventions such as MI are primarily designed to change health behaviors that influence the progression of disease or to help the patient cope with the stress and other negative affects related to the illness. Interventions may aim to reduce smoking behavior, to improve nutrition and dietary choices, or to increase physical activity. Psychological help may be provided in the form of individual or family therapy in which the patient or the patient's caregivers are provided with cognitive and behavioral skills to better cope with the illness.

A large number of interventions are designed to provide social support (Helgeson & Cohen, 1996). These can take the form of individually delivered support messages via health care worker visits, the telephone, or the Internet, but more often are through support groups. Support group members discuss issues of mutual concern, which helps to satisfy unmet needs, and provides support in addition to that provided by friends and family members. You have probably heard the phrase "misery loves company," an adage borne from early work on the social psychology of affiliation (Schachter, 1959). Groups also provide a form of public commitment to adhere to and change behaviors to help cope with the illness.

Groups do not always work for everyone. Helgeson, Cohen, Schulz, and Yasko (2000) determined the extent to which individual difference variables moderated the effects of an information-based educational group and how an emotion-focused peer discussion group helped women with breast cancer. Women who needed outside support (e.g., did not have strong personal connections) benefited the most from the educational group, and peer discussion groups were helpful for women who lacked support from their partners or doctors. Surprisingly, however, too much support can be detrimental. Helgeson et al. (2000) found that the discussion groups were harmful for women who already had high levels of personal support.

A number of recent reviews provide important insights into interventions to help people cope with chronic illnesses. In one review, Hoffman, Papas, Chatkoff, and Kerns (2007) conducted a meta-analysis of randomized controlled trials evaluating the efficacy of psychological interventions for adults with noncancerous chronic low back pain (CLBP). Hoffman et al. (2007) found that psychological interventions successfully reduced pain intensity, pain-related interference, and depression, and increased health-related quality of life. Cognitive-behavioral and self-regulatory treatments were particularly effective.

Another recent review of the research on chronic illness management interventions (Leventhal, Weinman, Leventhal, & Phillips, 2008) illustrates the state of the field:

a. Behavioral interventions have demonstrated effectiveness for improving health outcomes using biomedical indicators.

b. Current interventions are too costly and time consuming to be used in clinical and community settings.

c. Translating theory into practice especially focusing on cultural and institutional contexts suggest new avenues for developing effective and efficient cognitive-behavioral interventions.

d. The integration of the conceptual developments in self-management with new approaches to the design of clinical trials can generate tailored, behavioral interventions that will improve quality of care.

e. The development of theoretical concepts supported by substantial data show that patients represent specific chronic illnesses and treatments based upon their experience and perception of somatic changes in themselves and observations and exposure to information about illness in others. These exposures affect the behavioral strategies they perceive to be effective and within their competence to perform for the prevention and control of chronic illness. (Leventhal, Weinman, Leventhal, & Phillips, 2008, pp. 497.)

f. The translation of what has been learned about how patients self-regulate health into effective and usable interventions is in the beginning stages; interventions work for some diseases, though it is unclear which components are necessary and/or sufficient for success.

SYNTHESIZE, EVALUATE, APPLY

• How would you apply the different biopsychosocial models to the design of an intervention to help people cope with chronic illnesses?

- Map out the relationship between different sociocultural factors and coping with a chronic illness.
- Using the broad discussion of culture described in Chapter 1, what cultural groups do you think would cope better with chronic illnesses and why?

COPING WITH TERMINAL ILLNESS

The course of chronic illnesses can begin in childhood and can last a lifetime. Many chronic illnesses are treatable but not curable and some can be fatal. Some chronic illnesses, such as cancer or AIDS, are often referred to as advancing or **terminal illnesses** because people with these diseases often die after a relatively short time (although this time can range from months to a few years). Not only is coping with a weakening body difficult, but also facing the reality of approaching death is an even bigger psychological challenge.

What can be done to make the end of life easier? Problems with communication and visiting hours and too many administrative details can be trying to the patient and family members (Planalp & Trost, 2008). Care is highly fragmented in a hospital and up to 30 caregivers pass through a patient's room daily, monitoring the patient and performing different tests (Smith, Seplaki, Biagtan, Dupreez, & Cleary, 2008). In general, care should be taken to counter the effects of hospitalization. Patients and their families arrive with anxiety, and emotions are high if death is imminent. Health care practitioners need to be explicitly prepared to address these issues (Running, Girard, & Tolle, 2008). In particular, informed consent procedures should be closely followed whereby patients are told of their condition and the treatments available, if any. Patients should also be helped to accept their situation and prepare for death. This normally means helping patients to use their remaining time well.

Psychological counseling should be made available for both the patient and his or her family. The patient may need help in facing death and in making sense of life. The family may need help to cope both with their grief and with the strain of caregiving. Both the patient and his or her family may need also help communicating with each other, in saying goodbye, and in dealing with sometimes conflicting needs (the patient fearing death and the family unable to imagine living without the patient). One of the alternatives to dying in a hospital is hospices, described in detail at the end of this chapter.

THE ROLE OF RELIGION

Research supports the link between religion and health (Hill & Pargament, 2003; Miller & Thoresen, 2003; Powell, Shahabi, & Thoresen, 2003). One of the most salient aspects of culture, religion is intrinsically tied to the other major elements of culture such as race and ethnicity. It is important to keep in mind the diversity of religious beliefs between and within groups of people. For instance, different races often have different religious beliefs. Also, even though North America is primarily Christian, there are still a significant number of North Americans who have non-Christian beliefs. Regardless of beliefs, turning to one's spirituality can be a form of coping and can even help with pain management. However, this link is also an example of the differences between a correlational study and an experiment. Simply because people who are religious are also usually people who cope better with illness, does not allow us to conclude that religion causes better health. Nonetheless, what is important is that religion can help, and in the context of chronic and terminal illnesses, health psychologists should use any tool that can make a difference.

One of the growing number of studies on different ethnic groups illustrates this point well. Abraido-Lanza et al. (2004) tested for the link among religious, passive, and active coping, pain, and psychological adjustment in a sample of 200 Latinos with arthritis. The participants reported using high levels of religious coping that was correlated with active but not with passive coping. Religious coping was directly related to psychological well-being. Passive coping was associated with greater pain and worse adjustment (Abraido-Lanza et al., 2004). Traditional Latinos tend to be very religious, practicing Catholicism, curanderismo, or more often, a blend of both (as discussed in Chapter 2). With the growing number of North Americans who are Latino, the findings of Abraido-Lanza et al. (2004) and other such studies suggest a greater focus on the role of ethnicity and religion on coping.

A person's religious beliefs often become more important as the end of life nears. Religious beliefs vary regarding the role of pain and of the role and significance of death. Different religions even have different ways to treat death and distinct ways to treat the lifeless human body. The deeper your faith, the more likely you are to turn to it if you or someone you love is dying (Klass, 2007). The way death is treated within a culture can influence how well the patient copes (Corr & Corr, 2007). For example, for devout Catholics, suffering is related to original sin and a Catholic has to face suffering like Christ did. Death is the freeing of the soul to the father who is in heaven. A righteous, well-lived life serves as preparation for death. As death draws near, the family and the terminally ill patient can draw solace from the visitation of a priest who will help the patient finalize his or her earthly affairs. There is a final confession of sins, receiving of Holy Communion (a piece of bread or wafer that represents the body of Christ), an anointing, and a last blessing, known as the *last rites*. This scripted ritual goes a long way to help the terminally ill patient and family come to terms with the impending loss.

Muslims, or followers of Islam, see death as the termination of the soul's attachment to the body. Death is a blessing and a gift for the believer. To prepare, the person must do penance, and be careful to not be under obligation to any other human being—the patient should make sure that he or she pays any dues or debts owed. Cleanliness at the time of death is more important than at any other time. Especially important is the edict that the seriously ill must die at home. To Hindus, suffering is part of *maya*, or illusion. The only way to transcend suffering is to be free from the cycle of birth and death and rebirth. The Hindu tries to work off bad karma from an early point in life and the place of your karmic cycle is indicated by your status in the world; for example, if you sinned in your past lives you will be reborn as an animal or, even worse, as a worm. This belief in predetermined fate helps reduce the anxiety of death. Other Eastern religions share some of these beliefs. Buddhists speak of and contemplate death often, in stark contrast to many non-Buddhists. Pain is unavoidable, but attitudes and behavior influence suffering. According to Buddhists, the only way to avoid suffering is to free the self from desire, which is the cause of suffering. The Buddhist believes that as long as there is fear of death, life is not being lived to its fullest. Contemplating death can free us from fear, change the way we live and our attitude toward life, and help us face death healthily.

The sense that death can be joyous is also reflected in different religious traditions. The Irish funeral is often a rousing celebration of the recently departed's life and is accompanied by drinking and dancing. To the Sikhs of India, death is seen as a great opportunity to do something we put off all our lives. It is a chance to cleanse the soul of psychic fantasy, and life is an opportunity to practice dying, until one dies a death that will not have to be repeated. Death is not sad; friends chant and sing hymns near the dying to set a peaceful vibration and inspire the dying person to be in the best frame of mind. Hence, many religions downplay the sadness of death and emphasize the happiness coming from freedom and the unification with the creator.

DEATH

Different cultural groups face death differently, whether it is one's own death or the death of a close friend or family member (Corr & Corr, 2007; Irish, Lundquist, & Nelsen, 1993; Rosenblatt, 2007; Noppe & Noppe, 2008). In addition, it matters how and when death arrives; the major causes of death vary across the lifespan. How and when death occurs automatically influences how survivors cope.

Death across the Lifespan

Focusing on how we develop is important in understanding why mortality and morbidity varies across age groups. The main causes of death are not the same at each point of the life cycle (see Table 10.3). Birth defects are the leading cause of infant deaths in the United States. Other major causes include complications from low birth weight (LBW), sudden infant death syndrome, and problems from labor, delivery, and other maternal complications (National Center for Health Statistics, 2008). The trauma of losing a child and the way parents cope can vary with the ethnic group and the expectations they have, and many other cultural variables can play a role. Many Mexican American mothers tend to have higher levels of stress during pregnancy. The idea that pregnancy is stressful is actually rooted in the culture: the Spanish word for labor is *dolor*, which also is the root for the words "sorrow" and "pain." Other cultural variables beyond ethnicity can be important too. For example, prenatal care and nutrition vary by SES level and also influence development (Landry, Denson, & Swank, 1997). Many poor families do not have the health insurance or facilities to receive good prenatal care. Poor expecting mothers who are not well fed automatically have an increased chance of complications during labor and delivery (Giblin, Poland, & Ager, 1990; Sable, Stockbauer, Schramm, & Land, 1990).

TABLE **10.3**
Main Causes of Death across the Lifespan

Age	Top Three Leading Health-Related Causes of Death in 2006
1–4 years	1. Congenital malformations, deformations and chromosomal abnormalities. 2. Cancer 3. Diseases of heart
5–14 years	1. Cancer 2. Congenital malformations, deformations and chromosomal abnormalities. 3. Diseases of heart
15–24 years	1. Cancer 2. Diseases of heart 3. Congenital malformations, deformations and chromosomal abnormalities.
25–44 years	1. Cancer 2. Diseases of heart 3. Human immunodeficiency virus (HIV) disease
45–64 years	1. Cancer 2. Diseases of heart 3. Diabetes
65 years and over	1. Diseases of heart 2. Cancer 3. Cerebrovascular diseases

–Adapted from Table 7. Deaths and death rates for the 10 leading causes of death in specified age groups: United States, preliminary 2006; http://www.cdc.gov/nchs/data/nvsr/nvsr56/nvsr56_16.pdf. Page 30.

Injury and accidents are the leading causes of death for children, adolescents, and young adults (Irwin, Cataldo, Matheny, & Peterson, 1992; National Center for Health Statistics, 2008), and many of the primary predictors of such deaths are psychosocial. For example, mothers with high levels of stress, who worked more than 15 hours a week outside the home, and who had a negative attitude toward medical care providers, were more likely to have children with serious injuries (Horwitz, Morgenstern, DiPietro, & Morrison, 1998). Substance abuse and risky sexual behaviors are some of the other major predictors of adolescent mortality (Eisler et al., 1997).

As we age, we succumb to more diseases that are related to unhealthy behaviors. The top three killers of adults (age 25 to 55) and older adults (age 55 and older) are coronary heart disease, cancer, and stroke (National Center for Health Statistics, 2008), each exacerbated by eating badly, smoking, and overindulging in alcohol. Aging should not always be associated with illness and sickness either. A large-scale study conducted by researchers working with the MacArthur Foundation showed that eating well, getting physical activity, and giving and receiving a lot of social support are some of the factors that can provide many happy years of life for older adults (Berkman & Syme, 1994; Gurung, Taylor, & Seeman, 2003; Seeman et al., 1997). The physical deterioration of cells as discussed in Chapter 3 is related to specific diseases in adulthood. For example, many elderly adults experience marked problems in thinking and remembering or **dementia**. The most common problem is one that you will have heard about: Alzheimer's disease, a degenerative disease of the brain that leads to dementia, makes even simple everyday tasks like grocery shopping difficult. Other major causes of dementia include Parkinson's disease and stroke.

These differences in causes of mortality indicate how different areas of health psychological research will be applied at different times of the life cycle. Prevention of injuries should be a major goal when intervening with children, a decrease in unhealthy behaviors is a pertinent goal for children and young adults, and help in coping with chronic and terminal disease is a critical goal for elderly persons.

The Path to Death

As the moment of death approaches, some explicit physiological changes accompany the different psychological stages. Dying patients often experience incontinence, losing control of their bladder and other bodily functions. In particular, patients may be unable to control their salivation and will not be able to feed themselves or even eat solid food as their digestive systems reduce functioning. With cancer or CHD, there is often an increase in pain and medical practitioners prescribe high doses of morphine, even putting the delivery of morphine under the patient's own control. In this way patients can self-administer medication to alleviate their pain and suffering. Patients may now experience severe memory problems or have problems concentrating. Interactions with caregivers and hospital staff can become difficult, which can lead to misunderstandings and miscommunication. Friends and family often have trouble facing the patient in this state, and the patient may not want to be seen by anyone. Talking about death is taboo among many North Americans, the last few days of a patient's life can be very difficult as visitors and even medical personnel do not always know how to approach the topic. Consequently, death education is an important area of research. A variety of sources now exists to better educate different populations about death (DeSpelder & Strickland, 2007; Schuurman, 2008). Given the number of tragedies on college campuses, there is a special emphasis on helping students cope with grief (Stevenson, 2008).

Facilitating Death

Should life be terminated if a patient is in tremendous pain and discomfort or is comatose? This is on of the most controversial ethical issues regarding health care. **Euthanasia, physician-assisted suicide**, and the withdrawing of life-sustaining treatment are some of the most difficult moral and ethical dilemmas we face today. Euthanasia is the termination of life by the injection of a lethal drug. Assisted suicide involves a physician supplying a lethal drug while not actually administering it himself or herself. When life-sustaining treatment is withdrawn, the underlying disease takes its own course. All are subjects of intense national debate (Zucker, 2007).

Consider this scenario. By 2005, Terri Schiavo, a Florida woman, had been in a persistent vegetative state for 15 years. Her husband, Michael Schiavo, battled her parents over whether his wife should be allowed to die. He argued that because she was "brain dead," it would not be fair to keep her alive. Terri Schiavo suffered heart failure from a potassium imbalance in 1990. Her husband said his wife told him that she would not want to be kept alive artificially. Doctors who testified on behalf of Michael Schiavo said that his wife had no hope for recovery. She was fed through a tube, but breathed on her own. Terri Schiavo's parents, Bob and Mary Schindler, maintained that their daughter could be helped with therapy. After years of litigation and appeals, Terri Schiavo's feeding tube was removed in October 2004, only to be reinserted six days later after the Florida legislature, in emergency session, passed a law that affected only Terri Schiavo. The legislation gave Governor Jeb Bush the power to intervene in the case, and he ordered the feeding tube reinserted. In early 2005, the tube was removed again and Terri Schiavo died on March 31, 2005, of starvation and dehydration. What should have been done here? Should she have been kept alive? Was Terri conscious of the world around her? Did she experience psychological pain by being kept alive? Her vegetative state made it difficult to answer any of these questions.

Apart from this more recent case, the most publicized event that put these procedures into public consciousness was Dr. Jack Kevorkian's assistance in 44 suicides since 1990. This Michigan doctor helped patients end their own lives even in the face of threats to his own life. Three juries refused to convict him despite a Michigan statute established for that purpose. The uproar surrounding his case led to intense political movements with advocates on both sides of

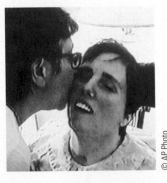

Terri Schiavo

Terri Schiavo from Florida had been in a coma for 15 years. Her husband wanted to turn off life support but her family wanted to keep her alive. She died in March 2005. What information can help decide what should have been done?

the issue, and Kevorkian was imprisoned. He served 8 years of a 10- to 25-year sentence for second-degree murder and was released in 2007. In 1994, Oregon became the first state to legalize forms of euthanasia.

There are interesting arguments on both sides. On one hand, one of the most important ethical principles in medicine is that the patient has autonomy (Angell, 1997). Terminally ill patients may spend months experiencing excruciating pain and discomfort in the process of dying. The extent of pain felt and the amount of cognition present are criteria that can be used to argue for allowing, or even mandating, a person to end his or her own life. It is still very hard to draw a line. Even if a person is in extreme pain, **palliative care** (a form of treatment aimed at alleviating symptoms without necessarily affecting the cause) could be used (see the Focus section at the end of this chapter). If a person is in a coma and has no measurable cognitive functioning, there is still no guarantee that cognition will not return or that the person is not thinking or feeling. Sometimes the decision to cut off life support is made easier by the patient having filled out a living will in which he or she clearly specifies the conditions under which life support should be terminated. A sample of a living will is shown in Table 10.4.

Families also play a major role in this issue (Mowery, 2007). However, research shows that surrogate preferences can inaccurately reflect patients' treatment wishes (Haley et al., 2002). Families provide the majority of care for individuals with chronic illness for many reasons, including a sense of attachment, cultural expectations, and preferences for avoiding institutional care. Although it is optimal for the families, patients, and health care providers to have ongoing discussions about goals of care, it is often only when the patient's condition worsens that decisions regarding end-of-life care take place. Research suggests that family members are often key decision makers for end-of-life issues regardless of patients' prior preferences concerning end-of-life care. Doctors tend to consult with family members even in the presence of written advance directives from their patients (Haley et al., 2002; Mowery, 2007). Because of family and ethical issues surrounding physician-assisted suicide and euthanasia, many doctors argue for an increase in ways to provide more competent care for the dying (Foley, 1997).

In relation, should one extend the life of a conscious and aware terminally ill patient (in contrast to the case described above)? There is some debate about whether a simple and low-cost intervention, such as having a volunteer visit, can extend the life of terminally ill patients. One study suggests this (Herbst-Damm & Kulik, 2005); others suggest it is critical to look beyond effects on longevity and assess the influence on quality of life (Hanoch, 2007).

Are There Stages?

Many in the lay population have heard of the concept of stages of death and that people who are dying experience a series of emotions. This somewhat inaccurate belief stems from work published by Elisabeth Kübler-Ross (1969). Kübler-Ross interviewed more than 200 dying patients and concluded that the process of dying involves five stages that vary in their emotional content and intensity. First comes denial, an initial reaction to the thought of death.

TABLE **10.4**

North Carolina Statutory Form, G.S. 90-321

NORTH CAROLINA COUNTY OF _____

DECLARATION OF A DESIRE FOR A NATURAL DEATH

I, _____, being of sound mind, desire that, as specified below, my life not be prolonged by extraordinary means or by artificial nutrition or hydration if my condition is determined to be terminal and incurable or if I am diagnosed as being in a persistent vegetative state. I am aware and understand that this writing authorizes a physician to withhold or discontinue extraordinary means or artificial nutrition or hydration, in accordance with my specifications set forth below:

(Initial any of the following, as desired):

____ If my condition is determined to be terminal and incurable, I authorize the following:

    ____ My physician may withhold or discontinue extraordinary means only.

    ____ In addition to withholding or discontinuing extraordinary means if such means are necessary, my physician may withhold or discontinue either artificial nutrition or hydration, or both.

____ If my physician determines that I am in a persistent vegetative state, I authorize the following:

    ____ My physician may withhold or discontinue extraordinary means only.

    ____ In addition to withholding or discontinuing extraordinary means if such means are necessary, my physician may withhold or discontinue either artificial nutrition or hydration, or both.

This the _____ day of _____

Signature: _____

I hereby state that the declarant, _____, being of sound mind signed the above declaration in my presence and that I am not related to the declarant by blood or marriage and that I do not know or have a reasonable expectation that I would be entitled to any portion of the estate of the declarant under any existing will or codicil of the declarant or as an heir under the Intestate Succession Act if the declarant died on this date without a will. I also state that I am not the declarant's attending physician or an employee of the declarant's attending physician, or an employee of a health facility in which the declarant is a patient or an employee of a nursing home or any group-care home where the declarant resides. I further state that I do not now have any claim against the declarant.

Witness: _____

Witness: _____

CERTIFICATE

I, _____, Clerk (Assistant Clerk) of Superior Court or Notary Public (circle one as appropriate) for _____ County hereby certify that _____, the declarant, appeared before me and swore to me and to the witnesses in my presence that this instrument is his/her Declaration Of A Desire For A Natural Death, and that he/she had willingly and voluntarily made and executed it as his/her free act and deed for the purposes expressed in it.

I further certify that _____ and _____, witnesses, appeared before me and swore that they witnessed _____, declarant, sign the attached declaration, believing him/her to be of sound mind; and also swore that at the time they witnessed the declaration (i) they were not related within the third degree to the declarant or to the declarant's spouse, and (ii) they did not know or have a reasonable expectation that they would be entitled to any portion of the estate of the declarant upon the declarant's death under any will of the declarant or codicil thereto then existing or under the Intestate Succession Act as it provides at that time, and (iii) they were not a physician attending the declarant or an employee of an attending physician or an employee of a health facility in which the declarant was a patient or an employee of a nursing home or any group-care home in which the declarant resided, and (iv) they did not have a claim against the declarant. I further certify that I am satisfied as to the genuineness and due execution of the declaration.

This stage lasts around two days, can be a form of emotional coping (see Chapter 5), and can mask anxiety without necessarily removing it. Next comes **anger,** a stage in which patients are upset that death is happening to them. In many ways, the fact that they are dying violates a sense of the world being just. Most people believe that they do not deserve to die because they have been good or at least have not been bad enough to be punished with death. There is often misplaced resentment and a lot of irritability. Next comes the **bargaining** stage. Patients try to restore their belief in a just world and may promise to be good or live life better (e.g., give a lot to charity) in exchange for life. This trading for life then gives way to depression. The patient feels a lack of control and now grieves in expectation of his or her death, a process known as **anticipatory grief.** The depression is often driven by a realization that a person will be losing his or her past and will also be losing all that was possible in a future. Finally, the patient may reach a stage of **acceptance** in which he or she fully acknowledges that death cannot be avoided. At this point the patient is often very weak and faces death with a peaceful calm.

Although these stages sound appropriate, and you probably can nod your head and see how a dying person could go through them, there is little empirical evidence for these stages. Kübler-Ross only used cross-sectional research and did not follow patients as they got closer to death. The fact is that people may experience these stages but not necessarily in the order just described. One constant feature in Kübler-Ross's stages of death is that most people will experience some depression just before death. How someone experiences death varies based on his or her culture, how much social support he or she has, the physiological progression of his or her disease, and other factors. Consequently, other researchers have attempted to explain the experience of dying (e.g., Pattison, 1977; Shneidman, 1980), although they only hypothesize variations on Kübler-Ross's five stages. The five emotions seem to represent the most relevant experiences of the dying patient.

CULTURAL VARIATIONS IN DEATH AND DYING

When the time of death draws closer and it is clear that little can be done for the dying patient, it is important to help the person and his or her family prepare for death. We have discussed already some of the traditional ways this has been done, such as psychological counseling. There is an important additional dimension to consider when you look beyond the biology and psychology surrounding dying: culture. From a psychological perspective, fear, depression, and even denial of death may be common for patients and their families, but the exact experiences vary significantly across cultural groups (Galanti, 2004; Parry & Ryan, 1995; Rosenblatt, 1993).

European American health practitioners are often unintentionally ethnocentric and this ethnocentricity makes it difficult for them to fully comprehend the experiences of people from other cultures. With an emotionally charged situation such as dying, this issue becomes even more important. Cultural differences become more evident from even a basic level of definition of key terms. It may seem clear what being "dead" is, but do not take death for granted. In many cultures, people are considered officially dead when

© Issouf Sanogo/AFP/Getty Images

Cultural Rituals for Death and Dying

Different cultures have very different rituals for death and dying. The caskets shown above are part of the burial rituals of the people of Ghana who use different shapes of coffins for different individuals.

Western biomedicine would consider them still alive and vice versa (Rosenblatt, 1993). There are correspondingly some significant differences in the expression and experience of emotions such as grief and loss. In some cultures it is normal for people to cut themselves or otherwise hurt themselves to express their loss. Some East Indians, for example, fast for weeks as a sign of grieving. There are also cultural differences in the fear of death. African Americans report higher levels of death anxiety than European Americans (Depaola, Griffin, Young, & Neimeyer, 2003).

Some of these cultural variations are seen in the rituals that accompany death. Making sure that the adequate ritual is conducted for the bereaved person is often critical to the health and coping of those left behind. Although they are not given any attention in the health psychological literature to date, cultural differences in dealing with the dead may have important implications for psychological adjustment. Many cultural beliefs may clash with the beliefs of Western biomedicine, and hospital policies may prohibit certain practices, but they are important practices nonetheless. For example, in the American Indian culture, the burning of sage and other herbs is often part of many religious ceremonies and is also used to prepare the soul of the dying person for the afterlife. Hospitals have nonsmoking policies and lighting a fire may seem clearly out of the question. But if sage is not burned, it could jeopardize the happiness of the dying patient's soul and greatly hurt his or her family. Health care professionals have to be aware of such cultural practices and negotiate a way to satisfy all concerned. For Muslims, there are also clear-cut practices that have to be followed at the time of death. As soon as a relative sees that the person is dead, he or she must turn the body to face Mecca (the site in the Middle East of the *Kaaba*, the Muslim's holy ground). They also have someone sitting close by read the Koran (the word of God as channeled through the prophet Mohammed), close the body's mouth and eyes and cover the face, and quickly bathe the body and cover it with white cotton (Gilanshah, 1993).

Sensitivity to different cultural traditions can make health practitioners more effective when helping individuals during the difficult time of coping with death. Many of the specific considerations needed are difficult for members of different ethnic groups to mention themselves. In the middle of coping with loss, it may be too much to expect a member of a different cultural group to explain exactly what is needed. It is likewise difficult for health care workers to know all the different cultural idiosyncrasies surrounding death, but both groups need to work toward ensuring an adaptive experience for all concerned.

For some groups, this sharing and explaining of cultural routines may be especially difficult. For example, given the negative points in the history of African Americans and American Indians in North America (Washington, 2007), both these ethnic groups have particularly strained relationships with European Americans and the health care institution in particular (Barrett, 1998). Consequently, there is an increase in the development of separate models to understand how different cultural groups understand death and dying (Corr & Corr, 2007). Barrett (1995, 1998), for example, has derived a list of special considerations for caregivers working with African Americans who experience loss (Table 10.5). Although devised for African Americans, these models serve as good reminders for health professionals working with any cultural group.

Sex, Gender, and Death

In the context of culture, it is also important to look at sex differences relating to the experience of death. Scholarship in death studies suggests that the different perceptions and experiences of men and women must also (in addition to cultural differences) be taken into consideration to best help those dying as well as those caring for the dead and grieving (Noppe, 2004). Martin and Doka (2000) remarked that the benchmark for grieving is normally set as how women handle loss. Women tend to show emotion, seek social support, talk about loss, and allow time to grieve openly, things not normally done by men (Cook, 1988). In a major review of gender differences

TABLE **10.5**
Critical Considerations for Helping African Americans Cope with Death and Dying

1. Understanding the sociocultural influences from both Western and African traditions that combine to influence the attitudes, beliefs, and values.
2. Acknowledge and appreciate the uniqueness of the subgroups of African Americans (when in doubt, ask).
3. Be sensitive to basic differences in quality of life and differences in death rates and causes for African Americans versus European Americans.
4. Understand the impact of collective losses that African Americans often grieve for.
5. Include a consideration of socioeconomic status as well as religion and spirituality.
6. Acknowledge the role of cultural mistrust regarding health.
7. Be sensitive to the value placed by African Americans on expressions of condolence.
8. Understand the role played by and expectations for the clergy and spiritual leaders (often higher expectations than for the medical community).

Source: Barret (1998).

in adjustment to bereavement, Stroebe, Stroebe, and Schut (2001) reported that women express their emotions more than men, although they found little evidence for the hypothesis that working through grief helps them recover faster. Particularly interesting is the fact that men suffer relatively greater health consequences when grieving than women, possibly because widowers get less support than widows (Stroebe & Stroebe, 1983). Specifically, widowers are significantly more distressed and depressed than widows and also have a higher incidence of mental illnesses. Widows have been found to suffer from fewer physical health problems and illnesses than widowers and are less likely to die during the period of acute grief after the loss of a spouse (Stroebe et al., 2001). Keeping these ethnic and sex differences in mind is clearly important in understanding how different subgroups of people experience the certainty of death.

SYNTHESIZE, EVALUATE, APPLY

- How does religion play a role in chronic and terminal illnesses and coping with death?
- Are there biopsychosocial factors that could be used to justify when euthanasia is appropriate?
- How can cultural variations in death and dying be translated into better health care?

FOCUS ON APPLICATIONS

Hospice

When it is clear that the end is fast approaching, how would you like to die? This may be a morbid thought; however, thinking about it now rather than later could influence how much discomfort you experience at life's end. For most terminal illnesses, the physical signs that death is near are relatively obvious (e.g., breathing and blood pressure changes or cognitive impairment). When the signs appear, patients are normally admitted into a hospital where they are monitored until they stop breathing. Sometimes hospitalized patients choose to be sent home to receive home care so that they can die in their own houses. Another choice that has gained popularity recently is hospice.

Hospice is a form of care that has its origins in medieval times. In the early nineteenth century, hospices were places where pilgrims, travelers, the homeless, and the destitute were offered lodging, usually by a religious group. In 1967, an English doctor, Cicely Saunders, felt that the terminally ill persons needed better care and began a new movement. The word **hospice** is derived from the words for hospitality and guesthouse, and hospices are also referred to as nursing homes for the dying. The hospice movement spread to the United States over the next ten years, and today there are hospices in every state and around the world. They tend to be small, residential institutions where the treatment is focused on the patient's QOL rather than on curing the illness.

Unlike in a hospital, hospices do not attempt to cure the patient or prolong life (Kastenbaum, 1999). The dying are comforted, and their pain and other symptoms are alleviated. Unlike hospitals, patients are urged to customize their surroundings and make them seem like home. Patients can wear their own clothes (no uncomfortable hospital gowns) and bring in pictures, paintings, or other personal effects. The patient and family are included in the care plan, and emotional, spiritual, and practical support is given based on the patient's wishes and family's needs. Similar to church-affiliated hospitals, some hospices have been started by churches and religious groups (sometimes in connection with their hospitals), but hospices

(continues)

FOCUS ON APPLICATIONS *(continued)*

serve a broad community and do not require patients to adhere to any particular set of beliefs. Most hospice patients are cancer patients, but hospices accept anyone regardless of age or type of illness.

Patients can ask to move to a hospice at any time during a terminal illness, although it is often the case that patients in a hospice do not have more than six months to live (and often much less). In America, the decision belongs to the patient although many people are not comfortable with the idea of stopping active efforts to beat the disease in the switch to palliative care. Hospice staff members are highly sensitive to this debate and facilitate discussions of the same with the patient and family. As you can guess, the decision-making process for hospice care has many components. In a study of patients with advanced cancer, Chen, Haley, Robinson, and Schonwetter (2003) found that patients receiving hospice care were significantly older, were less educated, and had more people in their households. Hospice patients had multiple health conditions and worse activities of daily living scores than nonhospice patients and were also more realistic about their disease course than their nonhospice counterparts.

Once the patient decides to go to hospice, the hospice program contacts the patient's physician to make sure he or she agrees that hospice care is appropriate for this patient at this time. The patient then signs consent and insurance forms, similar to the forms patients sign when they enter a hospital, acknowledging that the care is palliative (aimed to provide pain relief and symptom control) rather than curative. A hospice team then prepares an individualized care plan addressing the amount of caregiving needed by the patient, and staff visit regularly and are always accessible. Unlike in a hospital, in a hospice, family and friends deliver most of the care, but hospices provide volunteers to assist the families and to provide the primary caregivers with support. Hospice patients are also cared for by a team of physicians, nurses, social workers, counselors, hospice-certified nursing assistants, clergy, therapists, and volunteers—and each provides assistance based on his or her own area of expertise. In addition, hospices provide medications, supplies, equipment, and hospital services related to the terminal illness.

There is considerable empirical evidence for the efficacy of hospices. The National Hospice Work Group and the National Hospice and Palliative Care Organization both conducted one of the most comprehensive assessments of hospice. The two groups spearheaded a detailed two-year study of the efficacy of end-of-life care and studied more than 3,000 caregivers and patients. Some of the key results were that the majority of patients entering hospice in pain were made comfortable within days of admission, and caregivers' confidence in the care of their loved ones increased because of hospice services (Ryndes et al., 2001).

The hospice emphasis on palliative care can be seen in comparisons of pain relief (Azoulay, Hammerman-Rozenberg, Cialic, Ein Mor, Jacobs, & Stessman, 2008). Hospice patients are twice as likely as nonhospice patients to receive regular treatment for daily pain (Miller, Mor, Wu, Gozalo, & Lapane, 2002). For example, Miceli and Mylod (2003) looked at how satisfied family members were with the end-of-life care their loved ones received. Family satisfaction with hospice care was generally quite high, although the timing of the referral was critical. It was critical to get patients into hospice earlier rather than later. Families rated services lower almost across the board when the referral to hospice was deemed "too late."

Experiments comparing hospices to hospitals are hard to do and unethical (randomly assigning a dying loved one to a condition is clearly unpalatable), but some studies have compared the experiences of patients in each setting. Compared with patients in hospitals, patients in hospices and their families report more peace of mind and greater satisfaction with care (Ganzini et al., 2002; Kastenbaum, 1999; Lynn, 2001; Roscoe & Hyer, 2008). Note that in most cases there are few significant differences in pain symptoms and activities of daily living, although hospice patients report more overall psychological well-being (Gatchel & Oordt, 2003a; Viney, Walker, Robertson, Lilley, & Ewan, 1994). Patients in hospices do not necessarily live longer nor do they have significantly fewer physician visits (Kane, Klein, Bernstein, & Rothenberg, 1986).

(continues)

FOCUS ON APPLICATIONS *(continued)*

There are some significant cultural differences in hospice use as well. Colon and Lyke (2003) found that African Americans and Latinos both used hospice services at significantly lower rates than European Americans. In addition, African American use of hospices declined significantly during the study (1995 to 2001), whereas European American use increased. Similarly, Ngo-Metzger, Phillips, & McCarthy (2008) found that Asian Americans had lower rates of hospice use than European American patients. Japanese Americans had a shorter median length of stay (21 days), and Filipino Americans had a longer median length of stay (32 days) than European American patients (26 days).

SUMMARY

- Chronic illnesses are illnesses that persist over a long period of time. The most common chronic illnesses are cancer, cardiovascular disease, AIDS, back pain, diabetes, and arthritis. Some of these, such as cardiovascular disease, are reversible, but most are terminal. Most chronic diseases show varying incidence rates across different cultural groups.
- To help patients and their families cope with the changes in lifestyle from chronic illnesses, health psychologists often focus on improving the quality of life (QOL) of the individual. Quality of life is measured by assessing physical and psychological status together with functioning.
- Patients' cognitive appraisals of their situation and their own personal goals are critical components of coping with chronic illnesses. Common responses to the diagnosis of a chronic illness are denial, anxiety, and depression. Optimism is a powerful tool in coping with illness.
- Sociocultural factors play a major role in coping with chronic illnesses. The quality of one's close relationships, interactions with family and friends, and even the neighborhood one lives in can all influence QOL. Patients with strong religious beliefs or from certain ethnic groups may have different coping responses.
- A majority of health psychological interventions are designed to provide chronically ill patients with social support. Although many interventions show success, not all group support interventions work for everyone.
- The proximity of death brings its own specific challenges. Together with physiological and psychological deterioration, patients often experience denial, anger, depression, acceptance, or anticipatory grief and sometimes bargain (not always in this order).
- Physician-assisted suicide, euthanasia, and the withdrawal of life support are controversial issues in terminal care. Patients are urged to complete living wills that specify what they would like to be done if they are nonresponsive, in a coma, or receiving life support. Palliative care and hospice care are both commonly used forms of care that do not include attempts to cure the illness and prolong life.
- Not all cultures define death in the same way. Based on varying cultural philosophies regarding the purpose of life and the nature of the afterlife,

different cultures have different behaviors and procedures for coping with the impending death of a loved one.

TEST YOURSELF

Check your understanding of the topics in this chapter by answering the following questions. Answers appear in the Appendix.

1. Current life expectancy estimate for women born in 2006 is approximately _____ years.
   a. 65
   b. 72
   c. 78
   d. 82
2. The most prevalent chronic disease is also the nation's primary cause of death. That illness is_____.
   a. Coronary heart disease
   b. Cancer
   c. Diabetes
   d. Pneumonia
3. From a health psychologist's perspective, one of the main treatment goals for those with a chronic illness is:
   a. Increasing the quality of life.
   b. Preventing the spread of the disease.
   c. Safeguarding other family members.
   d. Curing the disease.
4. From a biological standpoint, chronic illnesses are difficult to cope with because they:
   a. Disrupt normal life functioning.
   b. Are often contagious.
   c. Always bring pain.
   d. Fluctuate unpredictably.
5. One of the most effective psychological resources that people with chronic illness have is:
   a. Self esteem.
   b. Appraisals of situations.
   c. Levels of extraversion.
   d. Hardiness.
6. One of the first psychological reactions to discovering you have a chronic illness is:
   a. Denial.
   b. Depression.

   c. Anxiety.
   d. Optimism.
7. One of the psychological reactions to a chronic illness that tends to be long term and increases as pain and disability increase is _____.
   a. Denial.
   b. Depression.
   c. Anxiety.
   d. Fear.
8. Psychological interventions to help people cope with chronic illnesses are primarily designed to:
   a. Change health behaviors that influence disease progression.
   b. Change personality traits to make the person more optimistic.
   c. Physically rehabilitate the person to make them live life normally.
   d. Help caregivers care for the patients.
9. Social support is good to help people cope, but Helgeson et al. (2000) warn that:
   a. Those who really do not need it benefit the most.
   b. Support is only helpful if people believe it will help.
   c. Getting more support if you already have enough can be harmful.
   d. Not providing enough support can hurt more than providing none at all.
10. _____ is the termination of life by a lethal drug administered by a physician.
    a. Euthanasia
    b. Mercy killing
    c. Self-suicide
    d. Assisted suicide

WEB RESOURCES

Visit the companion Web site at **www.cengage.com/psychology/gurung**, where you will find online resources for this book, including chapter-by-chapter quizzes, Web links, and more!

Association for Death Education and Counseling
http://www.adec.org

> This organization is one of the oldest interdisciplinary organizations in the field of dying, death, and bereavement. This Web site offers visitors relevant publications, conferences, and more information on how to be a thanatologist (one who studies death and dying).

Coping with Chronic Illness
www.nlm.nih.gov/medlineplus/copingwithchronicillness.html

This is a government site with links to patient information and publications by the National Institutes of Health.

Arthritis Foundation
http://www.arthritis.org

The Arthritis Foundation is the only national non-profit organization that supports the more than 100 types of arthritis and related conditions. This site has resources on coping with this chronic illness and information for you to learn more about this disease that someone you know may have.

KEY TERMS, CONCEPTS, AND PEOPLE

acceptance, 333

anger, 333

anticipatory grief, 333

anxiety, 316

appraisals, 315

bargaining, 333

chronic illnesses, 307

denial, 316

depression, 316

euthanasia, 329

hospice, 336

Kevorkian, Jack, 330

optimism, 317

palliative care, 331

physician-assisted suicide, 329

quality of life, 310

terminal illnesses, 325

ESSENTIAL READINGS

Gatchel, R. J., & Oordt, M. S. (2003). Clinical health psychology and primary care: Practical advice and clinical guidance for successful collaboration. Washington, DC: American Psychological Association.

Leventhal, H., Weinman, J., Leventhal, E. A., & Phillips, L. A. (2008). Health psychology: The search for pathways between behavior and health. *Annual Review of Psychology*, 59, 477–505.

Stanton, A. L., Collins, C. A., & Sworowski, L. (2001). Adjustment to chronic illness: Theory and research. In A. Baum, T. A. Revenson, and J. E. Singer (Eds). Handbook of health psychology (pp. 321–657). Mahwah, NJ: Lawrence Erlbaum.

Psychoneuroimmunology and HIV

pen your mouth, breathe in, and chew. Chew? You have probably heard stories about how we are surrounded by millions and millions of bacteria. You may have seen those television specials that show you just how many living things are harbored by your mouth or on a patch of your skin or on the surface of your pillow or in the carpet. Well, these are more than just stories. A microscopic examination of the air we breathe, the water we drink, and the world around us reveals a teeming multitude of life. Bacteria, viruses, and germs of various sorts cohabitate our world. Many of these viruses and bacteria can cause us to get sick. The common cold and the flu are some examples of what happens to the body when we are infected by viruses. However, given the number of infectious agents to which our bodies are exposed regularly, we do not get sick that often. Why is this? The answer is that we have a specialized arrangement of cells, organs, and processes that is designed to ward off such threats and protect the body from infection: the immune system.

When our immune system is strong, we are less susceptible to illness. When we are stressed or otherwise psychologically challenged and our immune system is weakened, we are more susceptible to disease and illness. In addition, some diseases such as lupus and AIDS can debilitate our immune defenses and threaten our health and our lives regardless of our psychological makeup. In Chapter 3, we introduced you to the key components of the immune system, discussed how the immune system works, and recounted what happens when it fails or is compromised. In this chapter we will explore the role played by cultural factors and the many differences in immune-related diseases across cultural groups. In particular, you will learn how sex and ethnicity, two major cultural aspects, play large roles in the experience and incidence of HIV infection and AIDS.

PSYCHONEUROIMMUNOLOGY

What biopsychological science has only discovered relatively recently is that the immune system is strongly influenced by the nervous system and correspondingly by our minds and thinking (Ader, Felten, & Cohen, 1991; Byrne-Davis, & Vedhara, 2008; Dunn, 1989; Irwin, 2008; Littrell, 2008). The influence of psychological processes on immune functioning (the "biopsycho" connection) can be seen in many ways. At the physiological level, there is evidence for direct explicit connections between the endocrine and autonomic systems and the immune system (see Chapter 3 and Figure 11.1). When we are stressed by physical (such as an infection) or psychological (such as living in a high-crime neighborhood) causes, the two systems act together. When we are well, the two are balanced. A disruption in the communication between the nervous and immune systems (caused by stress or illness) plays a major role in a wide range of disorders characterized by an over- or under-reactive immune

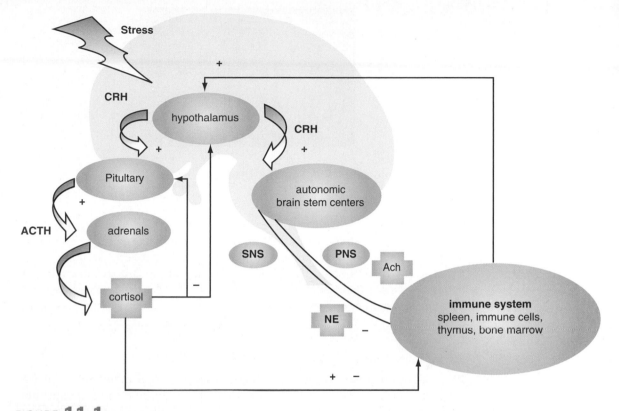

FIGURE **11.1**

A schematic showing the connection between the endocrine and nervous systems and the immune system. (SNS – sympathetic nervous system; PNS = parasympathetic nervous system; NE – nor-epinephrine; Ach = acetylcholine.)

system. For example, in multiple sclerosis (MS), a chronic inflammatory and neurodegenerative disease, there is growing evidence for a disturbed communication between the central nervous system (CNS) and the immune system as a crucial causative factor (Kern & Ziemssen, 2008).

Beyond the physiological link there is a clear psychological link (hence "psychoneuroimmuno"). A recent review shows that psychological interventions such as disclosure and hypnosis for children with asthma, HIV infection, or lupus, resulted in improvements in immune functioning (Nassau, Tien, & Fritz, 2008). In a particularly vivid demonstration, Futterman, Kemeny, Shapiro, and Fahey (1994) had an actor imagine that he was rejected for a part or had just won an acting award. Even the faked feelings of intense sadness led to an increase in immune cells in the bloodstream whereas the happy act led to a decrease. Findings such as these are all encompassed by the fascinating area of psychoneuroimmunology.

The field of **psychoneuroimmunology** (PNI) evolved out of the disciplines of biology and psychology and is dedicated to understanding the interplay between these disparate systems (Irwin, 2008). PNI developed in response to

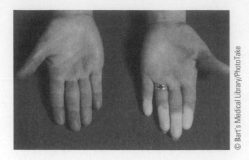

Features of Lupus, an Autoimmune Disease

research findings highlighting the fact that both psychological and physical factors (especially stress) can affect the functioning of the immune system. As the name implies, PNI researchers study interactions between the nervous system, the endocrine system, the immune system, and psychological activity and behavior. This collaboration of researchers is needed because the cells of the immune, endocrine, and nervous systems each bear receptors that respond to the same neurotransmitters, neurohormones, and neuropeptides.

Behavioral Conditioning and Immunity

From a health psychological perspective, there are two main pillars of PNI research. The first pillar is the observation that alterations of immune function can be linked to a conditioned stimulus (CS), such that the CS becomes able to instigate immune changes similar to those instigated by the unconditioned stimulus (UCS) with which it has been paired (Kusnecov, 2002). Whereas the UCS would be some immunosuppressive drug, the CS could be a sound, a light, or, more commonly, flavored water. Thus, similar to how Pavlov conditioned a dog to salivate to the sound of a bell, researchers found that they could condition the body's immune system to also respond to a CS. Ader and Cohen (1975) conducted the classic study in this area when they demonstrated a conditioned immune response in rats. They paired a novel-tasting solution (sweet water, the CS) with an illness-inducing drug (cyclophosphamide, the UCS). The drug served to suppress the immune system. After learning trials (pairing the CS and UCS), they gave one group of animals the CS only, gave another group plain water, and gave a third group the UCS again. All animals were then immunized with sheep red blood cells and the immune responses were measured. As predicted, both the groups that got the UCS and the one that got the CS showed a suppressed immune system demonstrating that the body could be conditioned to react as if it received a drug. Similar studies have been conducted in humans as well. For example, Buske-Kirschbaum, Kirschbaum, Stierle, Lehnert, and Hellhammer (1992) gave college students sherbet (the CS) paired with epinephrine (the UCS). The UCS caused an unconditioned response of increasing the number of natural killer (NK) cells. When given sherbet a few days later (without the UCS), the students experienced a similar increase in NK cell activity.

An active area of PNI research has fine tuned conditioning processes (Ader et al., 1991), and research is now getting closer to giving us an understanding of the neural mechanisms that account for conditioned immune responses. For example, we know that injecting morphine decreases natural killer (NK) cell activity and lymphocyte responsiveness (Saurer, Ijames, Carrigan, & Lysle, 2008). We also know that we can condition the immune alterations to environmental stimuli that predict morphine is going to be administered. We have learned from experiments involving rats and injections of chemical substances, such as Y1 receptor antagonist BIBP3226, into specific areas of the brain that the nucleus acumbens may play an important role in these conditioned immune modulations (Saurer et al., 2008).

Stress and Immunity

The second major pillar of PNI research is the association between the immune system and stress (Cohen & Herbert, 1996; Littrell, 2008). Knowledge of a stress-immune link can be traced back to the work of Hans Selye. Selye found that immune tissues such as the thymus atrophied in rats that were subjected to stress. For over ten years, health psychologists have accumulated significant evidence that stressful life events and psychological distress predict biologically verified infectious illnesses by impacting the immune system (Marsland, Bachen, Cohen, & Manuck, 2002). Upper respiratory infections such as the common cold have been the primary disease model used in the literature (Cohen et al., 1998), and a variety of inventive studies have provided insights into stress-immunity interactions (Stone et al., 1992; Turner, Cobb, & Steptoe, 1996). For example, Sheldon Cohen and colleagues have inoculated healthy individuals (volunteers for the study) with common cold or flu viruses after assessing for stress. The volunteers are kept in quarantine and monitored for the development of the illness. Sure enough, the volunteers who were more stressed (and consequently had a challenged immune system) were more likely to develop a cold (Cohen et al., 2008).

Stress in general has been reliably associated with the functioning of the immune system (Bachen, Marsland, Manuck, & Cohen, 1998; Herbert & Cohen, 1993; Kiecolt-Glaser & Glaser, 1991; Littrell, 2008). Stress is inversely related to circulating lymphocytes such that the more stress we experience, the fewer lymphocytes are produced by our bodies (Littrell, 2008; McEwen et al., 1997). Stress is also accompanied by a redistribution of lymphocytes and extended stress has been linked to the shrinking of the thymus (Sapolsky, 1991). Stress has been shown to kill T cells by a form of "suicide killing," in which cortisol damages the DNA of the T cell, mutating it and causing it to eat itself up from the inside out (Wyllie, 1980; Compton & Cidlowski, 1986). Acute stressors such as final exams and sleep deprivation have been found to suppress immune function, causing an increase in illness (e.g., Kiecolt-Glaser et al., 1984; Marshall et al., 1998) and even slower wound healing (Kiecolt-Glaser, Page, Marucha, MacCallum, & Glaser, 1998; Streblow, Dumortier, Moses, Orloff, & Nelson, 2008). Many life events are associated with immune system changes, such as job stress and unemployment (Arnetz et al., 1987), loss of a partner (Goodkin et al., 1996; Kemeny et al., 1995), separation (Kennedy, Kiecolt-Glaser, & Glaser, 1988), the strain of caregiving (Kiecolt-Glaser et al.,

1987; Light & Lebowitz, 1989), and natural disasters (Solomon, Segerstrom, Grohr, Kemeny, & Fahey, 1997). As can be expected, chronic illnesses negatively impact immunity as well (Nelson, 2008) and stress makes the immune system's ability to cope with chronic illnesses worse (Fang et al., 2008).

Note also, however, that acute stress may sometimes jump-start the **immune system**. In an inventive study, Schedlowski et al. (1993) wired 45 first-time parachutists and gathered measures of their stress chemicals and immune cells from one-half hour before their first jump, all the way through their jump, and then for some time after the jump. The numbers of both lymphocytes and NK cells significantly increased just after they jumped and then decreased greatly (to numbers below where they were before the whole process) one hour later. Thus, our immune responses are heavily tied to the context and chronicity of the stress. Why does chronic stress suppress the immune system? The best answer is that suppression prevents over-activity and consequently autoimmune diseases. Remember that one of the functions of the immune system is to distinguish "self" from "non-self." If this process fails, problems ensue. Sometimes it does fail. With multiple sclerosis, for example, part of the nervous system is attacked by the body's own immune cells. In lupus, the cartilage around joints is attacked by the body's immune cells. Table 11.1 summarizes the major autoimmune diseases. One of the most fatal autoimmune diseases is AIDS.

SYNTHESIZE, EVALUATE, APPLY	• How can conditioning be used to create an immune response greater than that stimulated by a certain dose of a drug? • What are the different ways in which stress and coping can influence the immune system's response? • How are psychological factors linked with immunity?

HIV AND AIDS

These are two short acronyms, but each is associated with large amounts of pain, fear, death, and sadness. **Acquired immunodeficiency syndrome** (AIDS) is one of the most well known of all the illnesses that cause death from complications with the immune system.

Since the beginning of the AIDS epidemic in the late 1970s, it is estimated that more than one-half million people have died of AIDS in the United States, and many millions have died worldwide (Centers for Disease Control and Prevention [CDC], 2003; World Health Organization [WHO], 2004). In this disorder, the immune system is gradually weakened and finally disabled by the **human immunodeficiency virus** (HIV). HIV infection is now clearly a world pandemic, and although great strides are being made in understanding the epidemiology of the disease, the number of infected people worldwide continues to grow at an alarming rate, as shown in Figure 11.2 (WHO, 2008). Recent surveys show that 56,300 people became newly infected with HIV in 2006 (Hall et al., 2008). Some areas of the world have much higher rates than others. For example, Africa is more heavily affected by HIV and AIDS than any other region of the world. An estimated 22 million people were living with HIV at the end of 2007 and approximately 1.9 million additional people were infected with HIV during that year (UNAIDS/WHO, 2008). There are cultural

TABLE **11.1**
Major Autoimmune Disorders

Symptoms and Tests of Diseases		
Disease	Symptoms	Tests to help find out if you have it
Hashimoto's thyroiditis (underactive thyroid)	• tiredness • depression • sensitivity to cold • weight gain • muscle weakness and cramps • dry hair • tough skin • constipation • sometimes there are no symptoms	• blood test for thyroid stimulating hormone (TSH)
Graves' disease (overactive thyroid)	• insomnia (not able to sleep) • irritability • weight loss without dieting • heat sensitivity • sweating • fine brittle hair • weakness in your muscles • light menstrual periods • bulging eyes • shaky hands • sometimes there are no symptoms	• blood test for thyroid stimulating hormone (TSH)
Lupus	• swelling and damage to the joints, skin, kidneys, heart, lungs, blood vessels, and brain • "butterfly" rash across the nose and cheeks • rashes on other parts of the body • painful and swollen joints • sensitivity to the sun	• exam of your lab tests (antinuclear antibody [ANA] test, blood tests, and urine tests)
Multiple sclerosis (MS)	• weakness and trouble with coordination, balance, speaking, and walking • paralysis • tremors • numbness and tingling feeling in arms, legs, hands, and feet	• exam of your body • exam of your brain, spinal cord, and nerves (neurological exam) • x-ray tests (magnetic resonance imaging [MRI] and magnetic resonance spectroscopy [MRS]) • other tests on the brain and spinal cord fluid to look for things linked to these diseases
Rheumatoid arthritis	• inflammation begins in the tissue lining your joints and then spreads to the whole joint (hand joints are the most common site, but it can affect most joints in the body)	• blood tests may show that you have anemia (when your body does not have enough red blood cells) and an antibody called rheumatoid factor (RF).

(continued)

TABLE **11.1** (*continued*)
Major Autoimmune Disorders

Symptoms and Tests of Diseases		
Disease	**Symptoms**	**Tests to help find out if you have it**
	• muscle pain • deformed joints • weakness • fatigue • loss of appetite • weight loss • becoming confined to bed in severe cases	(Some people with RF never get this disease, and others with the disease never have RF.)

Source: U.S. Department of Health and Human Services (2008). http://www.womenshealth.gov/faq/autoimmune.htm#1

differences among these diseases. Infection rates among African Americans are seven times as high as for European Americans (83.7 per 100,000 people versus 11.5 per 100,000) and almost three times as high as for Latino Americans (29.3 per 100,000 people), a group that was also disproportionately affected (CDC, 2008). Table 11.2 shows the number of people with AIDS worldwide.

The History of AIDS

The CDC coined the term *AIDS* in 1982, and HIV was discovered and named in 1984. Like most new diseases, the medical community first noticed similarities among the symptoms, such as fever, and pneumonia. In 1978 gay men in the United States and Sweden and heterosexuals in Tanzania and Haiti began showing symptoms of what would later come to be known as AIDS.

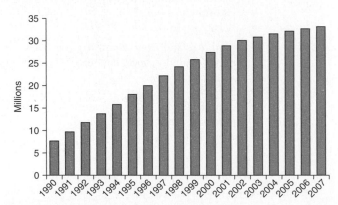

FIGURE **11.2** Trends in HIV/AIDS Incidence

The number of people living with HIV has risen from around 8 million in 1990 to 33 million today, and is still growing. Around 67% of people living with HIV are in sub-Saharan Africa.

TABLE **11.2**

Global HIV/AIDS Estimates, End of 2007

The latest statistics on the world epidemic of AIDS & HIV were published by UNAIDS/WHO in July 2008, and refer to the end of 2007.

	Estimate	Range
People living with HIV/AIDS in 2007	33.0 million	30.3–36.1 million
Adults living with HIV/AIDS in 2007	30.8 million	28.2–34.0 million
Women living with HIV/AIDS in 2007	15.5 million	14.2–16.9 million
Children living with HIV/AIDS in 2007	2.0 million	1.9–2.3 million
People newly infected with HIV in 2007	2.7 million	2.2–3.2 million
Children newly infected with HIV in 2007	0.37 million	0.33–0.41 million
AIDS deaths in 2007	2.0 million	1.8–2.3 million
Child AIDS deaths in 2007	0.27 million	0.25–0.29 million

The epidemic became evident in the year 1981. In June of that year, the CDC reported that five young men, all active homosexuals were treated for a special type of pneumonia (caused by *Pneumocystis carinii*) at three different hospitals in Los Angeles, California. At the same time, reports of 26 cases of a unique form of

The Faces of Those Impacted by AIDS

Not just a gay man's disease, AIDS can kill men, women, and children, and everyone is influenced by it.[*]

*The National Library of Medicine's Profiles in Science program has made every effort to secure proper permissions for ··sting items on the Web site. In this instance, however, it has not been possible to determine the current copyright owner. If you have information indicating who the copyright owner may be, please contact the NLM at profiles@nlm.nih.gov.

cancer (Kaposi's sarcoma) were also reported among gay men. Kaposi's sarcoma had been previously only a rare form of relatively benign cancer that tended to occur in older people. Because there was so little known about the transmission of what seemed to be a new disease, there was concern about contagion and whether the disease could be passed on by people who had no apparent signs or symptoms. For a long time, people believed that AIDS was just a disease seen in gay men and something that would not harm heterosexuals or women. AIDS was often referred to as a "gay disease," and gay men were subjected to even more societal wrath. Men who were infected with HIV and at risk for AIDS were often shunned. Hollywood star Tom Hanks illustrated the prejudice and discrimination experienced by gay men, both in the workplace and in everyday life, in his Oscar-winning performance in the movie *Philadelphia* (1993). You see how his character's coworkers and even some of his character's friends start to treat him differently once his symptoms start showing. The medical journal *Lancet* even called it the gay compromise syndrome, whereas at least one newspaper referred to it as GRID (gay-related immune deficiency). They were wrong. When it began turning up in children (since it can be transmitted from parent to child) and transfusion recipients, public perceptions began to change. Until then it was entirely an epidemic seen in gay men, and it was easy for the average person to think it would not happen to him or her. The number of people who could become infected was to widen again at the beginning of 1983, when it was reported that the disease could be passed on heterosexually from men to women.

Worldwide, researchers searched frantically to identify the cause. At the CDC researchers had been continuing to investigate the cause of AIDS through a study of the sexual contacts of homosexual men in Los Angeles and New York. They identified a man as the link between a number of different cases and they named him "patient O" for "Out of California" (some who read the published article on him misread the "O" as a "0" and referred to him as patient zero). He was a Canadian flight attendant named Gaetan Dugas, whose job and sexual habits caused him to spread the virus. A large number of individuals infected early in the epidemic had some sort of contact with Dugas. Between 1983 and 1984, researchers at the Pasteur Institute in France and at the CDC and National Cancer Institute managed to crack the mystery and identified two viruses they believed caused AIDS, lymphadenopathy virus (LAV) and human T-lymphotropic virus type III (HTLV-III). In 1985, it was clear that both viruses were the same and were referred to as HIV. For an account of the history of AIDS, read *And the Band Played On* (Shilts, 2000).

From where did this virus come in the first place? During the early years of the epidemic, it was assumed that HIV made the transition from animals to humans at some time during the 1970s. It was not until 1999 that research suggested HIV had "crossed over" into the human population from a particular species of chimpanzee, probably through blood contact that occurred during hunting and field dressing of the animals (Gao et al., 1999).

HIV is transmitted primarily through the exchange of bodily fluids (not by sitting on toilet seats that have been used by HIV carriers as was once believed). Blood contains the highest concentration of the virus, followed by semen, followed by vaginal fluids, followed by breast milk. The most common ways of passing on HIV are by unprotected sexual contact, particularly vaginal or anal intercourse, and direct blood contact including injection drug needles, blood transfusions, accidents in health care settings, or certain blood products. This is why blood donation centers are very careful about how they collect blood and why every needle is only used once and then discarded. For many years, people did not give blood because they feared HIV infection.

In 2008, the CDC introduced a new way to measure the incidence of HIV. New technology called the Serological Testing Algorithm for Recent HIV Seroconversion (STARHS) helps identify which HIV infections are new (CDC, 2008). STARHS determines which positive HIV tests represent new HIV infections (those that occurred within approximately the past five months). Before, HIV diagnosis data could only provide the best indication of recent trends in key populations. The problem was that diagnosis data only indicated when a person was diagnosed with HIV, not when an individual was actually infected, which can occur many years before a diagnosis. In 2008, using the new intricate statistics, data from 22 states (with specific HIV reporting systems) were extrapolated to the general population to provide the first national estimates of HIV incidence based on direct measurement. The method led to new estimates for national HIV (Hall et al., 2008), and are the estimates used in this chapter.

The Difference between HIV and AIDS

Remember that HIV is the virus that causes AIDS and that HIV and AIDS are not synonymous. The Centers for Disease Control and Prevention defines someone as having AIDS if he or she is HIV positive and meets one or both of these conditions: has had at least one of 21 AIDS-defining opportunistic infections; has had a CD4 cell count (T-cell count) of 200 cells or less (a normal CD4 count varies by laboratory, but usually is in the 600 to 1,500 range, CDC, 2008). A person can be HIV positive for a long time before developing AIDS. Currently, the average time between HIV infection and the appearance of signs that could lead to an AIDS diagnosis is 8 to 11 years. This time varies greatly from person to person and can depend on many factors including a person's health status and behaviors. Primary HIV infection is the first stage of HIV disease, when the virus first establishes itself in the body. Some researchers use the term acute HIV infection to describe the period of time between when a person is first infected with HIV and when antibodies against the virus are produced by the body (usually 6 to 12 weeks). Today, medical treatments that can slow down the rate at which HIV infection weakens the immune system are available. You may have heard about "protein cocktails," combinations of medications that slow down the progression of the disease. Considered to be one of the best treatments available, the cocktail or **highly active antiretroviral therapy** (HAART) involves a variety anti-HIV drugs that keep the virus from replicating. The utility of a combination of drugs is that if one certain combination does not work, another combination may. One of the most commonly used components of HAART is zidovudine (AZT). Other treatments can prevent or cure some of the illnesses associated with AIDS. As with other diseases, early detection offers more options for treatment and preventative health care.

AIDS research is actively working toward a cure and much is known about slowing down the disease. New data and considerations support initiating therapy before CD4 cell count declines to less than 350/microL (Hammer, et al., 2008). The International AIDS Society-USA panel recommends that for patients with 350 CD4 cells/microL or more, the decision to begin therapy should be individualized based on the presence of other illness diagnoses, risk factors for progression to AIDS and non-AIDS diseases, and patient readiness for treatment. In addition to the prior recommendation that a high plasma viral load and rapidly declining CD4 cell count should prompt treatment initiation, developing illnesses such as heart disease or other serious conditions should prompt earlier therapy (Hammer et al., 2008).

PHYSIOLOGICAL CORRELATES OF HIV/AIDS

HIV is a retrovirus, an RNA virus that secretes an enzyme that injects its own RNA into DNA inside the cells that it infects. DNA is where our genetic code is stored. When the HIV RNA manipulates the DNA of the host cell, the host cell functions improperly. HIV infects the cells of the immune system, specifically T_H. About 60 percent of T_H cells have a receptor known as CD4 whereas some T_H (Helper T) cells have CD8 receptors (each has specific activation and suppression functions in the system). Two of the main physiological symptoms of AIDS are low numbers of CD4 T cells and higher than average numbers of CD8 cells. If you are healthy you probably have about 1,000 CD4 T cells per milliliter of blood. The sickest AIDS patient will have an average of less than 50 of these cells. The lack of these cells corresponds to the AIDS patient being unable to mount an effective immune defense. This invasion of HIV into the system proceeds through four main stages as shown in Figure 11.3.

Some people newly infected with HIV experience some "flu-like" symptoms. These symptoms, which usually last no more than a few days, might include fevers, chills, night sweats, and rashes (not cold-like symptoms). Other people either do not experience "acute infection" or have symptoms so mild that they may not notice them. Given the general character of the symptoms of acute infection, they can easily have causes *other* than HIV, such as a flu infection. For example, if a person had some risk for HIV a few days ago and is now experiencing flu-like symptoms, it might be possible that HIV is responsible for the symptoms, but it is *also* possible that he or she has some other viral infection. Often some people with HIV have no symptoms, and studies of the effects of HIV normally include additional analyses to control for illness severity. HIV-positive patients can be either asymptomatic or symptomatic with or without an AIDS diagnosis. Classification as HIV/symptomatic requires the presence of at least one of the following symptoms in the last six months: diarrhea (one to six times per week or more), night sweats (one to six times per week or more), fevers (one to six times per week or more), yeast infections (two or more), weight loss of more than 10 pounds, thrush, or hairy leukoplakia, a precancerous condition that is seen as small thickened white patches, usually inside the mouth or vulva.

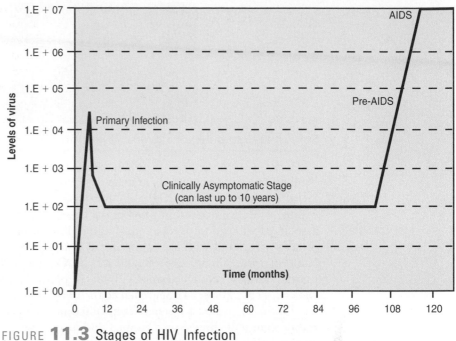

FIGURE **11.3** Stages of HIV Infection

There are no common symptoms for individuals who have AIDS. Classification as having AIDS requires the presence of fewer than 200 CD4 T cells and/or an AIDS-defining condition (e.g., toxoplasmosis or cryptococcosis). When immune system damage is more severe, people may experience **opportunistic infections** (called opportunistic because they are caused by organisms that cannot induce disease in people with normal immune systems, but take the "opportunity" to flourish in people with HIV infection). Most of these more severe infections, diseases, and symptoms fall under the CDC's definition of "full-blown AIDS." Again, the median time to receive an AIDS diagnosis among those infected with HIV is 7 to 10 years.

PSYCHOLOGICAL CORRELATES OF HIV/AIDS

The utility of the biopsychosocial approach of health psychology is especially clear when one is experiencing illnesses such as AIDS because both severe physiological and psychological problems are seen with the development of full-blown AIDS. Psychological factors can influence the acquisition of HIV, the development of HIV infection into AIDS, and the progression of AIDS. As with other chronic illnesses, HIV/AIDS is influenced by a variety of psychological factors. Some psychological factors help a person cope with HIV infection and AIDS whereas others can shorten the time one lives with AIDS. AIDS patients often experience severe depression and poor quality of life. Patients without depression had significantly healthier immune systems (e.g., lower plasma neopterin concentrations, higher CD4(+) cell counts and

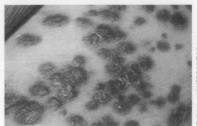

Skin rashes such as this are a common symptom of HIV infection.

hemoglobin concentrations) and better QoL scores than depressive patients (Schroecksnadel, et al., 2008). In particular, optimism, social support, and coping styles are important psychosocial resources that have been consistently associated with good psychological and physical outcomes and that have been directly associated with lower emotional distress in patients with HIV infection (Commerford, Gular, Orr, Reznikoff, & O'Dowd, 1994; Deichert, Fekete, Boarts, Druley, & Delahanty, 2008; Kaplan, Marks, & Mertens, 1997; Makoae et al., 2008; van Servellen et al., 1998).

Optimism refers to generalized outcome expectancies that good things, rather than bad things, will happen and is associated with boosts in immune systems in the presence of HIV infection (Littrell, 1996; Kalichman & Ramachandran, 1999), higher NK cell cytotoxicity during stress (Segerstrom, Taylor, Kemeny, & Fahey, 1998), and in some patients, protection against HIV exposure by decreasing intentions to engage in unsafe sex (Carvajal, Garner, & Evans, 1998). Optimists tend to cope better with stress, experience less negative mood effects, and may practice better health behaviors (Ironson, & Hayward, 2008; Taylor, Kemeny, Aspinwall, Schneider, Rodriguez, & Herbert, 1992). Optimists, in general, show better psychological well-being (Armor & Taylor, 1998), suggesting that optimism may be an important moderator of the likelihood of depression in response to a stressor such as HIV infection.

As discussed previously in Chapter 5, the presence of social support has been found to be health promoting and health restoring and is associated also with a decrease in mortality risk and progression of AIDS (Chesney & Darbes, 1998; Fasce, 2008; Galvan, Davis, Banks, & Bing, 2008; Hays, Turner, & Coats, 1992; Kalichman, Heckman, Kochman, Sikkema, & Bergholte, 2000; Mo & Coulson, 2008). Studies of populations with HIV infection suggest that social support from peers is critical for emotional well-being (Galvan et al., 2008) and, in periods of crisis, family support may become an especially important determinant of emotional well-being (Crystal & Kersting, 1998). In a clear example, Metts, Manns, and Kuzic (1996) showed that higher levels of emotional support from both friends and family made independent contributions to lower depression in a sample of persons infected with HIV. Furthermore, in a five-year study of HIV-positive patients, Theorell et al. (1995) found that participants who had more emotional support and reported better social networks showed significantly lesser declines in their T-cell counts over the course of the study. New work shows that social support can even be useful delivered over the Internet (Mo & Coulson, 2008).

The amount of social support one has can also influence the transition from being HIV positive to actually developing AIDS (Leserman et al., 2000). Paradoxically, social support is one thing that persons with HIV infection or AIDS find is harder to get because the label of being HIV positive or having AIDS often becomes stigmatizing, and people tend to avoid the patient (sometimes from the misplaced fear that HIV infection can be transmitted in the air or through casual contact).

Coping strategies, as described in Chapter 5, refer to the specific efforts, both behavioral and psychological, that people use to master, tolerate, reduce, or minimize stressful events (Lazarus & Launier, 1978). Among the coping strategies believed to relate to coping with HIV infection, three types of strategies stand out (Temoshok, Wald, Synowski, & Garzino-Demo, 2008). Problem-solving strategies include planning to confront the stressor and taking action; avoidance strategies include efforts to distract oneself from, ignore, or forget the stressor; and social support–seeking strategies include attempts to obtain emotional and information support. The first two categories map directly onto two major types of coping as analyzed in the literature—approach and avoidant coping (Lazarus & Folkman, 1991). An individual can approach a stressor and make active efforts to resolve it or he or she could try to avoid the problem (Moos & Schaefer, 1993). The third category emphasizes and incorporates the need for and importance of social support in the coping process (e.g., Sarason, Sarason, & Gurung, 2001). In general, patients with HIV infection who rely more on approach coping and who seek support tend to have a higher quality of life and experience less negative affect than those who make use of avoidant coping (Deichert et al., 2008; Kraaij, 2008; Mulder, de Vroome, van Griensven, Antoni, & Sandfort, 1999; Reed, Kemeny, Taylor, & Visscher, 1999). Despite the differences in health and health risk factors between minority and nonminority populations (Siegel, Karus, Raveis, & Hagan, 1998; Sikkema, Wagner, & Bogart, 2000; Sue, 2000), very few studies test for differences in psychosocial factors among ethnic groups. Some studies show that different ethnic groups vary in how social support is provided and utilized (Gant & Ostrow, 1995; Ulbrich & Bradsher, 1993), others show that different ethnic groups vary in coping styles in response to HIV infection (Heckman et al., 2000; Kaplan et al., 1997). Given that social support and coping have been shown to influence depression as discussed previously, any ethnic differences in these psychosocial factors could have significant implications for the life expectancy of HIV-positive individuals. For example, Schutte, Valerio, and Carrillo (1996) examined the relationship between optimism and socioeconomic status (SES) in European and Mexican Americans and found significant correlations between optimism and SES for European Americans, but not for Latinos.

Psychological Factors Influencing Progression

Using psychological factors and core elements of personality also provide insight into AIDS progression (Ironson & Hayward, 2008). Ironson, O'Cleirigh, Weiss, Schneiderman, and Costa (2008) examined the role of the big five personality domains (Neuroticism, Extraversion, Openness, Agreeableness, Conscientiousness) on change in CD4 cells and other indicators of immune health. The researchers used an ethnically diverse sample of HIV-seropositive patients who completed a personality assessment (NEO-PI-R), and underwent comprehensive psychological assessment and blood sampling every six months for four years. AIDS indicators and personality were strongly associated. Personality factors that were significantly associated with slower disease progression over four years included Openness, Extraversion, and Conscientiousness. Specific personality characteristics significantly related to slower disease progression were assertiveness, positive emotions, and gregariousness (Extraversion); ideas, esthetics (Openness); achievement striving and order (Conscientiousness). Personality styles which helped patients remain engaged (e.g., Creative Interactors, Upbeat Optimists, Welcomers, and Go Getters) had slower disease progression, whereas the "homebody" profile (Low Extraversion-Low Openness) was significantly associated with faster disease progression (Ironson et al., 2008).

Understandably, there is intense anxiety and maybe even some denial when a person first finds out he or she may be HIV positive, which is often followed by depression. AIDS patients who deny the reality of their being HIV positive often experience a more rapid development of symptoms (Ironson, Schneiderman, Kumar, & Antoni, 1994). There are some curious exceptions. Reed, Kemeny, Taylor, Wang, and Visscher (1994) found that HIV-positive men who denied their diagnosis actually survived longer than those who accepted their fate. Conflicting evidence such as this clearly demonstrates the need to better understand the ways different psychological constructs interact to influence coping. One psychological outcome of HIV infection and AIDS is unequivocally dangerous: depression. Depression is a critical psychosocial risk factor for individuals with compromised immune systems (Boland, 1997; Greeson et al., 2008). It is a common experience of AIDS patients (Griffin, Rabkin, Remien, & Williams, 1998) and is related to physical symptomatology, number of days spent in bed, and progression of HIV infection (e.g., Cole & Kemeny, 1997). Anxiety and depression also have physiological consequences (Leserman, 2008). For example, Greeson et al. (2008) found a significant relationship between higher distress levels and greater disease severity. This relationship was mediated by diminished natural killer (NK) cell count and cytotoxic function, as well as increased cytotoxic (CD8[+]) T-cell activation. As a testimony to the usefulness of using a biopsychosocial approach, Greeson et al. (2008) found that a psychoimmune model accounted for 67 percent of the variation in HIV disease severity.

Next, we will use the example of depression to highlight some important cultural differences in the experience of HIV infection and AIDS, especially focusing on the cultural components of sex and ethnicity.

SYNTHESIZE, EVALUATE, APPLY

- What factors in the history and nature of AIDS are most responsible for the worldwide health epidemic of this disease today?
- Compare and contrast coping with AIDS with coping with stress. What techniques would be more beneficial in this context?
- In what ways does the delivery of social support have to be modified in the context of AIDS?

CULTURAL VARIATIONS IN AIDS

Women and AIDS

Depression is more prevalent among women than men with HIV infection and many studies have focused on depressed women at risk for and with HIV (Fasce, 2008; Leserman, 2008; Wu et al., 2008). This is a change from even five years ago when much of what was known about the psychosocial concomitants of AIDS were provided by studies of gay men (Mays & Cochran, 1987). Gay men infected with HIV tend to be more economically advantaged, better educated, likely to be European American, and often have no dependents, relative to women infected with HIV (Siegel, Karus, Ravies, & Hagan, 1998). Women account for an increasing percentage of new cases of HIV infection (CDC, 2008; Siegel et al., 1998), and low-income women of color are especially at risk (Gurung, Taylor, Kemeny, & Myers, 2004; Wyatt, 1994). Differences between ethnic groups change with time. Ten years ago, Latina women were seven times more likely to get AIDS than European American women (Klevens, Diaz, Fleming, Mays, & Frey, 1999). In a recent report, Latina women represented 14 percent of new AIDS cases diagnosed in 2005 whereas European American women comprised 17 percent of new cases (CDC, 2008). Women account for 44 percent of all estimated HIV infections worldwide, and the proportion of women infected is rapidly increasing in every geographical area (Ickovics, Thayaparan, & Ethier, 2002). In North America, women account for 26 percent of HIV/AIDS diagnosed during 2005 (CDC, 2008).

Some key physiological differences between men and women increase women's likelihood to be infected. Women are more likely than men to be infected with HIV via heterosexual sex, and male to female transmission of HIV is eight times more likely than female to male transmission (Padian, Shiboski, Glass, & Vittinghoff, 1997). Whereas vaginal fluids can be easily washed off the male anatomy after sex, seminal fluids can reside within the female vagina for a long period, increasing the chance of infection. Furthermore, the tissue lining the walls of the vagina is fragile and prone to injury and related infection (Royce, Sena, Cates, & Cohen, 1997). Psychological power differentials are important as well (Thorburn, Harvey, & Ryan, 2005). It is also harder for women to raise the issue of condom use than it is for men, given the traditional power differentials in the sexes, the possibility of abuse, or cultures in which women are not "supposed" to admit to sexual knowledge (Abel & Chambers, 2004).

Women with HIV infection and chronic depressive symptoms are up to 2.4 times more likely to die even after controls were added for other clinical features known to be associated with morbidity and mortality (Ickovics et al., 2001). Such differences in incidence and in the responses (e.g., depression) compel a closer look at this group of individuals.

Ethnicity and AIDS

Together with gender, ethnicity may also be a critical variable in the relationship between depression, HIV status, and health (Ferreira, 2008; Warren, et al., 2008). There are some clear-cut differences in mortality patterns, health status, and health risk factors between ethnic minorities compared with each other and with the European American population (Sikkema et al., 2000; Sue, 2000). For example, African American and Latina women account for approximately 80 percent of AIDS cases diagnosed among women in the United States (CDC, 2008; Wortley & Fleming, 1997). African Americans and Latino Americans have been disproportionately affected by HIV infection, as is demonstrated by HIV seroprevalence and in the numbers of reported cases of AIDS (CDC, 2008; Jillson-Boostrom, 1992; Karon et al., 1996). Among women, as of 2005, African American women had the highest incidence rate of AIDS (66 percent), compared with European American women (17 percent, CDC, 2008). HIV incidence among African American women is more than 20 times that among European American women and more than 4 times that among Latinas (Tillerson, 2008). Figure 11.4 shows the differences in prevalence of HIV across ethnicities.

Ethnic and sex differences in HIV infection and AIDS also interact (Tedaldi, Absalon, Thomas, Shlay, & van den Berg-Wolf, 2008). Are psychological problems such as depression a greater risk factor for ethnic minority HIV-positive women? Additional knowledge on the concomitants of depression in women with HIV infection across different ethnic groups is sorely needed (Sikkema et al., 2000). To fill this need, Gurung, Taylor, Kemeny, and Myers (2004) studied an ethnically diverse sample of low-income women at risk for AIDS. The prospective design followed 350 African American, Latina, and European American women over a six-month period to assess the relationship of HIV status, SES, and chronic burden to depression and examine the moderation of these effects by psychosocial resources (social support, optimism, and coping style). HIV status and ethnicity were significantly associated with depressed mood at each point, but not with changes over time.

Gurung et al. (2004) paint a graphic picture of how ethnicity, SES, and sex can influence coping with HIV infection. Being seropositive for HIV was a significant stressor associated with depression, but it was also associated with a substantially greater number of chronic burdens affecting all aspects of life, including money, housing, work, vulnerability to crime, and relationships. The fact that these differences were found between the HIV-seropositive and

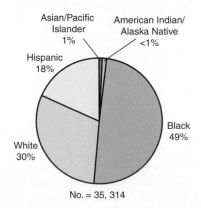

FIGURE **11.4** Race/Ethnicity of Persons with a New HIV Diagnosis in 2006

HIV-seronegative women after controlling for SES suggests that seropositivity confers risk for these additional burdens and highlights how biology and the social world directly interact. HIV infection thus increases vulnerability to depression both in its own right and secondarily by expanding the range of chronic burdens to which low-income seropositive women are vulnerable. Moreover, although HIV-positive women were significantly more depressed than HIV-negative women, changes in depression over the six-month period of the investigation were more strongly predicted by changes in the chronic burdens the women faced that are frequently associated with low SES.

Studies have begun to take a close look at the ethnicity by sex interaction. Tillerson (2008) examined key HIV risk factors (risky sex, drug use, inconsistent disclosure of same-sex behavior by male partners, and sexually transmitted diseases) to explain the higher incidence of HIV infection among African American women. A review of studies published between 1985 and 2006 showed that African American women are no more likely to have unprotected sex, have multiple sexual partners, or use drugs than women of other ethnic groups. Some studies did suggest that African American women are more likely to have risky sex partners and STDs and African American men are less likely to disclose their same-sex behavior to female partners (Tillerson, 2008).

There is also an interaction between ethnicity and health behaviors. By itself, poor health behaviors aggravate HIV by reducing immune functioning (e.g., cigarette smoke, Mian, Lauzon, Stämpfli, Mossman, & Ashkar, 2008). Different ethnic groups perform health behaviors to different extents, which further muddies the water. Take the case of drug use (sharing needles is a major cause of the spread of HIV). Between 1992 and 2004, the proportion of patients admitted to hospitals reporting using injections declined 44 percent among African Americans but only 14 percent for European Americans (Broz & Ouellet, 2008). Similarly, the peak age for heroin users in treatment increased 10 years for African Americans while declining over 10 years for European Americans.

These studies and others on other cultural variables (e.g., socioeconomic status, Werth, Borges, McNally, Maguire, & Britton, 2008) provide clear examples of why a biopsychosocial approach to understanding chronic illnesses such as HIV infection is critical.

Other Cultural Issues

Race, ethnicity, and nationality also influence the extent to which **sexual mixing** takes place (Catania, Binson, Dolcini, Moskowitz, & van der Straten, 2002; Wong et al., 2008). Sexual mixing, which has been found to have a central influence on HIV transmission rates (Garnett & Anderson, 1993; Tornesello, et al., 2008), is defined as the extent to which people engage in sexual activities with sexual partners from other sexual networks (dis-sortative mating) versus partners from their own network (assortative mixing). Heavy mixers form an important link in the spread of HIV infection. Laumann, Gagnon, Michael, and Michaels (1994) examined sexual mixing in a national sample of heterosexual adults aged 18 to 49. Their data indicated that for respondents with multiple sexual partners, women are more likely than men to be heavy mixers (14% versus 11%) and that Latino males (59% versus 17% African

American and 5% Caucasian) and females (33% versus 4% African American and 15% Caucasian) are more likely than other males and females to be heavy mixers with African American males and Caucasian females reporting moderate levels of mixing. Developmental state is important and these patterns vary by age group. Young adult Latino males and females report the heaviest mixing.

Advances in genetic research and the ability to hone in on specific parts of genes are providing new insights into cultural differences in diseases such as HIV infection and AIDS (Just et al., 1992; Kilpatrick, Hague, Yap, & Mok, 1991; Martin et al., 1998). For example, Mays et al. (2002) suggested that one useful area to consider in identifying ethnic differences in HIV infection is in the distribution of human leukocyte antigen (HLA). HLA molecules serve to initiate the immune response by how they present antigens to T cells, which, as described above, then clear the virus from the body. Ethnic variations in the genes encoding HLA molecules can affect antigen presentation and, correspondingly, how the host responds (Pérez et al., 2008). Variations in aspects of HLA molecules (the specific details of which are technically beyond the scope of this text) have been found across racial groups. Some aspects of HLA were four times more likely to be found in African Americans than in European Americans (Dunston, Henry, Christian, Ofosu, & Callendar, 1989). Osborne and Mason (1993) have also found aspects of HLA unique to the Latino population. The new discoveries are paving the way for the design of new genetic therapies targeting specific gene variations among individuals (McNicholl, 1997).

There are also important differences in social network use across cultural groups. Aitken, Higgs, & Bowden (2008) compared the social networks of Vietnamese Australian injecting drug users (IDUs) with those of other ethnicities. Results showed that the Vietnamese IDUs were more highly connected, intricate, and dense networks. The Vietnamese Australians were at greater risk for blood-borne infection (and had relatively high HIV prevalence, Aitken et al., 2008). Similarly, Ferreira (2008) explored how a South African community coped with living with HIV/AIDS. The study found that community members coped with HIV/AIDS by relying on culture and family, faith in God, religion and prayer. Inner strength, hope, optimism and expectancy appeared to be key resources for informal settlement residents (Ferreira, 2008).

The great ethnic discrepancies in incidence and prevalence of HIV and AIDS compel more cross-cultural research, but this has been slow in developing. Much research continues to be conducted using European American men (Mays et al., 2002) although researchers such as Wyatt et al. (2002) and Sikkema, Hansen, Kochman, Tate, and Difranciesco (2004) are focusing on mixed ethnic samples of women. African Americans, who made up 34 percent of all AIDS cases (Fahey & Flemming, 1997), previously made up only 7 percent of National Institutes of Health HIV studies (Ready, 1988). Similarly, Latinos represented 17 percent of AIDS cases but were only represented by 9 percent of research participants (Mays et al., 2002).

HEALTH PSYCHOLOGICAL MODELS RELATING TO HIV/AIDS

Given that one of the major ways of contracting HIV infection is via unprotected or risky sexual activity, you may think that one easy way to curtail

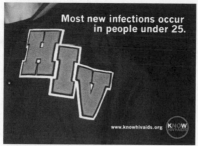

Public Service Ads Designed to Inform About HIV/AIDS

the spread of AIDS is to get people to have safe sex. Of course, that is easier said than done. For years, researchers have been trying to get men and women to have safe sex. These efforts range from educating individuals on the proper use of condoms to changing behavioral intentions. In a general sense, practicing safe sex can be considered analogous to any other health behavior and consequently most of the health behavior models that we discussed in Chapter 6 apply here as well. For example, researchers have used the Health Belief Model and the Theory of Planned Behavior to influence beliefs and intentions in regard to condom use and safe sex (Abraham, Sheeran, Spears, & Abrams, 1992; Aspinwall, Kemeny, Taylor, Schneider, & Dudley, 1991; Jemmott, Jemmott, & Hacker, 1992; Winslow, Franzini, & Hwang, 1992). Indeed most HIV interventions are adapted from existing theories and models such as the Transtheoretical model (Naar-King, et al., 2008) and other evidence-based interventions (EBIs) to save time and money. Wingood and DiClemente (2008) developed a framework for adapting HIV-related EBIs, known as the "ADAPT-ITT" model. The ADAPT-ITT model consists of eight sequential phases that inform HIV prevention providers and researchers of a prescriptive method for adapting EBIs.

There are also models designed specifically for HIV patients. For example the Information-Motivation-Behavioral Skills (IMB, Fisher & Fisher, 1992; Starace, Massa, Amico, & Fisher, 2006) model of health behavior provides a framework for guiding HIV risk reduction interventions and has been modified for many different subgroups (e.g., for men who have sex with men at high-risk for HIV infection, Kalichman, Picciano, & Roffman, 2008). In another example, Catania, Kegeles, and Coates (1990b) proposed the AIDS Risk Reduction Model (ARRM), which states that people must first understand the threat of HIV infection and recognize that their behaviors put them at risk for infection with the virus and consequently developing the disease.

Attitudes toward the protective behavior matter too. Using condoms can significantly reduce the risk of contracting a sexually transmitted disease, but many people believe that condoms reduce sexual pleasure, and this belief decreases condom use (Albarracin et al., 2000). Others may not be confident in their ability to properly use condoms (Catania, Kegeles & Coates, 1990a; Rosario, Nahler, Hunter, & Gwadz, 1999). As suggested by the social norms component of the Theory of Planned Behavior, people's attitudes toward condom use will also be influenced by what they think the norms are and what they believe their friends and partners think about it (Fischer, Fisher, & Rye, 1995). Other factors influencing condom use include concurrent alcohol or drug use (Gordon, Carey, & Carey, 1997; Leigh, Schafer, & Temple, 1995), level of commitment between the people having sex (Katz, Fortenberry, Zimet, Blythe, & Orr, 2000), level of sexual arousal—more arousal leads to less use of condoms (Galligan & Terry, 1993), and the type of relationship—women are more likely to practice safer sex in casual sexual relationships (Morrill, Ickovics, Golubchikov, Beren, & Rodin, 1996).

The first line of attack is most often education. If you can increase a person's knowledge about an illness, automatically their beliefs about their own susceptibility or vulnerability to it as well as their sense of the severity of the disease (factors from the Health Belief Model) will change. There are many misperceptions about HIV infection and who is most likely to get it. I already mentioned that people tend to believe that it is something just homosexuals get. In general, studies have found that although some segments of the population are well informed about AIDS (e.g., gay men), others such as adolescents are not (LeBlanc, 1993). Similarly, Murphy, Mann, O'Keefe, and Rotheram-Borus (1998) found that single, inner-city women often have little knowledge of AIDS or what behaviors place them at risk. Methods for providing education vary. General interventions that provide counseling about HIV infection seem to be effective to curtail the activity of those already infected with HIV, but are not as effective for those who are not (Weinhardt, Carey, Johnson, & Bickman, 1999). Instead, more targeted interventions (e.g., those aimed at very specific populations) have proved to be more effective (Jemmott, Jemmott, & Fong, 1992; Nyamathi, Stein, & Brecht, 1995).

Beyond education about AIDS, health psychological interventions have also targeted sexual activity. For most health behaviors, the best predictor of future behavior is past behavior. Old habits die hard. If a person has used condoms and practiced safe sex before, he or she is more likely to do it in the future. Modifying sexual behavior becomes especially difficult because it is linked to ideas of freedom and spontaneity. For many young men and women, being independent translates into not having to do anything (e.g., particularly have sex) in any specific way (even safely). Modification of sexual behavior has been found to be a threat to identity (McKusick, Horstman, & Coates, 1985). Consequently, many interventions are designed to vary different aspects of the process of indulging in sexual behavior. Some teach people how to exercise self-control and not rush into sex, which is more often unsafe (Miller, Bettencourt, DeBro, & Hoffman, 1993). Other interventions model skills to avoid high-risk behaviors (van der Velde & Van der Pligt, 1991).

Most interventions are designed to explicitly reduce sexual risk behavior (Gerressu, & Stephenson, 2008; Kalichman, Carey, & Johnson, 1996; Naar-King, et al., 2008). Noar (2008) examined 18 meta-analyses (9,423 participants, essentially a meta-meta-analysis) and found that all meta-analyses examining interventions aimed to reduce condom use and general sexual risk were statistically significant (Odds ratio = 1.34 and .78 respectively). A majority of the meta-analyses (9 of 11) showed interventions for reducing unprotected sex were significant (odds ratio = .76). Interventions for reducing

Yoga for AIDS

More and more groups are offering yoga classes specifically designed for people with AIDS. The postures and movements serve to relieve many of the physical symptoms, ease anxiety, and help with coping. The left panel shows a screenshot of a website specifically designed for AIDS patients.

numbers of sexual partners (odds ratio = .87) and reducing STDs (odds ratio = .74) were also effective. You may be surprised at what works. Albarracín, Leeper, Earl, and Durantini (2008) found that even having people read educational brochures increased the likelihood they would watch an educational video, which in turn increased participation in a counseling session designed to educate about reducing risky sexual behavior. People expecting the counseling to be useful were more likely to attend the session after watching the video (i.e., expectations was a mediator).

Being HIV positive does not signify the end of sexual activity. Safe sex does not mean no sex either. More than 70 percent of people infected with HIV continue to be sexually active (Kline & VanLandingham, 1994), and a large number of interventions seek to increase disclosure of status. Such interventions empower those with HIV infection to disclose their status to friends and family. Not only does this disclosure provide the patient with more opportunities for social support, but it also allows their sexual partners to make informed decisions about sexual activity with them. In addition, men who disclose their HIV status are more likely to practice safe sex (DeRosa & Marks, 1998).

The changing demographics of America and the ethnic differences in HIV incidence have led a number of researchers to focus on specific ethnic groups when designing interventions. In a recent meta-analysis, Albarracin, Albarracin, and Durantini (2008) examined data from studies (over 110,000 participants) assessing the efficacy of HIV-prevention interventions across samples with higher and lower concentrations of Latinos. Groups with higher percents of Latinos did not benefit from the interventions as much as groups with lower percents of Latinos (e.g., did not increase condom use). Interestingly, groups with more Latinos only benefited from intervention strategies that included threat-inducing arguments. Groups with greater percents of Latinos/ Latin Americans benefited from interventions conducted by a lay community member, whereas groups with lower percents of these groups increased condom use the most in response to experts. Supporting the subtext of this book, there were important differences by sex, acculturation, and nationality.

In a similar meta-analysis focused on an ethnic group, Darbes, Darbes, Crepaz, Lyles, Kennedy, and Rutherford (2008) reviewed HIV interventions for heterosexual African Americans to determine the overall efficacy in reducing HIV-risk sex behaviors and incident sexually transmitted diseases and identify intervention characteristics associated with efficacy. They found 38 randomized controlled trials (1988 to 2005) that showed that interventions significantly reduced unprotected sex (odds ratio = 0.75, see Chapter 1) and marginally decreased incidents of sexually transmitted diseases (odds ratio − 0.88; Darbes et al., 2008). Successful intervention components included cultural tailoring, aiming to influence social norms in promoting safe sex behavior, utilizing peer education, providing skills training on correct use of condoms and communication skills needed for negotiating safer sex, and multiple sessions and opportunities to practice learned skills (refer to Chapter 6 for intervention best practices).

To tackle health disparities head on is critical to ensure that interventions reflect cultural competence. For example, Latino Americans have unique cultural and social characteristics and norms that place them at risk for HIV exposure (Weidel, Provencio-Vasquez, Watson, & Gonzalez-Guarda, 2008). Correspondingly, there is now a group intervention designed for Latino patients living with HIV/AIDS in New York City (Acevedo, 2008). The intervention attempts to compensate for cultural influences on adherence, social isolation, stigma, disclosure, safer sex practices, and patient-provider communication. Similarly, Sister-to-Sister is a skill-building HIV/STD risk-reduction intervention for African American women that had significant effects in reducing self-reported sexual risk behavior and biologically confirmed STD incidence (O'Leary, Jemmott, & Jemmott, 2008). In analyses of mediating variables, O'Leary et al., (2008) found that self-efficacy for condom carrying was the critical factor. Apparently the skill-building sexual risk-reduction interventions on women's use of condoms worked to improve the women's belief that they would be successful using condoms. In fact, self-efficacy was more important than characteristics of male partners (e.g., their reactions to the woman wanting to use a condom).

Psychological Interventions for those with HIV

Focusing on psychological states is key. A review of psychological interventions for HIV-positive persons showed intervening can improve psychological adjustment and consequently positively effect neuroendocrine regulation and immune status (Carrico, & Antoni, 2008). It is possible that a large part of the effect is due to the intervention groups providing social support and a key research agenda item is a fine-tuned examination of the effects of individual components of complex psychological interventions.

Given that stress can also negatively impact the immune system (as discussed previously), stress management becomes even more important for people with HIV. Some interventions aimed at reducing the ill effects of HIV infection and AIDS have used physical activity and cognitive-behavioral approaches. For example, aerobic exercise training was found to lessen the drop in immune functioning that normally accompanies being informed of a positive HIV test (La Perriere et al., 1991). Cognitive-behavioral stress management interventions have similar effects (Antoni et al., 1991, 2000; Cruess et al., 2000), although not all such attempts are successful (Coates, McKusick, Kuno, & Stites, 1989).

There has been a lot of recent research designed to compare the role of stress management interventions in enhancing immune function. McCain, et al. (2008) conducted a randomized clinical trial to test effects of three 10-week stress management approaches—cognitive-behavioral relaxation training, tai chi training, and spiritual growth groups. Compared to the control group, both the relaxation and tai chi groups used less emotion-focused coping. Furthermore, all intervention groups showed better immune cell functioning. Scott-Sheldon, Kalichman, Carey, and Fielder (2008) evaluated interventions to reduce stress as a means to improve health among persons living with HIV. Their meta-analytic review integrated the results of 35 randomized controlled trials examining the efficacy of 46 separate stress management interventions for 3,077 HIV positive adults. Compared to control group participants, Scott-Sheldon, et al. (2008) found that stress-management interventions reduce anxiety, depression, distress, and fatigue and improve quality of life. In contrast, stress-management interventions did not appear to improve CD4+ counts, or viral load compared with controls. Clearly, this conclusion about the absence of effect on immune functioning is inconsistent with McCain et al. (2008). Why? The studies reviewed by Scott-Sheldon et al. (2008) had shorter assessment periods (measured typically within one-week of the interventions) and participants were in more advanced stages of HIV (HIV-positive for an average of five years). Furthermore, the sample was predominately male and European American.

SYNTHESIZE, EVALUATE, APPLY	• How do cultural factors influence the behaviors that put someone at risk for HIV infection and for its spread? • Given the fatal course of HIV infection, what psychological factors could explain why people would still continue to engage in unsafe sexual practices/drug use? • Compare and contrast interventions for HIV with interventions to improve health behaviors such as mammogram screenings.

FOCUS ON APPLICATIONS

Yoga and Coping with Illnesses Such as AIDS

Scientists are working hard to find the cures for chronic and terminal illnesses such as cancer and AIDS, and although advancements are being made, there are no absolute cures as yet. A large focus then is on how best to help the patient cope with the pain and discomfort of the illness. Health psychologists are very useful in this regard. Many cognitive and behavioral approaches are used, but a majority of techniques involve some form of relaxation training, such as guided imagery or meditation. One particular technique that has become popular with the North American general public and one that is growing in utility in the treatment of chronic illnesses as well is yoga (Galantino, Galbavy, & Quinn, 2008). In keeping with an increase in

(continues)

FOCUS ON APPLICATIONS *(continued)*

the use of complementary and alternative treatments, a recent survey of more than 30,000 Americans showed that 5 percent used yoga for health reasons (Barnes, Powell-Griner, McFann, & Nahin, 2004). Another study determined that yoga use was closer to 8 percent (Saper, Eisenberg, Davis, Culpepper, & Phillips, 2004).

Up to a few years ago (and maybe in the minds of some of you today as well) yoga conjured up images of people bent into twisted, uncomfortable shapes and was a lifestyle associated with hippies, flower children, and pacifism. There are many stereotypes about yoga, and this is a good time to look at the facts. Practices such as yoga are likely to become more accepted in public consciousness as the utility of using the mind to calm and relax the body gets even stronger empirical validation. To the millions of practitioners of yoga, the benefits are clear, and many people practice yoga daily. Given that a complete yoga lifestyle does include the practicing of many healthy behaviors like not smoking, limiting drinking alcohol, physical activity, relaxation and meditation, good eating, and getting enough sleep, the practice of yoga shows a potential for enhancing the quality of life of those with chronic illnesses.

Yoga originated in India approximately 4,000 years ago, and the word is derived from Sanskrit (an ancient Indian language), meaning "to unite." There are many different aspects in the practice of yoga. The physical postures are just one aspect. Derived from Hinduism and Buddhism, the practice of yoga has as its basic goal the transformation of the self and diminished cravings. Yoga is a part of the ayurvedic approach to health. Traditionally practitioners believed that a universal spirit pervades everything and used yoga to clear the mind and release this spirit. A stressed mind was compared with a turbid lake and yoga calmed the waters. There are four main types of yoga. Hatha yoga stresses purification, postures, relaxation, and diet. Hatha yoga and variations of it are the most common forms of yoga in North America. The most common variation is Iyengar yoga, which is characterized by precise poses often with the aid of various props, such as cushions, benches, wood blocks, straps, and even sand bags. Other variations are Astanga yoga (involving synchronizing of breath with a progressive series of postures) and Bhikram yoga (in which postures are done in a 100°F heated room). Other forms of yoga include Jnana yoga (yoga of wisdom involving a study of literature and striving for attainment of right views), Bhakti yoga (yoga of devotion, finding inner change through prayer or religious ecstasy), and Karma yoga (yoga of action and the pursuit of a higher social purpose).

Yoga involves a lot more than just striking poses. Traditional yoga has eight parts (angas or limbs). There are four practices and four experiences for which one should strive. The practices involve (1) attitude toward the world (abstinence, truthfulness, and chastity), (2) attitude toward self (purification and contentment), (3) posture (or asana, which is what you probably have heard of), and (4) breath regulation (pranayama). The four experiences are (1) withdrawal of senses (pratyaha), (2) fixed attention (dhyana), (3) contemplation (dharana), and (4) absolute concentration (superconsciousness/samadhi). A true yoga practitioner would not only do the physical components but also strive to live life in accordance with the moral and psychological components. Only a small number of the many Americans who practice yoga strive for (or even know about) the complete scope of the practice.

The use of yoga for the treatment of chronic illnesses is increasing, and empirical studies of its effectiveness for a range of illnesses have slowly begun to be reported. For example, patients with multiple sclerosis in a yoga class showed significant improvement in measures of fatigue compared with a control group of patients with similar levels of the disease (Oken et al., 2004). Similar successes have been found with cardiovascular functioning (Harinath et al., 2004) and diabetes (Manyam, 2004). Yoga has begun to be implemented in a number of different health care programs. For example, the Stanford Cancer Supportive Care Program (SCSCP) at the Center for Integrative Medicine at Stanford Hospitals offers yoga to both cancer patients and their families. A recent assessment showed that more than 90 percent

(continues)

FOCUS ON APPLICATIONS *(continued)*

of the patients using the SCSCP felt there was benefit to the program, and yoga was one of the classes with the highest number of participants (Rosenbaum et al., 2004).

In the context of HIV infection and AIDS, a number of AIDS patients use yoga to ease their pain and negative feelings (Bonadies, 2004). In a study of complementary and alternative medicine (CAM) use in a British Columbia HIV treatment center, 36 percent said they used yoga (Dhalla, Chan, Montaner, & Hogg, 2006). AIDS patient Steve McCeney (quoted in the *Yoga Journal*, 2001) provides a glimpse of what it is like. He said, "Sometimes I don't know what it's like to feel normal anymore, but I do know that after an hour of restorative poses, I feel like a new person mentally, spiritually, and physically." An international group of yoga therapists provides a variety of special resources and information for AIDS patients, and studies of the effects of yoga on HIV infection are being conducted.

Some yoga postures are thought to activate the hormonal system of the body, the ductless glands of the body, to start to balance their activities. For example, I talked earlier about the role of the thymus gland in the immune system. Open-chested poses such as Supta Baddha Konasana (reclining bound angle pose) or Setu Bandha over bolsters or a bench (bridge pose) stimulate the thymus gland (Kout, 1992). Yoga also can be a psychological booster, helping patients to strengthen their minds and build their resolve. In the words of another AIDS patient:

> Yoga is the main thing that makes me feel good, besides emotional things I can do with a partner or being in love. I really feel it if I don't have it every week. It is a big security blanket. Yoga does more for me than anything else I do. It makes so much sense, especially now that I am studying massage and learning about the organs. I'm feeling more in touch with my body than I thought I ever could. It helps me to slow down and look at life week by week, day by day; using what I have, not always wanting more; learning to live in the moment. (Kout, 1992)

SUMMARY

- Psychoneuroimmunology is a field that focuses on how psychological factors influence immune functioning. Research in PNI includes that done on behavioral conditioning of the immune response and the association between the immune system and stress. Stress has been reliably associated with the functioning of the immune system, mostly having a negative effect (e.g., in the long run) but sometimes activating it as well (in the short run).

- Acquired immunodeficiency syndrome (AIDS) and the human immunodeficiency virus (HIV), first noticed in the early 1980s, are a worldwide threat to health. Although a cure is yet to be found, health psychologists can be influential in helping change behaviors that can cause the spread of this disease. Originally thought to be a disease affecting only homosexual men, AIDS is now known to strike both heterosexuals and homosexuals alike. Low socioeconomic status individuals and those from some minority groups have a disproportionate risk for contracting this disease.

- Many psychological factors such as optimism and social support can be useful in helping a person with AIDS live a longer life. Similarly, problem-solving, avoidance, and support-seeking strategies all relate to coping with HIV infection.

- Specific health behavior change models such as the AIDS Risk Reduction Model (ARRM) have been designed to help combat the spread of AIDS, and research is now addressing understudied cultural populations such as women and minority groups.

TEST YOURSELF

Check your understanding of the topics in this chapter by answering the following questions. Answers appear in the Appendix.

1. A clear example of the connection between the mind and body, especially between psychology and immune functioning is that:
   a. Real emotional experience is related to immune changes.
   b. Any emotional experience, even faked, leads to immune changes.
   c. Only faked emotional experiences lead to immune changes.
   d. Thinking about increased immune activity can create it.

2. A girl with lupus was given a shot of a strong drug. At the same time she was exposed to the scent of rose perfume and the taste of cod liver oil. After a few pairings of these three (drug, oil, scent) her body had a physiological response to the rose scent even without the full dose of the strong drug. This is an example of:
   a. Conditioned immunity.
   b. Operant conditioning.
   c. Psychoneuroimmunological reactivity.
   d. Compensatory responding.

3. Why does chronic stress suppress the immune system?
   a. It conserves body resources
   b. It serves as a warning
   c. It prevents the organism from being too active
   d. It prevents overactivation

4. Which of the following statements is TRUE?
   a. AIDS and HIV are synonyms.
   b. A person can have AIDS without being HIV positive.
   c. A person who is HIV negative develops AIDS.

   d. A person can be HIV positive without having AIDS.

5. AIDS was first discovered and named in the:
   a. 1950s.
   b. 1960s.
   c. 1970s.
   d. 1980s.

6. Currently, the average time between HIV infection and the appearance of the first signs of AIDS is:
   a. 5–10 months.
   b. 1–2 years.
   c. 3–5 years.
   d. 8–11 years.

7. The most common cultural group to have HIV is:
   a. African Americans.
   b. Latino Americans.
   c. Minority women.
   d. Low SES men.

8. The extent to which people engage in sexual activities with sexual partners from other sexual networks is known as _____ and is a central influence on AIDS transmission.
   a. Miscegenation
   b. The contact hypothesis
   c. Sexual mixing
   d. Transgroup sexuality

9. People newly infected with HIV report:
   a. Depression.
   b. Hyperactivity.
   c. Flu-like symptoms.
   d. Cold-like symptoms.

10. One alternative medical treatment borrowed from a non-Western culture is increasing in popularity among AIDS patients and works on a biopsychosocial level. This is _____.

a. Sweat lodges.

b. Acupressure.

c. Tai chi.

d. Yoga.

WEB RESOURCES

Visit the companion Web site at **www.cengage.com/ psychology/gurung,** where you will find online resources for this book, including chapter-by-chapter quizzes, Web links, and more!

National Institute of Health AIDS Information
http://www.aidsinfo.nih.gov

> This is a site offering information on all aspects of HIV and AIDS including treatment options and the latest research on the topic.

Cousins Center for Psychoneuroimmunology
http://www.cousinspni.org

> This Web site for the UCLA Cousins Center is where research from the behavioral sciences, neuroscience and immunology combine to investigate how psychological and biological factors cause disease. It is a good psychoneuroimmunology resource.

National Center for Complementary and Alternative Medicine Yoga
http://nccam.nih.gov/health/yoga/

> This site offers complete introduction to yoga with links to the latest research on yoga including clinical trials.

KEY TERMS, CONCEPTS, AND PEOPLE

acquired immunodeficiency syndrome, 346

highly active antiretroviral therapy, 351

human immunodeficiency virus, 346

immune system, 346

opportunistic infections, 353

psychoneuro-immunology, 343

sexual mixing, 359

ESSENTIAL READINGS

Ader, R., Felten, D. L., & Cohen, N. (2001). *Psychoneuroimmunology*. San Diego, CA: Academic Press. (This edited volume has a collection of some of the best empirical work in the field of psychoneuroimmunology. Pay especially close attention to the chapter by Cole and Kemeny.)

Cohen, S., & Herbert, T. B. (1996). Health psychology: Psychological factors and physical disease from the perspective of human psychoneuroimmunology. *Annual Review of Psychology, 47*, 113–142.

Reed, G. M., Kemeny, M. E., Taylor, S. E., & Visscher, B. R. (1999). Negative HIV-specific expectancies and AIDS-related bereavement as predictors of symptom onset in asymptomatic HIV-positive gay men. *Health Psychology, 18*(4), 354–363.

Segerstrom, S. C., & Miller, G. E. (2004). Psychological stress and the human immune system: A meta-analytic study of 30 years of inquiry. *Psychological Bulletin, 130*(4), 601–630.

Culture and Cancer

I f you are reading this in a public place, observe the people around you. If you are reading this alone, think of the faces of your colleagues, students, or coworkers. Want to know some sobering facts? A high percentage of the people you see or the people you are thinking of have had a close encounter with cancer. They either know someone who has been diagnosed with it or may have been diagnosed with it themselves. Close to half of us are predicted to develop some form of cancer in our lifetimes. More than one million new cases of cancer are diagnosed every year, and cancer is the second leading cause of death in the United States (after heart disease, American Cancer Society, ACS, 2008). In 2008, over one-half million people will probably die from cancer and close to one and a half million people will be diagnosed with a cancer. You may know someone with cancer yourself—your mother, father, uncle, aunt, brother, or sister. You have probably heard of the cyclist Lance Armstrong, the golfer Arnold Palmer, the master chef Julia Child, the actresses Shirley Temple, Suzanne Somers, Kate Jackson, and Edie Falco, anchorman Peter Jennings, New York Yankee's manager Joe Torre, former first ladies Betty Ford and Nancy Reagan, the writer Gloria Steinem, and politicians Bob Dole, Colin Powell, John Kerry, and Rudy Guliani. All of them had cancer.

Even saying the word cancer conjures up images of sadness or dread. The fear of cancer has been so pervasive that finding a cure for it is often seen as the pinnacle of achievement, the truly ambitious child's dream. People jest about how the epitome of an impressive resume would be "found a cure for cancer" rating equally with "brokered world peace." The good news is that health psychology is demonstrating how preventative measures can greatly

Lance Armstrong—Cancer Survivor

reduce the incidence of cancer. What you do (and how much attention you paid to chapters 6 and 7 on health behaviors) can predict your likelihood of getting cancer. Want to hear some even better news? Health psychological research designed to improve cancer screening and increase early detection is helping more people survive what was once a terminal disease. Today there are more than 12 million cancer survivors. Nearly two-thirds of cancer patients can expect to live five years or longer after diagnosis and more than 80 percent of children with leukemia are cured (ACS, 2008). Most breast cancers, for example, are diagnosed at an early stage and up to 96 percent of those with localized disease survive five years (American Cancer Society, 2008).

What exactly is this dreadful disease? How do you get it? Who gets it? How is it treated? How can one survive it? These are just some of the questions we will answer in this chapter. We will also examine how cancer varies across cultural lines and is influenced by psychological factors.

PREVALENCE OF CANCER

As mentioned, unfortunately the chances of our developing some form of cancer in our lifetime are pretty high, and the chances get higher as we get older. For people between the ages of 60 and 70, there is a one in three chance (if you are male) or one in four chance (if you are female) of getting cancer. This incidence drops to a 1 in 12 and 1 in 11 chance for men and women between the ages of 40 and 59, respectively, and a 1 in 52 chance for men between the ages of 1 and 39 (1 in 73 for women in the same category). Culture is again very important. Prevalence rates vary across many levels of culture: by sex, ethnicity, and geography and are shown in Figure 12.1.

We are making strides in the fight against cancer. New results on the incidence of cancer show that it is not as common as it was before, although the good news is limited to European American populations. Jemal et al. (2008) collected cancer morbidity and mortality data from several government organizations like the Centers for Disease Control and Prevention (CDC), evaluated trends in cancer incidence and death rates, and compared survival rates over time and across racial/ethnic populations. The good news is that incidence rates for all cancers combined decreased from 1990 through 2004. Overall cancer death rates in 2004 compared with 1990 in men and 1991 in women decreased by 18.4 percent and 10.5 percent, respectively (Jemal et al., 2008). The bad news from a cultural perspective is that cancer-specific survival rates are lower and the risk of dying from cancer once it is diagnosed is higher in most minority populations compared with the European American population, as shown in Table 12.1 (Jemal et al., 2008). The relative risk of death from cancer (all types combined) compared with that for European American men and women was higher for both Latino men (1.16) and American Indian men (1.69). Another study showed that the breast cancer rate for Asian American women rose 6 percent per year from 1993 to 1997 compared with only 2 percent per year for European American women (Deapen, Lui, Perkins, Bernstein, & Ross, 2002).

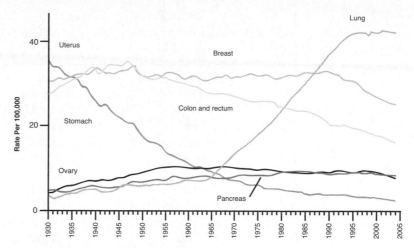

FIGURE **12.1** Cancer Death Rates for Women in the United States, 1930 to 2004

*Rates are age-adjusted to the 2000 U.S. standard population.

†Uterus includes uterine cervix and uterine corpus.

Note: Due to changes in ICD coding, numerator information has changed over time. Rates for cancers of the uterus, ovary, lung and bronchus, and colon and rectum are affected by these changes.

Source: U.S. Mortality Data, 1960 to 2004, U.S. Mortality Volumes 1930 to 1959, National Center for Health Statistics, Centers for Disease Control and Prevention, 2006.

WHAT IS CANCER?

Similar to stress and pain, the word cancer has many different forms and meanings. *Cancer* is derived from *carcinos* and *carcinoma*, terms first used by the Greek Hippocrates to describe nonulcer-forming and ulcer-forming tumors. The shape of a spreading cancer cell resembles the outstretching legs of a crab to which these words refer (in Greek the word for crab is *cancer*, think of the zodiac sign). Although typically discussed as one illness, cancer is a group of diseases that vary in terms of incidence and mortality rates, epidemiology, risk factors and causes, and treatments (American Cancer Society, 2008; Pecorino, 2008; Meyerowitz, Bull, & Perez, 2000; Weinberg, 2006). Also, understanding cancer and its effects through a cultural approach is an important area of health psychology because a comprehensive understanding of cancer requires a consideration of sex, gender, ethnicity, geographical location, sexual orientation, and all the other aspects of what makes up culture.

First, let's look at basic biology and some terminology. Cancer is the name given to the illness or condition caused by the presence of a malignant tumor. A malignant tumor or cancerous cell is identified as one showing uncontrollable cell growth that destroys healthy tissue. Cells that show abnormal growth are also referred to as **neoplasms**. Normally our cells grow, divide, and die in an orderly fashion, and cell growth is more pronounced when we are young. As we grow older, cells in most parts of the body divide only to replace worn-out or dying cells and to repair injuries. Because cancer cells continue to grow

TABLE **12.1**

Cancer Sites in Which African American Death Rates Exceed White Death Rates for Men in the United States, 1996 to 2000

Site	African American	White	Ratio of African American/White
All sites	356.2	249.5	1.4
Larynx	5.7	2.4	2.4
Prostate	73.0	30.2	2.4
Stomach	14.0	6.1	2.3
Myeloma	9.2	4.5	2.0
Oral cavity and pharynx	7.9	4.0	2.0
Esophagus	12.2	7.3	1.7
Liver	9.3	6.0	1.6
Lung and bronchus	107.0	78.1	1.4
Pancreas	16.4	12.0	1.4
Small intestine	0.7	0.5	1.4
Colon and rectum	34.6	25.3	1.4

Rates per 100,000, age-adjusted to the 2000 U.S. standard population.

Source: Surveillance, Epidemiology, and End Results Program, 1975–2000, Division of Cancer Control and Population Sciences, National Cancer Institute, 2003.

and divide, they are different from normal cells. Instead of dying, they outlive normal cells and continue to form new abnormal cells.

When a normal cell turns cancerous, it is often the result of a mutation in the cell's DNA that alters it and makes it grow uncontrollably, disrupting surrounding tissue and often spreading to organs all around the body (Hanahan & Weinberg, 2000; Pecorino, 2008; Weinberg, 2006). Most of the time when DNA becomes damaged, the body is able to repair it. In cancer cells, the damaged DNA cannot be repaired. Such genetic mutations can also be inherited, which accounts for why risk for cancer increases if someone in a person's family has had cancer. Many times though, a person's cancerous cell mutations occur because of exposure to environmental toxins such as cigarette smoke or other **carcinogens** (cancer-causing substances). The branch of medicine that concerns the study and treatment of cancer is referred to as oncology, and this is the term used more frequently in hospitals.

Types of Cancer

There are more than 100 different types of cancer, and even tumors within each type show a lot of variability. However, note that not all tumors are cancerous or **malignant. Benign** or noncancerous tumors do not **metastasize** or spread to other parts of the body and, with very rare exceptions, are not life threatening. Some cancers, such as leukemia, do not form tumors. Instead, these cancer cells involve the blood and blood-forming organs and circulate through other tissues

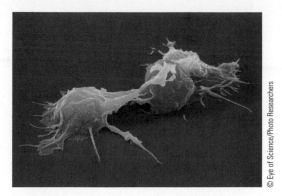

© Eye of Science/Photo Researchers

A Cancer Cell (Center) Being Attacked by Immune System Killer T Cells

Scanning electron microscope shows killer T cells attacking the cancer cell (with crab-like tentacles).

where they grow. The course of the disease and the likelihood of survival vary greatly with each type of cancer. Therefore, if someone just says he or she has cancer, you should not make any generalizations about his or her experiences until you have more details. Some cancers show very little deviation in patterns of disease course, and psychosocial influences on coping and treatment are minimal (Henderson & Baum, 2002). That said, psychosocial factors do relate to differences in disease progression (Antoni & Lutgendorf, 2007; Falagas, 2007).

The key variables that influence the interaction between biological, psychological, and social factors and the role each plays in cancer mortality or morbidity are cancer site, type, and severity. The most common sites for cancer are the lungs, breasts, prostate gland, colon, and rectum (the latter two are often affected together, which is referred to as colorectal cancer). The top 15 cancer sites and related incidence and mortality statistics for each are shown in Table 12.2.

There are four main types of cancer. The most common are **carcinomas** that start in the surface layers of the body or epithelial cells. This form of cancer accounts for the bulk of cancer cases and is seen in the most common sites. **Sarcomas** are cancers of the muscles, bones, and cartilage. **Lymphomas** are cancers of the lymphatic system and are referred to as Hodgkin's disease if the cancer spreads from a single lymph node (non-Hodgkin lymphomas are found at several sites). **Leukemias** are cancers that are found in the blood and bone marrow. In leukemia, white blood cells proliferate to displace red blood cells, which causes anemia (a shortage of red blood cells), bleeding, and other immune system problems.

The severity of cancer is determined by a multifactor assessment of stage. The **TNM system** is the most common method used to stage cancer (American Cancer Society, 2008). It provides three main pieces of information. The T describes the size of the tumor and whether cancer has spread to nearby tissues and organs. The N describes how far the cancer has spread to nearby lymph nodes. Given that the lymph nodes are critical components of the body's immune system, they are often heavily involved in fighting cancer cells.

TABLE **12.2**
Sites of Cancer and Incidence

2008 Estimated US Cancer Deaths*				
Lung and bronchus	31%	Men 290,890 · Women 272,810	26%	Lung and bronchus
Prostate	10%		15%	Breast
Colon and rectum	8%		9%	Colon and rectum
Pancreas	6%		6%	Ovary
Leukemia	4%		6%	Pancreas
Non-Hodgkin lymphoma	3%		3%	Leukemia
Esophagus	4%		3%	Non-Hodgkin lymphoma
Liver and intrahepatic bile duct	4%		3%	Uterine corpus
Urinary bladder	3%		2%	Liver and intrahepatic bile duct
Kidney and renal pelvis	3%		2%	Brain and other nervous system
All other sites	24%		25%	All other sites

Source: ©2008, American Cancer Society, Inc., Surveillance Research

The M indicates the extent to which the cancer has metastasized. Letters or numbers after the T, N, and M give more details about each of these factors. For example, a tumor classified as T1, N0, M0 is a tumor that is very small, has not spread to the lymph nodes, and has not spread to distant organs of the body. Once TNM descriptions have been established, they can be grouped together into a simpler set of stages, stages 0 through IV. In general, the lower the number, the less the cancer has spread. A higher number, such as stage IV, indicates a more serious, widespread cancer (American Cancer Society, 2008).

CULTURAL VARIATIONS IN THE INCIDENCE OF CANCER

Similar to the ethnic differences in incidence of HIV infection described in the previous chapter, there are large differences in the cultural makeup of people who have cancer (ACS, 2008; Gotay, Muraoka, & Holup, 2001; Meyerowitz, Richardson, Hudson, & Leedham, 1998; Stafford et al., 2008). In fact, there is a growing body of research clarifying the link between cancer and membership in certain ethnic groups (Elmore, Moceri, Carter, & Larson, 1998; Perkins, Cooksley, & Cox, 1996). Before looking at possible biological reasons why one ethnicity may be more at risk than another, let's first look at the different patterns of cancer across diverse ethnic groups.

There are two main statistics to bear in mind when studying the prevalence of cancer. The first is **incidence** or rates of newly diagnosed cases of the disease. The second is actual mortality. Keeping the two numbers separate is important because there are many people who are diagnosed with cancer who live

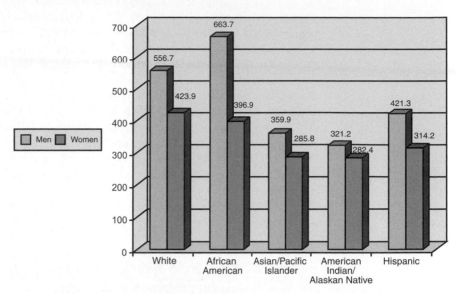

FIGURE **12.2** Cancer Incidence and Death Rates by Site, Race, and Ethnicity, United States, 2000 to 2004

Source: Adapted from TABLE 11 Cancer Incidence and Death Rates by Site, Race, and Ethnicity, United States, 2000 to 2004; http://caonline.amcancersoc.org/cgi/content/full/58/2/71#T11.

(remember there was good news), and the number of survivors varies across cultural groups. So even if there are two cultural groups who both have the same incidence levels for a certain type of cancer, they may not show the same mortality rates. Figure 12.2 shows the incidence and mortality rates for the main types of cancer broken down by two main cultural variables, sex and ethnicity.

As you can see, different ethnic groups and the two sexes do not get cancer or die from it in the same ways (Jemal et al., 2008). African Americans have the highest general cancer incidence rates and mortality rates of any population in the United States, with this difference being driven more by higher rates of cancer among African American men. Illustrating the difference between incidence and mortality, American Indians have greater mortality rates relative to their incidence rates, suggesting that if they have cancer they are more likely to die of it. Separating total cases of cancer from individual types of cancer is important too. Although Asian Americans show much lower rates of cancer than European Americans in general, their rates of colorectal cancer diagnoses are about the same. In contrast to some other ethnic differences, European American men are four times more likely to have testicular cancer than are African American men (Hawkins & Miaskowski, 1996).

In addition to these ethnic differences, there are significant sex differences in cancer incidence as well. Men experience higher incidences of cancer in general (American Cancer Society, 2008). The most common sites for male cancer are the prostate gland, the lungs, the colon, and the rectum (American Cancer Society, 2008). Testicular cancer is relatively uncommon among men in general, but it is one of the most common forms of cancer in younger men aged 15 to 35. For some time, male cancers did not receive as much research attention as female cancers and less is known about the etiology of most male cancers and men's psychological and social experiences with cancer (Gordon & Cerami, 2000).

The most common sites for female cancer for women of most ethnic groups are the breasts, lungs, colon, and rectum. In case you were wondering, men do get breast cancer although the rates are infinitesimal (and no, women cannot get testicular cancer although they do get ovarian cancer). Breast cancer incidence rates are somewhat counter to normal ethnic difference patterns: A higher incidence of breast cancer has been reported both in European American women and women of higher socioeconomic status (SES) compared to women of other ethnicities and lower SES (Vainshtein, 2008). Other common cancers tend to vary by ethnicity but usually include cancers of the reproductive organs (e.g., the uterus, cervix, and ovaries) and may be due to some ethnic groups such as Asian American and Latina women not getting screened for the cancers (Durvasula, Regan, Ureño, & Howell, 2008).

Cultural Differences in Beliefs and Knowledge about Cancer

Some of the cultural differences in cancer incidence are explained by cultural differences pertaining to beliefs held about cancer, people's attitudes toward cancer, and knowledge of cancer. Many studies have shown that low socioeconomic groups are less knowledgeable about cancer regardless of their sex, ethnicity, or religion (e.g., Breslow, Sorkin, Frey, & Kessler, 1997; Deibert et al., 2007; Hoffman-Goetz, & Friedman, 2006; Pendleton et al., 2008). Ethnically diverse groups have shown different levels of knowledge as well. African Americans (Griffith et al, 2007; Magnus, 2004; Miller & Champion, 1997), Arab Americans (Shah, Ayash, Pharaon, & Gany, 2008); Latinos (Deibert et al., 2007; Hall, Hall, Pfriemer, Wimberley, & Jones, 2007; Hubbell, Chavez, Mishra, & Valdez, 1996), Chinese Americans (Lee-Lin et al., 2007; Lee-Kin, Petit, et al., 2007; Liang et al., 2008; Mo, 1992), Vietnamese Americans (Pham & McPhee, 1992), Native Hawaiians (Blaisdell, 1998), American Samoans (Mishra, Luce-Aoelua, & Hubbell, 1998), and Korean Americans (Jo, Maxwell, Wong, & Bastani, 2008; Kim, Yu, Chen, Kim, & Brintnall, 1998; Lee, Tripp-Reimer, Miller, Sadler, & Lee, 2007) have all been found to have lower levels of knowledge about risk factors and cancer symptoms than European American groups.

Sometimes these cultural differences are linked to cultural beliefs and misconceptions about disease in general. Many religious individuals may believe that cancer is just punishment for sins or that cancer has spiritual meaning (Ashing-Giwa & Ganz, 1997; Koffman, Morgan, Edmonds, Speck, & Higginson, 2008; Martinez, Chavez, & Hubbell, 1997; Perez-Stable, Sabogal, Otero-Sabogal, Hiatt, & McPhee, 1992). The misperceived causes of cancer may also be more tangible. Vietnamese, Chinese, and Latino Americans (Garcia & Lee, 1989; Hubbell et al., 1996; Martinez et al., 1997; Pham & McPhee, 1992) reported poor hygiene or dirt as a cause for breast and cervical cancer. Another common cultural cancer belief is **fatalism**, the belief that a person with cancer cannot live a normal life and will die (Gotay et al., 2001; Pasick, & Burke, 2008). High levels of fatalism have been found in African Americans (Farmer, Reddick, D'Agostino, & Jackson, 2007),

Vietnamese and Chinese Americans (Liang et al., 2008), and Latinos (Champion & Menon, 1997; Demark-Wahnefried, Rimer, & Wimer, 1997; Lagos et al., 2008; Perez-Stable et al., 1992; Pham & McPhee, 1992).

A vivid example of how culture influences perceptions is seen in the views of American Indians. Many American Indians see cancer as a "White man's" disease and something that is a punishment for one's actions or the actions of a family member (Alvord & Van Pelt, 2000). Some of them see cancer as a natural part of life's pathway and as providing a lesson from which to learn. Many also see cancer as penance and a person with cancer must "wear the pain" to protect other members of the community (Burhansstipanov, 2000). A diagnosis of cancer is equivalent to a doctor shooting a hole through the spirit and thus results in depression and fear of the doctor instead of trust. Beliefs about how you can get cancer may seem outlandish to the ethnocentric non-Indians. Some American Indians believe cancer can result from a curse or from violating tribal mores like stepping on a frog or urinating on a spider. Others believe that it is contagious and that it can be caught from a mammography machine or from the child of someone who has cancer (Burhansstipanov, 2000). Some American Indians do not want to even talk about cancer for fear of catching the cancer spirit. Regardless of the extent to which you think these beliefs are far-fetched, they have to be respected and anticipated to optimize helping the American Indians who do hold them.

SYNTHESIZE, EVALUATE, APPLY	• What are the benefits and problems with celebrities speaking publicly about their cancers? • What can be done to demystify cancer? • How can coming from a different cultural background influence your risk of getting cancer? • How are different cultural beliefs and knowledge levels about cancer related to broader sociocultural differences such as cross-cultural approaches to health? • Do you think there is more or less stigma associated with having cancer than with having HIV/AIDS? Why?

DEVELOPMENTAL ISSUES IN CANCER

You are more likely to get cancer as you get older (Ukraintseva & Yashin, 2003). The rates for cancer increase dramatically over the lifespan. Incidence rates range from less than 15 per 100,000 for those younger than 15 years of age, but balloon to more than 2,000 per 100,000 for those older than 75 (Ries, 1996). Age is a cultural variable as well, and one that also needs to be attended to in understanding cancer.

Cancer can be considered a developmental disease (Meyerowitz et al., 2000). Why is this? Although cancer is primarily diagnosed in older adults, cancers actually develop when people are younger. Because there typically is a large gap between when a tumor starts to grow and when it is large enough to be diagnosed, exposure to many of the risk factors for cancer (described below) at a young age necessarily predict the occurrence of cancer at an older age. Significant risks for cancer are also associated with the different developmental milestones. (as described in chapter 3). There is a risk associated with girls starting to menstruate early (Colditz & Frazier, 1995) and dietary problems during the reproductive years have been linked to the development of oral and other cancers in older women years later (Muscat, Richie, Thompson, & Wynder, 1996). There are also risks associated with menopause and the ways that women cope with it. The biggest risk factor for cancer—smoking—also has a strong developmental link: smoking almost always begins in the teenage years; few adults initiate a regular smoking habit (Berman & Gritz, 1991).

Developmental age also influences how people, especially children, will cope with a cancer diagnosis. For example, Barrera et al. (2003) recruited preschool, school age, and adolescent patients and measured their psychological adjustment and quality of life (QOL), 3, 9, and 15 months after cancer was diagnosed. The children's age at diagnosis significantly affected both their adjustment and QOL. At 3 months after diagnosis, preschoolers had more externalizing behavior problems than did adolescents. Preschoolers had better QOL than adolescents did at all three assessments, suggesting that preschoolers with cancer are at risk for behavior problems and adolescents are at risk for poor QOL. Studies such as these are gentle reminders that the psychological reactions to cancer experienced by adults may be very different from those of children (Anderzén Carlsson, Sørlie, Gustafsson, Olsson, & Kihlgren, 2008; Katz, Kellerman, & Siegel, 1980). A developmental approach also helps us understand how family interactions change when one family member has cancer (Johnson, 1997; Jones et al., 2008; Weihs & Reiss, 1996).

PHYSIOLOGICAL CORRELATES OF CANCER

The physiological symptoms of cancer will depend on the size, location, and stage of cancer (Weinberg, 2006). If a cancer has reached a later stage and metastasizes, then symptoms may occur at different locations in the body. As the mutant cells divide, they exert pressure on the surrounding organs, blood vessels, and nerves that will be consciously felt by the individual (Pecorino, 2008). Some cancers, such as pancreatic cancer, are not felt until the cell has reached an advanced stage of development. Some of the general symptoms of cancer are fever, fatigue, pain, changes in the skin, and weight loss. Remember that having these symptoms does not necessarily mean a person has cancer, but suggests that something is not right (there are many other reasons for these same symptoms). Sometimes, cancer cells release substances into the bloodstream that cause symptoms not generally thought to result from cancers (American Cancer Society, 2008; Pecorino, 2008). For example, some cancers of the pancreas can release substances that cause blood clots to develop in veins of the legs. Some lung cancers produce hormone-like substances that change blood calcium levels, affecting nerves and muscles and causing weakness and dizziness.

Together with general symptoms, some symptoms are more specifically indicative of cancer. Any changes in your excretory functions could signify cancer of the colon (such as constant diarrhea) or bladder/prostate gland

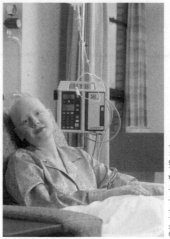

Coping with Cancer
Side-effects of chemotherapy include change in appearance; these changes have significant psychological coping implications.

(such as painful urination or blood in the urine). Sores that do not heal, especially in the mouth or on sexual organs, are signs of skin cancers. As a rule, the appearance of blood in fluids in which you do not normally see it like in the saliva, urine, stool, nonmenstrual vaginal fluids, or breast fluid should be reported to a doctor immediately. The appearance of lumps in the breast, testicles, or lymph nodes may also be a sign of cancer. In general, it is clear that the better you know your body, the more aware you will be of changes that may signify problems with it.

PSYCHOLOGICAL CORRELATES OF CANCER

You can divide the reality of cancer into three main phases: the period leading up to a diagnosis, the diagnosis and reactions to it, and the period following it. Psychological factors may play a role in all three, although the research evidence on how psychology influences progression is clearer than that on its role in the development of cancer.

Psychological Factors in Cancer Incidence

There is presently little unequivocal proof that psychological factors cause cancer (e.g., Bleiker, Hendriks, Otten, Verbeek, & van der Ploeg, 2008), except for the case of stress. We discuss this in more detail later. At least three general pathways through which psychological factors may influence the development of cancer have been identified: (1) direct effects of psychological processes on bodily systems, (2) healthy and unhealthy behaviors, and (3) responses to perceived or actual illness, such as screening behaviors or adherence to treatment recommendations (Henderson & Baum, 2002). The main psychological processes studied have been personality, social support, depression, stress, and health behaviors. Stress and health behaviors are perhaps the most pervasive and will be discussed later in the chapter.

Although receiving a lot of attention in the mid-1980s, the role of *personality* in cancer has been somewhat exaggerated. Morris, Greer, Pettingale, and Watson (1981) first found an association between breast cancer and anger suppression, leading to the hypothesis of a cancer-prone or **Type C personality** (Zozulya, Gabaeva, Sokolov, Surkina, & Kost, 2008). A Type C person was described as cooperative, appeasing, unassertive, and compliant and as someone who did not express negative emotions (Temoshok, 1987). Some later reviews (McKenna, Zevon, Corn, & Rounds, 1999) supported these early findings, but no correlation (Bleiker, Hendriks, Otten, Verbeek, & van der Ploeg, 2008) and some contradictory findings (e.g., Persky, Kempthorne-Rawson, & Shekelle, 1987) suggest that personality plays only a small role in cancer etiology.

Let's take a closer look at the role personality does or does not play with cancer. Nabi et al. (2008) looked at the responses of 14,445 participants age 39 to 54 who first completed measures of personality in 1993 (e.g., the Personality Stress Inventory that assesses cancer-prone, coronary heart disease (CHD)-prone, ambivalent, healthy, rational, and anti-social personality types. About 13 years later, the researchers followed up with the participants and found that mortality *was* predicted by hostility and CHD-prone, ambivalent, antisocial, and healthy personality types, but *not* by Type C personalities. Given the data, personality only plays a limited role in the progression of cancer.

If personality can have a limited effect, what about one's social environment? Social support has not been found to have a strong protective effect against cancer development (Fox, 1998) although it does play a significant role in coping with cancer (as discussed in the next section). To be fair, the social support research has been thwarted by the fact that there are many different types of social support (as described in chapter 5), and it has been operationalized in different ways, making study comparisons difficult (Sarason, Sarason, & Gurung, 2001). If your intuition says that social support must influence incidences of cancer, you are right (although don't let intuition get in the way of empirical evidence to the contrary). Women who were socially isolated were found to have a higher cancer incidence, although this relationship was not found in men (Reynolds & Kaplan, 1990).

There is slightly more evidence for the role of depression in cancer incidence than that for social support. Two literature reviews have shown depression to be a marginally significant risk factor for cancer (McGee, Williams, & Elwood, 1994; McKenna et al., 1999), and at least two prospective studies strengthen this conclusion (Gallo, Armenian, Ford, Eaton, & Khachaturian, 2000; Penninx et al., 1998). Gallo et al. (2000) used a large population-based sample in Baltimore, Maryland, following approximately 2,000 individuals for 13 years. Although there was no link between cancer and depression across the board, there was a significant association between depression and cancer for women. In conjunction with similar sex differences for social support, it is clear that the link between psychological factors and cancer may be very different for men and women. This difference may be linked to biological pathways or may be indicative of greater cultural differences between the sexes that have biopsychosocial components (e.g., Taylor, Kemeny, Reed, Bower, & Gruenewald, 2000).

Psychological Responses to Cancer Diagnosis

Even being screened for a potential cancer can be a fearful experience (Wardle & Pope, 1992). A positive diagnosis (i.e., that cells are cancerous) can be devastating and has been referred to as causing an "existential plight" (Weisman & Worden, 1972). In addition to anxiety, denial, and depression—the major responses to learning you have a chronic illness, as covered in chapter 9—a cancer diagnosis and its treatment result in stress and a lowered QOL (Anderson, Kiecolt-Glaser, & Glaser, 1994). The high emotions experienced right after diagnoses do lessen with time, and emotions actually improve as recovery begins after the end of treatment (Edgar, Rosberger, & Nowlis, 1992). Two other highly psychologically disturbing times occur during treatment, whether it is surgery or radiotherapy (Anderson & Tewfik, 1985; Gottesman & Lewis, 1982).

In general, depression is more common in those patients undergoing active treatment, rather than those in follow-up treatment, and those experiencing pain or with a history of stressors or low social support (Holland, 1989; Reich, Lesur, & Perdrizet-Chevallier, 2008). Approximately half of cancer patients meet the American Psychiatric Association's criteria for having a psychological disorder, the majority of them being related to emotional and/or behavioral problems resulting from having to adjust to cancer (Tope, Ahles, & Silberfarb, 1993). Over half of those treated for cancer experience fear, pain, insomnia, and related anxiety disorders (Derogatis et al., 1983).

Psychological Factors in Cancer Progression and Coping

Similar to HIV infection and other chronic illnesses, some psychological characteristics help one cope better with cancer and also influence the course of the disease. Similar to the factors associated with incidence, a person's personality, social support, depression, stress, and health behaviors again figure prominently (Fann et al., 2008; Helgeson, Snyder, & Steltman, 2004; Henderson & Baum, 2002).

Personality We have already discussed how personality relates to cancer *incidence*—meaning whether personality has any influence over whether someone will *get* cancer (its influence is very limited). In the late 1970s, the first positive links between personality and cancer *progression* were seen. How people coped with cancer seemed to be one of the most important factors. Patients who denied they had cancer had higher disease recurrence rates (Greer, Morris, & Pettingale, 1979). Other studies followed and have established that avoidant, repressive, or unexpressive personalities or coping styles are associated with poorer disease courses (Epping-Jordan, Compas, & Howell, 1994; Jensen, 1987). Other personality characteristics are important, too. For example, optimism is strongly and positively correlated with active coping and emotional regulation coping strategies and strongly negatively correlated with avoidant coping strategies (Scheier, Weintraub, & Carver, 1986). Optimists, in general, show better psychological well-being (Armor & Taylor, 1998). In the context of cancer, a number of studies show that optimism predicts better adjustment for a variety of cancers (early-stage breast cancer, Carver et al., 1994; Kurtz, Kurtz, Given, & Given, 2008; breast/ovarian or colorectal cancer, Geirdal, & Dahl, 2008).

Social Support The case for a positive correlation between social support and survival of cancer patients is very strong (Antoni, & Lutgendorf, 2008; Coughlin, 2008; Decker, 2007; Helgeson, Cohen, Schulz, & Yasko, 1999; Park, & Gaffey, 2007). Of course, some of the best studies to look at are prospective in nature. For example, Garssen and Goodkin (1999) reviewed 38 prospective studies assessing the role of psychological factors in cancer progression and found that low levels of social support consistently promoted cancer progression. In terms of specific aspects of social support, having a high number of confidants with which to discuss personal problems (Maunsell, Brisson, & Deschenes, 1995), having a high number of social connections (Reynolds & Kaplan, 1990), having more contact with friends and supportive others (Waxler-Morrison, Hislop, Mears, & Kan, 1991), and believing that you have a lot of emotional support (Ell, Nishomoto, Mediansky, Mantell, & Hamovitch, 1992) all have been linked to slower progression of cancer and higher rates of survival. A growing body of work suggests that spiritual sources, such as belief in a God and prayer, also provide social support, aiding adjustment and slowing cancer progression (Ahmadi, 2006; Chaturvedi, & Venkateswaran, 2008; Gall & Cornblat, 2002; Vachon, 2008).

Depression has also been linked to cancer progression (Fann et al., 2008; Siafaka et al., 2008; Spiegal, 1996) with a number of studies suggesting that depression and lower QOL in general have adverse effects on survival (Butow, Coates, & Dunn, 1999). We discuss further the role of social support and depression in the section about interventions later in this chapter.

Finding Meaning One of the active areas of psychosocial research in coping with cancer evolves around the notion of finding meaning or **benefit finding**. Taylor (1983) first reported that 53 percent of women in whom breast cancer was diagnosed reported that they experienced positive changes in their lives since their diagnosis, a finding since replicated (Antoni et al., 2001; Cordova, Cunningham, Carlson, & Andrykowski, 2001). Most of the research that followed linked benefit finding to positive outcomes (e.g., Davis, Nolen-Hoeksema, & Larson, 1998; Taylor, Lichtman, & Wood, 1984). Additional research suggests that there are many forms of benefit finding like social relationship and personal growth benefit finding (Weaver, Llabre, Lechner, Penedo, & Antoni, 2008). There are even therapies designed to help people find benefits in cancer that have been found to be effective (Lechner, Stoelb, & Antoni, 2008).

Now here's a twist. Some longitudinal studies of benefit finding (much of the previously cited work was cross-sectional) are suggesting that benefit finding may not always be good. Tomich and Helgeson (2004) followed 364 women for a six-month period and found that benefit finding was associated with more negative emotions although the negative associations with QOL were limited to those women with more severe disease. Some interesting cultural variations were found as well (Simon, & Wardle, 2008). Lower socioeconomic status (SES) women and African American and Latina women (independent of SES) were more likely to find benefit in their cancer than

European American women (Tomich & Helgeson, 2004). If it is useful to be optimistic, shouldn't finding benefit be good too? Research is under way to unravel this contradiction because nothing in the data collected offered a definite resolution (Tomich & Helgeson, 2004).

Although we have discussed the role of psychological factors in cancer progression, we would be remiss if we did not mention the effect cancer has on social relationships. The caregivers—spouses, friends, relatives, of cancer patients—often experience negative outcomes as well. For example, psychological interventions have been designed to help the spouses of women with breast cancer that reduce the spouse's anxiety and depression (Lewis et al., 2008; Kadmon, Ganz, Rom, & Woloski-Wruble, 2008). If one spouse has cancer, the other spouses' quality of life suffers unless both partners have a high quality marital relationship (Bergelt, Koch, & Petersen, 2008).

SYNTHESIZE, EVALUATE, APPLY	• Why should cancer be conceptualized as a "developmental disease"? How can this concept change how it is studied and the treatments for it? • What personality characteristics interact with health behaviors to influence risk of cancer? How do personality characteristics effect progression of cancer? • Evaluate the benefits and problems with benefit finding. At what stage do you think this process can be most helpful? When can it hurt and why?

CANCER, STRESS, AND IMMUNITY

Stress has been shown to influence both the incidence of cancer and its progression, although again, the link for the latter is stronger. There is no equivocation: stress-related psychosocial factors influence cancer. Chida, Wardle, Hammer, and Steptoe (2008) conducted a meta analysis of 165 studies and found that stress-related psychosocial factors were associated with higher cancer incidence in initially healthy populations, poorer survival in patients with diagnosed cancer, and higher cancer mortality. A cancer diagnosis sets up a negative cycle of experiences between stress and illness (see chapters 11 and 13 for other examples). The diagnosis and treatment cause stress that in turn influences the course of the disease by affecting the immune system (Nelson et al., 2008).

Stress has a direct effect on the activity of natural killer (NK) cells, which themselves are critical in the body's fight against cancer (Anderson et al., 1998; Weinberg, 2006). Patients with a variety of cancers have lowered NK cell activity in the blood to begin with (Whiteside & Herberman, 1994). Low NK cell activity in cancer patients is significantly associated with the spread of cancer and in patients treated for metastases, the survival time without metastasis correlates with NK cell activity. Correspondingly, the experience of any additional stress can have direct effects on the development of the cancer, complementing and antagonizing the low NK cell levels. Stress can also increase unhealthy behaviors that can accelerate illness progression (Carlson, Speca, Faris, & Patel, 2007). The patient may increase drug, tobacco, or alcohol use, get less sleep or physical activity, or eat badly, all behaviors that may further affect immunity (Friedman, Klein, & Specter, 1991).

It may be no surprise that cancer can stress you but can stress actually give you cancer? We discussed the negative impact stress can have on our minds and bodies in Chapter 4, so this is clearly a possibility. In fact, this question has been actively debated (Reiche, Nunes, Morimoto, 2004; Tez & Tez, 2008). Retrospective studies of stress and the onset of cancer have shown mixed results and are heavily criticized (Cooper, Cooper, & Faragher, 1986; Delahanty & Baum, 2001), but prospective studies show that, in general, patients with a subsequent diagnosis of cancer reported more severe stressful events than control groups (Cooper, 1989; Geyer, 1993). Stress has been shown to damage DNA, and this has been suggested as a general pathway through which stress can influence the development of cancer (Forlenxa & Baum, 2000; Pettingale, 1985). In a meta-analysis of 46 studies, McKenna et al. (1999) found that the relationship between stressful life events and cancer was only modest (see also Nielsen, N., Kristensen et al., 2008; Nielsen et al., 2007).

HEALTH BEHAVIORS AND CANCER

As mentioned in the introduction to this chapter, many of your health behaviors predict your likelihood of getting cancer and the course cancer takes (Anand et al., 2008; Beesley, Eakin, Janda, & Battistutta, 2008; James, Leone, Katz, McNeill, & Campbell, 2008). Figure 12.3 lists some of the main health behaviors that put you at risk for getting cancer. Take a moment to see how you fare. To some extent the results may surprise you. ("You mean doing *that* puts me at risk for cancer?" Yes, it may.) The usual unhealthy behaviors turn up again (see chapter 7) and, not surprisingly, cultural differences in the practice of some of these behaviors are significant in explaining cultural differences in cancer.

Tobacco Use

Do you want an easy way to decrease your risk of getting cancer? Make sure you do not smoke. Probably the most clear-cut cause of cancer is tobacco use (American Cancer Society, 2008; CDC, 2008; Fan, Yuan, Wang, Gao, & Yu, 2008; Varela-Lema et al., 2008). Smokers have nine times the risk of getting lung cancer compared with nonsmokers (Lubin, Richter, & Blot, 1984); only 10 percent of lung cancer patients have never smoked (Subramanian, & Govindan, 2007). Note that this risk is nine times—not double, not triple—but nine times. Talk about really playing with fire! Cigarette smoking accounts for at least 30 percent of all cancer deaths. As shown in Table 12.3 smoking is a major cause of cancers of the lung, larynx (voice box), oral cavity, pharynx (throat), and esophagus and is a contributing cause in the development of cancers of the bladder, pancreas, liver, uterine cervix, kidney, stomach, colon and rectum, and some leukemias.

The link between smoking and cancer is best illustrated when we look at populations that increased tobacco use. Smoking rates among women rose dramatically between the 1960s and the 1990s, and deaths due to lung cancer in women increased correspondingly (Berman & Gritz, 1991; CDC, 2008). Shopland (1996) showed that the risk of contracting lung cancer for women who smoke is 1,200 percent greater than that for women who do not smoke, and one-quarter of all cancer deaths among women can be attributed to smoking

Answer the following questions:

1. Do you protect your skin from overexposure to the sun? _____
2. Do you abstain from smoking or using tobacco in any form? _____
3. If you're over 40 or if family members have had colon cancer, do you get rou-tine digital rectal exams? _____
4. Do you eat a balanced diet that includes the RDA for vitamins A, B, and C? _____
5. If you're a woman, do you have regular Pap tests and pelvic exams? _____
6. If you're a man over 40, do you get regular prostate exams? _____
7. If you have burn scars or a history of chronic skin infections, do you get regular checkups? _____
8. Do you avoid smoked, salted, pickled and high-nitrate foods? _____
9. If your job exposes you to asbestos, radiation, cadmium, or other environmental hazards, do you get regular checkups?
_____
10. Do you limit your consumption of alcohol? _____
11. Do you avoid using tanning salons or home sunlamps? _____
12. If you're a woman, do you examine your breasts every month for lumps?
_____
13. Do you eat plenty of vegetables and other sources of fiber? _____
14. If you're a man do you perform regular testicular self-exams? _____
15. Do you wear protective sunglasses in sunlight? _____
16. Do you follow a low-fat diet? _____
17. Do you know the cancer warning signs?
_____

Making Changes
Cutting Your Cancer Risk
You may not be able to control every risk factor in your life or environment, but you can protect yourself from the obvious ones.

• *Avoid excessive exposure to ultraviolet light.* If you spend a lot of time outside you can protect your skin by using sunscreen and wearing long-sleeve shirts and a hat. Also, wear sunglasses to protect your eyes. Don't purposely put yourself at risk by binge-sun-bathing or by using sunlamps.

• *Avoid obvious cancer risks.* Besides ultraviolet light, other environmental factors that have been linked with cancer include tobacco, asbestos, and radiation.

• *Keep yourself as healthy as possible.* The healthier you are, the better able your body is to ward off diseases that can predispose you to cancer. Get regular exerciser; eat a balanced, high-fiber, low-fat diet; and avoid excessive alcohol use.

• *Be alert to changes in your body.* You know your body rhythms and appearance better than anyone else, and only you will know if certain things aren't right. Changes in bowel habits, skin changes, unusual lumps or discharges—anything out of the ordinary may be clues that require further medical investigation

• *Don't put off seeing your doctor if you detect any changes.* Procrastination can't hurt anyone but you.

FIGURE **12.3** Are You at Risk for Cancer?

If you answered no to any of the questions, your risk for developing various kinds of cancer may be increased.

Source: Hales (2000)

(Shopland, Eyre, & Pechacek, 1991). In men, almost 85 percent of lung cancers are related to cigarette smoking (CDC, 2008; Holland, 1989). The fact that men smoke more than women accounts for approximately 90 percent of the sex differences in lung cancer mortality (Mellström, & Svanborg, 1987; Waldron, 1995) and other carcinomas as well (Hassan et al., 2008). As men's and women's smoking rates become similar, their lung cancer rates also become similar. See Figure 12.4 for an illustration of how lung cancer rates and smoking rates have paralleled each other over the last 100 years.

TABLE **12.3**
Cancer and Smoking

Smoking and Cancer Mortality Table					
Type of Cancer	Gender	Relative Risk Among Smokers	Relative Risk Among Smokers	Mortality Attributable to Smoking	Mortality Attributable to Smoking
		Current	Former	Current	Former
Lung	Male	22.4	9.4	90	82,800
	Female	11.9	4.7	79	40,300
Larynx	Male	10.5	5.2	81	24,000
	Female	17.8	11.9	87	700
Oral Cavity	Male	27.5	8.8	92	4,900
	Female	5.6	2.9	61	1,800
Esophagus	Male	7.6	5.8	78	5,700
	Female	10.3	3.2	75	1,900
Pancreas	Male	2.1	1.1	29	3,500
	Female	2.3	1.8	34	4,500
Bladder	Male	2.9	1.9	47	3,000
	Female	2.6	1.9	37	1,200
Kidney	Male	3.0	2.0	48	3,000
	Female	1.4	1.2	12	500
Stomach	Male	1.5	?	17	1,400
	Female	1.5	?	25	1,300
Leukemia	Male	2.0	?	20	2,000
	Female	2.0	?	20	1,600
Cervix	Female	2.1	1.9	31	1,400
Endometrium	Female	0.7	1.0		

Note: Not all cancers are equally influenced by smoking. Notice the differences in relative risk from smoking for the different types of cancers and the sex differences.
Source: Centers for Disease Control, 2003.

Differences in tobacco use also highlight many of the cultural differences in cancer rates. Different ethnic groups have had different historical relationships with tobacco, serving to either increase or decrease their exposure to it. African Americans, for example, had heavy exposure to tobacco from the early 1600s when Africans were first brought to the Americas and were employed in southern tobacco-growing plantations and in tobacco manufacturing during the colonial period (Gately, 2003; Gotay et al., 2001). Tobacco was used in South America and Latin America even before the European colonization, and the *curanderismos* (see chapter 2) often used tobacco in religious and healing

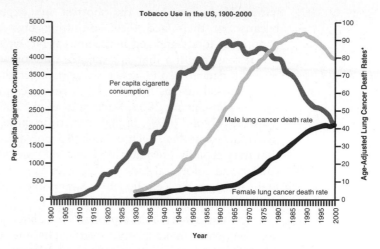

FIGURE **12.4** Tobacco Use in the United States, 1900 to 2000

*Rates age-adjusted to the 2000 U.S. standard population.

Source: U.S. Mortality Public Use Data Tapes 1960–2000, U.S. Mortality Volumes 1930–1959, National Center for Health Statistics, Centers for Disease Control and Prevention, 2002. Cigarette consumption: U.S. Department of Agriculture, 1900–2000.

practices. Even today, cigarette smoking is considered a "social activity" for Latinos, consistent with cultural values of *personalismo* (importance of personal relations) (Marin, Marin, Perez-Stable, Sabogal, & Otero-Sabogal, 1990). Not surprisingly, many Latin American countries show high rates of smoking (Müller, & Wehbe, 2008). Many Asian groups also have had a long history of smoking. In China, tobacco was mixed with opium and smoked and was used also medicinally. In India, the end of a hard day in the fields was often marked by the smoking of a *hookah*, a contraption that bubbled tobacco through water. Use of a hookah to smoke also has become a trendy habit in many New York and Los Angeles bars. Statistics are now proving that even exposure to second-hand smoke has been associated with cancer incidence (Miller et al., 2007).

Diet

For the majority of Americans who do not smoke, eating a nutritionally balanced diet and being physically active are the most important ways to reduce cancer risk. Evidence suggests that one-third of the 550,000 cancer deaths that occur in the United States each year are due to unhealthy diet and insufficient physical activity (Byers & Doyle, 2004). Different cultural groups have different eating habits (see chapter 7), which can accentuate their risk for cancer. There are a number of dietary features that are linked to an increased risk for cancer (Fan et al., 2008; Reedy et al., 2008; Singletary, & Milner, 2008; Willett & Trichopoulos, 1996). For example, eating too much fat and not getting enough fiber have been associated with increased cancer incidence (Steinmaus, Nunez, & Smith, 2000; Wynder et al., 1997). On the other hand, diets with high consumption of fruits and vegetables are associated with a lower risk for several types of cancer (Potter & Steinmetz, 1996). In Hawaii, native Hawaiians have the shortest life expectancy of any ethnic group because of their bad diets, including high consumption of cholesterol-containing foods and red meat, animal fat, eggs, milk, and cheese (the traditional roast pig at a luau is a mouth-watering example).

The data for some cancers are stronger than those for others. Eating a lot of animal fat has been linked to breast cancer (Freedman, Kipnis, Schatzkin, & Potischman, 2008; Kallianpur et al., 2008) and to colon cancer (Biasi, Mascia, & Poli, 2008), though not to prostrate cancer (Crowe et al., 2008). There are some fats, such as omega-3 polyunsaturated fat (found in salmon) that may actually prevent cancer and are associated with lower rates of breast cancer and colorectal cancer (Gogos et al., 1998; Greenwald, Clifford, Pilch, Heimendinger, & Kelloff, 1995; Simopoulos, 2008), but evidence supporting this finding is still mixed.

The diet-cancer link is probably mediated by obesity. Bad diets and eating too much make people overweight and obese. Obesity may promote breast cancer because of the effects of adipose tissue on epithelial cell growth (Guthrie & Carroll, 1999) or on the production and functioning of hormones such as estrogen (Mezzetti et al., 1998). Obesity has also been linked to a higher incidence of colon, endometrial, pancreatic, and gallbladder cancers (Ford, 1999; Pi-Sunyer, 1998; Stolzenberg-Solomon et al., 2008).

A wide variety of foods are supposed to help prevent cancer and also to cure it. Only a small percentage of the foods touted as curative have stood the test of scientific research (Table 12.4). Be warned that there are a lot of television and Internet reports of so-called cancer-busting foods for which there is no scientific basis. For example, eating grapes is supposed to be good, but the effects have not been proven. That said, eating a diet with high amounts of fruits and vegetables, especially those containing antioxidants, does seem to increase the cancer-fighting capacity of the body (Cao, Booth, Sadowski, & Prior, 1998). Also, eating soy products and broccoli actually does seem to help prevent some cancers (Fahey, Zhang, & Talalay, 1997; Moyad, 1999), and vegetarianism similarly has been linked to lower incidence of cancer (Hebert et al., 1998). As far as popular diets like South Beach and Atkins go, the Mediterranean diet, which is rich in nuts, grains, and olive oil, has shown the most promise for keeping cancer at bay (Benetou et al., 2008). For the rest of the things you may hear about, for example, vitamin A or C, the mineral selenium, and flavonoids (effective antioxidants that you'll hear more about in the next chapter), there is enough research to suggest that each is a potential cancer fighter (Knekt et al., 1997; Young et al., 1997), but we are far from having a guaranteed "perfect anticancer" diet. However, we are getting closer, as more and more nutrients are proving to be viable cancer fighters (Freeman et al., 2000; Norrish, Jackson, Sharpe, & Skeaff, 2000). As always, you should be a critical consumer of what claims you hear or read about.

Given that some foods may have the potential to reduce the risk for cancer, it follows that cultural differences in dietary patterns correspondingly explain cultural differences in cancer incidence and progression. For example, there is a lower incidence of breast cancer among Latinas than among non-Latino European American women. Can diet explain this? Murtaugh et al., (2008) examined the associations of dietary patterns (e.g., Western, Native

TABLE **12.4**

Foods Supposed to Help Prevent and Treat Cancer

Component	Food	Cancer Link
Fiber	Carrots, beets, onions and potatoes	Prevents colon, stomach
Folate and folic acid	Leafy vegetables, grains and legumes	Prevents breast
Antioxidants	Fruits, vegetables, nuts, grains	Potential
Beta-carotene	Carrots, cantaloupe, other orange foods	Potential
Vitamin E	Nuts, broccoli, corn oil	Potential
Vitamin A	Liver, egg yolks and milk, cabbage	No clear link
Vitamin C	Citrus fruits and leafy vegetables	No clear link
Selenium	Meat and bread	No clear link
Vitamin B	Brussels sprouts	No clear link
Flavones/Indoles	Broccoli, artichokes, celery	No clear link
Phytochemicals	Soy products	Potential
Omega-3 fatty acids	Fish oils, salmon	No clear link
Aspartame	Artificial sweetener	No clear link
High-fat diets		Increased risk of breast, colon, rectum, prostate, endometrium

Mexican, Mediterranean) with risk for breast cancer in Latinas (757 cases, 867 controls) and non-Latino European American women (1,524 cases, 1,598 controls) from the Four-Corners Breast Cancer Study. They found that it was the dietary pattern followed and not just the ethnicity that was important. The Western dietary pattern was associated with greater risk, and the Native Mexican and Mediterranean dietary patterns were associated with lower risk of breast cancer.

Physical Activity

The reasons for staying in shape (or getting in shape) continue to increase. A large body of evidence suggests that physical activity, especially during our younger years, can reduce the risk of breast (Bernstein, Henderson, Hanisch, Sullivan-Halley, & Ross, 1994) and endometrial cancer (Patel et al., 2008) in women, and colon cancer in men (Coups, Hay, & Ford, 2008; Longnecker, Gerhardsson, le Verdier, Frumkin, & Carpenter, 1995). Getting regular physical activity also lowers the risk for breast cancer for both pre- and postmenopausal women (Gilliland, Li, Baumgartner, Crumley, & Samet, 2001). Being active is good for men too. Physical activity reduces the rate of prostate cancer in men (Lee, Paffenbarger, & Hsieh, 1992; Thorsen, Courneya, Stevinson, & Fosså, 2008) and could protect both men and women from colon cancer (Batty & Thune, 2000). However, the relationship between physical activity and testicular cancer is a little inconsistent: some studies suggest there is no risk (Thune, & Lund, 1994), others suggest physical activity is a risk factor *for* testicular cancer (Srivastava, & Kreiger, 2000). For lung cancer, a relationship has yet to be fully established (Kubík et al., 2007; Thune & Furberg, 2001).

Sun Exposure

Few people lying on the beach soaking in the sun's rays are thinking about the fact that they have almost tripled their chances of getting squamous cell skin cancer (American Cancer Society, 2008; Thieden, 2008). Did you know that 45 percent of Americans who live to 65 years of age get skin cancer at least once? Prevention is again the key: 78 percent of skin cancers reported could have been prevented if people younger than age 18 had put on sunscreen. Even tanning booths are carcinogenic. A 15- to 20-minute session is equivalent in **ultraviolet (UV) ray** exposure to one full day at the beach. Although tanning salons often advertise that sun bed tanning is safer than sunbathing outside, the intensity of light in tanning beds is actually much greater. The customer not only has light rays above his or her body but also below it. Many of the older tanning beds emit short-wave UV rays, which burn the outer layers of the skin. The majority of the tanning beds used today, however, use long-wave UV rays, which actually penetrate deeper and weaken the skin's inner connective tissue. Tanning salon rays also increase the damage that is done by the sunlight, because the UV light from the tanning beds thins the skin, making it less able to heal. Both the sun and tanning beds produce a tan from UV rays. UV rays cause the skin to protect itself from burning by producing additional pigmentation and coloring. Overexposure to these UV rays can lead to eye injury, premature wrinkling, light-induced skin rashes, and increased chances of skin cancer. To get that nice tanned look without the risk, consumers are now flocking to risk-free tanning booths that use sprays.

So should you stay out of the sun altogether? No, that's not right, either. Although overexposure to sunlight can be very detrimental to one's health, we still need some amount of exposure to sunlight for both physical and psychological reasons. A lack of sunlight is associated with poor mood, as well as with a condition called seasonal affective disorder. Sunlight is also a major source of vitamin D in humans, because it produces vitamin D in the skin after exposure to UV radiation (Weinrich, Ellison, Weinrich, Ross, & Reis-Starr, 2001). Without vitamin D, diseases such as rickets occur. In direct relationship to this chapter, sunlight exposure has also been found to reduce the risk of advanced breast cancer among women with light skin pigmentation (John, Schwartz, Koo, Wang, & Ingles, 2007).

TREATMENT OPTIONS

Cancer need no longer be a death sentence, although many people still believe it is. Although earlier cancer detection increases its chances of being completely treated, even some cancers in their later stages can be successfully treated. Because cancer is essentially cells that are out of control, the main goal of

Courtesy of Lacey Moore

Courtesy of Lacey Moore

Tanning

A tanning booth (left) in which even a single visit can expose you to carcinogenic ultra-violet rays. A safer alternative for a "tanned" look is a spray-on tan (right) where you just step into the shower-like set-up and nozzles all around you coat you with a fine mist.

treatment is to get the cells out of the body. There are three major ways to treat cancer.

Surgery

The oldest and most straightforward way to treat cancer is *surgery*, during which the surgeon can remove the tumor. Surgery is most successful when the cancer has not spread because this provides the best chance of removing all the mutant cells. Surgery also has other uses in cancer. **Preventative surgery** is performed to remove tissue that is not malignant as yet but has a high chance of turning malignant. This happens in the case of women with a family history of breast cancer who also have a mutant breast cancer gene (*BRCA1* or *BRCA2*). Preventative surgery may also be used to remove parts of the colon if polyps, small stalk-shaped growths (not the little marine animals), are found. **Diagnostic surgery** is the process of removing a small amount of tissue to either identify a cancer or to make a diagnosis. If the patient does receive a positive diagnosis of cancer, sometimes **staging surgery** is needed to ascertain what stage of development the cancer is in. This form of surgery helps determine how far the cancer has spread and provides a *clinical stage* for the growth. If the cancer has been localized to a small area, **curative surgery** can be used to remove the growth. This is the primary form of treatment for cancer and is often used in conjunction with the other treatments. If it is not possible to remove the entire tumor without damaging the surrounding tissues, **debulking surgery** reduces the tumor mass. Finally, **palliative surgery** is used to treat complications of advanced disease (not as a cure), and **restorative surgery** is used to improve a person's appearance after curative surgery (e.g., after a **mastectomy** or breast removal).

Chemotherapy

The second major form of treatment for cancer involves taking medications with the aim of disabling the cancer growth, a process referred to as **chemotherapy**. The medications are either given in pill form, in the form of an injection, or in the form of an intravenous injection (medication delivered through a catheter right into a vein). The type of cancer and its severity determine the frequency of chemotherapy, and it can range from daily to monthly medication. This form of treatment often has very strong side effects but often results in successful outcomes. Patients who undergo chemotherapy (or "chemo" for short) often lose all their hair (not just the hair on their head as is commonly believed), experience severe nausea, and have a dry mouth and skin. Chemotherapy also has biopsychosocial effects. Biologically, the treatment lowers both red and white blood cell counts. Fewer red blood cells make a person anemic and feel weak and tired. A reduced number of white blood cells makes a person more prone to infection, and a person undergoing chemotherapy needs to take special care to not be exposed to germs or sources of contamination. Psychologically, the fatigue can lead to low moods and also a loss of sexual desire and low sociability. Social interactions become strained as well. The patient often feels embarrassed by not having any hair and may not want to be seen by other people or may be too tired to interact. Simultaneously, many visitors and friends feel uncomfortable at the sight of the hairless, fatigued patient. As with most chronic illnesses it is important for the patient's support networks to be prepared for and compensate for the effects of treatment.

Radiation Therapy

The third major form of treatment for cancer involves the use of radioactive particles aimed at the DNA of the cancer cells, a process referred to as **radiation therapy**. Radiation used for cancer treatment is called ionizing radiation because it forms ions as it passes through tissues and dislodges electrons from atoms. The ionization causes cell death or a genetic change in the cancerous cells (American Cancer Society, 2008). There are many different types of radiation treatments (e.g., electron beams, high-energy photons, protons, and neutrons), each sounding like something out of a science fiction movie and varying in intensity and energy. The process for getting radiation therapy is a little more complex than that for chemotherapy and surgery, although the preliminary stages are the same. Medical personnel first need to identify the location and size of the tumor and then pick the correct level of radiation. The key is to be able to do the most damage to the cancerous cells without damaging the normal cells. This is hard to do because the radiation stream cannot differentiate between types of cells, and normal cells often end up being affected as part of the process, resulting in side effects of treatment. The total dose of radiation, a rad, is often broken down into fractions, and delivered over several weeks. Radiation therapy is perhaps the most involved type of therapy, with treatments usually being given daily, five days a week, for five to seven weeks (American Cancer Society, 2008). The main side effects are fatigue and irritation of the body areas close to the radiation site, often accompanied by some disruption of functioning. For example, radiation to the throat area can cause difficulty in swallowing and a redness of the neck and surrounding areas.

Other Treatments

In addition to these three main forms of treatment, there are also a variety of other possible ways to treat cancer. For example, **immunotherapy** involves the activation of the body's own immune system to fight the cancer. There are also a number of alternative and complementary therapies that help people cope with cancer (some of which are believed to keep cancer at bay as well). These include aromatherapy, music therapy, yoga, massage therapy, meditation to reduce stress, special diets like taking peppermint tea for nausea, and acupuncture. There is growing public interest, especially among those living with cancer and/or the relatives of people with cancer, in obtaining information about complementary and alternative medicine (CAM) as discussed in Chapter 2 and methods of treatment. This interest is even more prevalent among individuals from different cultural groups who may have approaches and beliefs about cancer and its treatment that vary greatly from the view held by Western biomedicine. Very often cancer patients do not tell their doctors that they are also trying other treatments. Although there may be many treatments for cancer used by other cultures that are actually beneficial, very few methods have been tested by Western science and correspondingly North American health practitioners recommend very few alternative methods.

The stance of Western biomedicine is reflected particularly well in how the American Cancer Society refers to alternative and complementary medicine. The American Cancer Society (2008) defines alternative methods as "unproved or disproved methods, rather than evidence based or proven methods to prevent, diagnose, and treat cancer" and complementary methods as "those supportive methods used to complement evidence-based treatment." The American

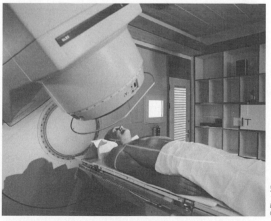

Person Preparing to Undergo Radiation Therapy

Cancer Society acknowledges that more research is needed to determine the safety and effectiveness of many of these methods and advocates for peer-reviewed scientific evidence of the safety and efficacy of these methods. Health care practitioners recognize the need to balance access to alternative and complementary therapies while protecting patients against methods that might be harmful to them. For example, the American Cancer Society supports patients having access to CAM but strongly encourages more oversight and accountability by governmental, public, and private entities to protect the public from harm. Part of the problem arises from the fact that harmful drug interactions may occur and must be recognized. In addition, sometimes use of the other treatments causes delays in starting standard therapies and are detrimental to the success of cancer treatment.

When treatments succeed in keeping cancer at bay, the health psychologist's job is not done. There is evidence that breast cancer survivors are at risk for developing secondary tumors (Sánchez et al., 2008). Similarly problematic, low levels of posttraumatic stress disorder (PTSD), and other stress-related problems have been seen in child cancer survivors (Erickson, Gerstle, & Montague, 2008; Schrag, McKeown, Jackson, Cuffe, & Neuberg, 2008). Many cancer survivors begin to (or continue to) use many complementary and alternative treatments. For example, Gansler, Kaw, Crammer, and Smith (2008) studied over 4,000 survivors and found the most frequently reported treatments were prayer/spiritual practice (61.4%), relaxation (44.3%), faith/spiritual healing (42.4%), nutritional supplements/vitamins (40.1%), meditation (15%), religious counseling (11.3%), massage (11.2%), and support groups (9.7%). Such treatments may provide the survivors with psychological benefits and prevent relapse, though this possibility has not been tested.

BEHAVIORAL INTERVENTIONS

The main way to reduce the death rates from cancer is to increase the practice of healthy behaviors and decrease other behavioral contributions to cancer risk (Given, 2003; Hiatt & Rimer, 1999; Thorogood, Simera, Dowler, Summerbell, Brunner, 2007). The general approaches to improving common behaviors—reduce tobacco use, eat a nutritionally balanced meal, and get physical activity—have been covered in some detail in chapters 6 and 7. Although challenging, interventions to get people to change old habits, such as what they eat, are beginning to be successful (Kumanyika et al., 2000). Another major health behavior not covered in as much detail before is getting routine screenings.

Aiding Prevention: Increasing Screening Behaviors

One of the strongest contributions of health psychological research has been to increase health behaviors that will ensure the early detection of cancer. The most direct early detection behavior is **screening**, and a number of interventions have attempted to increase cancer screenings especially for breast, cervical, and colorectal cancer (del Junco et al., 2008; Lairson et al., 2008; Rimer, 1994; Snell & Buck, 1996). Early detection ensures that the cancer can be treated in an early stage, almost literally "being nipped in the bud." Screening can take two main forms: screening that needs help from professionals and medical equipment such as mammograms, and screening that you can do at home such as testicular or breast self-examinations. The American Cancer Society has a clear set of recommendations for when and how often a person should be screened/should check for cancer (Table 12.5). The big question here is: Even if you know how often you should get screened, will you do it?

The **Health Belief Model** (**HBM**) described in Chapter 6 (Rosenstock, 1974) has been the model used most often to guide interventions to increase screening behavior (Aiken, Gerend, & Jackson, 2001; Henderson & Baum, 2002; Soskolne, Marie, & Manor, 2007). According to this model, the extent to which you see yourself as being susceptible to cancer, the extent to which you believe cancer to have severe consequences, the perceived barriers keeping you from getting screened, and the perceived benefits to getting screened all combine to predict your screening behavior. A number of interventions have included components especially designed to influence different parts of the HBM (e.g., Aiken, West, Woodward, Reno, & Reynolds, 1994; Farmer, Reddick, D'Agostino, & Jackson, 2007). The Focus section at the end of this chapter gives you a concrete example of an intervention aimed at increasing screening.

The model works well. Even increasing people's knowledge about cancer severity and the benefits of screening increases the likelihood that people will get screened (DiPlacido, Zauber, & Redd, 1998). Factors that influence perceptions of susceptibility or risk are important as well (Cole, Bryant, McDermott, Sorrell, & Flynn, 1997). Factors related to and probably influencing susceptibility are linked to screening. People with a family history of breast cancer and those who had breast problems are more likely to get screened (McCaul, Branstetter, Schroeder, & Glasgow, 1996). Susceptibility is not as predictive of self-examinations (Miller et al., 1996). Having strong perceived barriers to screening are some of the strongest predictors of self-examinations (Wyper, 1990). Other significant barriers to getting screened are the costs of tests, the

TABLE **12.5**

Screening Guidelines for the Early Detection of Breast Cancer, American Cancer Society, 2008

- Yearly mammograms are recommended starting at age 40 and continuing for as long as a woman is in good health.
- A clinical breast examination should be part of a periodic health examination, about every 3 years for women in their 20s and 30s and every year for women 40 and older.
- Women should know how their breasts normally feel and report any breast changes promptly to their health care providers. Breast self-examination is an option for women starting in their 20s.
- Women at increased risk (e.g., family history, genetic tendency, and past breast cancer) should talk with their doctors about the benefits and limitations of starting mammography screening earlier, having additional tests (i.e., breast ultrasound and MRI), or having more frequent examinations.

A Campaign to Increase Screening for Colorectal Cancer

Colorectal cancer is another cancer that can be successfully treated if it is detected early enough. This is one of the posters in a national campaign to increase screenings.

lack of health insurance, the lack of time, and an inconvenient test location (Friedman, Hall, & Harris, 1995; Maxwell, Bastani, & Warda, 1998; McPhee et al., 1997).

Paradoxically, believing yourself to be extremely susceptible to cancer (e.g., taking a genetic test showing you have a mutated gene) or having a strong knowledge of severity and the fact that the disease could be fatal sometimes keeps people from getting screened (Sutton, Bickler, Sancho-Aldridge, & Saidi, 1994). The fear of actually finding something can keep people from even getting the test (Bastani, Marcus, & Hollatz-Brown, 1991). This problem is amplified in some cultural groups. Fatalism, discussed previously, among older, low-income Mexican American women is associated with lower Pap smear rates (a test for uterine cancer) (Suarez, Rouche, Nichols, & Simpson, 1997).

Cultural Differences in Screening

Cultural differences arise once more in the use of preventative measures for cancer. Low SES women are less likely to get mammograms (CDC, 2008; National Center for Health Statistics, 1997). Non-European American groups do not use routine screening tests as frequently as European American groups and, consequently, have more severe cancer at diagnosis (Gotay et al., 2001). Hiatt et al. (1996) collected some of the best detailed information on ethnic differences in screening from a study of 4,228 individuals in the San Francisco Bay area. Illustrative data from Hiatt et al. (1996) and from the National Center for Health Statistics at the CDC collected around the same time are shown in Table 12.6.

As you can see, there are significant differences between African Americans, Latinos, European Americans, and Asian Americans. In terms of ever having a

TABLE **12.6**
Cultural Differences in Screening

Screening Test	African Americans	American Indians	Asian Americans	Latino	European American
Clinical breast examination	96		60	89	98
Mammogram	90		61	80	93
Pap test	98		56	76	99
Mammogram or Pap test in past 2 years	56	53	46	50	56
Pap test in past 3 years	84	73	66	74	76

Source: Hiatt, R. A., Pasick, R. J., Perez-Stable, E. J., McPhee, S. J., Engelstad, L., Lee, M., et al. (1996). Pathways to early cancer detection in the multiethnic population of San Francisco Bay area. *Health Education Quarterly, 23* (Suppl.), S10–S27; Gotay, C. C., Muraoka, M. Y., & Holup, J. (2001). Cultural aspects of cancer prevention and control. *Handbook of Cultural Health Psychology*, 163–193.

screening test for both breast and cervical cancer, Asian Americans reported significantly lower rates. Similar patterns can be seen for adherence to recommendations to get screening tests. Why is this? The main barriers to getting screened, described above, particularly affect low SES men and women across all ethnic groups (Hoffman-Goetz, Breen, & Meissner, 1998). For some cultural groups the embarrassment of having the test keeps them away. Asian American and Latina women, for example, are embarrassed when undergoing breast and cervical cancer screenings (Jennings, 1997; Maxwell et al., 1998). Cultural beliefs about modesty and who is allowed to see the naked body also have an influence. For members of many cultures it is inappropriate for an unknown member of the opposite sex, such as a doctor or nurse, to see the person's body (Galanti, 2004). Such issues are seen in the preferences of Vietnamese, Chinese, and Latina women to request service from a female physician (Galanti, 2004; Gotay et al., 2001).

The previously mentioned paradox between fear and screening (more fear of having cancer leads to avoiding the screening) has also been shown in both Latina and African American women (Friedman et al., 1995; Lobell, Bay, Rhoads, & Keske, 1998). In fact, the fear that the radiation from a mammogram is dangerous is higher among Asian and Latina women than among European American women (Dibble, Vanomi, & Miaskowski, 1997). African American and Latina women also report more fear of the pain associated with mammograms (Stein, Fox, & Murata, 1991). Finally, non-European American ethnic groups also report higher levels of incorrect knowledge about screening and cancer in general (Sung, Blumenthal, Coates, & Alema-Mensah, 1997; Yi, 1998). Some of this could be due to recent immigration-related issues, including a combination of inadequate English proficiency, acculturation problems, and potentially male-dominated family structures, which prevent some women from receiving community-based public health information (McPhee et al., 1996; Wismer et al., 1998; Yi, 1994).

Inhibiting Progression and Helping Patients Cope

Going beyond the prevention of cancer, another category of interventions has been designed to prolong life after diagnosis and to reduce patients' treatment anxiety (Anderson, 1992; Helgeson & Cohen, 1996; Meyer & Mark, 1995; Spiegel, 1996; Wallace, Priestman, Dunn, & Priestman, 1993; Yang, Brothers, & Andersen, 2008). Social support again figures prominently (Helgeson et al., 1999). In the classic demonstration of the effectiveness of social support, Spiegel;, Bloom, Kraemer, and Gottheil (1989) had women with breast cancer attend weekly supportive group therapy meetings. This group lived on average 36.6 months after the start of the intervention. In contrast, survival of the control patients who only received standard cancer care averaged 18.9 months. More recently, Fawzy et al. (1993) used a structured social support group to reduce distress and enhance the immune functioning in patients with newly diagnosed cancer. The group involved health education, illness-related problem solving, and relaxation, and members met weekly for six weeks. By six months, the intervention group showed lower levels of emotional distress, depression, confusion, and fatigue than the control group. Even their immune activity was higher. In general, such support groups are designed to promote the development of supportive relationships among group members and encourage expression of patients' feelings or disease-related anxieties (Henderson & Baum, 2002).

Some interventions focus directly on cancer pain. Ward et al., (2008) developed an intervention to decrease cancer pain (RIDcancerPain) and tested it using a classic randomized control trial. The main variables of interest, pain severity, pain interference with life, and overall quality of life and coping style, were measured three times (baseline, 1, and 2 months later). Participants in the intervention group who experienced pain related to metastatic cancer showed greater decreases in pain severity than those in control (Ward et al., 2008).

Other potentially useful psychological interventions involve relaxation training or hypnosis (Carlson, Speca, Patel, & Goodey, 2003; Sims, 1987; Spiegel et al., 1989) although neither method has received solid empirical support. For example, although relaxation is often recommended for cancer-related pain (Millard, 1993) and has been found to be a useful tool in pain management in general, (see chapter 9), a recent review found only two studies that used a controlled randomized design to directly examine the effectiveness of relaxation training (Redd & Jacobsen, 2001). Sloman, Brown, Aldana, and Chee (1994) used both progressive muscle relaxation and mental imagery to reduce patients' pain. Randomly assigned hospital patients were trained to relax by either a nurse or with the use of an audiotape. The intervention group reported significantly less pain and requested less pain medication. A similar study by Syrjala, Donaldson, Davis, Kippes, and Carr (1995) compared relaxation training with cognitive-behavioral coping training and found that both methods worked.

Keeping cultural differences in beliefs about cancer in mind, some interventions build on cultural values to change health behaviors that could cause cancer. For example, Lichtenstein and Lopez (1999) developed a program to reduce smoking in American Indian tribes in the Northwest by using American

Indian staff to ensure the target population that the intervention was at least partly Indian-owned. Distinctions were made between social uses of tobacco and ritualistic uses and tribal representatives were closely involved in the process of developing American Indian–specific materials on smoking cessation.

In general, a number of psychosocial interventions have shown promise for alleviating the pain and discomfort of cancer. When used in conjunction with medications, these interventions can help make life bearable and even enjoyable for the patient with cancer.

SYNTHESIZE, EVALUATE, APPLY	• Health behaviors play a large role in putting someone at risk for cancer. How does each behavior interact with the others? • What factors should go into the choice of a treatment? • How would you design an intervention to reduce risks for cancer? • Pick a health behavior change model and use it to increase screening behaviors. • What can be done to reduce the delay between identification of cancer symptoms and going in to a doctor?

FOCUS ON APPLICATIONS

Increasing Cancer Screening

A number of adages support the importance of early intervention for cancer. There is truth to the adages, "A stitch in time saves nine," "An ounce of prevention is worth a pound of cure," and so on. Many chronic illnesses take a long time to develop and are not always detectable in their early stages. That said, as described earlier in this chapter, cancer is a disease that can be cured if it is caught early enough. Consequently, one of the most common clinical applications of health psychological theory is in the design of interventions to increase health screening behaviors (Aiken et al., 2001). Interventions provide a wonderful window to look at theory in action. Let's take a close look at one intervention in particular to give you a better sense of the problem and a feel for how interventions are done.

A prototypical example of a screening intervention is one conducted by Leona Aiken and colleagues (Aiken et al., 1994). Although there are more recent interventions as discussed previously, this one served as a model for later research and bears close scrutiny. Their main goal was to increase mammography screening rates in accordance with American Cancer Society guidelines that suggest women should have a baseline mammogram between 35 and 39 years of age and then have a mammogram every year or two up to age 50 and yearly after age 50. There have been a lot of very public debates about these recommendations and about the effectiveness of screening in general. Health experts agree that women in their 50s should get mammograms. The debate centers on whether the tests reduce the risk of breast cancer for women in their 40s. Another factor is that mammograms can sometimes be inaccurate: nearly one in four women who regularly have a mammogram will have at least one false-positive result (Christiansen et al., 2000), but the benefits do seem to outweigh the costs.

Breast cancer has received some of the highest levels of funding of all cancer research, and, consequently, the majority of cancer research in the field of health psychology involves studies on the incidence and progression of this disease. Breast cancer is a malignant tumor that starts from cells of the breast. The breast itself is made up of lobules, ducts, fatty and connective tissue, blood vessels, and lymph vessels. When breast cancer cells reach the underarm lymph nodes and continue to grow, they cause the nodes to swell. Once cancer cells have reached these nodes they are more likely to spread to other organs of the body as

(continues)

FOCUS ON APPLICATIONS (continued)

well. There are several types of breast tumors. Most are abnormal benign growths. Some lumps are not really tumors at all. These lumps are often caused by the formation of scar tissue and are also benign. To detect the growth of cancers as early as possible, women in their 20s and 30s should have a clinical breast examination (CBE) as part of a regular physical examination by a health expert preferably every three years (American Cancer Society, 2008). Women are also urged to conduct regular breast self-examinations (BSE) to also detect abnormalities in changes. Unfortunately, growths have to be relatively large to be felt by BSEs or even CBEs. Mammograms, on the other hand, can detect extremely small particles in the breast and, consequently, it is important for women to go get screened.

The theory used by Aiken et al. (1994) was the Health Behavior Model (HBM). They designed an intervention that targeted each of the four components of the HBM: perceived susceptibility, severity, benefits, and barriers.

The sample comprised 295 primarily middle-class European American women. The authors sent out letters of invitation to 253 female support groups around the state of Arizona asking them if they would like to participate in a study. Forty-four groups replied. Each volunteer was given a pretest (before the intervention) and an assessment right after the intervention. She was then contacted three months later during the time when actual compliance was measured. At each assessment, the women's intention to get a screening and questions based on the model were used: What prevents you from getting a mammogram (barriers)? How susceptible do you think you are to getting breast cancer(vulnerability)?

There were three experimental groups. One group received an educational program. This group was given information about prevalence rates of breast cancer and its risk factors to increase perceived susceptibility. The pathological course of the disease and survival rates were described to increase severity and the advantages of early screening were described to increase perceived benefits. To decrease barriers, the authors stressed the minimal nature of the risks (women feared the radiation from the mammography machine could be dangerous) and low costs and presented a slide show of the procedure so it was clear what exactly was done.

The second experimental group received the educational program plus psychological training. The women were presented with counterarguments against mammography, actors modeled the process with a role-play, provided action steps for women to take (gave them the addresses and phone numbers of where to go to get a mammogram), made the women commit to calling and making an appointment by signing a form, and then mailed the women copies of the signed form and action steps two weeks later. The control group only completed the preintervention questionnaire.

What was the result? Not surprisingly, two to three times more women in the intervention groups went to get screened than women in the control group. In assessing the exact reasons behind the increase in compliance, Aiken et al. (1994) conducted a mediational analysis, which is a statistical procedure that illustrates links between chains of variables and tests for mediation as we discussed in Chapter 5. Essentially, they asked whether the HBM variables such as susceptibility, severity, benefits, and barriers served to mediate the connection between the intervention and the change in behavior (West & Aiken, 1997). In keeping with the predictions of the HBM model, strong mediational pathways were found between perceived susceptibility and perceived benefits to intentions, and there was a strong link between intentions to get screened and actually going in for a screening. Aiken et al. (1994) also found that perceived susceptibility played a substantial role in predicting behavior. In fact, the authors found that perceived susceptibility played both an indirect role in influencing behavior (intervention → susceptibility → benefits → intentions) and a direct role as well (intervention → susceptibility → intentions).

Such psychological interventions nicely demonstrate the effectiveness of health psychological research and the role it plays in health behavior change and the prevention of illness.

SUMMARY

- Cancer is the second leading cause of death, and the chances of being diagnosed with cancer increase with age. Cancer is the name given to a category of illnesses in which the main problem is the presence of a malignant tumor. Cancer cells form because of cell mutations in DNA caused by exposure to environmental toxins and unhealthy behaviors such as smoking.

- Tumors vary in where they are found, can be malignant or benign, and can vary in severity. The four main types of cancer are carcinomas (starting in surface layers of the body), sarcomas (in muscles, bones, or cartilage), lymphomas (in the lymphatic system), and leukemias (in the blood or bone marrow).

- There are large differences in the cultural makeup of people who have cancer. Both incidence rates and mortality rates vary across cultures. African Americans have the highest general cancer rates. Men experience higher incidences of cancer than women. These cultural differences also extend to beliefs and knowledge about cancer.

- Cancer can be considered a developmental disease because the chances of getting it increase as you age, and health behaviors at different stages of development may put one more at risk for having cancer.

- Psychological factors play a part in both the incidence of cancer and in responding to diagnosis although the effects are stronger for the latter. Personality traits such as optimism, the presence of social support, and finding meaning in the illness are all associated with coping with cancer and its progression.

- The key health behaviors associated with a higher incidence of cancer are tobacco use, poor diets, and a lack of physical activity. Sun exposure and the use of tanning beds also are associated with cancer incidence.

- The main treatments for cancer are surgery, chemotherapy, radiation therapy, and immunotherapy. A number of alternative and complementary therapies such as yoga, massage, meditation, and acupuncture are also being used to help patients cope with cancer.

- Health psychologists aid in the prevention of cancer by designing behavioral interventions to increase screening behaviors. There are a number of cultural differences in screening behaviors with low socioeconomic status individuals being the most likely to not get screened consistent with American Cancer Society guidelines. There are also significant differences in screening behaviors among African Americans, Latinos, European Americans, and Asian Americans.

- Some interventions are designed to inhibit the progression of cancer and help patients cope.

TEST YOURSELF

Check your understanding of the topics in this chapter by answering the following questions. Answers appear in the Appendix.

1. Cancer is the _____ cause of death in America.
   a. Leading
   b. Second leading
   c. Third leading
   d. Fourth leading
2. Cancer is best defined as:
   a. An illness caused by the presence of a malignant tumor.
   b. A mutated cell.
   c. A cell with retarded growth.
   d. A cell with accelerated growth.
3. Not all cells with abnormal cell growth are cancerous. The type that destroys healthy tissue is referred to as:
   a. Neoplasmic.
   b. Malignant.
   c. Benign.
   d. Mutant.
4. Cancer causing substances are referred to as:
   a. Carcinogens.
   b. Malignancies.
   c. Teratogens.
   d. Neoplasmas.
5. The most common site for cancer for men is the:
   a. Lungs.
   b. Prostrate gland.
   c. Colon.
   d. Pancreas.
6. Cancers that start at the surface layers of the body are called:
   a. Lymphomas.
   b. Carcinomas.

   c. Sarcomas.
   d. Leukemias.
7. _____ have the highest general cancer incidence rates in America.
   a. Asian Americans
   b. African Americans
   c. European Americans
   d. Latinos
8. _____ believe that cancer is punishment for one's actions or that of a family member and that one must bear the pain to protect other members of one's communities.
   a. African Americans
   b. Laotians
   c. American Indians
   d. Latinos
9. The single most dangerous health behavior in context of cancer is:
   a. Smoking.
   b. Drinking alcohol.
   c. Not exercising.
   d. Eating badly.
10. The health psychological model that is most commonly used to get people to get screened for cancer when they should is _____?
    a. The Health Beliefs Model
    b. The Theory of Planned Behavior
    c. The Transtheoretical Model
    d. Social Norm Marketing

WEB RESOURCES

Visit the companion Web site at **www.cengage.com/ psychology/gurung,** where you will find online resources for this book, including chapter-by-chapter quizzes, Web links, and more!

The American Cancer Society
www.cancer.org

This site has a variety of resources on and about cancer and its treatment.

Cancer Control
http://cancercontrolplanet.cancer.gov/atlas/timeall.jsp?
ap=1

> This is the National Cancer Institute site for
> graphing trends in cancer. Select by type of cancer,
> state, or ethnicity.

Cancer Support Groups
http://cissecure.nci.nih.gov/factsheet/

> This site helps one locate cancer support groups
> around the nation.

Locks of Love
http://www.locksoflove.org/

> If you want to help those with cancer, you may
> consider donating your hair to a good cause. This
> link has more details on what you can do.j

KEY TERMS, CONCEPTS, AND PEOPLE

benefit finding, 384

benign, 374

carcinogens, 374

carcinomas, 375

chemotherapy, 394

curative surgery, 393

debulking surgery, 393

diagnostic surgery, 393

fatalism, 378

Health Belief Model (HBM), 397

Immunotherapy, 395

incidence, 376

leukemias, 375

lymphomas, 375

malignant, 374

mastectomy, 394

metastasize, 374

neoplasms, 373

palliative surgery, 393

personality, 383

preventative surgery, 393

radiation therapy, 394

restorative surgery, 394

sarcomas, 375

screening, 396

social support, 384

Spiegel, David, 400

staging surgery, 393

TNM system, 375

Type C personality, 382

ultraviolet (UV) ray, 392

ESSENTIAL READINGS

Antoni, M., & Lutgendorf, S. (2007). Psychosocial Factors and Disease Progression in Cancer. *Current Directions in Psychological Science, 16*(1), 42–46.

Anderson, B. L., Kiecolt-Glaser, J., & Glaser, R. (1994). A biobehavioral model of cancer stress and disease course. *American Psychologist, 49*, 389–404.

Meyerowitz, B. E., Richardson, J., Hudson, S., & Leedham, B. (1998). Ethnicity and cancer outcomes: Behavioral and psychosocial considerations. *Psychological Bulletin, 123*, 47–70.

Spiegel, D., Sephton, S. E., Terr, A. I., & Stites, D. P. (1998). Effects of psychosocial treatment in prolonged survival may be mediated by neuroimmune pathways. *Annals of New York Academy of Science, 840*, 674–683.

Culture and Cardiovascular Disease

"Quick! Call 911. I think Pat is having a heart attack!" You have probably seen enough movies to imagine what this scenario must look like: a person writhing in pain on the floor, chest clutched between sweaty fingers. Perhaps this is in a crowded restaurant and worried onlookers are debating the best course of action. As you picture this scene, as yourself this question: What does Pat look like? You most likely picture "Pat" as an old or middle-aged Caucasian man, probably someone's grandfather or uncle named "Patrick." Heart problems are often expected of older men, but this stereotype is not accurate. In fact, heart-related diseases are common in older women as well and "Pat" in this scene could very well be "Patricia." There is a marked lack of awareness of the high risk for heart attack among women (Liewer, Mains, Lykens, & René, 2008). In addition, did you know that heart-related diseases are the third most common cause of death for children younger than age 15? Therefore, Pat could be a young boy or an older woman having a heart problem. But that's not all. Heart attacks are not always as dramatic as the scenario described here either.

This chapter describes the class of diseases that affect the heart and circulatory system and reviews the main biopsychosocial determinants and the factors that alleviate the illness. The core causes of most of the cardiovascular diseases (CVDs) are very similar. We focus on the most common: coronary heart disease, stroke, and hypertension. Figure 13.1 shows the prevalence of each in relation to the other. I will also highlight the many cultural factors that influence the effects and progression of heart diseases.

PREVALENCE OF CARDIOVASCULAR DISEASES

Heart disease death rates for the United States dropped 25.8 percent between 1999 and 2005—from 195 to 144 deaths for every 100,000 people—surpassing the American Heart Association's 25 percent target reduction (National Center

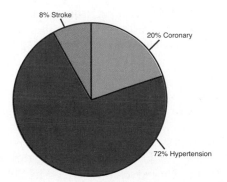

8% Stroke

20% Coronary

72% Hypertension

FIGURE **13.1** Frequency of Selected Circulatory Diseases: United States, 2006 for Health Statistics, 2008). Stroke deaths dropped 24.4 percent, from 61 to 47 deaths per 100,000 people. Deaths from cardiovascular disease have dropped also in some European countries (World Health Organization [WHO], 2008). Yet heart problems and those related to the circulatory system are still the leading causes of death globally (WHO, 2008; Figure 13.2) and problems due to heart disease vary from country to country (Anand & Yusuf, 1998). Fatality due to heart disease is affected also by differences among countries. Some of these varying major risk factors are blood pressure, blood cholesterol, smoking, physical activity, and diet. One-fifth of all deaths in developing countries such as India and Mexico and two-fifths of all deaths in developed countries such as the United States, Britain, and Canada are attributable to heart diseases (Murray & Lopez, 1997). The number of deaths from cardiovascular disease by sex and age is shown in Figure 13.3.

Much of our understanding of heart disease comes from a large-scope longitudinal study begun more than 50 years ago. In the late 1940s, the town of Framingham, Massachusetts, was selected by the U.S. Public Health Service as the site of a large-scale study to understand why heart disease had become North America's number one killer. A total of more than 5,000 healthy male and female residents between ages 30 and 60 were enrolled as the first cohort of participants. Every two to four years, study participants are given extensive medical examinations including a medical history, blood tests, and other tests of current health status. The **Framingham heart study** was the first to establish a relationship between levels of cholesterol and high blood pressure and their affect on heart disease risk (Apel at al., 1997). The researchers found that a lifestyle with a bad diet, sedentary living, smoking, and unrestrained weight gain accelerated the occurrence of cardiovascular problems. Even today, new information about heart disease is based on the latest assessments made with Framingham participants (Fox et al., 2008; Kannel, Evans, Piper, & Murabito, 2008; Parikh, Hwang, Larson, Levy, & Fox, 2008). The children and grandchildren of the original cohort participate today and are referred to as the "offspring" or "third generation" cohorts (Hamburg, et al., 2008; Kannel, Vasan, Keyes, Sullivan, & Robins, 2008). Let's take a closer look at these often fatal diseases.

WHAT IS CARDIOVASCULAR DISEASE?

Diseases resulting from problems with the heart and the circulatory system are all gathered under the general heading of **cardiovascular disease**, or CVD. The most common are coronary heart disease (CHD) and heart failure (both commonly referred to as heart attacks), strokes, and hypertension or high blood pressure (medically referred to as essential hypertension). Others include abnormal heart rhythms, congenital heart disease, heart valve failure, heart muscle disease (cardiomyopathy), rheumatic fever, pulmonary heart disease, cerebrovascular disease, and diseases of the veins, arteries, and lymph nodes (the last three collectively are called vascular diseases). To get a better feel for how CVDs develop, this is a good time to refresh yourself on the circulatory system (described in chapter 3).

Coronary heart disease (CHD) is a condition in which the small blood vessels that supply blood and oxygen to the heart narrow due the accumulation

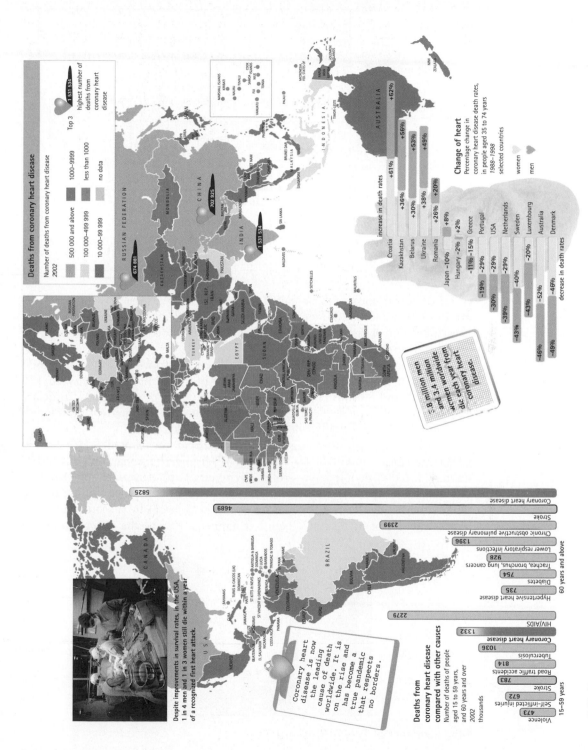

Deaths from coronary heart disease

Number of deaths from coronary heart disease 2002

- 500 000 and above
- 100 000–499 999
- 10 000–99 999
- 1000–9999
- less than 1000
- no data

Top 3 highest number of deaths from coronary heart disease

1 531 534

674 881

702 925

1 531 534

RUSSIAN FEDERATION

CHINA

MONGOLIA

INDIA

Change of heart

Percentage change in coronary heart disease death rates, in people aged 35 to 74 years 1988–1998 selected countries

women / men

increase in death rates

- Croatia +61%
- Kazakhstan +36%
- Belarus +30%
- Ukraine +38%
- Romania +26%
- Japan +8%
- Hungary +2%
- Greece –15%
- Portugal –11%
- USA –19%
- Netherlands –29%
- Sweden –30%
- Luxembourg –39%
- Australia –40%
- Denmark –43%

+62% +56% +53% +49% +20%

–2% –10% –29% –29% –29% –43% –46% –52% –49% –46%

decrease in death rates

≈ 8 million men and 3.4 million women worldwide die each year from coronary heart disease.

Despite improvements in survival rates, in the USA, 1 in 4 men and 1 in 3 women still die within a year of a recognised first heart attack.

CANADA

USA

BRAZIL

Coronary heart disease is now the leading cause of death worldwide. It is on the rise and has become a true pandemic that respects no borders.

Deaths from coronary heart disease compared with other causes

Number of deaths of people aged 15 to 59 years, and 60 years and over 2002 thousands

60 years and above

- Coronary heart disease 5825
- Stroke 4689
- Chronic obstructive pulmonary disease 2399
- Lower respiratory infections 1396
- Trachea, bronchus, lung cancers 754
- Diabetes 735
- Hypertensive heart disease

15–59 years

- HIV/AIDS 2279
- Coronary heart disease 1332
- Tuberculosis 1036
- Road traffic accidents 814
- Stroke 783
- Self-inflicted injuries 672
- Violence 473

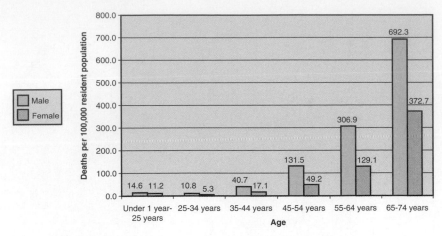

FIGURE **13.3** Death Rates for Diseases of the Heart by Age and Sex: United States, 2005

of fat or scar tissue. It is also called coronary artery disease. As the coronary arteries narrow, blood flow to the heart can slow down or even stop, causing chest pain, shortness of breath, or a heart attack. Coronary heart disease the leading cause of death in America.

Hypertension or high blood pressure is a condition in which the blood pressure remains chronically elevated. Blood pressure that stays between 120 and 139/80 and 89 mm Hg is considered prehypertension and blood pressure above this level (140/90 mm Hg or higher) is considered hypertension. Hypertension increases the risk for heart attack and stroke.

Stroke is the third-leading cause of death in the United States behind CHD and cancer and is the leading cause of disability among adults. Approximately 550,000 people have strokes each year, with approximately 150,000 of them fatal. Stroke is a type of CVD that affects the arteries leading to and within the brain. A stroke occurs when a blood vessel to the brain is either blocked by a clot or bursts. When that happens, part of the brain cannot get

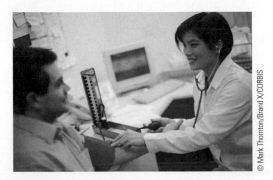

Measurement of Blood Pressure

High blood pressure is one of the easiest ways to detect a risk for heart problems and is associated with obesity, bad diets, and not enough physical activity.

the blood and oxygen it needs and it begins to die (American Stroke Association, 2008). We will discuss more of the physiological and psychological aspects of CVDs later in the chapter.

CULTURAL VARIATIONS IN THE INCIDENCE OF CARDIOVASCULAR DISEASE

As with other chronic illnesses, there are some significant cultural differences in the incidence of CVDs (Pleis & Lethbridge-Çejku, 2007). As shown in Figure 13.4, Asian or Pacific Islanders show the lowest numbers of deaths due to CVD followed by American Indians and Latinos and then by African Americans and European Americans who do not show large differences. Men experience more strokes than women, and all ethnic groups experience more strokes than European Americans (see Figure 13.5).

The incidence variations are often due to differences in the levels of knowledge about the disease, differences in health behaviors, and risk factors among different cultural groups (Hertz, McDonald, Unger, & Lustik, 2007). For example, Hamner, and Wilder (2008) used the Coronary Heart Disease Knowledge Test to measure knowledge of CVD in rural Alabama women. The average on the test was 8.50 (out of 20). The participants were at significant risk for CVD. The women recognized that smoking and obesity were issues, but were less aware of factors such as personality, oral contraceptive use, hypertension, diabetes, and family history. How you would fare on the test? You can assess the test using the Web links at the end of the chapter (and you should do pretty well once you get to the end of this chapter too).

There are many cultural differences that could account for higher CVD incidence. The higher risk for heart attack shown by South Asians is attributed, in part, to a higher prevalence of diabetes (Patel, et al., 2008) and other risk factors (e.g., Bathula, Francis, Hughes, & Chaturvedi, 2008) in some South Asian populations. Higher rates can also be due to the psychological

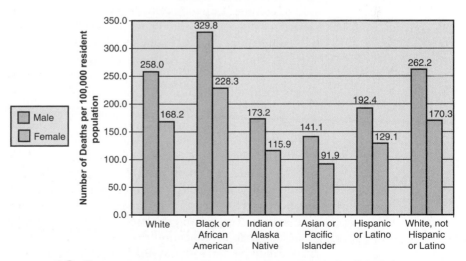

FIGURE **13.4** Death Rates for Diseases of the Heart by Ethnicity and Sex: United States, 2005

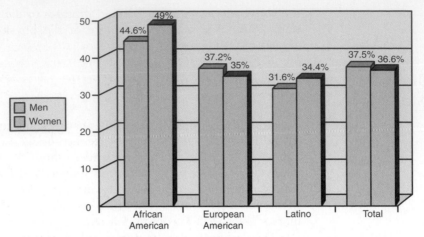

FIGURE **13.5** Ethnic and Sex Differences in the Incidence of Stroke (Percentage)

experiences of different groups that relate to CVD (Baker, Richter, & Anand, 2001). For example, hostility, anger, and social support, each of which play a key role in the development of CVD, also vary across cultures and map onto larger cultural dimensions (see Chapter 1).

Hypertension, a CVD, also shows strong cultural differences and is found at a higher rate in African Americans (Ng-Mak, 1999). Some evidence suggests an intriguing sociobiological reason. Gleiberman, Harburg, Frone, Russell, and Cooper (1995) showed that high blood pressure is positively correlated to dark skin color, which could induce more discrimination (i.e., because of being darker skinned) as a genetic marker.

Anger and other components of the Type A personality such as competitiveness and time urgency are closely tied to the individualistic/collectivistic dimension of culture. People in individualistic cultures are more competitive, which is viewed as a desirable trait. Those in collectivistic cultures are more cooperative, and competition against members of one's group is often discouraged. Social support, similarly, is seen more in collectivistic cultures (Sagrestano et al., 1999). Time orientation varies with another cultural dimension: **fluid time versus fixed time**. In most cultures in North America, time is fixed: when you say you will meet someone at 10:00 A.M., you mean exactly that. In fluid-time cultures, such as those in India and among American Indians, meeting someone at 10:00 A.M. really means you will show up anywhere between 10:15 A.M. and 10:30 A.M. This is understood and expected, and no one is frustrated when someone is late. In fact, in many East Indian American communities, people set appointments and specify whether they mean an exact time or Indian Style Time. Accelerated blood pressure due to time constraints is generally less common in such cultures, and the stress of being late accordingly is different as well.

There is some indication that increased risk of CHD in some ethnic populations may be due to basic differences in the epidemiology of **atherosclerosis,** the accumulation of fatty substances in the blood vessels. Some racial and ethnic populations are also inadequately prescribed antiplatelet therapy—daily aspirin doses—despite their higher risk (Saunders & Ofili, 2008). As discussed in Chapter 8, there are cultural differences in health care-seeking behavior and patient-practitioner interactions. For example, South Asians do not use ambulances as often when experiencing heart emergencies (reflecting cultural differences or possibly geographical proximity to hospitals), (Ben-Shlomo, Naqvi, & Baker, 2008). There is also evidence of differences in how doctors manage patients with chest pain according to their cultural backgrounds. Doctors may have a lower threshold for giving thrombolytic therapy (treatment that breaks up blood clots) to South Asian men with chest pain because they are aware of the increased risk of CHD in this population (Ben-Shlomo et al. 2008).

New areas of research are investigating more deeply into biological markers of CHD that may vary by culture. For example, **C-reactive protein** (CRP) concentrations are associated with risk of CHD. Kelley-Hedgepeth et al., (2008) conducted a cross-sectional study of 3,154 women enrolled in the Study of Women's Health across the Nation (SWAN), a culturally diverse prospective study. The study population was 47 percent European American, 28 percent African American, 17 percent Chinese American and Japanese American and 9 percent Latino. The African American women had the highest median CRP concentrations, followed by Latinas, European American, and then Asian American women.

In another detailed study of the links among culture, biology, and CHD, Nasir et al. (2008) assessed nearly 7,000 individuals in the Multi-Ethnic Study of Atherosclerosis (MESA). The researchers focused on different types of calcifications that correspond to atherosclerosis and CHD. Clear ethnic differences emerged. The highest prevalence of calcifications was observed in European Americans, followed by Latinos and African Americans with the lowest levels of calcification among Chinese Americans. The next step in such research is to see how these underlying differences map onto the differential incidence of CHD (Manolio et al., 2008).

Two other cultural dimensions beyond ethnicity can also influence CVD. In the **control versus constraint** dimension (Trompenaars, 1997), control cultures believe that they have absolute control of their outcomes (similar to having an internal locus of control). Contrastingly, people in constraint cultures believe everything is in the hands of God or fate. Those in control cultures may have higher levels of anxiety and stress and correspondingly have more risk for heart problems (Baker et al., 2001). Similarly, the level of emotionality may make a difference as well. **Neutral cultures**, such as that of Japan, do not sanction the open display of emotions. In contrast, **affect cultures**, such as that of Italy, place a premium on the display of emotions. Not expressing emotions could also lead to higher levels of CVD.

Sex differences, another element of culture, appear in not just the incidence of CVD (Ng, 2007) but also in patient-practitioner interactions. Adams et al. (2008) tested for the sources of uncertainty and sex bias in doctors' diagnoses and decision-making relating to CVD. They randomly selected male and female doctors in England and the United States and showed them video clips of actors portraying patients with CVD. They had "patients" of different ages, both sexes, and different ethnicities and socioeconomic status. The doctors were interviewed about their decision making. Adam et al found differences in male and female doctors' responses to different types of patient information. The female doctors remembered information differently than did the men (e.g., more patient cues). All doctors paid more attention to male patients' age and considered more age-related disease possibilities for men than women.

DEVELOPMENTAL ISSUES IN CARDIOVASCULAR DISEASE

A number of developmental issues connect to CVD. For example, low birth weight is now known to be associated with increased rates of CVD (Barker, 2008). Sub-optimal growth in infancy and rapid childhood weight gain exacerbate the effects of impaired prenatal growth. As we age we have a greater risk for developing CVDs. A large part of this risk is due to wear and tear on our arteries and the accumulation of plaque that increases with time, but this risk also has psychosocial correlates. People go through different stages of physical, social, and cognitive development. Erikson, for example, hypothesized that we progress through eight different stages, each with its own challenges and milestones. The life changes that accompany social development can serve as stressors that, in turn, can lead to higher risks for CVDs. Some milestones include puberty, graduation from high school or college, a first job, and perhaps losing a first job. Even relationships, dating, and marriage can be important correlates of CVDs (see the upcoming section on stress for more on the impact of transitions). Satisfying relationships can provide social support, and acrimonious relationships or divorces could raise blood pressure and otherwise negatively impact health. Important negative life events corresponding to developmental stages increase in frequency in the months before a heart attack (Welin et al., 1992). Although heart disease has been studied more extensively in men, studies of women also show that heart disease patients experience a significantly larger number of negative life changes, many of them related to family life (Orth-Gomer, Chesney, & Wegner, 1998).

Beyond developmentally related life events, it is also important to factor in development and take a lifespan approach to CVD because one of the main psychosocial correlates of CVD—social support—changes over time. Younger women with poor social networks have higher levels of heart problems (Orth-Gomer & Johnson, 1987). Surprisingly, older retired women with more extensive social networks also had a higher incidence of cardiac problems. The additional networks for older women could have come with more mental burdens. To understand conflicting data such as these, it is important to look at how social support changes over the lifespan (see Chapter 5 and Gurung, Taylor, & Seeman, 2003; Gurung & Von Dras, 2007).

SYNTHESIZE, EVALUATE, APPLY	<ul><li>Evaluate the pros and cons of basing a lot of information on studies such as the Framingham heart study. What concerns with the study do you have?</li><li>Each culture has factors that make people less likely or more likely to get CVD. Can you think of some examples from your own culture?</li><li>Trace the connections between different health behaviors and different heart diseases.</li><li>How can the different cultural variations that you have been exposed to in other chapters also explain differences in the incidence and progression of cardiovascular diseases?</li></ul>

PHYSIOLOGICAL CORRELATES OF CARDIOVASCULAR DISEASE

The primary physiological antecedent for the incidence of CVDs is atherosclerosis (American Heart Association, 2008; Giannoglou et al., 2008; Krantz & Lundgren, 1998). Microscopic accumulations of fats within artery walls progress to visible fatty streaks as early as childhood (Strong et al., 1999). This accumulation of fat, often in the form of plaque, reduces and sometimes blocks the arteries supplying blood to the heart. The plaque buildup can get so great as to tear the artery, creating a "snag" in which a blood clot can form to block the artery. Lesions are sometimes observed in adolescents and become increasingly common with age. This interference in blood flow to the heart is what causes heart attacks. A related condition is the hardening of the arteries, or **arteriosclerosis**, in which the arteries lose their elasticity and are more susceptible to blockages from clots or plaques (Liu et al., 2007; McEniery, & Cockcroft, 2007).

Some of the main physiological risk factors cannot be changed: age, sex, and family history. As mentioned, the risk for having a CVD increases as a person gets older, and men younger than 50 are more likely to develop a problem (Barker, 2008). At around 50 years of age, corresponding to when women reach menopause, women have a greater risk for CVDs than men (Mattar, Harharah, Su, Agarwal, Wong, & Choolani, 2008). It is also clear that having a parent or relative with a CVD greatly increases the incidence rates of CVDs (Nicolosi & Schaefer, 1992; Yamada, Ichihara, & Nishida, 2008). Although genetic linkage analyses of families and sibling pairs have implicated several loci and candidate genes in predisposition to CVD, the genes that contribute to genetic susceptibility to these conditions remain to be identified definitively.

Other physiological factors predicting the incidences of CVDs are high blood pressure, diabetes, high cholesterol level, inactivity, and being overweight or obese (Ockene, Kristeller, Goldberg, & Ockene, 1992). Men with diabetes, for example, are twice as likely to develop CVD whereas women with diabetes are up to seven times as likely to develop CVD (American Diabetic Association, 2008). In fact, coronary heart disease is the most common cause of death among diabetic patients. The increased risk of CHD in type 2

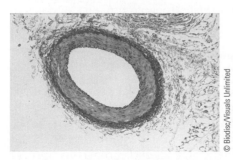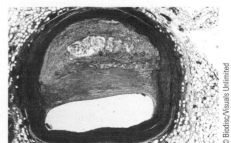

Cross-Sections of Human Arteries

The artery on the left is normal (clear wide opening). The artery on the right has a much smaller bore due to the accumulation of plaque (atherosclerosis).

diabetes is due, in part, to irregularities with fat storage and metabolism. Diabetic dyslipidemia, for example, is characterized by elevated triglycerides, low high-density lipoprotein cholesterol (HDL) and increased low-density lipoprotein cholesterol (LDL) particles (Karalis, 2008). As you can see, this second group of physiological factors can all be modified depending on a person's health behaviors (more on this later).

Another important issue in the modifiable physiological risk factors is the fact that different cultural groups vary in their genetic predispositions. Some ethnic groups are more prone to high blood pressure (Minor, Wofford, & Jones, 2008; Read, & Gorman, 2007). Some groups are more prone to be overweight. These underlying differences in risk factors could explain cultural differences in CVD. Hypertension is significantly higher in African Americans than European Americans and minority status is significantly associated with diabetes (Kurian & Cardarelli, 2007). For example, laboratory studies measuring participants' cardiovascular reactivity to different stressors have found that African Americans show higher blood pressure and epinephrine responses to tasks compared with European American participants (Mills, Berry, Dimsdale, & Neleson, 1993). Similarly, Salomon and Jagusztyn (2008) looked at the relationship between discrimination and cardiovascular responses to interpersonal incivility among African American, Latino, and European Americans. Participants completed a measure of past discrimination which was related to higher resting systolic blood pressure (SBP) among Latino participants and lower resting SBP among European American participants. Reporting being discriminated against was related to attenuated SBP and heart reactivity among Latino participants. Discrimination was not related to resting levels or reactivity among African American participants. Their findings suggest that the relationship between discrimination and cardiovascular risk differs by ethnicity. As testified to by this empirical evidence, **cardiovascular reactivity**—changes in heart rate and blood pressure in response to stress—varies greatly between individuals. This reactivity is a key physiological risk factor for the development of CVD (Holt-Lunstad, Smith, & Uchino, 2008; Nealey-Moore, Smith, Uchino, Hawkins, & Olson-Cerny, 2007; Rozanski, Blumenthal, & Kaplan, 1999).

As discussed in Chapter 6, there are also significant ethnic and geographical differences in obesity, tobacco use, diet, and activity levels—all key health behaviors related to CHD (discussed in detail below).

PSYCHOLOGICAL CORRELATES OF CARDIOVASCULAR DISEASE

There is strong evidence for a link between psychological characteristics and the development of CVDs (Nabi et al., 2008; Orth-Gomer, Rosengren, & Wilhelmsen, 1993; Turk Charles, Gatz, Kato, & Pedersen, 2008), making this set of diseases a prime candidate for use of the biopsychosocial approach of health psychology. Of all the chronic diseases, CVDs are perhaps most illustrative of the importance of focusing on psychological factors together with biological factors. Psychological factors, such as personality traits (e.g., hostility), anger, depression, social support, and stress, and health behaviors, such as dietary habits and physical activity, have all been intrinsically tied to the incidence and progression of CVDs (Krantz & Manuck, 1984; Nabi et al., 2008; Suchday, Tucker, & Krantz, 2002).

Perhaps the best-known controversy regarding the psychological causes of heart attacks revolves around a constellation of personality characteristics called the Type A personality (see Chapter 4). Friedman and Rosenman (1974) noted that heart patients who showed a sense of time urgency (always doing more than one thing at the same time), competitiveness, and hostility in their interactions with other people were found to have a higher risk for CHD. In contrast, the Type B personality is relaxed, patient, and easygoing. The original finding that was greeted with enthusiasm did not bear further examination (Shekelle et al., 1985). However, a number of people still believe that having a Type A personality, in general, is not necessarily a positive attribute. What seems more accurate is that being *hostile* is the problem (Boyle, Jackson, & Suarez, 2007; Scherwitz, Graham, & Ornish, 1985; Williams, 1987). Hostility and anger are negative emotions that can trigger a heart attack and even sudden death among individuals who are at risk (Muller, 1999; Willich, 1995). For example, in a study of patients at risk, Mittleman et al. (1995) found that episodes of anger occurred within two hours before the beginning of the heart attack. Hostility can also lessen the benefits of receiving social support (Holt-Lunstad et al., 2008). The role of hostility is so critical that for every dollar spent on anger-management treatments or hostility therapy, there is an approximate savings of two dollars in hospitalization costs in the following six months (Davidson, Gidron, Mostofsky, & Trudeau, 2007). How's that for a good deal?

The relationship between two variables is rarely straightforward. Research has begun to look for the factors that may mediate the relationship between hostility and the increased risk of CHD (see Chapter 5 for more on mediation). One such variable is carotenoid, a substance in most plants which is known to have antioxidant properties. Antioxidants, in turn may be mediators for atherosclerosis. Ohira et al., (2008) found that high hostility predicted future low levels of some serum carotenoids, which may help to explain the association of hostility and cardiovascular risk observed in epidemiologic studies.

Other negative emotions play a role in cardiac arrest too. Feeling sad and depressed may also increase your likelihood of heart problems and the progression of CVD (Boyle, Jackson, & Suarez, 2008; Cherr, Zimmerman, Wang, & Dosluoglu, 2008; Goldston, & Baillie, 2008; Hance, Carney, Freedland, & Skala, 1996). Anda et al. (1993) studied the relationship of both depressed affect and hopelessness to CHD incidence using data from a large cohort of 2,832 North American adults. The participants had no history of CHD or serious illness at baseline. Anda et al. (1993) found that people who were depressed were significantly more likely to have a fatal heart attack (relative risk 1.5). Depression was also associated with an increased risk of nonfatal heart attacks. In other studies of survivors of heart attacks, depression was found to be related to increased mortality in the six-month period after the first heart attack (Blumenthal, 2008; Frasure-Smith, Lesperance, & Talajic, 1995). Similarly, feeling hopeless, an emotion often accompanying depression, can independently predict the incidence of CVD as well (Gidron,

Levy, & Cwikel, 2007; Everson, Goldberg, Kaplan, & Cohen, 1996). A variety of different types of social supports also relate to CVD (Berkman, 1995; Seeman & Syme, 1987; Shumaker & Cjakowski, 1994), and social support is often a moderating factor (Orth-Gomer et al., 1993). Social support could influence the development of CVD by buffering the person from the effects of stress (the moderator role), consequently safeguarding the person from the deleterious effects that stress has on the circulatory system (Krantz & Lundgren, 1998). Supportive networks also ensure that a person is more likely to get help and to comply with doctor's orders. If a man is at risk for a heart attack and he is not supposed to eat fatty foods, smoke, or drink too much, a supportive partner and good friends are likely to make sure that he does not. In support of this link, studies of unmarried patients without close confidants showed them to be more likely to die over a five-year period (Case, Moss, Case, McDermott, & Eberly, 1992). Patients with large social networks are also more likely to cope better (such as attend rehab) after a cardiac incident (Molloy, Perkins-Porras, Strike, & Steptoe, 2008). Not having healthy social networks, another measure of social support, is also related to the incidence of CVD but some studies show this relationship is not always significant when demographic differences such as income level or marital status are accounted for (Morris, Wannamethee, Lennon, Thomas, & Whincup, 2008). In a sizable study on the power of social support, Sundquist, Lindstrom, Malmstrom, Johansson, and Sundquist (2004) examined whether low social participation predicted incidence rates of CHD. They followed 6,861 Swedish women and men for nearly 10 years and found that persons with low social participation (as measured by an interview) had the highest risk of CHD. They were more than twice as likely (relative risk 2.15) to have another heart attack than those with high social participation. This increased risk remained even after controls were added for education and smoking habits (Sundquist et al., 2004). In another large study, Ikeda et al., (2008) examined prospectively the association between social support and risk of coronary heart disease and stroke incidence and mortality within a cohort of 44,152 Japanese men and women. Low social support was associated with higher risk of stroke mortality in men.

Sometimes not getting social support can be fatal. Depressed patients in the Enhancing Recovery in Coronary Heart Disease (ENRICHD) trial and those with lower perceived social support (even without elevated depressive symptoms) were at increased risk for death (Lett, et al., 2007). Such findings have prompted a call for a form of special social support screening for depressed CVD patients (Thombs, 2008). Not having enough social support is often related to not having enough resources in general and is strongly linked to socioeconomic status (SES). Especially in developing countries, SES is negatively correlated with the risk of CVD (Adler et al., 1994; Kaplan & Keil, 1993). In a study of the relationship between SES and CVD, Marmot et al. (1991) studied British civil servants in the Whitehall part of London (the Whitehall studies). They showed that higher rates of CVD were seen in men of lower employment grade. At every rung of the bureaucratic ladder, men in the lower positions were worse off. There are other possible mediators. In a study of an ethnically diverse population, participants with more emotional social support showed higher high-density lipoprotein (HDL) cholesterol levels. The mediators? Physical activity and wine intake. These are but two health behaviors influenced by social support that may have the result of reducing cardiovascular disease risk (Fischer Aggarwal, Liao, & Mosca, 2008).

Stress

You may have heard of the television show and movie of the same title, *Sex and the City*, but have you considered that a show could be called *Stress and the City*? Studies in different cultures have shown that the stress from living in an urban environment can make you nine times more likely to develop CVD compared with living in a rural area (Gupta, Gupta, Jakovcic, & Zak, 1996). A little stress can go a long way. Not only does being stressed influence your health behaviors (as described in Chapter 7), but it also increases your likelihood of developing a number of diseases. In Chapter 4, we described how our body's reactions to short-term physical stressors are thought to have evolved to get us out of danger. You should also remember that these same responses, when activated for a long period of time (chronic stress), can begin to break down the body's systems (e.g., allostatic load). Cardiovascular problems are some of the most common ways that the body breaks down.

Superficially, the relationship is pretty intuitive. What happens when we get stressed? At the physiological core of the response, the catecholamines and cortisol pumped into the bloodstream increase blood flow, thus raising blood pressure. The heart is pumping faster, and blood is shunting around the body faster. There are also changes in how we metabolize food for energy. (details in chapter 4). This constellation of factors that accompany the experience and process of stress take a toll on the circulatory system and aid in the incidence of CVD (Lin et al., 2008). A sizeable body of research documents how various stressors, particularly those at work, accentuate CVD via effects on blood pressure (Brisson et al., 1999; Chandola et al., 2008). Together with the work front, environmental stress (especially that caused by low SES) and stress from interpersonal relationships at home have also been associated with the incidence of CVD.

Even watching sports can be stressful and lead to a heart attack! Wilbert-Lampen et al. (2008) examined the link between emotional stress and the incidence of heart attacks during the 2006 World Cup soccer games played in Germany. They found that watching a stressful soccer match more than doubles the risk of an acute cardiovascular event. On days of matches involving the German team, the incidence of cardiac emergencies was 2.66 times that during the control period. So take it easy during the NFL season!

Acute stress (e.g., a person's being the victim of an assault or having to deliver a very difficult presentation) can also trigger heart problems if the individual already is at risk because of atherosclerosis (Gottdiener et al., 1994; Muller, Tofler, & Stone, 1989). Early work showed that catastrophic events such as earthquakes and the death of a spouse could also initiate a heart attack (Cottington, Matthews, Talbott, & Kuller, 1980; Muller et al., 1989; Meisel et al., 1991). After the big Northridge earthquake outside Los Angeles, California, 1994, a significant increase in heart attacks was seen compared with the incidence in the previous week (Kloner, Leor, Poole, & Perritt, 1997).

The work-stress and CVD relationship has garnered the most research attention (Chandola et al., 2008; Schnall, Landsbergis, & Baker, 1994; Smith & Ruiz, 2002; Theorell & Harenstam, 2000). We can all acknowledge the fact that working can be stressful. Even if you enjoy your job, having to work can still challenge the body. The stress from work can be even more dangerous if you are overworked, have too many roles to fulfill, are not clear what your job role is, are bored with your job, or do not have support at work. No matter what the exact cause, work stress can accentuate the chances of developing CVD. Even job status is important. For example, Wamala, Mittleman, Horsten, Schenck-Gustafsson, & Orth-Gomer (2000) used data from the Stockholm Female Coronary Risk Study, a population-based case-control study comprising 292 women with CHD aged 65 years or younger and 292 age-matched healthy women, and found that unskilled women had four times the risk for CHD compared with the executive/professional women. Simultaneous adjustment for traditional risk factors and job stress lowered this risk to 2.45. Similar findings are found for men (Schnall et al., 1994).

There are also some interesting cultural differences in the work-stress relationship. Higher job strain was a major explanation for why Lithuanian men had four times the risk for CVD than Swedish men (Kristensen et al., 1998). In Japan, there is even a term for "death from overwork"—*karoshi* (Nishiyama & Johnson, 1997).

Researchers have only recently begun to look at the interaction of work stress and home stress. Orth-Gomer et al. (2000) followed women for an average of five years after hospitalization in one of the first studies to look at the longitudinal effects of marital stress and work stress in women patients. They found that stressful experiences from marital relationships may seriously affect prognosis in women with CHD, whereas living alone without a partner had no effect.

SYNTHESIZE, EVALUATE, APPLY	• What psychosocial factors explain why heart diseases are one of the biggest health issues in the twenty-first century? • Using what you know of the causes and types of stress (Chapter 4), which forms of stress do you think best explain CVD and which theory of stress would be most useful for this?

HEALTH BEHAVIORS AND CARDIOVASCULAR DISEASE

Tobacco Use

The number one behavior to avoid if you want to minimize your risk for cardiovascular diseases is smoking. You can see why we have spent so much time on this topic (see Chapter 7). Together with being an important risk factor for other chronic diseases such as cancer (see Chapter 12), cigarette smoking has also been identified as an important factor in the development of CVD (Woodward, Oliphant, Lowe, & Tunstall-Pedoe, 2003). In one of the clearest demonstrations of this link, Doll, Peto, Boreham, and Sutherland (2004) followed approximately 35,000 British doctors from 1951 to 2001 and found that the dangers of smoking varied with cohorts. Men born in 1900 through 1930 who smoked only cigarettes and continued smoking, died on average about 10 years sooner than

© Dennis MacDonald/Alamy Limited

Smoking and Cardiovascular Disease

Those who can quit smoking significantly reduce their risk for contracting a
Cardiovascular Disease.

lifelong nonsmokers. Quitting was beneficial regardless of the age at which it was
attempted. Men who quit when 60, 50, 40, or 30 years of age gained, respectively, about 3, 6, 9, or 10 years of life expectancy (Doll et al., 2004). Another
large study of 563,144 participants (82 percent of whom were Asian) showed
evidence that smoking aggravated blood pressure and together these two factors
substantially increased the risk of CVD (Nakamura et al., 2008). The risk of
CVD is almost three times as high for smokers as it is for nonsmokers, and the
risk for smokers is higher if they are younger (Baker et al., 2001).

What effects do smoking bans or governmental regulations to curb smoking have? Consider the following case. In 1993, the state of Massachusetts
introduced the Massachusetts Tobacco Control Program (MTCP) This
reduced how many people smoked in the state by 29 percent. That's not all.
There was a 31 percent decline in death rates due to CVD (from 1993 to
2003; 425 fewer CVD deaths, Kabir, Connolly, Clancy, Koh, & Capewell,
2008). C-reactive protein (CRP) levels (predictors of CVD as discussed earlier) also drop when a smoker quits the habit (Hastie, Haw, & Pell, 2008).

People around the world smoke. Smoking is more common in some cultures than in others, and the link between CVD and smoking is not the same
across cultures. For example, although there are relatively high rates of smoking in countries such as Japan and China, CVD mortality and morbidity are
not proportionally as high (WHO, 2008). In other countries, high levels of
other unhealthy behaviors also accompany high smoking rates. Europeans
tend to smoke more than Americans do in general and also consume diets
higher in saturated fats (Baker et al., 2001). Recent attention has turned to
the presence of risk factors that accentuate the effect of smoking, and some
of the most important are dietary factors and cholesterol.

Diet

Your food choices play a large role in your overall health and well-being. What
you eat determines the levels of nutrients available for your cells and ensures the

Dietary Recommendations to Minimize CVD

- Eat a variety of fruits and vegetables. Choose 5 or more servings per day.
- Eat a variety of grain products, including whole grains. Choose 6 or more servings per day.
- Include fat-free and low-fat milk products, fish, legumes (beans), skinless poultry, and lean meats.
- Choose fats and oils with 2 grams or less saturated fat per tablespoon, such as liquid and tub margarines, canola oil, and olive oil.
- Balance the number of calories you eat with the number you use each day. (To find that number multiply the number of pounds you weigh now by 15 calories. This represents the average number of calories used in one day if you're moderately active. If you get very little exercise, multiply your weight by 13 instead of 15. Less-active people burn fewer calories.)
- Maintain a level of physical activity that keeps you fit and matches the number of calories you eat. Walk or do other activities for at least 30 minutes on most days. To lose weight, do enough activity to use up more calories than you eat every day.
- Limit your intake of foods high in calories or low in nutrition, including foods like soft drinks and candy that have a lot of sugars.
- Limit foods high in saturated fat, trans fat, and/or cholesterol, such as full-fat milk products, fatty meats, tropical oils, partially hydrogenated vegetable oils, and egg yolks. Instead choose foods low in saturated fat, trans fat, and cholesterol from the first four points above.
- Eat less than 6 grams of salt (sodium chloride) per day (2,400 milligrams of sodium).
- Have no more than one alcoholic drink per day if you're a woman and no more than two if you're a man. "One drink" means it has no more than 1/2 ounce of pure alcohol. Examples of one drink are 12 oz. of beer, 4 oz. of wine, 1–1/2 oz. of 80-proof spirits or 1 oz. of 100-proof spirits.

FIGURE **13.6** Dietary Recommendations to Minimize Cardiovascular Disease

Source: American Heart Association (2005).

smooth and healthy functioning of your bodily symptoms. There are many dietary factors that influence the incidence and progression of CVD (Figure 13.6), and diet is a factor that affects the interaction between culture, psychology, and behavior (Van Horn et al., 2008). Your diet can influence your cholesterol level, your blood pressure, your tolerance for glucose (and consequently your risk for diabetes), your likelihood to be overweight, and even how your blood coagulates. Each of these factors is associated with the development of CVD (Brunner et al., 2008; Fung et al., 2008; Kesteloot, Sasaki, Xie, & Joossens, 1994).

The two most common risk factors for hypertension beyond age and family history are too much salt in the diet and obesity. The specific role diet plays with hypertension can be seen in a study of the Dietary Approaches to Stop Hypertension (DASH) diet (Fung et al., 2008). The diet of 88,517 female nurses was assessed seven times during (1980–2004). Researchers then calculated a DASH score based on eight food and nutrient components (fruits, vegetables, whole grains, nuts and legumes, low-fat dairy, red and processed meats, sweetened beverages, and sodium). There was a direct negative correlation between DASH scores and heart disease; the better the score the less likely a heart attack. The DASH score was also significantly associated with lower risk of stroke and lower levels of C-reactive protein.

In a similar analysis, Brunner et al., (2008) compared four dietary patterns: unhealthy (white bread, processed meat, fries, and full-cream milk); sweet (white bread, biscuits, cakes, processed meat, and high-fat dairy products); Mediterranean-like (fruit, vegetables, rice, pasta, and wine); and healthy (fruit, vegetables, whole-meal bread, low-fat dairy, and little alcohol) in nearly 8,000 participants. Compared with the unhealthy pattern, the healthy pattern reduced the risk of CVD and diabetes.

Similar to CHD, a lower risk of stroke has been related to the intake of fruits and vegetables (Hak et al., 2004). In an analysis of data from the Physicians' Health Study, a study of 22,071 U.S. male physicians, Hak et al. (2004) found that men who were in the bottom fifth for intake of antioxidants (such as alpha-carotene, beta-carotene, and lycopene) had the highest risk of stroke.

One of the most important risk factors for CVD is cholesterol level. Cholesterol is found in most animal products and is an important component of cell walls and membranes. It is also a main component of plaque. As discussed in Chapter 7, we have high-density lipoprotein and low-density lipoprotein (HDL) and (LDL) cholesterol, and if you want to prevent heart disease, you need to keep your total cholesterol level below 200 milligrams per deciliter (American Heart Association, 2008). As the level of cholesterol in the blood increases, the risk of CVD increases as well (Ballantyne, 2004; Dean, Borenstein, Henning, Knight, & Merz, 2004). LDLs seem to be the primary factor and a number of treatments (e.g., statins) aim to reduce the LDL levels in the bloodstream (Goldstein et al., 2008). A high cholesterol level is even more likely to cause CVD in people with other health issues such as diabetes (Tanasescu, Cho, Manson, & Hu, 2004). One other major risk factor may be a diet high in saturated fat, though this "lipid hypothesis" is being heavily contested (He, Xu, & Van Horn, 2007; Ravnskov, 2008).

Diets including fish (Streppel, Ocké, Boshuizen, Kok, & Kromhout, 2008; Whelton, He, Whelton, & Munter, 2004) and high levels of whole grains and fiber (Singh et al., 2002) are particularly good for you. Apparently fish oil is something everyone with cholesterol issues and at risk for CVD should be consuming (Leaf, Kang, & Xiao, 2008). In a recent intervention, Singh et al. recruited 1,000 patients with **angina pectoris** and **myocardial infarctions** and had half of them eat a diet rich in whole grains, fruits, vegetables, walnuts, and almonds (referred to as an **Indo-Mediterranean diet**). The control group ate a diet suggested by the National Cholesterol Education Program (NCEP). Interestingly, the intervention group had fewer heart problems, including heart attacks (both fatal and nonfatal) and showed lower cholesterol levels than the control group. The Indo-Mediterranean diet is one of the protective factors of culture: people in and from the southern part of Europe who follow it show lower incidence of CVD (Panagiotakos, Pitsavos, Chrysohoou, Skoumas, & Stefanadis, 2008; Trichopolou & Lagiou, 1997).

A related cultural diet component is alcohol. For example, the French have relatively low levels of CVD even though French food is known to be rich in saturated fats. This "French paradox" (see Chapter 7) has been linked to moderate consumption of alcohol. One or two glasses of wine per day seem to reduce the incidence of CVD (Rimm & Ellison, 1995; Saremi, & Arora, 2008). Too much alcohol (e.g., binge drinking) does not lessen your CVD risk (Bagnardi, Zatonski, Scotti, La Vecchia, & Corrao, 2008).

Physical Activity

In terms of physical activity, not only is exercising useful in reducing the risks of CVD, but being physically inactive actually increases the risks (Apullan et al.,

2008; Sofi, Capalbo, Cesari, Abbate, & Gensini, 2008). In this respect, standing still actually makes you slide backward on the continuum of health. For example, Yeager, Anda, Macera, Donehoo, and Eaker (1995) found a strong association between CHD mortality rates and the prevalence of a sedentary lifestyle that remained significant even after controls were added for the prevalence of diagnosed hypertension, smoking, and being overweight.

A key component of treatment and many behavioral interventions to reduce CVD hence includes some form of physical activity. Taylor, Lerner, Sage, Lehman, and Seeman (2004) presented a recent review of the effectiveness of exercise-based cardiac rehabilitation in patients with CHD. Their study included 48 trials with a total of 8,940 patients and found that compared with control subjects, exercise was associated both with fewer deaths from all causes and fewer deaths from heart attacks. Patients who exercised also showed greater reductions in total cholesterol level, systolic blood pressure, and smoking. In a specific example, Blumenthal et al. (2004) examined the link between physical exercise and CVD mortality and morbidity among 2,078 heart attack patients who were participating in the Enhancing Recovery in Coronary Heart Disease (ENRICHD) multicenter clinical trial. Patients reporting regular exercise had less than half the heart attacks of those patients who reported no regular exercise.

The most commonly recommended form of exercise is cardiovascular training, especially walking and increasing movement (American Cancer Society, 2008). Even though the recommendation is that patients with heart disease increase their levels of physical activity, this often does not happen. Zhao, Ford, Li, & Mokdad (2008) looked at the degree of compliance with national and/or American Heart Association and American College of Cardiology guidelines for physical activity in United States adults with coronary heart disease (CHD) in comparison with subjects without CHD using data from the 2005 Behavioral Risk Factor Surveillance System (BRFSS). The sample size was immense. A total of 297,145 participants were included. Unfortunately, patients with CVD were found to be less likely to comply with physical activity recommendations than those without CVD.

TREATMENT OPTIONS

The specific treatment for CVD is determined by the severity of the symptoms, the size and quantity of areas with **ischemias** (reduced blood flow), how well the left ventricle of the heart is pumping, and other medical factors such as severity of chest pain (American Heart Association, 2008). As you can tell from the previous sections, unhealthy lifestyles (e.g., bad eating habits and not getting enough physical activity) are key determinants of whether or not you will develop a CVD. Correspondingly, changing health behaviors is one of the most critical treatment options to prevent the development of symptoms, relieve the symptoms, and lower the risk of heart attack and death. The primary goal will be to change unhealthy behaviors. The patient is normally admitted to a **cardiac rehabilitation program**. Rehabilitation programs educate patients on the best way to change their lifestyles and use a combination of physical activity and social support to improve their overall functioning and prevent death (Bestehorn, Wegscheider, & Völler, 2008; Dafoe & Huston, 1997; Dusseldorp, van Elderen, Maes, Meulman, & Kraaij, 1999; Vossen et al., 2008). If the person smokes, a smoking cessation program will be prescribed. He or she will also receive consultations on how to change diet, reduce salt intake, and eat more nutritionally balanced meals. If excessive drinking or not enough physical activity is the issue, it is critical to tackle each of these problems. Patients may even be told to start taking aspirin. Aspirin, you say? That's right, not just any headache or pain killer, but aspirin. Many studies have shown that aspirin reduces the risk of heart attack in people with known CHD (Hayden, Pignone, Phillips, & Mulrow, 2002; Sofi, Marcucci, Gori, Abbate, & Gensini, 2008). In fact, for people at increased risk for CHD, studies have shown that aspirin therapy reduced the risk by 28 percent, although there are some risks associated with taking aspirin (Hayden et al., 2002). Major risks of aspirin therapy include bleeding inside the brain or gastrointestinal tract, and this treatment is not recommended for individuals with a low risk for CVD. It may be necessary to help restore the blood flow to the affected parts of the heart if the ischemias are serious or the disease continues to worsen despite measures to slow it down (sometimes because the person continues the unhealthy behaviors). In patients with critical conditions, surgery is often needed.

Surgery

There are two main forms of invasive surgery to deal with blockages: angioplasty and cardiac bypass surgery. **Angioplasty** is a procedure done to open a partially blocked blood vessel so that blood can flow through it more easily (Figure 13.7). It is most often done on arteries that deliver blood to the heart (coronary arteries) when they are narrowed by atherosclerosis. The procedure involves the insertion of a thin, flexible tube (catheter) through an artery in the groin or arm, which is carefully guided into the artery that is narrowed. This is not a comfortable procedure. Once the tube reaches the narrowed artery, a small balloon at the end of the tube is inflated. The balloon may remain inflated from 20 seconds to 3 minutes. The pressure from the inflated balloon pushes the plaque against the wall of the artery opening up the passageway to improve blood flow. Once the fat and calcium buildup is compressed, a small, expandable wire tube called a stent is sometimes inserted into the artery to keep it open.

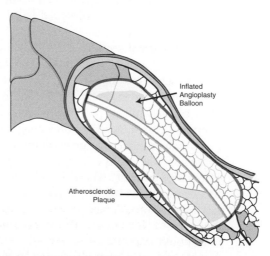

Inflated
Angioplasty
Balloon

Atherosclerotic
Plaque

FIGURE **13.7** Balloon Angioplasty

Another way to deal with the blockage is to just go around it. If you are driving to work, and you hear that there is a traffic jam ahead, you may take an alternative route. In the circulatory system there are few alternative routes for blood to take, so medical personnel create one. Cardiac bypass surgery involves taking a blood vessel from elsewhere in the body (usually the chest or leg) and using it to redirect blood flow around a severely blocked artery. Blood is redirected through the new blood vessel, bypassing the blocked artery and restoring blood flow to the affected portion of the heart muscle.

Behavioral Interventions

Most health psychological behavioral interventions for CVD take the form of cardiac rehabilitation programs (e.g., Gayda, Brun, Juneau, Levesque, & Nigam, 2008). These programs are hard to assess because they have many different components. If there is a change in risk, a decrease in mortality, or an increase in quality of life, any one of the components could have caused it (or even an interaction of several components). That said, meta-analytical studies have shown that rehabilitation programs in general have accounted for reductions in mortality compared with that for control groups (Fletcher, 1996). Programs building physical activity have been particularly effective (O'Conner et al., 1989).

Given the number of psychological factors involved in CVD, a number of interventions to reduce stress and negative emotions have also been tried, and the news is good (Koertge et al., 2008; Linden, Stossel, & Maurice, 1996; Rozanski et al., 1999). Linden et al. (1996) reviewed studies that collectively evaluated 2,024 patients who received psychosocial treatment versus 1,156 control subjects and found that the psychosocially treated patients showed greater reductions in psychological distress, systolic blood pressure, heart rate, and cholesterol level. Patients who did not receive psychosocial treatment were more likely to die earlier and had heart attacks reoccur during the first two years of follow up. The most common interventions attempted to modify personal characteristics such as hostility, stress, and social support.

One of the earliest and most ambitious interventions was conducted by Friedman et al. (1986). They observed 1,013 heart patients for 4½ years to determine whether their Type A behaviors could be altered. There were three experimental groups: a control section of 270 patients received group cardiac counseling, an experimental section of 592 patients received both group cardiac counseling and Type A behavioral counseling, and 151 patients served as a comparison group. The results were startling. At the end of the study, 35.1 percent of participants given cardiac and Type A behavior counseling reduced their Type A behavior compared with 9.8 percent of participants given only cardiac counseling, and the heart attack recurrence rate was only 12.9 percent. The recurrence rate in the control group was 21.2 percent, and the comparison group fared worse (recurrence rate of 28.2 percent). There was also a significant difference in the number of cardiac deaths between the experimental and control participants, clearly showing that altering Type A behavior reduces cardiac morbidity and mortality (Friedman et al., 1986). Given that the critical component of Type A behavior is hostility, you should expect that interventions designed specifically to reduce hostility should work even better (Friedman et al. 1996).

Diets low in carbohydrates have been shown to improve CVD risk factors.

Interventions to improve stress management and increase social support also reduce the effects of CVD (Cowan et al., 2008; Blumenthal et al., 2002a; Koertge, et al., 2008; Fischer et al., 2008). Blumenthal et al. (2002b) examined the effects of exercise and stress management training over a 5-year follow-up period in 94 male patients with established CVD. Patients either exercised (three times per week) or partook in a one and one-half-hour weekly class on stress management. Blumenthal et al. (2002b) found that stress management was associated with a significant reduction in heart attack episodes over each of the first two years of follow up and after five years. The stress management was even significantly cheaper than the exercise program.

Given the positive role played by a healthy diet (discussed previously), it is not surprising that many interventions focus on changing diets. The OmniHeart Trial compared three diets designed to reduce CVD risk (de Souza, Swain, Appel, & Sacks, 2008). One diet was high in carbohydrates. Two diets replaced carbohydrates with either unsaturated fat or protein. The lower carbohydrate diets improved the CVD risk factors.

SYNTHESIZE, EVALUATE, APPLY	• How would you make people more aware of the risks of smoking, bad eating, and not exercising in relation to CVD? • Design your optimal intervention to reduce risk for CVD. • Use the Health Belief Model and the transtheoretical model to design an intervention to reduce risks for CVD.

FOCUS ON APPLICATIONS

The Lifestyle Heart Trial

For many years, the first twangs of heart pains—evidence of atherosclerosis—and the eventual heart attack, signified the end of life. The prognosis was bad, and life would never be the same for the many thousand men and women who discovered that they had heart disease. Medical

(continues)

FOCUS ON APPLICATIONS *(continued)*

research had come up with ways to ease the pain and prolong life, but CHD was mostly seen to be a dead-end street—you venture down it and you will not be returning. Health psychologists helped engineer a number of interventions to help, for example, the Ischemic Heart Disease Life Stress Monitoring Program (Frasure-Smith & Prince, 1987) and the Recurrent Coronary Prevention Program (Friedman et al., 1986), but these were primarily designed to increase social support and decrease the stress of patients with CHD. Alleviation of suffering is a good thing, but could CHD actually be reversed? Dean Ornish surprised the health community by showing that it could.

Ornish et al. (1998) conducted one of the first multiple component interventions designed to change peoples' behaviors to reverse heart disease. Patients with CHD are especially susceptible to the effects of bad eating and insufficient exercise. If you can get people who have CHD to change these behaviors, will the physiological disease change as well? To test this, Ornish et al. randomly sampled 48 patients with moderate to severe CHD and randomly assigned them to one of two groups.

The 24 patients in the experimental group, an intensive lifestyle change group, were given special prescriptions of how to change their behaviors. As the name of the group implies, membership in this group was no walk in the park (although walks in the park were involved). This experimental group was told to severely restrict how much meat they ate and to switch to an essentially vegetarian diet. They were not to eat more than 10 percent fat (in contrast to the Atkins diet you may have heard a lot about that was discussed in Chapter 7). The rest of the diet was divided into 12 percent to 20 percent proteins and 70 percent to 75 percent carbohydrates, predominantly complex (meaning carbohydrates most often found in nuts and whole grains). All caffeine-containing beverages were eliminated, and alcohol consumption was discouraged. No animal products were allowed in the vegetarian diet except an egg white and one cup per day of nonfat milk or yogurt. Patients were also told to stop smoking (if they were smokers) and were helped with smoking cessation. Physical activity also had to be increased, and they were given a program of moderate levels of aerobic exercise to do. Each patient was told to exercise at least five times per week for a total of five hours. They could either walk or jog.

Together with these important health behaviors (nonsmoking, eating well, and getting physical activity), the Ornish program also aimed to reduce stress levels. We have discussed how emotional stress plays an important role in just about all illnesses. In CHD, stress makes arteries constrict and increases blood clot speed, both of which cause heart attacks. To make matters worse, stressed people are more likely to smoke, overeat, drink too much, and overwork. The Lifestyle trial included yoga exercises (primarily stretching), relaxation techniques involving breathing, meditation and mental imagery training, and social support groups. Patients in the control group were not asked to make lifestyle changes other than those recommended by their cardiologists (often similar though not in magnitude and not backed up by trained professionals with follow ups).

The results were astounding. After one year, patients in the experimental group showed a significant overall reduction of coronary atherosclerosis as measured by X-rays of heart blood vessels injected with radioactive chemicals (coronary angiography). The arteries went from being 40.0 percent blocked (stenosis) to 37.8 percent in the experimental group, but blockages increased from 42.7 percent to 46.1 percent in the control group. Overall, 82 percent of experimental patients experienced reduced blockages. The experimental group was able to make and maintain the lifestyle changes and also showed a 37 percent reduction in low-density lipoprotein level and a 91 percent reduction in cardiac problems. The control group showed a 165 percent increase in cardiac problems. Given that the control group was not doing as well, you would be right in wondering if it was ethical for the experiment to continue. The researchers did not explicitly address this, but one can assume that time period was a critical component in the intervention.

Was this a fluke? As good scientists should, Ornish et al. extended the study to confirm the findings and see if they persisted. One concern was that the lifestyle change was too drastic and would be difficult to maintain. Skip ahead four years. When assessing the health and behaviors of the original sample five years from the start of the original study, Ornish et al. (1998) found there was even more reduction and continued improvement. In the experimental

(continues)

FOCUS ON APPLICATIONS (continued)

group, the average percent diameter stenosis was 7.9 percent relative improvement after five years. In contrast, the average percent diameter stenosis in the control group was 27.7 percent relative worsening after five years. Twenty-five cardiac events occurred in the experimental group versus 45 events in the control group during the 5-year follow up. Even better, the people in the lifestyle change group showed better results than the people in the control group who were taking fat-lowering medications (none of the experimental group was taking any).

Similar positive effects of lifestyle change have also been shown in the Nurses' Health Study that followed 85,941 healthy women from 1980 to 1994. The women who did not smoke, were a healthy weight, ate well, and got sufficient physical activity had an 83 percent less risk of a heart attack (Stampfer et al., 2000). Other studies also varied dietary intake or increased exercise with similar results.

It is undoubtedly difficult to live a healthy life, and it definitely takes a lot of willpower and help to keep to a healthy regimen such as the one prescribed by the Lifestyle Heart Trial, but the results are clear. Not only can healthy behaviors keep heart disease from worsening, they can actually reverse it as well. Given that some people may not be able to tolerate lipid-lowering drugs, the fact that participants in this study showed improvement without the drugs is extremely important. It may be that the extremely rigorous levels of change are not needed, but why take a chance on your health? Be well aware of your behaviors and don't forget how many different benefits eating well, not smoking, and being physically active can have.

This is a wonderful example of how health behaviors can be changed to reverse heart disease, but there are a few caveats. It can be argued that these findings cannot easily be generalized to the population at large because the participants of Ornish et al. were highly motivated and compliant, both important attributes for a demanding intervention. Nevertheless, the point they make is clear: What you do with your lifestyle will determine how long you will live.

SUMMARY

- Cardiovascular diseases result from problems with the heart and the circulatory system. The most common are coronary heart disease or cardiovascular disease (CVD), heart failure, strokes, and high blood pressure or hypertension. Others include abnormal heart rhythms, pulmonary heart disease, and diseases of veins, arteries, and lymph nodes.

- American Indians show the lowest instances of deaths due to coronary heart disease followed by Asian Americans and Latinos. In contrast, all non-European ethnic groups have a higher risk for strokes. Anger, competitiveness, and time urgency are some of the main psychological differences among ethnic groups that could account for the differences in CVD.

- The accumulation of wear and tear on the circulatory system as we age accounts for significant developmental differences in the incidence of CVD. Social support networks also change as we age although the exact relationship is still unclear.

- The accumulation of fatty substances in the blood vessels and the thickening of the arteries are the most common precursors to CVD. The main physiological risk factors are age, sex, family history, obesity, diabetes, hypertension, high cholesterol levels, and inactivity. The main psychological predictors of CVD are stress, hostility, negative emotions, depression, and low social support.

- Changing unhealthy lifestyles is critical to preventing and treating CVD. Patients normally join cardiac rehabilitation programs to reduce stress and improve health behaviors such as quitting smoking, increasing physical activity, and eating better. Patients with severe CVD may need surgery, ranging from angioplasty to open blocked blood vessels to cardiac bypass surgery in which blood flow is redirected around blocked areas.

- Behavioral interventions such as the program of Dean Ornish and colleagues and those conducted by Friedman and colleagues demonstrate that CVD is reversible.

TEST YOURSELF

Check your understanding of the topics in this chapter by answering the following questions. Answers appear in the Appendix.

1. The largest percent of deaths from cardiovascular disease is due to:
   a. Coronary heart disease.
   b. Stroke.
   c. Congestive heart failure.
   d. High blood pressure.
2. One major source of information on the course and development of heart disease is the:
   a. Alameda County study.
   b. Berkeley Study.
   c. Framingham Study.
   d. MacArthur Study.
3. Heart-related diseases are more common in:
   a. Older men.
   b. Older women.
   c. Young adults.
   d. Infants.
4. The ethnic group with the lowest number of deaths due to coronary heart disease is:
   a. European Americans.
   b. Asian Americans.
   c. American Indians.
   d. Latinos.
5. A culture that is high in _____ is more likely to have stress-related heart problems.
   a. Collectivism
   b. Individualism
   c. Fluid time
   d. Constraint
6. Having high levels of _____ is one of the most important personality risk factors for CVD.
   a. Optimism.
   b. Time urgency.

c. Hostility.
d. Neuroticism.

7. The primary physiological precursor of CVD is:
   a. Stress.
   b. Phagocytosis.
   c. Angina pectoris.
   d. Atherosclerosis.
8. Certain cultural groups have greater genetic predispositions for CVD than others. _____, for example, show higher blood pressure reactivity to stressful tasks.
   a. European Americans
   b. American Indians
   c. African Americans
   d. Asian Americans
9. The number one behavior to avoid to minimize the risks for cardiovascular disease is:
   a. Bad eating.
   b. Smoking.
   c. Excessive drinking.
   d. Insufficient sleep.
10. The best diet to keep CVD at bay appears to be the:
    a. Atkins diet.
    b. South Beach diet.
    c. Indo-Mediterranean diet.
    d. Zone diet.

WEB RESOURCES

Visit the companion Web site at **www.cengage.com/psychology/gurung,** where you will find online resources for this book, including chapter-by-chapter quizzes, Web links, and more!

American Heart Association
www.americanheart.org

> This site is a key resource for those interested in heart disease and treatments. It is written to be understandable by those without medical or technical knowledge.

American Stroke Association
www.strokeassociation.org

> Similar to the AHA site above, this is a good site to learn about the incidence and treatment of stroke.

American Heart Association: Women and Cardiovascular Disease
http://www.americanheart.org/presenter.jhtml?identifier=1200011

This is asite that focuses on women and cardiovascular disease.

National Institute of Neurological Disorders and Stroke
http://www.ninds.nih.gov

> This is a good review of ongoing research in the field.

Test Your Knowledge about Cardiovascular Disease
http://www.healthsystem.virginia.edu/assets/UVAHealth/ssi/includes/wmhrtqiz.html

> Here you can find out how much you know about CVD and facts that could help you identify symptoms.

KEY TERMS, CONCEPTS, AND PEOPLE

affect cultures, 413

angina pectoris, 423

angioplasty, 425

arteriosclerosis, 415

atherosclerosis, 412

C-reactive protein, 413

cardiac rehabilitation program, 424

cardiovascular disease, 408

cardiovascular reactivity, 416

control versus constraint, 413

coronary heart disease (CHD), 408

fluid time versus fixed time, 412

Framingham heart study, 408

hypertension, 410

Indo-Mediterranean diet, 423

ischemias, 424

Lifestyle heart trial, 427

myocardial infarctions, 423

neutral cultures, 413

Ornish, Dean, 428

stroke, 410

ESSENTIAL READINGS

Baker, B., Richter, A., & Anand, S. S. (2001). From the heartland: Culture, psychological factors, and coronary heart disease. In S. S. Kazarian & D. R. Evans (Eds.). *Handbook of cultural health psychology* (pp. 141–162). San Diego, CA: Academic Press.

Linden, W., Stossel, C., & Maurice, J. (1996). Psychosocial interventions for patients with coronary artery disease: A meta-analysis. *Archives of Internal Medicine, 156*(7), 745–752.

Ornish, D., Scherwitz, L. W., Billings, J. H., Gould, K. L., Merritt, T. A., Sparler, S., et al. (1998). Intensive lifestyle changes for reversal of coronary heart disease. *Journal of the American Medical Association, 280*(23), 2001–2007.

Smith, T. W., & Ruiz, J. M. (2002). Psychosocial influences on the development and course of coronary heart disease: Current status and implications for research and practice. *Journal of Consulting & Clinical Psychology, 70*(3), 548–568.

The Future of Health Psychology

You may have heard people say, "don't miss the forest for the trees," referring to how we often miss the big picture when we focus too much on the small details. Hopefully by this point of the book, you have a very good sense of the many species of "trees" there are in the "forest" that is health psychology. This is a good time to step back and look at some of the bigger issues. We can actually take the forest analogy a long way. The field of health psychology is so vibrant, exciting, and sometimes wild (there are areas that still need a lot of cultivation), an invitation to learn more about it is akin to saying "welcome to the jungle." Like a forest, some areas of health psychology, such as stress and coping, are the old oaks that have been studied for many years. Other areas such as psychoneuroimmunology are the young saplings, new and still growing. Different parts of the forest can be used for many different purposes: the basic research in health psychology can be applied in many different ways and translated into interventions and programs that can be life saving as well as increase the quality of life. There are also areas of the forest that are enjoyable to be in, such as joining a team studying **positive psychology**— research findings that help us understand complex psychosocial issues and alleviate the pain and suffering of those with chronic illnesses. Some parts of the forest are dark and uninviting, the areas of health psychology that are rife with ethical concerns and difficult implications such as genetic testing and the design of some interventions or suggestions for policy change that may be perceived as compromising individual freedoms. There are also many areas of the forest yet to be discovered. What's next for the field of health psychology? What are the opportunities available for you as a burgeoning health psychologist?

LOOKING TO THE FUTURE

Health psychology has come a long way. In Chapter 1, we sketched the history of health psychology and the different organizations that cater to people using the health psychological approach. The Division of Health Psychology (**Division 38**) of the American Psychological Association (APA) recently celebrated 25 years of existence. The Society for Behavioral Medicine and the American Psychosomatic Society are even older (founded in 1978 and 1942, respectively). Times are changing, and the awareness of the role of psychology in health and well-being has become explicit and prominent. Even the APA modified its mission statement to include the advancement of psychology as a "means for promoting health, education, and human welfare" (APA, 2004).

You know an area of study has come a long way when there are published articles and special conferences designed to take stock of the field and set the agenda for its future growth. This has been the case for health psychology. In 2000, Kenneth Wallston and Janet Kiecolt-Glaser, the past President and the President of Division 38, presided over a conference to examine the state of the field. The proceedings of the conference resulted in many researchers taking a critical look at what health psychologists have achieved and what critical issues needed to be addressed. The results of this directed focus was a special issue of *Health Psychology* (Smith & Suls, 2004). Just a little before that, the *Journal of Consulting and Clinical Psychology* (Smith, Kendall, & Keefe, 2002) published a special issue on behavioral medicine and clinical health psychology that also gives us a good sense of what the important issues for the field are. In the first edition of this book, I had a chance to lay out some key issues as well (Gurung, 2006). As we contemplate the second decade of the millennium, let's take a look at where health psychology is going (and may need to go).

A Greater Focus on Sociocultural Issues and Health Disparities

This book was written with the explicit goal of increasing awareness of sociocultural issues. In looking back over the different chapters, you may have noticed that some chapters included a lot more "culture" in them than others. You may have thought we had swayed off course in the chapters without too much culture, but that's not so. The shortage of information on culture in some areas mirrors a sad lack of information of cultural differences in some areas of health psychology (Keefe, Buffington, Studts, & Ramble, 2002; Rüdell, & Diefenbach, 2008). To be fair, cultural research is not always easy to do and there are many barriers. Often language barriers necessitate the hiring of translators or bilingual researchers. English questionnaires have to be translated into the different languages and then translated back into English to establish reliability and validity. Many non-White ethnic groups are wary of White researchers and non-Christian individuals are often hesitant to share spiritual or folk medicinal practices. An examination of articles and books in the field show that *culture* and *health psychology* have not been common key words (Kazarian & Evans, 2001), and even reviews of *Health Psychology* (the journal) have shown a limited number of articles on culture and health (Landrine & Klonoff, 1992; Klonoff & Landrine, 2001), although the numbers are increasing.

One of the most pressing needs for health psychology is to spend more time and energy on examining how cultural differences influence health and behavior. A number of health psychologists have drawn attention to this problem (Eshun & Gurung, 2009; Kazarian & Evans, 2001; Landrine & Klonoff, 2001; Rüdell, & Diefenbach, 2008; Smith & Suls, 2004; Yali & Revenson, 2004). Many groups in addition to Division 38 are recognizing the need for a greater focus on culture. In 1995 a special issue of the *Journal of Behavioral Medicine* included the recommendations of the eight task groups of the National Conference on Behavioral and Sociocultural Perspectives on Ethnicity and Health that called for "future research, research funding and research training relevant to sociocultural and behavioral perspectives on ethnicity and health" (Anderson, 1995, p. 649). Similarly, Krantz (1995), in an editorial for *Health Psychology*, strongly encouraged the inclusion of women and minority groups in research.

There is a strong emphasis for academic curricula to be culturally diverse (Gurung & Prieto, 2009), so why has there not been enough cultural research? The limited focus on cultural differences arises from a number of different factors. One reason is that the majority of theories used by health psychologists were developed within other areas of psychology (Marks, 1996). Mainstream psychology has tended to be blind to culture, not so much because of some explicit prejudice (although it has been argued that the primarily European American male researchers were biased, Guthrie, 2003), but because of the belief that there are commonalities to human behavior that transcend culture. Early health psychological research also strove for depth versus breath, something necessary for a new field to establish itself (Kazarian & Evans, 2001). Furthermore, the field has had a tendency to focus on individuals out of context. Conceivably a function of the individualistic bias of mainstream psychology, health psychology has only recently begun to consider the theoretical implications of a focus on the collective context—the family, peers, community, and culture, of the individual.

In a move toward a greater focus on culture, certain key problems need to be avoided. There still appears to be a considerable amount of ambiguity surrounding the use of race and ethnicity in health research (Kazarian & Evans, 2001). For example, Williams (1995) identified 10 different terms used to refer to the concept of ethnicity (e.g., color, race or origin, racial and ethnic minority groups, minority status). Race and ethnicity are often used interchangeably (see Chapter 1 for why this is a problem). Many different cultural groups are often subsumed under single categories with little recognition of inherent differences (Phinney, 1996). For example, there are many different Asian Americans and Japanese Americans and East Indian Americans who will not necessarily behave in the same way or have the same beliefs regarding health (see Chapter 2).

Other problems relate to how culture is presently used. Most often ethnicity or race is used as a grouping variable in statistical analyses. As Wyatt (1994) has noted, large epidemiological studies often use traditional **grouping variables,** such as race, in studies of health and disease. Because ethnicity and socioeconomic status are correlated, when economic status is controlled, ethnic group comparisons sometimes suggest a high level of similarity (Murray, 1992; Zuckerman, 1990). Yet, the results of recent research (Gurung, Taylor, Kemeny, & Myers, 2004; Gurung, Dunkel-Shetter, Collins, Rini, & Hobel, 2005) suggest that controlling for ethnicity may obscure important group differences. For example, in analyses of changes in depression, Gurung et al. (2004) found that chronic burdens of African American women (when analyzed alone) predicted their depression over time, but when ethnicity was included as a control variable in analyses on the entire sample, it was not significantly related to depression. The separate analyses by ethnicity highlighted the fact that the African American women are vulnerable to socioeconomic status-related stressors (especially not having enough money to cover basic needs of life). Additionally, using social support to cope was not a significant variable when the entire sample was used but was significant for African American women. Likewise, optimism was not a significant predictor of

© Digital Vision/Getty Images

Health Varies Across Cultural Groups

These two women, who may lead very similar lives, could have very dissimilar health needs based simply on their differing ethnicities.

changes in depression for the entire sample but was significant for the Latina sample. Findings like these, which are obscured in overall analyses controlling for race, have important implications for understanding the particular circumstances that may be faced by different ethnic groups.

Why is this problem in urgent need of rectification? Now more than ever, health psychologists need to focus on cultural differences. As described in Chapter 1, North America today looks very different from the North America of even 20 years ago. The population is rapidly becoming more ethnically diverse and older. With major changes in population demographics come major changes in patterns of health (Whitfied, Weidner, Clark, & Anderson, 2002; Yali & Revenson, 2004). There is a sizeable amount of research already providing some answers (as the many chapters in this book bear testimony to), but much more is needed.

Related to a focus on sociocultural issues is the focus on health disparities. A major premise of this book has been that health varies across cultural groups. You have also been exposed to a lot of evidence of differences in health behaviors between different cultural groups. **Health disparities** are "differences in health that are not only unnecessary and avoidable, but in addition, are considered unfair and unjust" (Whitehead, 1992, p. 433). There are many examples of disparities: the infant death rate among African Americans is still more than double that of European Americans, heart disease death rates are more than 40 percent higher for African Americans than for European Americans (Healthy People 2010). In general, health care and disease incidence (e.g., tuberculosis) rates also vary significantly across ethnic groups as shown in Figures 14.1 and 14.2.

The fact that there are differences in health behaviors and health in general has not escaped the notice of the government, funding agencies, or health

Generally speaking, how often do you think our health care system treats people unfairly based on ...

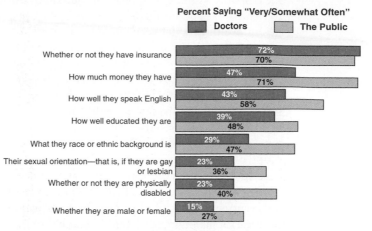

FIGURE **14.1** Disparities in Health Care System

Source: Kaiser Family Foundation, *National Survey of Physicians*, March 2002 (conducted March–October 2001). Kaiser Family Foundation, *Survey of Race, Ethnicity and Medical Care: Public Perceptions and Experiences*, October 1999 (Conducted July–Sept. 1999).

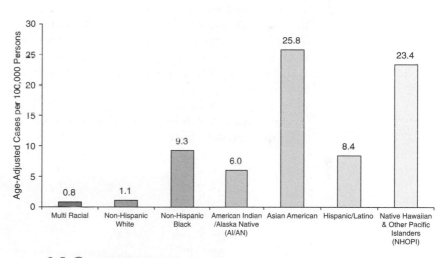

FIGURE **14.2** Age-Adjusted Case Rates Per 100,000 Persons by Race/ Ethnicity for Tuberculosis (TB): U.S., 2007

Source: CDC, MMWR, March 21, 2008/57(11), Trends in TB, US, 2007, Table: **http://www.cdc.gov/mmwr/ preview/mmwrhtml/mm5711a2.htm.**

psychology researchers (the latter can do research to better the support of the first two). In fact the Healthy People 2010 project (U.S. Department of Health and Human Services, 2008) described in Chapter 1, has eliminating health disparities as one of its two overarching goals (the other is increasing the number and quality of years of life). In parallel, the American Psychological

Association has also worked hard toward "… the elimination of racial and ethnic disparities in health access and outcomes through an increased commitment to behavioral and biomedical research, improved data systems, culturally competent health care delivery, and efforts to increase public awareness of the existence of health disparities and the resources that are available to improve minority health outcomes" (American Psychological Association, 2008). APA's Division 38 (Health Psychology) has a committee on Health Disparities that has developed a "Health Disparities webpage." The Health Disparities webpage introduces the key issues in health disparities research and provides resources to further aid research into this topic. As described on the division's Web page, the "overarching goals are to advance the understanding of 1) the nature and scope of health disparities and 2) the scientific study of health disparities, from description to intervention" (**http://www.health-psych.org/health_disparities/home.php**). Research specifically aimed to reduce health disparities, including interventions to reach out to negatively influenced parties is underway and holds promise for major improvements (Health disparities webpage removed Dec. 2008).

A Focus on Developmental Issues and the Lifespan

Older adults are the largest consumers of health care, and the number of older adults is increasing every year. As the population grows older and life expectancy increases, it becomes even more important to identify and change the behaviors that increase the incidence of chronic illnesses of middle and later adulthood (Siegler, Bastian, Steffens, Bosworth, & Costa, 2002; Smith et al., 2002; Spiro, 2007). Increased longevity affects men and women differently. Women tend to live longer, and this has its own unique implications. For example, there will be a large number of older women living with chronic but not life-threatening illnesses (e.g., arthritis). Ways to manage pain and stress are going to be especially important (Keefe et al., 2002; Spiro, 2007).

For each of the major chronic illnesses described in the preceding chapters, but especially for cancer and coronary heart disease, age is one of the

© Digital Vision/Getty Images

As the large generation known as the baby boomers moves into their senior citizen years, it becomes even more important for us to understand the health impacts of living a longer life. One of the best job opportunities is going to be in gerontology working with older adults.

biggest predictors of incidence. There are clear age-related increases in incidence for each. Research on the determinants of health behaviors among older adults will become even more important to complement similar research being conducted on younger age groups (Smith, Orleans, & Jenkins, 2004). The illnesses that manifest in adulthood often start to develop early in the lifespan and are accelerated by risky health behaviors (again more prominent in younger age groups). A developmental context is critical for a thorough understanding of chronic diseases (Berg, Smith, Henry, & Pearce, 2007; Williams, Holmbeck, & Greenley, 2002).

There are already large collections of research literature on aging and lifespan development and different parts of the life cycle are receiving specific attention. For example, adolescence is a pivotal period of development in respect to health and illness because this is the time that healthy behaviors are consolidated and unhealthy behaviors first become evident (Williams et al., 2002). Additionally, nearly 20 percent of adolescents have chronic physical conditions that will call for approaches to treatment that are different from those used with adults (Gortmaker, 1985). On the other end of the spectrum, older adults have unique needs and problems as well. Decreases in physical mobility and cognitive ability together with increases in pain severely influence the quality of life of the aging population (Siegler, Bastian, Steffens, Bosworth, & Costa, 2002). A key future direction for health psychology is to pay more attention to these different collections of literature as optimal approaches to behavior change will obviously vary across the lifespan (Wilcox & King, 1999).

A Focus on the Evidence

The field of medicine has for some time worked hard on translating research findings into evidence-based assessments and treatments—Evidence-Based Medicine. The field of psychology has similarly taken steps to join research with practice (Kazdin, 2008). Evidence-Based Behavioral Medicine is an extension of the Evidence-Based Medicine movement that identified the necessity of critically evaluating research to inform clinical practice (Rosenberg & Donald, 1995). In 2006, the flagship journal of APA's division 38 *Health Psychology*, launched a new series of articles titled "Evidence-Based Treatment Reviews." The initiators surmised that in addition to mentoring researchers in presenting their findings in a more user-friendly style (e.g., Consolidated Standards of Reporting Trials, or CONSORT, guidelines), teaching clinicians how to review the evidence (e.g., Evidence-Based Medicine Tool Kit), and compiling and summarizing the existing evidence for public consumption (e.g., the Cochrane Collaboration), it made sense to integrate these efforts by presenting research reviews with clinician commentary (Davidson, Trudeau, & Smith, 2006). Three to four evidence-based reviews are published per year in *Health Psychology* and each review is accompanied by a three- or four-page commentary by a clinical psychologist to aid in the application of the research to clinical practice (e.g., Thorn, Cross, & Walker, 2007). This new focus on the evidence to guide treatment makes good sense and promises to shape research agendas in the field as well.

Fine-Tuning the Biopsychosocial Model

By now you should be comfortable with the main health psychological approach, the biopsychosocial model (Matarazzo, 1980). Since its inception in the late 1970s, the biopsychosocial model has served as a guiding principle and has fueled dramatic advances in health psychological research (Boyer, 2008; Suls & Rothman, 2004). Clearly a useful and accurate model, it has been supported by a variety of research (Anderson 2002; Boyer, 2008; Niaura & Abrams, 2002; Smith & Ruiz, 2002). The success of the approach can also be seen in the number of organizations that serve and collect researchers and practitioners from biological and psychological perspectives and the increase in governmental support for health-related behavioral and psychological research. However, there is still a way to go.

Suls and Rothman (2004) calculated the frequency of citations of *biopsychosocial* in Medline (the database for medical science) and specifically in major medical journals such as *The New England Journal of Medicine* and *The Journal of the American Medical Association* (JAMA) and found that citations constituted only a small proportion of the absolute number. Even within health psychology, Suls and Rothman (2004) reported that although the *bio* and *psycho* components of the model are well represented, the *social* component is the least measured. Furthermore, assessments of people's social environments focused on subjective experiences of their relationships, or social information was restricted to demographic data and only used to describe the sample (and not as variables in the study). To fully capitalize on the strengths of a multidimensional approach, it is critical for health psychologists to pay more attention to the links between the different subsystems and improve the data collected to assess each subsystem. This may mean collecting physiological, self-report, and sociological data, possibly over a long period of time. There is a clear need to work toward greater applications of the biopsychosocial model and move it from the theoretical realm into a more practical one, while also ensuring that practice informs research and both (practice and research) inform policy changes (Keefe et al., 2002).

Still, there has been some development toward using a biopsychosocial approach on a large scale. Two new national evidence-based medical treatment guidelines, ODG (Official Disability Guidelines), and the ACOEM (American College of Occupational and Environmental Medicine), adopt a biopsychosocial treatment model, and recommend (and sometimes even REQUIRE) psychological evaluations for patients who need spinal surgery or who have chronic pain. Remarkably, some states have already passed legislation that give these guidelines legal status as medical regulations for work compensation, and other states are considering doing so. These guidelines are the first instances where biopsychosocial medical treatment guidelines have been developed with adherence to evidence-based medicine principles, reviewed by multiple medical societies and enacted into law (Bruns, 2008, personal communication). The point of these guidelines is to provide for good care while controlling costs by not spending money on treatments that don't work, and reducing controversy and litigation by setting a reasonable standard of care. These documents also illustrate how psychology is an integral pert of the medical treatment process, and address matters ranging from how many psych tests should be given to the business relationship between psychologists and physicians.

A Multidimensional Approach

Another aspect of fine-tuning the biopsychosocial model comes from the recognition and need for **multidimensional approaches** and more collaborative research. When you do try to include a consideration of biological, psychological, and societal processes you are automatically talking about different levels of measurement, different research methods, and different statistical analyses. No matter which illness you choose to study, you can see that many different bodily systems are involved and often more than one health behavior can influence the incidence or progression of the disease. Coronary heart disease, for example, can be influenced by what you eat and drink and whether you smoke or not. Your levels of physical activity can also influence it. Each of these health behaviors can vary based on the sociocultural environment the person lives in as well as with biological factors such as metabolic rates and family histories. Stress can also play a role in the development of heart disease, so now you have the interaction between your nervous system (stress) and circulatory system (heart disease) together with many other factors.

To complicate matters even more, some variables such as culture can play multiple roles within an investigation (Kelty, Hoffman, Ory, & Harden, 2000; Penn et al., 2000; Yali & Revenson, 2004). For example, a certain ethnic group may have biological predispositions for a certain illness (a biological component), and they may also experience more stress from prejudice or discrimination (a psychological component), but they may also have stronger social networks (a social component). Consequently, the researcher has to balance multiple systems, variables, and levels. One individual is rarely trained in all the necessary areas, hence it is important for researchers with different areas of expertise to collaborate. Each person contributes a different part of the puzzle so that the big picture can be made clearer. The complexity of the challenge can also be made more manageable with better tools. Fortunately, there have also been a number of methodological and technological innovations that are now available for health psychologists.

Technical Innovations

Medicine and health technology have been advancing at a rapid pace. We now have a good idea of constituents of the human genome, and techniques for the assessment of biological states and processes are giving us insights we could never have imagined possible. There are correspondingly a variety of implications of such advances for health psychology (Keefe et al., 2002; Saab et al., 2004).

The biggest area of innovation is in an area referred to as **behavioral telehealth** (Dellifraine, & Dansky, 2008; PausJenssen, Spooner, Wilson, & Wilson, 2008; Jerome et al., 2000; King et al., 2007; Suleiman, 2001; Whitten, Kingsley, Cook, Swirczynski, & Doolittle, 2001) in which health care is delivered over the telephone or through other technical means such as the Internet. Although it means no or little face-to-face contact with a health care provider,

Some doctors now give patients health information via online health websites, chat rooms, or even personalized emails.

it still allows individuals in remote locations a means to receive treatment. Procedures currently used include online treatment for weight management, pain relief, and smoking cessation, self-help chat rooms for cancer, assessments, strategies to increase adherence, and consultation services (Saab et al., 2004). Are these methods as effective as face-to-face contact? One study showed that an intervention to increase physical activity in older adults was as effective if delivered with the use of an automated telephone system versus by a trained human being (King et al., 2007). A range of another line of research shows that computerized decision support can be a significant help to patients making complex treatment decisions (Barnato et al., 2007; Col, Ngo, Fortin, Goldberg, & O'Connor, 2007; O'Connor et al., 2007). Further research is currently under way to assess this question.

An associated issue for health psychologists to be aware of is people's use of the Internet to get health information (Dart, 2008). If someone experiences a certain symptom or seems to be developing a certain illness, he or she can log onto the Internet and using sites such as WebMD, get a good idea of what he or she may (or may not) have. Parents are especially likely to also reach out to the internet when their kids show signs of sickness (Khoo, Bolt, Babl, Jury, & Goldman, 2008). There are some important cultural differences here too. Research shows that Latinos do not use the internet for health information as much as non-Latino European Americans (Peña-Purcell, 2008). Furthermore, Latinos have been found to view the internet as damaging to physician-patient relationships. Internet use has also been suggested as a plausible mediator of the relationship between SES and subjective health (Wangberg, Andreassen, Prokosch, Santana, Sørensen, & Chronaki, 2008).

Still, health care providers and health management organizations (HMOs) are setting up sites where members can access personalized health information before even seeing their primary care providers. This situation can be good and bad. The benefits are that patients can be forewarned and maybe learn enough to reduce treatment-seeking delays. The problem is that the same information can also increase some delays (see Chapter 8) because it may increase anxiety. Furthermore, not all health-related Web sites have reliable information.

And there are many sites too: it took my computer 0.12 seconds to come up with **135,000,000** sites that mention "health information." Inaccurate or misleading information can pose a risk by also undermining confidence in a provider's recommendations (Robinson, Patrick, Eng, & Gustafson, 1998). That said, studies of patient satisfaction show that up to 95 percent of the respondents who had used the Internet for health information rated such information between average to excellent (Ayantunde, Welch, & Parsons, 2007). More and more adults are looking online for health care information (see Figure 14.3).

The Internet can also greatly expand research opportunities and increase accessibility to personal medical information. Researchers can now conduct major surveys online with very little associated time or money, and large databases can be made available to research collaborations (more on this later). Even patients are going to have more control over their health information. The Health Insurance Portability and Accountability Act (HIPAA) that took effect in 2003 includes regulations that allow patients to examine their computerized medical records to correct mistakes and seek action against misuse of their records.

Two advances in medical science have direct implications for the work of health psychologists. First, living organ and tissue transplants are getting more and more common and more effective in treating diseases (Niklason & Langer, 2001; Shafer et al., 2008). Are you willing to be an organ donor? Would you give up your organs if you died (do you have an organ donor sticker on your driver's license)? There are many psychosocial factors that predict the answer to that question. In some cultures it may not be appropriate to donate organs or touch the deceased. Some individuals are not aware of the factors surrounding donations. Correspondingly, the aim of a body of psychological research is to identify transplant candidates and help people make donation decisions (Olbrisch, Benedict, Ashe, & Levenson, 2002). Second, more and more individuals now have access to genetic tests that can inform them of possible risks for chronic illnesses such as cancer. In the future, testing for risk may be as common as getting a cholesterol test, but it has a lot more implications (Collins &

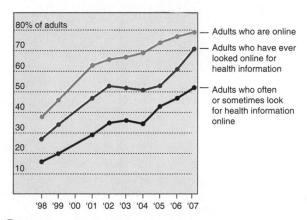

FIGURE **14.3** Looking for Answers

Note: Results are from a Harris Poll of 1,010 United States adults surveyed by telephone by Harris Interactive from July 10 and 16, 2007.
Source: *Harris Interactive*

McKusick, 2001). A high cholesterol level is not as anxiety provoking as finding out you have a high risk for cancer. What are the psychosocial consequences of being able to know? Consequently, health psychologists need to better understand the individual differences surrounding coping with the results of genetic testing (Ledbetter, & Faucett, 2008; Saab et al., 2004).

Interventions

It is clear that psychosocial interventions are valuable additions to traditional health care (Baban, & Craciun, 2007; Eldred, & Sykes, 2008; Leventhal, Weinman, Leventhal, & Phillips, 2008; Meyerowitz & Kerns, 2004; Smith et al., 2002; Smith et al., 2004; Wilfley et al., 2008). The good news is risky behaviors can be changed, and the large number of psychological and economical gains of using psychology to prevent illness and slow down the progression of illness means competition between health psychological interventions and medical treatments for attention and research funding. The development of both forms of interventions, preventative and those that restrict progression, now need more focused attention. It is becoming more important to be able to evaluate the clinical significance of each intervention (Kendall, 1999), and there is greater consideration of the associated costs (Kaplan & Groessl, 2002; Tovian, 2004).

In keeping with the refining of the biopsychosocial model, the design of interventions must also integrate interdisciplinary approaches and include different levels of analysis (Nicassio et al., 2004). Determinants of health behaviors, often the primary targets of interventions, range from biological processes and individual level processes to family and small-group processes as well as larger community and societal factors. A more comprehensive approach to interventions will be one that has at least four different dimensions: (1) recognition of the time course of the disease, including the stage of disease risk, disease development, and health outcome; (2) different levels of analysis; (3) consideration of cultural differences, and (4) a focus on risk and health threat across the life span (Nicassio et al., 2004; Smith et al., 2004). Already, interventions explicitly designed for women, the elderly, and minority groups have been implemented (Antoni et al., 2001; Lichstein, Riedel, Wilson, Lester, & Aguillard, 2001; Martin, Young, Billings, & Bross, 2007). Even more are needed.

There are also barriers that prevent interventions from reaching the clinical populations for whom they have been designed. Nicassio et al. (2004) suggested that the key barriers to be overcome are (1) researchers not always understanding the clinical applicability of their basic research; (2) a reluctance of clinicians to accept the value of basic research-driven interventions; and (3) various institutional-level constraints such as lack of time, training, or funding. The empirical evidence for the effectiveness of psychological interventions is strong; now the task is to disseminate the findings more and reach out to more people who need them.

Enhanced Training

Training in the areas of cultural competency and awareness of lifespan issues will also have to be enhanced (Gurung & Prieto, 2009). As discussed earlier, these are two critical areas for health psychologists to be cognizant of. Henderson and Springer-Littles (1996) have indicated that therapists often graduate ill prepared for their role within a culturally diverse society and could consequently do great harm. The same can be said of health psychologists. To keep up with the increasing diversification of the United States, health psychologists are going to need to be informed and aware of not only lifespan development issues (due to the aging population), but also culturally appropriate research methods (Smith & Suls, 2004). Present training programs give trainees very limited exposure to these two very important areas but, as with this book, the awareness and inclusion of these areas are growing.

Of course, sometimes it is not possible to train someone in all the needed areas of expertise to best use the biopsychosocial model. Most medical programs and psychological programs are already busy enough. Just getting through medical school or psychology graduate school can be very demanding. Where do you fit in developmental and cultural information? Where can you fit in the statistical training that is needed for dealing with complex multivariable data sets? The answer again is collaboration. Although postdoctoral training and special practicum experiences can give individuals exposure to the different areas needed for a comprehensive study of illness, it is more productive to have different researchers working together, each sharing their experience. Unfortunately, only a few existing programs provide the necessary training to facilitate the development of health collaborations (Suls & Rothman, 2004), and this is another key training area for the field to incorporate.

It is also going to be important for health psychologists to be able to spread the word about the effectiveness of a biopsychosocial approach. Health psychological content needs to make its way into the curricula of related areas such as medicine, public health, and health education. Even the public needs to be made more aware of the rich findings from the field.

To ensure that there is adequate funding for the continuing advancement of health psychological research, time and effort need to be allocated to the education of policymakers. This could lead to increased support for health psychological training and research. Some governmental changes are already under way, as you shall see in the next section.

RELATED DEVELOPMENTS

Mirroring the innovations and advancements within the field of health psychology, many different changes are taking place on national and international levels that will influence the health psychological agenda. On the national front, the National Institutes of Health (NIH) began a new initiative (first introduced in 2003) to speed up the process of improving public health. Director Zerhouni, together with more than 300 scientists, government and business representatives, and feedback from the public, mapped out a path of scientific discovery. In keeping with the need for multilevel investigations described above, the key goal of this initiative was to give scientists new ways to perform molecular-level research and translate the results from the same into clinical applications. Known as the **NIH Roadmap**, the plan sketches out 28 cross-institutional projects especially designed to tackle multifaceted issues such as obesity, which result from a variety of different biopsychosocial factors. The plan includes the creation of "molecular libraries"—publicly accessible databases documenting the properties and functions of minute organic compounds that can help the design of behavioral research conducted at the molecular level. The plan also includes the creation of a **National Electronic Clinical Trials and Research (NECTAR)** network, which will make the results of clinical trials easy to find and utilize. Because studies involving physiological measurement are expensive and time-consuming and require trained personnel, this sharing of data will reduce duplication among researchers and facilitate greater collaboration. These two collections of information will undoubtedly also speed up the rate of health psychological research. One more thing is needed—money helps the world go around, not to mention that it makes major studies possible. The NIH Roadmap also includes an incentive for researchers to collaborate: Directors of various suborganizations at NIH (e.g., the National Institute on Aging) are committed to funding more collaborative research.

Another form of collaboration is important: the collaboration between mind and body. To a large extent, even suggesting that the mind and body collaborate is to assume that the two are separate entities. The underlying and implicit assumption used by most health psychologists today is that the two are actually one; that is, the psyche of the mind is a creation of the physiology of the body. Mind-body medicine, the name often used for complementary and alternative medicine (CAM) (described in detail in Chapter 2) and treatments, are growing in popularity in America. In one study, more than half of the patients with depression and anxiety reported using alternative treatments (McFarland, Bigelow, Zani, Newsom, & Kaplan, 2002). As more alternative treatments such as acupuncture, yoga, and meditation are subjected to scientific tests, it is likely that more of them will be prescribed for and used by the general public. This use is going to call for a new series of interventions. Many CAM techniques are already components of the belief systems of different cultural groups. Many Chinese Americans are not waiting for research to demonstrate the effectiveness of Tai Chi or Qi Gong. They just do it. Once such health behaviors receive empirical validation, more and more individuals will want to practice them. Alternatively, if CAM is found to be effective, health psychologists will have the new challenge of finding the best ways to incorporate the techniques into people's lives to prevent unhealthy behavior.

Finally, let us go back to the question of money. Not being reimbursed by insurance companies has been one of the biggest reasons for not enough attention being paid to psychological factors and treatment—most patients cannot afford to take care of their mental or physical health if their insurance refuses to pay for the services they need; if health providers do not get paid, they cannot afford to conduct research. That situation is in the process of changing. In early 2002, the American Medical Association's **Current Procedural Terminology** (CPT) Manual was updated with new billing codes designed to capture behavioral services provided to patients to address physical health problems. The introduction of the health and behavior assessment and intervention codes and their acceptance by the federal Medicare program marked years of work by the APA Practice Organization (APAPO) and its members to advance the concept of psychologists as practitioners whose knowledge can help patients deal with physical as well as mental health issues (Richmond, 2004). The "health and behavior assessment and intervention" or H&B CPT codes, apply to psychological services that address behavioral, social, and psychophysiological conditions in the treatment or management of patients diagnosed with physical health problems (APA, 2008). The early years of implementation were a time of transition, with much work being done to ensure that Medicare carriers were properly reimbursing psychologists for health and behavior services. In 2006, local Medicare carriers in Florida began reimbursing for health and behavior assessment and intervention services. With the Florida coverage decision, which took effect April 11, 2006, all Medicare carriers now reimburse psychologists for services under the health and behavior codes. Now, the APA is expanding its work to get private insurance carriers to increase coverage as well. As more and more behavioral and psychological treatments are reimbursed (e.g., smoking cessation), the financial barriers to prevention will be eliminated.

The existence and use of H&B CPT codes highlights a practical element of health psychology. A significant number of health psychologists have their doctorates in clinical psychology and are practicing clinical psychologists (more on careers in the section at chapter's end). Reading the research cited in this book does not allow for much insight into the practice-side of health psychology, a realm where the use (or lack) of H&B codes has been problematic. Taking a glance into the politics may be useful, and the dynamics of code use also help highlight another side of the biopsychosocial nature of the field. First some details.

Battles rage around these CPT (Current Procedural Terminology) codes, because they are how all health professionals bill for their services and earn their income (Bruns, 2008 Personal communication). There is some turf battling: the American Medical Association literally owns the codes for all professions, meaning they wield enormous power. If the AMA decides to suddenly delete H&B or other codes with a wave of the hand, certain areas of clinical health psychology practice would be devastated. This did happen some years ago. The AMA deleted a code called "psychophysiological psychotherapy." This treatment used a combination of biofeedback, psychotherapy and related strategies. If that is what you use in your clinical practice, too bad; you could not bill for it anymore. The procedure no longer officially exists so you have to bill for it some other way (like using a biofeedback technician code that may pay half as much).

There are six codes clinical health psychologists can use and Medicare reimburses for five of them (code 96155: family intervention without the patient present). Some private health insurance plans have begun to pay for these codes as well; private insurance plans may have payment policies that are more or less restrictive than under Medicare. Psychologists, nurses, licensed clinical social workers, and other non-physician health care clinicians whose scope of practice permits can bill using these codes. Before being able to use the codes, however, health psychologists have to complete a number of "credentialing" forms, many of which ask for "certification" level status in various specialties. Many see the certification request by insurers as simply another obstacle to providing psychological health care. Physicians performing similar services use "Evaluation and Management" codes (APA, 2008). Psychologists are not allowed to use the E&M codes.

If health psychologists want to have a more direct impact on the health of patients, you can guess that being able to treat (and bill) patients (and get paid) is critical. Correspondingly, there is a lot of activity within APA to give clinical health psychologists a broader ability to bill their patients for services they have provided. But change is not easy. Making changes to billing codes is incredibly difficult. The H&B codes took six to seven years to push through. A subsequent tweaking of the H&B language took another three years or so. Psychology has only a handful of codes in a massive document and the AMA has historically blocked the APA from any direct involvement in creating it. APA has faced resistance on many fronts, with psychiatry (and other groups) lobbying intensively against it.

Despite these difficulties, slow progress is being made. In 2008, psychologists have been allowed to have a representative on key committees in the AMA, allowing for the first time ever the APA to have a vote. Having a seat at the table is an enormous step forward.

BIOPSYCHOCULTURAL HEALTH PSYCHOLOGY

Taken as a whole, health psychologists have made gigantic strides in the prevention of illness and in aiding those of us who do get sick. There is still more to be done, but the utility of a taking a biopsychosocial approach has already paid dividends. Now all we need is to expand our focus across the lifespan and to better incorporate diverse cultural backgrounds (Eshun & Gurung, 2009). The fact is that there really is not enough of a "social" focus in the biopsychosocial approach (Keefe et al., 2002). Indeed, what we do and why we do it are shaped by a variety of factors, and our health and well-being are no exceptions. A **biopsychocultural** approach might provide health psychology with stronger direction that not only incorporates the social nature of our interactions, but also explicitly acknowledges the role that culture plays in our lives.

SYNTHESIZE, EVALUATE, APPLY	
	• How would you summarize the state of the field of health psychology?
	• How would you prioritize the different future directions described above?
	• Generate your own description of health psychology, synthesizing what you have learned in this book.
	• Are there other areas of culture, development, and health that have not been discussed in this book?

FOCUS ON APPLICATIONS

Careers and Graduate Training in Health Psychology

Now that you have read about the spectrum of what constitutes health psychology, what do you do next? We hope that the research you have read has inspired you to consider working in this fascinating field. If so, you may wonder what your options are. Some of the main options are seen in Figure 14.4.

Most health psychologists work in either basic research settings or in applied settings. The former are academic psychologists who may be affiliated with a university or research center. The latter are clinicians who may be affiliated with hospitals or clinics. Researchers aim to determine the biopsychosocial factors involved in the many areas that we have discussed in

(continues)

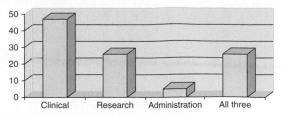

FIGURE **14.4** Approximate Percent of Job Advertisements in the APA Monitor for Health Psychologists.
Source: *Author*

FOCUS ON APPLICATIONS *(continued)*

this book such as stress, cardiovascular diseases, cancer, and HIV. Clinical activities include the conducting of a variety of tests such as cognitive and behavioral assessments, psychophysiological assessments, clinical interviews, demographic surveys, objective and projective personality assessments, and various other clinical and research-oriented protocols (*Health Psychology*, 2005). Health clinicians also implement interventions to change health behaviors, reduce stress, help people cope with chronic illnesses, and increase adherence to treatment. Many psychologists work in health care settings and many HMOs include psychologists as well. Health psychologists have also been employed in governmental agencies, rehabilitation centers, medical schools, and pain centers.

Although few undergraduate institutions offer specialized programs in health psychology, a growing number of graduate programs offer a degree or at least an emphasis in health psychology. The best preparation at the undergraduate level is a psychology major with many supporting courses in biology, statistics, and research methods. Many schools around the country are also adding an introductory health psychology course to the curriculum, but similar material may be covered in courses with titles such as behavioral health care, behavioral medicine, health behavior change, and health promotion. Because the biopsychosocial model incorporates many different subject areas you can cultivate your interest in health psychology by working in a variety of related fields. Many social workers, occupational and physical therapists, nutrition and exercise physiologists, dieticians, and other health care workers also utilize the health psychological approach even if not the explicit label. Many county, state, and national organizations also hire students with backgrounds and interests in health psychology to work with related departments. Even within the field of psychology many social, personality, clinical, and counseling psychologists (some of the classic and traditional areas of psychology) may also take a strong health psychological approach in their work.

After an undergraduate degree, most health psychologists enroll in graduate school and work toward a master's (M.S.) or doctoral degree (Ph.D.). These degrees can take from five to seven or more years and the content of the coursework will vary with the institution. Some graduate schools will focus more on the psychological aspects of the biopsychosocial model, including a greater number of advanced courses in psychology. Others will lean more heavily on the biological side of the model with more specialized courses in biology and medicine. If you use the most traditional way to look for graduate schools—the American Psychological Association's guide to graduate study—here is something to look for. There are a small (although growing) number of health psychology Ph.D. programs, but a larger number of clinical psychology programs that offer health psychology "tracks." There are also many schools that have a health psychology emphasis within their social psychology Ph.D. programs (e.g., UCLA). There are also schools with behavioral neuroscience or behavioral medicine programs whose curriculum is very close to that of health psychology programs. For one of the most up-to-date sources for programs with health psychology training, check the Society of Behavioral Medicine and health psychology education and training Web sites.

(continues)

FOCUS ON APPLICATIONS (continued)

Applied health psychologists have a doctoral or master's degree and are licensed for the independent practice of psychology in areas such as clinical and counseling psychology, and board certification is available in health psychology through the American Board of Professional Psychology. Clinical and counseling doctoral students are required to complete a one-year internship before obtaining their doctorates, and many of these programs offer some training in health psychology. After graduate school, a number of individuals choose to specialize in a particular area of the field and take on postdoctoral positions. Although these positions rarely pay much, they are excellent opportunities to work closely with experienced researchers in the field and learn much more about specific topics.

If this brief exposure of what is available to you has whet your appetite for more information about being a health psychologist, the best place to look is Health Psychology's (APA Division 38) education and training Web site or a similar site hosted by the Society for Behavioral Medicine. You will find a listing of doctoral programs in health psychology, a guide to internships in health psychology, and a listing of postdoctoral programs in health psychology. Commercial job searching sites carry health psychology jobs as well, but be careful of the terms you use (see Figure 14.5). This is an expanding, exciting field with a tremendous potential to change how long and how well we live. We hope you have enjoyed learning about it and we hope you will consider becoming a health psychologist.

SUMMARY

- Health psychology as a separate field has now been in existence for approximately 35 years, although its roots go back much farther. It has many areas of specialization and organizations that cater to individuals from different fields.
- There is a great need for health psychology to focus more on cultural issues. There are significant cultural differences in health behaviors and health in general. Health psychologists have only recently begun to focus explicitly on differences in cultural groups. This focus calls for more training and cultural awareness. With the increasing diversity in North America, there is an urgent need for more cross-cultural health psychology research.
- Although it is clear that health issues vary as we age and that the causes of death vary for different age groups, health psychologists have yet to focus on developmental issues and the lifespan. Disparate literature studies reporting on developmental issues should be initiated for studies of health as we age.
- Additional work needs to be done on refining the biopsychosocial model. Still used more in the theoretical realm, the biopsychosocial model needs to be put into practice more often.
- The need for more cultural and developmental research in health psychology is going to require more multilevel and interdisciplinary collaborations. These collaborations will foster the design of more powerful interventions.
- Technology is changing rapidly. Research designs and interventions need to keep abreast of novel ways to collect data and monitor individuals. The greater use of portable computers, the Internet, and even multifunction

cellular phones gives the health psychologist a wealth of new ways to reach people and change behavior.

- Interventions need to better account for the time course of diseases, different levels of analysis, cultural differences, and a focus on health threats across the lifespan.
- Training programs in health psychology need to be revised to keep up with the changing nature of the field and the increasing need for cultural competency.
- Health psychologists need to pay more attention to the use and utility of complementary and alternative medicines (CAMs). The uses of CAMs are growing, and they may prove to be effective aids to conventional treatments in addition to providing psychological buffers to illness.

TEST YOURSELF

Check your understanding of the topics in this chapter by answering the following questions. Answers appear in the Appendix.

1. Although a relatively new area of psychology, Health Psychology, as a division of the American Psychological Association has been around for over:
   a. 10 years.
   b. 15 years.
   c. 25 years.
   d. 50 years.
2. In many health psychological studies ethnicity is treated as a _____ variable, thereby downplaying its importance.
   a. Moderator
   b. Mediator
   c. Independent
   d. Control
3. Who are the largest consumers of health care?
   a. Latinos
   b. Older adults
   c. Infants and adolescents
   d. Asian Americans
4. Although the biopsychosocial model is well used, some aspects of it are favored over others. One component of it that is not studied as much is the _____ component.
   a. Cultural
   b. Biological
   c. Psychological
   d. Social

5. Given the specific training needed to be well versed with the different components of the biopsychosocial model, the future of health psychology will rely on:
   a. Better funding.
   b. International collaborations.
   c. Multidimensional collaborations.
   d. New graduate departments.
6. A new innovation in health psychology is the use of new forms of delivery of services. One such area is:
   a. Rural outreach.
   b. Behavioral telehealth.
   c. Intercultural consultation.
   d. Multimodal contact.
7. A challenge for health psychologists to face is the increasing role of _____ in health education.
   a. Movies
   b. Television
   c. The Internet
   d. Peers
8. An advance in medical science that has direct implications for health psychologists is the increasing use of:
   a. Living organ and tissue transplants.
   b. Cloning.
   c. Subcutaneous micropumps.
   d. Computerized diagnosis mechanisms.

9. The division of the American Psychological Association dedication to health psychology is:
   a. 2
   b. 8
   c. 38
   d. 45

10. The use of empirical proven research to guide treatment is referred to as:
    a. Emprical Behavioral Medicine.
    b. Evidence-Based Medicine.
    c. Pragmatic Science.
    d. Biobehavioral Treatments.

WEB RESOURCES

Visit the companion Web site at **www.cengage.com/psychology/gurung,** where you will find online resources for this book, including chapter-by-chapter quizzes, Web links, and more!

WebMD
http://www.webmd.com/

This site is an online source of information about health. Use the interactive symptom checker to see how the computer diagnosis system works.

The Society of Behavioral Medicine
http://www.sbm.org/

This website is for the Society of Behavioral Medicine, a multidisciplinary, nonprofit organization founded in 1978. Look at the education and training Web site for more information on careers and training in behavioral medicine.

The Health Disparities Webpage
http://www.health-psych.org/health_disparities/home.php (website removed at press time)

Division 38 and its committee on Health Disparities have developed this "Health Disparities Web page." The Health Disparities Web page is intended as an introduction to the key issues in health disparities research and as a guide to resources that can promote further investigation and advocacy.

Office of Minority Health and Health Disparities (OMHD)
http://www.cdc.gov/omhd/About/about.htm

OMHD aims to eliminate health disparities for vulnerable populations as defined by race/ethnicity, socio-economic status, geography, gender, age, disability status, risk status related to sex and gender, and among other populations identified to be at-risk for health disparities.

Health Psychology Education and Training
http://www.health-psych.org/EducationResources.cfm

This web site was created by the Education and Training Committee of Division 38 (Health Psychology). Together with housing information on resources for teaching psychology, the link also holds the directory of programs for further study in health psychology and information on internships.

NIH Road Map
http://nihroadmap.nih.gov/clinicalresearch/overview-networks.asp

This is a government-funded initiative to share clinical research findings with funded research listings to give you a sense of the active work in progress.

Health and Behavior Codes
http://www.apapractice.org/apo/health_and_behavior.html#

This site offers an introduction to the economics of how psychology and medicine interact. This site has information on the way that clinical psychologists can bill insurance companies for services provided.

KEY TERMS, CONCEPTS, AND PEOPLE

behavioral telehealth, 441

biopsychocultural, 448

Current Procedural Terminology, 446

Division 38, 433

grouping variables, 435

health disparities, 436

multidimensional approaches, 441

National Electronic Clinical Trials and Research (NECTAR), 446

NIH Roadmap, 445

positive psychology, 433

ESSENTIAL READINGS

Leventhal, H., Weinman, J., Leventhal, E., & Phillips, L. (2008). Health Psychology: The Search for Pathways between Behavior and Health. *Annual Review of Psychology*, *59*(1), 477–505.

Nicassio, P. M., Meyerowitz, B. E., & Kerns, R. D. (2004). The future of health psychology interventions. *Health Psychology*, *23*(2), 132–137.

Suls, J., & Rothman, A. (2004). Evolution of the biopsychosocial model: Prospects and challenges for health psychology. *Health Psychology*, *23*(2), 119–126.

Yali, A. M., & Revenson, T. A. (2004). How changes in population demographics will impact health psychology: Incorporating a broader notion of cultural competence into the field. *Health Psychology*, *23*(2), 147–155.

Chapter 1: Health Psychology: Setting the Stage

1. C
2. A
3. A
4. B
5. D
6. C
7. A
8. A
9. A
10. A

Chapter 2: Cultural Approaches to Health

1. A
2. A
3. A
4. A
5. B
6. C
7. B
8. A
9. A
10. B

Chapter 3: Essential Physiology

1. D
2. A
3. B
4. B
5. D
6. A
7. B
8. B
9. A
10. C

Chapter 4: Stress Across Cultures

1. D
2. A
3. A
4. D
5. A
6. D
7. B
8. A
9. B
10. B

Chapter 5: Coping and Social Support

1. A
2. B
3. D
4. A
5. C
6. C
7. D
8. C
9. B
10. D

Chapter 6: Models of Behavior Change

1. D
2. D
3. D
4. A
5. D
6. B
7. A
8. C
9. D
10. A

Chapter 7: Health Behaviors: Eating, Physical Activity, Smoking and Drinking

1. D
2. B
3. C
4. B
5. C
6. B
7. C
8. D
9. A
10. B

Chapter 8: Factors Surrounding Illness

1. B
2. B
3. D
4. C
5. A
6. C
7. A
8. A
9. C
10. D

Chapter 9: Pain

1. A
2. C
3. D
4. D
5. B
6. B
7. B
8. D
9. B
10. B

Chapter 10: Chronic Illness, Terminal Illness, and Death

1. D
2. A
3. A
4. A
5. B
6. A
7. B
8. A
9. C
10. A

Chapter 11: Psychoneuroimmunology and HIV

1. B
2. A
3. D
4. D
5. D
6. D
7. C
8. C
9. C
10. D

Chapter 12: Culture and Cancer

1. B
2. A
3. B
4. A
5. A
6. B
7. B
8. C
9. A
10. A

Chapter 13: Culture and Cardiovascular Disease

1. A
2. C
3. B
4. C
5. B
6. C
7. D
8. C
9. B
10. C

Chapter 14: The Future of Health Psychology

1. C
2. D
3. B
4. D
5. C
6. B
7. C
8. A
9. C
10. B

Acquired immunodeficiency syndrome illness resulting in a deficiency within the immune system, with a number of manifestations, rather than a single disease. Caused by HIV.

Action stage in the Transtheoretical Model where subjects are actually changing their behavior. The change has to have taken place over the last six months and should involve active efforts to change the behavior.

Acupuncture one of the most scientifically validated forms of alternative medicine that involves the use of fine needles inserted into specific points on the body. Acupuncture is theorized to keep the balance between yin and yang, thus allowing for the normal flow of qi throughout the body and restoring health to the mind and body.

ADAPT-ITT theoretical model consists of eight sequential phases that inform HIV prevention providers and researchers of a prescriptive method for adapting evidence based interventions.

Addiction state in which the body relies on a substance for normal functioning.

Adherence extent to which a patient's behavior matches with his or her practitioner's advice.

Affect cultures cultures such as Italy that place a premium on the display of emotions.

Afferent fibers sensory nerve fibers transmitting signals from the receptors to the spinal cord.

Alcohol abuse characterized by one or more of the following as a result of alcohol use: (1) failure to fulfill major role obligations; (2) recurrent physically hazardous use; (3) recurrent alcohol-related legal problems; or (4) continued use despite persistent alcohol-related social or interpersonal problems.

Allopathy conventional or Western medicine that treats disease by the use of remedies to produce effects different from those produced by the disease under treatment.

Allostasis the ability to achieve stability through change.

Analgesia pain relief or the inability to feel pain.

Analyses of variance (ANOVAs) statistical test that examines if group means vary from each other. It uses an *F-ratio* test.

Angina pectoris medical term for heart attacks or myocardial infarctions (or cardiac arrest). Chest pain is a common symptom.

Angioplasty treatment for cardiovascular disease involving a procedure done to open a partially blocked blood vessel so that blood can flow through it more easily.

Anorexia nervosa disorder defined by the following criteria: refusing to maintain body weight at or above a minimally normal weight for age and height; having an intense fear of gaining weight or becoming fat, even though underweight; having a disturbed view of the way in which one's body weight or shape is experienced, undue influence of body weight or shape on self evaluation, or denial of the seriousness of the current low body weight; and experiencing amenorrhea (the absence of at least three consecutive menstrual cycles).

Anticipatory grief process in which a dying patient feels a lack of control and now grieves in expectation of his or her death.

Antigens specific immune cells that are earmarked for specific germs or antigens. Also known as antibody generators.

Appraisal delay time taken to recognize one has symptoms after they first appear.

Appraisals way a potentially stressful event is interpreted. A significant component of Lazarus' psychological explanation of why we get stressed.

Approach coping form of coping where you actively attempt to solve the problem or address the stressor.

Atherosclerosis disease caused by the accumulation of fatty substances in the blood vessels.

Attributions cognitive process of assigning meaning to a symptom or behavior.

Avoidant coping form of coping where you focus more on emotions resulting from the stressor and ignore or avoid the stressful experience itself. It involves mental or behavioral methods to deal with the feelings resulting from the stress.

Ayurveda ancient system of medicine focuses on the body, the sense organs, the mind, and the soul. It originated in India approximately 4,000 years ago.

Bargaining stage of death in which patients try to restore their belief in a just world and may promise to be good or live life better in exchange for life.

Bariatric surgery weight loss surgery. There are many forms such as lap band surgery and gastric bypass surgery.

Behavioral cueing certain events, situations, people, locations, make act as stimuli that result in behaviors conditioned to be associated with them. When a smoker always smokes in his or her car, the car is a signal to the smoker's body that nicotine is coming and makes smoking more likely.

Behavioral involvement a patient's attitude toward self-care, specifically an active involvement in treatment.

Behavioral medicine interdisciplinary field of medicine that includes psychological, sociological, and biological views on health and illness.

Behavioral telehealth health care delivered over the telephone or through other technical means such as the Internet.

Benefit finding finding meaning in a chronic illness and growing.

Benign noncancerous tumors.

Binge drinkers men who have consumed five or more and women who have consumed four or more drinks in a row at least once during the previous two weeks.

Biofeedback procedure where a computer or other monitoring device measures heart rate and systolic and diastolic blood pressure in real-time allowing one to modify one's behavior and thinking to see resulting changes in cardiovascular reactions. A form of relaxation.

Biomedical approach An approach that sees health primarily as the state in which disease is absent.

Biopsychocultural approach to studying human behavior that incorporates biological, psychological, and cultural factors.

Biopsychosocial approach approach that focuses on the biology or physiology underlying health, the psychology or thoughts, feelings, and behaviors influencing health, and the ways that society and culture influence health.

Blended family family consisting of two parents, either or both of whom may have been previously married, with their children.

Body mass index standard measure of weight calculated by multiplying weight by 703 and dividing by the square of height measured in inches [BMI 5 (Wt 3 703)/(Ht 3 Ht)].

Broken families families consisting of divorced and/or single parents living with their kids.

Bulimia nervosa disorder characterized by the following criteria: recurrent episodes of binge eating; recurrent use of inappropriate compensatory behaviors in order to prevent weight gain; engaging in binge eating and inappropriate compensatory behaviors, on average, at least two times per week for three months; and having a self-evaluation that is unduly influenced by body shape and weight.

Carcinogens cancer-causing substances.

Carcinomas cancers that start in the surface layers of the body or epithelial cells. This form of cancer accounts for the bulk of cancer cases and is seen in the most common sites.

Cardiac rehabilitation program programs educate patients on the best way to change their lifestyles and use a combination of physical activity and social support to improve their overall functioning and prevent death.

Cardiovascular disease general category of diseases resulting from problems with the heart and the circulatory system. Includes coronary heart disease (CHD) (also referred to as coronary artery disease [CAD]) and heart failure (both commonly referred to as heart attacks), strokes, and hypertension or high blood pressure.

Cardiovascular reactivity changes in heart rate and blood pressure in response to stress. Reactivity varies greatly between individuals and is a key physiological risk factor for the development of cardiovascular disease.

Cell-mediated immunity form of immune reaction that takes place at the level of the cell. Cell mediated immunity involves the action of T cells although the first stages are similar to the process for humoral-mediated immunity.

Chemotherapy treatment involving taking medications with the aim of disabling cancer growth.

Chronic illnesses illnesses that persist over long periods of time.

Cognitive appraisal model Richard Lazarus' theory of why we get stressed and defined as the imbalance between the demands placed on the individual and that individual's resources to cope.

Complementary and alternative medicine any non-Western approach to health and wellness. Most common CAMs include acupuncture and reiki.

Conditioned immune response when the reaction of the body's immune system comes about via classical conditioning and not by direct stimulation of a drug or other factor.

Confirmation bias phenomenon by which when we believe something is true we often change the way we interpret new information and the way we look at the world because of it. We tend to try to confirm our belief and have a bias in how we process information.

Constraint cultures cultures where people believe everything is in the hands of God or is fate.

Contemplation stage in the Transtheoretical Model where people recognize they may be doing something unhealthy and then intend to change (within the next month)

Control cultures cultures where people believe that they have absolute control of their outcomes (similar to having an internal locus of control).

Coping process of making efforts to manage distressing problems and emotions that affect the physical and psychological outcomes of stress.

Coronary artery disease disease developing due to the build up of a combination of fat, salts, and scar tissue or plaque in the arteries that supply the heart with blood. The build up can lead to heart failure or heart attack.

Coronary heart disease disease developing due to the build up of a combination of fat, salts, and scar tissue or plaque in the arteries that supply the heart with blood. The build up can lead to heart failure or heart attack.

Correlation coefficient statistical measure of the association between two or more variables. It is represented by the

letter *r* and can range from +1.00 to
–1.00. Values closer to 1 (regardless of
sign) signifying stronger associations.
Values closer to 1 (regardless of sign)
signifying stronger associations.

Counterirritation process by which we
may try to reduce pain by itching or
poking a point on our skin around
where the pain is felt.

Creative nonadherence when patients
indirectly disobey their doctors' orders
often by modifying and supplementing
their treatment plans.

Cultural competency health care provider's understanding of patients' cultural
characteristics, values, and traditions.

Culture dynamic, yet stable, set of goals,
beliefs, and attitudes shared by a group
of people. Culture can also include similar physical characteristics (e.g., skin
color), psychological characteristics
(e.g., levels of hostility), and common
superficial features (e.g., hairstyle and
clothing).

Curanderismo holistic system of healing
practiced by Latin Americans and
blending spirituality and Western
approaches to health and healing.

Curative surgery treatment for cancer
used to remove the growth.

Current procedural terminology (CPT)
manual. The American Medical Association's policy specifying billing codes
designed to capture behavioral services
provided to patients to address physical
health problems.

Cytotoxicity the degree to which something is toxic to living cells and a measure of the strength of immune cells.

da Vinci, Leonardo da Vinci lived from
1452 to 1519. He was a Florentine artist, a painter, sculptor, architect, engineer, and scientist. Leonardo studied the
structure of the body using dissection
and created elaborate anatomical drawings of humans and animals that aided
medical research of the same.

Debulking surgery treatment to reduce
the tumor mass in cancer.

Dementia marked problems in thinking
and remembering often experienced by
older adults.

Denial one of the first psychological
reactions felt the moment a person is
informed that he or she has a chronic
illness or realizes he or she is dying.

Diabetes mellitus severe, chronic form
of diabetes caused by insufficient production of insulin and resulting in

disruption in the breaking down and
storage of carbohydrates, fats, and proteins. This disease often appears in
childhood and is characterized by
increased sugar levels in the blood and
urine and excessive thirst.

Diagnostic surgery process of removing
a small amount of tissue either to identify a cancer or to make a diagnosis.

Diathesis-stress model idea that some
individuals may have physiological predispositions to certain factors such as
depression, stress, or pain that interact
with psychological factors to cause those
outcomes.

Differentiation process by which a less
specialized cell becomes a more specialized cell. The extent to which differentiation occurs is an indicator of the
strength of one's immune system.

Eating disorders severe disturbance in
eating behaviors. Diagnostic criteria are
currently provided for two eating disorders, *anorexia nervosa* and *bulimia nervosa*, and a third general category,
eating disorder not otherwise specified.

Ecological theory a way of examining
behavior developed by Bronfenbrenner,
and which identifies different levels or
systems in which the individual acts
rather than just focusing on the
individual.

Effect size an objective and standardized
measure of the significance and magnitude of a result of a statistical test.

Efferent pathways sensory nerve fibers
transmitting signals from the spinal cord
to receptors in the skin and tissues.

Environmental tobacco smoke tobacco
smoke inhaled by nonsmokers who are
in the presence of smokers.

Epidemiology branch of medicine that
studies the frequency, distribution, and
causes of different diseases with an
emphasis on the role of the physical and
social environment.

Etiology the origin and causes of
diseases.

Euthanasia the termination of life by the
injection of a lethal drug.

Evidence-based treatments treatments
that are dependent on critically evaluated research and are essentially
empirically tested.

Exercise activity planned with the goal
of improving one or more aspects of
physical fitness.

Experiment form of research design
that helps us determine causality. In

experiments, the researcher manipulates
one variable, the independent variable,
and measures how changes in this variable influence another variable, the
dependent variable.

Extended family family consisting of a
blended or nuclear family plus grandparents or grandchildren, aunts, uncles,
and other relatives.

Familialism cultural value that emphasizes close family relationships, bonds,
and ties.

Fatalism the belief that a person with
cancer cannot live a normal life and will
die.

Fight-or-flight theory Walter Cannon's
theory of stress hypothesizing that
organism's respond to stressful events
with a nervous system activation that
prepares them to actively engage the
stressor. The body essentially is ener-
gized to either fight the stressor or flee.

Fixed time cultural orientation towards
time where individuals are exact with
regard to time and expect to be somewhere or start events at exactly the time
specified.

Fluid time cultural orientation towards
time where individuals are flexible with
regard to time and do not expect to be
someplace or start engagements or
events at exactly the time specified.

Food preferences biologically programmed inclinations toward certain
foods. Can be modified by experiences.

Framingham study large-scale longitudinal study following over 5,000 residents of Framingham, Massachusetts,
that has contributed to our understanding of heart disease.

French paradox the fact that most people in France have a diet that is high in
fat but still have lower rates of heart
disease.

Galen physician of the Emperor Marcus
Aurelius in Rome, Galen lived from 129
to 216. One of the most influential of the
Greek physicians he published a wide
body of work that shaped Western
biomedicine.

Gate control theory model of pain pro-
posing that key processes in the experience of pain take place in the dorsal
horn substantia gelatinosa of the spinal
cord and are influenced by the brain.

General adaptation syndrome Hans
Selye's theory of stress suggesting that
organisms have a general way of
responding to all stressors. When faced

with a stressor, the body first goes into a state of alarm, then attempts to cope during a period of resistance, and finally breaks down in a state of exhaustion.

Grouping variables variables such as race or ethnicity often statistically controlled for in analyses where culture is not the focus of the study.

Hardiness personality trait characterized by the ability to bounce back into action after facing a stressor.

Harvey, William British physician born (1578–1657). His 1628 *An Anatomical Study of the Motion of the Heart and of the Blood in Animals* first explained how blood was pumped from the heart throughout the body, then returned to the heart.

Health state of complete physical, mental, and social well-being.

Health belief model major theory of health behavior that suggests that our beliefs relating to the effectiveness, ease, and consequences of doing (or not doing) a certain behavior will determine whether we do (or not do) that behavior.

Health disparities differences in health that are not only unnecessary and avoidable, but in addition, are considered unfair and unjust.

Health education term for the collection of efforts to teach people to limit behaviors detrimental to their health and increase behaviors that are conducive to health. Health educators pay attention to a range of factors including the individual, interpersonal relationships, institutions, community, and public policy.

Health psychology section of psychology that focuses on how biological, psychological, and society factors can influence how we stay healthy, why we get sick, and how we cope best and recover from illness.

Healthy behaviors any specific behaviors that maintain and enhance health.

Healthy People 2010 science-based, 10-year national program designed to promote health and prevent disease.

Highly active antiretroviral therapy (HAART) most commonly used treatment for AIDS that involves many different anti-HIV drugs that keep the virus from replicating.

Hippocrates often referred to as the father of medicine, Hippocrates was a Greek physician who lived from 460 to 370 B.C. He based his medical practice on observations and on the study of the

human body. He held the belief that illness had a physical and a rational explanation.

Homeostasis an optimal level or ideal level of bodily functions. This varies for each individual and relates to blood glucose level, body temperature, rate of circulation, and breathing.

Hospice nursing homes for the dying, where the dying are comforted, and their pain and other symptoms are alleviated.

Human immunodeficiency virus HIV is the virus responsible for causing AIDS.

Humoral-medicated immunity form of immune reaction that takes place at the level of the tissue and involving immune cells circulating in the blood. Humoral-mediated immunity involves the action of B cells although the first stages are similar to the process for cell-mediated immunity.

Hypertension medical term for high blood pressure, a condition in which the blood pressure remains chronically elevated.

Hypochondriacs a psychological disorder characterized by excessive preoccupation with one's health and constant worry about developing physical illnesses.

Illness behaviors varying ways individuals respond to physiological symptoms, monitor internal states, define and interpret symptoms, make attributions, take remedial actions, and utilize various forms of informal and formal care.

Illness delay time between the recognition that one is ill to the decision to seek care.

Illusory correlation belief that our expectations have been correct more times than they actually have been.

Immunotherapy treatment involving the activation of the body's own immune system to fight cancer or other diseases.

Incidence rates frequency of new cases of the disease during a year.

Incidence rates of newly diagnosed cases of the disease.

Indo-Mediterranean diet diet rich in whole grains, fruits, vegetables, walnuts, and almonds.

Informational involvement measure of how much the patient wants to know about his or her illness and specific details of its treatment.

Information-motivation-behavioral skills theoretical model of health behav-

ior change devised primarily for reducing unhealthy practices associated with AIDS and which provides a framework for guiding HIV risk reduction interventions.

Insulin major endocrine hormone secreted by the islet cells of the pancreas. It facilitates the use of glucose by the body's cells and plays a major role in the metabolism of food.

Intention a person's subjective probability that he or she will perform the behavior in question.

Interventions specific programs designed to assess levels of behaviors, introduce ways to change them, measure whether change has occurred, and assess the impact of the change.

Ischemia condition in which the blood flow is restricted to a part of the body. For example, cardiac ischemia occurs when blood flow and oxygen to the heart muscle is disrupted. Ischemias often lead to heart attacks.

Lay-referral system nonprofessionals such as family, friends, and neighbors who patients rely on to help cope with illness symptoms instead of seeking biomedical treatment.

Leading health indicators the major health concerns in the United States at the beginning of the twenty-first century as reflected by the Healthy People 2010 program.

Leukemias cancers that are found in the blood and bone marrow.

Life expectancy the age at which you would be expected to die given biopsychosocial factors existing in society at that time.

Living will a legal document in which he or she clearly specifies the conditions under which life support should be terminated.

Logistic regression statistical analysis that predicts the probability of the occurrence of an event.

Lymphomas cancers of the lymphatic system.

Maintenance stage in the Transtheoretical Model where people try to not fall back into performing their unhealthy behaviors or relapsing. They may still be changing their behaviors and performing new behaviors, but they are not doing them as often as someone in the action stage.

Malignant cancerous tumors.

Mastectomy breast removal.

Mastery the extent to which one regards one's life chances as being under one's own control.

Mediation intervening process (variable) through which an antecedent variable influences an outcome variable. Mediation can be described as a relationship where an independent variable changes a mediating variable, which then changes a dependent variable.

Melatonin Melatonin is a hormone produced in the brain by the pineal gland. The production and release of melatonin is stimulated by darkness and suppressed by light.

Menopause stage when the female ovaries stop producing eggs. It occurs around the age of 50 for women and is accompanied by a drop in hormone levels.

Metastasize spread to other parts of the body.

Moderator variable that changes the *magnitude* (and sometimes the direction) of the relationship between an antecedent variable and an outcome variable.

Modulation the neural activity leading to the control of pain transmissions between the various parts of the brain.

Morbidity number of cases of a disease that exist at a given point in time.

Mortality number of deaths related to a specific cause.

Multidimensional approaches research that includes a consideration of biological, psychological, and societal processes incorporating different levels of measurement, different research methods, and different statistical analyses.

Multivariate analyses of variance (MANOVAs) a statistical test that examines if group means on a number of related variables vary from each other.

Myocardial infarctions also known as angina pectoris or cardiac arrest. Chest pain is a common symptom.

MyPyramid a schematic guide that offers personalized eating plans and interactive tools to help plan and assess food choices, and advice to find a balance between food and physical activity, and to get the most nutrition out of calories consumed.

National Electronic Clinical Trials and Research (NECTAR) electronic network that makes the results of clinical trials easy to find and utilize.

Neoplasms cells that show abnormal growth.

Neuropathic pain pure nociception without significant psychological pain.

Nociception technical name for pain, the activation of specialized nerve fibers that signal the occurrence of tissue damage.

Neutral cultures cultures such as that of Japan that do not sanction the open display of emotions.

NIH Roadmap government funded and organized plan that sketches out 28 cross-institutional projects especially designed to tackle multifaceted issues such as obesity that result from a variety of different biopsychosocial factors.

Nonimmunologic defenses body defenses and barriers that do not rely on the cells of the immune system and are referred to as nonimmunologic defenses. Examples include the skin, mucus, and the process of coughing.

Nonspecific immunity internal immune processes that do not differentiate between different types of germs or disease threats. These nonspecific immune defenses work on a wide variety of disease-causing microorganisms.

Normative beliefs what a person thinks others think about the behavior in question.

Nuclear family family consisting of a mother (female), a father (male), and unmarried children.

Obesity having a body mass index (BMI) of 30 or greater.

Odds ratio ratio of the odds of an event occurring in one group to the odds of it occurring in another group. An odds ratio of 1 suggests the phenomenon is equally likely in both groups. An odds ratio greater than 1 suggests the phenomenon is more likely to occur in the first group.

Opiates drug such as morphine or codeine containing or derived from opium and tending to induce sleep and alleviate pain.

Opioids substance produced in the body that has effects similar to opiates (such as morphine). Mainly associated with the relief of pain.

Opportunistic infections infections caused by organisms that cannot induce disease in people with normal immune systems, but take the "opportunity" to flourish in people with HIV infection.

Optimism personality trait where a person has a general tendency to expect that good things, rather than bad things, will happen.

Pain-prone personality personality type that predisposes a person to experience persistent pain.

Palliative care form of treatment aimed at alleviating symptoms without necessarily affecting the cause.

Palliative surgery treatment used to treat complications of advanced disease (not as a cure).

Pattern theory idea that pain results from a combination of impulses from nerve endings. Different patterns of stimulations caused different types of pain.

Personality an individual's unique set of consistent behavioral traits, where traits are durable dispositions to behave in a particular way in a variety of situations.

Phagocytosis process by which immune cells (e.g., macrophages) destroy germs or viruses by engulfing them and breaking them down.

Physical activity any bodily movement produced by contraction of the skeletal muscles that results in energy expenditure.

Physician-assisted suicide euthanasia involving a physician who supplies the actual drug although not actually administering it himself or herself.

Placebo an inactive substance that appears similar to the experimental drug.

Positive Psychology area of psychology that involves the scientific study of the strengths and virtues that enable individuals and communities to thrive. Major foci are emotions and individual traits.

Precontemplation stage in the Transtheoretical Model when people are not aware that they are practicing a behavior that is unhealthy or do not intend to take any action to change a behavior (especially not in the next six months).

Preparation stage in the Transtheoretical Model where people are ready to take action to change the behavior. They generate a plan and have specific ideas of how to change.

Pre-term birth a baby born before 37 weeks of pregnancy is considered to be born pre-term.

Prevalence rates proportion of the population that has a particular disease at a particular time (commonly reported as cases per 1,000 or 100,000 people).

Preventative surgery treatment to remove tissue that is not yet malignant but that has a high chance of turning malignant.

Primary appraisal first stage in Lazarus' cognitive appraisal model of stress where we determine the nature of an event, whether harmful, damaging, or challenging.

Private body consciousness degree to which one is sensitive to one's health states resulting in increased vigilance over the body.

Progressive illness chronic illnesses that get worse with time.

Proliferation extent to which the immune cells multiply and produce more cells. Proliferation is mostly seen as a sign of a strong immune system.

Psychogenic pain purely psychological pain without a physiological basis.

Psychoneuroimmunology a field of study that evolved out of the disciplines of biology and psychology and is dedicated to understanding the interplay between these disparate systems.

Qi Chinese word to describe the natural energy of the universe. The main goal of Traditional Chinese Medicine is to balance the Qi of the body and to increase Qi if needed when one is ill. It also translates to "life force" or "air."

Quality of life a measure of physical status and functioning, psychological status, social functioning, and the presence of the disease- or treatment-related symptoms.

Radiation therapy treatment involving the use of radioactive particles aimed at the DNA of the cancer cells in order to disable them.

Randomized clinical trials (RCTs) commonly used experimental method in health psychology research in which one group gets an experimental drug or intervention treatment and a second group unknowingly gets a placebo or nothing (the control group).

Reductionist process of explaining something by breaking it down to its smallest part.

Regression analysis statistical test in which an outcome is predicted from a set of variables.

Religiosity measure of how religious a person is commonly assessed by counting the frequency of temple/church/mosque/synagogue attendance, the average frequency of prayer, and the commitment to religious rituals.

Remitting illness an illness that eases with time and ends.

Risky families families in which a lot of arguing occurs between family members and in which relationships are cold, unsupportive, and neglectful.

Role ambiguity degree to which required information regarding role expectations are available, clear, and communicated to the individual playing the role (e.g. an employee).

Role conflict incompatibility of expectations for a given role and between different roles.

Role theory a role is the set of behaviors to be performed and is determined by one's own perceptions and the expectations of others. As an individual accumulates roles, the quantity and incompatibility of role demands increase. An individual experiences role strain that results in increased role conflict and ambiguity.

Sarcomas cancers of the muscles, bones, and cartilage.

Screening process of checking for cancer.

Secondary appraisal second stage in Lazarus' cognitive appraisal model of stress where we determine whether we have the resources to manage an event. Relates to primarily appraisal.

Secondhand smoke tobacco smoke inhaled by nonsmokers who are in the presence of smokers.

Self-efficacy conviction that one can successfully execute the behavior required to produce the outcome.

Self-fulfilling prophecy belief that if you believe something is going to happen, it is more likely to happen. Social psychologists suggest your expectancy of an outcome or behavior can subconsciously or consciously change your behavior to make the outcome more likely.

Self-management programs treatments for pain relief that make the patient with chronic pain the one with the major responsibility for making the change rather than the doctor or the health professional staff.

Sensory specific satiety when only one type of food is available at a meal people eat a moderate amount of it. If a second food is then introduced, the amount of the new food eaten will be more than if it was presented by itself.

Serological testing algorithm for recent HIV seroconversion new technology developed by the CDC that determines which positive HIV tests represent new HIV infections (those that occurred within approximately the past five months).

Sex an innate, biological characteristic. Men have an XY chromosome. Women have an XX sex chromosome.

Sexual mixing the extent to which people engage in sexual activities with sexual partners from other sexual networks (dis-sortative mating) versus partners from their own network (assortative mixing).

Shamans although a general term used for the practitioners of folk medicine, the word shaman originated in Eastern Europe and means "he (or she) who knows." Shamans are also referred to as "medicine men" and use a range of herbs and rituals to cure.

Social convoy model theory suggesting that people are motivated to maintain their social network sizes as they themselves age, despite changes in the composition of the networks. Individuals construct and maintain social relationships while becoming increasingly aware of specific strengths and weaknesses of particular members.

Social support feeling of being loved, esteemed, and cared for. Also emotional, informational, or instrumental assistance from others.

Socioeconomic status (SES) measure of an individual, family, or group's relative economic and social level most commonly measured by income and education level.

Socioemotional selectivity theory theory of social support change that proposes that people prune their social networks to maintain a desired emotional state depending on the extent to which time is perceived as limited. Basic functions of social interaction, such as maintaining a good mood, differ in respect to their relative importance for determining social preferences across the lifespan.

Somatic pain physiological pain without specific tissue damage.

Specificity idea that pain was a specific independent sensation such as heat or touch, with specialized receptors responding to specific stimuli.

Spillover transmission of stress from one domain of an individual's life into other domains of life.

Staging surgery treatment to ascertain in which stage of development the cancer is. This form of surgery helps determine how far the cancer has spread and provides a *clinical stage* for the growth.

Standard drink 12-ounce serving of beer (a standard bottle or can), a 5-ounce glass of wine, or a 1.5-ounce of gin, vodka, rum, or scotch, is a standard serving.

Stereotypes widely held beliefs that people have certain characteristics because of their membership in a particular group.

Stimulation-produced analgesia process by which electrically stimulating the brain can reduce pain.

Stress contagion effect when two or more domains or areas of a person's life are connected, stress from one area can spillover into the other area. If work and home are interconnected, stress from one area can influence the other.

Stress defined in a variety of ways but most simply as an upsetting of homeostasis. A state caused when the perceived demands on the organism exceeded the resources to meet those demands.

Stress-induced analgesia pain relief produced when our body releases opioids when we are stressed, a state that can also be induced by motor activity such as physical activity.

Stroke type of cardiovascular disease that affects the arteries leading to and within the brain. A stroke occurs when a blood vessel to the brain is blocked either by a clot or bursts. When that happens, part of the brain cannot get the blood (and oxygen) it needs, so it starts to die.

Synergistic effect phenomenon where two or more factors (e.g., smoking and drinking) act together to create an effect greater than that predicted by knowing only the separate effects of the individual factors.

Systematic desensitization form of classical conditioning in which stressful thoughts or events are paired with relaxation.

Tao major Chinese philosophical approach to life and the universe. Based on the *Tao Te Ching* written by Lao Tzu approximately 2,000 years ago, the Tao is translated to mean "way of life" "order of the Universe" and can be also seen as a state of being.

Tend-and-befriend Shelley Taylor's and colleagues' theory of how women when faced with a stressor may either tend to infants or others and befriend other females and cultivate female bonds as opposed to fighting or fleeing.

Terminal illnesses chronic illnesses such as cancer or AIDS are often referred to as advancing or terminal because people with these diseases often die after a relatively short time ranging from months to a few years.

Termination stage in the Transtheoretical Model where they are no longer tempted by the unhealthy behavior they have changed.

Thresholds level of stimuli needed to experience something such as pain or stress.

TNM system most common method used to stage cancer. The T describes the size of the tumor and whether cancer has spread to nearby tissues and organs. The N describes how far the cancer has spread to nearby lymph nodes. The M indicates the extent to which the cancer has metastasized.

Tolerance level amount beyond which pain becomes unbearable and intolerable.

Traditional Chinese Medicine holistic system of medicine and approach to health and healing originating in China

approximately 4,000 years ago. Major treatments include acupuncture and the use of herbs.

Transduction process taking place takes place at the level of the receptors where chemical, mechanical, or thermal energy is converted in electrochemical nerve impulses.

Transtheoretical Model major theory of health behavior change that identifies common themes across different intervention theories and notes that we process through different stages as we think about, attempt to, and finally change any specific behavior.

Triggers factors that increase the likelihood that a person will seek treatment.

Type C personality cancer-prone personality where the person is cooperative, appeasing, unassertive, and compliant and someone who does not express negative emotions.

Ultraviolet (UV) ray sunrays associated with skin cancer.

Utilization delays time between the decision to seek care and the actual behaviors to obtain medical health care.

Vesalius, Andreas Vesalius lived from 1514 to 1564 and was a Flemish anatomist and doctor. His dissections of the human body helped to correct misconceptions dating from ancient times.

Vital signs five basic measures that doctors get from patients (temperature, pulse, blood pressure, pain level, and respiration).

Yin and yang two opposing forces that, according to Traditional Chinese Medicine, combine to create everything in the universe. Yin and yang are mutually interdependent, constantly interactive, and potentially interchangeable forces.

Acevedo, V. (2008). Cultural competence in a group intervention designed for Latino patients living with HIV/AIDS. *Health and Social Work, 33*(2), 111–120.

Adams, A., Buckingham, C., Lindenmeyer, A., McKinlay, J., Link, C., Marceau, L., et al. (2008). The influence of patient and doctor gender on diagnosing coronary heart disease. *Sociology of Health and Illness, 30*(1), 1–18.

Adams, J., & White, M. (2007). Are the stages of change socioeconomically distributed? A scoping review. *American Journal of Health Promotion, 21*, 237–247.

Adams, K. F., Schatzkin, A., Harris, T. B., Kipnis, V., Mouw, T., Ballard-Barbash, R., et al. (2006). Overweight, obesity, and mortality in a large prospective cohort of persons 50 to 71 years old. *New England Journal of Medicine, 355*, 763–778.

Adams, P. F., Hendershot, G. E., Marano, M. A. (1999). Current estimates from the National Health Interview Survey, 1996. National Center for Health Statistics. *Vital Health Statistics, 10*, 1–203.

Adler, E., Hoon, M. A., Mueller, K. L., Chandrasekar, J., Ryba, N. J. P., & Zuker, C. S. (2000). A novel family of mammalian taste receptors. *Cell, 100*, 693–702.

Adler, N. E., & Rehkopf, D. H. (2008). U.S. Disparities in health: Descriptions, causes, and mechanisms. *Annual Review of Public Health, 29*, 235–252.

Adler, N. E., Singh Manoux, A., Schwartz, J., Stewart, J., Matthews, K., & Marmot, M. G. (2008). Social status and health: A comparison of British civil servants in Whitehall II with European- and African-Americans in CARDIA. *Social Science and Medicine, 66*, 1034–1045.

Aekplakorn, W., Hogan, M. C., Tiptaradol, S., Wibulpolprasert, S., Punyaratabandhu, P., & Lim, S. S. (2008). Tobacco and hazardous or harmful alcohol use in Thailand: Joint prevalence and associations with socioeconomic factors. *Addictive Behaviors, 33*, 503–514.

Ahmadi, F. (2006). *Culture, religion and spirituality in coping: The example of cancer patients in Sweden.* Uppsala, Sweden: Uppsala University Press.

Ahmed, N., Bestall, J. C., Ahmedzai, S. H., Payne, S. A., Clark, D., & Noble, B. (2007). Systematic review of the problems and issues of accessing specialist palliative care by patients, careers and health and social care professionals. *Palliative Medicine, 18*, 525–542.

Aiken, L. S., & West, S. G. (1991). *Multiple regression: Testing and interpreting interactions.* Newbury Park, CA: Sage.

Aitken, C., Higgs, P., & Bowden, S. (2008). Differences in the social networks of ethnic Vietnamese and non-Vietnamese injecting drug users and their implications for blood-borne virus transmission. *Epidemiology and Infection, 136*(3), 410–416.

Albarracín, D., Leeper, J., Earl, A., & Durantini, M. (2008). From brochures to videos to counseling: exposure to HIV-prevention programs. *AIDS and Behavior, 12*(3), 354–362.

Albarracín, J., Albarracín, D., & Durantini, M. (2008). Effects of HIV prevention interventions for samples with higher and lower percents of Latinos and Latin Americans: a meta-analysis of change in condom use and knowledge. *AIDS and Behavior, 12*(4), 521–543.

Al-Saffar, S., Borga, P., Edman, G., & Hallstrom, T. (2003). The etiology of post-traumatic stress disorder in four ethnic groups in outpatient psychiatry. *Social Psychiatry and Psychiatric Epidemiology, 38*, 456–462.

American Psychiatric Association. (2000). *Diagnostic and statistical manual of mental disorders, fourth edition, text revision.* Washington, DC: Author.

American Psychological Association (2008). Retrieved October 21, 2008, from www.apa.org/ppo/issues/phealthdis.html.

Anand, P., Kunnumakara, A., Sundaram, C., Harikumar, K.,

Tharakan, S., Lai, O., et al. (2008). Cancer is a preventable disease that requires major lifestyle changes. *Pharmaceutical Research*, 25(9), 2097–2116.

Andersen, R. M., Rice, T. H., & Kominski, G. F. (Eds.). (2007). *Changing the U.S. health care system: Key issues in health services policy and management* (3rd ed.). San Francisco: Jossey-Bass.

Anderson-Fye, E. P., & Becker, A. E. (2004). Sociocultural aspects of eating disorders. In J. K. Thompson, *Handbook of eating disorders and obesity* (pp. 565–589). Hoboken, NJ: John Wiley & Sons.

Anderzén Carlsson, A., Sørlie, V., Gustafsson, K., Olsson, M., & Kihlgren, M. (2008). Fear in children with cancer: observations at an outpatient visit. *Journal of Child Health Care: For Professionals Working with Children in the Hospital and Community*, 12(3), 191–208.

Andrews, G. J. (2002). Towards a more place-sensitive nursing research: An invitation to medical and health geography. *Nursing Inquiry*, 9, 221–238.

Antoni, M., & Lutgendorf, S. (2007). Psychosocial Factors and Disease Progression in Cancer. *Current Directions in Psychological Science*, 16(1), 42–46.

Apullan, F., Bourassa, M., Tardif, J., Fortier, A., Gayda, M., & Nigam, A. (2008). Usefulness of self-reported leisure-time physical activity to predict long-term survival in patients with coronary heart disease. *The American Journal of Cardiology*, 102(4), 375–379.

Atkinson, J. S., Schönnesson, L. N., Williams, M. L., & Timpson, S. C. (2008). Associations among correlates of schedule adherence to antiretroviral therapy (ART): A path analysis of a sample of crack cocaine using sexually active African-Americans with HIV infection. *AIDS Care*, 20, 260–269.

Avila, E., & Parker, J. (2000). *Woman who glows in the dark: A Curandera reveals traditional Aztec secrets of physical and spiritual health*. New York: Tarcher Penguin.

Ayantunde, A., Welch, N., & Parsons, S. (2007, March). A survey of patient satisfaction and use of the Internet for health information. *International Journal of Clinical Practice*, 61(3), 458–462.

Azoulay, D., Hammerman-Rozenberg, R., Cialic, R., Ein Mor, E., Jacobs, J., & Stessman, J. (2008). Increasing opioid therapy and survival in a hospice. *Journal of the American Geriatrics Society*, 56(2), 360–361.

Baban, A., & Craciun, C. (2007). Changing health-risk behaviors: A review of theory and evidence-based interventions in health psychology. *Journal of Cognitive and Behavioral Psychotherapies*, 7(1), 45–67.

Bagnardi, V., Zatonski, W., Scotti, L., La Vecchia, C., & Corrao, G. (2008). Does drinking pattern modify the effect of alcohol on the risk of coronary heart disease? Evidence from a meta-analysis. *Journal of Epidemiology and Community Health*, 62(7), 615–619.

Baker, M. K., Kennedy, D. J., Bohle, P. L., Campbell, D. S., Knapman, L., Grady, J., et al., (2007). Efficacy and feasibility of a novel tri-modal robust exercise prescription in a retirement community: A randomized, controlled trial. *Journal of the American Geriatrics Society*, 55, 1–10.

Balodhi, J. P. (1999). Traditional Indian system of medicine as applicable to treatment of mental illness. In A. Sahni (Ed.), *Mental health care in India* (pp. 132–138). Bangalore: Indian Society of Health Administrators.

Bandura, A. (1998). Health promotion from the perspective of Social Cognitive Theory. *Psychology and Health*, 13, 623–649.

Bandura, A. (2000). Cultivate self-efficacy for personal and organizational effectiveness. In E. A. Locke (Ed.), *The Blackwell handbook of principles of organizational behavior*. New York: Cambridge University Press.

Bantha, R., Moskowitz, J. T., Acree, M., & Folkman, S. (2007). Socioeconomic differences in the effects of prayer on physical symptoms and quality of life. *Journal of Health Psychology*, 12, 249–260.

Barker, D. (2008). Human growth and cardiovascular disease. *Nestlé Nutrition Workshop Series. Paediatric Programme*, 61, 21–38.

Barnato, A., Llewellyn-Thomas, H., Peters, E., Siminoff, L., Collins, E., & Barry, M. (2007). Communication and decision making in cancer care: Setting research priorities for decision support/patients' decision aids. *Medical Decision Making*, 27(5), 626–634.

Barnes, P.M., Adams, P.F., Powell-Griner, E. (2005). Health characteristics of the American Indian and Alaskan Native adult population: United States, 1999–2003. *Centers for Disease Control and Prevention*. Advance Data No. 356.

Barr-Anderson, D., van den Berg, P., Neumark-Sztainer, D., & Story, M. (2008). Characteristics associated with older adolescents who have a television in their bedrooms. *Pediatrics*, 121, 718–724.

Barrera, M., Strycker, L. A., MacKinnon, D. P., & Toobert, D. J. (2008). Social-ecological resources as mediators of two-year diet and physical activity outcomes in type 2 diabetes patients. *Health Psychology*, 27, S118–S125.

Barrera, M., Strycker, L. A., MacKinnon, D., P., & Toobert, D. J. (2008). Social-ecological resources as mediators of two-year diet and physical activity outcomes in type 2 diabetes patients. *Health Psychology*, 27, S118–S125.

Bartoshuk, L. M. (1993). The biological basis of food perception and acceptance. *Food Quality and Preference*, 4, 21–32.

Bates, L. M., Acevedo-Garcia, D., Alegría, M., & Krieger, N. (2008). Immigration and generational trends in body mass index and obesity in the United States: Results of the National Latino and Asian American Survey, 2002–2003. *American Journal of Public Health*, 98, 70–77.

Bathula, R., Francis, D., Hughes, A., & Chaturvedi, N. (2008). Ethnic differences in heart rate: can these be explained by conventional cardiovascular risk factors? *Clinical Autonomic Research: Official Journal of the Clinical Autonomic Research Society*, 18(2), 90–95.

Bau, P. F. D., Bau, C. H. D., Rosito, G. A., Manfroi, W. C., & Fuchs, F. D. (2007). Alcohol consumption, cardiovascular health, and endothelial function markers. *Alcohol*, 41, 479–488.

Beals, J., Novins, D. K., Whitesell, N. R., Spicer, P., Mitchell, C. M., & Manson, S. M. (2005). Prevalence of mental disorders and utilization of mental health services in two American Indian reservation populations. *American Journal of Psychiatry*, 162, 1723–1732.

Bearison, D. J., Minian, N., & Granowetter, L. (2002). Medical management of asthma and folk medicine in a Hispanic community. *Journal of Pediatric Psychology, 27,* 385–392.

Becker, A. E., Burwell, R. A., Gilman, S. E., Herzog, D. B., & Hamburg, P. (2002). Eating behaviors and attitudes following prolonged exposure to television among ethnic Fijian adolescent girls. *British Journal of Psychiatry, 180*(6), 509–514.

Bediako, S. M., Lavender, A. R., & Yasin, Z. (2007). Racial centrality and health care use among African American adults with sickle cell disease. *Journal of Black Psychology, 33,* 422–438.

Beesley, V., Eakin, E., Janda, M., & Battistutta, D. (2008). Gynecological cancer survivors' health behaviors and their associations with quality of life. *Cancer Causes and Control: CCC, 19*(7), 775–782.

Belar, C. D. (2008). Clinical health psychology: A health care specialty in professional psychology. *Professional Psychology: Research and Practice, 39,* 229–233.

Belar, C. D., McIntyre, T. M., & Matarazzo, J. D. (2003). Health psychology. *History of psychology, 4,* 451–464. New York: Wiley.

Benetou, V., Trichopoulou, A., Orfanos, P., Naska, A., Lagiou, P., Boffetta, P., et al. (2008). Conformity to traditional Mediterranean diet and cancer incidence: The Greek EPIC cohort. *British Journal of Cancer, 99*(1), 191–195.

Ben-Shlomo, Y., Naqvi, H., & Baker, I. (2008). Ethnic differences in healthcare-seeking behaviour and management for acute chest pain: secondary analysis of the MINAP dataset 2002–2003. *Heart (British Cardiac Society), 94*(3), 354–359.

Berg, C., Smith, T., Henry, N., & Pearce, G. (2007). A developmental approach to psychosocial risk factors and successful aging. In *Handbook of health psychology and aging* (pp. 30–53). New York: Guilford Press.

Bergelt, C., Koch, U., & Petersen, C. (2008). Quality of life in partners of patients with cancer. *Quality of Life Research: An International Journal of Quality of Life Aspects of Treatment, Care and Rehabilitation, 17*(5), 653–663.

Bernardes, S. F., Keogh, E., & Lima, M. L. (2008). Bridging the gap between pain and gender research: A selective literature review. *European Journal of Pain, 12,* 427–440.

Berthoud, H., & Morrison, C. (2008). The brain, appetite, and obesity. *Annual Review of Psychology, 59,* 55–92.

Bestehorn, K., Wegscheider, K., & Völler, H. (2008). Contemporary trends in cardiac rehabilitation in Germany: atient characteristics, drug treatment, and risk-factor management from 2000 to 2005. *European Journal of Cardiovascular Prevention and Rehabilitation, 15*(3), 312–318.

Biasi, F., Mascia, C., & Poli, G. (2008). The contribution of animal fat oxidation products to colon carcinogenesis, through modulation of TGF-beta1 signaling. *Carcinogenesis, 29*(5), 890–894.

Bjelakovic, G., Nikolova, D., Gluud, L. L., Simonetti, R. G., & Gluud, C. (2008). Antioxidant supplements for prevention of mortality in healthy participants and patients with various diseases. *Cochrane Database of Systematic Reviews, 2,* Art. No.: CD007176. DOI: 10.1002/14651858.CD007176.

Black, K., & Lobo, M. (2008). A conceptual review of family resilience factors. *Journal of Family Nursing, 14,* 33–55.

Blanchard, E. B., Lackner, J. M., Jaccard, J., Rowell, D., Carosella, A. M., & Powell, C., et al. (2008). The role of stress in symptom exacerbation among IBS patients. *Journal of Psychosomatic Research, 64,* 119–128.

Bleichhardt, G., Timmer, B., & Rief, W. (2005). Hypochondriasis among patients with multiple somatoform symptoms: Psychopathology and outcome of a cognitive-behavioral therapy. *Journal of Contemporary Psychotherapy, 35,* 239–249.

Bleiker, E., Hendriks, J., Otten, J., Verbeek, A., & van der Ploeg, H. (2008). Personality factors and breast cancer risk: A 13-year follow-up. *Journal of the National Cancer Institute, 100*(3), 213–218.

Bleuler, M. (1963). Conception of schizophrenia within the last fifty years and today. *Proceedings of the Royal Society of Medicine, 56,* 945–952.

Blomkvist, V., Eriksen, C. A., Theorell, T., Ulrich, R., & Rasmanis, G. (2005). Acoustics and psychosocial environment in intensive coronary care. *Occupational and Environmental Medicine, 62,* e1.

Blumenthal, J. (2008). Depression and coronary heart disease: association and implications for treatment. *Cleveland Clinic Journal of Medicine, 75,* S48–53.

Bonadies, V. (2004). A yoga therapy program for AIDS-related pain and anxiety: implications for therapeutic recreation. *Therapeutic Recreation Journal, 38*(2), 148–166.

Borkhoff, C. M., Hawker, G. A., Kreder, H. J., Glazier, R. H., Mahomed, N. N., & Wright, J. G. (2008). The effect of patients' sex on physicians' recommendations for total knee arthroplasty. *Canadian Medical Association Journal, 178,* 681–687.

Bova, C., Burwick, T. N., & Quinones, M. (2008). Improving women's adjustment to HIV infection: Results of the Positive Life Skills workshop project. *Journal of the Association of Nurses in AIDS Care, 19,* 58–65.

Boyer, B. (2008). Theoretical models of health psychology and the model for integrating medicine and psychology. In *Comprehensive handbook of clinical health psychology* (pp. 3–30). Hoboken, NJ: John Wiley & Sons.

Boyle, S., Jackson, W., & Suarez, E. (2007). Hostility, anger, and depression predict increases in C3 over a 10-year period. *Brain, Behavior, and Immunity, 21*(6), 816–823.

Brannon & Feist, (2007). Health psychology: An introduction to behavior and health. San Francisco: Wadsworth.

Braveman, P. (2006). Health disparities and health equity: concepts and measurement. *Annual Review of Public Health, 27,* 167–194.

Brendryen, H., & Kraft, P. (2008). Happy Ending: A randomized controlled trial of a digital multi-media smoking cessation intervention. *Addiction, 103,* 478–484.

Brown, D. L. (2008). African American resiliency: Examining racial socialization and social support as protective factors. *Journal of Black Psychology, 34,* 32–48.

Brown, R. T., Wiener, L., & Kupst, M. J. (2008). Single parents of children with chronic illness: An understudied phenomenon. *Journal of Pediatric Psychology, 33,* 408–421.

Broz, D., & Ouellet, L. (2008). Racial and ethnic changes in heroin injection in the United States: implications for the HIV/AIDS epidemic. *Drug and Alcohol Dependence, 94*(1-3), 221–233.

Bruchac, J. (1993). *The Native American sweat lodge: History and legends.* Freedom, CA: Crossing Press.

Bruss, M. B., Applegate, B., Quitugua, J., Palacios, R. T., & Morris, J. R. (2007). Ethnicity and diet of children: Development of culturally sensitive measures. *Health Education and Behavior, 34,* 735–747.

Buchanan, T. W., & Tranel, D. (2008). Stress and emotional memory retrieval: Effects of sex and cortisol response. *Neurobiology of Learning and Memory, 89,* 134–141.

Burke, A., Upchurch, D. M., Dye, C., & Chyu, L. (2006). Acupuncture use in the United States: Findings from the National Health Interview Survey. *Journal of Alternative and Complementary Medicine, 12,* 639–48.

Burke, G. L., Bertoni, A. G., Shea, S., Tracy, R., Watson, K. E., Blumenthal, R.S., et al. (2008). The impact of obesity on cardiovascular disease risk factors and subclinical vascular disease: The multi-ethnic study of atherosclerosis. *Archives of Internal Medicine, 168,* 928–935.

Burns, A. B., Brown, J. S., Sachs-Ericsson, N., Plant, E. A., Curtis, J. T., Fredrickson, B. L., & Joiner, T. E. (2008). Upward spirals of positive emotion and coping: Replication, extension, and initial exploration of neurochemical substrates. *Personality and Individual Differences, 44,* 360–370.

Butler, S. M., Black, D. R., Blue, C. L., Gretebeck, RJ. (2004). Change in diet, physical activity, and body weight in female college freshman. *American Journal of Health Behavior, 28,* 24–32.

Byrd-Williams, C., Kelly, L. A., Davis, J. N., Spruijt-Metz, D., Goran, M. I. (2007). Influence of gender, BMI and Hispanic ethnicity on physical activity in children. *International Journal of Pediatric Obesity, 2,* 159–166.

Byrne-Davis, L., & Vedhara, K. (2008). Psychoneuroimmunology. *Social and Personality Psychology Compass, 2*(2), 751–764.

Campaign for Tobacco-free Kids. (n.d.). Retrieved October 21, 2008, from www.tobaccofreekids.org.

Campbell, C. M., France, C. R., Robinson, M. E., Logan, H. L., Geffken, G. R., & Fillingim, R. B. (2008). Ethnic differences in the nociceptive flexion reflex (NFR). *Pain, 134,* 91–96.

Campbell, M. K., Hudson, M. A., Resnicow, K., Blakeney, N., Paxton, A., & Baskin, M. (2007). Church-based health promotion interventions: Evidence and lessons learned. *Annual Review of Public Health, 28,* 213–234.

Campbell, R., Greeson, M. R., Bybee, D., & Raja, S. (2008). The co-occurrence of childhood sexual abuse, adult sexual assault, intimate partner violence, and sexual harassment: A mediational model of post-traumatic stress disorder and physical health outcomes. *Journal of Consulting and Clinical Psychology, 76,* 194–207.

Campbell, T. A., Auerbach, S. M., & Kiesler, D. J. (2007). Relationship of interpersonal behaviors and health-related control appraisals to patient satisfaction and compliance in a university health center. *Journal of American College Health, 55,* 333–340.

Campos, B., Schetter, C. D., Abdou, C. M., Hobel, C. J., Glynn, L. M., & Sandman, C. A. (2008). Familialism, social support, and stress: Positive implications for pregnant Latinas. *Cultural Diversity and Ethnic Minority Psychology, 14,* 155–162.

Carlson, L. E., Speca, M., Patel, K. D., & Goodey, E. (2003). Mindfulness-based stress reduction in relation to quality of life, mood, symptoms of stress, and immune parameters in breast and prostate cancer outpatients. *Psychosomatic Medicine 65*(4), 571–581.

Carlson, L., Speca, M., Faris, P., & Patel, K. (2007). One year pre-post intervention follow-up of psychological, immune, endocrine and blood pressure outcomes of mindfulness-based stress reduction (MBSR) in breast and prostate cancer outpatients. *Brain, Behavior, And Immunity, 21*(8), 1038–1049.

Carnagey, N. L., Anderson. C. A., & Bushman, B. J. (2007). The effect of video game violence on physiological desensitization to real life violence. *Journal of Experimental Social Psychology, 43,* 489–496.

Carpenter, M. J., Strange, C., Jones, Y., Dickson, M. R., Carter, C.,

Moseley, M. A., et al. (2007). Does genetic testing result in behavioral health change? Changes in smoking behavior following testing for alpha-1 antitrypsin deficiency. *Annals of Behavioral Medicine, 33,* 22–28.

Carrico, A., & Antoni, M. (2008). Effects of psychological interventions on neuroendocrine hormone regulation and immune status in HIV-positive persons: a review of randomized controlled trials. *Psychosomatic Medicine, 70*(5), 575–584.

Cassetta, J. A., Boden-Albala, B., Sciacca, R. R., & Giardina, E. V. (2007). Association of education and race/ethnicity with physical activity in insured urban women. *Journal of Women's Health, 16,* 902–908.

Centers for Disease Control and Prevention. *HIV/AIDS Surveillance Report, 2006. Vol. 18.* Atlanta: U.S. Department of Health and Human Services, Centers for Disease Control and Prevention; 2008: [inclusive page numbers]. Retrieved October 21, 2008, from http://www.cdc.gov/hiv/topics/surveillance/resources/reports/.

Cerin, E., Vandelanotte, C., Leslie, E., & Merom, D. (2008). Recreational facilities and leisure-time physical activity: An analysis of moderators and self-efficacy as a mediator. *Health Psychology, 27,* S126–S135.

Cervone, D., Shadel, W. G., Smith, R. E., & Fiori, M. (2006). Self-regulation: reminders and suggestions from personality science. *Applied Psychology: An International Review 55*(3), 333–385.

Chafin, S., Christenfeld, N., & Gerin, W. (2008). Improving cardiovascular recovery from stress with brief post-stress exercise. *Health Psychology, 27,* S64–S72.

Chafin, S., Christenfeld, N., & Gerin, W. (2008). Improving cardiovascular recovery from stress with brief post-stress exercise. *Health Psychology, 27,* S64–S72.

Chandola, T., Britton, A., Brunner, E., Hemingway, H., Malik, M., Kumari, M., et al. (2008). Work stress and coronary heart disease: what are the mechanisms? *European Heart Journal, 29*(5), 640–648.

Chaturvedi, S., & Venkateswaran, C. (2008, March). New research in psychooncology. *Current Opinion in Psychiatry, 21*(2), 206–210.

Cherr, G., Zimmerman, P., Wang, J., & Dosluoglu, H. (2008). Patients with depression are at increased risk for secondary cardiovascular events after lower extremity revascularization. *Journal of General Internal Medicine, 23*(5), 629–634.

Chida, Y., Hamer, M., Wardle, J., & Steptoe, A. (2008). Do stress-related psychosocial factors contribute to cancer incidence and survival? *Nature Clinical Practice. Oncology, 5*(8), 466–475.

Choi, H. K., & Curhan, G. (2008). Soft drinks, fructose consumption, and the risk of gout in men: Prospective cohort study. *British Medical Journal, 336*, 309–312.

Choi, H., Meininger, J. C., & Roberts, R. E. (2006). Ethnic differences in adolescents' mental distress, social stress, and resources. *Adolescence, 41*, 263–283.

Choi, S., Rankin, S., Stewart, A., & Oka, R. (2008). Effects of acculturation on smoking behavior in Asian Americans: A meta-analysis. *Journal of Cardiovascular Nursing, 23*, 67–73.

Chopra, A., & Doiphode, V. (2002). Ayurvedic medicine: core concept, therapeutic principles, and current relevance. *Medical Clinics of North America, 86*, 75–89.

Chowdhury, R. I., Islam, M. A., Gulshan, J., & Chakraborty, N. (2007). Delivery complications and healthcare seeking behaviour: The Bangladesh Demographic Health Survey, 1999–2000. *Health and Social Care in the Community, 15*, 254–264.

Chung, H., & Breslau, N. (2008). The latent structure of post-traumatic stress disorder: Tests of invariance by gender and trauma type. *Psychological Medicine, 38*, 563–573.

Clark, N. M., Cabana, M. D., Nan, B., Gong, Z. M., Slish, K. K., Birk, N. A., & Kaciroti, N. (2008). The clinician-patient partnership paradigm: Outcomes associated with physician communication behavior. *Clinical Pediatrics, 47*, 49–57.

Clauss-Ehlers, C. S. (2008). Sociocultural factors, resilience, and coping: Support for a culturally sensitive measure of resilience. *Journal of Applied Developmental Psychology, 29*, 197–212.

Clifford, S., Barber, N., & Horne, R. (2008). Understanding different beliefs held by adherers, unintentional nonadherers, and intentional nonadherers: Application of the Necessity-Concerns Framework. *Journal of Psychosomatic Research, 64*, 41–46.

Cohen, K. (2003). *Honoring the medicine: The essential guide to Native American healing*. New York: Ballantine Books.

Cohen, S., Alper, C., Doyle, W., Adler, N., Treanor, J., & Turner, R. (2008). Objective and subjective socioeconomic status and susceptibility to the common cold. *Health Psychology: Official Journal of the Division of Health Psychology, American Psychological Association, 27*(2), 268–274.

Cokley, K. (2007). Critical issues in the measurement of ethnic and racial identity: A referendum on the state of the field. *Journal of Counseling Psychology, 54*, 224–234.

Col, N., Ngo, L., Fortin, J., Goldberg, R., & O'Connor, A. (2007). Can computerized decision support help patients make complex treatment decisions? A randomized controlled trial of an individualized menopause decision aid. *Medical Decision Making: An International Journal of the Society for Medical Decision Making, 27*(5), 585–598.

Cole, T.B. (2006). Rape at U.S. colleges often fueled by alcohol. *JAMA: Journal of the American Medical Association, 296*, 504–505.

Coleman, K., Koffman, J., & Daniels, C. (2007). Why is this happening to me? Illness beliefs held by haredi Jewish breast cancer patients: an exploratory study. *Spirituality and Health International, 8*, 121–134.

Collins, F. C. (2007). *The language of god: A scientist presents evidence for belief*. New York: Free Press.

Compas, B. E., Connor-Smith, J. K., Saltzman, H., Thomsen, A. H., & Wadsworth, M. E. (2001). Coping with stress during childhood and adolescence: Problems, progress, and potential in theory and research. *Psychological Bulletin, 127*, 87–127.

Contrada, R. J., Ashmore, R. D., Gary, M. L., Coups, E., Egeth, J. D., Sewell, A., et al. (2000). Ethnicity-related sources of stress and their effects on well-being. *Current Directions in Psychological Science, 9*(4), 136–139.

Cooke, L. (2007). The importance of exposure for healthy eating in childhood: A review. *Journal of Human Nutrition and Dietetics, 20*, 294–301.

Corr, C. A., & Corr, D. M. (2007). Culture, socialization, and dying. In D. Balk, C. Wogrin, G. Thornton, & D. Meagher (Eds.) *Handbook of thanatology: The essential body of knowledge for the student of death, dying, and bereavement* (3–10). Northbrook, IL: Association for Death Education and Counseling.

Coughlin, S. (2008). Surviving cancer or other serious illness: a review of individual and community resources. *CA: A Cancer Journal for Clinicians, 58*(1), 60–64.

Coups, E., Hay, J., & Ford, J. (2008). Awareness of the role of physical activity in colon cancer prevention. *Patient Education and Counseling, 72*(2), 246–251.

Covey, J. (2007). A meta-analysis of the effects of presenting treatment benefits in different formats. *Medical Decision Making, 27*, 638–654.

Cowan, M., Freedland, K., Burg, M., Saab, P., Youngblood, M., Cornell, C., et al. (2008). Predictors of treatment response for depression and inadequate social support—the ENRICHD randomized clinical trial. *Psychotherapy and Psychosomatics, 77*(1), 27–37.

Cramer, J. A., Roy, A., Burrell, A., Fairchild, C. J., Fuldeore, M. J., Ollendorf, D. A., et al. (2008). Medication compliance and persistence: Terminology and definitions. *Value in Health, 11*, 44–47.

Crow, T. M. (2001). *Native plants, native healing: Traditional Muskogee way*. Summertown, TN: Book Publishing Co.

Crowe, F., Key, T., Appleby, P., Travis, R., Overvad, K., Jakobsen, M., et al. (2008). Dietary fat intake and risk of prostate cancer in the European Prospective Investigation into Cancer and Nutrition. *The American Journal of Clinical Nutrition, 87*(5), 1405–1413.

Cunradi, C. B., Moore, R. S., & Ames, G. (2008). Contribution of occupational factors to current smoking among active-duty U.S. Navy careerists. *Nicotine and Tobacco Research, 10*, 429–437.

Curtis, L. H., Al-Khatib, S. M., Shea, A. M., Hammill, B. G., Hernandez, A. F., & Schulman, K. A. (2007). Sex differences in the use of implantable cardioverter-defibrillators for primary and secondary prevention of sudden cardiac death. *JAMA: Journal of the American Medical Association, 298*, 1517–1524.

Dalton, R., Scheeringa, M.S., & Zeanah, C.H. (2008). Did the prevalence of PTSD following Hurricane Katrina match a rapid needs assessment prediction? A template for future public planning after large-scale disasters. *Psychiatric Annals, 38*, 134–144.

Damschroder, L. J., Zikmund Fisher, B. J., & Ubel, P. A. (2008). Considering adaptation in preference elicitations. *Health Psychology, 27*, 394–399.

Darbes, L., Crepaz, N., Lyles, C., Kennedy, G., & Rutherford, G. (2008). The efficacy of behavioral interventions in reducing HIV risk behaviors and incident sexually transmitted diseases in heterosexual African Americans. *AIDS (London, England), 22*(10), 1177–1194.

Dart, J. (2008). The Internet as a source of health information in three disparate communities. *Australian Health Review: A Publication of the Australian Hospital Association, 32*(3), 559–569.

Daubenmier, J. J., Weidner, G., Sumner, M. D., Mendell, N., Merritt-Worden, T., Studley, J., & Ornish, D. (2007). The contribution of changes in diet, exercise, and stress management to changes in coronary risk in women and men in the multisite cardiac lifestyle intervention program. *Annals of Behavioral Medicine, 33*, 57–68.

Davidson, K. W., Trudeau, K. J., & Smith, T. W. (2006). Introducing the new health psychology series "Evidence-Based treatment reviews": Progress not perfection. *Health Psychology, 25*, 1–3.

Davidson, K., Gidron, Y., Mostofsky, E., & Trudeau, J. (2007). Hospitalization cost offset of a hostility intervention for coronary heart disease patients. *Journal of Consulting and Clinical Psychology, 75*(4), 657–662.

Davidson, K., Trudeau, K., & Smith, T. (2006). Introducing the new health psychology series evidence-based treatment reviews: Progress not perfection. *Health Psychology, 25*(1), 1–2.

de Jong, J. T. V. M. (2005). Commentary: Deconstructing critiques on the internationalization of PTSD. *Culture, Medicine, and Psychiatry, 29*, 361–370.

de Lapparent, M. (2008). Willingness to use safety belt and levels of injury in car accidents. *Accident Analysis and Prevention, 40*, 1023–1032.

de Souza, R., Swain, J., Appel, L., & Sacks, F. (2008). Alternatives for macronutrient intake and chronic disease: Comparison of the Omni-Heart diets with popular diets and with dietary recommendations. *The American Journal of Clinical Nutrition, 88*(1), 1–11.

DeBellonia, R. R., Marcus, S., Shih, R., Kashani, J., Rella, J.G., & Ruck B. (2008). Curanderismo: Consequences of folk medicine. *Pediatric Emergency Care, 24*, 228–229.

Decker, C. (2007). Social support and adolescent cancer survivors: A review of the literature. *Psycho-Oncology, 16*(1), 1–11.

DeGarmo, D. S., Patras, J., & Eap, S. (2008). Social support for divorced fathers' parenting: Testing a stress-buffering model. *Family Relations, 57*, 35–48.

Deibert, C., Maliski, S., Kwan, L., Fink, A., Connor, S., & Litwin, M. (2007). Prostate cancer knowledge among low-income minority men. *The Journal of Urology, 177*(5), 1851–1855.

Deichert, N., Fekete, E., Boarts, J., Druley, J., & Delahanty, D. (2008). Emotional support and affect: associations with health behaviors and active coping efforts in men living with HIV. *AIDS and Behavior, 12*(1), 139–145.

del Junco, D., Vernon, S., Coan, S., Tiro, J., Bastian, L., Savas, L., et al. (2008). Promoting regular mammography screening I. A systematic assessment of validity in a randomized trial. *Journal of The National Cancer Institute, 100*(5), 333–346.

Dellifraine, J., & Dansky, K. (2008). Home-based telehealth: a review and meta-analysis. *Journal of Telemedicine and Telecare, 14*(2), 62–66.

Delva, J., Johnston, L. D., & O'Malley, P. M. (2007). The epidemiology of overweight and related lifestyle behaviors: Racial/ethnic and socioeconomic status differences among American youth. *American Journal of Preventive Medicine, 33*, S178–S186.

DeSpelder, L. A., & Strickland, A. (2007). Culture, socialization, and death education. In D. Balk, C. Wogrin, G. Thornton, & D. Meagher (Eds.) *Handbook of thanatology: The essential body of knowledge for the student of death, dying, and bereavement* (303–314). Northbrook, IL: Association for Death Education and Counseling.

DeStefano, A. M. (2001). *Latino folk medicine: Healing herbal remedies from ancient traditions.* New York: Ballantine Books.

DeVol, R., Bedroussian, A., Charuworn, A., Chatterjee, A., Kim, I. K., Kim, S., & Klowden, K. (2007). An unhealthy America: The economic burden of chronic disease—charting a new course to save lives and increase productivity and economic growth. Report of the Milliken Institute. Retrieved July 28, 2008, from http://www.milkeninstitute. org/publications/publications.taf? function=detail&ID=38801020 &cat=ResRep.

Dhalla, S., Chan, K., Montaner, J., & Hogg, R. (2006). Complementary and alternative medicine use in British Columbia—A survey of HIV positive people on antiretroviral therapy. *Complementary Therapies in Clinical Practice, 12*(4), 242–248.

Diaz, R.M., Ayala, G., Bein, E., Henne, J., Marin, B.V. (2001). The impact of homophobia, poverty, and racism on the mental health of gay and bisexual Latino men: Findings from 3 US cities. *American Journal of Public Health, 91*, 927–932.

Ditzen, B., Schmidt, S., Strauss, B., Nater, U. M., Ehlert, U., & Heinrichs, M. (2008). Adult attachment and social support interact to reduce psychological but not cortisol responses to stress. *Journal of Psychosomatic Research, 64*, 479–486.

Duff, D. C., Levine, T. R., Beatty, M. J., Woolbright, J., & Park, H. S. (2007). Testing Public Anxiety Treatments against a Credible Placebo Control. *Communication Education, 56*, 72–88.

Durvasula, R., Regan, P., Ureño, O., & Howell, L. (2008). Predictors of cervical cancer screening in Asian and Latina university students. *College Student Journal, 42*(2), 243–253.

Eldred, C., & Sykes, C. (2008). Psychosocial interventions for carers of survivors of stroke: A systematic review of interventions based on psychological principles and theoretical frameworks. *British Journal of Health Psychology, 13*(3), 563–581.

Eliade, M. (1964). *Shamanism: Archaic techniques of ecstasy*. Princeton, NJ: Princeton University Press.

Erickson, S., Gerstle, M., & Montague, F. (2008). Repressive adaptive style and self-reported psychological functioning in adolescent cancer survivors. *Child Psychiatry and Human Development, 39*(3), 247–260.

Erlen, J. A., & Caruthers, D. (2007). Adherence to medical regimens. In P. Kennedy, *Psychological management of physical disabilities: A practitioner's guide* (pp. 203–232). New York: Routledge/Taylor & Francis.

Eshun, S., & Gurung, R. A. R. (Eds.). (2009). *Culture and mental health: Sociocultural influences on mental health*. Malden, MA: Blackwell.

Faith, M. S., Fontaine, K. R., Baskin, M. L., & Allison, D. (2007). Toward the reduction of population obesity: Macrolevel environmental approaches to the problems of food, eating, and obesity. *Psychological Bulletin, 133*, 205–226.

Falagas, M., Zarkadoulia, E., Ioannidou, E., Peppas, G., Christodoulou, C., & Rafailidis, P. (2007). The effect of psychosocial factors on breast cancer outcome: A systematic review. *Breast Cancer Research: BCR, 9*(4), R44–R44.

Fan, Y., Yuan, J., Wang, R., Gao, Y., & Yu, M. (2008). Alcohol, tobacco, and diet in relation to esophageal cancer: the Shanghai Cohort Study. *Nutrition and Cancer, 60*(3), 354–363.

Fang, C., Miller, S., Bovbjerg, D., Bergman, C., Edelson, M., Rosenblum, N., et al. (2008). Perceived stress is associated with impaired T-cell response to HPV16 in women with cervical dysplasia. *Annals of Behavioral Medicine, 35*(1), 87–96.

Fann, J., Thomas-Rich, A., Katon, W., Cowley, D., Pepping, M., McGregor, B., et al. (2008). Major depression after breast cancer: a review of epidemiology and treatment. *General Hospital Psychiatry, 30*(2), 112–126.

Farmer, D., Reddick, B., D'Agostino, R., & Jackson, S. (2007). Psychosocial correlates of mammography screening in older African American women. *Oncology Nursing Forum, 34*(1), 117–123.

Farmer, D., Reddick, B., D'Agostino, R., & Jackson, S. (2007, January). Psychosocial correlates of mammography screening in older African American women. *Oncology Nursing Forum, 34*(1), 117–123.

Farooqi, Y.N. (2006). Traditional healing practices sought by Muslim psychiatric patients in Lahore, Pakistan. *International Journal of Disability, Development and Education, 53*, 401–415.

Fasce, N. (2008). Depression and social support among men and women living with HIV. *Journal of Applied Biobehavioral Research, 12*(3), 221–236.

Ferrando, S., & Freyberg, Z. (2008). Treatment of depression in HIV positive individuals: a critical review. *International Review of Psychiatry (Abingdon, England), 20*(1), 61–71.

Ferreira, R. (2008, March). Culture at the heart of coping with HIV/AIDS. *Journal of Psychology in Africa, 18*(1), 97–104.

Field, A. (2005). *Discovering statistics using SPSS*. Thousand Oaks, CA: Sage.

Finch, B.K., Kolody, B., & Vega, W.A. (2000). Perceived discrimination and depression among Mexican-origin adults in California, *Journal of Health and Social Behavior, 41*, 295–313.

Finkelstein, E. A., Brown, D. S., & Evans, W. D. (2008). Do obese persons comprehend their personal health risks? *American Journal of Health Behavior, 32*, 508–516.

Finlayson, G., King, N., & Blundell, J. (2008). The role of implicit wanting in relation to explicit liking and wanting for food: Implications for appetite control. *Appetite, 50*, 120–127.

Fischer Aggarwal, B., Liao, M., & Mosca, L. (2008). Physical activity as a potential mechanism through which social support may reduce cardiovascular disease risk. *The Journal of Cardiovascular Nursing, 23*(2), 90–96.

Fisher, J.D., & Fisher, W. A. (1992). Changing AIDS-risk behavior. *Psychological Bulletin, 111*, 455–474.

Fisher, T. L., Burnet, D. L., Huang, E. S., Chin, M. H., & Cagney, K. A. (2007). Cultural leverage: Interventions using culture to narrow racial disparities in health care. *Medical Care Research and Review, 64*, 243S–282S.

Flum, D. R., Salem, L., Elrod, J. B., Dellinger, E. P., Cheadle, A., & Chan, L. (2005). Early mortality among Medicare beneficiaries undergoing bariatric surgical procedures. *JAMA: Journal of the American Medical Association, 294*, 1903–1908.

Folsom, D. P., Gilmer, T., Barrio, C., Moore, D. J., Bucardo, J., Lindamer, L. A., et al. (2007). A longitudinal study of the use of mental health services by persons with serious mental illness: Do Spanish-speaking Latinos differ from English-speaking Latinos and Caucasians? *American Journal of Psychiatry, 164*, 1173–1180.

Forcier, K., Stroud, L. R., Papandonatos, G. D., Hitsman, B., Reiches, M., Krishnamoorthy, J., & Niaura, R. (2006). Links between physical fitness and cardiovascular reactivity and recovery to psychological stressors: A meta-Analysis. *Health Psychology, 25*, 723–739.

Fowler, R. A., Sabur, N., Ping, L., Juurlink, D. N., Pinto, R., Hladunewich, M. A., et al. (2007). Sex- and age-based differences in the delivery and outcomes of critical care. *Canadian Medical Association Journal, 177*(12), doi:10.1503/cmaj.071112.

Fox, C., Pencina, M., Wilson, P., Paynter, N., Vasan, R., & D'Agostino, R. (2008). Lifetime risk of cardiovascular disease among individuals with and without diabetes stratified by obesity status in the Framingham heart study. *Diabetes Care, 31*(8), 1582–1584.

Franko, D. L., Thompson, D., Affenito, S. G., Barton, B. A., & Striegel-Moore, R. H. (2008). What mediates the relationship between family meals and adolescent health issues. *Health Psychology, 27*, S109–S117.

Franko, D. L., Thompson, D., Affenito, S. G., Barton, B. A., & Striegel-Moore, R. H. (2008). What mediates the relationship between family meals and adolescent health issues? *Health Psychology, 27*, S109–S117.

Fredrickson, B. L., Tugade, M. M., Waugh, C. E., & Larkin, G. R. (2003). What good are positive emotions in crisis? A prospective study of resilience and emotions following the terrorist attacks on the United States on September 11th, 2001. *Journal of Personality and Social Psychology, 84*, 365–376.

Freedman, L., Kipnis, V., Schatzkin, A., & Potischman, N. (2008). Methods of epidemiology: Evaluating the fat-breast cancer hypothesis–comparing dietary instruments and other developments. *Cancer Journal (Sudbury, Mass.)*, *14*(2), 69–74.

Friedman, H. (2008, July 18). The multiple linkages of personality and disease. *Brain, Behavior, and Immunity*, *22*(5), 668–675.

Fu, M. R., Xu, B., Liu, Y., & Haber, J. (2008). "Making the best of it": Chinese women's experiences of adjusting to breast cancer diagnosis and treatment. *Journal of Advanced Nursing*, *63*, 155–165.

Fuchs, F. D., & Chambless, L. E. (2007). Is the cardioprotective effect of alcohol real? *Alcohol*, *41*, 399–402.

Fuentes, M., Hart-Johnson, T., & Green, C. R. (2007). The association among neighborhood socioeconomic status, race, and chronic pain in Black and White older adults. *Journal of the National Medical Association*, *99*, 1160–1169.

Fung, T., Chiuve, S., McCullough, M., Rexrode, K., Logroscino, G., & Hu, F. (2008). Adherence to a DASH-style diet and risk of coronary heart disease and stroke in women. *Archives of Internal Medicine*, *168*(7), 713–720.

Galanti, G. A. (2004). *Caring for patients from diverse cultures*. State College: University of Pennsylvania Press.

Galantino, M., Galbavy, R., & Quinn, L. (2008). Therapeutic effects of yoga for children: a systematic review of the literature. *Pediatric Physical Therapy: The Official Publication of the Section on Pediatrics of the American Physical Therapy Association*, *20*(1), 66–80.

Galea, S., Brewin, C. R., Jones, R. T., King, D. W., King, L. A., McNally, R. J., et al. (2007). Exposure to hurricane-related stressors and mental illness after hurricane Katrina. *Archives of General Psychiatry*, *64*, 1427–1434.

Gallagher, S., Phillips, A. C., Ferraro, A. J., Drayson, M. T., & Carroll, D. (2008). Social support is positively associated with the immunoglobulin M response to vaccination with pneumococcal polysaccharides. *Biological Psychology*, *78*, 211–215.

Gallicchio, L., Hoffman, S. C., & Helzlsouer, K. J. (2007). The relationship between gender, social support, and health-related quality of life in a community-based study in Washington County, Maryland.

Quality of Life Research, *16*, 777–786.

Galvan, F., Davis, E., Banks, D., & Bing, E. (2008, May). HIV stigma and social support among African Americans. *AIDS Patient Care and Standards*, *22*(5), 423–436.

Gansler, T., Kaw, C., Crammer, C., & Smith, T. (2008). A population-based study of prevalence of complementary methods use by cancer survivors: a report from the American Cancer Society's studies of cancer survivors. *Cancer*, *113*(5), 1048–1057.

Garcia-Palacios, A., Hoffman, H. G., Richards, T. R., Seibel, E. J., & Sharar, S. R. (2007). Use of virtual reality distraction to reduce claustrophobia symptoms during a mock magnetic resonance imaging brain scan: A case report. *CyberPsychology and Behavior*, *10*, 485–488.

Gately, I. (2003). Tobacco: A cultural history of how an exotic plant seduced civilization. New York: Grove Press.

Gayda, M., Brun, C., Juneau, M., Levesque, S., & Nigam, A. (2008). Long-term cardiac rehabilitation and exercise training programs improve metabolic parameters in metabolic syndrome patients with and without coronary heart disease. *Nutrition, Metabolism, and Cardiovascular Diseases: NMCD*, *18*(2), 142–151.

Geirdal, A., & Dahl, A. (2008). The relationship between psychological distress and personality in women from families with familial breast/ovarian or hereditary non-polyposis colorectal cancer in the absence of demonstrated mutations. *Journal of Genetic Counseling*, *17*(4), 384–393.

Gerressu, M., & Stephenson, J. (2008). Sexual behaviour in young people. *Current Opinion in Infectious Diseases*, *21*(1), 37–41.

Giannoglou, G., Chatzizisis, Y., Zamboulis, C., Parcharidis, G., Mikhailidis, D., & Louridas, G. (2008). Elevated heart rate and atherosclerosis: an overview of the pathogenetic mechanisms. *International Journal of Cardiology*, *126*(3), 302–312.

Gidron, Y., Levy, A., & Cwikel, J. (2007). Psychosocial and reported inflammatory disease correlates of self-reported heart disease in women from south of Israel. *Women and Health*, *44*(4), 25–40.

Gilligan, R. (2008). Promoting resilience in young people in long-term care—the relevance of roles and relationships in the domains of recreation and work. *Journal of Social Work Practice*, *22*, 37–50.

Given, C. (2003). Introduction: The state of the knowledge of intervention research in cancer care. In *Evidence-based cancer care and prevention: Behavioral interventions* (pp. 1–16). New York: Springer.

Glanz, K., Halpern, A. C., & Saraiya, M. (2006). Behavioral and community interventions to prevent skin cancer: What works? *Archives of Dermatology*, *142*, 356–60.

Glanz, K., Rimer, B. K., & Viswanath, K. (Eds.) (2008). *Health behavior and health education: Theory, research, and practice* (4th ed.). San Francisco: Jossey-Bass.

Goldman, R. H., Stason, W. B., Park, S. K., Kim, R., Schnyer, R. N., Davis, R. B., Legedza, A. T. R., & Kaptchuk, Ted J. (2008). Acupuncture for treatment of persistent arm pain due to repetitive use: A randomized controlled clinical trial. *Clinical Journal of Pain*, *24*, 211–218.

Goldstein, L., Amarenco, P., Lamonte, M., Gilbert, S., Messig, M., Callahan, A., et al. (2008). Relative effects of statin therapy on stroke and cardiovascular events in men and women: Secondary analysis of the Stroke Prevention by Aggressive Reduction in Cholesterol Levels (SPARCL) Study. *Stroke; a Journal of Cerebral Circulation*, *39*(9), 2444–2448.

Goldston, K., & Baillie, A. (2008). Depression and coronary heart disease: A review of the epidemiological evidence, explanatory mechanisms and management approaches. *Clinical Psychology Review*, *28*(2), 288–306.

Goodman, E., Huang, B., Schafer-Kalkhoff, T., & Adler, N. E. (2007). Perceived socioeconomic status: A new type of identity which influences adolescents' self-rated health. *Journal of Adolescent Health*, *41*, 479–487.

Greenspan, J. D., Craft, R. M., LeResche, L., Arendt-Nielsen, L., Berkley, K. J., Fillingim, R. B., et al. (2007). Studying sex and gender differences in pain and analgesia: A consensus report. *Pain*, *132*, S26–S45.

Greeson, J., Hurwitz, B., Llabre, M., Schneiderman, N., Penedo, F., & Klimas, N. (2008, August 5). Psychological distress, killer lymphocytes and disease severity in HIV/AIDS. *Brain, Behavior, and Immunity, 22*(6), 901–911.

Griffith, D., Mason, M., Rodela, M., Matthews, D., Tran, A., Royster, M., et al. (2007). A structural approach to examining prostate cancer risk for rural southern African American men. *Journal of Health Care for the Poor and Underserved, 18*(4 Suppl), 73–101.

Guenole, N., Chernyshenko, S., Stark, S., McGregor, K., & Ganesh, S. (2008). Measuring stress reaction style: A construct validity investigation. *Personality and Individual Differences, 44,* 250–262.

Guo, Q., Johnson, C. A., Unger, J. B., Lee, L., Xie, B., Chou, C., et al. (2007). Chinese adolescent smoking. *Addictive Behaviors, 32,* 1066–1801.

Gurung, R. A. R., & Abhold, J. (2004). A report on the "You Know You Want To" campaign: Changing social norms to reduce college smoking. Technical report.

Gurung, R. A. R., & Prieto, L. (Eds.). (2009). *Getting culture: Incorporating diversity across the curriculum.* Sterling, VA: Stylus.

Gurung, R. A. R., & Roethel, A. (2009). Stress & culture. In S. Eshun & R A. R. Gurung (Eds.), *Sociocultural influences on mental health,* Malden, MA: Blackwell.

Gurung, R. A. R., & Von Dras, D. (2007). Social support and aging. In L. O. Randal (Ed.), *Aging and the elderly: Psychology, sociology, and health.* New York: Nova Science Publishers.

Gurung, R. A. R., Taylor, S. E., Kemeny, M., & Myers, H. (2004). HIV is not my biggest problem: Chronic burden, depression and ethnicity in women at risk for HIV. *Journal of Social and Clinical Psychology, 23,* 490–511.

Hagger-Johnson, G. E., & Whiteman, M. C. (2007). Conscientiousness facets and health behaviors: A latent variable modeling approach. *Personality and Individual Differences, 43,* 1235–1245.

Hall, C., Hall, J., Pfriemer, J., Wimberley, P., & Jones, C. (2007). Effects of a culturally sensitive education program on the breast cancer knowledge and beliefs of Hispanic women. *Oncology Nursing Forum, 34*(6), 1195–1202.

Hall, H. I., Song R., Rhodes P., Prejean J., An, Q., Lee, L.M., et al. (2008). Estimation of HIV incidence in the United States. *JAMA: Journal of the American Medical Association, 300*(5), 520–529.

Hall, J. D., Ashley, D. M., Bramlett, R. K., Dielmann, K. B., & Murphy, J. J. (2005). ADHD assessment: A comparison of negative versus positive symptom formats. *Journal of Applied School Psychology, 21,* 163–173.

Hamburg, N., Keyes, M., Larson, M., Vasan, R., Schnabel, R., Pryde, M., et al. (2008). Cross-sectional relations of digital vascular function to cardiovascular risk factors in the Framingham Heart Study. *Circulation, 117*(19), 2467–2474.

Hammen, C. (2003). Interpersonal stress and depression in women. *Journal of Affective Disorders, 74,* 49–57.

Hammer, S., Eron, J., Reiss, P., Schooley, R., Thompson, M., Walmsley, S., et al. (2008). Antiretroviral treatment of adult HIV infection: 2008 recommendations of the International AIDS Society-USA panel. *JAMA: The Journal of the American Medical Association, 300*(5), 555–570.

Hamner, J., & Wilder, B. (2008). Knowledge and risk of cardiovascular disease in rural Alabama women. *Journal of the American Academy of Nurse Practitioners, 20*(6), 333–338.

Hampson, S. E., Goldberg, L. R., Vogt, T. M., & Dubanoski, J. P. (2007). Mechanisms by which childhood personality traits influence adult health status: Educational attainment and healthy behaviors. *Health Psychology, 26,* 121–125.

Hanoch, Y. (2007). Terminally ill patients and volunteer support: Is it the right intervention? *Health Psychology, 26*(5), 537–538.

Hanoch, Y. (2007). Terminally ill patients and volunteer support: Is it the right intervention? *Health Psychology, 26,* 537–538.

Hanson, M. D., & Chen, E. (2007). Socioeconomic status and health behaviors in adolescence: A review of the literature. *Journal of Behavioral Medicine, 30,* 263–285.

Harkness, K. L., Bruce, A. E., & Lumley, M. N. (2006). The role of childhood abuse and neglect in the sensitization to stressful life events in adolescent depression. *Journal of Abnormal Psychology, 115,* 730–741.

Harris, J. B., Schwartz, S. M., & Thompson, B. (2008). Characteristics associated with self-identification as a regular smoker and desire to quit among college students who smoke cigarettes. *Nicotine and Tobacco Research, 10,* 69–76.

Harris, K. M, Edlund, M. J., & Larson, S. (2005). Racial and ethnic differences in the mental health problems and use of mental health care, *Medical Care, 43,* 775–784.

Harrison, K., & Bond, B. J. (2007). Gaming magazines and the drive for muscularity in preadolescent boys: A longitudinal examination. *Body Image, 4,* 269–277.

Harrison, K., Taylor, L. D., & Marske, A. L. (2006). Women's and men's eating behavior following exposure to ideal-body images and text. *Communication Research, 33,* 507–529.

Harvey, I. S. (2008). Assessing self management and spirituality practices among older women. *American Journal of Health Behavior, 32,* 157–168.

Harvey, M. R., & Tummala-Narra, P. (2007). Sources and expression of resilience in trauma survivors: Ecological theory, multicultural perspectives. *Journal of Aggression, Maltreatment and Trauma, 14,* 1–7.

Haskell, W. L., Lee, I., Pate, R. R., Powell, K. E., Blair, S. N., Franklin, B. A., et al. (2007). Physical Activity and Public Health: Updated Recommendation for Adults from the American College of Sports Medicine and the American Heart Association. *Medical Science Sports Exercise, 39,* 1423–1434.

Hassan, M., Spitz, M., Thomas, M., El-Deeb, A., Glover, K., Nguyen, N., et al. (2008). Effect of different types of smoking and synergism with hepatitis C virus on risk of hepatocellular carcinoma in American men and women: case-control study. *International Journal of Cancer, 123*(8), 1883–1891.

Hastie, C., Haw, S., & Pell, J. (2008). Impact of smoking cessation and lifetime exposure on C-reactive protein. *Nicotine and Tobacco Research: Official Journal of the Society for Research on Nicotine and Tobacco, 10*(4), 637–642.

Haven, J., Burns, A., Britten, P., & Davis, C. (2006). Developing the consumer interface for the MyPyramid food guidance system. *Journal of Nutrition and Educational Behavior, 38*, S124–S135.

Hawkes, C. (2007). Regulating food marketing to young people worldwide: Trends and policy drivers. *American Journal of Public Health, 97*, 1962–1973.

He, K., Xu, Y., & Van Horn, L. (2007). The puzzle of dietary fat intake and risk of ischemic stroke: A brief review of epidemiologic data. *Journal of the American Dietetic Association, 107*(2), 287–295.

Healy, K. M. (2000). Cultural perspectives. Concepts of alternative healing systems: an overview of Mexican curanderismo. *Perspective on Physician Assistant Education, 11*, 51–55.

Heiss, G., Wallace, R., Anderson, G. L., Aragaki, A., Beresford, S. A. A., Brzyski, R., et al. (2008). Health risks and benefits 3 years after stopping randomized treatment with estrogen and progestin. *JAMA: Journal of the American Medical Association, 299*, 1036–1045.

Helsley, J. D. (2008). Post-traumatic stress disorder. In J. R. Vanin & J. D. Helsley (Eds.), *Anxiety disorders: A pocket guide for primary care. Current clinical practice* (pp. 175–181). Totowa, NJ: Humana Press.

Henriksen, L., Feighery, E. C., Schleicher, N. C., & Fortmann, S. P. (2008). Receptivity to alcohol marketing predicts initiation of alcohol use. *Journal of Adolescent Health, 42*, 28–35.

Hertz, R., McDonald, M., Unger, A., & Lustik, M. (2007). Racial and ethnic disparities in the prevalence and management of cardiovascular risk factors in the United States workforce. *Journal of Occupational and Environmental Medicine/American College of Occupational and Environmental Medicine, 49*(10), 1165–1175.

Hillman, C. H., Erickson, K. I., & Kramer, A. F. (2008). Be smart, exercise your heart: Exercise effects on brain and cognition. *Nature Reviews Neuroscience, 9*, 58–65.

Hodge, C. N., Jackson, L. A., Sullivan, L. A. (1993) The freshman 15—facts and fantasies about weight-gain in college women. *Psychology of Women Quarterly, 17*, 119–126.

Hoffman, B. M., Papas, R. K., Chatkoff, D. K., Kerns, R. D. (2007). Meta-Analysis of Psychological Interventions for Chronic Low Back Pain. *Health Psychology, 26*, 1–9.

Hoffman, H. G., Patterson, D. R., Carrougher, G. J., & Sharar, S. R. (2001). Effectiveness of virtual reality-based pain control with multiple treatments. *Clinical Journal of Pain, 17*, 229–235.

Hoffman, H. G., Patterson, D. R., Seibel, E., Soltani, M., Jewett-Leahy, L., & Sharar, S. R. (2008). Virtual reality pain control during burn wound debridement in the hydrotank. *Clinical Journal of Pain, 24*, 299–304.

Hoffman-Goetz, L., & Friedman, D. (2006). A systematic review of culturally sensitive cancer prevention resources for ethnic minorities. *Ethnicity and Disease, 16*(4), 971–977.

Hojsted, J. & Sjogren, P. (2007). Addiction to opioids in chronic pain patients: A literature review. *European Journal of Pain, 11*, 490–518.

Holm-Denoma, J. M., Joiner, T. E., Vohs, K. D., & Heatherton, T. F. (2008). The "freshman fifteen" (the "freshman five" actually): Predictors and possible explanations. *Health Psychology, 27*, S3–S9.

Holt-Lunstad, J., Smith, T., & Uchino, B. (2008). Can hostility interfere with the health benefits of giving and receiving social support? The impact of cynical hostility on cardiovascular reactivity during social support interactions among friends. *Annals of Behavioral Medicine: A Publication of the Society of Behavioral Medicine, 35*(3), 319–330.

Hon, K. L. E., Leung, T. F., Ng, P.C., Lam, M.C.A., Kam, W.Y.C., Wong, K.Y., et al. (2007). Efficacy and tolerability of a Chinese herbal medicine concoction for treatment of atopic dermatitis: A randomized, double-blind, placebo-controlled study. *British Journal of Dermatology, 157*, 357–363.

Hovell, M. F., Mewborn, C. R., Randle, Y., Fowler-Johnson, S. (1985) Risk of excess weight gain in university women: a three-year community controlled analysis. *Addictive Behavior, 10*, 15–28.

Howard, J. H., & Willie, L. (1984). *Oklahoma Seminoles: Medicine, magic, and religion.* Norman: Oklahoma University Press.

Hsiao, A., Wong, M. D., Goldstein, M. S., Becerra, L. D., Cheng, E. M., & Wenger, N. S. (2006). Complementary and alternative medicine use among Asian-American subgroups: Prevalence, predictors, and lack of relationship to acculturation and access to conventional health care. *Journal of Alternative and Complementary Medicine, 12*, 1003–1010.

Hu, F. B., Manson, J. E., Stampfer, M.J., Colditz, G., Liu, S., Solomon, C. G., & Willett, W. C. (2001). Diet, lifestyle, and the risk of type 2 diabetes mellitus in women. *New England Journal of Medicine, 345*, 790–797.

Ikeda, A., Iso, H., Kawachi, I., Yamagishi, K., Inoue, M., & Tsugane, S. (2008). Social support and stroke and coronary heart disease: The JPHC study cohorts II. *Stroke; a Journal of Cerebral Circulation, 39*(3), 768–775.

Ikeda, A., Iso, H., Kawachi, I., Yamagishi, K., Inoue, M., & Tsugane, S. (2008). Social support and stroke and coronary heart disease: the JPHC study cohorts II. *Stroke; a Journal of Cerebral Circulation, 39*(3), 768–775.

Ironson, G., & Hayward, H. (2008, June). Do positive psychosocial factors predict disease progression in HIV-1? A review of the evidence. *Psychosomatic Medicine, 70*(5), 546–554.

Ironson, G., O'Cleirigh, C., Weiss, A., Schneiderman, N., & Costa, P. (2008). Personality and HIV disease progression: role of NEO-PI-R openness, extraversion, and profiles of engagement. *Psychosomatic Medicine, 70*(2), 245–253.

Irwin, M. (2008). Human psychoneuroimmunology: 20 years of discovery. *Brain, Behavior, and Immunity, 22*(2), 129–139.

James, A., Leone, L., Katz, M., McNeill, L., & Campbell, M. (2008). Multiple health behaviors among overweight, class I obese, and class II obese persons. *Ethnicity and Disease, 18*(2), 157–162.

Jasso, G., Massey, D. S., Rosenzweig, M. R., Smith, J. P. (2004). *Immigrant health: selectivity and acculturation.* Working paper 04/23, Institute for Fiscal Studies, London.

Jemal, A., Siegel, R., Ward, E., Hao, Y., Xu, J., Murray, T., et al. (2008). Cancer statistics, 2008. *CA: A Cancer Journal for Clinicians, 58*(2), 71–96.

Jo, A., Maxwell, A., Wong, W., & Bastani, R. (2008). Colorectal cancer screening among underserved Korean Americans in Los Angeles County. *Journal of Immigrant and Minority Health/Center for Minority Public Health*, 10(2), 119–126.

Johansson, M., Hassmén, P., & Jouper, J. (2008). Acute effects of qigong exercise on mood and anxiety. *International Journal of Stress Management*, 15, 199–207.

John, E., Schwartz, G., Koo, J., Wang, W., & Ingles, S. (2007). Sun exposure, vitamin D receptor gene polymorphisms, and breast cancer risk in a multiethnic population. *American Journal of Epidemiology*, 166(12), 1409–1419.

Johnson, S. K. (2008). Biology of medically unexplained illness. In S. K., Johnson (Ed.), *Medically unexplained illness: Gender and biopsychosocial implications* (pp. 49–60). Washington, DC: American Psychological Association.

Johnson-Greene, D., & Denning, J. (2008). Neuropsychology of alcoholism. In A. M. Horton & D. Wedding (Eds.), *The neuropsychology handbook* (3rd ed., pp. 729–752). New York: Springer.

Johnston, D. W., Tuomisto, M. T., Patching, G. R. (2008). The relationship between cardiac reactivity in the laboratory and in real life. *Health Psychology*, 27, 34–42.

Jones, C. H. (2005). The spectrum of therapeutic influences and integrative health care: Classifying health care practices by mode of therapeutic action. *Journal of Alternative and Complementary Medicine*, 11, 937–944.

Jones, R., Taylor, A., Bourguignon, C., Steeves, R., Fraser, G., Lippert, M., et al. (2008). Family interactions among African American prostate cancer survivors. *Family and Community Health*, 31(3), 213–220.

Joseph, A. M., Hecht, S. S., Murphy, S. E., Lando, H., Carmella, S. G., Gross, M., Bliss, R., Le, C. T., & Hatsukami, D. K. (2008). Smoking reduction fails to improve clinical and biological markers of cardiac disease: A randomized controlled trial. *Nicotine and Tobacco Research*, 10, 471–481.

Kabir, Z., Connolly, G., Clancy, L., Koh, H., & Capewell, S. (2008). Coronary heart disease deaths and decreased smoking prevalence in Massachusetts, 1993–2003. *American Journal of Public Health*, 98(8), 1468–1469.

Kadmon, I., Ganz, F., Rom, M., & Woloski-Wruble, A. (2008). Social, marital, and sexual adjustment of Israeli men whose wives were diagnosed with breast cancer. *Oncology Nursing Forum*, 35(1), 131–135.

Kalichman, S., Picciano, J., & Roffman, R. (2008). Motivation to reduce HIV risk behaviors in the context of the information, motivation and behavioral skills (IMB) model of HIV prevention. *Journal of Health Psychology*, 13(5), 680–689.

Kallianpur, A., Lee, S., Gao, Y., Lu, W., Zheng, Y., Ruan, Z., et al. (2008). Dietary animal-derived iron and fat intake and breast cancer risk in the Shanghai Breast Cancer Study. *Breast Cancer Research and Treatment*, 107(1), 123–132.

Kannel, W., Evans, J., Piper, S., & Murabito, J. (2008). Angina pectoris is a stronger indicator of diffuse vascular atherosclerosis than intermittent claudication: Framingham study. *Journal of Clinical Epidemiology*, 61(9), 951–957.

Kannel, W., Vasan, R., Keyes, M., Sullivan, L., & Robins, S. (2008). Usefulness of the triglyceride-high-density lipoprotein versus the cholesterol-high-density lipoprotein ratio for predicting insulin resistance and cardiometabolic risk (from the Framingham Offspring Cohort). *The American Journal of Cardiology*, 101(4), 497–501.

Kapur, N. K., (2007). Rosuvastatin: A highly potent statin for the prevention and management of coronary artery disease. *Expert Review of Cardiovascular Therapy*, 5, 161–175.

Kapur, R.L. (1979). The role of traditional healers in mental health care in rural India. *Social Sciences and Medicine*, 13B, 27–31.

Karalis, D. (2008). The role of lipid-lowering therapy in preventing coronary heart disease in patients with type 2 diabetes. *Clinical Cardiology*, 31(6), 241–248.

Karim, K., Bailey, M., & Tunna, K. (2000). Nonwhite ethnicity and the provision of specialist palliative care services: Factors affecting doctors' referral patterns. *Palliative Medicine*, 14, 471–478.

Karim, S., Saeed, K., Rana, M.H., Mubbashar, M.H., & Jenkins, R. (2004). Pakistan mental health country profile. *International Review of Psychiatry*, 16, 83–92.

Katzman, M. A., Hermans, K. M. E., Van Hoeken, D., & Hoek, H. W. (2004). Not your "typical island woman": Anorexia nervosa is reported only in subcultures in Curacao. *Culture, Medicine, and Psychiatry*, 28(4), 463–492.

Kavasch, E. B., & Baar, K. (1999). *American Indian healing arts: Herbs, rituals, and remedies for every season of life*. New York: Bantam Books.

Kazdin, A. (2008). Evidence-based treatment and practice: New opportunities to bridge clinical research and practice, enhance the knowledge base, and improve patient care. *American Psychologist*, 63(3), 146–159.

Keel, P. K., & Klump, K. L. (2003). Are eating disorders culture-bound syndromes? Implications for conceptualizing their etiology. *Psychological Bulletin*, 129(5), 747–769.

Kelley-Hedgepeth, A., Lloyd-Jones, D., Colvin, A., Matthews, K., Johnston, J., Sowers, M., et al. (2008). Ethnic differences in C-reactive protein concentrations. *Clinical Chemistry*, 54(6), 1027–1037.

Kern, S., & Ziemssen, T. (2008). Brain-immune communication psychoneuroimmunology of multiple sclerosis. *Multiple Sclerosis (Houndmills, Basingstoke, England)*, 14(1), 6–21.

Kessing, Lars V., Harhoff, M., & Andersen, P. K. (2008). Increased rate of treatment with antidepressants in patients with multiple sclerosis. *International Clinical Psychopharmacology*, 23, 54–59.

Kessler, R.C., Mickelson, K.D., & Williams, D.R. (1999). The prevalence, distribution, and mental health correlates of perceived discrimination in the United States. *Journal of Health and Social Behavior*, 40, 208–230.

Khoo, K., Bolt, P., Babl, F., Jury, S., & Goldman, R. (2008). Health information seeking by parents in the Internet age. *Journal of Paediatrics and Child Health*, 44(7–8), 419–423.

Kiecolt-Glaser, J. K., Bane, C., Glaser, R., & Malarkey, W. B. (2003). Love, marriage, and divorce: Newlyweds' stress hormones foreshadow relationship changes. *Journal of Consulting and Clinical Psychology*, 71, 176–188.

Kiesler, D. J., & Auerbach, S. M. (2006). Optimal matches of patient preferences for information, decision-making and interpersonal behavior: Evidence, models and interventions. *Patient Education and Counseling, 61*, 319–341.

Kim, H. S., Sherman, D. K., & Taylor, S. E. (in press). Culture and social support. *American Psychologist.*

Klass, D. (2007). Religion, spirituality in loss, grief, and mourning. In D. Balk, C. Wogrin, G. Thornton, & D. Meagher (Eds.) *Handbook of thanatology: The essential body of knowledge for the student of death, dying, and bereavement* (121–131). Northbrook, IL: Association for Death Education and Counseling.

Kline, K. A., Fekete, E. M., & Sears, C. M. (2008). Hostility, emotional expression, and hemodynamic responses to laboratory stressors: Reactivity attenuating effects of a tendency to express emotion interpersonally. *International Journal of Psychophysiology, 68*, 177–185.

Koenig, L. J., Pals, S. L., Bush, T., Pratt Palmore, M., Stratford, D., & Ellerbrock, T. V. (2008). Randomized controlled trial of an intervention to prevent adherence failure among HIV-infected patients initiating antiretroviral therapy. *Health Psychology, 27*, 159–169.

Koertge, J., Janszky, I., Sundin, O., Blom, M., Georgiades, A., László, K., et al. (2008). Effects of a stress management program on vital exhaustion and depression in women with coronary heart disease: a randomized controlled intervention study. *Journal Of Internal Medicine, 263*(3), 281–293.

Koffman, J., Morgan, M., Edmonds, P., Speck, P., & Higginson, I. (2008). I know he controls cancer: The meanings of religion among Black Caribbean and White British patients with advanced cancer. *Social Science and Medicine* (1982), *67*(5), 780–789.

Komiyama, O., Kawara, M., & De Laat, A. (2007). Ethnic differences regarding tactile and pain thresholds in the trigeminal region. *The Journal of Pain, 8*, 363–369.

Konijn, E. A., Nije Bijvank, M., & Bushman, B. J. (2007). I wish I were a warrior: The role of wishful identification in effects of violent video games on aggression in adolescent boys. *Developmental Psychology, 43*, 1038–1044.

Korte, S. M., Koolhaas, J. M., Wingfield, J. C., & McEwen, B. S. (2005). The Darwinian concept of stress: Benefits of allostasis and costs of allostatic load and the trade-offs in health and disease. *Neuroscience and Biobehavioral Reviews, 29*, 3–38.

Kraaij, V., Garnefski, N., Schroevers, M., van der Veek, S., Witlox, R., & Maes, S. (2008). Cognitive coping, goal self-efficacy and personal growth in HIV-infected men who have sex with men. *Patient Education and Counseling, 72*(2), 301–304.

Kraemer, H. C., Kiernan, M., Essex, M., & Kupfer, D. J. (2008). How and why criteria defining moderators and mediators differ between the Baron & Kenny and MacArthur approaches. *Health Psychology, 27*, S101–S109.

Kroenke, K., Bair, M., Damush, T., Hoke, S., Nicholas, G., Kempf, C., et al., (2007). Stepped Care for Affective Disorders and Musculoskeletal Pain (SCAMP) study: Design and practical implications of an intervention for comorbid pain and depression. *General Hospital Psychiatry, 29*, 506–517.

Kubík, A., Zatloukal, P., Tomásek, L., Pauk, N., Havel, L., Dolezal, J., et al. (2007). Interactions between smoking and other exposures associated with lung cancer risk in women: Diet and physical activity. *Neoplasma, 54*(1), 83–88.

Kurian, A., & Cardarelli, K. (2007). Racial and ethnic differences in cardiovascular disease risk factors: a systematic review. *Ethnicity and Disease, 17*(1), 143–152.

Kurtz, M., Kurtz, J., Given, C., & Given, B. (2008). Patient optimism and mastery-do they play a role in cancer patients' management of pain and fatigue? *Journal of Pain and Symptom Management, 36*(1), 1–10.

Laban, C. J., Gernaat, H. B. P. E., Komproe, I. H., van der Tweel, I. & de Jong, J. T. V. M. (2005). Postmigration living problems and common psychiatric disorders in Iraqi asylum seekers in the Netherlands. *Journal of Nervous and Mental Disease, 193*, 825–832.

Lagos, V., Perez, M., Ricker, C., Blazer, K., Santiago, N., Feldman, N., et al. (2008). Social-cognitive aspects of underserved Latinas preparing to undergo genetic cancer risk assessment for hereditary breast and ovarian cancer. *Psycho-Oncology, 17*(8), 774–782.

Lairson, D., DiCarlo, M., Myers, R., Wolf, T., Cocroft, J., Sifri, R., et al. (2008). Cost-effectiveness of targeted and tailored interventions on colorectal cancer screening use. *Cancer, 112*(4), 779–788.

Lauver, L. S. (2008). Parenting foster children with chronic illness and complex medical needs. *Journal of Family Nursing, 14*, 74–96.

Leaf, A., Kang, J., & Xiao, Y. (2008). Fish oil fatty acids as cardiovascular drugs. *Current Vascular Pharmacology, 6*(1), 1–12.

Lechner, S., Stoelb, B., & Antoni, M. (2008). Group-based therapies for benefit finding in cancer. In *Trauma, recovery, and growth: Positive psychological perspectives on post-traumatic stress* (pp. 207–231). Hoboken, NJ: John Wiley & Sons.

Ledbetter, D., & Faucett, W. (2008). Issues in genetic testing for ultra-rare diseases: background and introduction. *Genetics in Medicine: Official Journal of the American College of Medical Genetics, 10*(5), 309–313.

Lederer, D. J., Benn, E. K., Barr, R.G., Wilt, J. S., Reilly, G., Sonett, J. R., et al. (2008). Racial differences in waiting list outcomes in chronic obstructive pulmonary disease. *American Journal of Respiratory and Critical Care Medicine, 177*, 450–454.

Lee, E., Tripp-Reimer, T., Miller, A., Sadler, G., & Lee, S. (2007). Korean American women's beliefs about breast and cervical cancer and associated symbolic meanings. *Oncology Nursing Forum, 34*(3), 713–720.

Lee, M. S., Pittler, M. H., & Ernst, E. (2007). External qigong for pain conditions: A systematic review of randomized clinical trials. *The Journal of Pain, 8*, 827–831.

Lee, M. S., Pittler, M. H., Shin, B., Kong, J. C., & Ernst, E. (2008). Bee venom acupuncture for musculoskeletal pain: A review. *The Journal of Pain, 9*, 289–297.

Lee, S. M. (2005). Physical activity among minority populations: What health promotion practitioners should know—a commentary. *Health Promotion Practice, 6*, 447–452.

Lee-Lin, F., Menon, U., Pett, M., Nail, L., Lee, S., & Mooney, K. (2007). Breast cancer beliefs and mammography screening practices among Chinese American immigrants. *Journal of Obstetric, Gynecologic, and Neonatal Nursing: JOGNN/ NAACOG, 36*(3), 212–221.

Lee-Lin, F., Pett, M., Menon, U., Lee, S., Nail, L., Mooney, K., et al. (2007). Cervical cancer beliefs and pap test screening practices among Chinese American immigrants. *Oncology Nursing Forum, 34*(6), 1203–1209.

Leserman, J. (2008). Role of depression, stress, and trauma in HIV disease progression. *Psychosomatic Medicine, 70*(5), 539–545.

Lett, H. S., Blumenthal, J. A., Babyak, M. A., Catellier, D. J., Carney, R. M., Berkman, L. F., et al. (2007). Social support and prognosis in patients at increased psychosocial risk recovering from myocardial infarction. *Health Psychology, 26*, 418–427.

Lett, H., Blumenthal, J., Babyak, M., Catellier, D., Carney, R., Berkman, L., et al. (2007). Social support and prognosis in patients at increased psychosocial risk recovering from myocardial infarction. *Health Psychology: Official Journal of the Division of Health Psychology, American Psychological Association, 26*(4), 418–427.

Levenson, J. L. (2007). Psychiatric issues in gastrointestinal disorders. *Primary Psychiatry, 14*, 35–38.

Leventhal, H., Musumeci, T. J., & Contrada, R. J. (2007). Current issues and new directions in psychology and health: Theory, translation, and evidence-based practice. *Psychology and Health, 22*(4), 381–386.

Leventhal, H., Weinman, J., Leventhal, E. A., & Phillips, L. A. (2008). Health psychology: The search for pathways between behavior and health. *Annual Review of Psychology, 59*, 477–505.

Leventhal, H., Weinman, J., Leventhal, E. A., & Phillips, L. A. (2008). Health psychology: The search for pathways between behavior and health. *Annual Review of Psychology, 59*, 477–505.

Leventhal, H., Weinman, J., Leventhal, E., & Phillips, L. (2008). Health psychology: The search for pathways between behavior and health.

Annual Review of Psychology, 59(1), 477–505.

Levitsky, D. A., Halbmaier, C. A., Mrdjenovic, G. (2004) The freshman weight gain: a model for the study of the epidemic of obesity. *International Journal of Obesity Related Metabolic Disorders, 28*, 1435–1442.

Lewinsohn, P. M., Joiner, T. E., & Rohde, P. (2001). Evaluation of cognitive diathesis-stress models in predicting major depressive disorder in adolescents. *Journal of Abnormal Psychology, 110*, 203–215.

Lewis, F., Cochrane, B., Fletcher, K., Zahlis, E., Shands, M., Gralow, J., et al. (2008). Helping her heal: a pilot study of an educational counseling intervention for spouses of women with breast cancer. *Psycho-Oncology, 17*(2), 131–137.

Lewis, T. H. (1990). *The medicine men: Oglala Sioux ceremony and healing.* Lincoln: Nebraska Press.

Lewy, A. J., Lefler, B. J., Emens, J. S., & Bauer, V. K. (2006). The circadian basis of winter depression. *Proceedings of the National Academy of Sciences, 103*, 7414–7419.

Li, D., Puntillo, K., & Miaskowski, C. (2008). A review of objective pain measures for use with critical care adult patients unable to self-report. *The Journal of Pain, 9*, 2–10.

Liang, W., Wang, J., Chen, M., Feng, S., Lee, M., Schwartz, M., et al. (2008). Developing and validating a measure of Chinese cultural views of health and cancer. *Health Education and Behavior: The Official Publication of the Society for Public Health Education, 35*(3), 361–375.

Liang, W., Wang, J., Chen, M., Feng, S., Lee, M., Schwartz, M., et al. (2008). Developing and validating a measure of Chinese cultural views of health and cancer. *Health Education and Behavior, 35*(3), 361–375.

Licciardone, J. C. (2003). Perceptions of drinking and related findings from the Nationwide Campuses Study. *Journal of American College Health, 51*, 238–246.

Lichtenstein, A. H., Rasmussen, H., Yu, W. W., Epstein, S. R., & Russell, R. M. (2008). Modified MyPyramid for older adults. *Journal of Nutrition, 138*, 5–11.

Liewer, L., Mains, D., Lykens, K., & René, A. (2008). Barriers to women's cardiovascular risk

knowledge. *Health Care for Women International, 29*(1), 23–38.

Lin, F., Shaw, L., Berman, D., Callister, T., Weinsaft, J., Wong, F., et al. (2008). Multidetector computed tomography coronary artery plaque predictors of stress-induced myocardial ischemia by SPECT. *Atherosclerosis, 197*(2), 700–709.

Linn, S., & Novosat, C. L. (2008). Calories for sale: Food marketing to children in the twenty-first century. *Annals of the American Academy of Political and Social Science, 615*, 133–155.

Lipkus, I. M. (2007). Numeric, verbal, and visual formats of conveying health risks: Suggested best practices and future recommendations. *Medical Decision Making, 27*, 696–713.

Littrell, J. (2008). The mind-body connection: not just a theory anymore. *Social Work in Health Care, 46*(4), 17–37.

Liu, X., Gao, H., Li, B., Cheng, M., Ma, Y., Zhang, Z., et al. (2007). Pulse wave velocity as a marker of arteriosclerosis and its comorbidities in Chinese patients. *Hypertension Research: Official Journal of the Japanese Society of Hypertension, 30*(3), 237–242.

Livingston, E. H. (2007). Obesity, mortality, and bariatric surgery death rates. *JAMA: Journal of the American Medical Association, 298*, 2406–2408.

Llorca, P. (2008). Monitoring patients to improve physical health and treatment outcome. *European Neuropsychopharmacology, 18*, S140–S145.

Lolak, S., Connors, G. L., Sheridan, M. J., & Wise, T. N. (2008). Effects of progressive muscle relaxation training on anxiety and depression in patients enrolled in an outpatient pulmonary rehabilitation program. *Psychotherapy and Psychosomatics, 77*, 119–125.

Looks for Buffalo Hand, F. (1998). *Learning journey on the Red Road.* Toronto, Ontario: Learning Journey Communications.

Lopez, R. A. (2005). Use of alternative folk medicine by Mexican American women. *Journal of Immigrant Health, 7*, 23–31.

Lucas, T., Michalopoulou, G., Falzarano, P., Menon, S., & Cunningham, W. (2008). Healthcare provider cultural competency: Development and initial validation of a patient report measure. *Health Psychology, 27*, 185–193.

Lynch, A. M., Kashikar-Zuck, S., Goldschneider, K. R., & Jones, B. A. (2007). Sex and age differences in coping styles among children with chronic pain. *Journal of Pain and Symptom Management, 33*, 208–216.

Lyssenko, V. (2004). The human body composition in statics and dynamics: Ayurveda and the philosophical schools of Vaisesika and Samkhya. *Journal of Indian Philosophy, 32*, 31–56.

Macario, A., Richmond, C., Auster, M., & Pergolizzi, J. V. (2008). Treatment of 94 outpatients with chronic discogenic low back pain with the DRX9000: A retrospective chart review. *Pain Practice, 8*, 11–17.

Macintyre, S., Hunt, K., & Sweeting, H. (1996). Gender differences in health: Are things really as simple as they seem? *Social Science and Medicine, 42*, 617–624.

MacKinnon, D. P. (2008). *Introduction to statistical mediation analysis.* Mahwah, NJ: Erlbaum.

MacKinnon, D. P., & Luecken, L. J. (2008). How and for whom? Mediation and moderation in health psychology. *Health Psychology, 27*, S99–S100.

Magnus, M. (2004). Prostate cancer knowledge among multiethnic black men. *Journal of the National Medical Association, 96*(5), 650–656.

Mailis-Cagnon, A., Yegneswaran, B., Nicholson, K., Lakha, S., Papagapiou, M., Steiman, A. J., et al., (2007). Ethnocultural and sex characteristics of patients attending a tertiary care pain clinic in Toronto, Ontario. *Pain Research and Management, 12*, 100–106.

Makoae, L., Greeff, M., Phetlhu, R., Uys, L., Naidoo, J., Kohi, T., et al. (2008). Coping with HIV-related stigma in five African countries. *The Journal of the Association of Nurses in AIDS Care: JANAC, 19*(2), 137–146.

Malenbaum, S., Keefe, F. J., de C. Williams, A. C., Ulrich, R., & Somers, T. J. (2008). Pain in its environmental context: Implications for designing environments to enhance pain control. *Pain, 134*, 241–244.

Mann, T., Tomiyama, A.J., Westling, E., Lew, A., Samuels, B., & Chatman, J. (2007). Medicare's search for effective obesity treatments: Diets are not the answer. *American Psychologist, 62*, 220–233.

Manolio, T., Arnold, A., Post, W., Bertoni, A., Schreiner, P., Sacco, R., et al. (2008). Ethnic differences in the relationship of carotid atherosclerosis to coronary calcification: the Multi-Ethnic Study of Atherosclerosis. *Atherosclerosis, 197*(1), 132–138.

Manson, J. E., Hsia, J., Johnson, K. C., Rossouw, J. E., Assaf, A. R., Lasser, N. L. et al. (2003). Estrogen plus progestin and the risk of coronary heart disease. *New England Journal of Medicine, 349*, 523–534.

Margolin, A., Avants, S. K., & Kleber, H. D. (1998). Investigating Alternative Medicine Therapies in Randomized Controlled Trials. *JAMA: Journal of the American Medical Association, 280*, 1626–1628.

Margolin, A., Kleber, H. D., Avants, S. K., Konefal, J., Gawin, F., Stark, E., et al. (2002). Acupuncture for the treatment of cocaine addiction: A randomized controlled trial. *JAMA: Journal of the American Medical Association, 287*, 55–63.

Markey, C. N., Markey, P. M., Ericksen, A. J., & Tinsley, B. J. (2006). Children's behavioral patterns, the Five-Factor model of personality, and risk behaviors. *Personality and Individual Differences, 41*, 1503–1513.

Markey, M. A., Vander Wal, J. S., & Gibbons, J. L. (2009). Culture and eating disorders. In S. Eshun & R. A. R. Gurung (Eds.), *Sociocultural factors influencing mental health.* Malden, MA: Blackwell-Wiley.

Marsella, A. J., & Christopher, M. A. (2004). Ethnocultural considerations in disasters: An overview of research, issues, and directions. *Psychiatric Clinics of North America, 27*, 521–539.

Marshall, R. D., Bryant, R. A., Amsel, L., Suh, E. J., Cook, J. M., & Neria, Y. (2007). The psychology of ongoing threat: Relative risk appraisal, the September 11 attacks, and terrorism-related fears. *American Psychologist, 62*, 304–316.

Martin, S., Young, S., Billings, D., & Bross, C. (2007). Health care-based interventions for women who have experienced sexual violence: a review of the literature. *Trauma, Violence and Abuse, 8*(1), 3–18.

Mason, V. L., Skevington, S. M., & Osborn, M. (2008). The quality of life of people in chronic pain: Developing a pain and discomfort module for use with the WHOQOL. *Psychology and Health, 23*, 135–154.

Matsumoto, D. (2009). Teaching about culture. In R. A. R. Gurung & L. Prieto (Eds.), *Getting culture: Incorporating diversity across the curriculum.* Arlington, VA: Stylus.

Mattar, C., Harharah, L., Su, I., Agarwal, A., Wong, P., & Choolani, M. (2008). Menopause, hormone therapy and cardiovascular and cerebrovascular disease. *Annals of the Academy of Medicine, Singapore, 37*(1), 54–62.

Mausbach, B. T., von Kanel, R., Patterson, T. L., Dimsdale, J. E., Depp, C. A., Aschbacher, K., et al. (2008). *Health Psychology, 27*, S172–S179.

Mayes, V. O., & Lacy, B. B. (1989). *Nanise: A Navajo herbal–one hundred plants from the Navajo reservation.* Tsaile, AZ: Navajo Community College Press.

Mays, V. M., Cochran, S. D., & Barnes, N. W. (2007). Race, race-based discrimination, and health outcomes among African Americans. *Annual Reviews of Psychology, 58*, 201–225.

Mazure, C. M. (1998). Life stressors as risk factors in depression. *Clinical Psychology: Science and Practice, 5*, 291–313.

McCaffery, K., Irwig, L., & Bossuyt, P. (2007). Patient decision aids to support clinical decision making: Evaluating the decision or the outcomes of decision. *Medical Decision Making, 27*, 619–625.

McCain, N., Gray, D., Elswick, R., Robins, J., Tuck, I., Walter, J., et al. (2008). A randomized clinical trial of alternative stress management interventions in persons with HIV infection. *Journal of Consulting and Clinical Psychology, 76*(3), 431–441.

McClure, F. H., Chavez, D. V., Agars, M. D., Peacock, M. J., & Matosian, A. (2008). Resilience in sexually abused women: Risk and protective factors. *Journal of Family Violence, 23*, 81–88.

McEniery, C., & Cockcroft, J. (2007). Does arterial stiffness predict atherosclerotic coronary events? *Advances in Cardiology, 44*, 160–172.

Mellström, D., & Svanborg, A. (1987). Tobacco smoking—a major cause of sex differences in health. *Comprehensive Gerontology. Section A, Clinical and Laboratory Sciences*, 1(1), 34–39.

Meyer, I. H. (2003). Prejudice, social stress, and mental health in lesbian, gay, and bisexual populations: Conceptual issues and research evidence, *Psychological Bulletin, 129*, 674–697.

Meyler, D., Stimpson, J. P., & Peek, M. K. (2007). Health concordance within couples: A systematic review. *Social Science and Medicine, 64*, 2297–2310.

Mian, M., Lauzon, N., Stämpfli, M., Mossman, K., & Ashkar, A. (2008). Impairment of human NK cell cytotoxic activity and cytokine release by cigarette smoke. *Journal of Leukocyte Biology, 83*(3), 774–784.

Michel, G. (2007). Daily patterns of symptom reporting in families with adolescent children. *British Journal of Health Psychology, 12*, 245–260.

Michie S., Hardeman W., Fanshawe T., Prevost A. T., Taylor L., Kinmonth A. L. (2008). Investigating theoretical explanations for behaviour change: The case of ProActive. *Psychology and Health, 23*, 25–39.

Michie, S., Hardeman, W., Fanshawe, T., Prevost, A. T., Taylor, L., & Kinmonth, A. L. (2008). Investigating theoretical explanations for behaviour change: The case study of ProActive. *Psychology and Health, 23, 25–39*.

Michie, S., Rothman, A. J., & Sheeran, P. (2007). Current issues and new direction in psychology and health: Advancing the science of behavior change. *Psychology and Health, 22*, 249–253.

Miller, M., Marty, M., Broadwin, R., Johnson, K., Salmon, A., Winder, B., et al. (2007). The association between exposure to environmental tobacco smoke and breast cancer: a review by the California Environmental Protection Agency. *Preventive Medicine, 44*(2), 93–106.

Minor, D., Wofford, M., & Jones, D. (2008). Racial and ethnic differences in hypertension. *Current Atherosclerosis Reports, 10*(2), 121–127.

Mo, P., & Coulson, N. (2008). Exploring the communication of social support within virtual communities: a content analysis of messages posted to an online HIV/AIDS support group. *Cyberpsychology and Behavior: The Impact of the Internet, Multimedia and Virtual Reality on Behavior and Society, 11*(3), 371–374.

Modi, A. C., Marciel, K. K., Slater, S. K., Drotar, D., & Quittner, A. L. (2008). The influence of parental supervision on medical adherence in adolescents with cystic fibrosis: Developmental shifts from pre to late adolescence. *Children's Health Care, 37*, 78–82.

Mokdad, A. H., Marks, J. S., Stroup, D. F., & Gerberding, J. L. (2005). Correction: Actual causes of death in the United States. *JAMA: Journal of the American Medical Association, 293*, 293–294.

Molloy, G. J., Perkins-Porras, L., Strike, P. C., & Steptoe, A. (2008). Social networks and partner stress as predictors of adherence to medication, rehabilitation attendance, and quality of life following acute coronary syndrome. *Health Psychology, 27*, 52–58.

Molloy, G., Perkins-Porras, L., Strike, P., & Steptoe, A. (2008). Social networks and partner stress as predictors of adherence to medication, rehabilitation attendance, and quality of life following acute coronary syndrome. *Health Psychology, 27*(1), 52–58.

Monroe, S. M., & Harkness, K. L. (2005). Life stress, the "kindling" hypothesis, and the recurrence of depression: Considerations from a life stress perspective. *Psychological Review, 112*, 417–445.

Monroe, S. M., & Simons, A. D. (1991). Diathesis-stress theories in the context of life stress research: Implications for the depressive disorders, *Psychological Bulletin, 110*, 406–425.

Monteleone, P., Tortorella, A., Castaldo, E., Di Filippo, C., & Maj, M. (2007). The Leu 72Met polymorphism of the ghrelin gene is significantly associated with binge eating disorder. *Psychiatric Genetics, 17*, 13–16.

Moos, R. H. (2008). Active ingredients of substance use-focused self-help groups. *Addiction, 103*, 387–396.

Moradi, B., & Risco, C. (2006). Perceived discrimination experiences and mental health of Latina/o American persons. *Journal of Counseling Psychology, 53*, 411–421.

Morone, N. E., Greco, C. M., & Weiner, D. K. (2008). Mindfulness meditation for the treatment of chronic low back pain in older adults: A randomized controlled pilot study. *Pain, 134*, 310–319.

Morris, R., Wannamethee, G., Lennon, L., Thomas, M., & Whincup, P. (2008). Do socioeconomic characteristics of neighbourhood of residence independently influence incidence of coronary heart disease and all-cause mortality in older British men? *European Journal of Cardiovascular Prevention and Rehabilitation, 15*(1), 19–25.

Morrow, M. L., Heesch, K. C., Dinger, M. K., Hull, H.R., Kneehans, A. W., & Fields, D. A. (2006). Freshman 15: Fact or fiction? *Obesity, 14*, 1438–1443.

Moseley, K. L., Freed, G. L., Bullard, C. M. & Goold, S. D. (2007). Measuring African-American parents' cultural mistrust while in a healthcare setting: A pilot study. *Journal of the National Medical Association, 99*, 15–21.

Moskowitz, J. T., Epel, E. S., & Acree, M. (2008). Positive affect uniquely predicts lower risk of mortality in people with diabetes. *Health Psychology, 27*, S73–S82.

Moskowitz, J. T., Epel, E. S., & Acree, M. (2008). Positive affect uniquely predicts lower risk of mortality in people with diabetes. *Health Psychology, 27*, S73–S82.

Mottram, S., Peat, G., Thomas, E., Wilkie, R., & Croft, P. (2008). Patterns of pain and mobility limitation in older people: Cross-sectional findings from a population survey of 18,497 adults aged 50 years and over. *Quality of Life Research, 17*, 529–539.

Moumjid, N., Gafni, A., Brémond, A., & Carrère, M. (2007). Shared decision making in the medical encounter: Are we all talking about the same thing? *Medical Decision Making, 27*, 539–546.

Mowery, R. L. (2007). The family, larger systems, and end-of-life decision making. In D. Balk, C. Wogrin, G. Thornton, & D. Meagher (Eds.), *Handbook of thanatology: The essential body of knowledge for the student of death, dying, and bereavement* (93–102). Northbrook, IL: Association for Death Education and Counseling.

Müller, B., Nordt, C., Lauber, C., & Rössler, W. (2007). Changes in social network diversity and perceived social support after psychiatric hospitalization: Results from a longitudinal study. *International Journal of Social Psychiatry, 53,* 564–575.

Müller, F., & Wehbe, L. (2008). Smoking and smoking cessation in Latin America: A review of the current situation and available treatments. *International Journal of Chronic Obstructive Pulmonary Disease, 3(2),* 285–293.

Murtaugh, M., Sweeney, C., Giuliano, A., Herrick, J., Hines, L., Byers, T., et al. (2008). Diet patterns and breast cancer risk in Hispanic and non-Hispanic white women: the Four-Corners Breast Cancer Study. *The American Journal of Clinical Nutrition, 87(4),* 978–984.

Naar-King, S., Rongkavilit, C., Wang, B., Wright, K., Chuenyam, T., Lam, P., et al. (2008). Transtheoretical model and risky sexual behaviour in HIV + youth in Thailand. *AIDS Care, 20(2),* 205–211.

Nabi, H., Kivimäki, M., Zins, M., Elovainio, M., Consoli, S., Cordier, S., et al. (2008). Does personality predict mortality? Results from the GAZEL French prospective cohort study. *International Journal of Epidemiology, 37(2),* 386–396.

Nabi, H., Kivimäki, M., Zins, M., Elovainio, M., Consoli, S., Cordier, S., et al. (2008). Does personality predict mortality? Results from the GAZEL French prospective cohort study. *International Journal of Epidemiology, 37(2),* 386–396.

Nahin, R. L., & Straus, S. E. (2001). Research into complementary and alternative medicine: Problems and potential. *British Medical Journal, 20,* 322(7279), 161–164.

Nakamura, K., Barzi, F., Lam, T., Huxley, R., Feigin, V., Ueshima, H., et al. (2008). Cigarette smoking, systolic blood pressure, and cardiovascular diseases in the Asia-Pacific region. *Stroke; a Journal of Cerebral Circulation, 39(6),* 1694–1702.

Nasir, K., Katz, R., Takasu, J., Shavelle, D., Detrano, R., Lima, J., et al. (2008). Ethnic differences between extra-coronary measures on cardiac computed tomography: multi-ethnic study of atherosclerosis (MESA). *Atherosclerosis, 198(1),* 104–114.

Nassau, J., Tien, K., & Fritz, G. (2008). Review of the literature: Integrating psychoneuroimmunology into pediatric chronic illness interventions.

Journal of Pediatric Psychology, 33(2), 195–207.

National Center for Health Statistics. (2006). *Chartbook on trends in the health of Americans. Health, United States, 2006.* Hyattsville, MD: Public Health Service.

National Diabetes Information Clearinghouse. (2008). Retrieved April 30, 2008, from http://diabetes. niddk.nih.gov/dm/pubs/statistics/ index htm#7.

National Digestive Diseases Information Clearinghouse. (2008). Retrieved may 10, 2008, from http://digestive. niddk.nih.gov/index.htm.

National Highway Traffic Safety Administration (2008). Retrieved June 2, 2008, from www.nhtsa.gov/ portal/site/nhtsa/menuitem.9fa154a 4d39f02e770f6df1020008a0c/.

National Research Council. (2004). *Eliminating health disparities: Measurement and data needs.* Washington, DC: The National Academies Press.

National vital statistics reports (2008). Hyattsville, MD: National Center for Health Statistics. 2008.

Nealey-Moore, J., Smith, T., Uchino, B., Hawkins, M., & Olson-Cerny, C. (2007). Cardiovascular reactivity during positive and negative marital interactions. *Journal Of Behavioral Medicine, 30(6),* 505–519.

Negoianu, D., & Goldfarb, S. (2008). Just add water. *Journal of the American Society of Nephrology, 19,* 1041–1043.

Nelson, E. L., Wenzel, L. B., Osann, K., Dogan-Ates, A., Chantana, N., Reina-Patton, A., et al. (2008). Stress, immunity, and cervical cancer: Biobehavioral outcomes of a randomized clinical trail. *Clinical Cancer Research, 14,* 2111–2118.

Nelson, E., Wenzel, L., Osann, K., Dogan-Ates, A., Chantana, N., Reina-Patton, A., et al. (2008). Stress, immunity, and cervical cancer: Biobehavioral outcomes of a randomized clinical trial [corrected]. *Clinical Cancer Research, 14(7),* 2111–2118.

Nelson, S., McCoy, G., Stetter, M., & Vanderwagen, W. C. (1992). An overview of mental health services for American Indians and Alaska Natives in the 1990's. *Hospital and Community Psychiatry, 43,* 257–261.

Ng, M. (2007). New perspectives on Mars and Venus: Unravelling the role of androgens in gender differences in cardiovascular biology and

disease. *Heart, Lung and Circulation, 16(3),* 185–192.

Ngo-Metzger, Q., Massagli, M. P., Clarridge, B. R., Manocchia, M., Davis, R. B., Iezzoni, L. I., et al. (2003). Linguistic and cultural barriers to care. *Journal of Internal Medicine, 18,* 44–52.

Ngo-Metzger, Q., Phillips, R., & McCarthy, E. (2008). Ethnic disparities in hospice use among Asian-American and Pacific Islander patients dying with cancer. *Journal of the American Geriatrics Society, 56(1),* 139–144.

Nicolson, P., Kopp, Z., Chapple, C. R., & Kelleher, C. (2008). It's just the worry about not being able to control it! A qualitative study of living with overactive bladder. *British Journal of Health Psychology, 13,* 343–359.

Nielsen, N., Kristensen, T., Strandberg-Larsen, K., Zhang, Z., Schnohr, P., & Grønbaek, M. (2008). Perceived stress and risk of colorectal cancer in men and women: A prospective cohort study. *Journal of Internal Medicine, 263(2),* 192–202.

Nielsen, N., Strandberg-Larsen, K., Grønbaek, M., Kristensen, T., Schnohr, P., & Zhang, Z. (2007). Self-reported stress and risk of endometrial cancer: a prospective cohort study. *Psychosomatic Medicine, 69(4),* 383–389.

Noar, S. (2008). Behavioral interventions to reduce HIV-related sexual risk behavior: Review and synthesis of meta-analytic evidence. *AIDS and Behavior, 12(3),* 335–353.

Noar, S. M. (2005). A health educator's guide to theories of health behavior. *International Quarterly of Community Health Education, 24,* 75–92.

Noar, S. M. (2006). A 10-year retrospective of research in health mass media campaigns: Where do we go from here? *Journal of Health Communication, 11(1),* 21–42.

Noar, S. M., & Zimmerman, R. S. (2005). Health Behavior Theory and cumulative knowledge regarding health behaviors: Are we moving in the right direction? *Health Education Research, 20,* 275–290.

Noar, S. M., Benac, C. N., & Harris, M. S. (2007). Does tailoring matter? Meta-analytic review of tailored print health behavior change interventions. *Psychological Bulletin, 133,* 673–693.

Noble, M., Tregear, S. J., Treadwell, J, R, & Schoelles, K. (2008). Long-term opioid therapy for chronic noncancer pain: A systematic review and meta-analysis of efficacy and safety. *Journal of Pain and Symptom Management*, 35, 214–228.

Noda, H., Iso, H., Toyoshima, H., Date, C., Yamamoto, A., Kikuchi, S., et al. (2008). Smoking status, sports participation and mortality from coronary heart disease. *Heart (British Cardiac Society)*, 94(4), 471–475.

Noh, S., & Kaspar, B. (2003). Perceived discrimination and depression: Moderating effects of coping, acculturation, and ethnic support. *American Journal of Public Health*, 93, 232–238.

Noh, S., Beiser, M., Kaspar, V., Hou, F., & Rummens, J. (1999). Perceived racial discrimination, depression, and coping: A study of Southeast Asian refugees in Canada. *Journal of Health and Social Behavior*, 40, 193–207.

Nolte, S., Elsworth, G. R., Sinclair, A. J., Osborne, R. H. (2007). The extent and breadth of benefits from participating in chronic disease self-management courses: A national patient-reported outcomes survey. *Patient Education and Counseling*, 65, 351–360.

Noppe, I. C., & Noppe, L. D. (2008). When a friend dies. In K. J. Doka, & A. S. Tucci, (Eds.) *Living with grief: Children and adolescents* (175–192). Washington, DC: Hospice Foundation of America.

Norris, F. H., Perilla, J. L., Ibanez, G. E. & Murphy, A. D. (2001). Sex differences in symptoms of post-traumatic stress: Does culture play a role? *Journal of Traumatic Stress*, 14, 7–28.

Nurses health study. (2008). Retrieved October 16, 2008, from http://www.channing.harvard.edu/nhs/index.html.

O'Brien, E. M., Atchison, J. W., Gremillion, H. A., Waxenberg, L. B., & Robinson, M. E. (2008). Somatic focus/awareness: Relationship to negative affect and pain in chronic pain patients. *European Journal of Pain*, 12, 104–115.

O'Connor, A., Bennett, C., Stacey, D., Barry, M., Col, N., Eden, K., et al. (2007). Do patient decision aids meet effectiveness criteria of the international patient decision aid standards collaboration? A systematic review and meta-analysis. *Medical Decision Making*, 27(5), 554–574.

O'Connor, D. B., Jones, F., Conner, M., McMillan, B., & Ferguson, E. (2008). Effects of daily hassles and eating style on eating behavior. *Health Psychology*, 27, S20–S31.

O'Donovan, A., & Hughes, B. M. (2008). Factors that moderate the effect of laboratory-based social support on cardiovascular reactivity to stress. *International Journal of Psychology and Psychological Therapy*, 8, 85–102.

O'Leary, A., Jemmott, L., & Jemmott, J. (2008). Mediation analysis of an effective sexual risk-reduction intervention for women: The importance of self-efficacy. *Health Psychology: Official Journal of the Division of Health Psychology, American Psychological Association*, 27(2 Suppl), S180–4.

Ogden, C. L., Carroll, M. D., & Flegal, K. M. (2008). High body mass index for age among US children and adolescents, 2003–2006. *Journal of the American Medical Association*, 299, 2401–2405.

Ogden, C. L., Carroll, M. D., Curtin, L.R., McDowell, M. A., Tabak C. J., & Flegal, K. M. (2006). Prevalence of overweight and obesity in the United States, 1999–2004. *Journal of the American Medical Association*, 295, 1549–1555.

Ohira, T., Hozawa, A., Iribarren, C., Daviglus, M., Matthews, K., Gross, M., et al. (2008). Longitudinal association of serum carotenoids and tocopherols with hostility: The CARDIA study. *American Journal of Epidemiology*, 167(1), 42–50.

Ortega, S., Beauchemin, A., & Kaniskan, R. B. (2008). Building resiliency in families with young children exposed to violence: The safe start initiative pilot study. *Best Practices in Mental Health: An International Journal*, 4, 48–64.

Ortiz, I. E., & Torres, E. C. (2007). Curanderismo and the treatment of alcoholism: findings from a focus group of Mexican curanderos... folk healers. *Alcoholism Treatment Quarterly*, 25, 79–90.

Oxlad, M., & Wade, T. D. (2008). Longitudinal risk factors for adverse psychological functioning six months after coronary artery bypass graft surgery. *Journal of Health Psychology*, 13, 79–92.

Ozer, E. J., Best, S. R., Lipsey, T. L., & Weiss, D. S. (2007). Predictors of post-traumatic stress disorder and symptoms in adults: A meta-analysis. *Psychological Bulletin*, 129, 52–73.

Pacquiao, D. (2007). The relationship between cultural competence education and increasing diversity in nursing schools and practice settings. *Journal of Transcultural Nursing*, 18, 28S–37S.

Paez, K. A., Allen, J. K., Carson, K. A., & Cooper, L. A. (2008). Provider and clinic cultural competence in a primary care setting. *Social Science and Medicine*, 66, 1204–1216.

Panagiotakos, D., Pitsavos, C., Chrysohoou, C., Skoumas, I., & Stefanadis, C. (2008). Five-year incidence of cardiovascular disease and its predictors in Greece: The ATTICA study. *Vascular Medicine (London, England)*, 13(2), 113–121.

Parikh, N., Hwang, S., Larson, M., Levy, D., & Fox, C. (2008). Chronic kidney disease as a predictor of cardiovascular disease (from the Framingham Heart Study). *The American Journal of Cardiology*, 102(1), 47–53.

Park, C. L., & Gaffey, A. E. (2007). Relationships between psychosocial factors and health behavior change in cancer survivors: An integrative review. *Annals of Behavioral Medicine*, 34, 115–134.

Park, C., & Gaffey, A. (2007). Relationships between psychosocial factors and health behavior change in cancer survivors: An integrative review. *Annals of Behavioral Medicine: A Publication of the Society of Behavioral Medicine*, 34(2), 115–134.

Pasick, R., & Burke, N. (2008). A critical review of theory in breast cancer screening promotion across cultures. *Annual Review of Public Health*, 29, 351–368.

Pate, R. R., Pratt, M., Blair, M. N., et al. (1995). Physical activity and public health: a recommendation from the Centers for Disease Control and Prevention and the American College of Sports Medicine. *JAMA: Journal of American Medical Association*, 273, 402–407.

Patel, A., Feigelson, H., Talbot, J., McCullough, M., Rodriguez, C., Patel, R., et al. (2008). The role of body weight in the relationship between physical activity and endometrial cancer: Results from a large cohort of U.S. women. *International Journal of Cancer, 123*(8), 1877–1882.

Patel, J., Lim, H., Gunarathne, A., Tracey, I., Durrington, P., Hughes, E., et al. (2008). Ethnic differences in myocardial infarction in patients with hypertension: Effects of diabetes mellitus. *QJM: Monthly Journal of the Association of Physicians, 101*(3), 231–236.

PausJenssen, A., Spooner, B., Wilson, M., & Wilson, T. (2008). Cardiovascular risk reduction via telehealth: A feasibility study. *The Canadian Journal of Cardiology, 24*(1), 57–60.

Payman, V., George, K., & Ryburn, B. (2008). Religiosity of depressed elderly inpatients. *International Journal of Geriatric Psychiatry, 23*, 16–21.

Pecorino, L. (2008). *Molecular biology of cancer: Mechanisms, targets, and therapeutics.* New York: Oxford University Press.

Peña-Purcell, N. (2008). Hispanics' use of Internet health information: An exploratory study. *Journal of the Medical Library Association: JMLA, 96*(2), 101–107.

Pendleton, J., Hopkins, C., Anai, S., Nakamura, K., Chang, M., Grissett, A., et al. (2008). Prostate cancer knowledge and screening attitudes of inner-city men. *Journal of Cancer Education: The Official Journal of the American Association for Cancer Education, 23*(3), 172–179.

Pérez, C., Larsen, M., Gustafsson, R., Norström, M., Atlas, A., Nixon, D., et al. (2008). Broadly immunogenic HLA class I supertype-restricted elite CTL epitopes recognized in a diverse population infected with different HIV-1 subtypes. *Journal of Immunology, 180*(7), 5092–5100.

Perloff, R. M., Bonder, B., Ray, G. B., Ray, E. B. & Siminoff, L. A. (2006). Doctor-patient communication, cultural competence and minority health: Theoretical and empirical perspectives. *American Behavioral Scientist, 49*, 835–852.

Pesek, T.J., Helton, L.R., & Nair, M. (2006). Healing across cultures: Learning from Traditions. *EcoHealth, 3*, 114–118.

Pinckney, R. (2003). *Blue roots: African American folk magic of the Gullah people.* Orangeburg, SC: Sandlapper Publishing CO.

Planalp, S., & Trost, M. (2008). Communication issues at the end of life: Reports from Hospice Volunteers. *Health Communication, 23*(3), 222–233.

Pleis JR, & Lethbridge-Çejku M. (2007). Summary health statistics for U.S. adults: National Health Interview Survey, 2006. *National Center for Health Statistics. Vital Health Statistics, 10*(235).

Pletcher, M. J., Kertesz, S. G., Kohn, M. A., & Gonzales, R. (2008). Trends in opioid prescribing by race/ethnicity for patients seeking care in us emergency departments. *JAMA: Journal of the American Medical Association, 299*, 70–78.

Politi, M. C., Han, P. K. J., & Col, N. F. (2007). Communicating the uncertainty of harms and benefits of medical interventions. *Medical Decision Making, 27*, 681–695.

Polyakova, S. A., & Pacquiao, D. F. (2006). Psychological and mental illness among elder immigrants from the former Soviet Union. *Journal of Transcultural Nursing, 17*, 40–49.

Porter, N. (2003). *Report of focus group findings for messages development related to CDC/ACSM physical activity guidelines.* Contract No.: GS- 23F-0231N. Washington, DC: Centers for Disease Control and Prevention.

Prasadarao, P. S. D. V., & Sudhir, P.M. (2001). Clinical Psychology in India. *Journal of Clinical Psychology in Medical Settings, 8*, 31–38.

Protheroe, J., Bower, P., Chew-Graham, C., Peters, T., & Fahey, T. (2007). Effectiveness of a computerized decision aid in primary care on decision making and quality of life in menorrhagia: results of the MENTIP randomized controlled trial. *Medical Decision Making, 27*(5), 575–584.

Racette, S. B., Deusinger, S. S., Strube, M. J., Highstein, G. R., Deusinger, RH. (2005) Weight changes, exercise, and dietary patterns during freshman and sophomore years of college. *Journal of American College Health, 53*, 245–251.

Rahim-Williams, F. B., Riley, J. L., Herrera, D., Campbell, C. M., Hastie, B. A., & Fillingim, R. B. (2007). Ethnic identity predicts experimental pain sensitivity in African Americans and Hispanics. *Pain, 129*, 177–184.

Rashid, M., & Zimring, C. (2008). A review of the empirical literature on the relationship between indoor environment and stress in health care and office settings: Problems and prospects of sharing evidence. *Environment and Behavior, 40*, 151–190.

Ravnskov, U. (2008). The fallacies of the lipid hypothesis. *Scandinavian Cardiovascular Journal: SCJ, 42*(4), 236–239.

Read, J., & Gorman, B. (2007). Racial/ethnic differences in hypertension and depression among US adult women. *Ethnicity and Disease, 17*(2), 389–396.

Reedy, J., Mitrou, P., Krebs-Smith, S., Wirfält, E., Flood, A., Kipnis, V., et al. (2008). Index-based dietary patterns and risk of colorectal cancer: the NIH-AARP Diet and Health Study. *American Journal of Epidemiology, 168*(1), 38–48.

Reich, M., Lesur, A., & Perdrizet-Chevallier, C. (2008). Depression, quality of life and breast cancer: A review of the literature. *Breast Cancer Research and Treatment, 110*(1), 9–17.

Reiche, E. M. V., Nunes, S. Morimoto, H. (2004). Stress, depression, the immune system, and cancer. *The Lancet Oncology, 5*, 617–625.

Renahy, E., Parizot, I., & Chauvin, P. (2008). Health information seeking on the Internet: A double divide? Results from a representative survey in the Paris metropolitan area, France, 2005–2006. *BMC Public Health, 8*, 69–69.

Reyes-Gibby, C. C., Aday, L. A., Todd, K. H., Cleeland, C., Anderson, K. O. (2007). Pain in aging community-dwelling adults in the United States: Non-Hispanic Whites, Non-Hispanic Blacks, and Hispanics. *The Journal of Pain, 8*, 75–84.

Richards, R., & Smith, C. (2007). Environmental, parental, and personal influences on food choice, access, and overweight status among homeless children. *Social Science and Medicine, 65*, 1572–1583.

Richman, L. S., Kohn-Wood, L. P., & Williams, D. R. (2007). The role of discrimination and racial identity for mental health service utilization. *Journal of Social and Clinical Psychology, 26*, 960–981.

Roach, M. (2006). *Spook: Science tackles the afterlife.* New York: Norton.

Roethel, A., & Gurung, R. A. R. (2007, August). *Managing stress: Which techniques are the most effective?*

Poster presented at the annual meeting of the American Psychological Association: San Francisco, CA.

Rollnick, S., William, W.R., & Butler, C.C. (2008). *Motivational Interviewing in Health Care: Helping patients change behavior.* New York: Guilford Press.

Roscoe, L., & Hyer, K. (2008). Quality of life at the end of life for nursing home residents: Perceptions of hospice and nursing home staff members. *Journal of Pain and Symptom Management, 35*(1), 1–9.

Rosen, D., Spencer, M. S., Tolman, R. M., Williams, D. R., & Jackson, J. S. (2003). Psychiatric disorders and substance dependence among unmarried low-income mothers. *Health and Social Work, 28,* 157–65.

Rosenblatt, P. C. (2007). Culture, socialization, and loss, grief and mourning. In D. Balk, C. Wogrin, G. Thornton, & D. Meagher (Eds.), *Handbook of thanatology: The essential body of knowledge for the student of death, dying, and bereavement* (pp. 115–120). Northbrook, IL: Association for Death Education and Counseling.

Rosenthal, D. (1970). *Genetic theory and abnormal behavior.* New York: McGraw-Hill.

Roter, D., & Hall, J. A. (2006). *Doctors talking with patients/patients talking with doctors* (2e). Westport, CT: Greenwood Publishing Press.

Rothman, A. J., Hertel, A. W., Baldwin, A. S., & Bartels, R. D. (2008). Understanding the determinants of health behavior change: Integrating theory and practice. In J. Y. Shah & W. L. Gardner (Eds.), *Handbook of motivation science* (pp. 494–507). New York: Guilford Press.

Rüdell, K., & Diefenbach, M. (2008). Current issues and new directions in psychology and health: Culture and health psychology. Why health psychologists should care about culture. *Psychology and Health, 23*(4), 387–390.

Rudolph, K. D., & Hammen. C. (1999) Age and gender as determinants of stress exposure, generation, and reactions in youngsters: A transactional perspective. *Child Development, 70,* 660–677.

Running, A., Girard, D., & Tolle, L. (2008). When there is nothing left to do, there is everything left to do. *American Journal of Hospice and Palliative Medicine, 24*(6), 451–454.

Ruthig, J. C., Chipperfield, J. G., Newall, N. E., Perry, R. P., Hall, N. C. (2007). Detrimental effects of falling on health and well-being in later life: The mediating roles of perceived control and optimism. *Journal of Health Psychology, 12,* 231–248.

Salomon, K., & Jagusztyn, N. (2008). Resting cardiovascular levels and reactivity to interpersonal incivility among Black, Latina/o, and White individuals: The moderating role of ethnic discrimination. *Health Psychology: 27*(4), 473–481.

Sampson, R. J., Morenoff, J. D., & Gannon-Rowley, T. (2002). Assessing "neighborhood effects": social processes and new directions in research. *Annual Review of Sociology, 28,* 443–478.

Samson, A., & Siam H. (2008). Adapting to major chronic illness: a proposal for a comprehensive task-model approach. *Patient Education and Counseling, 70,* 426–429.

Sánchez, L., Lana, A., Hidalgo, A., Rodríguez, J., Del Valle, M., Cueto, A., et al. (2008). Risk factors for second primary tumours in breast cancer survivors. *European Journal of Cancer Prevention: The Official Journal of the European Cancer Prevention Organisation (ECP), 17*(5), 406–413.

Santry, H. P., Gillen, D. L., & Lauderdale, D. S. (2005). Trends in bariatric surgical procedures. *JAMA. Journal of the American Medical Association, 294,* 1909–1917.

Saremi, A., & Arora, R. (2008). The cardiovascular implications of alcohol and red wine. *American Journal of Therapeutics, 15*(3), 265–277.

Saunders, E., & Ofili, E. (2008). Epidemiology of atherothrombotic disease and the effectiveness and risks of antiplatelet therapy: Race and ethnicity considerations. *Cardiology in Review, 16*(2), 82–88.

Saurer, T., Ijames, S., Carrigan, K., & Lysle, D. (2008). Neuroimmune mechanisms of opioid-mediated conditioned immunomodulation. *Brain, Behavior, and Immunity, 22*(1), 89–97.

Schrag, N., McKeown, R., Jackson, K., Cuffe, S., & Neuberg, R. (2008). Stress-related mental disorders in childhood cancer survivors. *Pediatric Blood and Cancer, 50*(1), 98–103.

Schroecksnadel, K., Sarcletti, M., Winkler, C., Mumelter, B., Weiss, G., Fuchs, D., et al. (2008). Quality of life and immune activation in patients with HIV-infection. *Brain, Behavior, and Immunity, 22*(6), 881–889.

Schure, M. B., Christopher, J., & Christopher, S. (2008). Mind-body medicine and the art of self-care: Teaching mindfulness to counseling students through yoga, meditation, and Qigong. *Journal of Counseling and Development, 86,* 47–56.

Schuurman, D. (2008). Grief groups for grieving children and adolescents. In K. J. Doka & A. S. Tucci (Eds.), *Living with grief: Children and adolescents* (pp. 255–268). Washington, DC: Hospice Foundation of America.

Schwartz, L. M., Woloshin, S., & Welch, H. G. (2007). The drug facts box: Providing consumers with simple tabular data on drug benefit and harm. *Medical Decision Making, 27,* 655–662.

Schwarzer, R. (2008). Modeling health behavior change: How to predict and modify the adoption and maintenance of health behaviors. *Applied Psychology: An International Review, 57,* 1–29.

Scott-Sheldon, L. A. J., Kalichman, S. C., Carey, M. P., & Fielder, R. L. (2008). Stress management interventions for HIV+ adults: A meta-analysis of randomized controlled trials, 1989 to 2006. *Health Psychology, 27,* 129–139.

Segerstrom, S. C. (2007). Stress, energy, and immunity: An ecological view. *Current Directions in Psychological Science, 16,* 326–330.

Segrin, C. (1999). Social skills, stressful life events, and the development of psychosocial problems. *Journal of Social and Clinical Psychology, 19,* 14–34.

Shafer, T., Wagner, D., Chessare, J., Schall, M., McBride, V., Zampiello, F., et al. (2008). US organ donation breakthrough collaborative increases organ donation. *Critical Care Nursing Quarterly, 31*(3), 190–210.

Shah, S., Ayash, C., Pharaon, N., & Gany, F. (2008). Arab American immigrants in New York: Health care and cancer knowledge, attitudes, and beliefs. *Journal of Immigrant and Minority Health/Center for Minority Public Health, 10*(5), 429–436.

Sheeran, P. (2002). Intention-behavior relations: A conceptual and empirical review. *European Review of Social Psychology, 12,* 1–36.

Shields, C. A., Spink, K. S., Chad, K., Muhajarine, N., Humbert, L., & Odnokon, P. (2008). Youth and adolescent physical activity lapsers: Examining self-efficacy as a mediator of the relationship between family social influence and physical activity. *Journal of Health Psychology, 13,* 121–130.

Siafaka, V., Hyphantis, T., Alamanos, I., Fountzilas, G., Skarlos, D., Pectasides, D., et al. (2008). Personality factors associated with psychological distress in testicular cancer survivors. *Journal of Personality Assessment, 90*(4), 348–355.

Siegrist, J., & Marmot, M. (2004). Health inequalities and the psychosocial environment: Two scientific challenges. *Social Science and Medicine, 58,* 1463–1473.

Simon, A., & Wardle, J. (2008). Socioeconomic disparities in psychosocial well-being in cancer patients. *European Journal of Cancer (Oxford, England: 1990), 44*(4), 572–578.

Simopoulos, A. (2008). The importance of the omega-6/omega-3 fatty acid ratio in cardiovascular disease and other chronic diseases. *Experimental Biology and Medicine (Maywood, N.J.), 233*(6), 674–688.

Singh, A. (2007). Action and reason in the theory of Ayurveda. *AI & Society, 21,* 27–46.

Singletary, K., & Milner, J. (2008, July). Diet, autophagy, and cancer: a review. *Cancer Epidemiology, Biomarkers and Prevention: A Publication of the American Association for Cancer Research, Cosponsored by the American Society of Preventive Oncology, 17*(7), 1596–1610.

Sjösten, N., & Kivelä, S. (2006). The effects of physical exercise on depressive symptoms among the aged: A systematic review. *International Journal of Geriatric Psychiatry,* (5), 410–418.

Smith, M., Seplaki, C., Biagtan, M., Dupreez, A., & Cleary, J. (2008). Characterizing Hospice Services in the United States. *Gerontologist, 48*(1), 25–31.

Sofi, F., Capalbo, A., Cesari, F., Abbate, R., & Gensini, G. (2008). Physical activity during leisure time and primary prevention of coronary heart disease: An updated meta-analysis of cohort studies. *European Journal of Cardiovascular Prevention and Rehabilitation, 15*(3), 247–257.

Sofi, F., Marcucci, R., Gori, A., Abbate, R., & Gensini, G. (2008). Residual platelet reactivity on aspirin therapy and recurrent cardiovascular events—a meta-analysis. *International Journal of Cardiology, 128*(2), 166–171.

Soskolne, V., Marie, S., & Manor, O. (2007). Beliefs, recommendations and intentions are important explanatory factors of mammography screening behavior among Muslim Arab women in Israel. *Health Education Research, 22*(5), 665–676.

Spiro, A. (2007). The relevance of a lifespan developmental approach to health. In *Handbook of health psychology and aging* (pp. 75–93). New York: Guilford Press.

Srivastava, A., & Kreiger, N. (2000). Relation of physical activity to risk of testicular cancer. *American Journal of Epidemiology, 151*(1), 78–87.

Stafford, H., Saltzstein, S., Shimasaki, S., Sanders, C., Downs, T., & Robins Sadler, G. (2008). Racial/ethnic and gender disparities in renal cell carcinoma incidence and survival. *The Journal of Urology, 179*(5), 1704–1708.

Starace, F., Massa, A., Amico, K., & Fisher, J. (2006). Adherence to antiretroviral therapy: an empirical test of the information-motivation-behavioral skills model. *Health Psychology: Official Journal of the Division of Health Psychology, American Psychological Association, 25*(2), 153–162.

Starr, C., & McMillan, B. (2006). *Human Biology* (6th ed.). Pacific Grove, CA: Brooks/Cole.

Staton, L. J., Panda, M., Chen, I., Genao, I., Kurz, J., Pasanen, M., et al. (2007). When race matters: Disagreement in pain perception between patients and their physicians in primary care. *Journal of the National Medical Association, 99,* 532–537.

Stekelenburg, J., Jager, B.E., Kolk, P.R., Westen, E.H.M.N., van der Kwaak, A., & Wolffers, I.N. (2005). Health care seeking behaviour and utilization of traditional healers in Kalabo, Zambia. *Health Policy, 71,* 67–81.

Stevenson, R. G. (2008). Helping students cope with grief. In K. J. Doka & A. S. Tucci (Eds.) *Living with Grief: Children and adolescents* (317–334). Washington, DC: Hospice Foundation of America.

Stewart, D. E., Abbey, S. E., Shnek, Z. M., Irvine, J., & Grace, S. L. (2004). Gender differences in health information needs and decisional preferences in patients recovering from an acute ischemic coronary event. *Psychosomatic Medicine 66,* 42–48.

Stice, E. (2002). Risk and maintenance factors for eating pathology: A meta-analytic review. *Psychological Bulletin, 128,* 825–848.

Stice, E., Shaw, H., & Marti, C. N. (2006). A meta-analytic review of obesity prevention programs for children and adolescents: The skinny on interventions that work. *Psychological Bulletin, 132,* 667–691.

Stice, E., Shaw, H., & Marti, C. N. (2006). A meta-analytic review of obesity prevention programs for children and adolescents: The skinny on interventions that work. *Psychological Bulletin, 132,* 667–691.

Stickel, F., Egerer, G., & Seitz, H. K. (2002). Hepatotoxity of botanicals. *Public Health Nutrition, 3,* 113–124.

Stinson, D. A., Logel, C., Zanna, M. P., Holmes, J. G., Cameron, J. J., Wood, J. V., et al. (2008). The cost of lower self-esteem: Testing a self- and social-bonds model of health. *Journal of Personality and Social Psychology, 94,* 412–428.

Stinson, J., Yamada, J., Dickson, A., Lamba, J., & Stevens, B. (2008). Review of systematic reviews on acute procedural pain in children in the hospital setting. *Pain Research and Management, 13,* 51–57.

Stolzenberg-Solomon, R., Adams, K., Leitzmann, M., Schairer, C., Michaud, D., Hollenbeck, A., et al. (2008). Adiposity, physical activity, and pancreatic cancer in the National Institutes of Health-AARP Diet and Health Cohort. *American Journal of Epidemiology, 167*(5), 586–597.

Streblow, D., Dumortier, J., Moses, A., Orloff, S., & Nelson, J. (2008). Mechanisms of cytomegalovirus-accelerated vascular disease: induction of paracrine factors that promote angiogenesis and wound healing. *Current Topics in Microbiology and Immunology, 325,* 397–415.

Streppel, M., Ocké, M., Boshuizen, H., Kok, F., & Kromhout, D. (2008). Long-term fish consumption and n-3 fatty acid intake in relation to (sudden) coronary heart disease death: The Zutphen study. *European Heart Journal, 29*(16), 2024–2030.

Stroebe, W. (2008). *Dieting, overweight, and obesity: Self-regulation in a food-rich environment.* Washington, DC: American Psychological Association.

Su, D., Li, L., & Pagán, J. A. (2008). Acculturation and the use of complementary and alternative medicine. *Social Science and Medicine, 66,* 439–453.

Subramanian, J., & Govindan, R. (2007). Lung cancer in never smokers: A review. *Journal of Clinical Oncology: Official Journal of the American Society of Clinical Oncology, 25*(5), 561–570.

Sue, S. (2006). Cultural competency: From philosophy to research and practice. *Journal of Community Psychology, 34,* 237–245.

Suominen–Taipale, A. L., Martelin, T., Koskinen, S., Holmen, J., & Johnsen, R. (2006). Gender differences in health care use among the elderly population in areas of Norway and Finland. A cross-sectional analysis based on the HUNT study and the FINRISK Senior Survey. *BMC Health Services Research, 6*:110, DOI:10.1186/1472-6963-6-110.

Sutton, S. (2005). Stage theories of health behavior. In M. Conner & P. Norman (Eds.) *Predicting health behaviour: Research and practice with social cognition models* (2nd ed.). Buckingham, United Kingdom: Open University Press.

Swartz, A., Strath, S., Parker, S., Miller, N., & Cieslik, L. (2007). Ambulatory activity and body mass index in White and non-White older adults. *Journal of Physical Activity and Health, 4,* 294–304.

Tamimi, R. M., Hankinson, S. E., Campos, H., Spiegelman, D., Zhang, S., Colditz, G. A., et al. (2005). Plasma carotenoids, retinol, and tocopherols and risk of breast cancer. *American Journal of Epidemiology, 161,* 153–160.

Tarn, D. M., Meredith, L.S., Kagawa-Singer, M., Matsumura, S., Bito, S., Oye, R. K., et al. (2005). Trust in one's physician: the role of ethnic match, autonomy, acculturation, and religiosity among Japanese and Japanese Americans. *Annals of Family Medicine, 3,* 339–347.

Taylor, R. M., Gibson, F., & Franck, L. S. (2008). A concept analysis of health-related quality of life in young people with chronic illness. *Journal of Clinical Nursing, 17,* 1823–1833.

Taylor, S. E. (1990). Health psychology. *American Psychologist, 45*(1), 40–50.

Taylor, S. E., Welch, W., Kim, H. S., Sherman, D. K. (2007). Cultural differences in the impact of social support on psychological and biological stress responses. *Psychological Science, 18,* 831–837.

Tedaldi, E., Absalon, J., Thomas, A., Shlay, J., & van den Berg-Wolf, M. (2008). Ethnicity, race, and gender. Differences in serious adverse events among participants in an antiretroviral initiation trial: results of CPCRA 058 (FIRST Study). *Journal of Acquired Immune Deficiency Syndromes (1999), 47*(4), 441–448.

Temoshok, L., Wald, R., Synowski, S., & Garzino-Demo, A. (2008). Coping as a multisystem construct associated with pathways mediating HIV-relevant immune function and disease progression. *Psychosomatic Medicine, 70*(5), 555–561.

Tez, M., & Tez, S. (2008). Is cancer an adaptation mechanism to stress? *Cell Biology International, 32*(6), 713–713.

Thieden, E. (2008). Sun exposure behaviour among subgroups of the Danish population. Based on personal electronic UVR dosimetry and corresponding exposure diaries. *Danish Medical Bulletin, 55*(1), 47–68.

Thombs, B. (2008). Perceived social support predicts outcomes following myocardial infarction: A call for screening? *Health Psychology, 27*(1), 1–1.

Thompson, B., Coronado, G., Chen, L., Thompson, L. A., Halperin, A., Jaffe, R., et al. (2007). Prevalence and characteristics of smokers at 30 Pacific Northwest colleges and universities. *Nicotine and Tobacco Research, 9,* 429–438.

Thorn, B., Cross, T., & Walker, B. (2007). Meta-analyses and systematic reviews of psychological treatments for chronic pain: Relevance to an evidence-based practice. *Health Psychology, 26*(1), 10–12.

Thornicroft, G., Rose, D., & Kassam, A. (2007). Discrimination in health care against people with mental illness. *International Review of Psychiatry, 19,* 113–122.

Thorogood, M., Simera, I., Dowler, E., Summerbell, C., & Brunner, E. (2007). A systematic review of population and community dietary interventions to prevent cancer, *Nutrition Research Reviews, 20,* 74–88.

Thorsen, L., Courneya, K., Stevinson, C., & Fosså, S. (2008). A systematic review of physical activity in prostate cancer survivors: outcomes, prevalence, and determinants. *Supportive Care in Cancer: Official Journal of the Multinational Association of Supportive Care in Cancer, 16*(9), 987–997.

Thune, I., & Lund, E. (1994). Physical activity and the risk of prostate and testicular cancer: A cohort study of 53,000 Norwegian men. *Cancer Causes & Control: CCC, 5*(6), 549–556.

Tillerson, K. (2008). Explaining racial disparities in HIV/AIDS incidence among women in the U.S.: A systematic review. *Statistics in Medicine, 27*(20), 4132–4143.

Tod, A. M., Craven, J., & Allmark, P. (2008). Diagnostic delay in lung cancer: A qualitative study. *Journal of Advanced Nursing, 61,* 336–343.

Tornesello, M., Duraturo, M., Giorgi-Rossi, P., Sansone, M., Piccoli, R., Buonaguro, L., et al. (2008). Human papillomavirus (HPV) genotypes and HPV16 variants in human immunodeficiency virus-positive Italian women. *The Journal of General Virology, 89*(Pt 6), 1380–1389.

Torres, E., & Sawyer, T. L. (2005). *Curandero: A Life in Mexican Folk Healing.* Albuquerque: University of New Mexico Press.

Tremblay, P. F., Graham, K., & Wells, S. (2008). Severity of physical aggression reported by university students: A test of the interaction between trait aggression and alcohol consumption. *Personality and Individual Differences, 45,* 3–9.

Triest-Robertson, S. (2008, April). Pain management: A multidisciplinary approach. Presentation given at the University of Wisconsin, Green Bay.

Trotter, R. T. (2001). Curanderismo: A picture of Mexican-American folk healing. *Journal of Alternative and Complementary Medicine, 7,* 129–131.

Tse, M. M. Y., Ng, J. K. F., Chung, J. W. Y., & Wong, T. K. S. (2002). The effect of visual stimulation via the eyeglass display and the perception of pain. *CyberPsychology and Behavior, 5,* 65–75.

Tsenkova, V. K., Love, G. D., Singer, B. H., and Ryff, C. D. (2008). Coping and positive affect predict longitudinal change in glycosylated hemoglobin. *Health Psychology, 27,* S163–S171.

Tugade, M. M., Fredrickson, B. L., & Barrett, L. F. (2004). Psychological resilience and positive emotional granularity: Examining the benefits of positive emotions on coping and health. *Journal of Personality, 72,* 1161–1190.

Tullmann, D. F., Haugh, K. H., Dracup, K. A., & Bourguignon, C. (2007). A randomized controlled trial to reduce delay in older adults seeking help for symptoms of acute myocardial infarction. *Research in Nursing and Health, 30,* 485–497.

Turk Charles, S., Gatz, M., Kato, K., & Pedersen, N. (2008). Physical health 25 years later: The predictive ability of neuroticism. *Health Psychology: Official Journal of the Division of Health Psychology, American Psychological Association, 27*(3), 369–378.

U.S. Department of Health & Human Services. (2008). *Healthy People 2010.* Retrieved October 21, 2008, from http://www.healthypeople.gov/.

U.S. Department of Health and Human Services. (2000, 12 January). *Healthy People 2010 Fact Sheet* [Online]. Office of Disease Prevention and Health Promotion.

U.S. Department of Health and Human Services. (2001). *Mental Health: Culture, Race, and Ethnicity—A Supplement to Mental Health: A Report of the Surgeon General.* Rockville, MD: U.S. Department of Health and Human Services, Substance Abuse and Mental Health Services Administration, Center for Mental Health Services.

U.S. Department of Health and Human Services. (2007). Health, United States 2007.

U.S. Department of Justice. (2006). 2006 National Crime Victimization Survey.

Ukraintseva, S., & Yashin, A. I. (2003). Individual aging and cancer risk: How are they related? *Demographic Research, 9,* 164–196.

Ulrich, R. (2004). The role of the physical environment in the hospital of the 21st century: A once-in-a-lifetime opportunity. Report to the Center for Health Design for the *Designing the 21st Century Hospital Project.*

Ulrich, R. S., Simons, R. F., & Miles, M. A. (2003). Effects of environmental simulations and television on blood donor stress. *Journal of Architectural and Planning Research, 20,* 38–47.

Upchurch, D. M., Chyu, L., Greendale, G.A., Utts, J., Bair, Y. A., Zhang, G., et al. (2007). Complementary and alternative medicine use among American women: findings from the National Health Interview Survey, 2002. *Journal of Women's Health, 16*(1), 102–113.

Utsey, S. O., Payne, Y. A., Jackson, E. S., & Jones, A. M. (2002). Race-related stress, quality of life indicators, and life satisfaction among elderly African Americans. *Cultural Diversity and Ethnic Minority Psychology, 8,* 224–233.

Vachon, M. (2008). Meaning, spirituality, and wellness in cancer survivors. *Seminars in Oncology Nursing, 24*(3), 218–225.

Vainshtein, J. (2008). Disparities in breast cancer incidence across racial/ethnic strata and socioeconomic status: A systematic review. *Journal of the National Medical Association, 100*(7), 833–839.

Van Horn, L., McCoin, M., Kris-Etherton, P., Burke, F., Carson, J., Champagne, C., et al. (2008). The evidence for dietary prevention and treatment of cardiovascular disease. *Journal of the American Dietetic Association, 108*(2), 287–331.

Varela-Lema, L., Taioli, E., Ruano-Ravina, A., Barros-Dios, J., Anantharaman, D., Benhamou, S., et al. (2008). Meta-analysis and pooled analysis of GSTM1 and CYP1A1 polymorphisms and oral and pharyngeal cancers: a HuGE-GSEC review. *Genetics in Medicine: Official Journal of the American College of Medical Genetics, 10*(6), 369–384.

Vella, E. J., Kamarck, T. W., & Shiffman, S. (2008). Hostility moderates the effects of social support and intimacy on blood pressure in daily social interactions. *Health Psychology, 27,* S155–S162.

Ventura, J., Nuechterlein, K. H., Lukoff, D., & Hardesty, J. P. (1989). A prospective study of stressful life events and schizophrenic relapse. *Journal of Abnormal Psychology, 4,* 407–411.

Vossen, C., Hoffmann, M., Hahmann, H., Wüsten, B., Rothenbacher, D., & Brenner, H. (2008). Effect of APOE genotype on lipid levels in patients with coronary heart disease during a 3-week inpatient rehabilitation program. *Clinical Pharmacology and Therapeutics, 84*(2), 222–227.

Wachholtz, A. B., Pearce, M. J., & Koenig, H. (2007). Exploring the relationship between spirituality, coping, and pain. *Journal of Behavioral Medicine, 30,* 311–318.

Walsh, R., & Shapiro, S. L. (2006). The meeting of meditative disciplines and Western psychology: A mutually enriching dialogue. *American Psychologist, 61,* 227–239.

Wang, D., & Audette, J. F. (2008). Acupuncture in pain management. In J. F. Audette & A. Bailey (Eds.), *Integrative pain medicine: The science and practice of complementary and alternative medicine in pain management. Contemporary pain medicine* (pp. 379–416). Totowa, NJ: Humana Press.

Wang, H. X., Leineweber, C., Kirkeeide, R., Svane, B., Schenck-Gustafsson, K., Theorell, T., & Orth-Gomér, K. (2007). Psychosocial stress and atherosclerosis: family and work stress accelerate progression of coronary disease in women. The Stockholm Female Coronary Angiography Study. *Journal of Internal Medicine 261,* 245–254.

Wang, M., Lightsey, O. R., Pietruszka, T., Uruk, A. C., & Wells, A. G. (2007). Purpose in life and reasons for living as mediators of the relationship between stress, coping, and suicidal behavior. *The Journal of Positive Psychology, 2,* 195–204.

Wangberg, S., Andreassen, H., Prokosch, H., Santana, S., Sørensen, T., & Chronaki, C. (2008). Relations between Internet use, socioeconomic status (SES), social support and subjective health. *Health Promotion International, 23*(1), 70–77.

Wansink, B., & Sobal, J. (2007). Mindless eating: The 200 daily food decisions we overlook. *Environment and Behavior, 39,* 106–123.

Wansink, B., van Ittersum, K., & Painter, J. E. (2006). Ice cream illusions: Bowls, spoons, and self-served portion sizes. *American Journal of Preventive Medicine, 31,* 240–243.

Ward, S., Donovan, H., Gunnarsdottir, S., Serlin, R. C., Shapiro, G. R., & Hughes, S. (2008). A randomized trial of a representational intervention to decrease cancer pain (RID-CancerPain). *Health Psychology, 27,* 59–67.

Warren, J., Fernández, M., Harper, G., Hidalgo, M., Jamil, O., & Torres, R. (2008). Predictors of unprotected sex among young sexually active African American, Hispanic, and White MSM: the importance of ethnicity and culture. *AIDS and Behavior, 12*(3), 459–468.

Weaver, K., Llabre, M., Lechner, S., Penedo, F., & Antoni, M. (2008). Comparing unidimensional and multidimensional models of benefit finding in breast and prostate cancer. *Quality of Life Research: An International Journal of Quality of Life Aspects of Treatment, Care and Rehabilitation, 17*(5), 771–781.

Webb, M. S., & Carey, M. P. (2008). Tobacco smoking among low-income black women: Demographic and psychosocial correlates in a community sample. *Nicotine and Tobacco Research, 10,* 219–229.

Weidel, J., Provencio-Vasquez, E., Watson, S., & Gonzalez-Guarda, R. (2008). Cultural considerations for intimate partner violence and HIV risk in Hispanics. *The Journal of the Association of Nurses in AIDS Care: JANAC, 19*(4), 247–251.

Weinberg, R. A. (2006). *Biology of Cancer.* New York: Garland Science.

Weinstein, N. D. (2007). Misleading tests of health behavior theories. *Annals of Behavioral Medicine, 33,* 1–10.

Werth, J. L., Borges, N. J., McNally, C. J., Maguire, C. P., & Britton, P. J. (2008). The intersections of work, health, diversity, and social justice: Helping people living with HIV disease. *Counseling Psychologist, 36,* 16–41.

Whitbeck, L. B., McMorris, B. J., Hoyt, D. R., Stubben, J. D., LaFramboise, T. (2002). Perceived discrimination, traditional practices, and depressive symptoms among American Indians in the Upper Midwest. *Journal of Health and Social Behavior, 43,* 400–418.

Whitehead, M. (1992). The concepts and principles of equity and health. *International Journal of Health Services, 22,* 429–45.

Whitehead, M. The concepts and principles of equity and health.

International Journal of Health Service: 1992, 22, 429–45.

Whittemore, R., & Dixon, J. (2008). Chronic illness: The process of integration. *Journal of Clinical Nursing, 17,* 177–187.

Wiederhold, M. D., & Wiederhold, B. K. (2007). Virtual reality and interactive simulation for pain distraction. *Pain Medicine, 8,* S182–S188.

Wilbert-Lampen, U., Leistner, D., Greven, S., Pohl, T., Sper, S., Völker, C., et al. (2008). Cardiovascular events during World Cup soccer. *The New England Journal of Medicine, 358*(5), 475–483.

Wilfley, D., Tibbs, T., Van Buren, D., Reach, K., Walker, M., & Epstein, L. (2007). Lifestyle interventions in the treatment of childhood overweight: A meta-analytic review of randomized controlled trials. *Health Psychology, 26*(5), 521–532.

Willi, C., Bodenmann, P., Ghali, W. A., Faris, P. D., & Cornuz, J. (2007). Active smoking and the risk of type 2 diabetes: A systematic review and meta-analysis. *JAMA: Journal of the American Medical Association, 298,* 2654–2664.

Williams, A., & Manias, E. (2008). A structured literature review of pain assessment and management of patients with chronic kidney disease. *Journal of Clinical Nursing, 17,* 69–81.

Williams, L., O'Connor, R. C., Howard, S., Hughes, B. M., Johnston, D. W., Hay, J. L., et al. (2008). Type-D personality mechanisms of effect: The role of health-related behavior and social support. *Journal of Psychosomatic Research, 64,* 63–69.

Williamson, D. A., Martin, C. K., Anton, S. D., York-Crowe, E., Han, H., Redman, L., et al. (2008). Is caloric restriction associated with development of eating-disorder symptoms? Results from the CALERIE trial. *Health Psychology, 27,* S32–S42.

Wilson, D. K. (2008). Commentary for health psychology special issue: Theoretical advances in diet and physical activity interventions. *Health Psychology, 27,* S1–S2.

Wilson, R. S., Schneider, J. A., Boyle, P. A., Arnold, S. E., Tang, Y., & Bennett, D. A. (2007). Chronic distress and incidence of mild cognitive impairment. *Neurology, 68,* 2085–2092.

Windich-Biermeier, A., Sjoberg, I., Dale, J. C., Eshelman, D., & Guzzetta, C. E. (2007). Effects of distraction on pain, fear, and distress during venous port access and venipuncture in children and adolescents with cancer. *Journal of Pediatric Oncology Nursing, 24,* 8–19.

Wingood, G., & DiClemente, R. (2008). The ADAPT-ITT model: a novel method of adapting evidence-based HIV Interventions. *Journal of Acquired Immune Deficiency Syndromes (1999), 47* Suppl 1, S40–6.

Wong, F., Huang, Z., He, N., Smith, B., Ding, Y., Fu, C., et al. (2008). HIV risks among gay- and non-gay-identified migrant money boys in Shanghai, China. *AIDS Care, 20*(2), 170–180.

Wu, D., Munoz, M., Espiritu, B., Zeladita, J., Sanchez, E., Callacna, M., et al. (2008). Burden of depression among impoverished HIV-positive women in Peru. *Journal of Acquired Immune Deficiency Syndromes (1999), 48*(4), 500–504.

Xiaoxing, Z. H., & Baker, D. W. (2007). Differences in leisure-time, household, and work-related physical activity by race, ethnicity, and education. *Journal of General Internal Medicine, 20,* 259–266.

Xu, Y. (2007). Adaptation strategies of Asian nurses working in Western countries. *Home Health Care Management & Practice, 19,* 146–148.

Yahav, R., & Cohen, M. (2008). Evaluation of a cognitive-behavioral intervention for adolescents. *International Journal of Stress Management, 15,* 173–188.

Yamada, Y., Ichihara, S., & Nishida, T. (2008). Molecular genetics of myocardial infarction. *Genomic Medicine, 2*(1–2), 7–22.

Yang, H., Brothers, B., & Andersen, B. (2008). Stress and quality of life in breast cancer recurrence: Moderation or mediation of coping? *Annals of Behavioral Medicine, 35*(2), 188–197.

Yeoman, P. D., & Forman, E. M. (2009). Cultural factors in traumatic stress. In S. Eshun & R. A. R. Gurung (Eds.), *Sociocultural issues in mental health.* Malden, MA: Wiley-Blackwell.

Yuh, J., Neiderhiser, J. M., Spotts, E. L., Pedersen, N. L. Lichtenstein, P., Hansson, K., et al. (2008). The role of temperament and social support in depressive symptoms: A twin study of mid-aged women. *Journal of Affective Disorders, 106,* 99–105.

Zhao, G., Ford, E., Li, C., & Mokdad, A. (2008). Are United States adults with coronary heart disease meeting physical activity recommendations? *The American Journal of Cardiology, 101*(5), 557–561.

Zozulya, A. A., Gabaeva, M.V., Sokolov, O. Y., Surkina, I. D., & Kost, N. V. (2008). Personality, coping style, and constitutional neuroimmunology. *Journal of Immunotoxicology, 5,* 221–225.

Zucker, A. (2007). Ethical and legal issues and end-of-life decision making. In D. Balk, C. Wogrin, G. Thornton, & D. Meagher (Eds.) *Handbook of thanatology: The essential body of knowledge for the student of death, dying, and bereavement* (pp. 103–112). Northbrook, IL: Association for Death Education and Counseling.

NAME INDEX